Microsoft®
PowerPoint®
2002

MINUTE
GUIDE

MW00909596

201 West 103rd Street
Indianapolis, IN 46290

Joe Habraken

Ten Minute Guide to Microsoft® PowerPoint® 2002
©2002 by Que® Corporation

International Standard Book Number: 0-7897-2637-8

Library of Congress Catalog Card Number: 2001090294

Printed in the United States of America

First Printing: November, 2001

04 03 02   4

Trademarks

Warning and Disclaimer

Associate Publisher
Greg Wiegand

Acquisitions Editor
Stephanie J. McComb

Managing Editor
Thomas Hayes

Project Editor
Tonya Simpson

Indexer
Ken Johnson

Proofreader
Melissa Lynch

Technical Editor
Dallas Releford

Team Coordinator
Sharry Gregory

Interior Designer
Gary Adair

Cover Designer
Sandra Schroeder

Page Layout
Gloria Schurick

Contents at a Glance

TABLE OF CONTENTS

DEDICATION

To all of humanity, in the hopes that a time will come when we realize world peace, love, and understanding.

ACKNOWLEDGMENTS

Creating books like this takes a real team effort. I would like to thank Stephanie McComb, our acquisitions editor, who worked very hard to assemble the team that made this book a reality. Also a tip of the hat and a thanks to Dallas Releford, who as the technical editor for the project did a fantastic job making sure that everything was correct and suggested a number of additions that made the book even more technically sound. Finally, a great big thanks to our project editor, Tonya Simpson, who ran the last leg of the race and made sure the book made it to press on time—what a great team of professionals!

TELL US WHAT YOU THINK!

As the reader of this book, *you* are our most important critic and commentator. We value your opinion and want to know what we're doing right, what we could do better, what areas you'd like to see us publish in, and any other words of wisdom you're willing to pass our way.

As an associate publisher for Que, I welcome your comments. You can fax, email, or write me directly to let me know what you did or didn't like about this book—as well as what we can do to make our books stronger.

Please note that I cannot help you with technical problems related to the topic of this book, and that due to the high volume of mail I receive, I might not be able to reply to every message.

When you write, please be sure to include this book's title and author as well as your name and phone or fax number. I will carefully review your comments and share them with the author and editors who worked on the book.

Fax: 317-581-4666

E-mail: feedback@quepublishing.com

Mail: Greg Wiegand
           Que
           201 West 103rd Street
           Indianapolis, IN 46290 USA

Introduction

Microsoft PowerPoint 2002 is a powerful presentation software application that provides an easy-to-use interface and all the tools you need to build personal and business presentations. You have the option to create your presentations from scratch or to use the AutoContent Wizard and design templates that help you build a variety of different presentation types.

The What and Why of Microsoft PowerPoint

Microsoft PowerPoint not only enables you to create your own presentations; it also provides features and tools that enable you to easily enhance the slides in your presentation and rearrange the slides as needed. You will be able to quickly create exciting presentations using the following features:

- The AutoContent Wizard walks you through each step of creating a new presentation and supplies dummy text that you can replace with your own information.

- Views such as the Outline view and the Slide Sorter make it easy to arrange your presentation slides in a logical order.

- Design templates enable you to add color, background patterns, and special fonts to the slides in your presentation.

- Animation schemes can be used to add transitions as you move from slide to slide that add visual impact to your presentation.

- You can add clip art to your slides to provide visual interest. The Clipart library also includes motion clips and sounds.

While providing you with many complex features, Microsoft PowerPoint is easy to learn. It enables you to build presentations that can be shown on a computer, printed, or saved in a format so that the presentation can be viewed on the World Wide Web. This book will help you understand the possibilities awaiting you with Microsoft PowerPoint 2002.

WHY QUE'S *10 MINUTE GUIDE TO MICROSOFT POWERPOINT 2002*?

The *10 Minute Guide to Microsoft PowerPoint 2002* can save you precious time while you get to know the different features provided by Microsoft PowerPoint. Each lesson is designed to be completed in 10 minutes or less, so you'll be up to snuff on basic and advanced PowerPoint features and skills quickly.

Although you can jump around among lessons, starting at the beginning is a good plan. The bare-bones basics are covered first, and more advanced topics are covered later. Following the lessons sequentially will allow you to walk through all the steps of creating and enhancing personal and business presentations.

INSTALLING POWERPOINT

You can install Microsoft PowerPoint 2002 on a computer running Microsoft Windows 98, Windows NT 4.0, Windows 2000, and Windows XP. Microsoft PowerPoint can be purchased as a standalone product on its own CD-ROM, or it can be purchased as part of the Microsoft Office XP suite (which comes on several CD-ROMs). Whether you are installing PowerPoint as a standalone product or as part of the Microsoft Office XP suite, the installation steps are basically the same.

To install PowerPoint, follow these steps:

1. Start your computer, and then insert the PowerPoint or Microsoft XP Office CD in the CD-ROM drive. The CD-ROM should autostart, showing you the opening installation screen (for either PowerPoint or Office, depending on the CD you are working with).

2. If the CD-ROM does not autostart, choose **Start**, **Run**. In the Run dialog box, type the letter of the CD-ROM drive, followed by `setup` (for example, `d:\setup`). If necessary, click the **Browse** button to locate and select the CD-ROM drive and the setup.exe program.

3. When the Setup Wizard prompts you, enter your name, organization, and CD key in the appropriate box.

4. Choose **Next** to continue.

5. The next wizard screen provides instructions to finish the installation. Complete the installation, and select **Next** to advance from screen to screen after providing the appropriate information requested by the wizard.

After you complete the installation from the CD, icons for PowerPoint and any other Office applications you have installed will be provided on the Windows Start menu. Lesson 2 in this book provides you with a step-by-step guide to starting PowerPoint 2002.

CONVENTIONS USED IN THIS BOOK

To help you move through the lessons easily, these conventions are used:

On-screen text	On-screen text appears in bold type.
`Text you should type`	Information you need to type appears in bold monospaced type.
Items you select	Commands, options, and icons you should select and keys you should press appear in bold type.

In telling you to choose menu commands, this book uses the format *menu title*, *menu command*. For example, the statement "Choose **File**, **Properties**" means to open the File menu and select the Properties command.

In addition to those conventions, the *10 Minute Guide to Microsoft PowerPoint 2002* uses the following icons to identify helpful information:

PLAIN ENGLISH

> **Plain English**   New or unfamiliar terms are defined in term sidebars.

TIP

> **Tips**   Read these tips for ideas that cut corners and confusion.

CAUTION

> **Cautions**   Cautions identify areas where new users often run into trouble; these tips offer practical solutions to those problems.

LESSON 1
What's New in PowerPoint 2002?

In this lesson, you are introduced to PowerPoint's powerful presentation features, and you learn what's new in PowerPoint 2002.

GETTING THE MOST OUT OF POWERPOINT 2002

PowerPoint is a powerful presentation application that enables you to create presentations that can be viewed on a computer. Using PowerPoint, you can print handouts or create film slides for a presentation. PowerPoint also enables you to add animation and sound to your presentations, which makes it the perfect presentation tool for business presentations or classroom lectures.

PowerPoint provides several features to help you create personal and business presentations. These features range from the AutoContent Wizard and design templates, which help you create slides for your presentation, to tools such as the Outline and Slide Sorter views, which make it easy for you to rearrange the slides in your presentation. You can add images, sounds, and many different types of objects to your slides as you create informative and visually interesting presentations.

Whether you are new to PowerPoint or are familiar with previous versions of PowerPoint, this book will walk you through the basics of creating a new presentation in PowerPoint 2002 and look at several different ways to enhance your PowerPoint slides. You can even save your PowerPoint presentations in HTML format so they can be viewed on the World Wide Web.

New Features in PowerPoint 2002

PowerPoint 2002 embraces a number of features that were first introduced with the release of PowerPoint 2000. For example, PowerPoint 2002 uses the same adaptive menu and toolbar system found in PowerPoint 2000 that customizes the commands and icons listed based on the commands you use most frequently.

PowerPoint 2002 also builds on the features found in the previous version of PowerPoint by offering many new features that make it easier for you to create, arrange, and format the slides in your presentation. New features in PowerPoint 2002 range from the different views that you can use to display your presentation, to voice dictation, to new ways to quickly get help.

For example, you will find that getting help in PowerPoint 2002 is even easier than in previous versions of PowerPoint. A new feature, the Ask a Question Box, has been added to the top left of the PowerPoint application window, making it easier for you to get help on a particular topic as you work. The various ways to get help in PowerPoint are covered in Lesson 10, "Getting Help in Microsoft PowerPoint." Let's take a survey of some of the other new features that are provided by PowerPoint 2002.

Introducing Task Panes

One of the biggest changes to the PowerPoint environment (and all the Microsoft Office XP member applications, such as Word 2002, Excel 2002, and Access 2002) is the introduction of the Office task pane. The task pane is a special pane that appears on the right side of the PowerPoint application window. It is used to provide access to many PowerPoint features that formerly were controlled using dialog boxes.

For example, when you want to add slides to a presentation or change the layout of a slide already in the presentation, you will use the Slide Layout task pane. This task pane appears in Figure 1.1. Creating new slides is discussed in Lesson 6, "Inserting, Deleting, and Copying Slides."

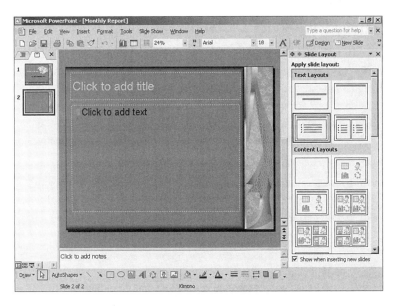

FIGURE 1.1
The Slide Layout task pane enables you to select the layout for the current slide.

Other task panes that you will run across as you use PowerPoint are the Slide Design task pane, the Office Clipboard, and the Clip Gallery. The Slide Design task pane enables you to select the design template for the presentation and the color or animation scheme used on a particular slide (this task pane is discussed in Lesson 5, "Changing a Presentation's Look").

The Office Clipboard enables you to copy or cut multiple items from a slide and then paste them onto an existing or new slide. The Clip Gallery enables you to insert clip art, sounds, and animated content onto your slides. Task panes are discussed throughout this book as you explore the various PowerPoint features.

INTRODUCING VOICE DICTATION AND VOICE COMMANDS

One of the most exciting new features in PowerPoint 2002 (and the entire Office XP suite) is voice dictation and voice-activated commands. If your computer is outfitted with a sound card, speakers, and a microphone (or a microphone with an earphone headset), you can dictate information into your PowerPoint presentations. You also can use voice commands to activate the menu system in that application.

Before you can really take advantage of the Speech feature, you must train it so that it can more easily recognize your speech patterns and intonation. After the Speech feature is trained, you can effectively use it to dictate text entries or access various application commands without a keyboard or mouse.

CAUTION

> **Requirements for Getting the Most Out of the Speech Feature**   To make the Speech feature useful, you will need a fairly high-quality microphone. Microsoft suggests a microphone/headset combination. The Speech feature also requires a more powerful computer. Microsoft suggests using a computer with 128MB of RAM and a Pentium II (or later) processor running at a minimum of 400MHz. A computer that meets or exceeds these higher standards should be capable of getting the most out of the Speech feature.

You might want to explore the other lessons in this book if you are new to PowerPoint before you attempt to use the Speech feature. Having a good understanding of how PowerPoint operates and the features that it provides will allow you to get the most out of the Speech feature.

TRAINING THE SPEECH FEATURE

The first time you start the Speech feature in PowerPoint, you are
required to configure and train it. Follow these steps to get the Speech
feature up and running:

1. In PowerPoint, select the **Tools** menu and select **Speech**. The
   Welcome to Office Speech Recognition dialog box appears.
   To begin the process of setting up your microphone and train-
   ing the Speech feature, click the **Next** button.

2. The first screen of the Microphone Wizard appears. It asks
   you to be sure that your microphone and speakers are connected to your computer. If you have a headset microphone,
   this screen shows you how to adjust the microphone for use.
   Click **Next** to continue.

3. The next wizard screen asks you to read a short text passage
   so that your microphone volume level can be adjusted (see
   Figure 1.2). When you have finished reading the text, click
   Next to continue.

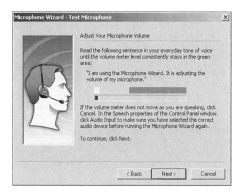

FIGURE 1.2
The Microphone Wizard adjusts the volume of your microphone.

4. On the next screen, you are told that if you have a headset microphone, you can click **Finish** and proceed to the speech recognition training. If you have a different type of microphone, you are asked to read another text passage. The text then is played back to you to determine whether the microphone is placed at an appropriate distance from your mouth. When you get a satisfactory playback, click **Finish**.

When you finish working with the Microphone Wizard, the Voice Training Wizard appears. This wizard collects samples of your speech and, in essence, educates the Speech feature as to how you speak.

To complete the voice training process, follow these steps:

1. After reading the information on the opening screen, click **Next** to begin the voice training process.

2. On the next screen, you are asked to provide your gender and age (see Figure 1.3). After specifying the correct information, click **Next**.

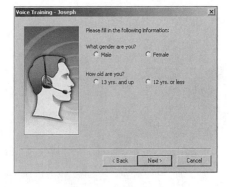

FIGURE 1.3
Supply the voice trainer with your gender and age.

3. The next wizard screen provides an overview of how the voice training will proceed. You also are provided with directions for how to pause the training session. Click **Next**.

4. The next wizard screen reminds you to adjust your microphone. You also are reminded that you need a quiet room when training the Speech feature. When you are ready to begin training the speech recognition feature, click **Next**.

5. On the next screen, you are asked to read some text. As the wizard recognizes each word, the word is highlighted. After finishing with this screen, continue by clicking **Next**.

6. You are asked to read text on several subsequent screens. Words are selected as the wizard recognizes them.

7. Your profile is updated when you complete the training screens. Click **Finish** on the wizard's final screen.

You are now ready to use the Speech feature. The next two sections discuss using the Voice Dictation and Voice Command features.

CAUTION

> **The Speech Feature Works Better Over Time**   Be advised that the voice feature's performance improves as you use it. As you learn to pronounce your words more carefully, the Speech feature tunes itself to your speech patterns. You might need to do additional training sessions to fine-tune the Speech feature.

USING VOICE DICTATION

When you are ready to start dictating text into a PowerPoint slide, put on your headset microphone or place your standalone microphone in the proper position that you determined when you used the Microphone Wizard. When you're ready to go, select the **Tools** menu, and then select **Speech**. The Language bar appears, as shown in Figure 1.4. If necessary, click the **Dictation** button on the toolbar (if the Dictation button is not already activated or depressed).

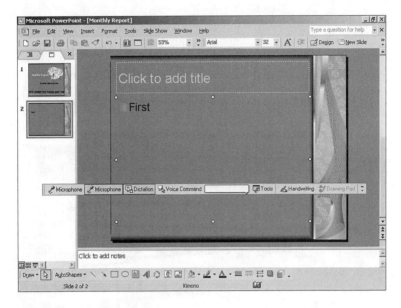

FIGURE 1.4
Dictating text into a PowerPoint slide.

After you enable the Dictation button, you can begin dictating your text. Figure 1.4 shows text being dictated into a PowerPoint slide. When you want to put a line break into the text, say "New line." You can place punctuation in the document by saying the name of a particular punctuation mark, such as "period" or "comma."

> **CAUTION**
>
> **How Do I Insert the Word "Comma" Rather Than the Punctuation Mark?**   Because certain keywords, such as "period" or "comma," are used to insert punctuation during dictation, you must spell these words out if you want to include them in the text. To do this, say "spelling mode," and then spell out the word, such as c-o-m-m-a. As soon as you dictate an entire word, the spelling mode is ended.

When you have finished dictating into the document, click the **Micro-phone** button on the Language bar (the second Microphone button from the left; the first is used to select the current speech driver, which you can leave as the default). When you click the **Microphone** button, the Language bar collapses, hiding the **Dictation** and the **Voice Command** buttons. You also can stop Dictation mode by saying "microphone."

You can minimize the Language bar by clicking the **Minimize** button on the right end of the bar. This sends the Language bar to the Windows System Tray (it appears as a small square icon marked EN, if you are using the English version of Office).

With the Language bar minimized in the System Tray, you can quickly open it when you need it. Click the **Language Bar** icon in the System Tray, and then select **Show the Language Bar** (which is the only choice provided when you click on the Language Bar icon).

Using the Dictation feature correctly requires that you know how to get the Speech feature to place the correct text or characters into PowerPoint. For more help with the dictation feature, consult the Microsoft PowerPoint Help system (discussed in Lesson 10).

USING VOICE COMMANDS

Another tool the Speech feature provides is voice commands. You can open and select menus in an application, and even navigate dialog boxes, using voice commands.

To use voice commands, open the Language bar (click **Tools, Speech**). Click the **Microphone** icon, if necessary, to expand the Language bar. Then, click the **Voice Command** icon on the bar (or say "voice command").

To open a particular menu, such as the Format menu, say "format." Then, to open a particular submenu, such as Font, say "font." In the case of these voice commands, the Font dialog box opens.

You then can navigate a particular dialog box using voice commands. In the Font dialog box, for example, to change the size of the font, say "size"; this activates the Size box that controls font size. Then, say the size of the font, such as "14." You can activate other font attributes in the dialog box in this manner. Say the name of the area of the dialog box you want to use, and then say the name of the feature you want to turn on or select.

When you have finished working with a particular dialog box, say "OK" (or "Cancel" or "Apply," as needed), and the dialog box closes and provides you with the features you selected in the dialog box. When you have finished using voice commands, say "microphone," or click the **Microphone** icon on the Language bar.

Believe it or not, you also can activate buttons on the various toolbars using voice commands. For example, you could turn on bold by saying "bold." The Bold button on the Formatting toolbar becomes active. To turn bold off, say "bold" again.

In this lesson, you were introduced to PowerPoint 2002 and some of the new features available in this latest version of Microsoft PowerPoint, such as task panes and the Speech feature. In the next lesson, you learn how to start PowerPoint and work in the application window.

LESSON 2
Working in PowerPoint

In this lesson, you learn how to start and exit PowerPoint. You also learn about the PowerPoint presentation window.

STARTING POWERPOINT

PowerPoint provides a complete environment for creating, managing, and viewing presentation slides. To start PowerPoint, follow these steps:

1. Click the **Start** button.

2. Move your mouse pointer to **Programs**. A menu of programs appears.

3. Move your mouse pointer to the **Microsoft PowerPoint** icon and click it. The PowerPoint application window opens, as shown in Figure 2.1.

Outline and Slides pane   Slide pane   Notes pane   Task pane

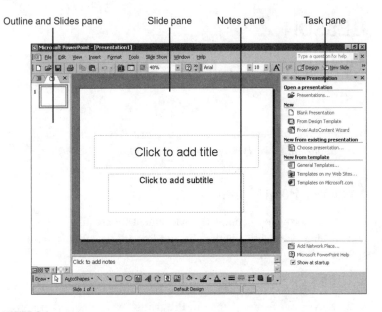

FIGURE 2.1
The PowerPoint window is divided into several panes.

The first thing you see when you open PowerPoint is that the application window is divided into different areas. The default view for PowerPoint is the Normal view (you learn about the different PowerPoint views in Lesson 4, "Working with Slides in Different Views"). On the left of the screen is a pane that can be used to switch between an Outline and Slides view of the current presentation. In the center of the PowerPoint application window is the Slide pane; this is where you work individually on each slide in the presentation.

Below the Slide pane is the Notes pane, which enables you to add notes to the presentation for each slide. On the far right of the application window is the New Presentation task pane. The task pane provides different commands and features depending on what you are currently doing in PowerPoint.

GETTING COMFORTABLE WITH THE POWERPOINT WINDOW

Although PowerPoint looks a little different from the other Office applications, such as Word and Excel, all the standard Office application com-
ponents, such as the menu bar and various toolbars, are available to you
as you design your presentations. The basic element of a presentation is
a slide, to which you add text and other objects, such as images, using
the Slide pane (which is discussed in the next lesson). PowerPoint provides several slide layouts; each layout provides the necessary text boxes
or clip-art boxes for creating a particular type of slide.

Adding text to a slide is very straightforward. Each slide that you add
to a presentation (Lesson 6, "Inserting, Deleting, and Copying Slides,"
discusses inserting slides into a presentation) contains placeholder text
that tells you what to type into a particular text box on the slide. For
example, Figure 2.2 shows a title slide. Note that the top text box on
the slide says Click to Add Title.

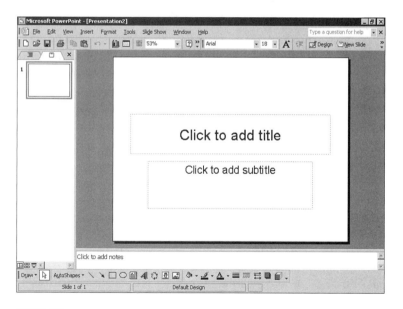

FIGURE 2.2
Click the placeholder text to input text into a slide.

To replace the placeholder text with your own text, just click the placeholder text. Then, you can type your entry into that text box.

Because a presentation consists of several slides, PowerPoint provides a thumbnail view of each slide in the presentation to the left of the Slides pane. Figure 2.3 shows an example of a complete presentation with a series of these thumbnail slides. This view can be used to keep track of your slides as you add them to the presentation and can even be used to rearrange slides in the presentation.

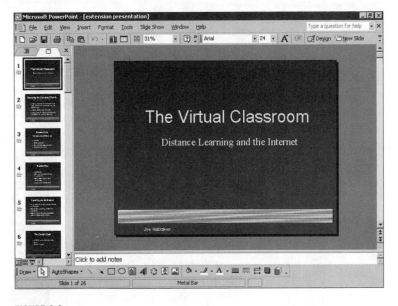

FIGURE 2.3
The Slides pane enables you to view thumbnails of the slides in the presentation.

Because presentations require a certain logical arrangement of information, you can view the slides in the presentation as an outline. This enables you to make sure that you have the facts presented by each slide in the proper order for the presentation. The Outline pane also enables you to move topics within the presentation and even move information from slide to slide. Figure 2.4 shows the Outline pane for a presentation that contains several slides.

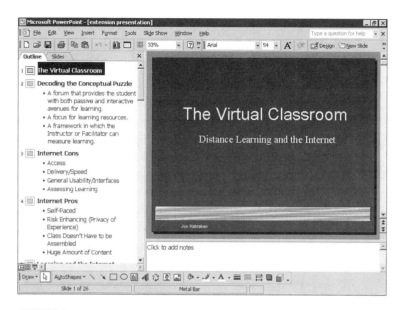

FIGURE 2.4
The Outline pane enables you to view the topic of each slide and each piece of text information included in a slide.

You learn about using the Slides and Outline pane in Lesson 4, "Working with Slides in Different Views." Lesson 4 shows you how you can edit the presentation's text in either the Outline or the Slide pane. Changes in one pane are reflected in the other pane. When you want to place a nontext object on a slide (such as a graphic), you do so in the Slide pane.

EXITING POWERPOINT

When you finish using PowerPoint, you can exit the application. This closes any open presentations (PowerPoint might prompt you to save changes to those presentations).

To exit PowerPoint, perform one of the following:

• Click the PowerPoint window's **Close** (**x**) button.

- Double-click the **Control Menu** icon in the left corner of the title bar, or click it once to open the **Control** menu and then select **Close**.

- Open the **File** menu and select **Exit**.

- Press **Alt+F4**.

In this lesson, you learned how to start and exit PowerPoint. In addition, you learned about the PowerPoint application window. In the next lesson, you learn how to create a new presentation.

LESSON 3
Creating a New Presentation

In this lesson, you learn several ways to create a presentation. You also learn how to save, close, and open an existing presentation.

THREE CHOICES FOR STARTING A NEW PRESENTATION

PowerPoint offers several ways to create a new presentation. Before you begin, decide which method is right for you:

- The AutoContent Wizard offers the highest degree of help. It walks you through each step of creating the new presentation. When you're finished, you have a standardized group of slides, all with a similar look and feel, for a particular situation. Each slide created includes dummy text that you can replace with your own text.

- A design template provides a professionally designed color, background, and font scheme that applies to the slides you create yourself. It does not provide sample slides.

- You can start from scratch and create a totally blank presentation. The means that you build the presentation from the ground up and create each slide in the presentation (beginners might want to use the wizard or templates until they get a feel for the overall design approach used to create a cohesive slide presentation).

PLAIN ENGLISH

Design Template   A design template is a preformatted presentation file (without any slides in it). When you select a template, PowerPoint applies the color scheme and general layout of the template to each slide you create for the presentation.

CREATING A NEW PRESENTATION WITH THE AUTOCONTENT WIZARD

With the AutoContent Wizard, you select the type of presentation you want to create (such as corporate, sales, or various projects), and PowerPoint creates an outline for the presentation.

The following steps describe how you use the AutoContent Wizard:

1. Select the **File** menu and select **New**. The New Presentation task pane appears on the right of the PowerPoint window, as shown in Figure 3.1 (if the Presentation task pane was already open in the window, you can skip to step 2).

FIGURE 3.1
Start the AutoContent Wizard from the task pane.

2. Click the **From AutoContent Wizard** link on the task pane.

3. The AutoContent Wizard starts. The opening wizard screen summarizes the process you should follow to create a new presentation. Click **Next** to continue.

4. The wizard provides you with category buttons for different categories of presentations: General, Corporate, Projects, Sales/Marketing, and Carnegie Coach. Select a category by

selecting the appropriate button (see Figure 3.2). To see all
the presentations available, click the **All** button.

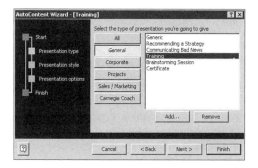

FIGURE 3.2
Select a category button to view a list of presentation types.

PLAIN ENGLISH

> **What Is the Carnegie Coach?**   The Carnegie Coach pro-
> vides presentations that can be used to sell your ideas
> or motivate a team; they are named after Dale Carnegie,
> the motivational speaker and author.

5. After selecting a particular category of presentations, select a
   presentation type in the list provided, and click **Next** to
   continue.

6. On the next screen, you select how you will give the presentation. Select one of the following options:

   • **Onscreen Presentation** — Choose this if you plan to
     use a computer and your PowerPoint file to present the
     show.

   • **Web Presentation**—Choose this if you are planning to
     distribute the presentation as a self-running or user-
     interactive show.

- **Black-and-White Overheads**—Choose this if you plan to make black-and-white transparencies for your show.

- **Color Overheads**—Choose this if you plan to make color transparencies for your show.

- **35mm Slides**—Choose this if you plan to send your PowerPoint presentation to a service bureau to have 35mm slides made. (You probably don't have such expensive and specialized equipment in your own company.)

7. After selecting how you will give the presentation, click **Next** to continue.

8. On the next screen, type the presentation title into the text box provided (see Figure 3.3). If you want to add a footer (such as your name) that will appear at the bottom of each slide of the presentation, click in the Footer box and type the appropriate text. If you do not want a date and/or slide number on each slide, deselect the **Date Last Updated** and/or **Slide Number** check boxes.

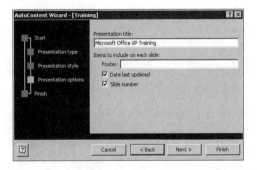

FIGURE 3.3
Provide a title for the presentation.

9. After supplying the presentation title and any optional information, click **Next** to continue.

10. PowerPoint takes you to the last wizard screen, where you
    should simply click **Finish**.

The title slide of your new presentation appears in the Slide pane. The
entire presentation, including the dummy text placed on each slide,
appears in the Outline pane on the left of the PowerPoint window (see
Figure 3.4).

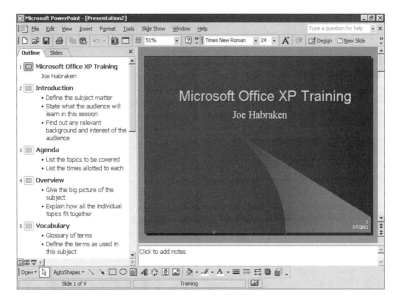

FIGURE 3.4
Your new presentation appears in the PowerPoint window.

You can start working on your presentation right away by replacing
the dummy text on the slides with your own text. Just select the
existing text in a text box and type right over it. You learn about
editing text in slide text boxes in Lesson 8, "Adding and Modifying
Slide Text."

CREATING A NEW PRESENTATION WITH A DESIGN TEMPLATE

A template is the middle ground between maximum hand-holding (the AutoContent Wizard) and no help at all (Blank Presentation). Two kinds of templates are available: presentation templates and design templates.

When you use the AutoContent Wizard, you use a presentation template. It contains not only formatting, but also sample slides that contain placeholder text. The other kind of template is a design template. It contains the overall formatting for the slides of the presentation but does not actually create any slides. If you want to use a presentation template, use the AutoContent Wizard, as explained in the preceding section.

To start a new presentation using a design template, follow these steps:

1. Select the **File** menu and select **New**. The New Presentation task pane appears on the right of the PowerPoint window.

TIP

> **Select Your Task Pane**   If the task pane is already open for another PowerPoint feature, click the drop-down arrow on its title bar and select **New Presentation** from the list that appears.

2. On the New Presentation task pane, click the **From Design Template** link. PowerPoint switches to the Slide Design side pane, which displays a list of design templates, as shown in Figure 3.5. A blank title slide for the presentation appears in the Slide pane.

FIGURE 3.5
Design templates are listed in the task pane.

3. Click a template from the Available for Use section of the
   task pane. PowerPoint then formats the title slide in the Slide
   pane using the selected template.

You can select different templates to determine the best look for your
presentation. When you have found the design template that you want
to use, you can immediately start working on the slides for the
presentation.

PLAIN ENGLISH

> **The Next Step?**   Add more slides by clicking the **New
> Slide** button on the toolbar. Inserting slides into a pre-
> sentation is covered in Lesson 6, "Inserting, Deleting,
> and Copying Slides."

CREATING A BLANK PRESENTATION

Your third option for creating a new presentation is to create a blank
presentation. This means that you have to create all the slides from

scratch. You then can select a design for the slides using the Slide Design task pane. You open this task pane by selecting **Format**, **Slide Design**. In the Slide Design task pane, be sure that the **Design Templates** icon is selected.

 Creating a new, blank presentation takes only a click: Click the **New** button on the Standard toolbar or click the **Blank Presentation** link on the New Presentation task pane. The new presentation appears in the PowerPoint window. A blank title slide is ready for you to edit.

SAVING A PRESENTATION

After you create a new presentation, it makes sense to save it. To save a presentation for the first time, follow these steps:

 1. Select **File**, **Save**, or just click the **Save** button on the Standard toolbar. The Save As dialog box appears (see Figure 3.6).

FIGURE 3.6
Type a name for your presentation into the Save As dialog box.

2. In the **File Name** text box, type the name you want to assign to the presentation. Your filenames can be as long as 255 characters and can include spaces.

3. The Save In box shows in which folder the file will be saved. The default is My Documents. To select a different drive location for the file, click the Save In drop-down arrow and select one from the list that appears. To save to a specific folder in the drive location you've selected, double-click the folder in which you want to store the file.

4. Click **Save**.

Now that you have named the file and saved it to a disk, you can save any changes you make simply by pressing **Ctrl+S** or clicking the **Save** button on the Standard toolbar. Your data is saved under the filename you assigned the presentation in the Save As dialog box.

To create a copy of a presentation under a different filename or location, select **File**, **Save As**. The Save As dialog box reappears; follow steps 2 to 4 as discussed in this section to give the file a new name or location.

CLOSING A PRESENTATION

You can close a presentation at any time. Note that although this closes the presentation window, it does not exit PowerPoint as with the methods discussed in Lesson 1. To close a presentation, follow these steps:

1. If more than one presentation is open, click a presentation's button on the Windows taskbar to make it the active presentation, or select the **Window** menu and select the presentation from the list provided.

2. Select **File** and then select **Close**, or click the presentation's **Close** (x) button. (It's the lower of the two Close buttons; the upper one is for the PowerPoint window.) If you haven't saved the presentation or if you haven't saved since you last made changes, a dialog box appears, asking whether you want to save.

3. To save your changes, click **Yes**. If this is a new presentation that has never been saved, refer to the steps in the preceding section for saving a presentation. If you have saved the file previously, the presentation window closes.

OPENING A PRESENTATION

Because a presentation, like Rome, is not built in a day, you probably will fine-tune a presentation over time. To open a saved presentation file that you want to work on, follow these steps:

1. Select **File**, **Open**, or click the **Open** button on the Standard toolbar. The Open dialog box appears (see Figure 3.7).

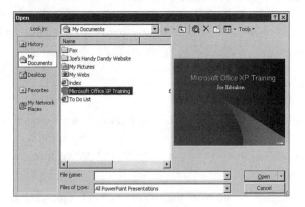

FIGURE 3.7
Select the presentation you want to open.

2. If the file isn't in the currently displayed folder, select the **Look In** drop-down arrow to choose from a list of other drives and/or folders.

3. Browse to the location containing the file, and double-click it to open it in PowerPoint.

FINDING A PRESENTATION FILE

If you're having trouble locating your file, PowerPoint can help you look. Follow these steps to find a file:

1. Select the **File** menu, and then select **Open** (if the Open dialog box is not already open).

2. Click the **Tools** drop-down button in the Open dialog box and select **Search**. The Search dialog box appears (see Figure 3.8).

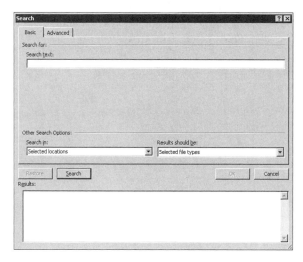

FIGURE 3.8
Use the Search dialog box to find a presentation on your computer.

3. In the **Search Text** box, type text that is contained in the presentation's filename. Use the Search In box to specify where you want the search to be conducted. In the Results Should Be box, specify the file types you want to be included in the search.

4. When you are ready to conduct the search, click the **Search** button.

5. Files that meet the search criteria are listed in the Results box (if you see your file in the Results box and the search is continuing, click the **Stop** button).

6. To open a file in the Results box, double-click the filename.

7. You are returned to the Open dialog box with the file listed in the File Name box. Click **OK** to open the file. A PowerPoint presentation then opens in the PowerPoint window.

In this lesson, you learned how to create a new presentation. You also learned how to save, close, open, and find presentations. In the next lesson, you learn how to work with slides in different views.

LESSON 4

Working with Slides in Different Views

In this lesson, you learn how to display a presentation in different views and how to edit slides in the Outline and Slide views.

UNDERSTANDING POWERPOINT'S DIFFERENT VIEWS

PowerPoint can display your presentation in different views. Each of these views is designed for you to perform certain tasks as you create and edit a presentation. For example, Normal view has the Outline/Slides, Slide, and Notes panes; it provides an ideal environment for creating your presentation slides and to quickly view the organization of the slides or the information in the presentation (using the Outline or the Slides tabs). Another view, the Slide Sorter view, enables you to quickly rearrange the slides in the presentation (and is similar to the Slides view that shares the pane with the Outline tab when you are in the Normal view).

To change views, open the **View** menu and choose the desired view: **Normal**, **Slide Sorter**, **Slide Show**, or **Notes Page**.

- **Normal**—The default, three-pane view (which is discussed in Lesson 2, "Working in PowerPoint").

- **Slide Sorter**—This view shows all the slides as thumbnails so that you can easily rearrange them by dragging slides to new positions in the presentation (Figure 4.1 shows the Slide Sorter).

- **Slide Show**—A specialized view that enables you to preview and present your show onscreen. It enables you to test the presentation as you add slides, and it is used later when your presentation is complete.

- **Notes Page**—This view provides a large pane for creating notes for your speech. You also can type these notes in Normal view, but Notes Page view gives you more room and allows you to concentrate on your note text.

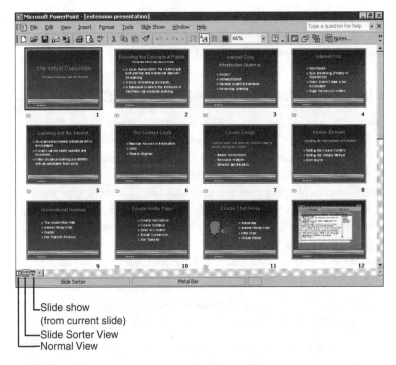

LSlide show
(from current slide)
Slide Sorter View
Normal View

FIGURE 4.1
The Slide Sorter view is used to rearrange the slides in a presentation.

An even faster way to switch to certain views is to use the view buttons that are provided along the lower-left corner of the PowerPoint window. These buttons, from left to right, are Normal View, Slide Sorter View, and Slide Show (from current slide) button. A button is not provided for the Notes view.

MOVING FROM SLIDE TO SLIDE

PowerPoint provides several ways to move from slide to slide in the presentation. The particular view you are in somewhat controls the procedure for moving to a specific slide.

In the Normal view, you can move from slide to slide using these techniques:

- Click the **Outline** tab on the far left of the window. To go to a particular slide in the outline, click the slide icon next to the slide number (see Figure 4.2). The slide opens in the Slide pane.

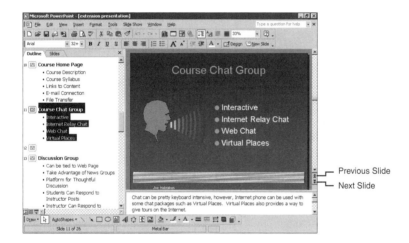

FIGURE 4.2
The Outline view can be used to quickly move to a particular slide.

- Press the **Page Up** or **Page Down** keys to move to the previous or next slide, respectively.

- Click the **Previous Slide** or **Next Slide** button just below the vertical scrollbar (refer to Figure 4.2), or drag the scroll box inside the vertical scrollbar until the desired slide number is displayed.

- Click the **Slides** tab on the far left of the PowerPoint window. This enables you to move from slide to slide in the Normal view by selecting a particular slide's thumbnail. When you click the thumbnail, the slide appears in the Slide pane.

You also can move from slide to slide in other views, such as the Slide Sorter view or the Slide Show view. In the Slide Sorter view (refer to Figure 4.1), just click a slide's thumbnail to move to that slide. You then can use any of the tools that PowerPoint provides to format the selected slide (or delete it). If you want to actually open a slide when you are working in the Slide Sorter view, so that you can edit the text it contains, double-click the slide. You are returned to the Normal view.

When you are actually showing a presentation in the Slide Show view, you can use the **Page Up** or **Page Down** keys to move from slide to slide (unless you have set up timers to change slides). You also can click a slide with the mouse to move to the next slide. You learn more about the Slide Show view in Lesson 16, "Presenting an Onscreen Slideshow."

INTRODUCTION TO INSERTING SLIDE TEXT

If you created a presentation in Lesson 3 using the AutoContent Wizard, you already have a presentation that contains several slides, but they won't contain the text you want to use. Slides created by the wizard contain placeholder text that you must replace. If you created a blank presentation or based a new presentation on a design template, you have only a title slide in that presentation, which, of course, needs to be personalized for your particular presentation. This means that additional slides will need to be added to the presentation. Lesson 6, "Inserting, Deleting, and Copying Slides," covers the creation of new slides for a presentation.

The sections that follow in this lesson look at the basics of inserting text into the text boxes provided on slides. You will look at adding new text boxes and formatting text in text boxes in Lesson 8, "Adding and Modifying Slide Text." Upcoming lessons also discuss how to add pictures and other objects to your PowerPoint slides.

PLAIN ENGLISH

> **Object**   An object is any item on a slide, including text, graphics, and charts.

EDITING TEXT IN THE SLIDE PANE

The text on your slides resides within boxes (all objects appear on a slide in their own boxes for easy manipulation). As shown in Figure 4.3, to edit text on a slide, click the text box to select it, and then click where you want the insertion point moved or select the text you want to replace.

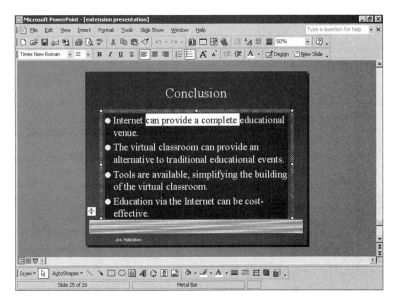

FIGURE 4.3
You can edit your text directly on the slide in the Slide pane.

When you work with the Slide pane, you might want to close the Outline/Slides pane. Just click the pane's **Close** button (**x**) to provide the Slide pane with the entire PowerPoint window (refer to Figure 4.3). In Lesson 8, "Adding and Modifying Slide Text," you'll learn more about adding text to a slide, including creating your own text boxes on a slide.

TIP

Opening the Outline Pane   If you close the Outline pane to concentrate on the Slide pane, click **View**, **Normal (Restore Panes)** to restore it to the application window.

EDITING TEXT IN THE OUTLINE PANE

The Outline pane provides another way to edit text in a slide. To switch to the Outline view on the Outline/Slides pane, click the **Outline** tab. You simply click to move the insertion point where you want it (or select the range of text you want to replace) in the outline, and then type your text (see Figure 4.4). If you've placed the insertion point in the slide text (without selecting a range), press the **Del** key to delete characters to the right of the insertion point or press the **Backspace** key to delete characters to the left. If you've selected a range of text, either of these keys deletes the text. If you want to move the highlighted text, simply drag it to where you want it moved.

PLAIN ENGLISH

Larger Outline   You might want to enlarge the Outline pane by dragging its divider to the right in the Normal view.

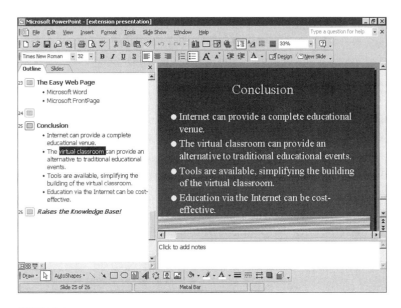

FIGURE 4.4
You can edit your text in Outline view.

TIP

> **Auto Word Select**   When you select text, PowerPoint
> selects whole words. If you want to select individual
> characters, open the **Tools** menu, select **Options**, click
> the **Edit** tab, and click the **When Selecting**, **Automatically
> Select Entire Word** check box to turn it off. Click **OK**.

MOVING TEXT IN THE OUTLINE PANE

As you work in the Normal view, you also can view your presentation
slides as an outline using the Outline pane. This provides you with a
quick way to move text items around on a slide or move them from
slide to slide. Just select the text and drag it to a new position.

As already mentioned, you also can drag text from one slide to another. All you have to do is select a line of text in the Outline pane and drag it to another slide. You also can move a slide in the Outline pane. Drag the slide's icon in the Outline pane to a new position (under the heading for another slide).

If you aren't that confident with your dragging skills, PowerPoint provides help in the form of the Outlining toolbar. It provides buttons that make it easy to move text up or down on a slide (with respect to other text on the slide) or to move a slide up or down in the presentation.

To turn on the Outlining toolbar, right-click one of the PowerPoint toolbars and select **Outlining**. Figure 4.5 shows the Outlining toolbar on the left side of the Outline pane (the Outline pane has also been expanded to take up more of the PowerPoint window).

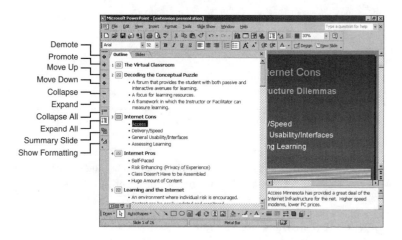

FIGURE 4.5
You can use the Outlining toolbar to move text and slides in the presentation.

- To move a paragraph or text line up in a slide, select it and click the **Move Up** button.

- To move a paragraph or text down in a slide, select it and click the **Move Down** button.

You also can use the **Move Up** and **Move Down** buttons to move entire slides up or down in the presentation. Click the slide's icon, and then use the appropriate button (it might take several clicks to move a slide up or down with respect to another slide).

If you want to see how the text is actually formatted on the slides that you are viewing in the Outline pane, click the **Show Formatting** button on the Outlining toolbar. Viewing the text as it is formatted can help you determine where the text should appear on a slide as you move the text (or whether you will have to reformat the text later).

REARRANGING TEXT IN THE OUTLINE PANE

As you can see from Figure 4.5, your presentation is organized in a multilevel outline format. The slides are at the top level of the outline, and each slide's contents are subordinate under that slide. Some slides have multiple levels of subordination (for example, a bulleted list within a bulleted list).

You can easily change an object's level in Outline view with the Tab key or the Outlining toolbar:

- To demote a paragraph in the outline, click the text, and then press the **Tab** key or click the **Demote** button on the Outlining toolbar.

- To promote a paragraph in the outline, click the text, and then press **Shift+Tab** or click the **Promote** button on the Outlining toolbar.

In most cases, subordinate items on a slide appear as items in a bulleted list. In Lesson 9, "Creating Columns, Tables, and Lists," you learn how to change the appearance of the bullet and the size and formatting of text for each entry, as well as how much the text is indented for each level.

TIP

Create Summary Slides in the Outline Pane   If you would like to create a summary slide for your presentation that contains the headings from several slides, select those slides in the Outline pane (click the first slide, and then hold down the Shift key and click the last slide you want to select). Then, click the **Summary Slide** button on the Outlining toolbar. A new slide appears at the beginning of the selected slides containing the headings from the selected slides. You then can position the Summary slide anywhere in the presentation as you would any other slide.

In this lesson, you learned how to change views for a presentation, move from slide to slide, and edit text. In the next lesson, you learn how to change the look of your slides and the presentation.

LESSON 5

Changing a Presentation's Look

In this lesson, you learn various ways to give your presentation a professional and consistent look.

GIVING YOUR SLIDES A PROFESSIONAL LOOK

PowerPoint comes with dozens of professionally created designs and color schemes that you can apply to your presentations. These designs include background patterns, color choices, font choices, and more. When you apply a design template to your presentation, it applies its formatting to a special slide called the Slide Master.

The Slide Master is not really a slide, but it looks like one. It is a master design grid to which you make changes; these changes affect every slide in the presentation. When you apply a template, you actually are applying the template to the Slide Master, which in turn applies it to each slide in the presentation.

> **PLAIN ENGLISH**
>
> **Slide Master** A slide that contains the master layout and color scheme for the slides in a presentation.

You don't have to work with the Slide Master itself when you apply template or color scheme changes to your presentations. Just be aware that you can open the Slide Master (select **View**, point at **Master**, and then select **Slide Master**) and change the style and fonts used by the text boxes in a presentation (see Figure 5.1). You also can select a custom background color for the slides in the presentation. Any changes

that you make to the Slide Master affect all the slides in the
presentation.

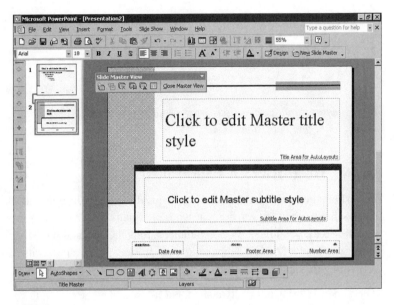

FIGURE 5.1
*The Slide Master holds the default design and color options for the entire
presentation.*

You probably will find that PowerPoint provides enough template and
color scheme options that you won't need to format the Slide Master
itself very often. Edit its properties only if you have a very strict formatting need for the presentation that isn't covered in the templates
and color schemes provided. For example, one good reason to edit the
Slide Master would be a situation in which you want a graphic to
appear on every slide (such as a company logo); you can place the
image on the Slide Master instead of pasting it onto each slide
individually.

**PLAIN ENGLISH**

> **Close the Slide Master**   If you open the Slide Master, you can close it by clicking **Close Master View** on the Master View toolbar.

APPLYING A DIFFERENT DESIGN TEMPLATE

You can apply a different template to your presentation at any time, no matter how you originally created the presentation. To change the design template, follow these steps:

1. Select **Format**, **Slide Design** to open the Slide Design task pane. Then, if necessary, click the **Design Templates** icon at the top of the task pane. This provides a listing of PowerPoint's many design templates (see Figure 5.2).

FIGURE 5.2
Choose a different template from the Design Templates task pane.

2. Click the template that you want to use in the list. The template is immediately applied to the slide in the Slide pane.

3. When you have decided on a particular template (you can click on any number of templates to see how they affect your slides), save the presentation (click the **Save** button on the toolbar).

CAUTION

The Design Template Changes Custom Formatting   If you spent time bolding text items on a slide or changing font colors, these changes are affected (lost) when you select a new design template. For example, if you have customized bold items in black in your original design template and switch to another template that uses white text, you lose your customizations. You should choose your design template early in the process of creating your presentation. Then, you can do any customized formatting at the end of the process so that it is not affected by a design template change.

When you work with design templates, you can apply them to all the slides in the presentation (as discussed in the steps provided in this section), or you can apply the template to selected slides in the presentation. Follow these steps to apply a template to a selected group of slides in a presentation:

1. Switch to the Slide Sorter view (select **View, Slide Sorter**).

2. Open the Slide Design task pane as outlined in the previous steps.

3. Now you must select the slide (or slides) to which you want to apply the template. Click the first slide you want to select, and then hold down the **Ctrl** key as you click other slides you want to select.

4. Point at the design template you want to use in the Slide Design task pane; a drop-down arrow appears.

5. Click the template's drop-down arrow and select **Apply to Selected Slides** (see Figure 5.3).

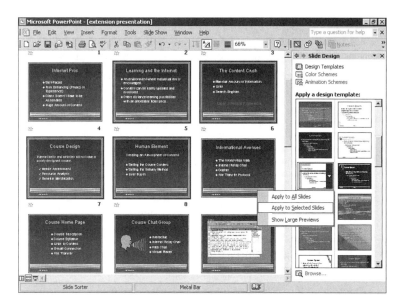

FIGURE 5.3
Design templates can be assigned to selected slides in a presentation.

The template's design then is applied to the selected slides.

TIP

View a Larger Design Sample   To expand the view of the design templates, click the drop-down arrow on the template and select **Show Large Previews**.

USING COLOR SCHEMES

Design templates enable you to change the overall design and color scheme applied to the slides in the presentation (or selected slides in the presentation, as discussed in the previous section). If you like the overall design of the slides in the presentation but would like to explore some other color options, you can select a different color scheme for the particular template you are using.

The number of color schemes available for a particular design template depends on the template itself. Some templates provide only three or four color schemes, whereas other templates provide more. As with design templates, you can assign a new color scheme to all the slides in the presentation or to selected slides.

To change the color scheme for the presentation or selected slides, follow these steps:

1. In the Normal or Slide Sorter view (use the Slide Sorter view if you want to change the color scheme for selected slides), open the task pane by selecting **View**, **Task Pane**. (If the task pane is already open, skip to the next step.)

2. Select the task pane's drop-down arrow, and then select **Slide Design-Color Schemes**. This switches to the Color Schemes section of the Slide Design task pane. The color schemes available for the design template that you are using appear in the Apply a Color Scheme section (see Figure 5.4).

3. (Optional) If you are in the Slide Sorter view and want to assign a new color scheme only to selected slides, select those slides (click the first slide and then hold down **Ctrl** and click additional slides).

4. To assign the new color scheme to all the slides in the presentation, click a scheme in the Slide Design task pane. If you are assigning the color scheme only to selected slides, point at the color scheme and click its drop-down arrow. Select **Apply to Selected Slides**.

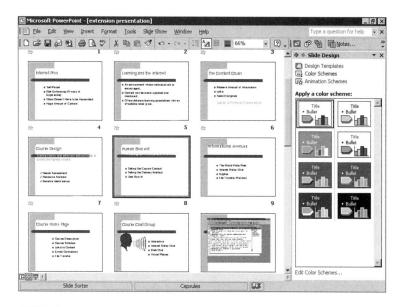

FIGURE 5.4
You can choose from a list of color schemes for the presentation or selected slides.

The new color scheme is applied to the slides in the presentation (or selected slides in the presentation). If you decide you don't like the color scheme, select another scheme from the task pane.

CHANGING THE BACKGROUND FILL

You can fine-tune the color scheme that you add to a slide or slides by changing the background fill. This works best in cases where the design template and color scheme that you selected don't provide a background color for the slide or slides. You must be careful, however, because you don't want to pick a background color that obscures the texts and graphics that you place on the slide or slides.

To change the background fill on a slide or slides, follow these steps:

1. Switch to the Slide Sorter view (select **View, Slide Sorter**).

2. (Optional) If you are going to change the background fill for selected slides, select those slides in the Slide Sorter window.

3. Select the **Format** menu, and then select **Background**. The Background dialog box appears (see Figure 5.5).

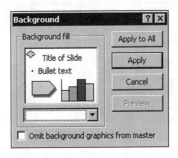

FIGURE 5.5
Use the Background dialog box to add a fill color to a slide or slides.

4. Click the drop-down arrow at the bottom of the dialog box and choose a fill color from the color palette that appears.

5. To assign the fill color to all the slides in the presentation, click **Apply to All**. To assign the fill color to selected slides (if you selected slides in step 2), click **Apply**.

In this lesson, you learned how to give your presentation a consistent look with design templates and color schemes. You also learned how add a fill color to a slide or slides. In the next lesson, you learn how to insert, delete, and copy slides, and you learn to add slides from another presentation.

LESSON 6
Inserting, Deleting, and Copying Slides

In this lesson, you learn how to insert new slides, delete slides, and copy slides in a presentation.

INSERTING A NEW SLIDE

You can insert a slide into a presentation at any time and at any position in the presentation. To insert a new slide, follow these steps:

1. On the Outline or Slides panes, select the slide that appears just before the place you want to insert the new slide (you also can insert a new slide in the Slide Sorter view).

2. Choose the **Insert** menu and then **New Slide**, or click the **New Slide** button on the PowerPoint toolbar. A new blank slide appears in the PowerPoint window, along with the Slide Layout task pane (see Figure 6.1).

3. In the Slide Layout task pane, select the slide layout that you want to use for the new slide. Several text slide layouts and layouts for slides that contain graphics are provided.

New Slide button

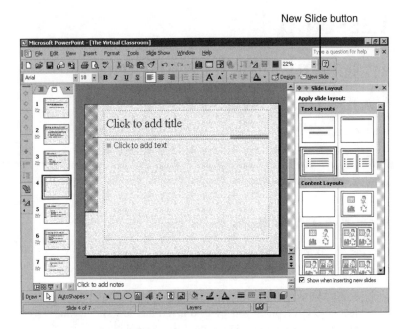

FIGURE 6.1
Your new slide appears in the PowerPoint window.

4. Follow the directions indicated on the slide in the Slide pane to add text or other objects. For text boxes, click an area to select it and then type in your text. For other object placeholders, double-click the placeholder.

PLAIN ENGLISH

Cloning a Slide   To create an exact replica of an existing slide (in any view), select the slide you want to duplicate. Click **Insert**, and then select **Duplicate Slide**. The new slide is inserted after the original slide. You then can choose a different layout for the slide if you want.

INSERTING SLIDES FROM ANOTHER PRESENTATION

If you want to insert some or all of the slides from another presentation into the current presentation, perform these steps:

1. Open the presentation into which you want to insert the slides.

2. Select the slide located before the position where you want to insert the slides.

3. Select the **Insert** menu and select **Slides from Files**. The Slide Finder dialog box appears (see Figure 6.2).

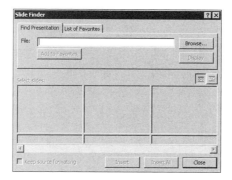

FIGURE 6.2
Use the Slide Finder dialog box to insert slides from another presentation.

4. Click the **Browse** button to display the Browse dialog box. In the Browse dialog box, locate the presentation that contains the slides that you want to insert into the current presentation (use the **Look In** drop-down arrow to switch drives, if necessary).

5. When you locate the presentation, double-click it.

6. The slides in the presentation appear in the Slide Finder's Select Slides box. To select the slides that you want to insert into the current presentation, click the first slide, and then hold down **Ctrl** and click any subsequent slides.

7. When you have selected all the slides you want to insert, click **Insert** (if you want to insert all the slides, click **Insert All**).

8. PowerPoint inserts the slides into the presentation at the point you originally selected. Click **OK** to close the Slide Finder dialog box.

CREATING SLIDES FROM A DOCUMENT OUTLINE

If you have created a document in Word that includes outline-style headings and numbered or bulleted lists, PowerPoint can pull the headings and the text from the document and create slides. To create slides from a document outline, follow these steps:

1. Choose the **Insert** menu, and then choose **Slides from Outline**. The Insert Outline dialog box appears (it is similar to the Open dialog box used to open a presentation or other file).

2. Use the Insert Outline dialog box to locate the document file you want to use.

3. Double-click the name of the document file.

PowerPoint then uses all the first-level headings to create slides for your presentation. Any text in the document below a first-level outline heading is added to the slide in an additional text box.

SELECTING SLIDES

In the following sections, you learn how to delete, copy, and move slides. However, before you can do anything with a slide, you must select it. To select slides, follow these directions:

• To select a single slide, click it.

• To select two or more contiguous slides in the Outline pane, click the first slide, and then hold down the **Shift** key while you click the last slide in the group.

- To select two or more contiguous slides in the Slides pane or the Slide Sorter view, place the mouse pointer in front of the first slide you want to select (not on it), and drag to select additional slides.

CAUTION

Don't Drag the Slide   If you are trying to select multiple, contiguous slides by dragging with the mouse, drag from in front of the first slide. Don't start dragging while pointing directly at the first slide because it will move the slide rather than highlight the remaining slides that you want to select.

- To select multiple noncontiguous slides in Slide Sorter view, click the first slide and hold down the **Ctrl** key while clicking subsequent slides in the group.

DELETING SLIDES

You can delete a slide from any view. To delete a slide, perform the following steps:

1. Select the slide you want to delete. You can delete multiple slides by selecting more than one slide (on the Outline or Slides pane or in the Slide Sorter view).

2. Choose the **Edit** menu, and then choose **Delete Slide**. The slide is removed from the presentation.

TIP

Use the Delete Key   You can quickly delete slides by selecting the slide or slides and then pressing the **Delete** key on the keyboard.

CAUTION

Oops! If you deleted a slide by mistake, you can get it back. Select **Edit**, **Undo**, or press **Ctrl+Z**. This works only if you do it immediately. You cannot undo the change if you exit PowerPoint and restart the application.

CUTTING, COPYING, AND PASTING SLIDES

In Lesson 7, "Rearranging Slides in a Presentation," you learn how to rearrange slides using the Slide Sorter and the Outline/Slides pane. Although dragging slides to new positions in the Slide Sorter is probably the easiest way to move slides, you can use the Cut, Copy, and Paste commands to move or copy slides in the presentation. Follow these steps:

1. Change to Slide Sorter view, or display Normal view and work with the Outline or Slides panes.

2. Select the slides you want to copy or cut.

3. Open the **Edit** menu and select **Cut** or **Copy** to either move or copy the slides, respectively, or you can use the **Cut** or **Copy** toolbar buttons.

TIP

Quick Cut or Copy From the keyboard, press **Ctrl+C** to copy or **Ctrl+X** to cut.

4. In Slide Sorter view, select the slide after which you want to place the cut or copied slides, or on the Outline pane, move the insertion point to the end of the text in the slide after which you want to insert the cut or copied slides.

5. Choose the **Edit** menu and choose **Paste**, or click the **Paste** toolbar button. PowerPoint inserts the cut or copied slides.

TIP

Keyboard Shortcut   You also can press **Ctrl+V** to paste an item that you cut or copied.

In this lesson, you learned how to insert, delete, cut, copy, and paste slides. In the next lesson, you learn how to rearrange the slides in your presentation.

LESSON 7

Rearranging Slides in a Presentation

In this lesson, you learn how to rearrange your slides using the Slide Sorter view and the Outline/Slides pane.

REARRANGING SLIDES IN SLIDE SORTER VIEW

Slide Sorter view shows thumbnails of the slides in your presentation. This enables you to view many if not all slides in the presentation at one time. Slide Sorter view provides the ideal environment for arranging slides in the appropriate order for your presentation. To rearrange slides in Slide Sorter view, perform the following steps:

1. If necessary, switch to Slide Sorter view by selecting **View** and then choosing **Slide Sorter**.

2. Place the mouse pointer on the slide you want to move.

3. Hold down the left mouse button and drag the slide to a new position in the presentation. The mouse pointer becomes a small slide box.

4. To position the slide, place the mouse before or after another slide in the presentation. A vertical line appears before or after the slide (see Figure 7.1).

FIGURE 7.1
Drag a slide in the presentation to a new position.

> **CAUTION**
>
> **Destination Not in View?** If you have more than just a few slides in your presentation, you might not be able to see the slide's final destination in the Slide Sorter. Don't worry; just drag the slide in the direction of the destination, and the Slide Sorter pane scrolls in that direction.

5. Release the mouse button. PowerPoint places the slide into its new position and shifts the surrounding slides to make room for the inserted slide.

You can copy a slide in Slide Sorter view as easily as you can move a slide. Simply hold down the **Ctrl** key while you drag the slide. When you release the mouse, PowerPoint inserts a copy of the selected slide into the presentation.

Although the Slides pane on the left side of the Normal view window does not provide as much workspace as the Slide Sorter, you can use the techniques discussed in this section to move or copy a slide. The Slides pane probably works best when you have only a few slides in the presentation. When you have a large number of slides, you might want to switch from the Normal view to the Slide Sorter view.

REARRANGING SLIDES IN THE OUTLINE PANE

In the Outline pane of the Normal view, you see the presentation as an outline that numbers each slide and shows its title and slide text. This provides you with a pretty good picture of the content and overall organization of your presentation. To rearrange the slides in your presentation using the Outline pane, follow these steps:

1. Switch to the Normal view by selecting **View**, **Normal**, or by clicking the **Normal** button on the bottom left of the PowerPoint window.

2. Click the slide number you want to move. This highlights the contents of the entire slide.

3. Place the mouse on the slide icon for that particular slide and drag the slide up or down within the presentation; then release the mouse.

TIP

Use the Up or Down Buttons   You also can move a slide in the outline by selecting the slide and then using the **Move Up** or **Move Down** buttons on the Outlining toolbar.

HIDING SLIDES

Before you give a presentation, you should try to anticipate any questions that your audience might have and be prepared to answer those questions. You might even want to create slides to support your answers to these questions and then keep the slides hidden until you need them. To hide one or more slides, perform the following steps:

1. In the Slide Sorter view or the Slides pane of the Normal view, select the slides you want to hide.

2. Select the **Slide Show** menu, and then select **Hide Slide**. In the Slide Sorter view and in the Slides pane, the hidden slide's number appears in a box with a line through it (see Figure 7.2).

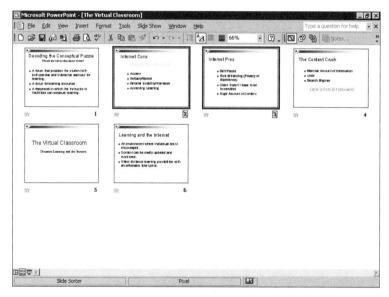

FIGURE 7.2
Hidden slides are denoted by a line through the slide number (slides 2 and 3 in this figure).

3. To unhide the slides, display or select the hidden slides, choose the **Slide Show** menu, and then select **Hide Slide**.

TIP

> **Right-Click Shortcut**   To quickly hide a slide, you can right-click it and select **Hide Slide** from the shortcut menu that appears. To unhide the slide, right-click it again and select **Hide Slide** again.

In this lesson, you learned how to rearrange the slides in a presentation and how to hide slides. In the next lesson, you learn how to add text to a slide and how to modify the text in text boxes.

LESSON 8
Adding and Modifying Slide Text

In this lesson, you learn how to add text boxes to a slide and change the text alignment and line spacing.

CREATING A TEXT BOX

As you learned in Lesson 4, "Working with Slides in Different Views," the text on slides resides in various text boxes. To edit the text in a text box, click in the box to place the insertion point, and then enter or edit the text within the box. If you want to add additional text to a slide that will not be contained in one of the text boxes already on the slide, you must create a new text box.

> **PLAIN ENGLISH**
>
> **Text Box** A text box acts as a receptacle for the text. Text boxes often contain bulleted lists, notes, and labels (used to point to important parts of illustrations).

To create a text box, perform the following steps:

1. If necessary, switch to the Normal view (select **View**, **Normal**). Use the Slides or Outline tab on the left of the workspace to select the slide on which you want to work. The slide appears in the Slide pane.

2. Click the **Text Box** button on the Drawing toolbar (if the Drawing toolbar isn't visible, right-click any toolbar and select **Drawing**).

3. Click the slide where you want the text box to appear. A
   small text box appears (see Figure 8.1). (It will expand as
   you type in it.)

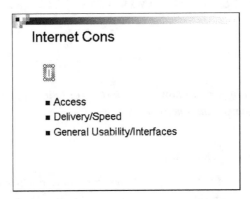

Internet Cons

■ Access
■ Delivery/Speed
■ General Usability/Interfaces

FIGURE 8.1
Text boxes can be inserted from the Drawing toolbar.

4. Type the text that you want to appear in the text box. Press
   Enter to start a new paragraph. Don't worry if the text box
   becomes too wide; you can resize it when you are finished
   typing.

5. When you are finished, click anywhere outside the text box
   to see how the text appears on the finished slide.

6. If you want, drag the text box's selection handles to resize it.
   If you make the box narrower, text within a paragraph might
   wrap to the next line.

If the text does not align correctly in the text box, see the section
"Changing the Text Alignment and Line Spacing," later in this lesson,
to learn how to change it.

TIP

> **Rotate a Text Box**   You can rotate a text box using the green rotation handle that appears at the top center of a selected text box. Place the mouse pointer on the handle, and the rotation icon appears. Use the mouse to drag the rotation handle to the desired position to rotate the box.

Changing Font Attributes

You can enhance your text by using the Font dialog box or by using various tools on the Formatting toolbar. Use the Font dialog box if you want to add several enhancements to your text at one time. Use the Formatting toolbar to add one font enhancement at a time.

PLAIN ENGLISH

> **Fonts, Styles, and Effects**   In PowerPoint, a font is a family of text that has the same design or typeface (for example, Arial or Courier). A style is a standard enhancement, such as bold or italic. An effect is a special enhancement, such as shadow or underline.

Using the Font Dialog Box

The font dialog box offers you control over all the attributes you can apply to text. Attributes such as strikethrough, superscript, subscript, and shadow are available as check boxes in this dialog box.

You can change the font of existing text or of text you are about to type by performing the following steps:

1. To change the font of existing text, select text by clicking and dragging the I-beam pointer over the text in a particular text box. If you want to change font attributes for all the text in a text box, select the text box (do not place the insertion point within the text box).

2. Choose the **Format** menu, and then choose **Font**. The Font dialog box appears, as shown in Figure 8.2.

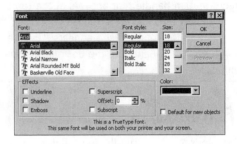

FIGURE 8.2
The Font dialog box enables you to change all the text attributes for selected text.

 TIP

> **Right-Click Quick**   You can right-click the text and select **Font** from the shortcut menu to open the Font dialog box.

3. From the Font list, select the font you want to use.

4. From the Font Style list, select any style you want to apply to the text, such as Bold or Italic. (To remove styles from text, select **Regular**.)

5. From the Size list, select any size in the list, or type a size directly into the box. (With TrueType fonts—the fonts marked with the TT logo—you can type any point size, even sizes that do not appear on the list.)

6. In the Effects box, select any special effects you want to add to the text, such as **Underline**, **Shadow**, or **Emboss**. You also can choose **Superscript** or **Subscript**, although these are less common.

7. To change the color of your text, click the arrow button to the right of the Color list and click the desired color. (For more

colors, click the **More Colors** option at the bottom of the
Color drop-down list; to select a color, use the dialog box
that appears.)

8. Click **OK** to apply the new look to your selected text.

TIP

> **Title and Object Area Text**   If you change a font on an
> individual slide, the font change applies only to that
> slide. To change the font for all the slides in the presen-
> tation, you must change the font on the Slide Master.
> Select **View**, point at **Master**, and then select **Slide
> Master**. Select a text area and perform the preceding
> steps to change the look of the text on all slides. Be
> careful, however, because these changes override any
> font styles that are supplied by the design template
> assigned to the presentation.

FORMATTING TEXT WITH THE FORMATTING TOOLBAR

The Formatting toolbar provides several buttons that enable you to
change font attributes for the text on your slides. It makes it easy for
you to quickly bold selected text or to change the color of text in a
text box.

To use the different Formatting toolbar font tools, follow these steps:

1. To change the look of existing text, select the text, or select a
   particular text box to change the look of all the text within
   that box.

2. To change fonts, open the **Font** drop-down list and click the
   desired font.

3. To change font size, open the **Font Size** drop-down list, click
   the desired size or type a size directly into the box, and then
   press **Enter**.

TIP

Incrementing the Type Size   To increase or decrease the text size to the next size up or down, click the **Increase Font Size** or **Decrease Font Size** buttons on the Formatting toolbar.

4. To add a style or effect to the text (bold, italic, underline, and/or shadow), click the appropriate button(s):

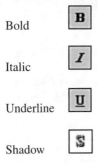

Bold

Italic

Underline

Shadow

As you have already seen, you can change the font color through the Font dialog box. You also can change it with the **Font Color** button on the Formatting toolbar. Just do the following:

1. Select the text for which you want to change the color.

2. Click the down-pointing arrow next to the **Font Color** button on the Formatting toolbar. A color palette appears (see Figure 8.3).

3. Do one of the following:

• Click a color on the palette to change the color of the selected text or the text box (the colors available are based on the design template and color scheme you have selected for the presentation).

• Click the **More Font Colors** option to display a Colors dialog box. Click a color on the Standard tab or use the Custom tab to create your own color. Then click **OK**. The color is applied to the text.

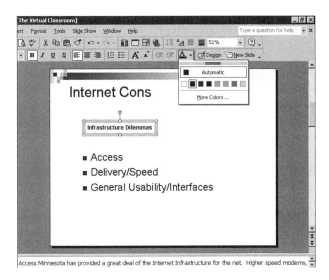

FIGURE 8.3
When you click the arrow next to the Font Colors button, a color palette appears.

COPYING TEXT FORMATS

If your presentation contains text with a format you want to use, you can copy that text's format and apply it to other text on the slide (or other slides). To copy text formats, perform the following steps:

1. Highlight the text with the format you want to use.

2. Click the **Format Painter** button on the toolbar. PowerPoint copies the format.

3. Drag the mouse pointer (which now looks like the Format Painter icon) across the text to which you want to apply the format.

If you want to apply a format to different text lines or even different text boxes on a slide or slides, double-click the **Format Painter** button. Use the mouse to apply styles to as many text items as you want. Then, click the **Format Painter** button again to turn off the feature.

CHANGING THE TEXT ALIGNMENT AND LINE SPACING

When you first type text, PowerPoint automatically places it against the left edge of the text box. To change the paragraph alignment, perform the following steps:

1. Click anywhere inside the paragraph you want to realign (a paragraph is any text line or wrapped text lines followed by a line break—created when you press the **Enter** key).

2. Select the **Format** menu, and then select **Alignment**. The Alignment submenu appears (see Figure 8.4).

3. Select **Align Left**, **Center**, **Align Right**, or **Justify** to align the paragraph as required.

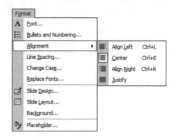

FIGURE 8.4
You can align each text line or paragraph in a text box.

TIP

Some Alignment Shortcuts   To quickly set left alignment, press **Ctrl+L** or click the **Align Left** button on the Formatting toolbar. For centered alignment, press **Ctrl+C** or click the **Center** button. For right alignment, press **Ctrl+R** or click the **Align Right** button.

If you want to align all the text in a text box in the same way (rather than aligning the text line by line), select the entire text box (click the box border), and then use the Alignment menu selection or the alignment buttons on the Formatting toolbar.

You also can change the spacing between text lines (remember, PowerPoint considers these to be paragraphs) in a text box. The default setting for line spacing is single space. To change the line spacing in a paragraph, perform these steps:

1. Click inside the paragraph you want to change, or select all the paragraphs you want to change by selecting the entire text box.

2. Select **Format**, **Line Spacing**. The Line Spacing dialog box appears, as shown in Figure 8.5.

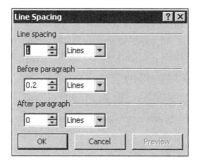

FIGURE 8.5
Select Format, Line Spacing to open the Line Spacing dialog box.

3. Click the arrow buttons to the right of any of the following text boxes to change the spacing for the following:

   • **Line Spacing**—This setting controls the space between the lines in a paragraph.

   • **Before Paragraph**—This setting controls the space between this paragraph and the paragraph that comes before it.

   • **After Paragraph**—This setting controls the space between this paragraph and the paragraph that comes after it.

4. After you make your selections, click **OK**.

PLAIN ENGLISH

Lines or Points?   The drop-down list box that appears to the right of each setting enables you to set the line spacing in lines or points. A line is the current line height (based on the current text size). A point is a unit commonly used to measure text. One point is 1/72 of an inch.

SELECTING, DELETING, AND MOVING A TEXT BOX

If you go back and click anywhere inside the text box, a selection box appears around it. If you click the selection box border, handles appear around the text box. You can drag the box's border to move the box or drag a handle to resize it. PowerPoint wraps the text automatically as needed to fit inside the box.

To delete a text box, select it (so that handles appear around it and no insertion point appears inside it), and then press the **Delete** key.

ADDING A WORDART OBJECT

PowerPoint comes with an add-on program called WordArt (which also is available in other Office applications, such as Word and Excel) that can help you create graphical text effects. You can create text wrapped in a circle and text that has 3D effects and other special alignment options. To insert a WordArt object onto a slide, perform the following steps:

1. In the Slide view, display the slide on which you want to place the WordArt object.

2. Click the **Insert** menu, point at **Picture**, and then select **WordArt**. The WordArt Gallery dialog box appears, showing many samples of WordArt types.

3. Click the sample that best represents the WordArt type you want, and click **OK**. The Edit WordArt Text dialog box appears (see Figure 8.6).

FIGURE 8.6
Enter the text, size, and font to be used into the Edit WordArt Text dialog box.

4. Choose a font and size from the respective drop-down lists.

5. Type the text you want to use into the Text box.

6. Click **OK**. PowerPoint creates the WordArt text on your slide, as shown in Figure 8.7.

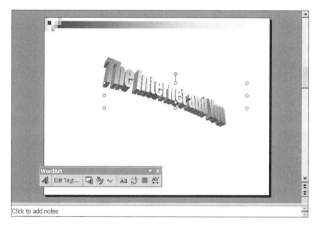

FIGURE 8.7
The WordArt toolbar is available when your WordArt object is selected.

After you have created WordArt, you have access to the WordArt toolbar, shown in Figure 8.7. You can use it to modify your WordArt. Table 8.1 summarizes the toolbar's buttons.

Table 8.1 Buttons on the WordArt Toolbar

To Do This	Click This
Insert a new WordArt object	
Edit the text, size, and font of the selected WordArt object	Edit Text...
Change the style of the current WordArt object in the WordArt Gallery	
Open a Format WordArt dialog box	
Change the shape of the WordArt	Abc
Make all the letters the same height	Aa
Toggle between vertical and horizontal text orientation	Ab b
Change the text alignment	
Change the spacing between letters	AV

You can rotate a WordArt object by dragging the rotation handle on the WordArt box. To edit the WordArt object, double-click it to display the WordArt toolbar and text entry box. Enter your changes, and then click outside the WordArt object. You can move the object by dragging its border or resize it by dragging a handle.

In this lesson, you learned how to add text to a slide, how to change the text alignment and spacing, and how to add WordArt objects. You also learned how to change the appearance of text by changing its font, size, style, and color. In addition, you learned how to copy text formats. In the next lesson, you learn how to use tables and tabs to create columns and lists.

LESSONS 9
Creating Columns, Tables, and Lists

In this lesson, you learn how to use tabs to create columns of text, bulleted lists, numbered lists, and other types of lists.

WORKING IN MULTIPLE COLUMNS

Depending on the type of slide you are creating, you might find the occasion to arrange text on a slide in multiple columns. PowerPoint provides three options for placing text into columns on a slide:

- You can use the Title and 2 Column slide layout to create a slide with side-by-side text columns.

- You can place tab stops in a single text box and press Tab to create columns for your text.

- You can use a table to create a two- or multiple-column text grid.

In this lesson, you learn about all these methods.

CREATING COLUMNS WITH A SLIDE LAYOUT

The easiest way to create columns of text is to change a slide's layout so that it provides side-by-side text boxes. Because the default layout for slides is a slide with a title box and a single text box, you probably will need to use the Slide Layout task pane to change its format to include two text columns. Follow these steps:

1. Create a new slide or select a slide that you want to format with the two-column layout (using the Outline or Slides pane).

2. Open the task pane (select **View**, **Task Pane**).

3. Select the task pane drop-down arrow and select **Slide Layout**.

4. Click the **Title and 2 Column** slide layout from the Text Layouts section of the Slide Layout task pane to format the slide (see Figure 9.1).

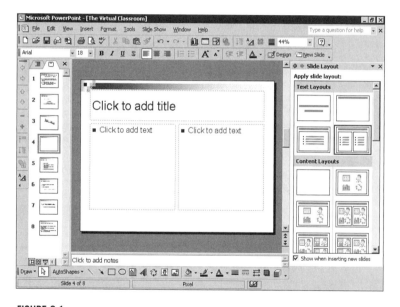

FIGURE 9.1
A two-column slide layout provides two panes in which to enter text.

You then can type the text that you want to appear in the two text boxes provided on the slide.

TIP

> **Place the Mouse on a Slide Layout to See Its Description**
> If you place the mouse on any of the slide layouts in the Slide Layout task pane, a tip appears, describing the layout.

USING TABS TO CREATE COLUMNS

You can create multiple columns in a text box using tab stops. To set the tabs for a multicolumn list, perform the following steps:

1. Open the presentation and select the slide with which you want to work in Slide view.

2. Create a text box for the text if one does not already exist (use the **Text Box** icon on the Drawing toolbar to create the text box).

TIP

> **Disappearing Text Box**   If you are creating a brand-new text box in step 2, type a few characters in it to anchor it to the slide. Otherwise, it disappears when you click outside it, meaning it no longer exists and you will have to insert it all over again.

3. Click anywhere inside the text box. After the insertion point is in the text box, you can set the tabs.

4. If you already typed text inside the text box, select the text.

5. If the ruler is not onscreen, select the **View** menu, and then select **Ruler** to display the ruler.

6. Click the **Tab** button at the left end of the ruler until it represents the type of tab you want to set (see Table 9.1 for more information on the type of tabs available).

7. Click in various positions on the ruler to place a tab stop using the type of tab you currently have selected. Figure 9.2 shows several tab stops that have been placed in a text box.

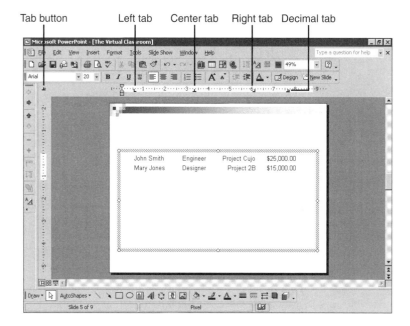

FIGURE 9.2
The ruler enables you to create tab stops for a text box.

8. Repeat steps 6 and 7 if you want to set different types of tab stops at different positions.

9. To change the position of an existing tab stop setting, drag it on the ruler to the desired position. To delete an existing tab stop setting, drag it off the ruler.

10. (Optional) To hide the ruler, select the **View** menu and then select **Ruler**.

Table 9.1   Tab Button Stop Types

Button Appearance	Tab Stop Type
L	Aligns the left end of the line against the tab stop.
⊥	Centers the text on the tab stop.
⅃	Aligns the right end of the line against the tab stop.
⊥	Aligns the tab stop on a period. This is called a decimal tab and is useful for aligning a column of numbers that uses decimal points.

CREATING A TABLE

Tables can also be used to place text in side-by-side columns. You can create tables that provide two columns, three columns, or any number of columns that you require. Tables are also very useful when you want to display numerical information in a grid layout or information that you want to arrange in rows. A table is a collection of intersecting columns and rows. The block created when a column and a row intersects often is referred to as a *cell*. The easiest way to create a table on a slide is to use the Table layout. Follow these steps:

1. Create a new slide or select a slide that you want to format with the Table layout (using the Outline or Slides pane).

2. Open the task pane (select **View**, **Task Pane**).

3. Select the task pane drop-down arrow and select **Slide Layout**.

4. Scroll down through the slide layouts in the task pane, and then click the **Title and Table** layout. This assigns the Title and Table layout to the current slide (see Figure 9.3).

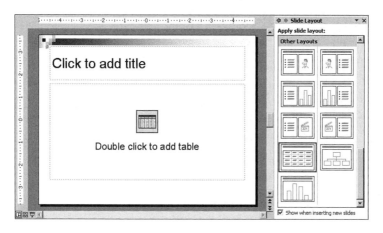

FIGURE 9.3
The Table layout enables you to place a table on a slide.

5. After you assign the Title and Table layout to the slide, you can set the number of columns and rows for the table. Double-click the Table icon on the slide. The Insert dialog box appears.

6. Specify the number of columns and rows that you want in the table, and then click **OK**. The table is placed on the slide.

You also can insert a table onto an existing slide. This enables you to include a table on a slide where you don't want to change the slide's layout as discussed in the preceding steps. Follow these steps:

1. Display the slide on which you want to place the table.

2. Select the **Insert** menu and choose **Table**. The Insert Table dialog box appears.

3. Enter the number of columns and rows that you want to have in the table.

4. Click **OK**. The table appears on the slide.

When the table appears on the slide, the Tables and Borders toolbar also appears in the PowerPoint window (we will use this toolbar in a moment). After you have a table on a slide, you can work with it like this:

- Click inside a table cell and enter your text. You can move from cell to cell by pressing **Tab** to go forward or **Shift+Tab** to go back. Enter text as needed.

- If you need to resize the table, drag a selection handle, the same as you would any object.

- To adjust the row height or column width, position the mouse pointer on a line between two rows or columns and drag. The mouse pointer becomes a sizing tool when you place it on any column or row border.

- If you want to change the style of the borders around certain cells on the table (or the entire table), select the cells (drag the mouse across the cells to select them). You then can use the buttons on the Tables and Borders toolbar to change the border attributes (see Figure 9.4). Use the Border Style button and the Border Width button to change the border style and border line weight, respectively. If you want to change the border color, use the Border Color button. The buttons on the Tables and Borders toolbar adjust the thickness and style of the table gridlines.

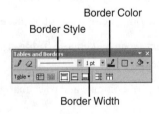

FIGURE 9.4
Border attributes for the table can be changed using the buttons on the Tables and Borders toolbar.

To make a table appear to be multiple columns of text without the table borders, turn off all the gridlines in the table. To do so, select all the cells in the table; then, right-click and choose **Borders and Fill**. In the Format Table dialog box that appears (see Figure 9.5), click each of the border buttons provided on the table diagram to turn the border off for each side of each cell in the table. Click **OK** to return to the table.

FIGURE 9.5
The Format Table dialog box can be used to control border lines and other table attributes.

MAKING A BULLETED LIST

When you enter new slides into a presentation, the default layout provides a title box and a text box that is set up as a simple bulleted list. Therefore, just creating a new slide creates a bulleted list.

You can turn off the bullets in front of any paragraphs by selecting the paragraphs and clicking the **Bullets** button on the Formatting toolbar to toggle the bullets off. If you want to remove the bullets from all the paragraphs (remember, a text line followed by the Enter key is a paragraph), select the entire text box and click the **Bullets** button.

When you insert your own text boxes using the Text Box button on the Drawing toolbar, the text does not have bullets by default. You can add your own bullets by following these steps:

1. Click the text line (paragraph) that you want to format for bullets. If you want to add bullets to all the text lines in a text box, select the text box.

2. Select the **Format** menu, and then select **Bullets and Numbering**. The Bullets and Numbering dialog box appears (see Figure 9.6).

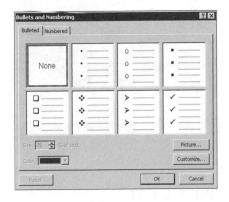

FIGURE 9.6
The Bullets and Numbering dialog box enables you to select the bullets for your bulleted items.

TIP

Quick Bullets   To bypass the dialog box, click the **Bullets** button on the Formatting toolbar to insert a bullet, or right-click and select **Bullet** from the shortcut menu. You can click the **Bullets** button again to remove the bullet.

3. Select the bullet style you want to use from the list Power-Point provides.

4. Click **OK**. PowerPoint formats the selected text into a bulleted list. (If you press **Enter** at the end of a bulleted paragraph, the next paragraph starts with a bullet.)

TIP

Create Your Own Bullets   You can select from a number of pictures and symbols for the bullets that you apply to text in PowerPoint. In the Bullets and Numbering dialog box, select **Picture** to choose from several bullet pictures. Select **Customize** to select from several bullet symbols.

WORKING WITH NUMBERED LISTS

Numbered lists are like bulleted lists, except they have sequential numbers instead of symbols. You can convert any paragraphs to a numbered list by selecting them and clicking the **Numbering** button on the Formatting toolbar. Select the paragraphs again and click the **Numbering** button again to toggle the numbering off.

You also can create numbered lists with the Bullets and Numbering dialog box, the same as you did with bullets. Follow these steps:

1. Select the paragraphs that you want to convert to a numbered list.

2. Choose **Format**, and then select **Bullets and Numbering**.

3. Click the **Numbered** tab on the dialog box. The numbered list styles appear (see Figure 9.7).

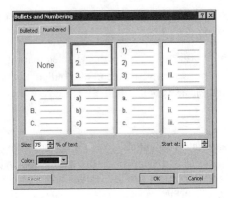

FIGURE 9.7
*Choose the numbering style you want or turn numbering off by choosing **None**.*

4. Click the number style you want for your list.

5. (Optional) Change the Size and/or Color of the numbers.

6. (Optional) If you want the list to start at a number other than 1, enter it into the **Start At** text box.

7. Click **OK**.

In this lesson, you learned how to create columns with slide layouts, tabs, and tables, and how to work with bulleted and numbered lists. In the next lesson, you learn how to get help in PowerPoint.

LESSON 10
Getting Help in Microsoft PowerPoint

In this lesson, you learn how to access and use the Help system in Microsoft PowerPoint.

HELP: WHAT'S AVAILABLE?

Microsoft PowerPoint supplies a Help system that makes it easy for you to look up information on PowerPoint commands and features as you work on your presentations. Because every person is different, the Help system can be accessed in several ways. You can

- Ask a question in the Ask a Question box.

- Ask the Office Assistant for help.

- Get help on a particular element you see onscreen with the What's This? tool.

- Use the Contents, Answer Wizard, and Index tabs in the Help window to get help.

- Access the Office on the Web feature to view Web pages containing help information (if you are connected to the Internet

USING THE ASK A QUESTION BOX

The Ask a Question box is a new way to access the PowerPoint Help system. It also is the easiest way to quickly get help. An Ask a Question box resides at the top right of the PowerPoint window.

For example, if you are working in PowerPoint and want to view information on how to create a chart, type **How do I create a chart?** into the Ask a Question box. Then, press the **Enter** key. A shortcut menu appears below the Ask a Question box, as shown in Figure 10.1.

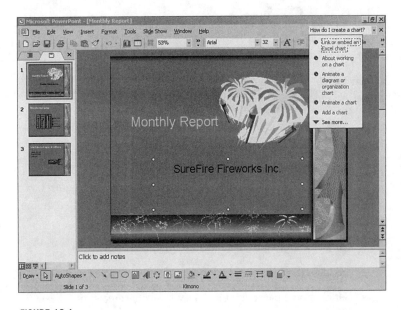

FIGURE 10.1
The Ask a Question box provides a list of Help topics that you can quickly access.

To access one of the Help topics supplied on the shortcut menu, click that particular topic. The Help window opens with topical matches for that keyword or phrase displayed.

In the case of the chart question used in Figure 10.1, you could select **Add a chart** from the shortcut menu that appears. This opens the help window and displays help on how to add a chart to a slide (see Figure 10.2).

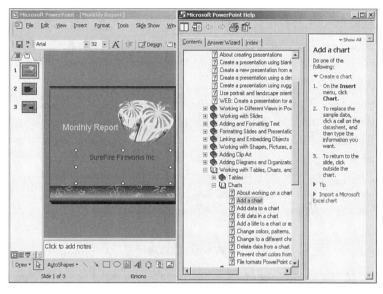

FIGURE 10.2
The Ask a Question box provides a quick way to access the Help window.

In the Help window, you can use the links provided to navigate the Help system. You also can use the Contents, Answer Wizard, and Index tabs to find additional information or look for new information in the Help window. You learn more about these different Help window tabs later in this lesson.

USING THE OFFICE ASSISTANT

Another way to get help in PowerPoint is to use the Office Assistant. The Office Assistant supplies the same type of access to the Help system as the Ask a Question box. You ask the Office Assistant a question, and it supplies you with a list of possible answers that provide links to various Help topics. The next two sections discuss how to use the Office Assistant.

TURNING THE OFFICE ASSISTANT ON AND OFF

By default, the Office Assistant is off. To show the Office Assistant in your application window, select the **Help** menu, and then select **Show the Office Assistant**.

You also can quickly hide the Office Assistant if you no longer want it in your application window. Right-click the Office Assistant and select **Hide**. If you want to get rid of the Office Assistant completely so it isn't activated when you select the Help feature, right-click the Office Assistant and select **Options**. Clear the **Use the Office Assistant** check box, and then click **OK**. You can always get the Office Assistant back by selecting **Help**, **Show Office Assistant**.

ASKING THE OFFICE ASSISTANT A QUESTION

When you click the Office Assistant, a balloon appears above it. Type a question into the text box. For example, you might type `How do I print?` for help printing your work. Click the **Search** button.

The Office Assistant provides some topics that reference Help topics in the Help system. Click the option that best describes what you're trying to do. The Help window appears, containing more detailed information. Use the Help window to get the exact information you need.

Although not everyone likes the Office Assistant because having it enabled means it is always sitting in your PowerPoint window, it can be useful at times. For example, when you access particular features in PowerPoint, the Office Assistant can automatically provide you with context-sensitive help on that particular feature. If you are brand new to Microsoft PowerPoint, you might want to use the Office Assistant to help you learn the various features that PowerPoint provides.

TIP

Select Your Own Office Assistant   Several different Office
Assistants are available in Microsoft Office. To select
your favorite, click the Office Assistant and select the
Options button. On the Office Assistant dialog box that
appears, select the **Gallery** tab. Click the **Next** button
repeatedly to see the different Office Assistants that are
available. When you locate the assistant you want to
use, click **OK**.

USING THE HELP WINDOW

You can forgo either the Type a Question box or the Office Assistant
and get your help directly from the Help window. To directly access
the Help window, select **Help** and then **Microsoft PowerPoint Help**.
You also can press the **F1** key to make the Help window appear.

The Help window provides two panes. The pane on the left provides
three tabs: Contents, Answer Wizard, and Index. The right pane of the
Help window provides either help subject matter or links to different
Help topics. It functions a great deal like a Web browser window. You
click a link to a particular body of information and that information
appears in the right pane.

The first thing you should do is maximize the Help window by clicking its **Maximize** button. This makes it easier to locate and read the
information that the Help system provides (see Figure 10.3).

When you first open the Help window, a group of links in the right
pane provides you with access to information about new PowerPoint
features and other links, such as a link to Microsoft's Office Web site.
Next, take a look at how you can take advantage of different ways to
find information in the Help window: the Contents tab, the Answer
Wizard tab, and the Index tab.

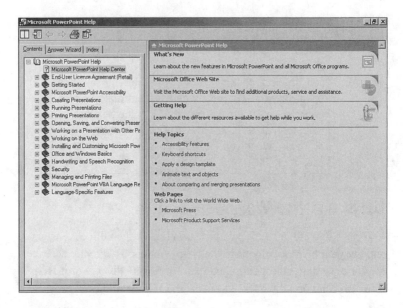

FIGURE 10.3
The Help window provides access to all the help information provided for PowerPoint.

TIP

> **View the Help Window Tabs**   If you don't see the different tabs in the Help window, click the **Show** button on the Help window toolbar.

USING THE CONTENTS TAB

The Contents tab of the Help system is a series of books you can open. Each book has one or more Help topics in it, which appear as pages or chapters. To select a Help topic from the Contents tab, follow these steps:

1. In the Help window, click the **Contents** tab on the left side of the Help window.

2. Find the book that describes, in broad terms, the subject for which you need help.

3. Double-click the book, and a list of Help topics appears below the book, as shown in Figure 10.4.

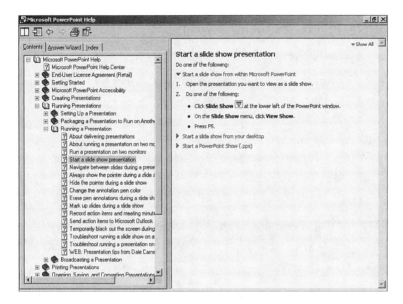

FIGURE 10.4
Use the Contents tab to browse through the various Help topics.

4. Click one of the pages (the pages contain a question mark) under a Help topic to display it in the right pane of the Help window.

5. When you finish reading a topic, select another topic on the Contents tab or click the Help window's **Close** (**x**) button to exit Help.

USING THE ANSWER WIZARD

Another way to get help in the Help window is to use the Answer Wizard. The Answer Wizard works the same as the Ask a Question box or the Office Assistant; you ask the wizard questions and it supplies you with a list of topics that relate to your question. You click one of the choices provided to view help in the Help window.

To get help using the Answer Wizard, follow these steps:

1. Click the **Answer Wizard** tab in the Help window.

2. Type your question into the What Would You Like to Do? box. For example, you might type the question, `How do I insert a new slide?`

3. After typing your question, click the **Search** button. A list of topics appears in the Select Topic to Display box. Select a particular topic, and its information appears in the right pane of the Help window, as shown in Figure 10.5.

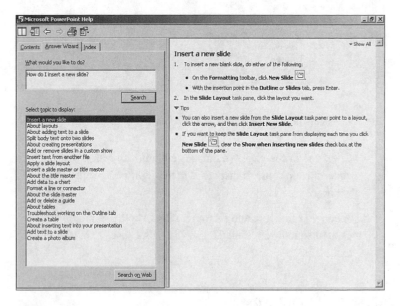

FIGURE 10.5
Search for help in the Help window using the Answer Wizard tab.

TIP

> **Print Help**   If you want to print information provided in the Help window, click the **Print** icon on the Help toolbar.

USING THE INDEX

The index is an alphabetical listing of every Help topic available. It's like an index in a book.

Follow these steps to use the index:

1. In the Help window, click the **Index** tab.

2. Type the first few letters of the topic for which you are look-ing. The Or Choose Keywords box jumps quickly to a key-word that contains the characters you have typed.

3. Double-click the appropriate keyword in the keywords box. Topics for that keyword appear in the Choose a Topic box.

4. Click a topic to view help in the right pane of the Help window.

TIP

> **Navigation Help Topics**   You can move from topic to topic in the right pane of the Help window by clicking the various links that are provided there. Some topics are collapsed. Click the triangle next to the topic to expand the topic and view the help provided.

GETTING HELP WITH SCREEN ELEMENTS

If you wonder about the function of a particular button or tool on the PowerPoint screen, wonder no more. Just follow these steps to learn about this part of Help:

1. Select **Help** and then **What's This?** or press **Shift+F1**. The mouse pointer changes to an arrow with a question mark.

2. Click the screen element for which you want help. A box
   appears explaining the element.

TIP

Take Advantage of ScreenTips   Another Help feature provided by the Office applications is the ScreenTip. All the
buttons on the different toolbars provided by PowerPoint
have a ScreenTip. Place the mouse on a particular button or icon, and the name of the item (which often helps
you determine its function) appears in a ScreenTip.

In this lesson you learned how to access the PowerPoint Help feature.
In the next lesson you will learn how to add clip art to your slides.

LESSON 11
Adding Graphics to a Slide

In this lesson, you learn how to add PowerPoint clip art to your presentations and how to add images from other sources.

INTRODUCING THE INSERT CLIP ART TASK PANE

With the introduction of the task pane in Office XP, accessing clip art and other graphics for use on your PowerPoint slides has changed dramatically from earlier versions of Office. The Insert Clip Art task pane provides you with a search engine that you can use to search for clip art, photographs, movies, and sounds that are stored on your computer. You also can search for clip art and other items using Microsoft's online clip library. (You must be connected to the Internet when using PowerPoint to access the Microsoft online library.)

Figure 11.1 shows the Insert Clip Art task pane. You can use this task pane to search for and insert images onto your slides, or you can take advantage of slides that use a layout that contains a placeholder for images and clip art.

You learn about using the Clip Art task pane and slide layouts that provide image placeholders in this lesson. In Lesson 12, "Adding Sounds and Movies to a Slide," you take a look at using the Clip Art task pane to add movies and slides to your PowerPoint slides.

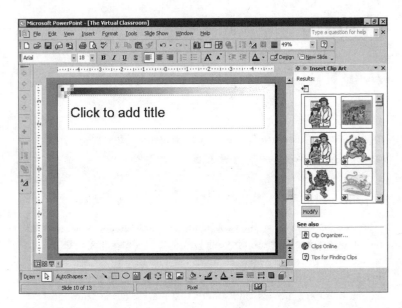

FIGURE 11.1
The Insert Clip Art task pane manages pictures, motion clips, and sounds—all in one convenient place.

> **PLAIN ENGLISH**
>
> **Clip Art**   A collection of previously created images or pictures that you can place on a slide. Microsoft Office provides clip art and other media types, such as movies and sounds.

You can open the Clip Art task pane in any of these ways:

- Click the **Insert Clip Art** button on the Drawing toolbar.

- Select the **Insert** menu, point at **Picture**, and then choose **Clip Art**.

- Open the task pane, click the task pane drop-down arrow, and then select **Insert Clip Art** to switch to the Insert Clip Art task pane.

When you use the Insert Clip Art task pane, you search for images by keywords. In the following sections, you take a look at inserting clip art from the task pane and learn how you can insert clip art using some of the slide layouts (that provide a clip art placeholder on the slide).

TIP

Clip Organizer Scan   The first time you open the Insert Clip Art task pane, PowerPoint prompts you to allow the Clip Organizer (which is discussed later in the lesson) to search your hard drive. Clip Organizer then creates category folders and image indexes from the clip art and images that it finds there. Click **Yes** to allow this process to take place.

INSERTING AN IMAGE FROM THE TASK PANE

As previously mentioned, the Insert Clip Art task pane allows you to search for clip art files using keywords. If you wanted to search for clip art of cats, you would search for the word "cats." To insert a piece of the clip art using the task pane, follow these steps:

1. Select the slide on which you want to place the image so that it appears in the Slide pane.

2. Select **Insert**, point at **Picture**, and then select **Clip Art**. The Insert Clip Art task pane appears.

3. Type keywords into the Search Text box in the task pane that will be used to find your clip art images.

4. Click the **Search** button. Images that match your search criteria appear in the task pane as thumbnails.

5. In the Results list, locate the image that you want to place on the slide. Then click the image, and the clip art is placed on the slidementioned, (see Figure 11.2).

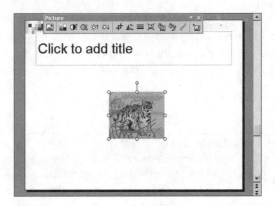

FIGURE 11.2
Click the clip art thumbnail to place the image onto the current slide.

You can use the sizing handles on the image to size the clip art box. Or you can drag the clip art box to a new location on the slide.

INSERTING AN IMAGE FROM AN IMAGE BOX

Another way you can add clip art images to a slide in your presentation is to create the slide using a slide format that supplies a clip art placeholder box on the slide. These slide layout types are called content layouts because they make it easy to insert objects such as clip art, charts, and other items onto a slide. You then can use the object placeholder on the slide to access the clip art library and insert a particular image onto the slide.

Follow these steps:

1. Create a new slide or select the slide to which you want to assign a layout that contains a clip art placeholder box.

2. Open the task pane (**View**, **Task Pane**), and then click the task pane drop-down menu and select **Slide Layout** (the Slide Layout task pane automatically opens if you've just created a new slide).

3. Scroll down through the layouts provided until you locate either the Content layout or the Text and Content layout. Both of these layout categories provide slide layouts that contain object placeholders or object placeholders and text boxes, respectively.

4. Select the layout that best suits the purpose of your slide (see Figure 11.3).

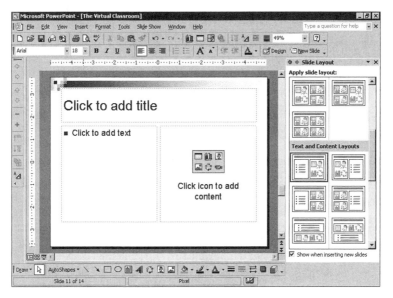

FIGURE 11.3
Select a slide layout that contains an object placeholder.

5. The slide layout you choose provides you with a placeholder box that contains icons for tables, charts, clip art, and other objects. Click the **Insert Clip Art** icon in the placeholder box. The Select Picture dialog box appears (see Figure 11.4).

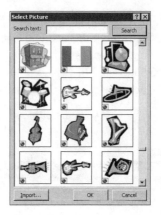

FIGURE 11.4
*The Select Picture dialog box enables you to scroll through or search through the
entire clip art and image library on your computer.*

6. Scroll down through the list of clip art and other images to
   find a particular image (the list will be lengthy because it
   includes all the Office Clip Art and any other images that
   were located on your computer when the Clip Organizer cata-
   loged the images on your computer).

7. You can search for particular images by keyword. Type the
   search criteria into the Search Text box, and then click
   Search. Images that match the search criteria appear in the
   Select Picture dialog box.

8. Click the picture thumbnail that you want to place on the
   slide. Then click **OK**.

PowerPoint places the image on the slide in the object placeholder
box. You can size the box or move it on the slide.

INSERTING A CLIP FROM A FILE

If you have an image stored on your computer that you would like to
place on a slide, you can insert the picture directly from the file. This

means that you don't have to use the Insert Clip Art task pane to search for and then insert the image.

To place a graphical image on a slide directly from a file, follow these steps:

1. Select the slide on which the image will be placed.

2. Select the **Insert** menu, point at **Picture**, and then select **From File**. The Insert Picture dialog box appears (see Figure 11.5).

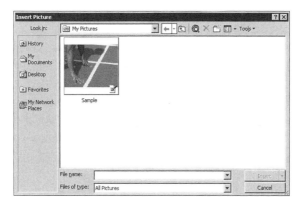

FIGURE 11.5
Use the Insert Picture dialog box to place images on a slide.

3. Select the picture you want to use. You can view all the picture files in a particular location as thumbnails. Select the **Views** button, and then select **Thumbnails** on the menu that appears.

4. Click **Insert** to place the image on the slide.

If the picture is too big or too small, you can drag the selection handles (the small squares) around the edge of the image to resize it. Hold down the **Shift** key to proportionally resize the image (this maintains the height/width ratio of the image so that you cannot stretch or distort it). See Lesson 13, "Working with PowerPoint Objects," for more details about resizing and cropping images and other objects on a slide.

TIP

> **Link It Up**   You can link a graphic to the presentation so that, whenever the original changes, the version in the presentation changes, too. Just open the drop-down list on the **Insert** button in the Insert Picture dialog box (refer to Figure 11.5) and choose **Link to File**.

MANAGING IMAGES IN THE CLIP ORGANIZER

Occasionally, you might want to add or delete clip art images from folders on your computer. Managing images is accomplished using the Clip Organizer. When you install Microsoft PowerPoint or Microsoft Office XP (using the default installation), a fairly large library of clip art is placed on your hard drive in different category folders. You can manage these clip art images and other images on your computer, such as scanned images or pictures from a digital camera. To open the Clip Organizer, follow these steps:

1. With the Insert Clip Art task pane open in the PowerPoint window, click the **Clip Organizer** link near the bottom of the task pane to open the Clip Organizer.

2. To view the clip art categories PowerPoint (or Office) has provided, click the plus sign (+) to the left of the Office Collections folder in the Collection list (this folder is located on the left side of the Clip Organizer window). Category folders such as Academic, Agriculture, and so on will appear in the Collection list.

3. Click one of the category folders to view the clip art that it holds (for example, click **Food**). The clip art in that category folder appears in the Clip Organizer window (see Figure 11.6).

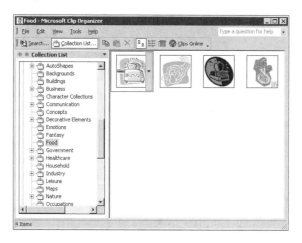

FIGURE 11.6
Use the Clip Organizer to manage your clip art and image files.

Not only does the Clip Organizer allow you to browse the various clip art and other images on your computer, it allows you to copy, delete, or move images. For example, if you find an image you no longer want to store on your computer, select the image in the Clip Organizer window and press **Delete**. A dialog box appears, letting you know that this image will be removed from all collections on the computer. Click **OK** to delete the image.

You also can use the Clip Organizer to copy or move clip art images from a location on your hard drive to one of the clip art collections. Locate the images you want to move or copy to a particular collection, and then select them.

To move the images to a collection, Select the **Edit** menu, and then **Move to Collection**. The Move to Collection dialog box appears (see Figure 11.7). Select a location in the dialog box and click **OK** to move the selected image or images.

FIGURE 11.7
You can move images from one location to another using the Clip Organizer.

You also can copy images to a new location using the Copy to Collection command. Select the images in a particular folder on your computer using the Clip Organizer window. Select the **Edit** menu and then **Copy to Collection**. Select a location in the Copy to Collection dialog box where you would like to place copies of the images, and then click **OK**.

In this lesson, you learned how to add clip art and other images to your slides. In the next lesson, you learn how to add sounds and videos to your PowerPoint slides.

Lesson 12
Adding Sounds and Movies to a Slide

In this lesson, you learn how to add sound and video clips to a PowerPoint presentation.

Working with Sounds and Movies

A great way to add some interest to your PowerPoint presentations is to add sounds and movies to your slides. Sounds enable you to emphasize certain slides, and movie animations can add humor and style to your presentations. Next, you take a look at adding sounds and then adding movie animations to your slides.

Including Sounds in a Presentation

Sounds can be used to add emphasis to information on slides or to add some auditory interest to your presentation. You can place sound files on your slides in two different ways:

- You can insert a sound clip as an icon on a slide. When you click the icon, the sound plays.

- You can assign a sound to another object on a slide so that the sound plays when you click the object. For example, you could assign a sound to an image. When you click the image, the sound plays (sounds added to PowerPoint animations play when the animation plays).

INSERTING A SOUND ONTO A SLIDE

To insert a sound clip as an object onto a slide, you can either use the Insert Clip Art task pane or insert the sound as a file. The Clip Art task pane can provide you only with sound files that have been included in the Office clip art library or sound files that you have added to your collection using the Clip Organizer (which is discussed in the previous lesson). Any sound file that you have recorded or otherwise acquired can be inserted as a file.

To insert a sound clip from the Clip Art task pane, follow these steps:

1. Select the slide on which you will place the sound, so that it appears in the Slide pane.

2. Select **Insert**, point at **Movies and Sounds**, and then select **Sound from Media Gallery**. The Insert Clip Art task pane appears with a list of sound files.

3. To preview a particular sound file, point at the file and click the menu arrow that appears. Select **Preview/Properties** from the menu. The Preview/Properties dialog box for that sound file appears (see Figure 12.1).

FIGURE 12.1
Preview a sound clip before placing it onto a slide.

4. To play the sound, click the **Play** button on the left side of the dialog box. When you have finished previewing a sound file, click **Close** to close the Preview/Properties dialog box.

5. When you are ready to insert a sound file onto the slide, click the sound file on the task pane.

6. A dialog box opens, asking you whether you want the sound to play automatically when you run the slide show. Click **Yes** to have the sound played automatically. Click **No** to set up the sound so that you will have to click it during the slide show to play the sound.

Regardless of whether you choose to have PowerPoint play the sound automatically, it appears as a sound icon on the slide.

If you have recorded a sound file or have acquired a sound file that you want to use on a slide without using the Insert Clip Art task pane, you can insert it as a file. To insert a sound clip from a file, follow these steps:

1. Choose the **Insert** menu, point at **Movies and Sounds**, and then choose **Sound from File**.

2. In the Insert Sound dialog box, navigate to the drive and folder containing the sound you want to use (see Figure 12.2).

3. Select the sound clip and click **OK**.

4. A dialog box opens, asking you whether you want the sound to play automatically when you run the slide show. As with the earlier steps, you can click **Yes** to have the sound played automatically or **No** to set up the sound so that you will have to click it during the slide show to play the sound.

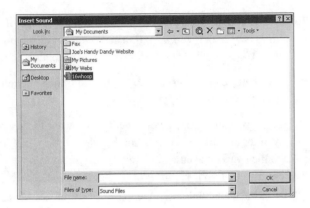

FIGURE 12.2
Choose the sound clip you want to include on your slide.

Like before, the sound file appears on the slide as a sound icon. If you want to play the sound file on the slide, right-click the sound icon and select **Play Sound** from the shortcut menu.

ASSOCIATING A SOUND WITH ANOTHER OBJECT ON THE SLIDE

If you want to avoid having a sound icon on your slide, you can associate the sound with some other object already on the slide, such as a graphic. To do so, follow these steps:

1. Right-click the object (such as a clip art image) to which you want to assign the sound.

2. Choose **Action Settings** from the shortcut menu. The Actions Settings dialog box appears.

3. If you want the sound to play when the object is pointed at, click the **Mouse Over** tab. Otherwise, click the **Mouse Click** tab. The Mouse Click option requires that the sound icon be clicked on for the sound to play.

4. Click the **Play Sound** check box. A drop-down list of sounds becomes available (see Figure 12.3).

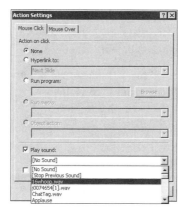

FIGURE 12.3
Choose a sound to be associated with the object.

5. Open the **Play Sound** drop-down list and choose the sound
   you want.

   If the sound you want is not on the list, choose **Other Sound**
   and locate the sound using the Add Sound dialog box that
   appears. Select the sound from there, and click **OK**.

6. When you have chosen the sound you want, click **OK** to
   close the Action Settings dialog box.

Now, when you are giving the presentation, you can play the sound
by either clicking or pointing at the object (depending on how you
configured the sound to play). To test this, jump to the Slide Show
view (Select the **View** menu and click **Slide Show**) and try it out.
Press **Esc** to return to the Normal view when you are finished testing
the sound file.

PLACING A MOVIE ONTO A SLIDE

The procedure for placing a movie onto a slide is very much the same
as that for a sound. You can place a movie using the Insert Clip Art

task pane or from a file. You will find that the task pane Clip Gallery provides several movies that can be used to add interest to your slides. To insert a movie onto a slide, follow these steps:

1. Choose the **Insert** menu, point at **Movies and Sounds**, and then select **Movies from Clip Gallery**.

2. Scroll through the movies listed on the Insert Clip Art task pane.

3. Point at a movie clip you want to preview. Click the menu arrow that appears and select **Preview/Properties**. The Preview Properties dialog box for the movie appears.

4. PowerPoint previews the movie on the left side of the dialog box (see Figure 12.4). If you want to place a caption onto the movie clip, click in the **Caption** box below the Preview pane and type a caption.

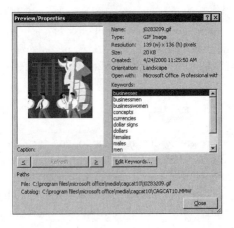

FIGURE 12.4
Preview a movie in the Preview/Properties dialog box.

5. Click **Close** to close the Preview/Properties dialog box. To insert the movie into your slide, click the movie in the task pane.

After the movie icon is in place on your slide, you can size the movie box using the usual sizing handles or move it to another position on the slide. If you want to test view the movie on the slide, jump to the Slide Show view (select the **View** menu and then click **Slide Show**) and try it out. Press **Esc** to return to the Normal view when you are finished testing the movie.

PLAIN ENGLISH

> **Clip Gallery Movies Really Aren't Movies**   The clip gallery movies provided by Microsoft Office are really just animations. They are designed to play automatically when the slide containing the image is opened during a slide show.

You can also place actual videos on a slide as a file. This enables you to place video captures that you have created or video files from other sources. Follow these steps:

1. Choose the **Insert** menu, point at **Movies and Sounds**, and then choose **Movie from File**.

2. In the Insert Sound dialog box that appears, navigate to the drive and folder containing the movie file you want to use.

3. Select the file and click **OK** to place it on the slide.

4. A dialog box appears (see Figure 12.5) that allows you to have the movie play when the slide appears in the slide show. Click **Yes**. To require that you click the movie's icon to make it play during the slide show, click **No**.

FIGURE 12.5
You can choose how the movie will be handled during the slide show.

After you make your selection in step 4, PowerPoint places the movie onto the slide. To preview the video file on the slide, right-click the video icon and select **Play Movie**.

In this lesson, you learned how to place sounds and movies in your presentation for great multimedia effects. In the next lesson, you learn how to select objects; work with object layers; and cut, copy, and paste objects.

LESSON 13
Working with PowerPoint Objects

In this lesson, you learn how to manipulate objects on your slides, such as clip art and other items, to create impressive presentations.

SELECTING OBJECTS

In the previous two lessons, you learned about inserting clip art, image files, sound files, and movie files onto the slides of your PowerPoint presentation. Any type of special content that you place on a slide is called an *object*. In addition to the object types just listed, objects could also be items from other Office applications. For example, you could create an object on a slide that actually is an Excel worksheet or chart (for more about sharing information between Office applications see Lesson 14, "Using Microsoft Office Objects in Presentations.")

After you select an object, you can do all kinds of things to it, such as copying, moving, deleting, or resizing it. The following is a review of ways you can select objects on a PowerPoint slide:

- To select a single object, click it. (If you click text, a frame appears around the text. Click the frame to select the text object.)

- To select more than one object, hold down the **Ctrl** or **Shift** key while clicking each object. Handles appear around the selected objects, as shown in Figure 13.1 (this temporarily groups the objects so that you can move them all simultaneously on the slide).

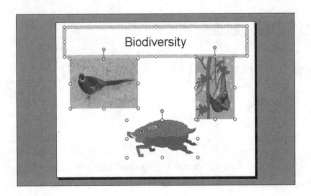

FIGURE 13.1
You can select multiple objects on a slide.

• To deselect selected objects, click anywhere outside the
  selected object or objects.

TIP

Select Objects Tool   Use the Select Objects tool on the
Drawing toolbar to drag a selection box around several
objects you want to select. When you release the mouse
button, PowerPoint selects all the objects inside the box.

WORKING WITH LAYERS OF OBJECTS

As you place objects onscreen, they might start to overlap, creating
layers of objects where the lower layers are often difficult or impossible to select. To move objects in layers, perform the following steps:

1. Click the object you want to move up or down in the stack. If
   the Drawing toolbar is not available in the PowerPoint window, right-click on any toolbar and select **Drawing** from the
   menu that appears.

2. Click the **Draw** button on the Drawing toolbar to open the
   Draw menu, and select **Order**, as shown in Figure 13.2.

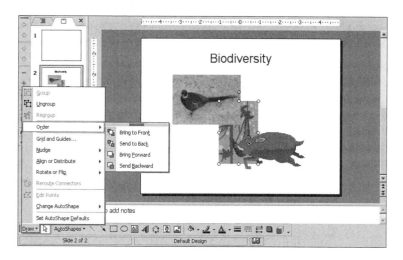

FIGURE 13.2
Use the Draw menu on the Drawing toolbar to change the layer on which a graphic appears on your slide.

3. Select one of the following options:

- **Bring to Front**—Brings the object to the top of the stack.

- **Send to Back**—Sends the object to the bottom of the stack.

- **Bring Forward**—Brings the object up one layer.

- **Send Backward**—Sends the object back one layer.

GROUPING AND UNGROUPING OBJECTS

Each object on a slide, including text boxes, is an individual object. However, sometimes you want two or more objects to act as a group. For example, you might want to make the lines of several objects the same thickness or group several objects so that they can easily be moved together on the slide. If you want to treat two or more objects as a group, perform the following steps:

1. Select the objects you want to group. Remember, to select more than one object, hold down the **Shift** or **Ctrl** key as you click each one.

2. Click the **Draw** button on the Drawing toolbar to open the Draw menu, and then select **Group**.

3. To ungroup the objects, select any object in the group and select **Draw**, and then choose **Ungroup**.

Cutting, Copying, and Pasting Objects

You can cut, copy, and paste objects onto a slide (or onto another slide) the same as you would normal text. When you cut an object, PowerPoint removes the object from the slide and places it in a temporary holding area called the Office Clipboard. When you copy or cut an object, a copy of the object, or the object itself when you use Cut, is placed on the Office Clipboard. You can place multiple objects onto the Clipboard and paste them as needed onto a slide or slides in your presentation.

To view the Office Clipboard, select **View**, **Task Pane**. Then, on the task pane drop-down menu, select **Clipboard**. Figure 13.3 shows the Clipboard task pane.

FIGURE 13.3
Use the Clipboard to keep track of objects that you have cut or copied.

To cut or copy an object, perform the following steps:

1. Select the object(s) you want to cut, copy, or move.

2. Select the **Edit** menu and then choose **Cut** or **Copy**, or click the **Cut** or **Copy** buttons on the Standard toolbar.

TIP

> **Right-Click Shortcut**   Right-click a selection to choose **Cut** or **Copy** from the shortcut menu.

3. Display the slide on which you want to paste the cut or copied objects.

4. Select **Edit** and then choose **Paste**, or click the **Paste** button on the Standard toolbar. PowerPoint pastes the objects onto the slide.

To remove an object without placing it on the Clipboard, select the object and press the **Delete** key.

ROTATING AN OBJECT

When you select an object on a slide, a handle with a green end on it appears at the top center of the object. This is the rotation handle, and it can be used to rotate any object on a slide. The rotation handle enables you to revolve an object around a center point.

To rotate an object, do the following:

1. Click the object you want to rotate.

2. Place the mouse pointer on the object's Rotation handle (the green dot) until the Rotation icon appears.

3. Hold down the mouse button and drag the Rotation handle until the object is in the position you want.

4. Release the mouse button.

The Draw menu (on the Drawing toolbar) also enables you to rotate or flip an object. You can flip an object horizontally left or right or flip the object vertically from top to bottom. To flip an object, click the **Draw** button on the Drawing toolbar, and then point at **Rotate and Flip**. Select either **Flip Horizontal** or **Flip Vertical** from the menu that appears.

TIP

> **Can't Find the Drawing Toolbar?** If the Drawing toolbar
> does not appear at the bottom of the PowerPoint appli-
> cation window, right-click any visible toolbar and select
> **Drawing**.

RESIZING OBJECTS

You will find that objects such as pictures and clip art are not always
inserted onto a slide in the correct size. You can resize the object by
performing these steps:

1. Select the object to resize. Selection handles appear.

2. Drag one of the following handles (the squares that surround
   the object) until the object is the desired size:

   • Drag a corner handle to change both the height and
     width of an object. PowerPoint retains the object's
     height-to-width ratio.

   • Drag a side, top, or bottom handle to change the height
     or width alone.

   • To keep the original center of the object stationary
     while sizing, hold down the **Ctrl** key while dragging a
     sizing handle.

3. Release the mouse button when you have finished resizing
   the object.

CROPPING A PICTURE

Besides resizing a picture, you can crop it; that is, you can trim a side
or a corner off the picture to remove an element from the picture or
cut off some whitespace. This enables you to clean up the picture
within the object box.

To crop a picture, perform the following steps:

1. Click the picture you want to crop.

2. To crop the picture, you need the Picture toolbar. Right-click any toolbar currently showing in the PowerPoint window and select **Picture**. The Picture toolbar appears.

3. Click the **Crop** button on the Picture toolbar. Cropping handles appear around the picture (see Figure 13.4).

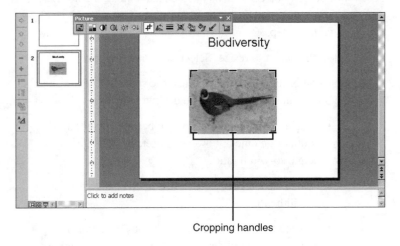

Cropping handles

FIGURE 13.4
Use the cropping handles on the figure to crop portions of the picture.

4. Move the mouse pointer over one of the cropping handles. The mouse pointer becomes the same shape as the cropping handle. (Use a corner handle to crop two sides at once. Use a side, top, or bottom handle to crop only one side.)

5. Hold down the mouse button and drag the pointer until the crop lines are where you want them.

6. Release the mouse button. PowerPoint crops the image.

7. After cropping that image, move or resize the picture as needed.

CAUTION

Stop That Crop!   To undo the cropping of a picture immediately after you crop it, select **Edit** and then choose **Undo Crop Picture**.

In this lesson, you learned how to select, copy, move, rotate, and resize an object on a slide. You also learned how to crop an image. In the next lesson, you learn how to insert objects from other Microsoft applications into PowerPoint presentations.

LESSON 14
Adding Charts to PowerPoint Slides

In this lesson, you learn how to add charts to PowerPoint slides and how to enhance those charts.

USING CHARTS IN PRESENTATIONS

Because your PowerPoint presentations serve the basic purpose of allowing your audience to visualize the subject matter that you are presenting, the use of charts is a great way to visually represent numerical data. Although many people find tables of statistics intimidating, providing a "picture" of the data in a form of a chart will greatly enhance audience understanding of important information as you give your presentation.

PowerPoint provides a Chart feature that enables you to create several different chart types. The following are some of the commonly used chart types:

- **Pie**—Use this chart type to show the relationship among parts of a whole.

- **Bar**—Use this chart type to compare values at a given point in time.

- **Column**—Similar to the bar chart; use this chart type to emphasize the difference between items.

- **Line**—Use this chart type to emphasize trends and the change of values over time.

- **Scatter**—Similar to a line chart; use this chart type to emphasize the difference between two sets of values.

- **Area**—Similar to the line chart; use this chart type to emphasize the amount of change in values over time.

The data represented by the chart is placed in a datasheet that is similar to the worksheets provided by spreadsheet software such as Microsoft Excel. This means that you enter the numerical information that creates the chart in a series of rows and columns. Each block created by the intersection of a row and column is referred to as a *cell*.

PLAIN ENGLISH

Cell—The block created by the intersection of a row and column in the chart datasheet.

The data you place in the datasheet appears on the chart along a particular axis of the chart. A two-dimensional chart has an x-axis (horizontal) and a y-axis (vertical). The x-axis typically contains the text description found in the chart (which would be the column headings found on the datasheet). The y-axis typically reflects the values of the bars, lines, or plot points. The y-axis information would the numerical data that you place under each column heading in the datasheet.

PLAIN ENGLISH

Axis—One side of a chart. A two-dimensional chart has an x-axis (horizontal) and a y-axis (vertical).

Not only will a chart contain an x- and y-axis; it also will contain a legend. The legend defines the separate data series of a chart. For example, the legend for a pie chart shows what each piece of the pie represents. The legend information typically would be the same as the row headings that you place in the datasheet.

PLAIN ENGLISH

> **Legend**—Defines the separate numerical series of a
> chart. For example, the legend for a column chart shows
> what each column in the chart represents.

You can add a chart to an existing slide using the Chart command on
the Insert menu. You also can place a chart on a slide by creating a
new slide that uses a slide layout that includes a chart object. Let's
take a look at both these possibilities, and then we can look at some
ways in which you can enhance a chart to maximum its visual impact
in your PowerPoint presentation.

TIP

> **Using Charts From Excel**   PowerPoint enables you to cre-
> ate charts by entering information into a datasheet, but
> you also can opt to paste charts from Excel onto a
> PowerPoint slide. This certainly makes sense if you have
> already entered the data in an Excel worksheet and cre-
> ated a chart. Open Excel and PowerPoint and use the
> Copy and Paste commands to place a copy of the Excel
> chart on any PowerPoint slide. For information about
> copying objects, see Lesson 13, "Working with
> PowerPoint Objects."

INSERTING A CHART ON AN EXISTING SLIDE

PowerPoint enables you to insert a chart on any existing slide. When
the chart appears on the slide, it will be in the default format, which is
a column chart (a vertical bar chart). We will discuss how to change
the chart type later in this lesson.

To insert a chart on a slide, follow these steps:

1. Open the slide on which you will place the chart.

2. Select the **Insert** menu, and then select **Chart**. The chart will appear on the slide, and the chart's datasheet also will appear in the PowerPoint window, as shown in Figure 14.1.

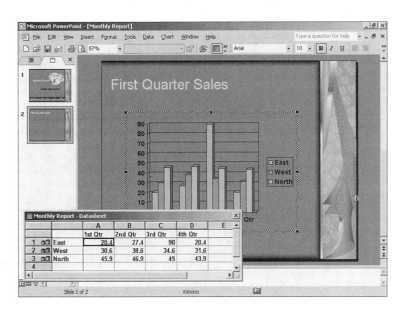

FIGURE 14.1
The chart and the chart's datasheet appear in the PowerPoint window.

3. To establish the x-axis text labels for the chart, click in the cell that currently contains the text **1st Qtr**. Type the new column heading that you will use for your chart. For example, if you are doing a summary of the first quarter's profit for your business, type `January`.

4. Press the **Tab** key to move to the next cell (or click in the cell using the mouse) and change the column heading as needed. If you need to delete a row or column of the default information on the datasheet, click the row number or column letter to select that row or column, respectively. Then, press the **Delete** key to clear the data.

5. Change the row headings to reflect the information you want to place on the chart's legend. Figure 14.2 shows a modified datasheet for a chart.

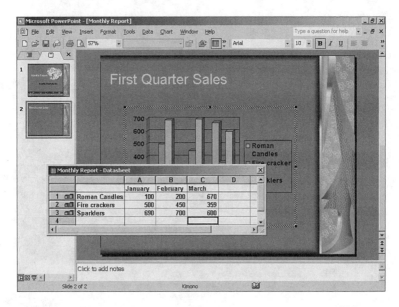

FIGURE 14.2
Modify the datasheet information to create your chart.

6. When you have finished entering the data for the chart, you can close the datasheet by clicking its **Close** button.

 TIP

> **Widening Datasheet Columns**   When you are adding text descriptions to your column headings in the datasheet, you might find that the headings are cut off. To widen the columns, place the mouse on the dividing line between the columns and use the sizing tool that appears to resize the column width so that it accommodates the text.

As already mentioned, the default chart type is a column chart. We will take a look at how you change the chart type in a moment.

CREATING A NEW SLIDE CONTAINING A CHART

An alternative to inserting a chart in an existing slide is to create a new slide that contains a placeholder for a chart. PowerPoint provides three different slide layouts that contain a chart placeholder object. You can create a slide that contains a title, bulleted list, and chart in two variations, with either the chart on the left or right of the slide. A third alternative provides a slide layout that contains a title and a chart only.

To create a new slide containing a chart, follow these steps:

1. Select the slide in the Slides pane (or Outline pane) that will provide the position in the presentation for the new slide (the new slide will be inserted after the selected slide).

2. Select the **Insert** menu, and then select **New Slide**. The New slide will appear in the presentation and open in the Slide view. The Slide Layout task pane also will open in the PowerPoint window.

3. Scroll down through the layouts provided in the task pane and select a slide layout that contains a chart placeholder (the layout icon will contain an image of a column chart).

4. The Chart layout will be changed to a slide that contains a chart (see Figure 14.3).

5. Double-click on the chart placeholder on the slide (it says "Double click to add chart").

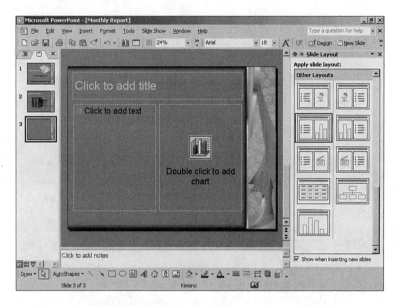

FIGURE 14.3
Create a new slide that contains a chart placeholder.

6. The datasheet for the chart will appear. Enter your data and row and column headings for the chart as discussed in the previous section.

7. Close the datasheet when you have finished entering your data.

SELECTING THE CHART TYPE

After you have created a chart on a slide, either by inserting the chart or by creating a new slide containing a chart (and filled in your data on the datasheet), you will want to be able to select the chart type that is used. As mentioned in the opening of this lesson, several different chart types are available.

To select the chart type, follow these steps:

1. Be sure the chart is selected on the slide.

2. Select the **Chart** menu, and then select **Chart Type**. The Chart Type dialog box will appear (see Figure 14.4).

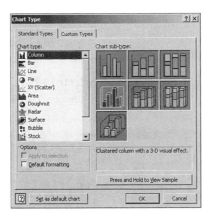

FIGURE 14.4
Use the Chart Type dialog box to specify your chart type.

3. In the Chart type box, select the chart type you wish to use (such as Bar, Line, or Pie).

4. Each chart type will provide several subtypes. Use the subtype box to select the "look" of your chart.

5. (Optional) If you want to view a sample of a particular chart type (and the selected subtype) click and hold the **Press and Hold to View Sample** button.

6. When you have selected the type and subtype for your chart, click **OK**.

You will be returned to your slide and your chart will appear on the slide. If you want to change the chart type, you can select the chart, and then follow the preceding steps to edit the chart type or the subtype.

MODIFYING THE CHART'S ATTRIBUTES

You can change the look of your chart by modifying the chart's border. You can change the color or add a shadow to the chart border. You also can modify the font used on the chart.

To modify the chart, follow these steps:

1. Select the chart on the slide.

2. Select **Format**, and then select **Selected Chart Area**. The Format Chart Area dialog box will appear (see Figure 14.5).

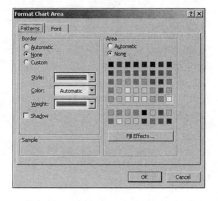

FIGURE 14.5
The Format Chart Area dialog box enables you to change the chart's border and font.

3. On the Patterns tab, select the **Custom** option button. Use the **Style**, **Color**, and **Weight** drop-down boxes to set the various attributes for the chart's border. If you wish to include a shadow on the border, select the **Shadow** check box.

4. To change the font attributes for the chart, click the **Font** tab of the Format Chart Area dialog box.

5. Use the various font attribute drop-down boxes and check boxes to select the custom font settings for the chart (the font attributes provided are the same as those available in the Font dialog box we discussed in Lesson 8, "Adding and Modifying Slide Text").

6. After you have finished making your border and font changes to the chart, click **OK**. You will be returned to the slide.

 TIP

> **You Can Modify the Look of Chart Parts**   You can modify the border and font used in specific parts of the chart, such as the legend. Double-click on the particular chart area and the Format dialog box for that particular area will appear. Change the attributes as needed.

In this lesson, you learned how to place a chart on a PowerPoint slide. You also learned how to enhance the chart's attributes, such as the font and border color. In the next lesson, you learn how to add an organizational chart and other diagrams to a PowerPoint slide.

LESSON 15

Adding Organizational Charts to PowerPoint Slides

In this lesson, you learn how to add organizational charts to PowerPoint slides and then edit them.

WORKING WITH ORGANIZATIONAL CHARTS

We have looked at several different object types that you can add to your PowerPoint slides, including clip art, sounds, and charts that display numerical data, such as column charts and pie charts. Another very useful visual object that you can add to your PowerPoint slides is the organizational chart.

Organizational charts often are used to display the report structure for a business or institution. They also can be used to diagram business processes, such as the different steps in a marketing or business plan, and they can be used to create a family tree.

Organizational charts can be added to an existing slide, or you can create a new slide that contains an organizational chart placeholder (when this object is double-clicked, you are provided with the tools that you use to create the chart). When you have an organizational chart on a slide, PowerPoint also provides you with different formatting options for that chart.

INSERTING AN ORGANIZATIONAL CHART ON A SLIDE

You can place an organizational chart on any slide in your presentation. All you need is the appropriate blank space on the slide to accommodate the chart object. To insert an organizational chart onto an existing slide, follow these steps:

1. Display the slide on which you want to place the organizational chart.

2. Select the **Insert** menu, then point at **Picture**, and then select **Organization Chart**. A new chart appears on the slide (as does the Organization Chart toolbar, as shown in Figure 15.1).

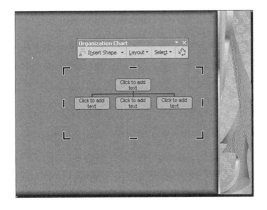

FIGURE 15.1
The organizational chart is placed on the slide.

3. Click on a box in a chart to add text. Enter the appropriate information, such as the name, title, and up to two optional comments about the person in the organization who will appear at that level in the chart. Press **Enter** to start a new line after typing each item. Press **Esc** when you complete the entry for that person.

4. Repeat step 3 for each person or item you want to include in the organizational chart.

5. To add another box to the chart, select a box in the chart to which you want to attach the new box. Then, click the drop-down arrow on the right of the **Insert Shape** button on the Organization Chart toolbar.

6. Select either **Subordinate**, **Coworker**, or **Assistant** from the Insert Shape list. Selecting **Subordinate** will place a new box below (subordinate to) the currently selected box. **Coworker** will place a new box at the same level of the selected box, and **Assistant** will place a new box subordinate to the selected box using a line with an elbow (this is used to differentiate between a subordinate and an assistant).

7. Select the new box that you created and type the appropriate text.

8. When you have finished working with the chart, you can click anywhere on the slide to deselect the chart. This also closes the Organization Chart toolbar.

CREATING A NEW SLIDE CONTAINING AN ORGANIZATIONAL CHART

You can create a new slide that contains a placeholder for an organizational chart. Follow these steps:

1. Select the slide in the Slides pane (or Outline pane) that will provide the position in the presentation for the new slide (the new slide will be inserted after the selected slide).

2. Select the **Insert** menu, and then select **New Slide**. The new slide will appear in the presentation and open in the Slide view. The Slide Layout task pane will also open in the PowerPoint window.

3. Scroll down through the layouts provided in the task pane and select the slide layout that contains Organizational Chart placeholder (it is the second to last layout provided in the task pane). The layout will be assigned to the slide (see Figure 15.2).

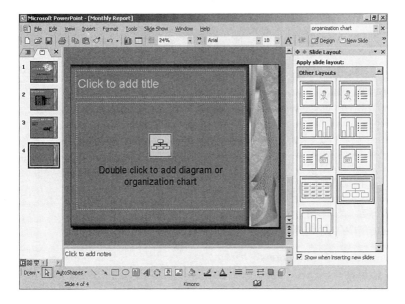

FIGURE 15.2
You can create a new slide that contains an organizational chart.

4. To create the organizational chart, double-click the placeholder box containing the text "Double click to add diagram or organization chart."

5. The Diagram Gallery dialog box will appear (see Figure 15.3). Double-click the **Organizational Chart** button in the dialog box.

FIGURE 15.3
Organizational charts can be placed on a new slide.

6. The organizational chart will be placed on the slide. Place your text entries in the appropriate boxes using the techniques discussed in the previous section.

EDITING AN ORGANIZATIONAL CHART

Editing an organizational chart really is no different than initially creating the chart. Follow these steps:

1. Select the slide containing the chart so that it is displayed in the Slide view.

2. Click on the chart to select it.

3. Select any of the chart boxes to edit the text. You can delete a box by selecting the box and then pressing the **Delete** key.

TIP

Zoom In on Your Chart   As you work on the chart, you can zoom in or out to see more or less of the chart at once. Just open the **View** menu and select a different view percentage.

Another aspect of editing an organizational chart relates to changing the fonts or the color of the chart box borders or background. Before we look at how you change the font for a single box or several selected boxes or work with color attributes, let's look at some strategies for how you can select multiple boxes in a chart:

- To select a single box, click it.

- To select more than one box, hold down the **Shift** key while clicking on each box.

- To select all the boxes at a particular level, select the **Select** drop-down arrow on the Organization Chart toolbar, and then select **Level**.

- To select all the assistants for a selected box, select the **Select** drop-down arrow on the Organization Chart toolbar, and then select **Assistants**.

After you select a box or boxes you can change the font, line, or color attributes for that box or boxes. For example, to change the font for selected boxes, select the **Format** menu and then select **Font**. You then can use the Font dialog box to make any changes to the font for the selected boxes (you would use the Font dialog box just as you would to change regular text on a slide, as discussed in Lesson 8, "Adding and Modifying Slide Text").

FORMATTING BOX LINES AND FILL COLORS

You also might want to change the attributes for a box or boxes in an organizational chart, such as the line style or the fill color. Follow these steps:

1. Select the boxes you want to format (as discussed in the previous section).

2. Select the **Format** menu, and then select **AutoShape**. The Format AutoShape dialog box appears (see Figure 15.4).

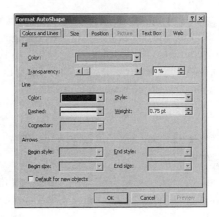

FIGURE 15.4
You can change the border line attributes and the fill color for boxes in the chart.

3. To change the fill color for the box or boxes, click the **Color** drop-down box in the Fill area of the dialog box. Select a new color from the color palette that appears.

4. If you wish to increase the transparency of the box or boxes, move the **Transparency** slider bar to the right (the greater the transparency percentage, the lighter the fill color becomes).

5. To change the line color, style, or weight use the appropriate drop-down box in the **Line** area of the dialog box.

6. When you have finished changing the fill color or the line settings, click **OK** to close the dialog box and return to the slide.

TIP

> **Formatting Connecting Lines**   You can change the line style and color of the connecting lines on your organizational chart. Select a connecting line or lines (to select multiple lines hold down the **Shift** key). Then, right-click on the selected lines and select **Format AutoShape** on the shortcut menu that appears. The Format AutoShape dialog box will open; it can be used to change the formatting for the selected connecting lines.

CHANGING THE ORGANIZATIONAL CHART STYLE

PowerPoint provides several different styles for your organizational charts. These styles provide different color schemes, box types, and even 3-D effects.

To change the style for your chart, follow these steps:

1. Select the organizational chart on the slide.

2. Click the **AutoFormat** button on the Organization Chart toolbar. The Organization Chart Style Gallery dialog box appears (see Figure 15.5).

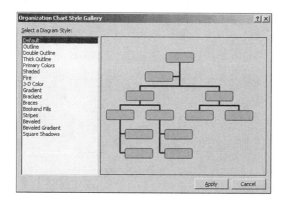

FIGURE 15.5

You can change the overall style of the chart using the Organization Chart Style Gallery.

3. Select one of the styles provided. A preview is provided on the right side of the dialog box.

4. When you have found the style you wish to use for your chart, click the **Apply** button.

The dialog box will close and the style will be applied to your organizational chart.

In this lesson, you learned how to place an organizational chart on a PowerPoint slide. You also learned how to edit a chart. In the next lesson, you learn how to present your slideshow onscreen.

Lesson 16
Presenting an Onscreen Slide Show

In this lesson, you learn how to view a slide show onscreen, how to make basic movements within a presentation, and how to set show options. You also learn how to create a self-running show with timings and how to work with slide transitions.

Viewing an Onscreen Slide Show

Before you show your presentation to an audience, you should run through it several times on your own computer, checking that all the slides are in the right order and that the timings and transitions between the slides work correctly. This also enables you to fine-tune any monologue you might have to give as you show the slides so that what you are saying at any point in the presentation is synchronized with the slide that is being shown at that moment.

You can preview a slide show at any time; follow these steps:

1. Open the presentation you want to view.

2. Choose the **Slide Show** menu and choose **View Show**. The first slide in the presentation appears full screen (see Figure 16.1).

The Virtual Classroom

Distance Learning and the Internet

FIGURE 16.1
When you run your slide show, the entire screen is used to display the slides.

3. To display the next or the previous slide, do one of the following:

- To display the next slide, click the left mouse button, press the **Page Down** key, or press the right-arrow or down-arrow key.

- To display the previous slide, click the right mouse button, press the **Page Up** key, or press the left-arrow or up-arrow key.

4. When you have finished running the slide show, press the **Esc** key.

TIP

> **Start the Show!**   You also can start a slide show by clicking the **Slide Show** button in the bottom-left corner of the presentation window or by pressing **F5**.

SETTING SLIDE ANIMATION SCHEMES

After running the slide show a few times, you might find that the presentation doesn't really provide the visual impact that you had hoped. Even though you have designed your slides well and created slides that include images and movies, you are still looking for something with a more "artsy" feel. A great way to add visual impact to the presentation is to assign an animation scheme to a slide or slides in the presentation.

An animation scheme controls how the text in the text boxes on the slide appear or materialize on the slide during the presentation. For example, you can select a slide animation scheme called Bounce, where the various text on the slide "bounces" onto the slide when it appears onscreen during the slide show.

PLAIN ENGLISH

> **Animation Scheme**   A scheme that controls how objects materialize onto the slide during the slide show.

PowerPoint provides three categories of animation schemes that you can assign to a slide: Subtle, Moderate, and Exciting. Each of these categories provides several animation schemes. The great thing about the animation schemes is that you can assign them to a slide or slides and then try them out in the Normal view. If you don't like the animation scheme, you can select another.

To assign an animation scheme to a slide in the presentation, follow these steps:

1. Select the slide to which you will assign the animation scheme so that it appears in the Slide pane in the Normal view.

2. Select the **Slide Show** menu and select **Animation Schemes**. The Animation Schemes list appears in the Slide Design task pane on the right side of the PowerPoint window (see Figure 16.2).

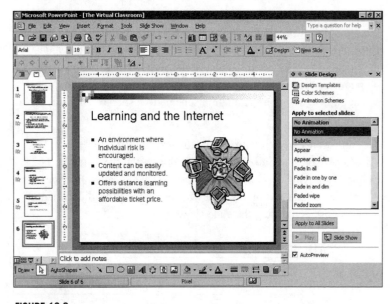

FIGURE 16.2
The task pane houses the animation schemes that you can assign to the slides in your presentation.

3. Scroll through the list of animation schemes. When you find a scheme that you want to try, select the scheme in the list box.

4. To try the scheme, click the **Play** button in the task pane.

5. If you don't like the scheme, select another.

6. If you find a scheme that you would like to apply to all the slides in the presentation, click the **Apply to All Slides** button.

TIP

> **Assign Animation Schemes to Selected Slides**   You can select several slides in the Slide Sorter view and then use the Slide Design task pane to assign the same animation scheme to all the selected slides.

Setting Up a Self-Running Show

In a self-running show, the slide show runs itself. Each slide advances after a specified period of time. This allows you to concentrate on the narrative aspects of the presentation as you use the slide show for a speech or classroom presentation. For a self-running show, you must set timings. You can set the same timing for all slides (for example, a 20-second delay between each slide), or you can set a separate timing for each slide individually.

When you set up a self-running show, you also can select different slide transitions. A slide transition is a special effect that is executed when the slide appears during the slide show. For example, you can have a slide dissolve onto the screen, or you can have the slide appear on the screen using a checkerboard effect.

To configure the show to use timings and transitions, follow these steps:

1. Open the presentation you want to view.

2. Select the slide to which you would like to apply a timing or transition so that it appears in the Slides pane in the Normal view.

3. Select **Slide Show** and click **Slide Transition**. The Slide Transition task pane opens containing controls for the type of transition you want to use, the speed with which that transition executes, and the length of time the slide should remain onscreen (see Figure 16.3).

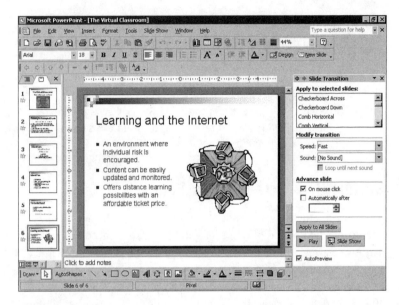

FIGURE 16.3
The Slide Transition task pane houses the controls necessary for tailoring the way a slide transitions onto the screen during a presentation.

4. To select a transition for the slide, select one of the transitions supplied in the Apply to Selected Slides box.

5. To test the transition, click the **Play** button.

6. If you want to change the speed of the transition, click the Speed drop-down list and select **Slow**, **Medium**, or **Fast** (Fast is the default).

7. (Optional) If you want to select a sound to accompany the slide transition (such as Applause, Drum Roll, or Laser), click the **Sound** drop-down list and select one of the supplied sounds.

8. To set the timing for the slide in the Advance Slide section of the task pane, click the **Automatically After** check box. Use the click box below the check box to enter the number of seconds for the slide's automatic timing.

9. If you want to apply the selected transition and the timing to all the slides in the presentation, click the **Apply to All Slides** button.

CAUTION

My Slides Don't Advance Using the Timings   If you find when you run the slide show that the slides don't advance using the timings that you have set, select **Slide Show**, **Set Up Show**. In the Set Up Show dialog box, be sure that the **Using Timings, If Present** option button is selected. Then click **OK**.

When you run the slide show, the slides advance according to the timings that you have set. The slides also use any transitions that you have selected for them. Take the time to run the slide show several times so that you can gauge whether the transitions and timings work well. Remember that the slide must be onscreen long enough for your audience to read and understand the text on the slide.

TIP

Assign Transitions and Timings to Selected Slides   You can select several slides in the Slide Sorter view and then use the Slide Transition task pane to assign the same transition and/or timing to the selected slides.

CAUTION

Don't Get Too Fancy!   If you are going to use slide transitions and animation schemes on each and every slide, you might find that your slide show is becoming "too exciting," like a film with too many explosions, car chases, and other special effects. Viewers of the slide show likely will have trouble concentrating on the text on the slides if too many things are going on at once. Remember, everything in moderation.

USING THE SLIDE SHOW MENU TOOLS

PowerPoint also provides some other features that you will find very useful when you are running your slide show. For example, you can turn the mouse pointer into a pen that enables you to draw on a particular slide, enabling you to quickly emphasize a particular point visually. A Meeting Minder feature enables you to take notes during the actual presentation, which is a great way to record audience questions or comments concerning the presentation as you actually show it.

These tools are found on a menu that you can access during a slide show by right-clicking the screen. Figure 16.4 shows the menu. Three of the most useful tools are discussed in the following sections of this lesson.

FIGURE 16.4
You can access the pen and other tools, such as your Speaker Notes, from the menu on the Slide Show screen.

DRAWING WITH THE PEN

An extremely useful tool is the pen, which enables you to draw on a particular slide. This is great for highlighting information on a slide to emphasize a particular point.

To use the pen during the slide show, follow these steps:

1. With the slide show running, right-click anywhere on the screen. The Slide Show menu appears.

2. Point at **Pointer Options** on the menu, and then choose **Pen**. The mouse pointer becomes a pen.

3. Press the left mouse button and draw on the slide as needed (see Figure 16.5).

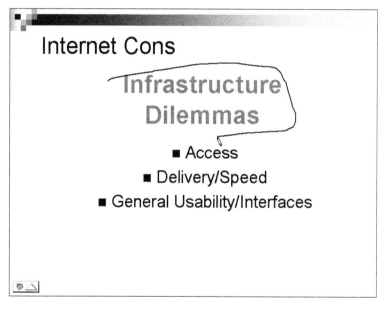

FIGURE 16.5
The pen provides you with an easy way to highlight a particular item on a slide.

4. After you've finished working with the pen, you can return to the arrow pointer. Right-click on the screen, point at **Pointer Options** on the menu, and then select **Arrow**. You now can use the mouse to advance to the next slide.

You also can choose the pen color that you use to draw on the slides. This option is available on the Slide Show menu (point at **Pointer Options**, point at **Pen Color**, and then select the pen color you want to use from the cascading menu).

TAKING NOTES WITH THE MEETING MINDER

Another useful tool that you can take advantage of while showing your slide presentation is the Meeting Minder. The Meeting Minder enables you to quickly take notes or create action related to the discussion or to audience comments made during your presentation.

To use the Meeting Minder, follow these steps:

1. With the slide show running, right-click anywhere on the screen. The Slide Show menu appears.

2. Click **Meeting Minder**. The Meeting Minder dialog box opens (see Figure 16.6.)

FIGURE 16.6
The Meeting Minder makes it easy for you to record notes or a task related to your presentation.

3. Type your notes onto the **Meeting Minutes** tab of the dialog box.

4. If you want to create an action item, click the **Action Items** tab on the dialog box. Type a description into the **Description** box, and type the name of the person who will work on

the item into the **Assigned To** box. After filling in this information, click the **Add** button to add the item to the Action Items list on the tab.

5. When you have finished adding notes or creating action items related to the slide presentation, click the **OK** button to close the dialog box.

FINDING A PARTICULAR SLIDE DURING THE SHOW

As you reach the end of a presentation, you might be asked to reshow a particular slide or subset of slides that you included in your slide show. The easiest way to go to a particular slide when you are in the Slide Show view is by using the Slide Navigator. The Slide Navigator lists all the slides in the current slide show.

To use the Slide Navigator, follow these steps:

1. With the slide show running, right-click anywhere on the screen. The Slide Show menu appears.

2. Point at **Go** and then click **Slide Navigator**. The Slide Navigator dialog box opens.

3. To move to a particular slide, click the slide's title in the Slide Navigator's slide list and then click **Go To**. PowerPoint takes you to the selected slide.

ADDING ACTION BUTTONS TO USER-INTERACTIVE SHOWS

You may create slide show presentations that will be played on a computer where your audience actually interacts with the slide show (for example, a computer at a trade show that tells potential customers about your company). This means that you need to give the audience some means of controlling the show. You can simply provide access to a keyboard and/or mouse and let the user control the show in the same way you learned earlier in this lesson, or you can provide action buttons onscreen that make it easy to jump to specific slides.

Action buttons are like controls on an audio CD player; they enable you to jump to any slide quickly, to go backward, to go forward, or even to stop the presentation.

TIP

> **The Same Controls on All Slides?**   If you want to add the same action buttons to all slides in the presentation, add the action buttons to the Slide Master. To display the Slide Master, select **View**, point at **Master**, and then choose **Slide Master**.

To add an action button to a slide, follow these steps:

1. Display the slide in Normal view.

2. Select **Slide Show**, point at **Action Buttons**, and pick a button from the palette that appears. For example, if you want to create a button that advances to the next slide, you might choose the button with the arrow pointing to the right.

TIP

> **Which Button Should I Choose?**   Consider the action that you want the button to perform, and then pick a button picture that matches it well. To change the button picture, you must delete the button and create a new one.

3. Your mouse pointer turns into a crosshair. Drag to draw a box on the slide where you want the button to appear. (You can resize it later if you want.) PowerPoint draws the button on the slide and opens the Action Settings dialog box (see Figure 16.7).

FIGURE 16.7
Set the action for your button in the Action Settings dialog box.

4. Select either **Mouse Click** or **Mouse Over** to set the action for the button (Mouse Click options require a click; Mouse Over requires only that the mouse pointer be placed on the button).

5. Choose the type of action you want to happen when the user clicks the button. Click the **Hyperlink To** drop-down list and select an action such as **Next Slide**.

6. (Optional) If you want a sound to play when the user clicks the button, select the **Play Sound** check box and choose a sound from the drop-down list.

7. Click **OK**. Your button appears on the slide.

8. View the presentation (as you learned at the beginning of this lesson) to try out the button.

If you do use buttons on your slides so that users can run the slide show, be sure you use the same style of button on each of your slides for a particular action. This kind of consistency gives the viewer of the presentation a feeling of comfort and control.

TIP

Buttons Can Do Many Things   You also can create action buttons that run a program or fire off a macro that has been created using the Visual Basic for Applications programming language. Although these are very advanced features not covered in this book, keep in mind as you learn more about PowerPoint that many possibilities exist for making very creative and complex slide show presentations.

SETTING SLIDE SHOW OPTIONS

Depending on the type of show you're presenting, you might find it useful to make some adjustments to the way the show runs, such as making it run in a window (the default is full screen) or showing only certain slides. You'll find these controls and more in the Set Up Show dialog box, which you can open by clicking the **Slide Show** menu and selecting **Set Up Show** (see Figure 16.8).

FIGURE 16.8
Use the Set Up Show dialog box to give PowerPoint some basic instructions about how to present your slide show.

In this dialog box, you can choose from several options, including the following:

- Choose the medium for showing the presentation. Your choices are **Presented by a Speaker (Full Screen)**, **Browsed by an Individual (Window)**, and **Browsed at a Kiosk (Full Screen)**.

- Choose whether to loop the slide show continuously or to show it only once. You might want to loop it continuously so that it operates unaided at a kiosk at a trade show, for example.

- Show all the slides or a range of them (enter the range into the **From** and **To** boxes).

- Choose whether to advance slides manually or to use timings you set up.

- Choose a pen color. Use the Pen Color drop-down box to select a color.

In this lesson, you learned how to display a slide presentation onscreen, how to move between slides, and how to set slideshow options. You also learned to set timings and transitions for your slides and add animation schemes to the slide in the presentation. In the next lesson you learn how to print a presentation, speaker's notes, and presentation handouts.

LESSON 17

Printing Presentations, Notes, and Handouts

In this lesson, you learn how to select a size and orientation for the slides in your presentation and how to print the slides, notes, and handouts you create.

USING POWERPOINT NOTES AND HANDOUTS

Although PowerPoint presentations are designed to be shown on a computer screen, you might want to print some items related to the presentation. For example, as you design your presentation, you can enter notes related to each slide that you create in the Notes pane. These notes can then be printed out and used during the presentation.

Using speaker notes helps you keep on track during the presentation and provides you with the information that you want to present related to each slide in the presentation. When you print your notes, each slide is printed on a separate page with the notes printed below the slide.

If you want to make it easier for your presentation audience to follow the presentation and perhaps take notes of their own, you can print out handouts. Handouts provide a hard copy of each slide. The number of slides printed on each page of the handout can range from 1 to 9 slides. If you choose to print three slides per page (this is set up in the Print dialog box, which is discussed later in this lesson), PowerPoint automatically places note lines on the printout pages to the right of each slide (which makes it even easier for your audience to take notes related to the slides in the presentation).

This lesson covers the options related to printing hard copies of your slides, notes, and handouts. Let's start with a look at printing out presentation slides.

QUICK PRINTING WITH NO OPTIONS

You can quickly print all the slides in the presentation. You don't get to make any decisions about your output, but you do get your printout without delay.

To print a quick copy of each slide in the presentation, choose one of these methods:

- Click the **Print** button on the Standard toolbar.
- Choose the **File** menu, choose **Print**, and click **OK**.
- Press **Ctrl+P** and click **OK**.

The downside of printing the presentation in this way is that you will get a printout of only one slide per page in the landscape orientation. It doesn't matter what view you are in—you just get the slides. This uses up a lot of printer ink or toner, and if you want to print the presentation as an outline or print the presentation so that you can see the presentation notes that you've made, you need to access printing options that provide more control over the printout.

One way to fine-tune some of the settings that control how pages will be printed is the Page Setup dialog box.

CHANGING THE PAGE SETUP

The Page Setup dialog box enables you to select how slides, notes, and handouts should be oriented on the page (Portrait or Landscape) and the type of page that the slides should be formatted for, such as On-Screen Show, overhead sheets, or regular 8 ½-inch by 11-inch paper.

To customize the Page Setup settings, follow these steps:

1. Select the **File** menu and select **Page Setup**. The Page Setup dialog box appears as shown in Figure 17.1.

FIGURE 17.1

The Page Setup dialog box enables you to set the paper type and the orientation of slides and notes on the page.

2. Perform one of the following procedures to set the slide size:

   - To use a standard size, select a size from the **Slides Sized For** drop-down list. For example, you can have slides sized for regular 8 ½-inch by 11-inch paper, overheads, or 35mm slides (if you have a special printer that can create slides).

   - To create a custom size, enter the dimensions into the **Width** and **Height** text boxes.

TIP

Spin Boxes   The arrows to the right of the Width and Height text boxes enable you to adjust the settings in those boxes. Click the up arrow to increase the setting by .1 inch or the down arrow to decrease it by .1 inch.

3. In the **Number Slides From** text box, type the number with which you want to start numbering slides. (This usually is **1**, but you might want to start with a different number if the presentation is a continuation of another.)

4. Under the Slides heading, choose **Portrait** or **Landscape** orientation for your slides.

5. In the Notes, Handouts & Outline section, choose **Portrait** or **Landscape** for those items.

6. Click **OK**. If you changed the orientation of your slides, you might have to wait a moment while PowerPoint repositions the slides.

CHOOSING WHAT AND HOW TO PRINT

To really control your printouts related to a particular presentation, use the various options supplied in the Print dialog box. The Print dialog box enables you to specify what to print, such as handouts or the presentation as an outline; it also enables you to specify the printer to use for the printout. For example, you might want to use a color printer for overhead transparencies and a black-and-white printer for your handouts. To set your print options, follow these steps:

1. Select the **File** menu and select **Print**. The Print dialog box appears with the name of the currently selected printer in the Name box (see Figure 17.2).

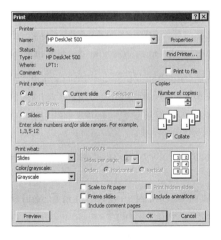

FIGURE 17.2
The Print dialog box enables you to control the printer and the printouts.

2. If you want to use a different printer, open the Name drop-down list and select the printer you want.

TIP

Printer Properties The Properties button enables you to adjust graphics quality, select paper size, and choose which paper tray to use, among other things.

3. Choose what to print in the Print Range section:

   • Choose **All** to print all the slides in the presentation.

   • Choose **Current Slide** to print only the currently displayed slide.

   • Enter a range of slide numbers into the **Slides** text box; for example, enter **2-4** to print slides 2, 3, and 4.

4. Open the **Print What** drop-down list and choose what you want to print. You can print slides, handouts, notes, or outlines.

5. If you want more than one copy, enter the number of copies you want into the **Number of Copies** box.

6. Use the Color/Grayscale drop-down box to specify whether the printout should be in color, grayscale, or black and white.

7. If you are printing handouts, use the Handouts box on the dialog box to specify the number of slides that should be printed per page and the orientation used for the printed page (Portrait or Landscape).

8. Select or deselect any of these check boxes in the dialog box, as required:

   • **Print to File**—Select this option to send the output to a file rather than to your printer.

   • **Collate**—If you are printing more than one copy, select this check box to collate (1, 2, 3, 1, 2, 3) each printed copy instead of printing all the copies of each page at once (1, 1, 2, 2, 3, 3).

- **Scale to Fit Paper**—If the slide (or whatever you're printing) is too large to fit on the page, select this check box to decrease the size of the slide to make it fit on the page. Now you won't have to paste two pieces of paper together to see the whole slide.

- **Frame Slides**—Select this check box if you want to print a border around each slide.

- **Print Hidden Slides**—If you have any hidden slides, you can choose whether to print them. If you don't have any hidden slides, this check box will be unavailable.

- **Include Animations**—If you have any animated elements on the slide, mark this check box and PowerPoint will do its best to approximate them in still form.

- **Include Comment Pages**—Prints all the comments on the slides of the presentation on a separate comments page.

TIP

> **Preview Your Printout Selection**   After specifying the various options in the Print dialog box, you might want to preview the printout before you send it to the printer. Click the **Preview** button. You are taken to the Print Preview screen. If things look good on the Print Preview screen, click **Print** to send the printout to the printer.

9. Click **OK** to print.

In this lesson, you learned how to print your presentations and how to set options in the Page Setup and Print dialog boxes. In the next lesson, you learn how to save a PowerPoint presentation for use on the World Wide Web.

LESSON **18**

Designing a Presentation for the Internet

In this lesson, you'll learn how PowerPoint makes it easy to publish your presentations on the World Wide Web or your corporate intranet.

POWERPOINT AND THE WORLD WIDE WEB

The World Wide Web is the most popular and graphical component of the Internet, a worldwide network of computers. Many businesses maintain Web sites containing information about their products and services for public reading. Still other businesses maintain an internal version of the Web that's strictly for employee use, and they use the company's local area network to make it available to its staff. These are called *intranets*.

PLAIN ENGLISH

Intranet   A private corporate network that uses Internet protocols and services to share information. Intranets can use Web pages to share information among corporate intranet users.

Sooner or later, you might be asked to prepare a PowerPoint presentation for use on a Web site or an intranet. Taking a PowerPoint presentation and converting it to Web-ready content is much easier than you might think.

SPECIAL CONSIDERATIONS FOR DESIGNING WEB SHOWS

Creating a presentation for Web distribution is much like creating any other user-interactive presentation. However, consider these factors when dealing with the Web:

- For your viewers' convenience, keep the file size as small as possible. That means don't use graphics, sounds, or movies that don't serve an obvious purpose (other than providing a few additional bells and whistles in the presentation).

- Include action buttons on each slide that enable the user to jump to the previous and next slides, and possibly other action buttons, too.

- If you want the users to be able to jump from your presentation to other Web sites, be sure you include the appropriate hyperlinks. See the following section for details.

- If you convert the presentation to HTML (Web) format, anyone with a Web browser can view it on the Internet, but the presentation might not be exactly the same as the PowerPoint version of it. Depending on the Web browser used to view it, sounds, movies, transitions, and other features might not play correctly.

- If you distribute the file in PowerPoint format, your audience must have PowerPoint installed on their PCs or must download a special PowerPoint viewer (discussed later in this lesson).

ADDING URL HYPERLINKS

One way to add some Web connectivity to a PowerPoint slide presentation is by adding hyperlinks to a slide. A *hyperlink* is a link to a particular Web page, file on your computer, or even a person's e-mail address. In PowerPoint, hyperlinks can be added to a slide as text or you can create action buttons that serve as a hyperlink. For example, you might have a button that takes you to your company's home page (the top page at its Internet site) at the bottom of every slide.

PLAIN ENGLISH

Hyperlink   A graphic, text entry, or button that supplies a quick link to a Web page, a file on your computer, or an e-mail address. Hyperlinks that specify URLs (Uniform Resource Locators, or Web addresses) are used to navigate from page to page on the World Wide Web.

A hyperlink can be attached to an action button (action buttons that move you from slide to slide are hyperlinks, too) or to some other graphic, or it can be attached to a string of text characters.

ASSIGNING A HYPERLINK TO AN ACTION BUTTON

The following steps show you how to assign a hyperlink to an action button:

1. Open the slide in the slide view to which you will add the hyperlink. Select the **Slide Show** menu, and then select **Action Buttons**. Select the button you wish to place on the slide from the button palette that appears. For example, use the one that looks like a house to hyperlink to your company's home page.

2. When the Action Settings dialog box appears, click the **Hyperlink To** option, button (see Figure 18.1).

3. Open the **Hyperlink To** drop-down list and select **URL**. The Hyperlink to URL dialog box appears.

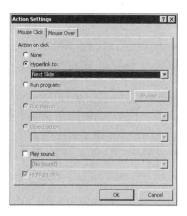

FIGURE 18.1
The Action settings dialog box allows you to determine the action of the button you have created.

4. Enter the Web address in the **URL** text box (see Figure 18.2). Then click **OK**.

FIGURE 18.2
Enter the URL (the Web address) for the hyperlink.

5. Click **OK** to close the Action Settings dialog box.

If you have already created an action button and you want to change its hyperlink, select the button and select **Slide Show** then **Action Settings**. Then start at step 2 in the preceding steps to change the URL for the action button. You also can assign a hyperlink to any graphic in this same way—select the graphic and then select **Slide Show, Action Settings**. Use the Action Settings dialog box to select the hyperlink address for the graphic as listed in steps 2 through 5.

CREATING A TEXT-BASED HYPERLINK

You can insert a hyperlink on a slide as text by typing the actual URL of a site, such as `www.quehelp.com`. It will automatically be formatted as a hyperlink to the Web site. If you want to assign a hyperlink to existing text (for example, you might want to assign the `www.que-help.com` URL to text that says, "Que Help Site"), you need to assign the URL to the text as you assigned a URL hyperlink to an action button or image (discussed in the previous section).

To assign a hyperlink to text on a slide, follow these steps:

1. (Optional) To use existing text on a slide, select it.

2. Select the **Insert** menu, and then select **Hyperlink**. The Insert Hyperlink dialog box opens (see Figure 18.3).

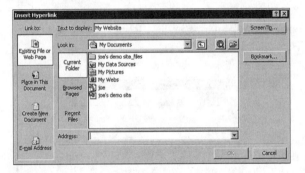

FIGURE 18.3
Use the Insert Hyperlink dialog box to assign a hyperlink to your text.

3. The text you selected in step 1 appears in the Text to Display box. If you want to change it, do so. If you didn't select any text in step 1, type the text to which you will assign the hyperlink. For example, if the URL will take them to your home page, you might type `Click here to visit my home page`.

4. If you know the address of the Web site you wish to use as the hyperlink, type the URL in the **Address** box. If you wish

to select the URL from a list of Web sites that you recently visited, click the **Browsed Pages** link in the Look In box to the left of the dialog box. Select a Web site in the list and it will appear in the Address box.

5. When you have placed a URL in the Address box, click **OK**. This will close the dialog box.

The text that you selected in step 1 or typed in step 3 will be underlined and appear in blue (typically the default color for hyperlinks). When this text is clicked on the slide during a slide show, a browser window will open displaying the Web site.

TIP

> **Auto URL Entry**   If you don't know the Web page's address, open your Web browser. Navigate to the page to which you want to link, and then jump back to PowerPoint (by clicking the PowerPoint presentation's name on the Windows taskbar). The URL is automatically entered for you in the Address box.

To test your hyperlink, view the slide in Slide Show view (discussed in Lesson 16, "Presenting an Onscreen Slide Show"), and click the button with your mouse. Your Web browser should start and the selected URL should load in it. If it doesn't work, check to be sure you entered the URL correctly. If it is correct, check your Internet connection or try again later. (Sometimes a Web page might be temporarily unavailable.)

Saving a Presentation in HTML Format

PowerPointhas the capability to save a presentation in HTML format so it can be viewed using any Web browser. PowerPoint saves in a Web format that allows your sounds, movies, animations, and other special effects to be seen just as you intended.

PLAIN ENGLISH

HTML   HyperText Markup Language (HTML) is the coding language used to build a Web page.

To save a presentation in HTML format, follow these steps:

1. Select the **File** menu, and then select **Save As Web Page**.
   The Save As dialog box appears (see Figure 18.4).

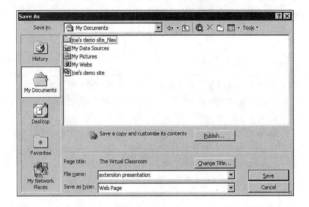

FIGURE 18.4
Choose a name for your saved Web presentation.

2. In the **File Name** text box, enter a filename for the first page
   of the presentation (the title slide). By default this is the name
   of your presentation file.

3. (Optional) If you want the page title (the name in the title bar
   when the page is displayed in a Web browser) to be different
   than the one shown, click the **Change Title** button and enter
   a different title in the Set Page Title box that appears. Click
   OK to return to the Save In dialog box.

4. Click **Save**. Your presentation is saved as an HTML file.

You might have noticed in the Save As dialog box (Figure 18.4) that there is a Publish button. This button takes you to the Publish as Web Page dialog box, in which you can set all kinds of options related to your HTML presentation, including which Web browser your audience will likely use and which slides to include. You are not required to set all these options to have your presentation saved for use on the Web.

A saved HTML presentation actually consists of several files, not just a single HTML file. PowerPoint creates a home page (an entry point) with the same name as the original presentation. (This is the file you were naming when you chose a name in step 2.) For example, if the presentation file was named Broadway.ppt, the home page would be named Broadway.htm.

A folder is also created for the HTML presentation, which is given the name of the presentation (for example, Broadway Files). This folder contains all the other HTML, graphics, and other files needed to display the complete presentation. If you are transferring the HTML presentation to another PC (which is very likely, if you are going to make it available on the Internet through a Web server), you must transfer not only the lone HTML home page but also the entire associated folder.

Viewing Your Web Presentation

As you work on a slide presentation that you plan on making part of a Web page (and have it viewed online), you can preview your presentation in Internet Explorer (or any compatible Web browser) to see how the slides look and operate as Web content. Viewing the presentation in Internet Explorer can really help you fine-tune the presentation for the Web before you actually make it available to your audience.

To view your current presentation in Internet Explorer (or your default Web browser), follow these steps:

1. Select the **File** menu, and then choose **Web Page Preview**. The Internet Explorer Window will appear showing the first slide in your presentation (see Figure 18.5).

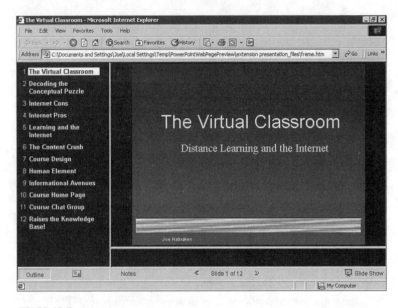

FIGURE 18.5
You can preview your presentation for the Web.

2. Use the navigation pane (on the left side of the Explorer window) to view each slide in the presentation. You also can navigate the presentation using the navigation buttons found below the main slide pane.

3. When you have finished previewing the presentation in Internet Explorer, click the Explorer **Close** button.

When you close the Internet Explorer window, you will be returned to the PowerPoint window. You can now fine-tune the presentation for the Web and preview it as needed.

In this lesson, you learned about PowerPoint's capabilities in helping you present your slides on the Web.

Index

P

Page Setup command
(PowerPoint File menu), 160
paragraphs, spacing, 71
Paste command (PowerPoint
Edit menu), 56
pasting
charts to slides, 126
objects, 118-120
slides, 56-57
pen (PowerPoint slide shows),
150-152
Picture command (PowerPoint
Insert menu), 72, 98-99, 103
Picture toolbar (PowerPoint)
Crop button, 122
pie charts. *See* charts
Pointer Options command
. (PowerPoint Slide Show
menu), 151-152
PowerPoint
Action Settings dialog box,
155
Background dialog box, 50
Borders and tables, 83
Bullets and Numbering
dialog box, 84-86
charts, 129
axis, 125
cells, 125
Chart Type, 130
copying, 126
creating, 124-133
creating new slides
containing chart
placeholders, 129

creating new slides
containing charts,
129
creating new slides
containing
Organizational
charts, 136-137
datasheets, 128
Format Chart Area,
132
Format menu, 139
Insert menu, 126, 136
legends, 126
modifying attributes,
132-133
Organization Chart,
134-141
cropping graphics, 121-123
design templates, 45-47
Draw menu
Group command, 118
Order command,
116-117
Rotate and Flip com-
mand, 120
Drawing toolbar
Draw button, 116-120
Insert Clip Art button,
98
Select Objects Tool,
116
Text Box button, 63, 78
Edit menu
Copy command, 56
Copy to Collection
command, 106
Cut command, 56

Microsoft® Word 2002

MINUTE

GUIDE

201 West 103rd Street
Indianapolis, IN 46290

Joe Habraken

10 Minute Guide to Microsoft® Word 2002

Copyright © 2002 by Que® Corporation

International Standard Book Number: 0-7897-2636-x

Library of Congress Catalog Card Number: 20-01090295

Printed in the United States of America

First Printing: August 2001

04   03   02   8   7   6

Trademarks

Warning and Disclaimer

Associate Publisher
Greg Wiegand

Managing Editor
Thomas Hayes

Acquisitions Editor
Stephanie J. McComb

Development Editor
Stephanie J. McComb

Project Editor
Tricia Liebig

Indexer
Sheila Schroeder

Proofreader
Amy Jay

Team Coordinator
Sharry Lee Gregory

Interior Designer
Gary Adair

Cover Designer
Alan Clements

Page Layout
Susan Geiselman

Contents

Dedication

To my nieces, Ryland and Lena.

Acknowledgments

Creating books like this takes a real team effort. I would like to thank Stephanie McComb, our acquisitions editor, who worked very hard to assemble the team that made this book a reality and also served as the development editor for this book—coming up with many great ideas for improving the content of the book. Also, a great big thanks to our project editor, Tricia Liebig, who ran the last leg of the race and made sure the book made it to press on time—what a great team of professionals.

TELL US WHAT YOU THINK!

As the reader of this book, *you* are our most important critic and commentator. We value your opinion and want to know what we're doing right, what we could do better, what areas you'd like to see us publish in, and any other words of wisdom you're willing to pass our way.

As an Associate Publisher for Que, I welcome your comments. You can fax, e-mail, or write me directly to let me know what you did or didn't like about this book—as well as what we can do to make our books stronger.

Please note that I cannot help you with technical problems related to the topic of this book, and that due to the high volume of mail I receive, I might not be able to reply to every message.

When you write, please be sure to include this book's title and author as well as your name and phone or fax number. I will carefully review your comments and share them with the author and editors who worked on the book.

Fax: 317-581-4666

E-mail: feedback@quepublishing.com

Mail: Greg Wiegand
            Que
            201 West 103rd Street
            Indianapolis, IN 46290 USA

Introduction

Microsoft Word 2002 is an incredibly versatile and easy-to-use word processing program that can help you create business and personal documents. You can create simple documents, such as memos and outlines, and complex documents, such as newsletters and Internet-ready Web pages.

THE WHAT AND WHY OF MICROSOFT WORD

Word provides you with all the tools you need to quickly create many different types of word processing documents. Whether you work at home or in a busy office, Microsoft Word can provide you with the ability to do any of the following:

- Create memos and letters
- Build complex documents like brochures, reports, and even legal pleadings
- Use clipart, pictures, borders, and colors to add interest to your documents
- Create your own Web pages and Web site using the different Web Wizards

Additionally, Word provides a number of features that make it easy for you to create great looking documents whether you are working on a simple memo or a complex Web page. You can

- Quickly format text using Word Styles.
- Use the Autoformat feature to quickly format an entire document.
- Use sections in large documents to provide formatting for different document parts.
- Use the new speech feature for voice dictation and voice commands.

While providing you with many complex features, Microsoft Word is easy to learn. This book will help you understand the possibilities awaiting you with Microsoft Word 2002.

WHY QUE'S *10 MINUTE GUIDE TO MICROSOFT WORD 2002?*

The 10 Minute Guide to Microsoft Word 2002 can save you precious time while you get to know the different features provided by Microsoft Word. Each lesson is designed to be completed in 10 minutes or less, so you'll be up to snuff on basic and advanced Word skills quickly.

Although you can jump around among lessons, starting at the beginning is a good plan. The bare-bones basics are covered first, and more advanced topics are covered later. If you need help installing Word, see the next section for instructions.

CONVENTIONS USED IN THIS BOOK

The *10 Minute Guide to Microsoft Word 2002* includes step-by-step instructions for performing specific tasks. To help you as you work through these steps and help you move through the lessons easily, additional information is included and identified by the following icons.

PLAIN ENGLISH

New or unfamiliar terms are defined to help you as you work through the various steps in the lesson.

TIP

Read these tips for ideas that cut corners and confusion.

CAUTION

This icon identifies areas where new users often run into trouble; these hints offer practical solutions to those problems.

LESSON 1

What's New in Word 2002?

In this lesson, you are introduced to Word's powerful word processing and desktop publishing features, and you learn what's new in Word 2002.

GETTING THE MOST OUT OF WORD 2002

Microsoft Word is an efficient and full-featured word processor that provides you with all the tools you need to produce a tremendous variety of document types—everything from simple documents, such as memos and outlines, to complex documents, such as newsletters and Internet-ready Web pages.

Word provides a number of features to help you create personal and business documents. These features range from document wizards to easy document formatting options such as styles and the AutoFormat feature. Some of the Word features that you will explore in this book are:

- Wizards: Wizards such as the Memo Wizard, Mailing Label Wizard, and Web Page Wizard make it easy for you to create complex documents in Word. A wizard walks you through the creation of a particular document type using a step-by-step process. Wizards are covered in Lesson 3, "Working with Documents."

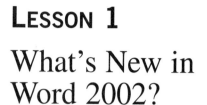

PLAIN ENGLISH

Wizard A feature that guides you step by step through a particular process in Word, such as creating a new document.

- Styles: A style is a grouping of formatting attributes identified by a style name. Styles can contain character-formatting attributes such as bold, or a particular font size. Styles can also contain attributes, such as alignment information, indents, and line spacing. Styles are covered in Lesson 12, "Working with Styles."

PLAIN ENGLISH

> **Style** A collection of formatting attributes that is identified by a style name. Styles can quickly be assigned to text in your documents rather than adding each attribute individually to the text.

- AutoFormat: No matter what type of document you create, you can have Word add formatting to all the text in the document, providing you with a unified and professional look for any document. AutoFormat is covered in Lesson 13, "Using AutoFormatting to Change Text Attributes."

Whether you are a new Word user or are familiar with previous versions of Word, Word 2002 provides the proper level of features and help for you to immediately begin the document creation process.

NEW FEATURES IN WORD 2002

Word 2002 embraces a number of features that were first introduced with the release of Word 2000. For example, Word 2002 uses the same adaptive menu and toolbar system found in Word 2000 that customizes the commands and icons listed based on the commands you use most frequently.

Word 2002 also builds on the features found in the previous version of Word. It offers a number of new features that make it easier for you to input information into your Word documents and perform tasks related to the use of graphics in your documents and features, such as the Word Mail Merge. New features in Word 2002 range from smart tags to voice dictation to new ways to quickly get help.

For example, you will find that it is even easier to get help in Word 2002 than in previous versions of Word. A new feature—the Ask a Question Box—has been added to the top left of the Word application window, making it easier for you to get help on a particular topic as you work in Word. The various ways to get help in Word are covered in Lesson 5, "Getting Help in Microsoft Word." Let's take a survey of some of the other new features that are provided by Word 2002.

INTRODUCING TASK PANES

One of the biggest changes to the Word environment (and all the Microsoft Office XP member applications such as Word 2002, Excel 2002, and PowerPoint 2002) is the introduction of the Office task pane. The task pane is a special pane that appears on the right side of the Word application window. It is used to provide access to a number of Word features that were formerly controlled using dialog boxes.

For example, when you work with styles to format text in your Word document, you will access the various styles available in your document and create new styles using the Styles and Formatting task pane, which is shown in Figure 1.1.

Other task panes that you will run across as you use Word are the Office Clipboard and the Clip Gallery. The Office Clipboard allows you to copy or cut multiple items from a Word document and then paste them into a new location in the current or a new document. The Clip Gallery provides you with the ability to insert clip art into your Word document. Task panes are discussed throughout this book as you explore the various Word features.

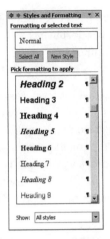

FIGURE 1.1
The Styles and Formatting task pane is used to manage and create styles for a Word document.

SMART TAGS PROVIDE QUICK OPTIONS

Another new enhancement that Word 2002 provides is the smart tag. A smart tag is a special shortcut menu that provides you with additional options related to a particular feature. There are a number of smart tags including Paste smart tags and AutoCorrect smart tags.

For example, in cases where you cut or copy information from a Word document and paste it into a new location, you will find that a Paste smart tag appears at the bottom of the pasted item. This enables you to access options related to your paste job, such as whether the information pasted should maintain its original formatting or be formatted the same as text or numbers that are in the same part of the document where you pasted the new information. Figure 1.2 shows the smart tag that appears when an item is pasted in a Word document.

Smart tags are discussed throughout this book as you encounter them in relation to the various Word features.

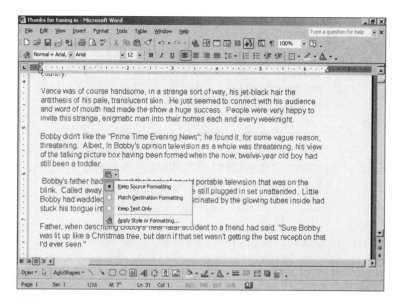

FIGURE 1.2
The Paste smart tag allows you to choose how the text is pasted into a Word document.

Introducing Voice Dictation and Voice Commands

Some of the most exciting new features in Word 2002 (and the entire Office XP suite) are voice dictation and voice-activated commands. If your computer is outfitted with a sound card, speakers, and a microphone (or a microphone with an earphone headset), you can dictate information into your Word documents. You also can use voice commands to activate the menu system in that application.

Before you can really take advantage of the Speech feature, you must provide it with some training so that it can more easily recognize your speech patterns and intonation. After the Speech feature is trained, you can effectively use it to dictate text entries or access various application commands without a keyboard or mouse.

CAUTION

> **Requirements for Getting the Most Out of the Speech Feature**   To make the Speech feature useful, you will need a fairly high-quality microphone. Microsoft suggests a microphone/headset combination. The Speech feature also requires a more powerful computer. Microsoft suggests using a computer with 128MB of RAM and a Pentium II (or later) processor running at a minimum of 400MHz. A computer that meets or exceeds these high standards should be capable of getting the most out of the Speech feature.

You might wish to explore the other lessons in this book, if you are new to Word, before you attempt to use the Speech feature. Having a good understanding of how Word operates and the features that it provides will allow you to get the most out of using the Speech feature.

TRAINING THE SPEECH FEATURE

The first time you start the Speech feature in Word, you are required to configure and train the feature. Follow these steps to get the Speech feature up and running:

1. In Word, select the **Tools** menu and select **Speech**. The Welcome to Office Speech Recognition dialog box appears. To begin setting up your microphone and training the Speech feature, click the **Next** button.

2. The first screen of the Microphone Wizard appears. It asks you to make sure that your microphone and speakers are connected to your computer. If you have a headset microphone, this screen shows you how to adjust the microphone for use. Click **Next** to continue.

3. The next wizard screen asks you to read a short text passage so that your microphone volume level can be adjusted (see Figure 1.3). When you have finished reading the text, click **Next** to continue.

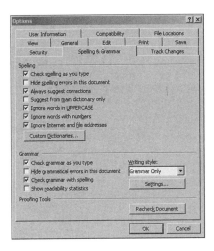

FIGURE 1.3
The Microphone Wizard adjusts the volume of your microphone.

4. On the next screen, you are told that if you have a headset microphone, you can click **Finish** and proceed to the speech recognition training. If you have a different type of microphone, you are asked to read another text passage. The text is then played back to you. This is to determine whether the microphone is placed at an appropriate distance from your mouth. When you get a satisfactory playback, click **Finish**.

When you finish working with the Microphone Wizard, the Voice Training Wizard appears. This wizard collects samples of your speech and educates the Speech feature as to how you speak.

To complete the voice training process, follow these steps:

1. After reading the information on the opening screen, click **Next** to begin the voice training process.

2. On the next screen, you are asked to provide your gender and age (see Figure 1.4). After specifying the correct information, click **Next**.

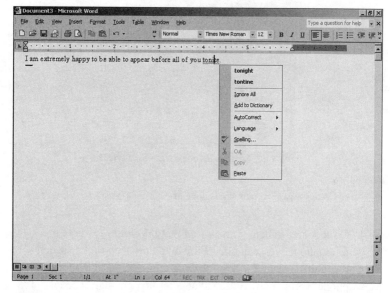

FIGURE 1.4
Supply the voice trainer with your gender and age.

3. On the next wizard screen, you are provided an overview of how the voice training will proceed. You are also provided with directions for how to pause the training session. Click **Next**.

4. The next wizard screen reminds you to adjust your microphone. You are also reminded that you need a quiet room when training the Speech feature. When you are ready to begin training the Speech Recognition feature, click **Next**.

5. On the next screen, you are asked to read text. As the wizard recognizes each word, the word is highlighted. After finishing with this screen, continue by clicking **Next**.

6. You are asked to read text on several subsequent screens. Words are selected as the wizard recognizes them.

7. When you complete the training screens, your profile is updated. Click **Finish** on the wizard's final screen.

You are now ready to use the Speech feature. The next two sections discuss using the Voice Dictation and Voice Command features.

CAUTION

> **The Speech Feature Works Better Over Time** Be advised that the voice feature's performance improves as you use it. As you learn to pronounce your words more carefully, the Speech feature tunes itself to your speech patterns. You might need to do additional training sessions to fine-tune the Speech feature.

USING VOICE DICTATION

When you are ready to start dictating text into a Word document, put on your headset microphone or place your standalone microphone in the proper position that you determined when you used the Microphone Wizard. When you're ready to go, select the **Tools** menu and then select **Speech**. The Language bar appears, as shown in Figure 1.5. If necessary, click the **Dictation** button on the toolbar (if the Dictation button is not already activated or depressed).

After you enable the Dictation button, you can begin dictating your text into the Office document. Figure 1.5 shows text being dictated into a Word document. When you want to put a line break into the text, say "new line." Punctuation is placed in the document by saying the name of a particular punctuation mark, such as "period" or "comma."

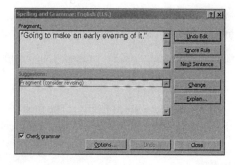

FIGURE 1.5
Dictating text into a Word document.

CAUTION

> **How Do I Insert the Word "Comma" Rather Than the Punctuation Mark?**   Because certain keywords, such as "period" or "comma," are used to insert punctuation during dictation, you must spell these words out if you want to include them in the text. To do this, say "spelling mode," and then spell out the word, such as c-o-m-m-a. As soon as you dictate an entire word, the spelling mode is ended.

When you have finished dictating into the document, click the **Microphone** button on the Language bar (the second Microphone button from the left; the first is used to select the current speech driver, which you can leave as the default). When you click the **Microphone** button, the Language bar collapses and hides the Dictation and the Voice Command buttons. You can also stop Dictation mode by saying "microphone."

You can minimize the Language bar by clicking the **Minimize** button on the right end of the bar. This sends the Language bar to the Windows System Tray (it appears as a small square icon marked EN, if you are using the English version of Office).

With the Language bar minimized in the System Tray, you can quickly open it when you need it. Click the **Language Bar** icon in the

System Tray, and then select **Show the Language Bar** (which is the only choice provided when you click on the Language Bar icon).

Correctly using the Dictation feature requires you to know how to make the Speech feature place the correct text or characters into a Word document. For more help with the Dictation feature, consult the Microsoft Word Help system (discussed in Lesson 5).

USING VOICE COMMANDS

Another tool the Speech feature provides is voice commands. You can open and select menus in an application and even navigate dialog boxes using voice commands.

To use voice commands, open the Language bar (click **Tools, Speech**). Click the **Microphone** icon, if necessary, to expand the Language bar. Then, click the **Voice Command** icon on the bar (or say "voice command").

To open a particular menu such as the Format menu, say "format." Then, to open a particular submenu such as Font, say "font." In the case of these voice commands, the Font dialog box opens.

You can then navigate a particular dialog box using voice commands. You can also activate other font attributes in the dialog box in this manner. Say the name of the area of the dialog box you want to use, and then say the name of the feature you want to turn on or select.

When you have finished working with a particular dialog box, say "OK", and the dialog box closes and provides you with the features you selected in the dialog box. When you have finished using voice commands, say "microphone," or click the **Microphone** icon on the Language bar.

Believe it or not, you can also activate buttons on the various toolbars using voice commands!

In this lesson, you were introduced to Word 2002 and some of the new features available. In the next lesson, you will learn how to start Word and navigate the Word application window.

LESSON 2
Working in Word

In this lesson, you learn how to start Microsoft Word and navigate the Word window. You also learn how to use common tools such as menus, toolbars, and dialog boxes.

STARTING WORD

You create your documents in the Word window, which provides easy access to all the tools you need to create different types of Word documents including memos, letters, and even Web pages.

Before you can take advantage of Word's proficient document processing features, you must open the Word application window. To start the Word program, follow these steps:

1. From the Windows desktop, click **Start**, **Programs**. The Programs menu appears (see Figure 2.1).

2. To start Word, click the **Word** icon. The Word program window appears.

TIP

> **Create a Desktop Shortcut** You can create a shortcut icon for Word on your desktop. Then, you can double-click this icon to start Word. Select the **Start** button, and point at **Programs**. Right-click the **Word** icon and select **Create Shortcut** from the menu that appears.

FIGURE 2.1
Open the Programs menu and click the Word icon to start Word.

Understanding the Word Environment

When you start the Word program, the Word application window opens (see Figure 2.2). You create your documents in the Word window. The Word window also provides items that help you navigate and operate the application itself.

TIP

Control the View   If your view differs from the view shown in Figure 2.2 (the Normal view), or if you don't see all the Word window elements shown in that figure (particularly the ruler), you can easily change your view. Select **View**, then choose the menu selection (such as **Normal** or **Ruler**) that matches your view to the figure.

Notice that the largest area of the window is blank; this is where you create your new document. All the other areas—the menu bar, the toolbar, and the status bar—either provide a fast way to access the various commands and features that you use in Word, or they supply you with information concerning your document, such as what page you are on and where the insertion point is currently located in your document.

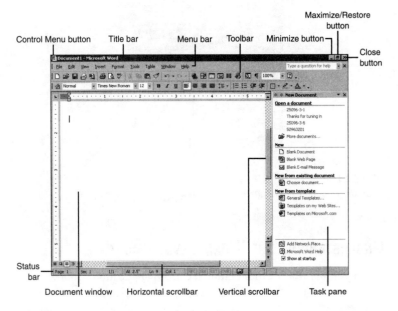

FIGURE 2.2
Create your documents and access Word's features and commands in the Word window.

Table 2.1 describes the elements you see in the Word application window.

TABLE 2.1   Elements of the Word Window

Element	Description
Title bar	Includes the name of the application and the current document, as well as the Minimize, Maximize, and Close buttons.

TABLE 2.1   (continued)

Element	Description
Control Menu button	Opens the Control menu, which provides such commands as Restore, Minimize, and Close.
Minimize button	Reduces the Word window to a button on the taskbar; to restore the window to its original size, click the button on the taskbar.
Maximize/Restore button	Enlarges the Word window to cover the Windows desktop. When the window is maximized, the Maximize button changes to a Restore button that you can click to return the window to its previous size.
Close (x) button	Closes the Word program. "x" is the icon for closing any window.
Menu bar	Contains menus of commands you can use to perform tasks in the program, such as Edit, Format, and Tools.
Toolbar	Includes icons that serve as shortcuts for common commands, such as Save, Print, and Spelling.
Status bar	Displays information about the current page number, the document section in which you are located, and the current location of the insertion point (inches, line, and column). The status bar also shows you other information, such as whether you have turned on the Typeover (OVR) mode by pressing the Insert key on the keyboard.
Document window	Where you type and format your documents.

TABLE 2.1   (continued)

Element	Description
Scrollbars	The horizontal scrollbar is used to scroll your view of the current document in a left-to-right motion. The vertical scrollbar is used to scroll up and down through the current document.
Task pane	The column of information on the right side of the document is the task pane. This is where you can access features such as the Clipboard, styles, and formatting; you can also open another document or mail merge.

USING MENUS AND TOOLBARS

Word provides several ways to access the commands and features you use as you create your documents. You can access these commands by using the menus on the menu bar and the buttons on the various toolbars.

You can also access many Word commands using shortcut menus. Right-clicking a particular document element (a word or a paragraph, for example) opens these menus, which contain a list of commands related to the item on which you are currently working.

THE WORD MENU BAR

The Word menu bar gives you access to all the commands and features that Word provides. Like all Windows applications, Word's menus reside below the title bar and are activated by clicking a particular menu choice. The menu then drops open, providing you with a set of command choices.

Word (and the other Office applications) adopted a menu system called personalized menus that enables you to quickly access the commands you use most often. When you first choose a particular menu, you find a short list of Word's most commonly used menu commands. This list of commands will actually be the ones that you have used most recently on that particular menu.

If a menu has a small double arrow at the bottom of its command list, you can click that to gain access to other, less commonly needed commands. As you use hidden commands, Word adds them to the normal menu list. This means that you are basically building the list of commands available on the menu as you use Word.

This personalized strategy is also employed by the toolbar system. As you use commands, they are added to the toolbar. However, this personalized toolbar feature is available only when you have the Standard toolbar and the Formatting toolbar on the same line in an application window. This provides you with customized menus and toolbars that are personalized for you.

To access a particular menu, follow these steps:

1. Select the menu by clicking its title (such as **View**), as shown in Figure 2.3. The most recently used commands appear; wait just a moment for all the commands on a particular menu to appear (if the commands do not appear, click the down arrow at the bottom of the menu).
2. Select the command on the menu that invokes a particular feature (such as **Header** and **Footer**).

You will find that many of the commands found on Word's menus are followed by an ellipsis (...). These commands, when selected, open a dialog box that requires you to provide Word with additional information before the particular feature or command can be used. More information about understanding dialog boxes is included later in this lesson.

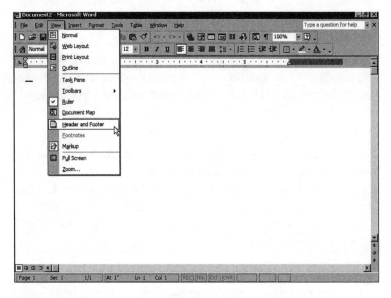

FIGURE 2.3
Select a particular menu to view, and then point to a Word command.

Some of the menus also contain a submenu or cascading menu from which you make choices. The menu commands that produce a sub-menu are indicated by an arrow to the right of the menu choice. When a submenu is present, point at the command (marked with the arrow) on the main menu to open the submenu.

The menu system itself provides a logical grouping of the Word commands and features. For example, commands related to files, such as Open, Save, and Print, are all found on the File menu.

TIP

> **Activating Menus with the Keyboard**   You can activate a
> particular menu by holding down the **Alt** key and then
> pressing the keyboard key that matches the underscored
> letter in the menu's name. This underscored letter is
> called the hotkeyFor example, to activate the File menu
> in Word, press **Alt+F**.

If you find that you would rather have access to all the menu commands (rather than accessing only those you've used recently), you
can turn off the personalized menu system. To do this, follow these
steps:

1. Click the **Tools** menu, and then click **Customize**.

2. In the Customize dialog box, click the **Options** tab.

3. To show all the commands on the menus, click the **Always
   Show Full Menus** check box.

4. Click **OK** to close the dialog box.

SHORTCUT MENUS

A fast way to access commands related to a particular document element is to select that document object and then right-click. This opens
a shortcut menu that contains commands related to the particular
object with which you are working.

PLAIN ENGLISH

> **Object**   Any element found in a document, such as text,
> a graphic, a hyperlink, or other inserted item.

For example, if you select a line of text in a document, right-clicking
the selected text (see Figure 2.4) opens a shortcut menu with commands such as Cut, Copy, and Paste, or it provides you with quick
access to formatting commands, such as Font and Paragraph.

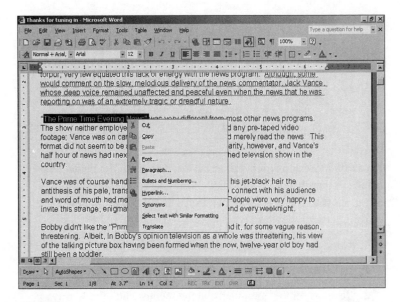

FIGURE 2.4
You can quickly access Word commands using shortcut menus.

WORD TOOLBARS

The Word toolbars provide a very quick and straightforward way to access commands and features. When you first start Word, you are provided with the Standard and Formatting toolbars, which reside as one continuous toolbar found directly below the menu bar.

To access a particular command using a toolbar button, click the button. Depending on the command, you see either an immediate result in your document (such as the removal of selected text when you click the **Cut** button) or the appearance of a dialog box requesting additional information from you.

TIP

Finding a Toolbar Button's Purpose   You can hover (but do not click) the mouse pointer on any toolbar button to view a description of that tool's function.

Word offers several toolbars; many of them contain buttons for a specific group of tasks. For example, the Drawing toolbar provides buttons that give you access to tools that enable you to draw graphical elements in your documents (such as text boxes, lines, and rectangles).

To place additional toolbars in the Word window, right-click any toolbar currently shown and select from the list that appears. Specific toolbars exist for working with tables, pictures, and the World Wide Web.

You can also easily add or remove buttons from any of the toolbars present in the Word window. Each toolbar is equipped with a Toolbar Options button that you can use to modify the buttons shown on that particular toolbar.

To add or remove buttons from a toolbar, follow these steps:

1. Click the **Toolbar Options** button on any toolbar; a drop-down area appears.

2. Click **Add or Remove Buttons** and then select the name of the toolbar that appears on the pop-up menu. A list of all the buttons for the current toolbar appears, as shown in Figure 2.5.

3. For a button to appear on the toolbar, a check mark must appear to the left of the button in this list. For buttons without a check mark next to them, clicking this space puts the button on the toolbar. These buttons work as toggle switches; one click adds the check mark, another click removes it.

4. When you have completed your changes to the current toolbar, click outside the button list to close it.

The Word toolbars provide fast access to the commands you need most often. Buttons exist for all the commands that are available on the Word menu system.

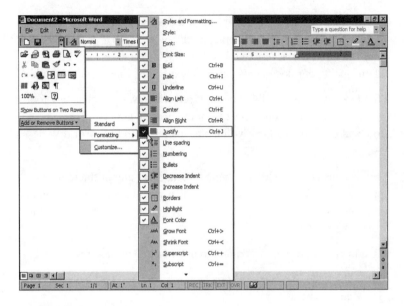

FIGURE 2.5
You can easily add or remove buttons from a toolbar using the button list.

TIP

Give the Standard Toolbar More Space   Another way to provide more space for buttons on the toolbars is to place the Formatting toolbar below the Standard toolbar. Then, both toolbars have the width of the screen on which to display their respective buttons. Select the **Toolbar Options** button on a toolbar, and then select **Show Buttons on Two Rows**.

EXITING WORD

When you have completed your initial survey of the Word application window or have completed your work in the program, exit the software. More than one way exists to close the Word window, which is the same as exiting the program.

You can exit Word by selecting the **File** menu and then **Exit**, or you can close Word with one click of the mouse by clicking the Word **Close** (x) button in the upper-right corner of the application window.

When you close Word, you might be prompted to save any work that you have done in the application window. If you were just experimenting as you read through this lesson, you can click **No**. The current document will not be saved, and the Word application window closes. All the ins and outs of saving your documents are covered in Lesson 3, "Working with Documents."

In this lesson, you learned how to start Word and explored the various parts of the Word window. You also learned how to work with the menu system, toolbars, and dialog boxes. Finally, you also learned how to exit the Word program. In the next lesson, you will learn how to create a new document and save your work.

LESSON 3
Working with Documents

In this lesson, you learn how to start a new document and enter text. You also learn how to take advantage of Word document templates and Word document wizards.

STARTING A NEW DOCUMENT

When you choose to start a new document in Word, you can take three routes. You can

- Create a blank new document using Word's default template.

- Create a document using one of Word's many other templates or a custom one you created yourself.

- Create a document using one of the Word *wizards*, such as the Fax or Envelope Wizard.

The amount of software assistance you get in creating your new document is greatly increased when you choose the template or wizard option.

PLAIN ENGLISH

> **Template**   A blueprint for a document that may already contain certain formatting options and text.

When you create a new document from scratch, you are actually using a template—the Blank Document template. Documents based on the Blank Document template do not contain any premade text (as some of the other templates do), and the formatting contained in the document reflects Word's default settings for margins, fonts, and other document attributes (including any you customized specifically to your needs or preferences). To find more information on default Word settings involving font and document attributes, see Lesson 7, "Changing How Text Looks," and Lesson 11, "Working with Margins, Pages, and Line Spacing," respectively).

As covered in Lesson 2, "Working in Word," Word automatically opens a new blank document for you when you start the Word software. You can also open a new document when you are already in the Word application window.

To open a new document, follow these steps:

1. Select **File**, and then **New**. The task pane opens on the right side of your screen. Under **New from Template**, select **General Templates** and Word opens the Templates dialog box with a range of templates from which to choose (see Figure 3.1).

2. Make sure that the General tab is selected in the Templates dialog box, and then double-click the Word **Blank Document** icon. A new document appears in the Word application window.

Although the steps shown here are designed for you to create a new blank document, you could have chosen any of the templates available in the Templates dialog box to create a new document. The fastest way to create a new blank document is to click the **New Blank Document** icon on the Word Standard toolbar.

CAUTION

> **What Happened to My Previous Document?** If you were already working on a document, the new document will, in effect, open on top of the document you were previously working on. You can get back to the previous document by clicking the appropriately named document icon on the Windows taskbar (if you haven't yet named the first document, it might appear as Document1 on the taskbar). You can also select the **Windows** menu to see a list of currently opened documents. Click any document in the list to switch to it.

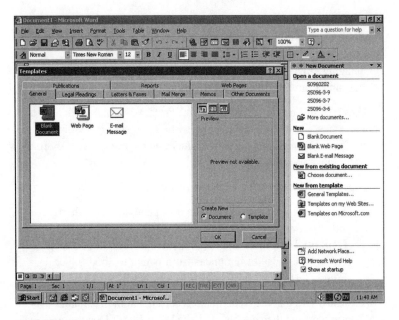

FIGURE 3.1
When you choose New on the File menu, the task pane opens and you can choose General Templates.

TIP

> **Removing Multiple Document Icons from the Taskbar**   If you prefer not to see the open document icons on the taskbar, select the **Tools** menu, select **Options**, and click the **View** tab. Clear the **Windows in Taskbar** check box. You must then use the Windows menu to switch between documents.

ENTERING TEXT

After you have opened a new document, you are ready to start entering text. Notice that a blinking vertical element called the *insertion point* appears in the upper-left corner of your new document. This is where new text will be entered.

Begin typing text from the keyboard. The insertion point moves to the right as you type. As soon as you reach the end of the line, the text automatically wraps to the next line if you are using word wrap.

When you reach the end of a paragraph in Word, you must press the **Enter** key to manually insert a line break. If you want to view the manually placed line breaks (called paragraph marks) in your document, click the **Show/Hide** button on the Word Standard toolbar.

If the Show/Hide button is not visible on the Word toolbar, click the **Tool Options** button located at the end of the Standard toolbar. From the shortcut menu that appears, select **Add or Remove Buttons** and then **Standard**. A drop-down box of other buttons, including the Show/Hide button, appears. Clicking this button adds it to the Standard toolbar. When you are finished, click outside the drop-down box to return to your document. Now you can turn the Show/Hide option on and off as previously described.

How Word Views Paragraphs   Word considers any line or series of lines followed by a line break (created when you press the Enter key) a separate paragraph. This concept becomes very important when you deal with paragraph formatting issues, such as line spacing, indents, and paragraph borders.

USING DOCUMENT TEMPLATES

You don't have to base your new documents on a blank template. Instead, you can take advantage of one of the special document templates that Word provides. These templates make it easy for you to create everything from memos to newsletters.

Templates contain special text and document attributes; therefore, the look and layout of the document you create using a template are predetermined by the options contained in the template. This can include margins, fonts, graphics, and other document layout attributes.

To base a new document on a Word template, follow these steps:

1. Select the **File** menu, and then click **New**. The task pane opens in your current document window.

2. Several template category links are available under the **New from Template** heading. These links include categories such as Normal, General Templates, and Templates on Microsoft.com. Select the category link for the type of document you want to create. For example, to create a new memo, click the **General Templates** link. In the Templates dialog box that appears, choose the **Memos** tab (see Figure 3.2). Select your favorite style of memo and click **OK** (or double-click the icon of choice).

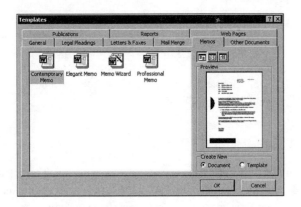

FIGURE 3.2
The document category tabs in the Templates dialog box contain templates for different document types.

3. The new document based on the template appears as shown in Figure 3.3.

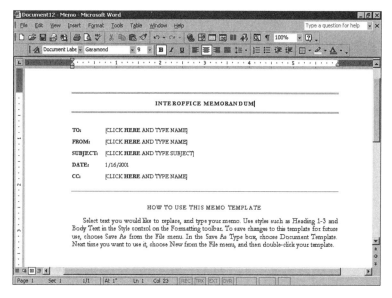

FIGURE 3.3
The new document contains predetermined text and formatting attributes derived from the template.

Most new documents based on templates already contain text, such as headings, as well as a variety of document layouts and text attributes, such as a particular font. For example, the document based on the Elegant Memo template already contains the layout for a memo, and it automatically enters the current date in the memo for you.

Text can easily be entered into the document using the Click Here and Type boxes that are placed in the document. Just click anywhere on the bracketed box and type the text you want to enter.

Many templates (the Elegant Memo template, for example) contain text that gives you advice on how to use the template. Any of this explanatory text can be selected and removed or replaced with your own text (for more about selecting text, see Lesson 4, "Editing Documents").

USING WORD WIZARDS

If you find that you would like even more help as you create a new document, you can use any of a number of Word document wizards. These wizards actually walk you through the document creation process, and in many cases, they make sure that you enter the appropriate text in the proper place in the new document.

The wizards are found on the same tabs that housed the templates located in the Templates dialog box (reached through the task pane). The wizards can be differentiated from standard templates by a small wizard's wand that appears over a template's icon.

To create a new document using one of the wizards, follow these steps:

1. Select the **File** menu, and then click **New** to open the task pane.

2. Under the **New from Template** heading, select the link for the document category you want to create (many useful templates are under the **General Templates** link). In the Templates dialog box that appears, choose the new document tab of your choice.

3. To start the document creation process using the wizard, double-click the appropriate wizard icon (for example, the Memo Wizard on the Memos tab).

When you double-click the wizard icon, the wizard dialog box opens with an introductory screen and outlines the document creation process for the type of document you want to create. For example, the Memo Wizard shown in Figure 3.4 details the memo creation process on the left side of the wizard dialog box.

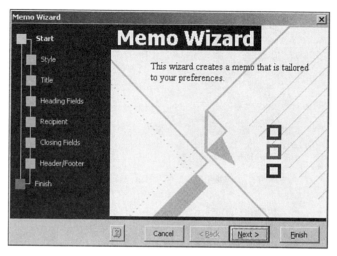

FIGURE 3.4
The various document wizards, such as the Memo Wizard, outline the new creation process and then walk you through the steps of creating the document.

If you find that you need help as you work with a wizard, you can click the **Office Assistant** button on the wizard dialog box. The Office Assistant, which appears as an animated paper clip by default, appears with context-sensitive help related to the wizard screen on which you are currently working. If the button is not available, cancel the wizard, select the **Help** menu, and then **Show the Office Assistant**; then repeat the steps necessary to open the particular document wizard.

To move to the next step in the document creation process, click the **Next** button at the bottom of the wizard screen.

The various document wizards walk you through the entire document creation process. After completing the steps for document creation, click the **Finish** button to close the wizard. A new document appears in the Word window based on the choices you made as you worked with the wizard. Figure 3.5 shows a new document created using the Memo Wizard.

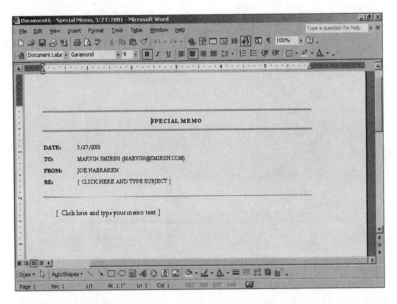

FIGURE 3.5
The Memo Wizard prompts you to input the appropriate information for a memo and provides the formatting for the new document.

The wizards you use vary in look and feel, depending on the type of document you are trying to create. For example, the Resume Wizard produces a decidedly different product than the Envelope Wizard does. A good rule to follow is to read each wizard screen carefully. Remember that you can always back up a step by clicking the **Back** button if you find that you've made an inappropriate choice (or you can close the unwanted document and start over).

SAVING A DOCUMENT

Whether you create your new document using the Blank Document template, a Word template, or a document wizard, at some point you will want to save the new document. Saving your work is one of the most important aspects of working with any software application. If you don't save your Word documents, you could lose them.

CAUTION

Save and Save Often   You don't want to lose your valuable documents as you create them in Word. Power failures, an accidentally kicked-out power cord, or your computer locking up as you work can all lead to lost work. If you are really absent-minded about periodically saving your work, use the AutoSave feature. Select the **Tools** menu, then **Options**. Click the **Save** tab on the dialog box. Make sure the **Save AutoRecover Info Every** check box is selected. Use the minutes box to set the time interval between autosaves. This feature doesn't replace periodically saving your document using the Save command, but it will help you recover more of your document if there is a problem such as a power failure.

To save a document, follow these steps:

1. Click the **Save** button on the Word toolbar, or select the **File** menu and then **Save**. The first time you save your new document, the Save As dialog box appears.

2. Type a filename into the File Name box. If you want to save the file in a format other than a Word document (.doc), such as a text file (.txt), click the **Save As Type** drop-down arrow and select a different file type.

3. To save the file to a different location (the default location is My Documents), click the **Save In** drop-down arrow. After you select a particular drive, all the folders on that drive appear.

4. Double-click the desired folder in the Save In box to open that folder.

5. After you have specified a name and a location for your new document, select the **Save** button to save the file. Word then returns you to the document window.

 As you edit and enhance your new document, you should make a habit of frequently saving any changes that you make. To save changes to a document that has already been saved under a filename, just click the **Save** button.

If you would like to keep a backup of a document (the version as it appeared the last time you saved it) each time you save changes to it, you need to set the backup option.

1. Click the **Tools** command on the toolbar, and then select **Options**.

2. In the Options dialog box, click the **Save** tab and then the **Always Create Backup Copy** check box. Click **OK** to return to the document.

3. Name your file and save it for the first time to an appropriate location.

Now, when you use the Save command to save changes you've made to the document, a backup copy of the file (with the extension.wbk) is also saved. This backup copy is the previous version of the document before you made the changes. Each subsequent saving of the document replaces the backup file with the previous version of the document.

There might be occasions when, rather than using the backup option, you want to save the current document under a new filename or drive location. This can be done using the Save As command. To save your document with a new filename, follow these steps:

1. Select **File**, and then **Save As**.

2. In the Save As dialog box, type the new filename into the File Name box (make sure that you are saving the document in the desired path).

3. Click **Save**. The file is saved under the new name.

CLOSING A DOCUMENT

When you have finished working with a document, you need to save your changes and then close the document. To close a document, select the **File** menu and then select **Close**. You can also close a document by clicking the **Close (x)** button on the right side of the document window. If you are working with multiple documents, closing one of the documents does not close the Word application. If you want to completely end your Word session, select the **File** menu, and then select **Exit**. Before closing a document, Word checks to see whether it has changed since it was last saved. If it has, Word asks whether you want to save these changes before closing. If you don't want to lose any recent changes, click **Yes** to save the document.

OPENING A DOCUMENT

Opening an existing document is a straightforward process. You will find that the Open dialog box shares many of the attributes that you saw in the Save As dialog box.

To open an existing Word file, follow these steps:

1. Select the **File** menu, and then **Open**. The Open dialog box appears.

2. By default, Word begins showing the files and folders in your My Documents folder. If the document you need is located elsewhere on your computer, click the **Look In** drop-down arrow to select the drive on which the file is located, and navigate to the folder containing the document you need.

3. To open the file, click the file, and then click the **Open** button (you can also double-click the file). The file appears in a Word document window.

If you are working with text files or documents that have been saved in a format other than the Word document format (.doc), you must select the file type in the **Files of Type** drop-down box to see them.

In this lesson, you learned how to create a new blank document and base a new document on a Word template. You also learned how to create a new document using the Word wizards, how to open an existing document, and how to save your documents. In the next lesson, you will learn how to edit your document and delete, copy, and move text. You also will learn how to save your document under a new filename.

LESSON 4
Editing Documents

*In this lesson, you learn how to do basic text
editing in Word, including moving and copying text; you work with the
mouse and keyboard to move your document, and you learn how to
save existing documents under a new filename.*

ADDING OR REPLACING TEXT AND MOVING IN THE DOCUMENT

After you have completed a draft of your document, you probably will
find yourself in a situation where you want to add and delete text in
the document as you edit your work. Word makes it very easy for you
to add new text and delete text that you don't want. You also will find
that, whether you use the mouse or the keyboard to move around in
your document as you edit, Word offers a number of special keystrokes and other tricks that make moving within the document a
breeze. Figure 4.1 highlights some of these tools and Word screen
areas.

ADDING NEW TEXT

You actually have two possibilities for adding text to the document:
insert and *typeover*. To insert text into the document and adjust the
position of the existing text, place the *I-beam* mouse pointer where
you want to insert the new text. Click the mouse to place the insertion
point at the chosen position. Make sure that the OVR indicator on the
Status bar is not active (it will be gray rather than bolded). This means
that you are in the insert mode.

I-beam: Used to place the
insertion point in the document.

Vertical scrollbar: Scroll up
and down in a document.

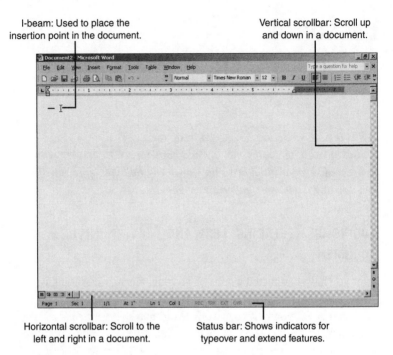

Horizontal scrollbar: Scroll to the
left and right in a document.

Status bar: Shows indicators for
typeover and extend features.

FIGURE 4.1
A number of different tools and approaches are available for editing and select-ing text in Word and moving around in your Word documents.

PLAIN ENGLISH

I-beam   The shape that the mouse pointer takes when you place it over any text in a Word document. Use it to place the insertion point at a particular position in a document.

PLAIN ENGLISH

Insert Mode   The default text mode in Word. New text is added at the insertion point and existing text is pushed forward in the document so that it remains as part of the document.

Type your new text. It is added at the insertion point, and existing text (the text to the right of the inserted text) is pushed forward in the document.

REPLACING TEXT

If you want to add new text to a document and simultaneously delete text to the right of the insertion point, use the mouse to place the insertion point where you want to start typing over the existing text. Press the **Insert** key on the keyboard and add your new text. The added text types over the existing text, deleting it (see Figure 4.2). When you switch to Typeover mode using the **Insert** key, the Word status bar displays the message OVR. This means that you are currently in Typeover mode.

Typeover indicator

FIGURE 4.2
When you are in Typeover mode, existing text is overwritten by the new text.

 **PLAIN ENGLISH**

Typeover Mode   Press the **Insert** key to enter this mode; new text is added at the insertion point and types over the existing text, deleting it.

If you want to return to Insert mode, press the **Insert** key again (it toggles Word between the Insert and Typeover modes) and the OVR message on the status bar is dimmed (you can also double-click **OVR** on the status bar to toggle this feature on and off).

CAUTION

> **Undo That Typeover**   If you inadvertently type over text
> in a document because you are in the Typeover mode,
> click the **Undo** button (it might take several clicks in
> cases where you have added several words to the docu-
> ment) on the toolbar to return the deleted text to the
> document (or press **Ctrl+Z**).

MOVING AROUND THE DOCUMENT

Whether you are a mouse aficionado or prefer to stick close to your
keyboard, Word provides several shortcuts and tools for moving
around a document that you are trying to edit.

When you use the mouse, you can move to a different position in the
current page by placing the mouse pointer (the I-beam) over a particular text entry and then clicking. This places the insertion point where
you clicked.

You also can use the mouse to move through your document using the
vertical and horizontal scrollbars. For example, clicking the up-
scroll arrow on the vertical scrollbar moves you up through the document. Clicking the down-scroll arrow moves you down through the
document. If you want to quickly move to a particular page in the
document, you can drag the scroll box to a particular place on the vertical scrollbar. As soon as you click the scrollbox, a page indicator box
appears that you can use to keep track of what page you are on as you
drag the scroll box up or down on the vertical scrollbar.

The vertical scrollbar also provides Previous Page and Next Page buttons (the double-up arrow and double-down arrow buttons on the bottom of the scrollbar) that can be used to move to the previous page
and next page, respectively. Use the mouse to click the appropriate
button to move in the direction that you want to go in your document.

The horizontal scrollbar operates much the same as the vertical scrollbar; however, it offers the capability to scroll only to the left and the right of a document page. This is particularly useful when you have zoomed in on a document and want to scrutinize an area of the page in great detail.

You should be aware that clicking the mouse on the vertical scrollbar to change your position in a document allows you to view a different portion of a page or a different part of the document; however, it does not move the insertion point to that position on the page. To actually place the insertion point, you must move to a specific place or position in the document, and then click the mouse I-beam where you want to place the insertion point.

When you're typing or editing text, you might find that the fastest way to move through the document is with the help of the keyboard shortcuts shown in Table 4.1. Keeping your hands on the keyboard, rather than reaching out for the mouse, can be a more efficient way to move in a document while you compose or edit.

TIP

> **Scroll Quickly with a Wheel Mouse**   You might want to purchase a wheel mouse, such as Microsoft's IntelliMouse, which provides a rolling device on the top of mouse (between the click buttons). With your finger on the wheel device, you can literally "roll" the vertical scrollbar through the document at the pace of your choice—rapidly or slowly.

TABLE 4.1   Using the Keyboard to Move Through the Document

Key Combination	Movement
Home	Move to the beginning of a line
End	Move to the end of a line
Ctrl+Right arrow	Move one word to the right

TABLE 4.1 (continued)

Key Combination	Movement
Ctrl+Left arrow	Move one word to the left
Ctrl+Up arrow	Move to the previous paragraph
Ctrl+Down arrow	Move to the next paragraph
PgUp	Move up one window
PgDn	Move down one window
Ctrl+PgUp	Move up one page
Ctrl+PgDn	Move down one page
Ctrl+Home	Move to the top of a document
Ctrl+End	Move to the bottom of a document

SELECTING TEXT

Having a good handle on the different methods for selecting text in a document makes it easy for you to take advantage of many features, including deleting, moving, and formatting text. You can select text with either the mouse or the keyboard. Both methods have their own advantages and disadvantages as you work on your documents.

SELECTING TEXT WITH THE MOUSE

The mouse is an excellent tool for selecting text in your document during the editing process. You can double-click a word to select it and also use different numbers of mouse clicks (quickly pressing the left mouse button) or the mouse in combination with the Shift key to select sentences, paragraphs, or other blocks of text. You also can hold the left mouse button down and drag it across a block of text that you want to select.

How you use the mouse to select the text depends on whether the mouse pointer is in the document itself or along the left side of the document in the *selection bar*. The selection bar is the whitespace on the left edge of your document window, just in front of your text paragraphs. When you place the mouse in the selection bar, the mouse pointer becomes an arrow (in contrast to placing the mouse in the document where the pointer appears as an I-beam).

Selecting text lines and paragraphs from the selection bar makes it easy for you to quickly select either a single line or the entire document. Table 4.2 shows you how to select different text items using the mouse. Figure 4.3 shows the mouse pointer in the selection bar with a selected sentence.

TABLE 4.2   Using the Mouse to Quickly Select Text in the Document

Text Selection	Mouse Action
Selects the word	Double-click a word
Selects text block	Click and drag
	Or
	Click at beginning of text, and then hold down Shift key and click at the end of text block
Selects line	Click in selection bar next to line
Selects multiple lines	Click in selection bar and drag down through multiple lines
Selects the sentence	Hold Ctrl and click a sentence
Selects paragraph	Double-click in selection bar next to paragraph
	Or
	Triple-click in the paragraph
Selects entire document	Hold down Ctrl and click in selection bar

You will find these mouse manipulations are particularly useful when you are editing the document. Selected text can be quickly deleted, moved, or copied.

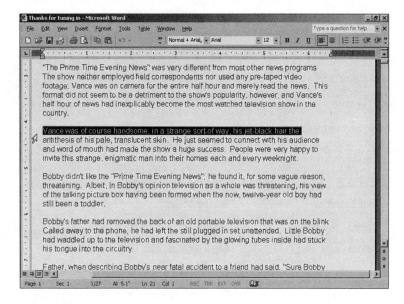

FIGURE 4.3
Place the mouse pointer in the selection bar to quickly select a line, a para-graph, or other text block.

SELECTING TEXT WITH THE KEYBOARD

You can also select text using only the keyboard. Press the **F8** function key to turn on the extend (or select) feature; the EXT indicator becomes active on the Word status bar (meaning it is no longer "grayed" out).

To select text using the extend feature, use the arrow keys to move over and highlight characters, words, or sentences you want to select. You can quickly select entire words by pressing **F8** and then pressing the spacebar. To select an entire sentence, turn on the extend feature, and then press the period (.) key. Entire paragraphs can be selected using this method by pressing the **Enter** key. To turn off the extend feature, press the **Esc** key.

Finally, you can select text by pressing only the F8 function key. Press **F8** once to turn on the select feature where you want it, press it twice to select a word, three times to highlight an entire sentence, four times to select a paragraph, and five times to select your entire document.

Deleting, Copying, and Moving Text

Another important aspect of editing is being able to delete, move, or copy text in your document. Each of these tasks can be easily accomplished in Word and uses the mouse or the keyboard to select the text that you want to delete, move, or copy. Then, it's just a matter of invoking the correct command to delete, move, or copy the selected text.

Deleting Text

Deleting text can be accomplished in more than one way. The simplest way to remove characters as you type is with the Backspace key or the Delete key. With no selected text

- **Delete**—Deletes the character to the right of the insertion point.
- **Backspace**—Deletes the character to the left of the insertion point.

You will probably find, however, that when you delete text you want to remove more than just one character, so use the keyboard or the mouse to select the text you want to delete. After the text is selected, press the **Delete** key. The text is then removed from the document.

You can also delete text and replace it with new text in one step. After the text is selected, type the new text. It replaces the entire existing, selected text.

CAUTION

> **Delete and Cut Are Different**   When you want to erase a
> text block forever, use the **Delete** key. When you want to
> remove text from a particular place in the document but
> want to have access to it again to place it somewhere
> else, use the **Cut** command on the **Edit** menu. When you
> cut an item, it is automatically placed on the Office
> Clipboard. These steps are covered later in this lesson.

COPYING, CUTTING, AND PASTING TEXT

Copying or cutting text and then pasting the copied or cut item to a
new location is very straightforward. All you have to do is select the
text as we have discussed earlier in this lesson and then invoke the
appropriate commands. Use the following steps to copy and paste text
in your document:

1. Using the mouse or the keyboard, select the text that you
   want to copy.

2. Select the **Edit** menu and then select **Copy**, or press **Ctrl+C**
   to copy the text.

3. Place the insertion point in the document where you want to
   place a copy of the copied text.

4. Select the **Edit** menu and then select **Paste**, or press **Ctrl+V**.
   A copy of the text is inserted at the insertion point.

TIP

> 🔲 ✂ 📋 **Use the Copy, Cut, and Paste Icons**   To
> quickly access the copy, cut, and paste features, use
> the Copy, Cut, and Paste icons on the Word toolbar,
> respectively.

After pasting your selected text, the Paste smart tag icon appears just below the text that you have pasted. When you click this icon, it provides a shortcut menu that allows you to keep the formatting that was applied to the source text that you copied, match the formatting supplied by the destination for the text (the paragraph in which the text is placed), or just paste the text into the new location with no formatting at all (which means it will assume the formatting that is provided at the current location).

Smart tags are a new feature found in Word 2002. Figure 4.4 shows pasted text and the Paste smart tag provided for the text.

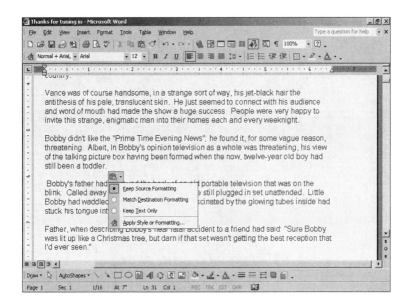

FIGURE 4.4
The Paste smart tag allows you to choose how the text is pasted into the new location.

Cutting text from the document and then pasting it to a new location is every bit as straightforward as using copy and paste. Select the text, and then press **Ctrl+X** or click the **Cut** button on the Standard toolbar. Click the I-beam to place the insertion point on the document, and then you can then use **Ctrl+V** or the **Paste** button on the Standard toolbar to place the text in a new location. A Paste smart tag will appear below the pasted text as shown in Figure 4.4.

USING THE OFFICE CLIPBOARD TO COPY AND MOVE MULTIPLE ITEMS

The Office Clipboard feature now resides in the task pane of your Office application windows. If you want to copy or cut more than one item and then be able to paste them into different places in the document, you must use the Office Clipboard. Follow these steps:

1. To open the Clipboard task pane, select the **Edit** menu and select **Office Clipboard**. The Clipboard appears in the task pane.

2. As shown in Figure 4.5, select and copy each item to the Clipboard.

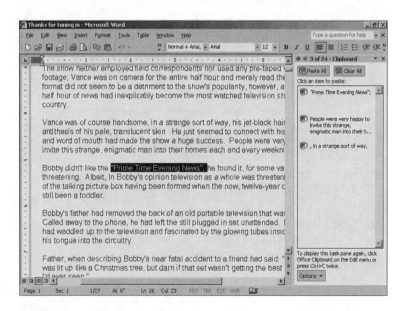

FIGURE 4.5
The Clipboard can hold up to 24 separate items.

3. After you have copied your items onto the Clipboard, place the insertion point where you want the first item to be pasted. Then, return to the Clipboard and with the mouse, point to your first item and click; Word automatically inserts the item into the document.

4. Repeat step 3 as needed to paste other items from the Clipboard into your document.

If you want to cut and paste (or move) multiple items, you must use the Office Clipboard. Follow these steps:

1. To open the Clipboard, select the **Edit** menu and select **Clipboard**. The Clipboard appears in the task pane.

2. Select and cut each item to the Clipboard.

3. After you have your cut items on the Clipboard, place the insertion point where you want the first item to be pasted. Then, return to the Clipboard and with the mouse, point to your first item and click; it will automatically be inserted into the document.

4. Repeat step 3 as needed to paste other items from the Clipboard into your document.

USING DRAG AND DROP

One other way to move text is by selecting it and dragging it to a new location. This is called drag and drop. After the text is selected, place the mouse on the text block and hold down the left mouse button. A Move pointer appears, as shown in Figure 4.6.

Drag the Move pointer to the new location for the text. A dotted insertion point appears in the text. Place this insertion point in the appropriate position and release the mouse button. The text is moved to the new location.

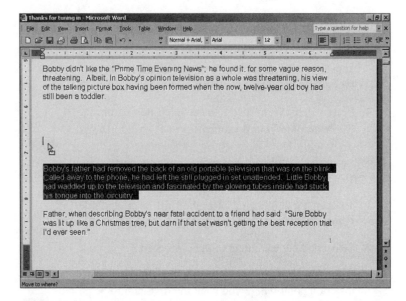

FIGURE 4.6
Drag a block of selected text to a new location with drag and drop.

COPYING AND MOVING TEXT BETWEEN DOCUMENTS

You can copy and move text easily between documents. All you have to do is open the appropriate documents and then use the methods already discussed for copying or moving text. You can even use drag and drop to move information from one document to another.

To copy information from one document to another, follow these steps:

1. Open the document you want to copy information from and the one you want to copy that information to (see Lesson 3, "Working with Documents," for more information on opening documents).

2. Switch to the document that contains the text you want to copy by clicking the document's button on the **Taskbar** or selecting the **Windows** menu and then the name of the document.

3. Select the text you want to copy, select the **Edit** menu, and then select the **Copy** command.

4. Using the instructions in step 3, switch to the document into which you want to paste the text.

5. Select the **Edit** menu and then select **Paste**. The text is pasted into your document.

You can also use the preceding steps to move text from one document to another by substituting the Cut command for the Copy command. You can also use drag and drop to move text from one document to another. Working with multiple document windows can be tricky. You probably won't want to have more than two documents open at a time if you want to use drag and drop. (There won't be enough space in the Word workspace to scroll through the documents and find the text you want to move or the final resting place for the text in the other document.)

To view multiple document windows, open the desired documents. Select the **Windows** menu and then select **Arrange All**. Each document is placed in a separate window in the Word workspace. The windows might be small if you have several documents open. Locate the text you want to move and select it. Drag it from the current document window to the document window and position where you want to place it.

In this lesson, you learned basic editing techniques including the deleting, copying, and moving of text. You also learned to move around your documents and various ways to select text. You also worked with multiple documents and copied text from one document to another. In the next lesson you will learn how to get help in Word.

LESSON 5

Getting Help in Microsoft Word

In this lesson, you learn how to access and use the Help system in Microsoft Word.

HELP: WHAT'S AVAILABLE?

Microsoft Word supplies a Help system that makes it easy for you to look up information on Word commands and features as you work on your documents. Because every person is different, the Help system can be accessed in several ways. You can

- Ask a question in the Ask a Question box.

- Ask the Office Assistant for help.

- Get help on a particular element you see onscreen with the What's This? tool.

- Use the Contents, Answer Wizard, and Index tabs in the Help window to get help.

- Access the Office on the Web feature to view Web pages containing help information (if you are connected to the Internet).

USING THE ASK A QUESTION BOX

The Ask a Question box is a new way to access the Word Help system. It is also the easiest way to quickly get help. An Ask a Question box resides at the top right of the Word window.

For example, if you are working in Word and wish to view information on how to create a style, type **How do I create a style?** into the
Ask a Question box. Then press the **Enter** key. A shortcut menu
appears below the Ask a Question box, as shown in Figure 5.1.

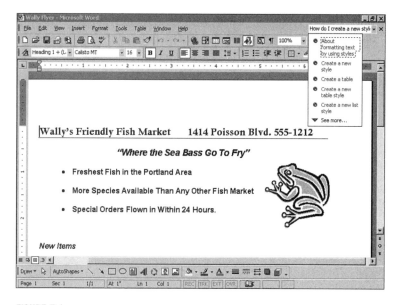

FIGURE 5.1
*The Ask a Question box provides a list of Help topics that you can quickly
access.*

To access one of the Help topics supplied on the shortcut menu, click
that particular topic. The Help window opens with topical matches for
the keyword or phrase displayed.

In the case of the "styles" question used in Figure 5.1 you could select
Create a new style from the shortcut menu that appears. This opens
the help window and displays help on how to create a Word style (see
Figure 5.2).

In the Help window, you can use the links provided to navigate the
Help system. You can also use the Contents, Answer Wizard, and
Index tabs to find additional information or look for new information

in the Help window. You will learn more about these different Help window tabs later in this lesson.

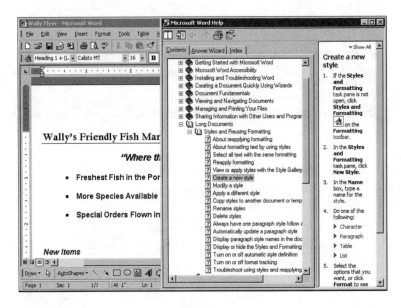

FIGURE 5.2
The Ask a Question box provides a quick way to access the Help window.

USING THE OFFICE ASSISTANT

Another way to get help in Word is to use the Office Assistant. The Office Assistant supplies the same type of access to the Help system as the Ask a Question box. You ask the Office Assistant a question, and it supplies you with a list of possible answers that provide links to various Help topics. The next two sections discuss how to use the Office Assistant.

TURNING THE OFFICE ASSISTANT ON AND OFF

By default, the Office Assistant is off. To show the Office Assistant in your application window, select the **Help** menu and then select **Show the Office Assistant**.

You can also quickly hide the Office Assistant if you no longer want it in your application window. Right-click the Office Assistant and select **Hide**. If you want to get rid of the Office Assistant completely so it isn't activated when you select the Help feature, right-click the Office Assistant and select **Options**. Clear the **Use the Office Assistant** check box, and then click **OK**. You can always get the Office Assistant back by selecting **Help** and then **Show Office Assistant**.

ASKING THE OFFICE ASSISTANT A QUESTION

When you click the Office Assistant, a balloon appears above it. Type a question into the text box. For example, you might type **How do I print?** for help printing your work. Click the **Search** button.

The Office Assistant provides some topics that reference Help topics in the Help system. Click the option that best describes what you're trying to do. The Help window appears, containing more detailed information. Use the Help window to get the exact information that you need.

Although not everyone likes the Office Assistant because having it enabled means that it is always sitting in your Word window, it can be useful at times. For example, when you access particular features in Word, the Office Assistant can automatically provide you with context-sensitive help on that particular feature. If you are brand new to Microsoft Word, you might want to use the Office Assistant to help you learn the various provides.

TIP

> **Select Your Own Office Assistant**   Several different Office Assistants are available in Microsoft Office. To select your favorite, click the Office Assistant and select the **Options** button. On the Office Assistant dialog box that appears, select the **Gallery** tab. Click the **Next** button repeatedly to see the different Office Assistants that are available. When you locate the assistant you want to use, click **OK**.

USING THE HELP WINDOW

You can also forgo either the Type a Question box or the Office Assistant and get your help directly from the Help window. To directly access the Help window, select **Help** and then the help command for the application you are using, such as **Microsoft Word Help.** You can also press the **F1** key to make the Help window appear.

The Help window provides two panes. The pane on the left provides three tabs: Contents, Answer Wizard, and Index. The right pane of the Help window provides either help subject matter or links to different Help topics. It functions a great deal like a Web browser window. Click a link to a particular body of information and that information appears in the right pane.

The first thing that you should do is maximize the Help window by clicking its **Maximize** button. This makes it easier to locate and read the information that the Help system provides (see Figure 5.3).

When you first open the Help window, a group of links in the right pane provides you with access to information about new Word features and other links, such as a link to Microsoft's Office Web site. Next, take a look at how you can take advantage of different ways to find information in the Help window: the Contents tab, the Answer Wizard tab, and the Index tab.

TIP

View the Help Window Tabs   If you don't see the different tabs in the Help window, click the **Show** button on the Help window toolbar.

USING THE CONTENTS TAB

The Contents tab of the Help system is a series of books you can open. Each book has one or more Help topics in it, which appear as pages or chapters. To select a Help topic from the Contents tab, follow these steps:

1. In the Help window, click the **Contents** tab on the left side of the Help window.

2. Find the book that describes, in broad terms, the subject for which you need help.

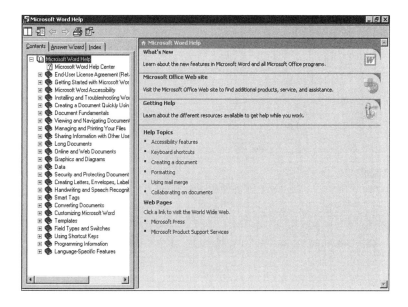

FIGURE 5.3
The Help window provides access to all the help information provided for Word.

3. Double-click the book, and a list of Help topics appears below the book, as shown in Figure 5.4.

4. Click one of the pages (the pages contain a question mark) under a Help topic to display it in the right pane of the Help window.

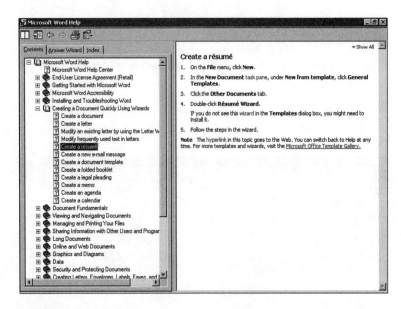

FIGURE 5.4
Use the Contents tab to browse through the various Help topics.

5. When you finish reading a topic, select another topic on the Contents tab or click the Help window's **Close** (**x**) button to exit Help.

Using the Answer Wizard

Another way to get help in the Help window is to use the Answer Wizard. The Answer Wizard works the same as the Ask a Question box or the Office Assistant; you ask the wizard questions and it supplies you with a list of topics that relate to your question. Click one of the choices provided to view help in the Help window.

To get help using the Answer Wizard, follow these steps:

1. Click the **Answer Wizard** tab in the Help window.

2. Type your question into the What Would You Like to Do? box. For example, you might type the question, **How do I format text?**

3. After typing your question, click the **Search** button. A list of topics appears in the Select Topic to Display box. Select a particular topic, and its information appears in the right pane of the Help window, as shown in Figure 5.5.

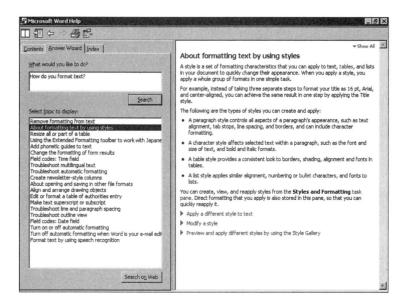

FIGURE 5.5
Search for help in the Help window using the Answer Wizard tab.

TIP

> **Print Help**   If you want to print information provided in the Help window, click the **Print** icon on the Help toolbar.

USING THE INDEX

The Index is an alphabetical listing of every Help topic available. It's like an index in a book.

Follow these steps to use the index:

1. In the Help window, click the **Index** tab.

2. Type the first few letters of the topic for which you are looking. The Or Choose Keywords box jumps quickly to a keyword that contains the characters you have typed.

3. Double-click the appropriate keyword in the keywords box. Topics for that keyword appear in the Choose a Topic box.

4. Click a topic to view help in the right pane of the Help window (see Figure 5.6).

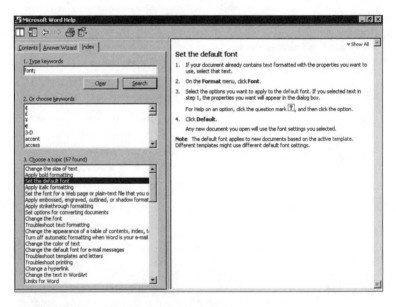

FIGURE 5.6
Use the Index tab to get help in the Help window.

TIP

> **Navigation Help Topics**   You can move from topic to topic in the right pane of the Help window by clicking the various links that are provided there. Some topics are collapsed. Click the triangle next to the topic to expand the topic and view the help provided.

GETTING HELP WITH SCREEN ELEMENTS

If you wonder about the function of a particular button or tool on the Word screen, wonder no more. Just follow these steps to learn about this part of Help:

1. Select **Help** and then **What's This?** or press **Shift+F1**. The mouse pointer changes to an arrow with a question mark.

2. Click the screen element for which you want help. A box appears explaining the element.

TIP

> **Take Advantage of ScreenTips**   Another Help feature provided by the Office applications is the ScreenTip. All the buttons on the different toolbars provided by Word have a ScreenTip. Place the mouse on a particular button or icon, and the name of the item (which often helps you determine its function) appears in a ScreenTip.

In this lesson you learned how to access the Word Help feature. In the next lesson you will work with proofreading tools such as the Word spell checker, grammar checker, and the AutoCorrect feature.

LESSON 6
Using Proofreading Tools

In this lesson, you learn to check your documents for errors such as misspellings and improper grammar. You work with the spell checker and grammar checker and learn how to find synonyms with the thesaurus, how to proof your document as you type, and how to use the AutoCorrect feature.

PROOFING AS YOU TYPE

Word offers several excellent features for helping you to create error-free documents. Each of these features—the spell checker, the grammar checker, and the thesaurus—are explored in this lesson. Word also gives you the option of checking your spelling and grammar automatically as you type. You can also use the AutoCorrect feature to automatically make some proofing changes for you (for more about AutoCorrect, see "Working with AutoCorrect" in this lesson).

Proofing as you type simply means that errors in spelling and grammar can be automatically flagged as you enter text into your document. This enables you to quickly and immediately correct errors as you build your document.

When you proof as you type, spelling errors—words not found in the Word dictionary file or in your custom dictionary file—are flagged with a wavy red underline. Errors in grammar are underlined with a wavy green line. Spelling and grammar errors marked in this way can be corrected immediately, or you can correct them collectively by running the spelling and grammar checking features after you have finished entering all the text. For information on using the Spelling and

Grammar Checker on a completed document, see the section "Using the Spelling and Grammar Checker," found later in this lesson.

The check-as-you-type features are turned on in Word by default. To change the defaults associated with the automatic spelling and grammar checking features (or to turn them off completely), follow these steps:

1. Select the **Tools** menu and then choose **Options**. The Options dialog box opens.

2. Make sure the **Spelling and Grammar** tab is selected, as shown in Figure 6.1.

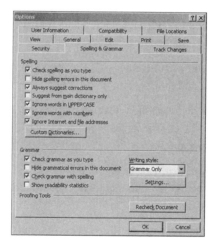

FIGURE 6.1
You can turn the automatic spelling and grammar checking options on or off in the Options dialog box.

3. To toggle the automatic spelling checker on or off, click the **Check Spelling As You Type** check box in the Spelling area of the dialog box.

4. To toggle the automatic grammar checker on or off, click the **Check Grammar As You Type** check box in the Grammar area of the dialog box (near the bottom).

Several other options are also available in this dialog box that relate to how the Spelling and Grammar features operate when you use them in Word.

- **Hide spelling errors in this document**—This option hides the wavy red lines that flag misspellings in the document.

- **Always suggest corrections**—This option provides a list of suggested corrections for each misspelled word when the spell checker is used.

- **Suggest from main dictionary only**—This option uses only the main dictionary for spell checking the document. Any customized dictionaries that have been created are ignored.

- **Ignore words in UPPERCASE**—This option ignores upper-case words in the document.

- **Ignore words with numbers**—This option ignores combinations of text and numbers in the document.

- **Ignore Internet and file addresses**—This option ignores Web addresses and filenames (such as C:\my documents\joe.doc).

- **Hide grammatical errors in the document**—This option hides the wavy green line that marks potential grammatical errors in the document.

- **Check grammar with spelling**—This option is used to check the grammar in the document when you run the spell checker.

- **Show readability statistics**—This option is used to display different readability statistics that show you the readability level and grade level of your text.

After you have finished making your selections in the Options dialog box, click **OK**.

With the check-as-you-type options enabled, suspected misspellings and grammatical errors are flagged with the appropriate colored wavy line.

CORRECTING INDIVIDUAL SPELLING ERRORS

As mentioned, Word marks all words not found in its dictionary with a wavy red line. Because Word's dictionary isn't entirely complete, you might find that it marks correct words as misspelled. To correct words flagged as misspelled (whether they are or not), follow these steps:

1. Place the mouse pointer on the flagged word and click the right mouse button. A shortcut menu appears, as shown in Figure 6.2.

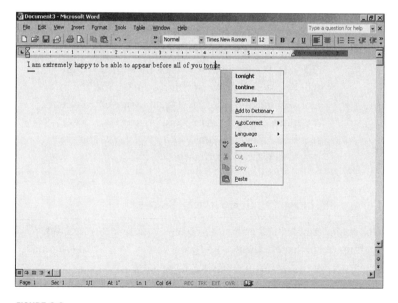

FIGURE 6.2
Right-click any flagged word to get a list of suggested spellings.

2. Word provides a list of possible correct spellings when it encounters a word not in its dictionary. If the correct spelling

for the word you want appears in the list, simply click it, and Word replaces the incorrect spelling with the correct one.

If the flagged word is correctly spelled (and just not in Word's dictionary) or the correct spelling is not in the suggestions list, you have three other options:

- If the word is correct and you don't want it flagged at all in the current document, you can click **Ignore All** and the wavy red line will be removed from all occurrences of the word.

- If the word is correct and you don't want it flagged in this or any other document, you can add the word to the dictionary file; click **Add**.

- If you find that you constantly misspell the word as it currently appears in your document, you can add the word to the AutoCorrect list (discussed later in this chapter). Point to **AutoCorrect**. Suggested spellings will be listed. Select a spelling from the list; the incorrect spelling and the correct spelling are entered into the AutoCorrect list. The word in your document is corrected, and the next time you type the word incorrectly, it is automatically corrected.

CORRECTING INDIVIDUAL GRAMMATICAL ERRORS

Correcting grammatical errors as you type is similar to correcting spelling errors that are flagged in the document. Suspected grammatical errors are marked with a green wavy line.

To correct a suspected grammatical error, follow these steps:

1. Right-click text blocks marked with the green wavy line.

2. The shortcut menu that appears might offer you a list of grammatically correct phrases. Select the phrase that corrects your text entry.

3. If your text is not incorrect grammatically or requires that you manually make any necessary changes, click **Ignore**.

As soon as you make a selection from the shortcut menu or click **Ignore**, the shortcut menu closes. You can then continue working on your document.

USING THE SPELLING AND GRAMMAR CHECKER

You might prefer not to correct spelling and grammatical errors as you type. If you're a touch typist, you might not even notice Word has flagged a word or sentence as incorrect. Waiting to correct the document until you have finished composing enables you to concentrate on getting your thoughts down without interruption. Then, you can check the entire document upon completion.

To use the Word Spelling and Grammar feature, follow these steps:

1. Select **Tools**, **Spelling and Grammar**, or click the **Spelling and Grammar** button on the toolbar. The Spelling and Grammar dialog box appears as shown in Figure 6.3.

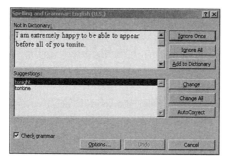

FIGURE 6.3
The Spelling and Grammar dialog box displays the suspected spelling and grammar errors in your document and offers you options for correcting them.

2. Words not found in the dictionary are flagged, and the text in which the word is contained is displayed in the Not in Dictionary box. You can manually correct the highlighted word in the box and then click **Change** to correct the word in the document. The following are other options available for the flagged word:

   - Select the appropriate selection for the flagged word from the Suggestion box and click **Change**. If you want to correct all occurrences of the misspelled word (assuming you have consistently and knowingly mis-spelled it), click **Change All**.

   - Ignore the flagged word if it is correctly spelled. Click **Ignore Once** to ignore this occurrence of the word, or click **Ignore All** to ignore all occurrences of the word in the document.

   - You can also add the word to the dictionary; just click **Add**.

   - If you would rather add the misspelled word and an appropriate correct spelling to the AutoCorrect feature, click **AutoCorrect**; the word is corrected, and future insertions of the word (even in other documents when they're opened) with the incorrect spelling are automatically corrected.

Whichever selection you make, the word is dealt with appropriately and the spelling checker moves on to the next flagged word. Make your selection either to correct or to ignore the word, as previously outlined.

If the Check Grammar check box in the Spelling and Grammar dialog box is selected, Word also checks the grammar in your document.

When the Spelling and Grammar dialog box flags a grammatical error in the document, the suspected error appears in the text box at the top of the Spelling and Grammar dialog box with a heading that describes the type of error. Figure 6.4 shows a sentence fragment that has been caught by the grammar checker.

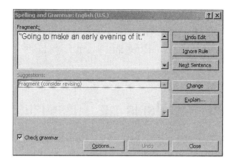

FIGURE 6.4
The grammar checker flags suspected grammatical errors and offers suggestions and possible fixes for the problem.

Suggested corrections, if available, appear in the Suggestions box. In the case of the fragment, the suggestion is to consider revising the fragment. In other cases, more suggestions with actual sentence revisions might appear in this box. If present, select the appropriate revision and click **Change**.

You are also presented with different ignore options for flagged grammatical errors:

- You can choose to ignore the suspected grammatical error by clicking **Ignore**. This ignores only the currently flagged error.

- In some cases, **Ignore All** is also an option. If you click **Ignore All**, the grammar checker ignores all occurrences of this same grammatical error in the rest of the document.

- Word also provides you with the option of ignoring the actual grammar rule that was used to flag the current grammatical error; click **Ignore Rule** to do this throughout the document. This means that any error (not just the current error) that is flagged because of that particular rule (fragment or long sentence, for example is not flagged as a grammatical error.

Use the Grammar feature to check the entire document using the options discussed in this section. When you reach the end of the document and the Grammar check is complete, a dialog box will appear letting you know that the spelling and grammar check has been completed.

FINDING SYNONYMS USING THE THESAURUS

The Word thesaurus provides you with a tool that can be used to find synonyms for the words in your document. Synonyms are words that mean the same thing. Because the thesaurus can generate a list of synonyms for nearly any word in your document, you can avoid the constant use of a particular descriptive adjective (such as "excellent") and add some depth to the vocabulary that appears in your document.

TIP

The Thesaurus Also Lists Antonyms   Depending on the word you select to find synonyms, you might find that a list of antonyms—words that mean the opposite—are also provided. Antonyms are marked with (antonym) to the right of the suggested word.

To use the thesaurus, follow these steps:

1. Place the insertion point on the word for which you want to find a synonym.

2. Select the **Tools** menu, point at **Language**, and then select **Thesaurus**. The Thesaurus dialog box appears as shown in Figure 6.5.

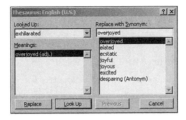

FIGURE 6.5
The Thesaurus dialog box offers a list of synonyms for the selected word.

3. To replace the word with a synonym, select the synonym in the synonym list, and then click **Replace**.

4. You can also choose to see a list of synonyms for any of the words listed in the synonym list. Select the word, and then click **Look Up**. This can provide a greater number of possible words to use when you replace the particular word in your document. The word in your document might be less close in meaning to the synonyms provided on the synonym list.

After you have selected a synonym and clicked **Replace**, the word is replaced in the document and the Thesaurus dialog box closes.

TIP

> **Right-Click for Synonyms**   A quick way to check for a list of synonyms for a word is to right-click that word in your document and then select **Synonyms** from the shortcut menu. A list of synonyms (if available for that word) appears. Select the appropriate word on the list to replace the currently selected word. Words flagged as misspelled or in a sentence marked as a grammatical error will not provide a list of synonyms when you right-click them.

WORKING WITH AUTOCORRECT

Some of your misspelled words are automatically corrected as you type. This is done by the AutoCorrect feature that uses a list of common spelling errors and typos to correct entries in your documents. For example, Word has already arranged to have the incorrect spelling of "t-e-h" to be replaced with "the." You can also add your own words to the AutoCorrect feature. For example, if you always spell aardvark as ardvark, you can set up AutoCorrect to correct this spelling error every time you type it.

You've already seen that the Spelling feature provides you with the option of placing misspelled words into the AutoCorrect library. You can also manually enter pairs of words (the incorrect and correct spellings) into the AutoCorrect dialog box.

To place words in the AutoCorrect list, follow these steps:

1. Click the **Tools** menu, and then click **AutoCorrect Options**. The AutoCorrect dialog box appears as shown in Figure 6.6.

FIGURE 6.6
The AutoCorrect feature enables you to build a list of commonly misspelled words for automatic correction.

2. In the **Replace** box, enter the word as you misspell it. In the **With** box enter the correct spelling of the word.

3. Click **Add** to add the entry to the AutoCorrect list.

4. When you have completed adding entries, click **OK** to close the dialog box.

Now when you misspell the word, Word corrects it for you automatically. You can also use the AutoCorrect dialog box to delete AutoCorrect entries that you do not use (highlight the entry and click **Delete**) or that inadvertently correct items that you want to have in your document (clear the applicable check box).

This feature can also be used to help speed your typing along. For example, suppose that you are writing a technical paper that includes a long organizational name, such as the National Museum of American Art. If you tell the AutoCorrect feature to replace "nmaa" with "National Museum of American Art," it saves you a lot of typing.

 TIP

> **Override the AutoCorrect Feature**   If you type a text entry that is automatically changed by the AutoCorrect feature but you want it spelled your original way, immediately place your mouse on the corrected text. The AutoCorrect smart tag (it has a lightning bolt symbol on it) appears. When you click this smart tag's arrow, you can choose to return the word to its original text, among other options.

In this lesson, you learned how to proof your documents as you type. You also learned to use the Spelling and Grammar feature and select synonyms for words in your document using the thesaurus. You also explored the use of the AutoCorrect feature. In the next lesson, you will learn how to change the look of your documents using fonts and how to align text in your documents.

LESSON 7
Changing How Text Looks

In this lesson, you learn basic ways to change the look of your text. You work with fonts and learn how to change font attributes. You also work with text alignment, such as centering and right justification.

UNDERSTANDING FONTS

When you work in Word, you want to be able to control the look of the text in the documents that you create. The size and appearance of the text is controlled for the most part by the font or fonts you choose to use in the document. Each available font has a particular style or typeface. A variety of fonts exists, with names such as Arial, Courier, Times New Roman, CG Times, Bookman Old Style, and so on; the fonts you can choose depend on the fonts that have been installed on your computer (Windows offers a large number of default fonts; other font families are added when you install Office, and you can purchase software for special lettering and printing projects). Each font has a particular look and feel that makes it unique.

TIP

> **Keep Your Business Documents Standard** The standard point size for most business documents is 12 point, which is 1/6 of an inch tall. So, when selecting a new font, it's generally a good idea to make sure that you use 12 point for documents such as business letters and memos.

You can change the font or fonts used in a document whenever you have the need, and you can also manipulate the size of the characters and their attributes, including bold, underlining, and italic. You can select a new font before you begin typing your document, or you can select text and change its fonts and text attributes at any time.

CHANGING FONT ATTRIBUTES

The easiest way to change font attributes is through the use of the buttons provided on the Word Formatting toolbar. Figure 7.1 shows the Word Formatting toolbar with some of the most common font attribute buttons displayed.

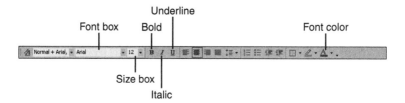

FIGURE 7.1
The Word Formatting toolbar gives you quick access to control the font attributes in your documents.

You can quickly change the font of selected text by clicking the **Font** box and selecting a new font from the list that appears. Other attributes, such as bold, italic, and underline, require that you select the text and then click the appropriate button once to add that attribute to the text. For example, you might want to apply special formatting to a heading so that it stands out from the rest of the text. You can do that by adding bold to the text.

To add bold to text in a document, follow these steps:

1. **Select** the word or other text to be bold.

2. Click the **Bold** button on the Formatting toolbar. The text appears in bold.

B

3. Click any other part of the document to deselect the text and view the results of your formatting.

You can use this same technique to underline and italicize text in your documents.

TIP

> **I Don't Have Those Buttons on My Toolbar**   Click the **Toolbar Options** drop-down arrow, point at **Add or Remove Buttons,** and then select the name of the toolbar to which you want to add the buttons (such as the Formatting toolbar). From the drop-down list, select the buttons that you want to add to the Formatting toolbar. If you don't see the Formatting toolbar at all, right-click any of the toolbars and select **Formatting** on the menu that appears.

You can also use the various font buttons to select font attributes for the new text you type into a new document or insert into an existing document. Select the appropriate font attributes on the Formatting toolbar, and then type the text. To turn off a particular attribute, such as bold or italic, click the appropriate button a second time. To change to a new font or size, use the appropriate drop-down box.

When you are typing in a document, you might find that selecting font attributes from the toolbar actually slows you down because you must remove one hand from the keyboard to use the mouse to make your selection. You can also turn on or off a number of the formatting attributes using shortcut keys on the keyboard. Table 7.1 shows some of the common keyboard shortcuts for formatting attributes.

TABLE 7.1   Font Attribute Shortcut Keys

Attribute	Shortcut Keys
Bold	Ctrl+B
Italic	Ctrl+I

TABLE 7.1   (continued)

Attribute	Shortcut Keys
Underline	Ctrl+U
Double underline	Ctrl+Shift+D
Subscript	Ctrl+equal sign (=)
Superscript	Ctrl+Shift+plus sign (+)

To use any of the shortcut key combinations, press the keys shown simultaneously to turn the attribute on, and then repeat the key sequence to turn the attribute off. For example, to turn on bold while you are typing, press the **Ctrl** key and the **B** key at the same time. Press these keys again to turn the bold off.

WORKING IN THE FONT DIALOG BOX

Although the Formatting toolbar certainly provides the quickest avenue for controlling various font attributes, such as the font and the font size, you can access several more font attributes in the Font dialog box. The Font dialog box gives you control over common attributes, such as font, font size, bold, and so on, and it also provides you with control over special font attributes, such as superscript, subscript, and strikethrough.

To open the Font dialog box, click the **Format** menu and then select **Font**. The Font dialog box appears, as shown in Figure 7.2.

As you can see, the Font dialog box enables you to choose from several font attributes. You can control the font, the font style, and other character attributes such as strikethrough, superscript, and shadow, as shown next.

- To change the font, click the **Font** drop-down box and select the new font by name.

- To change the font style to italic, bold, or bold italic, make the appropriate selection in the **Font Style** box.

- To change the size of the font, select the appropriate size in the **Size** scroll box.

- For underlining, click the **Underline Style** drop-down box and select an underlining style.

- To change the color of the font, click the **Font Color** drop-down box and select a new color.

- To select any special effects, such as strikethrough, super-script, or shadow, select the appropriate check box in the lower half of the dialog box.

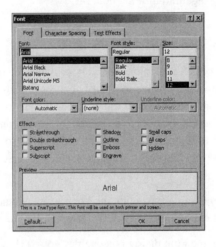

FIGURE 7.2
The Font dialog box provides you with control over several font attributes not found on the Formatting toolbar.

As you make the various selections in the Font dialog box, a sample of what the text will look like appears in the Preview box at the bottom of the dialog box. After you have made all your selections in the Font dialog box, click **OK**.

TIP

> **Change the Default Font**   To change the default font that you use for your documents (those created using the current or desired template), select the font attributes in the Font dialog box and then click the **Default** button at the lower left of the dialog box. Click **Yes** when Word asks for a confirmation of the change.

ALIGNING TEXT

Another important basic attribute of the text in your documents is how that text is oriented on the page. When you first start typing in a new document, all the text begins at the left margin and moves to the right as you type; this means the text is left-justified using the default align left feature. Left-justified text is characterized by text that is straight or unvarying on the left margin but has a ragged right-edged margin.

Text that serves a special function in a document, such as a heading, would probably stand out better in the document if it were placed differently than the rest of the text. Word makes it easy for you to change the alignment of any text paragraph. Several alignment possibilities are available:

- **Align Left**—The default margin placement for normal text that is aligned on the left.

- **Align Right**—Text is aligned at the right margin and text lines show a ragged left edge.

- **Center**—The text is centered between the left and right margins of the page (with both margins having irregular edges).

- **Justify**—The text is spaced irregularly across each line so that both the left and the right margins are straight edged and uniform (often used in printed publications such as the daily newspapers).

CAUTION

> **Remember How Word Sees a Paragraph**　Any text fol-
> lowed by a paragraph mark—created when you press the
> **Enter** key—is considered a separate paragraph in Word.
> This means that when you use alignment features, such
> as those discussed in this section, only the paragraph
> that currently holds the insertion point will be affected
> by the alignment command that you select (such as
> Center). If you need to align multiple lines that are in
> separate paragraphs, select that text before selecting the
> alignment command.

Figure 7.3 shows examples of each of the alignment possibilities.

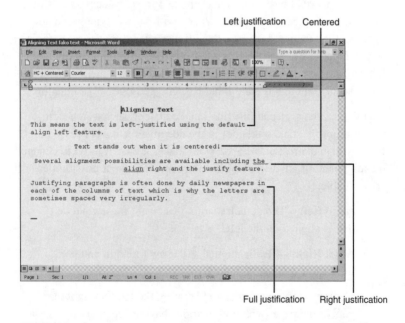

FIGURE 7.3
*You can align the text in your document to suit your particular needs on a
document page.*

The easiest way to change the alignment of text in the document is to use the alignment buttons on the Formatting toolbar. Also, a button exists in the Paragraph dialog box for each of the alignment possibilities. Table 7.2 shows the buttons and their functions.

TABLE 7.2   Alignment Icons on the Formatting Toolbar

Button	Justification
	Align left
	Center
	Align right
	Justify (full justification)

These justification buttons can be used to align new text or selected text. Again, if you are typing new text with a particular justification, your selected justification will still be in force even after you press Enter. You must change the justification as needed.

ALIGNING TEXT WITH CLICK AND TYPE

Word offers a unique and quick way to insert and align text (or to insert graphics, tables, and other items) in a blank area of a document. Before entering text or another item, place the mouse pointer on a blank line on the page. As you move the mouse pointer from right to left on the blank line, the pointer (or I-beam, in this case) changes shapes as you move it, denoting a particular line alignment. This makes it very easy to center or right align the insertion point before you insert the text or other item.

CAUTION

Click and Type Option Must Be On   To use Click and Type, you must also make sure that the **Enable Click and Type** box is selected on the **Edit** tab of the Options dialog box (select **Tools** and then **Options** to open this dialog box).

To use the Click and Type feature, you must be in the Print Layout or Web Layout view. The feature is not available in the Normal view. To switch to the Print Layout or Web Layout view, select **View**, and then select the appropriate view from the View menu.

Then, to use Click and Type to align your new text, follow these steps:

1. Move the mouse pointer toward the area of the page where you want to place the insertion point. The pointer icon changes to

   - Center (the centering pointer appears)

   - Right (the align-right pointer appears)

2. After the mouse pointer shows the centering or right-align icon, double-click in the document. The insertion point moves to the selected justification.

3. Type your new text.

After you've typed the centered or right-aligned text and you've pressed **Enter** to create a new line, you can return to left justification by placing the mouse to the left of the line (the align-left icon appears on the mouse pointer) and double-clicking.

AUTOMATICALLY DETECTING FORMATTING INCONSISTENCIES

Word 2002 offers a new feature that marks formatting inconsistencies in your document. This allows you to make sure that the text in your document is formatted as you intended. The Detect Formatting feature keeps track of the formatting in your document and can also be configured to flag any formatting inconsistencies.

To configure the Detect Formatting feature to flag formatting inconsistencies, follow these steps:

1. Select **Tools** and then select **Options**. The Options dialog box opens.

2. On the Options dialog box, select the **Edit** tab.

3. Under Editing options, select the **Keep track of Formatting** check box, if it is not already selected. Also select the **Mark Formatting Inconsistencies** check box.

4. Click **OK** to close the Options dialog box.

Now, formatting inconsistencies will be marked with a wavy blue line as you type. When you find a word or paragraph that has been flagged with the wavy blue line, right-click the word or paragraph. A shortcut menu appears as shown in Figure 7.4.

Use the menu choices on the shortcut menu to either replace the direct formatting with an available style or ignore the direct formatting occurrence. To ignore this formatting occurrence, click **Ignore Once**. If you want all formatting occurrences that have been flagged by the Detect Formatting feature to be ignored in the document, click the **Ignore Rule** choice on the shortcut menu.

Be advised that the Detect Formatting feature doesn't always catch formatting errors. For example, if you have most of your text in a 12-point font, some font that you might have inadvertently formatted for 14 point won't necessarily be flagged. Word assumes you might be using the 14 point for a heading or other special text.

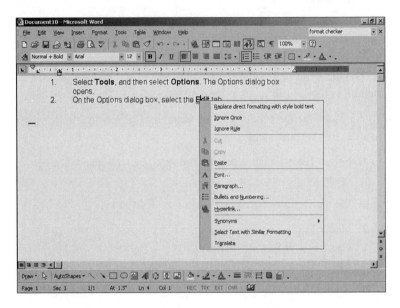

FIGURE 7.4
You can have formatting inconsistencies flagged in your documents.

The Detect Formatting feature is best at detecting direct formatting changes that you have made to text in a document (such as directly adding bold to text, as shown in Figure 7.4), where other text that has been bolded has been formatted using a "bold" style that you created (styles are covered in Lesson 12, "Working with Styles"). The inconsistency that Word picks up on is that you didn't use the style to bold the item as you had done in the rest of the document.

In this lesson, you learned how change the font and font size in your document and work with various font attributes, such as bold, italic, and underline. You also learned how to align text in your document and worked with the various justification options. In the next lesson, you will learn how to use borders and colors to emphasize text in your documents.

Lesson 8
Using Borders and Colors

In this lesson, you learn how to use borders and colors to emphasize text in your documents.

Adding Borders to Text

In Lesson 7, "Changing How Text Looks," you learned that you can use various font attributes, such as font size, bold, italic, and underline, to emphasize and otherwise denote certain text in your document. You also learned that alignment, such as centering, can be used to set off certain text lines on a page. Word provides you with the capability to add borders to your text and even place a shadow on the edge of a border for greater emphasis.

A border can be placed around any text paragraph (any line followed by a paragraph mark). This means that one line of text or several lines of text can have a border placed around them.

TIP

> ¶ **Remember How Word Views a Paragraph** Whenever you type a line or several lines of text and then press **Enter**, you are placing an end-of-paragraph mark at the end of the text. Word views any line or lines followed by a paragraph mark as a separate paragraph. If you need to view the paragraph marks in your document, click the **Show/Hide** button on the Word Standard toolbar.

To place a border around a text paragraph, follow these steps:

1. Place the insertion point in the paragraph that you want to place the border around. If you want to place a border around multiple paragraphs, select all the paragraphs.

2. Select the **Format** menu, and then **Borders and Shading**. The Borders and Shading dialog box appears, as shown in Figure 8.1.

FIGURE 8.1

Click here to put a line over the text.

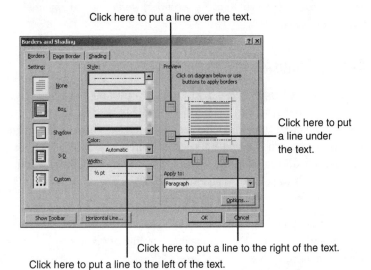

Click here to put a line under the text.

Click here to put a line to the right of the text.

Click here to put a line to the left of the text.

The Borders and Shading dialog box enables you to place a border around your text.

3. Make sure the **Borders** tab is selected on the dialog box. You are provided with several settings for how the border should appear around the text.

4. In the Setting area of the dialog box, select the type of box you want around your text; choose **Box, Shadow, 3-D**, or **Custom** by clicking the appropriate setting sample. The Custom option enables you to create a border that uses different line styles for the various sides of the border.

TIP

> **Removing a Border from a Paragraph**   If you want to remove the border from a paragraph, choose **None** in the Setting area of the Borders and Shading dialog box.

5. Several line styles are available for your border. Click the **Style** scroll box to scroll through the various line styles, and then click the style you want to use.

6. To change the color of the border lines, click the **Color** drop-down arrow and select a color from the color palette that appears.

7. As you select the various parameters for your border (in cases where you have selected Box, Shadow, or 3-D as the border setting), you can view a preview of the border in the Preview box. The Preview box also makes it easy for you to place an incomplete border around a paragraph in cases where you might only want a line above or below the text (refer to Figure 8.1).

8. When you have finished selecting the settings for the border, click the **OK** button. The border appears around the paragraph or paragraphs in the document, as shown in Figure 8.2.

You also can quickly place a border around a paragraph or other selected text by using the Tables and Borders toolbar. Right-click anywhere on one of the currently shown toolbars and select **Tables and Borders** from the toolbar list. The Tables and Borders toolbar appears in the document window. Figure 8.3 shows the Tables and Borders toolbar.

CAUTION

> **Borders Around More Than One Paragraph**   If you select several paragraphs that are using the same style and indents, Word places one border around all the paragraphs. If you want separate borders around the paragraphs, assign a border to them one at a time. For more discussion about indents, see Lesson 9, "Working with Tabs and Indents." You can find more information about styles in Lesson 11, "Working with Margins, Pages, and Line Spacing."

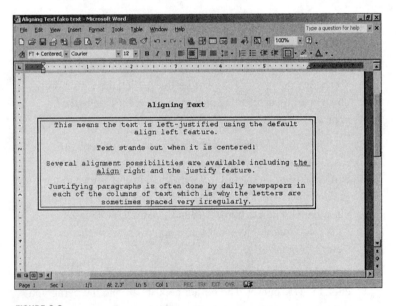

FIGURE 8.2
A border appears around the selected paragraph after you set the border parameters in the Borders and Shading dialog box.

 To apply a border to a paragraph, make sure the insertion point is in the paragraph, and then click the **Borders** drop-down button on the Tables and Borders toolbar. From the border list provided, select the type of border you want to place around the text.

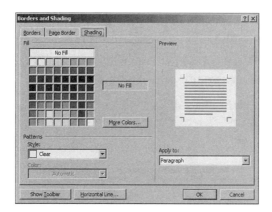

FIGURE 8.3
You can add borders to selected text using the Tables and Borders toolbar.

PLACING A BORDER AROUND A PAGE

If you find that you would like to place a border around an entire page or pages in your document, you need to use the Page Border feature.

Follow these steps to place a border around the entire page:

1. Open the Borders and Shading dialog box (click the **Format** menu and select **Borders and Shading**) and click the **Page Border** tab (see Figure 8.4).

2. Select the **Border** setting and style as you would for a paragraph border.

3. Click the **Apply To** list drop-down arrow and select one of the following:

   • **Whole Document**—Places a border around each page in the document.

- **This Section**—Places a border around each page in the current section of the document.

- **This Section-First Page Only**—Places a border around the first page of the current section.

- **This Section-All Except First Page**—Places a border around each page of the current section except the first page.

FIGURE 8.4
Borders can be placed around an entire page.

To put a border around pages in a section, you must place sections in your document. Sections enable you to break a large document into smaller parts that can have radically different formatting attributes. For more about sections and how to create them, see Lesson 21, "Working with Larger Documents."

PLAIN ENGLISH

Section   A portion of a document that has been defined as a discrete part. Each section can then have different formatting and even headers and footers defined for the section.

ADDING SHADING TO THE PARAGRAPH

You can place a color or a grayscale pattern behind the text in a paragraph or paragraphs. This color or pattern is called shading and can be used with or without a border around the text.

To add shading to text, you must select the text for a particular paragraph—just make sure the insertion point is in the paragraph.

After you've designated the text that you want to place the shading behind, follow these steps:

1. Select **Format**, **Borders and Shading**. The Borders and Shading dialog box appears.

2. Select the **Shading** tab, as shown in Figure 8.5.

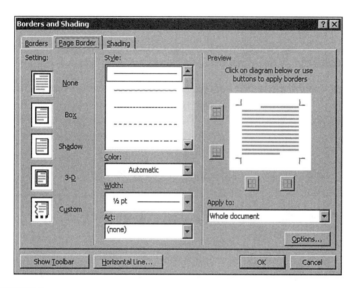

FIGURE 8.5
You can apply shading to a paragraph or selected text.

3. To select a fill color, click one of the colors on the color palette in the **Fill** area.

4. To select a pattern for the fill color, click the **Style** drop-down arrow and select a pattern from the list.

5. Use the **Apply To** drop-down arrow to designate whether the current paragraph or selected text should be shaded.

6. When you have completed your selections, click **OK**.

Your selected text or paragraph will now be shaded.

Take Advantage of More Colors If the color you want to use is not shown on the Shading tab, click the **More Colors** button. This opens the Colors dialog box, which provides a huge number of colors on a color palette. You can even click the **Custom** tab on this dialog box and mix your own custom colors.

CHANGING FONT COLORS

When using the shading options, you might find that the current text color does not show up that well on the fill color or pattern that you selected.

To change the color of text, follow these steps:

1. Select the text that you want to change to a different font color.

2. Select the **Format** menu and select **Font**. The Font dialog box appears.

3. In the Font dialog box, click the **Font Color** drop-down arrow and select the color you want to use (Word automatically defaults to black-colored fonts because this is typically what you use in business documents that you print).

4. When you have completed your selection, click **OK**.

You might find that you have to play around with the fill color and the font color to get an ideal combination on the page. Intensity of color typically varies between color printers.

In this lesson, you learned how to place a border around your text and place shading behind text. You also learned how to change the font color for selected text. In the next lesson, you will learn how to set tabs and indents in your documents.

LESSON 9
Working with Tabs and Indents

In this lesson, you learn how to set and use tabs and indents in your documents.

ALIGNING TEXT WITH TABS

Although the left and right alignment of text in your document is governed by the margins set in the document, there are times when you want to align the text to emphasize a list of items or otherwise offset text from the rest of the items on the page. In Lesson 7, "Changing How Text Looks," you worked with centering and justification as a way to change the alignment of text. Another way to align text in a document is to use tabs. Tabs are set every half inch by default in a new document. Every time you press the Tab key on the keyboard, you offset the text line from the left margin one tab stop.

You can use tab stops to align text lines in columns. Word gives you complete control over where the tab stops are set in your document. Word also provides different tabs that enable you to align text in different ways:

- **Left Tab**—Aligns the beginning of the text line at the tab stop
- **Center Tab**—Centers the text line at the tab stop
- **Right Tab**—Right-aligns the text line at the tab stop
- **Decimal Tab**—Lines up numerical entries at their decimal point

Each of these tab types makes it easy for you to create lists that are offset from other text elements in the document. Your tab stops fall between the left and right margins on each page of the document. Each paragraph in the document can potentially have a different set of tab stops with different kinds of tabs set at the stops.

One way to set tabs in your document is using the Tabs dialog box. Select the **Format** menu, and then select **Tabs**. The Tabs dialog box requires that you specify a tab position in the Tab stop position box (the position you specify is the number of inches from the left margin); use the spinner box arrows to specify the position for the tab or type a position directly in the box.

After the tab stop position is set, click the appropriate Alignment option button to select the type of tab you want to create at the tab stop (see Figure 9.1). If you want to have a leader (a repeating element, such as a dash), fill the empty space to the left of the tab stop and select one of the leader option buttons in the Leader box. After you have specified a position and a tab type (and an optional leader), add the tab by clicking **Set**.

As you create the tabs, they will appear in the Tabs list on the left of the dialog box. If you want to remove a particular tab from the list, select it, and then click the **Clear** button. If you want to clear all the tabs listed (and start over), click the **Clear All** button.

After you have finished setting your tabs, click **OK**. Although you can certainly set all the tabs for a document or section in the Tabs dialog box, it is not necessarily the best place to quickly set the tabs for your documents. It does not really provide you with a visual display of how the tabs will look in the document. However, if you are creating tabs that include leading characters (such as dot leaders often seen in a table of contents) and you want to precisely set the tab positions to previously determined settings, the Tabs dialog box gives you complete control over all the settings.

FIGURE 9.1
You can set and remove tab stops in the Tabs dialog box.

SETTING TABS ON THE RULER

An excellent alternative to setting tabs in the Tabs dialog box is to use the Word Ruler and actually set the tabs on the Ruler itself. This enables you to visually check the position of the tab stops and makes it easy for you to change the type of tab at a particular tab stop and delete unwanted tabs.

To view the Ruler in the Word document window, select **View** and then **Ruler**. The Ruler appears at the top of your document.

TIP

> **Quickly View the Ruler**   If the Ruler is not displayed in the Word window, place the mouse pointer at the top of your current document, below the toolbars. If you wait for just a moment, the Ruler drops down onto the document. This allows you to view current tab settings. When you remove the mouse, the Ruler folds up.

To set a tab on the Ruler, click the **Tab** button on the far left of the Ruler to select the tab type (Left, Center, Right, or Decimal). Each time you click the Tab button, you are cycled to the next tab type. If you go past the type of tab you want to set, keep clicking until the tab type appears on the Tab button.

After you have the appropriate tab type selected on the Tab button, place the mouse pointer on the ruler where you want to create the tab stop. Click the mouse and the tab is placed on the ruler. It's that simple.

Figure 9.2 shows the Ruler with each of the tab types set. The figure also shows how text aligns at each of the tab types.

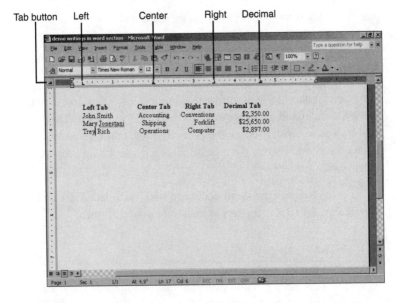

FIGURE 9.2
Setting tabs on the Ruler allows you to view their position and type.

TIP

Moving or Removing Tabs   If you want to delete a tab on the Ruler, use the mouse to drag the tab off the Ruler. If you need to reposition a particular tab, drag it to a new location on the Ruler.

Working with Indents

Although tabs enable you to align text at various tab stops on the
Ruler, you might want to indent or offset lines and paragraphs from
the left or right margins. Word provides different indent settings that
indent the text at particular settings on the Ruler.

 **PLAIN ENGLISH**

> **Indent**   The offset of a particular paragraph or line of
> text from the left or right margin.

The easiest way to indent a paragraph from the left margin is to use
the **Increase Indent** button on the Formatting toolbar. Place the insertion point in the paragraph you want to indent, and then click the
Increase Indent button on the toolbar. Remember that you can also
use the Click and Type feature for left indents (see the previous
Lesson 8, "Using Borders and Colors").

Each time you click the button, you are increasing the indent one-half
inch. You can also decrease the left indent on a particular paragraph.
Click the **Decrease Indent** button on the Formatting toolbar.

Setting Indents on the Ruler

You can also indent a paragraph from both the left and right margins
using the Ruler. The Ruler has a left and right indent marker on the far
left and far right, respectively (see Figure 9.3).

To indent a paragraph from the left margin, use the mouse to drag the
Left Indent marker to the appropriate position. Grab the marker at the
very bottom because the top of the marker is the First Line Indent
marker. You can also indent a paragraph from the right margin using
the Right Indent marker.

Left Indent marker

First Line Indent marker

Right Indent marker

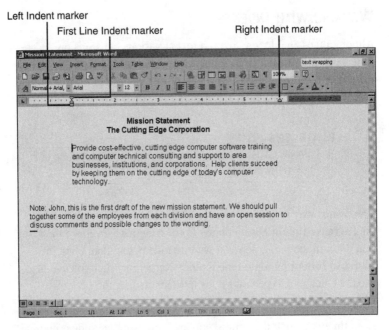

FIGURE 9.3
The Left Indent and Right Indent markers can be used to indent paragraphs from the left and right margins, respectively.

CREATING HANGING INDENTS

The hanging indent is a special kind of indent. The text that wraps under the first line of the paragraph is indented more than the first line. Hanging indents are created by separating the First Line Indent marker from the Left Indent marker on the ruler.

To create a hanging indent, follow these steps:

1. Place the insertion point in the paragraph that you want to indent.

2. Drag the **Left Indent marker** (drag it by the square bottom of the marker) to the position where you want to indent the second and subsequent lines of the paragraph.

3. Drag the **First Line Indent marker** (drag it by the top of the marker) back to the position where you want the first line to begin.

Figure 9.4 shows a paragraph with a hanging indent. You can increase or decrease the offset between the first line and the rest of the paragraph by dragging either the First Line Marker or the Left Indent marker. If you prefer to enter numerical information for your hanging indents, choose the **Indents and Spacing** tab (select **Format** menu and then **Paragraph**) and in the **Special** list under **Indentation**, select **Hanging**. Then, set the amount of space for the hanging indent in the **By** box.

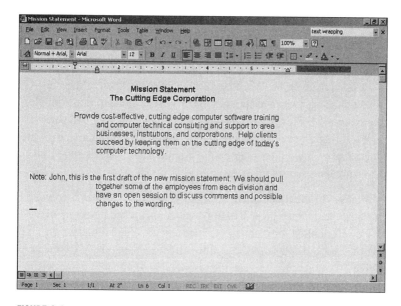

FIGURE 9.4
Hanging indents enable you to offset the indent on the first line of a paragraph and the remainder of the paragraph.

In this lesson, you learned to set tabs in your document using the Tabs dialog box and the Ruler. You also learned how to set indents for your paragraphs. In the next lesson, you will learn how to change the view of your document in the Word window.

LESSON 10

Examining Your Documents in Different Views

In this lesson, you learn how to examine your document using the different document displays offered in Word.

CHANGING THE DOCUMENT DISPLAY

Word provides you with several viewing possibilities as you work on your documents in the Word application window. Each of these display modes provides a different look at your document. For example, the Normal view provides you with a look at all the font and paragraph formatting in the document, but does not give you a view of the document as it would appear on the printed page. Instead, the Print Layout view supplies this viewpoint.

Using the different document views to your advantage can help you visualize and create great-looking documents in Word. Special views are even supplied for creating outlines and creating Web pages in Word. Take advantage of these different views using the View menu. Table 10.1 shows the various views available to you and describes, in general terms, for what they are best used.

TABLE 10.1 The Word Views

View	Typical Use
Normal	Use for general word processing tasks
Web Layout	Use for designing HTML documents and viewing Web pages

TABLE 10.1 (continued)

View	Typical Use
Print Layout	Use for document layout and documents containing graphics and embedded or linked objects
Outline	Use to view document as an outline
Full Screen	Use when you want to use the entire screen to view the document and avoid seeing the toolbars and other marginal information

THE NORMAL VIEW

The Normal view provides you with a view that is perfect for most word processing tasks. It is the default view for Word; however, to change to the Normal view from another view, select **View** and then **Normal**.

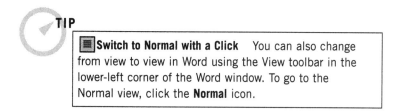

TIP

Switch to Normal with a Click   You can also change from view to view in Word using the View toolbar in the lower-left corner of the Word window. To go to the Normal view, click the **Normal** icon.

This view displays character and paragraph formatting that you place in the document (see Figure 10.1). Normal view, however, does not display the document headers and footers or show graphics in the document as they will print. Also, items created using the Drawing toolbar are not displayed in the Normal view.

In the Normal view, you see the following:

- Page breaks appear as dashed lines.

- Headers and footers are displayed in a header/footer editing pane (when **Header and Footer** is selected on the **View** menu). Only the header or footer can be edited at this point.

- Footnotes and endnotes are displayed in a footnote or end-note editing pane (when **Footnotes** is selected on the **View** menu). Only the footnote or endnote can be edited at this point.

- Margins and column borders are not displayed in this view.

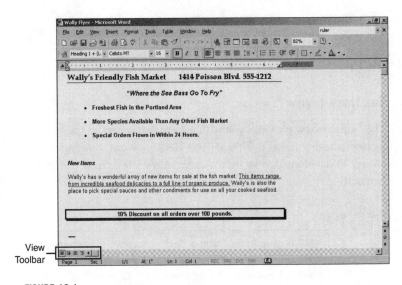

FIGURE 10.1
The Normal view shows all the formatting in the document but does not show graphics, margins, and other special elements as they will appear on the printed page.

WEB LAYOUT VIEW

The Web Layout view is perfect for designing *HTML* documents that you want to use as Web pages. The Web Layout view displays your document as it would appear in your Web browser window. To switch to the Web Layout view, select **View**, and then **Web Layout**.

In the Web Layout view, text is wrapped to fit in the window and graphics are placed as they will appear online. Any backgrounds present on the page are also seen in this view. Figure 10.2 shows a Web page in the Web Layout view.

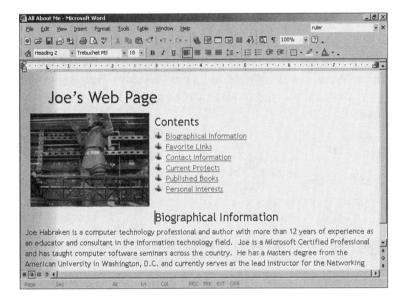

FIGURE 10.2
The Web Layout view allows you to look at and edit your HTML documents as they will appear in a Web browser.

 TIP

> **Switch to Web Layout View Quickly**   To switch to the Web Layout view, click the **Web Layout** icon on the **View** toolbar.

The Web Layout view is the perfect view for designing your personal Web pages or for viewing Web pages using the Web Page Wizard.

PRINT LAYOUT VIEW

The Print Layout view shows your document exactly as it will appear on the printed page. Working in this view allows you to fine-tune your document and work with graphic placement and text formatting as you prepare your document for printing.

To switch to the Print Layout view, select **View, Print Layout**. This enables you to view headers, footers, footnotes, endnotes, and the margins in your document. Graphics are also positioned and sized as they will appear on the printed page. Figure 10.3 shows the same document that appeared in Figure 10.1 but notice that in Page Layout view, the margins of the document and a graphic in the document appears.

TIP

> 🔲 **Switch to Print Layout View Quickly**   To switch to the Print Layout view, click the **Print Layout** icon on the **View** toolbar.

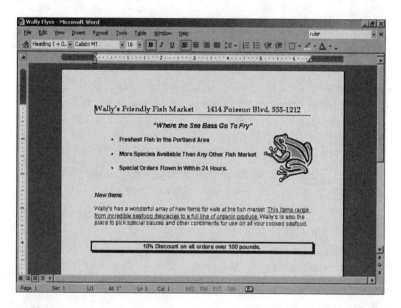

FIGURE 10.3
The Print Layout view enables you to fine-tune your document for printing.

OUTLINE VIEW

The Outline view allows you to create and edit your document in an outline format. Using the Word built-in heading styles is the key to creating the document in this view (for more about styles, see Lesson 11, "Working with Margins, Pages, and Line Spacing"). Each heading (Headings 1, 2, 3, and so on) is treated as a different level in the outline. For example, a heading assigned the Heading 1 style would be a Level 1 heading in the outline. You can promote and demote headings using the appropriate buttons on the Outline toolbar (a special toolbar that appears when you are in Outline view).

The Outline toolbar also provides an Outline Levels drop-down box that allows you to quickly change the level of the text where the insertion point currently resides. These levels coincide with different styles used by the outline feature. For example, Level 1 is equivalent to the Heading 1 style.

You can also collapse and expand the outline to better organize your document. Collapsing the document to all Level 1 Headings allows you to ignore the body text in the document and concentrate on the overall organization of the document.

TIP

> **Move a Heading and Associated Text**   When you drag a heading to a new position, the subheading and body text associated with the heading move to the new position as well. This makes it very easy for you to reorganize the text in your document.

To change to the Outline view, select **View** and then click **Outline**. You can easily select a heading and the text that is subordinate to it by clicking the hollow plus symbol (+) to the left of the text (see Figure 10.4). After the text is selected, it can be dragged to a new position.

When you have finished creating and editing a document in the Outline view, you can switch to any of the other views (such as the Print Layout view) to see your document in a more typical format.

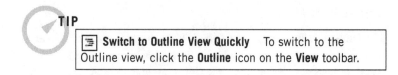

TIP

⊞ **Switch to Outline View Quickly**   To switch to the Outline view, click the **Outline** icon on the **View** toolbar.

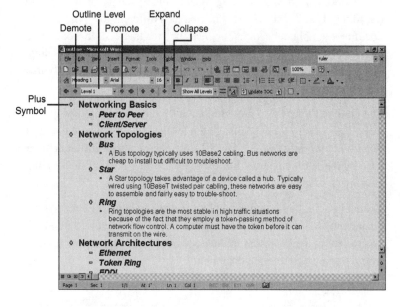

FIGURE 10.4
The Outline view makes it very easy to organize your document by collapsing and expanding different levels.

USING THE FULL SCREEN VIEW

In situations where you want to concentrate on the text and other items in your document, it is great to be able to clear all the visual clutter from the screen (toolbars, scrollbars, and other Word tools) and view only your document. For example, you might be proofreading a particular page and want to place as much of the page's text on the screen as you can. You can switch to a view where your document occupies all the space available on the screen. Select **View** and then **Full Screen**.

You can still add or edit the text in your document when you are in the Full Screen view. You can also quickly return to the previous view you were using (such as Normal view or Print Layout view) before you switched to the Full Screen view. Click the **Close Full Screen** box that appears in the document window to return to the previous view.

ZOOMING IN AND OUT ON YOUR DOCUMENT

You can use the Zoom command to zoom in and out on your documents. This allows you to increase the magnification of items on the page, such as small fonts, and allows you to step back (zoom out) from the document to view its general layout.

You can use Zoom in any of the Word views. In Normal, Web Layout, and Outline views, the effect of zooming in or out just changes the magnification of the onscreen elements. When you use Zoom on the Print Layout view, you get a good look at how the document is laid out on the printed page.

To zoom in or out on your current document, select **View**, **Zoom**. The Zoom dialog box appears (see Figure 10.5).

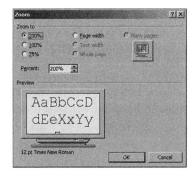

FIGURE 10.5
The Zoom dialog box can be used to change the current zoom level of your document.

A series of option buttons is used to change the zoom setting for the current document. When you click a particular option button (such as the 200% option button), you see a preview of this magnification in the Preview box.

You can also set a custom zoom level in the Percent box. Use the click arrows in the box to increase or decrease the current Zoom percentage. When you have selected the zoom level for the current document, click **OK**.

> **View Multiple Pages on Your Screen**   When you are in the Print Layout view, you can use the Zoom dialog box to view two or more pages at the same time. Click the **Many Pages** option button (when in Zoom option), and then click the **Computer** icon below the option button. Drag over the page boxes to select the number of pages you want to display, and then click **OK**.

You can also quickly change the zoom level in your current document using the Zoom drop-down box on the Word Standard toolbar. Click the drop-down arrow on the **Zoom** box and select the appropriate zoom level. If you want to set a custom zoom level, select the current zoom percentage on the Zoom box and then type your own value.

Working with the Document Map

The Document Map view is somewhat similar to the Outline view in that it gives you a quick reference to the overall structure of your document. A special pane appears in the document window (on the left) that shows the headings in your document. The Document Map can be used to quickly move from one area of a document to another by clicking the appropriate heading.

To open the Document Map, select **View**, **Document Map**; the map pane appears in the document window (see Figure 10.6). You can change the width of the Document Map pane by placing the mouse on the border between the pane and your document. The mouse arrow changes to a sizing tool—a double-headed arrow. Drag the sizing tool to create a custom Document Map width.

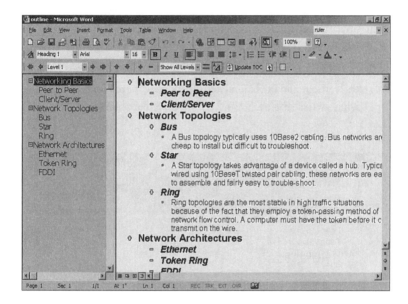

FIGURE 10.6
The Document Map view makes it easy to jump to a particular part of a document by clicking the appropriate heading.

The Document Map pane is available in any of the Word views. When you want to close the Document Map, select **View**, and then **Document Map** to deselect it.

SPLITTING THE DOCUMENT WINDOW

Another useful way to view your documents is to split the current document window into two panes. This allows you to view the same document in both panes, which is particularly useful when you want to view two different parts of the same document.

You can use the two panes to drag and drop information from one part of a document into another. Remember that changes you make in either of the split panes will affect the document.

To split the document screen into two panes, select **Window, Split**. A horizontal split appears across the document window. Notice that as you move the mouse in the document window, the split bar moves with it. Place the mouse where you want to split the document window, and then click the left mouse button.

A set of vertical and horizontal scrollbars appears for each pane in the split window (see Figure 10.7). Use the scrollbars in each pane as needed.

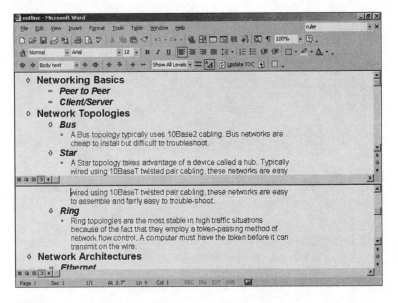

FIGURE 10.7
You can split the document screen to view different areas of a long document.

When you have finished working in the split document window, select **Window** and then **Remove Split**. The splitter bar is removed from the document.

TIP

Split a Window Using the Splitter Bar   You can split a document window by manually dragging the splitter bar down into the document window. Place the mouse just above the Up arrow on the vertical scrollbar on the splitter bar. Your mouse becomes a splitter sizing tool. Drag to split the window as needed, and then click the mouse to set the bar.

In this lesson, you learned to take advantage of the various views offered to you by Word. You also learned to zoom in and out on your document and split the document window. In the next lesson, you will learn how to work with margins, line spacing, and line breaks.

LESSON 11
Working with Margins, Pages, and Line Spacing

In this lesson, you learn how to set margins, insert page breaks into your documents, and control line spacing and line breaks in your documents.

SETTING MARGINS

Margins control the amount of whitespace between your text and the edge of a printed page. Four margins—Left, Right, Top, and Bottom—can be set for your pages. The default margin settings for documents based on the Word Normal template are shown in Table 11.1.

TABLE 11.1 Default Margin Settings for the Normal Template

Margin	Setting (in Inches)
Left	1.25
Right	1.25
Top	1
Bottom	1

You can change any of the margin settings for your document or a portion of your document at any time. The Page Setup dialog box provides you with access to all these margin settings. You also have control over how your margins affect the layout of multiple pages in a document. For example, you can set up your pages to be laid out in book folio fashion (two pages arranged horizontally on each piece of paper) or two pages per sheet arranged vertically.

To change the margin settings for your document, follow these steps:

1. Select **File**, **Page Setup**. The Page Setup dialog box appears as shown in Figure 11.1.

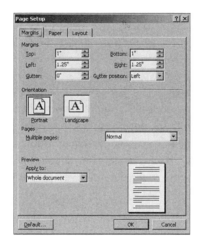

FIGURE 11.1
Use the Margins tab of the Page Setup dialog box to set your document margins and arrange them on multiple pages if necessary.

 TIP

> **Margins Can Be Different for Different Parts of the Document**
> You can set different margin settings for different por-
> tions of your document. The easiest way to do this is to
> divide your document into sections. Each section can
> then have a different set of margins. For information on
> creating sections in your documents, see Lesson 21,
> "Working with Larger Documents."

2. Click the **Margins** tab if necessary. You can also double-click in any of the boxes and type in a new value.

CAUTION

> **Maximum and Minimum Margins**   Be advised that your printer defines the minimum margins for a page. Most inkjet printers limit you to a minimum top and bottom margins of .25" and .5", and left and right margins of .25". If you set margins less than the minimum, a dialog box appears letting you know that your margins are outside the printable area of the page. Click the **Fix** button to set the margins to the minimum for your printer.

3. After you have selected the new margin settings, you can apply the margins to the entire document, to a section of the document, or to the document from the current page forward in the document. Using the last choice allows you to have different margin settings in the same document without requiring you to divide the document into sections (for more about sections, see Lesson 21). Click the **Apply To** drop-down box and select **Whole Document** (the default setting), **This Point Forward**, or **This Section** (if available).

4. After you have finished selecting your new margin settings and the amount of the document that they will affect, click **OK**.

TIP

> **Set a Gutter for Bound Documents**   If your document will be bound (left or top) or placed into a three-ring notebook, set a value in the Gutter box to provide extra space for the binding or punch holes. Setting the Mirror Margins (under multiple pages) ensures that margins on facing pages are similar.

The new margins take effect in your document. The best way to view how they will look when you print is to switch to the Print Layout view (if you are not already in this view). Select **View, Print Layout**. The margins you've selected appear on the top, left, right, and bottom of your document in the Word document window.

When you are in the Print Layout view, you can adjust the margins in your document using the Ruler. To view the Ruler, select **View, Ruler**. The vertical ruler is visible in the Print Layout View only.

In the Print Layout view, horizontal and vertical rulers appear in the document window. The margins appear as shaded areas on the edge of the respective ruler. For example, the left margin is a gray-shaded area on the left side of the horizontal ruler (see Figure 11.2).

FIGURE 11.2
Drag the respective margin-sizing arrow to increase or decrease a margin.

TIP

> **Open the Page Setup Dialog Box Using the Ruler**   Double-click any of the margins shown on the vertical or horizontal ruler. This opens the Page Setup dialog box.

To adjust a margin, place the mouse pointer between the gray margin and the white document area on the ruler. A margin-sizing arrow appears. Drag the gray margin to increase or decrease the respective margin. Figure 11.2 shows the margin-sizing arrow on the top margin on the vertical ruler.

CONTROLLING PAPER TYPES AND ORIENTATION

Other page attributes that you need to control in your documents are the paper size and the page orientation. Word's default settings assume that you will print to paper that is a standard 8.5×11 inches. The default page orientation is portrait, meaning that the maximum distance from the left edge to the right edge of the page is 8.5 inches.

You can select different paper sizes, which is particularly important if you want to print to envelopes or a different paper size. You can also change the orientation of your text and images as they appear on a page from portrait to landscape, where the page contents are rotated so that the distance between the left and right edges on a standard sheet of paper would be 11 inches.

Paper size and page orientation are both set in the Page Setup dialog box. Follow these steps to edit the settings for these page attributes:

1. Select **File**, **Page Setup**. The Page Setup dialog box opens.

2. Click the **Paper** tab on the dialog box (see Figure 11.3).

3. To select a new paper size, click the **Paper Size** drop-down box and select the paper type. For nonstandard paper sizes, select **Custom Size** in the **Page Size** box and then type the

paper's width into the **Width** box and its height into the
Height box.

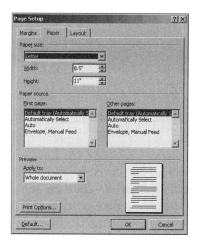

FIGURE 11.3
*The Paper tab of the Page Setup dialog box enables you to set your paper size
and source.*

4. To change the orientation of the page to portrait or landscape,
   select the **Margins** tab and click the **Portrait** or the
   Landscape option button as needed (refer to Figure 11.1).

5. Finally, in the Apply To drop-down box, select **Whole
   Document** to apply the new settings to the new document or
   This Point Forward to apply the settings to the document
   from the current page forward.

6. When you complete editing the settings, click **OK**.

INSERTING PAGE BREAKS

As you create your document, Word automatically starts a new page
when you fill the current page with text or other document items (such

as graphics, tables, and so on). However, you can insert your own page breaks in the document as needed. These types of page breaks are often referred to as *hard*, or *manual*, page breaks.

To insert a page break into your document, follow these steps:

1. Place the insertion point in the document where you want to force a page break.

2. Select **Insert**, **Break**. The Break dialog box appears.

3. Make sure the Page Break option button is selected, and then click **OK**.

A page break is placed in your document. In the Normal view, the page break appears as a dashed line across the page, with "page break" denoted at the center of the line. In the Print Layout view, you can move to the new page by clicking the **Next Page** button on the bottom of the vertical scrollbar.

TIP

> **Use the Keyboard to Place a Page Break**   You can also place a page break in your document using the keyboard. Hold down the **Ctrl** key, and then press the **Enter** key.

To remove a page break, switch to the Normal view (select **View**, **Normal**). The page break appears as a dotted line in the document and is denoted as a "page break." Select the page break with a mouse, and press **Delete** to remove it.

CHANGING LINE SPACING

Another setting that greatly influences the amount of whitespace on the page is line spacing. When you consider whether you want your text single-spaced or double-spaced, those text attributes are controlled by changing the line spacing.

Line spacing can be set for each paragraph in the document or for selected text. Setting line spacing for a blank document allows you to set a default line spacing for all text paragraphs that will be placed in the document.

To set the line spacing for a new document, a paragraph, or selected text, follow these steps:

1. Select **Format, Paragraph**. The Paragraph dialog box appears (see Figure 11.4).

2. Make sure the **Indents and Spacing** tab on the dialog box is selected.

3. To change the line spacing, click the **Line Spacing** drop-down box and select one of the following choices:

   - **Single**—Spacing accommodates the largest font size found on the lines and adds a small amount of white-space (depending on the font used) between lines.

   - **1.5**—The line spacing is 1 and 1/2 times greater than single spacing.

   - **Double**—Twice the size of single line spacing.

   - **At Least**—(The default setting) Line spacing adjusts to accommodate the largest font on the line and special items, such as graphics.

   - **Exactly**—All lines are equally spaced, and special font sizes or items such as graphics are not accommodated. These items, if larger than the setting used here, appear cut off in the text. You can still accommodate these items by using the Multiple box.

   - **Multiple**—You specify the line spacing by a particular percentage. This feature is used in conjunction with the Exactly option to set a line spacing percentage that accommodates special font sizes or graphics found in the document. For example, if you want to decrease the line spacing by 20%, enter the number 0.8. To increase the line spacing by 50%, enter 1.5.

4. The **Line Spacing** option selected in step 3 is influenced by the point size entered in the **At** box (this applies only when you have selected At Least, Exactly, or Multiple). Use the click arrows to increase or decrease the point size of the line spacing, if needed.

TIP

Set Spacing Before and After a Paragraph   You can also set special spacing Before and After a particular paragraph. This is particularly useful for headings or other special text items.

5. When you complete setting the line spacing parameters, click **OK**.

If you find that you don't like the new line spacing settings for a particular paragraph, click the **Undo** button on the Standard toolbar to reverse the changes that you have made.

In this lesson, you learned to set margins for your documents, change the paper size and page orientation, and place page breaks in your documents. You also learned how to control line spacing in your paragraphs. In the next lesson, you will learn how to create and apply styles to the text in your documents.

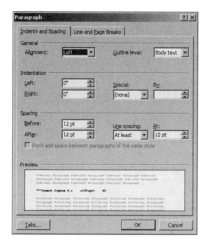

FIGURE 11.4

The Paragraph dialog box allows you to control the line spacing in your text.

Lesson 12
Working with Styles

In this lesson, you learn how to create text and paragraph styles. You also learn how to edit your styles and take advantage of the styles in the Style Gallery.

Understanding Styles

Word styles provide an excellent way to manage the character and paragraph formatting in a document. A *style* is a grouping of formatting attributes identified by a style name. You can create styles for text that contain character-formatting attributes such as bold, italic, or a particular font size; these types of styles are called *character styles*. You can also create styles for paragraphs that include paragraph attributes, such as alignment information, indents, and line spacing; this type of style is called a *paragraph style*.

You view the style names in the Styles and Formatting task pane (see Figure 12.1). To open the Styles and Formatting task pane, select the **Format** command and then click **Styles and Formatting**.

TIP

> Select Styles and Formatting at the Touch of a Button
> The easiest way to access the Styles and Formatting task pane is to use the **Styles and Formatting** button on the Formatting toolbar.

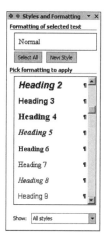

FIGURE 12.1

The Styles and Formatting task pane is the starting place for creating, editing, and managing the styles and formatting in your documents.

Word includes several built-in styles, such as the headings, that you can take advantage of in your documents. Styles are particularly useful because if you use them to format text or paragraphs in the document, you can change the attributes saved in the style at any time. These changes immediately take effect on all the text that has been assigned that style.

CAUTION

> **Paragraph Styles Versus Text Styles**   Paragraph styles (the more commonly used option) assign both character and paragraph attributes to the paragraph containing the insertion point. Text styles affect only the word or words you select before you apply the style.

CREATING TEXT STYLES

Creating text styles is extremely easy. Select the text you want to emphasize with special character formatting and assign it all the character attributes (font type, bold, underline, italic, and so on) that you want to include in the style. You may assign the attributes using either the Font dialog box (by selecting **Format**, **Font**) or the appropriate buttons on the Formatting toolbar. Fonts are covered in Lesson 7, "Changing How Text Looks."

Make sure that the desired text is selected, and then follow these steps:

1. Select the **Styles and Formatting** task pane and then **New Style**; the New Style dialog box appears.

2. Click the **Style Type** drop-down box and select **Character** for the style type.

3. Look in the Formatting of Selected Text area of the Styles and Formatting task pane. Here you can see the text attributes that you have assigned to your selected text. Note that the new style is based on the current style (the default paragraph style or the normal style) plus your added attributes.

4. Type a name for your new style into the Name box.

5. Click **OK** to conclude the style creation process. You are returned to the Styles and Formatting task pane. Notice that your new style now appears in the Pick Formatting to Apply list in the task pane.

You can now assign the new character style to text in your document as needed. Simply select the text to which you want to assign this unique style, and then select the **Styles and Formatting** task pane. Select your unique style from the list provided. The style is applied to the selected text.

TIP

> **View All the Text Assigned a Particular Style**   If you would like to select all the different text items that you assigned a particular style, select the style in the Styles and Formatting task pane and then click the Select All button.

CREATING PARAGRAPH STYLES

Creating paragraph styles is similar to creating text styles. Apply to a paragraph the formatting that you want to include in the style (you can use alignment settings, indents, and all the paragraph attributes that you are familiar with). Make sure the insertion point is in the paragraph. You can create the style by following these steps:

1. Select the **Styles and Formatting** task pane and then **New Style**; the New Style dialog box appears.

2. Click the **Style Type** drop-down box and select **Paragraph** for the style type.

3. Type a unique name into the **Name** box for the style.

4. Click **OK** to return to the Styles and Formatting task pane. The style is now available on the Style list. You can now apply the style to any paragraph in the document by placing the insertion point in the paragraph.

EDITING STYLES

You can also edit or modify the attributes found in any of your styles or the default styles in the document. You edit styles using the Styles and Formatting task pane. Remember that when you edit a style, all the text to which the style was applied reflects the new text and paragraph attributes of your edited style.

To edit a style, follow these steps:

1. Select the **Styles and Formatting** task pane.

2. Under **Pick Formatting to Apply**, select the style you want to edit and place the mouse pointer on it until you see the box outline and down arrow appear. Then, click the down arrow and press **Modify**. The Modify Style dialog box appears as shown in Figure 12.2.

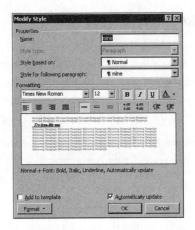

FIGURE 12.2
The Modify Style dialog box allows you to edit the name of a style and modify all the attributes found in the style.

3. To modify the style, select the **Format** button. A menu appears, allowing you to modify the following attributes in the style:

   - Font
   - Paragraph
   - Tabs
   - Borders
   - Language
   - Frame
   - Numbering

4. Select one of the choices provided in the Format box. The appropriate dialog box appears, allowing you to edit the settings for the chosen attributes. For example, if you want to modify the font attributes for the style, click the **Format** arrow and select **Font** from the list provided. The Font dialog box appears.

5. When you have finished modifying the Font attributes for the style (or for whichever style type you chose to modify), click **OK**. You are returned to the **Modify Style** dialog box.

6. Modify other attributes of the style as needed by making the appropriate choices from the menus.

7. When you have completed your style modifications, click **OK** in the Modify Style dialog box and you return to the task pane with the changes made.

TIP

> **You Can Delete Unwanted Styles**   You can delete styles that you've created that you no longer need. Open the **Styles and Formatting** task pane and place the mouse pointer on the style in the **Pick Formatting to Apply** list. Wait for the box outline and down arrow to appear, and then click the **Delete** button under the down arrow. The style is removed from the Style list.

USING THE STYLE ORGANIZER

Word also has the capability to copy styles from other documents and templates into your current document. This provides you with an easy way to add already existing styles to a document (rather than reinventing the wheel or style).

To copy styles from another document or template, follow these steps:

1. Select the **Tools** command, and then choose **Templates and Add-Ins**.

2. In the Templates and Add-Ins dialog box, click the **Organizer** button. The Organizer dialog box appears as shown in Figure 12.3.

3. The styles in the current document appear on the left side of the Organizer dialog box. Styles in the template that your current document was based on are shown on the right side of the Organizer dialog box (all documents are based on a template, even if it is just the Word Normal template). To close the template file on the right side of the dialog box, click the **Close File** button (in Figure 12.3, click **Close File** under the Normal.dot template on the right of the dialog box).

4. Now you can open a new template or document and copy the styles that it contains to the current document (shown on the left of the dialog box). Click **Open File** on the right side of the Organizer dialog box. Locate the document or template from which you want to copy the styles. Double-click the file in the Open dialog box to open the file.

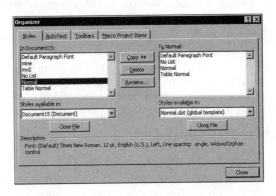

FIGURE 12.3
The Organizer dialog box makes it easy for you to copy a style or styles from one document to another.

5. You are returned to the Organizer dialog box, and the styles for the recently opened template or document are listed on the right side of the dialog box. To copy a style or styles, select the style and click the **Copy** button. The style is copied to the styles in your current document.

TIP

> **Copy More Than One Style at a Time**   To select several styles to copy to your document simultaneously, click the first style you want to copy and then hold down the **Shift** key and click the last style you want to copy. All the styles in between these two are also selected. To select styles that are not in a series, click the first style you want to copy, and then hold down the **Ctrl** key and click any other styles you want to select.

6. When you have finished copying styles (styles can be copied from either of the documents in the Organizer dialog box), click **Close** to close the Organizer dialog box.

As you can see, the Organizer makes it very easy for you to share the styles that you create between your documents. Remember, styles that you create reside only in the document where you create them. The only way to copy those styles to another document is to use the Style Organizer.

In this lesson, you learned to create and assign character and paragraph styles. You also learned to modify your styles and learned how to copy styles from one document to another using the Organizer dialog box. In the next lesson, you will learn how to use AutoFormat to quickly change the way text and paragraphs look in your documents.

LESSON 13

Using AutoFormatting to Change Text Attributes

In this lesson, you learn how to quickly change the look of your text with AutoFormat and apply text attributes automatically as you type.

UNDERSTANDING AUTOFORMATTING

AutoFormat is a great feature that helps you create professional-looking documents. AutoFormatting actually examines the text elements that you have placed in your document (such as headings, tables, lists, regular body text, and other items) and then automatically formats these elements using an appropriate Word style. Even though this formatting is automatic, you can accept or reject the changes AutoFormatting makes. You can also make additional changes to the document as you see fit by using other styles or font and paragraph formatting attributes (for more about styles, see Lesson 12, "Working with Styles").

You will also find that AutoFormat does more than just apply styles to your document elements. It can remove extra line breaks between paragraphs and apply the hyperlink styles to e-mail addresses or Web addresses that you place in your documents.

You can use AutoFormat in two ways. You can turn on AutoFormatting so that items are formatted as you type, or you can create a new document and then use AutoFormat to format the entire document at once.

FORMATTING AS YOU TYPE

You can have your document elements formatted as you type.
However, this feature requires that you supply Word with certain cues
so that the correct formatting is applied to the text. For example, if
you turn on AutoFormat As You Type and want to create a bulleted list
that is automatically formatted by the AutoFormat feature, you must
begin the bulleted line with a dash, an asterisk, or a lowercase "o" so
that Word knows to apply the bulleted list formatting.

Many AutoFormat As You Type features are enabled by default; others
are not. To customize the AutoFormat As You Type feature, follow
these steps:

1. Select **Tools**, **AutoCorrect Options**. The AutoCorrect dialog
   box appears.

2. Select the **AutoFormat As You Type** tab on the dialog box
   (see Figure 13.1).

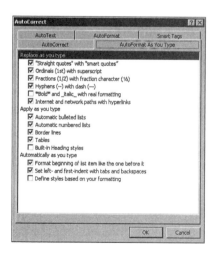

FIGURE 13.1

*The AutoFormat As You Type tab of the AutoCorrect Options dialog box allows
you to select which document elements will be formatted automatically as you
type.*

3. A series of check boxes on the AutoFormat As You Type tab allows you to select which document elements will be formatted as you type. Again, you need to type certain characters for a particular element so that the AutoFormat feature recognizes and then formats the text.

- **Built-In Heading Styles**—All headings that you apply to an outline or a legal document are automatically assigned the appropriate built-in heading style (using Headings 1–9).

- **Border Lines**—Borders are automatically placed between paragraphs. You must type three dashes (-) for a thin border, three underscores (_) for a bold line, or three equal signs (=) for a double-line border.

- **Tables**—Automatically creates tables. You must type a series of plus symbols (+) and dashes (-) to signify the number of columns (+) and the distance between the columns (-).

- **Automatic Bulleted Lists**—Creates bulleted lists automatically. Start each line in the list with an asterisk (*), a dash (-), or a lowercase "o."

- **Automatic Numbered Lists**—Creates numbered lists. Start a line with a letter or number and it is turned into a numbered list item. Paragraphs following the first numbered line are numbered sequentially if the Format Beginning of List Item Like the One Before It check box is selected.

Other AutoFormatting check boxes include features that format your quotation marks, ordinals (1st), and fractions (1/2). Select (or deselect) the various AutoFormat As You Type options and then click **OK** to close the dialog box.

TIP

Create Styles As You Type   If you select the Define
Styles Based on Your Formatting check box, Word automatically takes your character and paragraph formatting
attributes and turns them into styles. You can then use
the created styles to format other paragraphs.

Although formatting as you type might seem like a real timesaver, you
must remember which special characters to use to automatically begin
a particular formatting type.

APPLYING AUTOFORMAT TO A DOCUMENT

The alternative to AutoFormatting as you type is to create the document and then format it after the fact with AutoFormat. Waiting to format a document until after its completion allows you to concentrate on
the document content as you type. You then can concentrate on the
look and feel of the document by selecting from the various
AutoFormatting options. Heads, numbered or bulleted lists, and other
items you have designated throughout the text are identified and formatted.

To AutoFormat a document, follow these steps:

1. Make sure that you are in the Print Layout view (select **View**,
   and then **Print Layout**—this allows you to see the various
   formatting tags applied to the document when you review the
   Autoformat changes). Select **Format**, **AutoFormat**. The
   AutoFormat dialog box appears (see Figure 13.2).

2. You can increase the accuracy of the formatting process by
   choosing a particular document type. Click the General
   Document type drop-down arrow and select from the document types listed on the drop-down list (the default setting is
   General Document; you can also select **Letter** or **Memo** as
   the document type from the list).

FIGURE 13.2
The AutoFormat dialog box allows you to immediately format the document or review each of the suggested formatting changes.

3. Now you can AutoFormat the document. If you want to AutoFormat the current document without reviewing the formatting changes, click the **AutoFormat Now** option button and then click **OK**. The document is automatically formatted.

4. If you want to review the AutoFormatting process after the changes are made, click the **AutoFormat and Review Each Change** option button. Then click **OK**.

5. The document is formatted and then the AutoFormat/Review Changes dialog box appears. If you already know whether you are happy with the results, choose to **Accept All** or **Reject All** using the appropriate button in the dialog box. You can also click **Review Changes** to review the changes to your document so that you can decide whether you're happy with the results on a change-by-change basis. The Review AutoFormat Changes dialog box appears (see Figure 13.3).

6. Click the **Find** (forward) button (this button has a right-pointing arrow) to begin the review process. Notice that all the changes that AutoFormat has made to the document are tagged with a red line and a description box in the document.

7. When you are asked to review a particular change (the change appears in the Changes box), either select **Reject** to reject the change or click the **Find** button to skip to the next

formatting change in the document. You can also choose to **Accept All** or **Reject All** using the appropriate button in the dialog box.

FIGURE 13.3
This dialog box enables you to review each of the formatting changes made in the document.

8. When you reach the bottom of the document, Word notifies you that it can start searching for changes at the top of the document. If you had the insertion point at the top of the document when you began the review process, click **Cancel**. Then, click **Cancel** to close the two subsequent dialog boxes as well.

To safeguard any automatic formatting changes that have been made, be sure to immediately save your document.

CHANGING AUTOFORMAT OPTIONS

You can customize certain options related to the AutoFormat feature. This dialog box can be reached by selecting the **Tools** menu and then **AutoCorrect**. Make sure that the **AutoFormat** tab is selected.

The options that you have control over on the AutoFormat tab are similar to those found on the AutoFormat As You Type tab. You can choose check boxes that automatically format headings, lists, and so on (see Figure 13.4).

You can also choose to have Word retain the style that you have already placed in the document (prior to running AutoFormat). Select the **Styles** check box to do so.

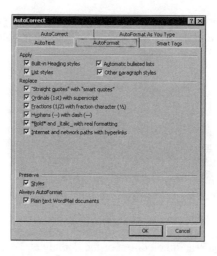

FIGURE 13.4
You can set the various options for automatic formatting on the AutoFormat tab of the AutoCorrect dialog box.

TIP

AutoFormat Text-Only E-mail Automatically   If you use Word as your e-mail editor for Outlook, you can have any text-only e-mail messages that you receive automatically formatted to look better when you read them. Select the **Plain Text Wordmail Document** check box at the bottom of the AutoFormat tab.

After you select the options you want to set for AutoFormat, select **OK**. You can now run AutoFormat and your options will be in force as your document is formatted.

In this lesson, you learned to AutoFormat your text as you typed and also to use AutoFormat to format a completed document. In the next lesson, you will learn how to use the AutoText feature and add special characters to your documents.

LESSON 14

Adding Document Text with AutoText and Using Special Characters

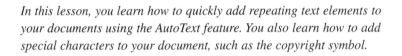

In this lesson, you learn how to quickly add repeating text elements to your documents using the AutoText feature. You also learn how to add special characters to your document, such as the copyright symbol.

UNDERSTANDING AUTOTEXT

AutoText provides you with a way to build a library of words and text phrases that you use often in your documents. An AutoText entry can consist of a company name, your name, or an entire paragraph that you commonly place in your documents.

AutoText makes it easy for you to quickly insert items from your AutoText list into any document. Creating AutoText entries is also very straightforward.

CREATING AUTOTEXT ENTRIES

You can create an AutoText entry using text from an existing docu-ment, or you can type the text that you want to add to the AutoText list in a blank document. It's then just a matter of copying the text to your AutoText list.

To create an AutoText entry, follow these steps:

1. Type the text you want to use for the AutoText entry or open the document containing the text that will serve as the AutoText entry.

2. Select the text.

3. Select the **Insert** menu, point at **AutoText,** and then select **New** from the cascading menu. The Create AutoText dialog box appears as shown in Figure 14.1.

TIP

> **AutoText Isn't on My Insert Menu**   Remember that Word uses a personalized menu system that places your most recently used commands on the various menus. If you click a menu and don't see a particular command, rest your pointer in the menu for a moment; the menu will expand and provide a list of all the commands available on that particular menu.

FIGURE 14.1
Type a name for your new AutoText entry into the Create AutoText dialog box.

4. Type the name that you want to use to retrieve this AutoText entry in the text box provided (for one-word text entries, the selected text can also serve as the entry name).

5. After providing the name for the AutoText entry, click **OK**.

Your selected text is added to the AutoText list. You can repeat this procedure and add as many text items to the AutoText list as you want.

INSERTING AUTOTEXT ENTRIES

After you add an AutoText entry or entries to the list, you can insert them into any Word document. One method of inserting an AutoText entry into the current document is to pull the entry directly from the AutoText list.

To insert an AutoText entry into a document, follow these steps:

1. Place the insertion point in the document where you want to insert the AutoText entry.

2. Select the **Insert** menu, point at **AutoText**, and then select **AutoText**. The AutoCorrect dialog box appears as shown in Figure 14.2.

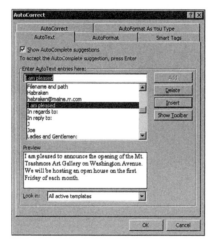

FIGURE 14.2
Insert your AutoText entries from the AutoCorrect dialog box.

3. The AutoText tab of the AutoCorrect dialog box displays an alphabetical list (as well as various default entries that Word provides) of the AutoText entries that you have added to the AutoText list. Select the entry you want to insert and click

Insert, or double-click any entry on the list to insert it into the document.

An alternative to manually inserting AutoText into the document is using the AutoComplete feature to automatically insert an entry into your document. For example, if you have an entry in your AutoText list that reads "I am pleased to announce," you can automatically insert this entry into your document by beginning to type the entry. As you type the first few letters in the AutoText entry, an AutoComplete box appears containing the complete AutoText entry, as shown in Figure 14.3.

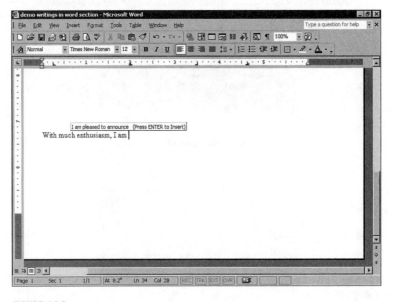

FIGURE 14.3
AutoComplete automatically places entries from your AutoText list into your documents.

To insert the entry into the document, press the **Enter** key. AutoComplete also helps you enter items that are not included on your AutoText list into your document. These items include the current date, days of the week, and names of months. For example, as you begin to type the name of a month, the AutoComplete box message appears telling you to press **Enter** to insert the complete word.

TIP

> **Use the AutoText Toolbar to Quickly Insert AutoText Entries**
> Right-click any toolbar and then select **AutoText** from the menu. To add an entry into the current document, click the **All Entries** button on the AutoText toolbar and select your AutoText from the list.

DELETING AUTOTEXT ENTRIES

You can easily delete items on the AutoText list when you no longer need them. This is done on the AutoText tab of the AutoCorrect dialog box.

To delete an AutoText entry, follow these steps:

1. Select the **Insert** menu, point at **AutoText**, and then select **AutoText** from the cascading menu. The AutoCorrect dialog box appears.

2. Select any of the entries in the AutoText list.

3. Click **Delete** to remove the entry from the list.

After you have completed your deletion of AutoText entries, click **OK** to close the AutoText dialog box.

USING SPECIAL CHARACTERS AND SYMBOLS

Special characters and symbols are characters that can't be found on your keyboard and that are not part of what is considered to be the standard character set. Characters such as the German "u" with an umlaut (Ü) are special characters, and an item such as the trademark is an example of a symbol.

Many special characters and symbols exist. Table 14.1 lists some of the commonly used special characters and symbols.

TABLE 14.1　Common Special Characters and Symbols

Special Character or Symbol	Use
Copyright symbol ©	Used in a copyright notice in a document.
Trademark symbol ™	Placed to the right of official trademarks in a document.
Em dash —	Used to bracket asides or sudden changes in emphasis in a sentence—rather than using a comma. It appears as a long dash.
En dash –	Slightly shorter than an em dash; this dash is commonly used to separate numbers from capital letters, such as Figure B–1.
Wingdings	A group of special icons that can be used in your documents for emphasis or as bullets.
Foreign language font (é)	Characters that include special accents.

The basic special characters and symbols are held in three groups:

- **Symbol**—This group contains mathematical symbols, arrows, trademark and copyright symbols, and letters from the Greek alphabet.

- **Normal Text**—This group provides you with characters containing accents and other special marks.

- **Wingdings**—Special icons and symbols for many purposes.

Additional special character sets might be available to you, depending on which fonts have been installed on your computer (you can purchase software with unique fonts and symbols, as well).

TIP

> **Shortcut to Making an Em Dash**   As you are typing, you
> may quickly insert an em dash into the text by pressing
> **Ctrl+Alt+**the minus sign on the number pad. The em
> dash appears.

You can easily insert special characters and symbols into your documents using the Insert Symbol feature. To insert a special character or
symbol, follow these steps:

1. Place the insertion point in your document where you want to
   insert the special character or symbol. Select **Insert**, **Symbol**.
   The Symbol dialog box appears as shown in Figure 14.4.

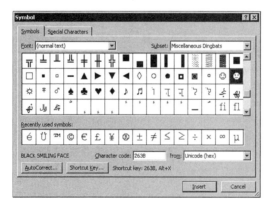

FIGURE 14.4
*The Symbol dialog box gives you access to symbols and special characters that
you can insert into your document.*

2. To insert a symbol, make sure the Symbol tab is selected on
   the Insert dialog box (if you want to insert a special character, go to step 5). Use the Font drop-down box to select the
   symbol set from which you want to choose your symbol. The
   symbol set that you choose dictates which symbols are available, so select a symbol set that provides the symbol you

want to insert. You will find that the normal text symbol set provides most of the commonly used symbols, such as copyright and trademark.

3. After you select the symbol set (such as normal text, Symbol, Wingdings, or another font family), click to select the symbol you want to insert.

4. After selecting the symbol, click the **Insert** button.

5. If you want to insert a special character, such as the copyright symbol or an em dash, click the **Special Characters** tab on the Symbol dialog box.

6. Select the special character and then click **Insert**.

7. When you have finished inserting your symbol or special character, click the **Close** button on the Symbol dialog box.

CAUTION

> **My Key Combination Turns into a Symbol** The Word AutoCorrect feature is set up to replace several character combinations with special characters. You can override these changes made by the AutoCorrect feature by immediately pressing the **Backspace** key. For more on AutoCorrect, see Lesson 6, "Using Proofreading Tools."

After you've inserted the symbol or special character into the document, you can continue typing or editing your text. Symbols and special characters give your document a finished, typeset look.

In this lesson, you learned how to create an AutoText entry list and insert AutoText entries into your documents. You also learned to add special characters to your documents. In the next lesson, you will learn how to add headers, footers, and page numbers to your Word documents.

LESSON 15
Adding Headers, Footers, and Page Numbers

In this lesson, you learn how to add headers, footers, and page numbers to your documents.

UNDERSTANDING HEADERS AND FOOTERS

Another aspect of creating a document is using headers and footers to insert information that you want repeated on every page of the document or in the pages of a particular document section.

> **PLAIN ENGLISH**
>
> **Header/Footer** The header resides inside the top margin on the page; it holds information such as the date or draft number that appears at the top of every page of the document. Every section of a document could potentially have a separate header.
>
> The footer resides inside the bottom margin of the page; it holds information such as the page number or other information that appears at the bottom of every page of the document. Every section of a document could potentially have a separate footer.

Headers and footers provide you with a way to include a document title, the current date, or the current page number on the top or bottom of each page in the document. Headers can include text, graphics, or other items.

ADDING HEADERS AND FOOTERS

You can add a header or footer to a document in any view. To add a
header or footer, follow these steps:

1. Select **View, Header and Footer**. You are temporarily
    switched to the Print Layout mode and placed in the header
    area of the document (see Figure 15.1). The regular text area
    is dimmed and unavailable while you work in the header or
    footer box.

2. Type your text into the header area. If you want to create a
    footer, click the **Switch Between Header and Footer** button
    on the Header and Footer toolbar. The toolbar is also avail-
    able in the document window.

3. You can add a page number, the current date, the current
    time, and other elements using the appropriate buttons on the
    Header and Footer toolbar (see Table 15.1).

4. In cases where you need to align or format the text, use the
    appropriate buttons on the Word Formatting toolbar (while in
    the header/footer areas) as you would for text on the docu-
    ment page.

5. When you have finished entering your header and footer text,
    click the **Close** button on the Header and Footer toolbar.

You are returned to your document text. In the Normal view, you are
not able to see your header or footer. In the Print Layout view, however, header and footer text appears dimmed.

You can edit your headers and footers by selecting **View, Header and
Footer**. Move to the appropriate header or footer using the navigation
buttons on the Header and Footer toolbar, shown in Table 15.1. To
quickly enter a header or footer box in the Print Layout view, double-
click the header or footer text.

Header area   Header and Footer toolbar

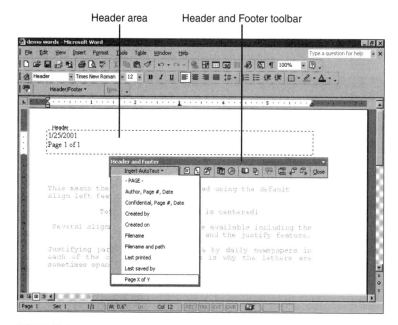

FIGURE 15.1
The header area of the page is where you type your header text. The Header and Footer toolbar provides you with tools to insert page numbers, insert the date, and to switch between your headers and footers.

TABLE 15.1   The Header and Footer Toolbar Buttons

Button	Purpose
⊞	Inserts the page number
⊕	Inserts the page count or number of total pages
🗗	Edits the format of the page number
🗓	Inserts the current date
🕐	Inserts the current time

TABLE 15.1   (continued)

Button	Purpose
📖	Opens the Page Setup dialog box to the Layout tab, where you can change the header and footer settings
🗐	Hides the document text while you work on your header and footer
🖼	Sets up the next header the same as the current header (or footer)
🖼	Switches between your header and footer
🖼	Moves to the previous header or footer in the document
🖼	Moves to the next header or footer in the document

Several toolbar choices, such as Same As Previous and Move to Previous or Next (header or footer), relate to documents that have several sections and so have different headers or footers within the same document. You can also have more than one header or footer in the document if you choose to have different headers or footers for odd- and even-numbered pages.

Using Odd- and Even-Numbered Page Headers and Footers

By default, the header and footer layout settings in Word assume that one header or footer appears on all the pages of a document (except in cases where the document is divided into more than one section; each section can have different headers and footers). You can change the header and footer settings so that different headers and/or footers appear on the odd- and even-numbered pages of your document (or the odd- and even-numbered pages of a document section).

To change the layout settings for Word Headers and Footers, follow these steps:

1. After activating the Header and Footer view (so that the Header and Footer toolbar appears), click the **Page Setup** button.

2. In the Page Setup dialog box, click the **Different Odd and Even** check box to enable odd and even headers and/or footers in the current document (or document section).

 TIP

> **Changing Header and Footer Layout When You Aren't in the Header or Footer**   To get to the header and footer layout options when you don't have the header or footer displayed, select **File**, **Page Setup**. The Page Setup dialog box appears. If it is not already selected, click the **Layout** tab.

3. If you want to have a header or footer (or none) on the first page of your document that is different from subsequent pages in the document, click the **Different First Page** check box (see Figure 15.2).

4. Click **OK** to close the Page Setup dialog box. If you are returned to your document, select **View**, **Header and Footer** to add the odd- or even-numbered page headers to the document otherwise you are returned to the current header and footer.

5. If you want to specify how close the header or footer is to the margin edge of the top or bottom of the document, respectively, use the Header or Footer spin boxes to set the distance.

FIGURE 15.2
On the Layout tab of the Page Setup dialog box, you can select whether to have different odd- and even-numbered page headers/footers or a different header/footer on the first page of the document.

6. When you have finished adding your odd- and even-numbered page headers and/or footers or your first page and subsequent page headers, click the **Close** button on the Header and Footer toolbar.

Odd- and even-numbered page headers and footers are set up exactly the way you would typically set up a header or footer in the document. Use the **Show Next** or **Show Previous** button to move between the odd- and even-numbered page headers or footers and enter the text you want to appear on them.

ADDING PAGE NUMBERING TO A DOCUMENT

Headers and footers enable you to place repeating information in your documents, including the date, other important text, and most importantly—page numbers. When you want to place only page numbers on your document pages, you can forgo the Header and Footer command and quickly add page numbers using the Insert menu.

To place page numbers in your document, follow these steps:

1. Select **Insert**, **Page Numbers**. The Page Numbers dialog box appears (see Figure 15.3).

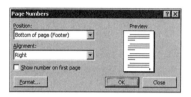

FIGURE 15.3
Use the Page Numbers dialog box to select the position and alignment of page numbers in your document.

2. To select the position for your page numbers, select the **Position** drop-down arrow and select **Top of Page (Header)** or **Bottom of Page (Footer)**.

3. You can select the alignment for the page numbers using the **Alignment** drop-down box. Select **Center**, **Left**, or **Right** to position the page numbers. When you are using mirror margins on a document that will be printed on both sides of the paper, select **Inside** or **Outside** (relative to a central binding—like that of a book) to position your page numbers.

4. To select the format for your page numbers, click the **Format** button. The Format dialog box appears.

5. Use the **Page Number Format** drop-down box (shown in Figure 15.4) to choose the format for your page numbers (Arabic numerals—1, 2, 3—is the default). When you have selected your number format, click **OK** to return to the Format dialog box.

FIGURE 15.4
Use the Page Number Format drop-down box to choose the format for your page numbers.

6. To have the page numbering start on a specific page in the document, click the **Start at** option button and then use the spinner box to specify the page number.

7. Click **OK** to close the Page Number Format dialog box.

The page numbers are placed in the header or footer of your document according to your positioning and formatting choices. You can edit the page numbers and add text if you want by selecting **View**, **Header and Footer**.

In this lesson, you learned to place headers and footers in your documents and you also learned how to add page numbering to your documents using the Insert menu. In the next lesson, you will learn how to print your documents and work with the various print options.

LESSON 16
Printing Documents

In this lesson, you learn how to preview your documents and then print them.

SENDING YOUR DOCUMENT TO THE PRINTER

When you have finished a particular document and are ready to generate a hard copy, Word gives you three choices. You can send the document directly to the printer by clicking the **Print** button on the Standard toolbar. You can open the Print dialog box (select **File**, **Print**) and set any print options that you want, such as printing a particular range of pages or printing multiple copies of the same document. You also have the option of previewing your hard copy before printing. This enables you to view your document exactly as it will appear on the printed page.

To preview your document before printing, click the **Print Preview** button on the Word Standard toolbar. The Print Preview window opens for the current document (see Figure 16.1).

You will find that the Print Preview window provides several viewing tools that you can use to examine your document before printing.

- **Zoom In or Out**—In the Print Preview window, the mouse pointer appears as a magnifying glass. Click once on your document to zoom in, and then click a second time to zoom out. To turn this feature off (or on again), click the **Magnifier** button.

- **Zoom by Percentage**—You can change to different zoom levels on the current document by using the **Zoom** drop-down arrow.

- **View Multiple Pages**—You can also zoom out and view several pages at once in the Preview window. Click **Multiple Pages**, and then drag to select the number of pages to be shown at once.

- **Shrink to Fit**—In cases where you have a two-page document and only a small amount of text appears on the second page, you can condense all the text to fit on the first page by clicking the **Shrink to Fit** button.

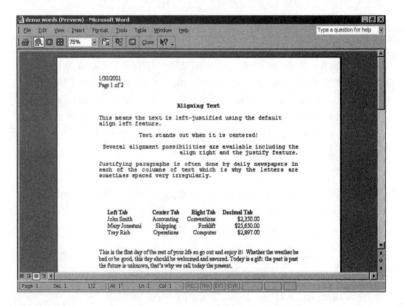

FIGURE 16.1
The Print Preview mode enables you to view your document the way it will print.

When you have completed viewing your document in the Print Preview mode, you can either click the **Print** button to print the document, or, if you want to edit the document before printing, click the **Close** button on the toolbar.

CHANGING PRINT SETTINGS

The Print dialog box supplies you with several options, including the printer to which you send the print job, the number of copies desired, and the page range to be printed.

To open the Print dialog box, select **File, Print**. The Print dialog box is shown in Figure 16.2.

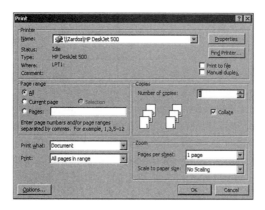

FIGURE 16.2
The Print dialog box gives you control over the various print options for your document.

Depending on your home or office situation, you might have your computer connected to more than one printer. The Print dialog box has a drop-down box that lists all the printers to which you have access. To select a printer other than the current printer, click the drop-down arrow in the **Name** box and choose your printer from the list.

The Print dialog box also enables you to select the range to be printed:

- **All Pages**—To print all the pages in the document, make sure the **All** option button is selected.

- **Current Page**—To print a single page, click the **Current Page** option button (this prints the page that the insertion point is parked on).

- **Page Range**—To designate a range of pages, click the **Pages** option button and type the page numbers into the Pages box.

TIP

> **Specifying Page Ranges**   To print a continuous range of pages, use the 1–5 format (where 1 is the start and 5 is the end of the range). For pages not in a continuous range, use the 5,9,11 format (where each distinct page number to be printed is separated by a comma). You can also mix the two formats. For example, you could specify 1–5,9,11.

- **Number of Copies**—In the Copies area of the Print dialog box, use the increment buttons in the Number of Copies box to select the number of copies you want to print. You can also double-click inside the Number of Copies box and type in a particular value for the number of copies you want.

- **Collate**—In addition to specifying the number of copies, you can collate your document by checking the Collate box in the copies area. *Collate* means that the document is printed in the proper order for stapling or binding.

You can also choose to print all the pages in a chosen range or print only the odd or even pages. Click the **Print** drop-down box (near the bottom left of the dialog box) and select **All Pages in Range**, **Odd Pages**, or **Even Pages**, as required.

Another print option worth mentioning is the Zoom print option in the Print dialog box. This feature enables you to place several document pages on one sheet of paper. To use Zoom print, click the **Pages per Sheet** drop-down box in the **Zoom** area of the Print dialog box and select the number of document pages you want to place on a sheet of paper. To select a scale for the print job (the scale is the relative size of the mini-pages on the printout page, such as 8.5 × 11 inches or legal size), click the **Scale to Paper Size** drop-down box.

After you select these two options, proceed with your print job. Be advised, however, that the more pages you place on a single sheet, the smaller the text appears.

Finally, you can print special items that you have placed in your document, such as comments, styles, and AutoText entries. When you choose to print one of these items, you are supplied with a page or pages separate from the main document that list the comments, styles, or other items you've selected.

Select the **Print What** drop-down arrow and select from the list of items (**Document**, **Document Properties**, **Document Showing Markup**, **List of Markup**, **Styles**, **AutoText Entries**, or **Key Assignments**). If you want to print more than one of these optional items with the document printout, you must select them in the Print Options dialog box.

Selecting Paper Trays, Draft Quality, and Other Options

Several additional print options are also available from the Print dialog box. To access these options, click the **Options** button on the bottom left of the Print dialog box (see Figure 16.3).

The Print options dialog box gives you control over the output of the print job, as well as other options. You can also select the paper tray in your printer that you want to use for the print job (this is very useful in cases where you have a specific tray for letterhead, envelopes, and so on). Several of these options are described in Table 16.1.

FIGURE 16.3
In the Print options dialog box, you can select or deselect certain options associated with your print job.

TABLE 16.1 Print Options on the Print Dialog Box

Option	Purpose
Draft Output	Prints the document faster with less resolution
Reverse Print Order	Prints pages last to first, collating your document on printers that output documents face up
Background Printing	Prints the document quickly to a memory buffer so that you can work while the output is actually sent out to the printer
Document Properties	Prints the document properties

When you have finished selecting the various options for printing your document, click the **OK** button. You are returned to the Print dialog box. When you are ready to print the document, click **OK**.

In this lesson, you learned how to preview and print your Word documents. In the next lesson, you will learn how to create bulleted and numbered lists.

LESSON 17
Creating Numbered and Bulleted Lists

In this lesson, you learn how to create and edit numbered and bulleted lists.

UNDERSTANDING NUMBERED AND BULLETED LISTS

You can add emphasis to a list of points or delineate a list of items in a document by adding numbers or bullets to the items in the list. Numbered lists are great for steps that should be read in order. Bulleted lists work best when you want to separate and highlight different items, but they do not have to appear in any order.

The style of the numbers or bullets that you apply to a list can easily be edited, and you can even change the starting number for a numbered list. The list then renumbers itself automatically. Also, as you add new lines to numbered or bulleted lists, the items are automatically set up with the same numbering style (with the proper number in the list sequence) or bullet style.

CREATING A NUMBERED OR A BULLETED LIST

You can create numbered or bulleted lists from scratch or add numbers or bullets to an existing list.

To create a new numbered list, follow these steps:

1. Place the insertion point where you want to begin the numbered list in your document.

2. Select **Format, Bullets and Numbering**. The Bullets and Numbering dialog box appears.

3. For a numbered list, select the **Numbered** tab (see
   Figure 17.1).

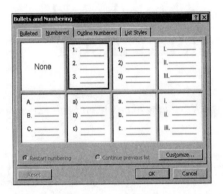

FIGURE 17.1
*Use the Numbered tab on the Bullets and Numbering dialog box to select
a number style for your numbered list.*

 TIP

> ▤ ▤ **Quickly Start a Numbered or Bulleted List**   To
> start a numbered or bulleted list using the default num-
> ber or bullet style, click the **Numbering** or **Bullets** button
> on the Formatting toolbar. To turn off the numbers or
> bullets, click the appropriate button on the toolbar.

4. On the **Numbered** tab, click the style box for the style that
   you want to use. If you want to customize any of the default
   styles offered, select the style box and then click the
   Customize button. The Customize Numbered List dialog box
   appears (see Figure 17.2).

5. Use this dialog box to change the number style, the format,
   the start number, the font for the numbers, or the number
   position. A preview of your changes appears at the bottom of
   the dialog box.

FIGURE 17.2
The Customize Numbered List dialog box enables you to set the number style, format, and start number for the list.

6. When you have selected your options for the number style for your list, click **OK**. You are returned to the Bullets and Numbering dialog box. Click **OK** to return to the document.

You can also easily create a bulleted list using the Bullets and Numbering dialog box; follow these steps:

1. To start a bulleted list, open the Bullets and Numbering dialog box, as previously discussed (select **Format, Bullets and Numbering**). Click the **Bulleted** tab.

2. Select the bullet style you want to use by clicking the appropriate box. If you need to customize your bullet style, click the **Customize** button (see Figure 17.3).

3. The Customize dialog box enables you to select any symbol available in the various font symbol sets or create your button from a graphic available in the Office clip art library. Use the

Font and **Character** buttons to select your bullet style from
the various symbol sets (as discussed in Lesson 14, "Adding
Document Text with AutoText and Using Special
Characters"). If you want to use a graphic as the bullet, click
the **Picture** button. Use the Picture Bullet dialog box that
appears to select the bullet graphic you want to use, and then
click **OK** (see Figure 17.4).

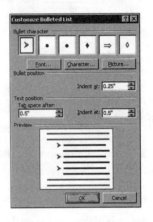

FIGURE 17.3
*Use the Customize Bulleted List dialog box to select the bullet style or shape for
your bulleted list.*

4. Your new bullet style will appear in the Customize Bulleted
   List dialog box. Click **OK** to return to the Bullets and
   Numbering dialog box.

5. When you are ready to begin the bulleted list, click **OK** to
   close the Bullets and Numbering dialog box. The first bullet
   for the list will appear in your document.

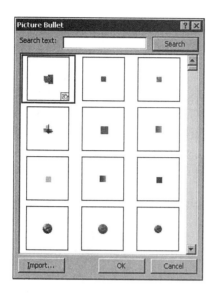

FIGURE 17.4
You can select from several bullet graphics using the Picture Bullet dialog box.

ADDING ITEMS TO THE LIST

After you've turned on numbering or bulleting, you will notice that a number or a bullet appears at the beginning of the line that holds the insertion point. Type the text for this numbered or bulleted item.

Press the **Enter** key to begin a new line. The numbering (sequentially) or bulleting continues with each subsequent line. Just add the needed text and press **Enter** whenever you are ready to move to the next new item in the list.

You can turn off the numbering or bulleting when you have finished creating your list. Click the **Numbering** button or the **Bullets** button, as appropriate, on the Formatting toolbar.

CREATING A NUMBERED OR A BULLETED LIST FROM EXISTING TEXT

You can also add numbers or bullets to existing text. Select the text list, as shown in Figure 17.5, and then select **Format**, **Bullets and Numbering**. Select the appropriate tab on the Bullets and Numbering dialog box and select the style of bullets or numbers you want to use.

When you have completed making your selection, click **OK**. The numbers or bullets appear on the text list.

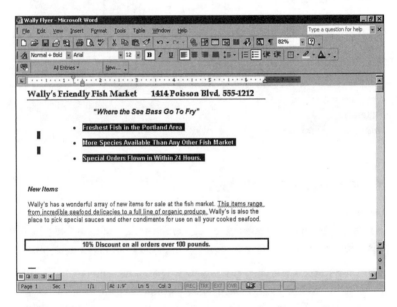

FIGURE 17.5
Select an existing text list and then add numbers or bullets to the list.

TIP

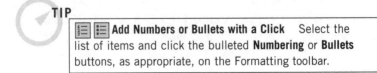

Add Numbers or Bullets with a Click   Select the list of items and click the bulleted **Numbering** or **Bullets** buttons, as appropriate, on the Formatting toolbar.

CREATING MULTILEVEL LISTS

You can also create multilevel lists by using the numbering and bullet
feature. Multilevel lists contain two or more levels within a particular
list. For example, a multilevel list might number primary items in the
list, but secondary items (which fall under a particular primary item)
in the list are denoted by sequential letters of the alphabet. Figure 17.6
shows a numbered, multilevel list.

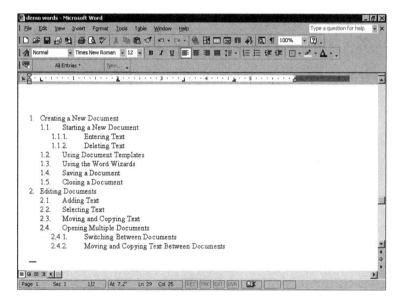

FIGURE 17.6
A multilevel numbered list uses several levels of numbering, as an outline does.

To create a multilevel list, follow these steps:

1. Place the insertion point where you want to begin the list or
   select text in an already existing list.

2. Select **Format**, **Bullets and Numbering**. The Bullets and
   Numbering dialog box opens.

3. Click the **Outline Numbered** tab to view the multilevel
   options (see Figure 17.7).

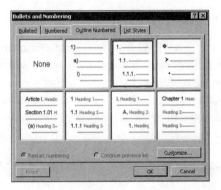

FIGURE 17.7
Use the Outline Numbered tabto select the outline style for your multilevel list.

4. Select the style of multilevel list for your document.

5. After customizing the list options in the Customize Outline Numbered list, click **OK** to return to the Outline Numbered tab.

6. Click **OK** to close the Bullets and Numbering dialog box and return to the document.

7. To enter first-level items in the list, type the item (it will be automatically numbered as is appropriate). Press **Enter** to move to the following line.

8. To demote the next line to the next sublevel (the next level of numbering), press the **Tab** key. Then, type your text. Press **Enter** to move to the following line.

9. If you decide to promote a line that you have demoted using the **Tab** key, be sure the insertion point is on that line, and then press **Shift+Tab**. When you have finished with the current line, press **Enter** to continue.

When you have completed your list, you can turn off the numbering by clicking the **Numbering** button on the Formatting toolbar.

 In this lesson, you learned how to create numbered, bulleted, and multilevel lists. In the next lesson, you will learn how to work with Word tables.

Lesson 18
Using Word Tables

In this lesson, you learn how to create and format tables in your Word document. You also learn how to place math formulas in a table.

Understanding Tables and Cells

A Word table is made up of vertical columns and horizontal rows—a tabular format. The intersection of a row and a column in a table is called a *cell*. A tabular format gives you flexibility to arrange text and graphics in an organized fashion. Tables enable you to enter and work with information in a self-contained grid.

Word makes it easy for you to create and edit a table of any size with any number of columns and rows. In addition to editing text or graphics in a table, you have access to several formatting options related to the table itself, such as row and column attributes and the capability to easily add or delete rows and columns from the table.

Word also offers you several approaches for actually placing the table into the document. You can insert the table into the document or draw the table using the Draw Table command.

Inserting a Table

One option for placing a table into your document is inserting the table. Inserting a table enables you to select the number of rows and columns in the table. The height and width of the rows and columns are set to the default (one line space—based on the current font height—for the row height and 1.23 inches for the column width). Using the Insert command for a new table is the simplest way to select the number of rows and columns in the table. To place the table, you need only to place the insertion point at the position where the new table is to be inserted. The insertion point marks the top-left starting point of the table.

Inserted tables are static; you can move them to a new location in a document simply by selecting the entire table and then using cut and paste. If you want to have better control over the placement of the table, you might want to draw a table (as described in the next section). The drawn table can be dragged to any location in the document because it is created inside a portable frame.

To insert a table into your document, follow these steps:

1. Place the insertion point in the document where you want to place the table; select **Table**, and then point to **Insert**. Select **Table** from the cascading menu. The Insert Table dialog box appears (see Figure 18.1).

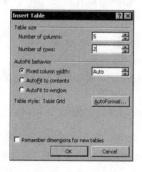

FIGURE 18.1
The Insert Table dialog box enables you to specify the number of columns and rows in your new table.

2. Use the click arrows in the **Number of Columns** text box to set the number of columns. Use the click arrows in the **Number of Rows** text box to set the number of rows.

3. If you want to set the number of columns and rows as the default for subsequent tables, click the **Set As Default for New Tables** check box.

4. To set the table so that it automatically adjusts the column widths to accommodate the text that you type in the column, select the **AutoFit to Contents** option button. If you are going to save the Word document containing the table as a Web document (and use it on a Web site), select the **AutoFit to Window** option button. This allows the table to automatically adjust within a Web browser window so that it can be viewed when the browser window is sized.

5. When you have completed your settings for the table, click **OK**.

The table is inserted into your document.

TIP

 Use the Toolbar to Insert a Table   Click the **Insert Table** button on the Standard toolbar, and then drag down and to the right to select the number of rows and columns (a column and row counter shows you the number selected). Release the mouse to insert the table (or click cancel if you change your mind).

DRAWING A TABLE

An alternative to inserting a table into your document is to draw the table. This method creates a table that resides inside a table cell. (This cell is not the same thing as the intersection of a column and a row, but a movable box that the table lives inside—much like a frame. It can be dragged to any position in the document.) You actually draw the table with a drawing tool and use the tool to add rows and columns to the table.

When you draw the table, you will find that it is created without any rows or columns. You then must manually insert the rows and columns using the Table Drawing tool. Although you can build a highly customized table using this method, it is not as fast as inserting a table with a prescribed number of rows and columns, as described in the previous section.

To draw a table in your document, follow these steps:

1. Select **Table, Draw Table**. The mouse pointer becomes a "pencil" drawing tool. The Tables and Borders toolbar also appears in the document window.

2. Click and drag to create the table's outside borders (its box shape). Release the mouse when you have the outside perimeter of the table completed.

3. To add rows and columns to the table, use the pencil to draw (hold down the left mouse button and drag the mouse) the row and column lines (see Figure 18.2).

 4. When you have completed your table, click the **Tables and Borders** button on the standard toolbar to deactivate the Draw Tables feature.

 TIP

> **Use the Tables and Borders Button to Show Draw Tables Tools**   Click the **Tables and Borders** button on the Standard toolbar, and the Draw Table pencil pointer appears on your screen. Click the button again when you are finished drawing.

The Tables and Borders toolbar provides you with buttons that enable you to edit the attributes of the table. Several of the buttons on the Tables and Borders toolbar are useful for customizing your table:

 • **Distribute Rows Evenly**—Makes the row heights in the table consistent.

 • **Distribute Columns Evenly**—Makes all the column widths consistent.

 • **Eraser**—Enables you to turn on the eraser; drag the eraser across any row or column line in the table to erase it.

• **Line Style**—Enables you to change the weight and style of the row or column lines you create.

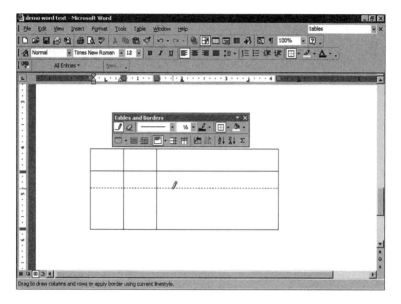

FIGURE 18.2
With the table drawing tool, you can draw a table in your document, and then draw in the row and column lines. The borders all snap to right-angled lines on an unseen grid so your table will always have straight lines.

You can also move the table anywhere on the document page (it's not anchored in one place like tables that are placed on the page using the Insert Table command). Place the mouse on the upper-left edge of the table and a Move icon (a four-headed arrow) appears. Drag the icon to a new location on the page. When you release the mouse, the table is placed in the new location.

> ### CAUTION
> **When I Insert or Draw a Table, My Screen View Changes**
> For you to be able to see the table formatting as it occurs, Word automatically sets your document view to Print Layout. If you had previously been in the Normal view, your screen will look different because it is now showing all layout instructions. To switch back, select your desired page view under the **View** menu.

ENTERING TEXT AND NAVIGATING IN A TABLE

Entering text into the table is very straightforward. Click in the first cell of the table (the open box where the first column and first row of the table meet) and enter the appropriate text. To move to the next cell (horizontally, then vertically), press the **Tab** key. You can continue to move through the cells in the tables by pressing **Tab** and entering your text. If you want to back up a cell, press **Shift+Tab**. This moves you to the cell to the left of the current cell and selects any text entered in that cell.

Several other keyboard combinations are useful as you work in your table:

- **Alt+Home**—Takes you to the first cell in the current row
- **Alt+Page Up**—Takes you to the top cell in the current column
- **Alt+End**—Takes you to the last cell in the current row
- **Alt+Page Down**—Takes you to the last cell in the current column

Of course, you can use the mouse to click any cell of the table at any time.

Deleting text in the table is really no different from deleting text in your document. Select text in the table and press **Delete** to remove it. If you want to delete text in an entire row, but you want to keep the row in the table, place the mouse pointer at the left edge of the particular row. The mouse arrow pointer appears in the selection area. Click to select the entire row. When you press Delete, all the text in the cells in that particular row is deleted. You can also use a column pointer (a solid black arrow; place the mouse at the top of any column) to select an entire column and delete text using the Delete key.

INSERTING AND DELETING ROWS AND COLUMNS

You also have complete control over the number of rows and columns in your table. You can delete empty or filled rows and columns depending on your particular need.

To insert a row or column into the table, place the insertion point in a cell that is in the row or column next to where you want to place a new row or column. Select **Table** and then point to **Insert** to see the available options. Options can be selected from a cascading menu:

- **Rows Above**—Insert a new row above the selected row.

- **Rows Below**—Insert a new row below the selected row.

- **Columns to the Left**—Insert a new column to the left of the selected column.

- **Columns to the Right**—Insert a new column to the right of the selected column.

You can also easily delete columns or rows from your table. Select the rows or columns, and then select the **Table** menu. Point at **Delete**, and then select **Columns** or **Rows** from the cascading menu, as appropriate. The columns or rows selected are removed from the table.

TIP

> **Quick Select Multiple Columns**   To select several cells, drag the mouse across them. You can also click the first cell in the series and then hold down the **Shift** key as you click the last cell you want to select.

FORMATTING A TABLE

Formatting a table can involve several things—you can change the width of a column or the height of a row and can also format the various table borders with different line weights or colors. Some of the table attributes can be modified directly on the table, but other attributes are best handled by modifying settings in the Table Properties dialog box or by using the AutoFormat dialog box.

MODIFYING CELL SIZE

An important aspect of working with your rows and columns is adjusting column widths and row heights to fit the needs of the information that you place inside the table cells. Both of these formatting tasks are mouse work. However, in cases where you want to enter an actual value for all the column widths or row heights, you can use the Table Properties dialog box discussed in this section.

Place the mouse pointer on the border between any columns in your table. A sizing tool appears (see Figure 18.3). Drag the sizing tool to adjust the width of the column.

TIP

> **Use the Ruler As Your Guide**   You can also use the column border markers on the ruler to adjust the width of a column or columns in your table. This provides a method of sizing columns using the ruler as a measurement guide. Drag the marker on the ruler to the appropriate width. To view the ruler, select **View, Ruler**.

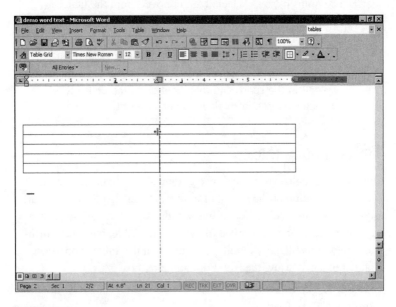

FIGURE 18.3
Use the column sizing tool to adjust the width of a column.

CAUTION

> **Be Careful When Sizing Columns If a Cell Is Selected**   If
> a cell is selected anywhere in a column and you attempt
> to drag the sizing tool to change the column width,
> only the width of the row holding the selected cell is
> changed. Make sure no cells are selected if you want
> to size the entire column.

You can also adjust the column widths and the row heights in the table using the Table Properties dialog box. If you want to adjust the row or column attributes for just one row or column, make sure the insertion point is in that row or column. If you want to adjust the values for the entire table, click anywhere in the table, choose the **Table** menu, point at **Select**, and then choose **Table**. This selects the entire table.

Follow these steps to open the dialog box and adjust the various properties associated with the current table:

1. Select **Table, Table Properties**. The Table Properties dialog box appears.

2. To adjust column widths using the dialog box, select the **Column** tab.

3. Make sure the **Specify Width** check box is selected, and then use the width click arrows to adjust the width (see Figure 18.4).

4. If you want to change the width of the next column, click the **Next Column** button. The **Previous Column** button enables you to adjust the width of the previous column.

5. When you have completed adjusting column widths, click the **OK** button.

You can adjust row heights in a like manner. Use the **Row** tab of the Table Properties dialog box. You can use the Specify Height box to specify the row height and Previous Row and Next Row buttons to specify the row for which you want to adjust the height.

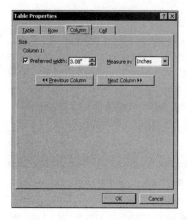

FIGURE 18.4
Adjust your column widths using the Column tab of the Table Properties dialog box.

TIP

> **Working with Drawn Tables**   If you've created your table using the Draw Table command and then inserted your rows and columns with the Drawing tool, you might find it faster to align any irregularly sized elements (such as rows or columns) with the mouse rather than using the Table Properties dialog box.

FORMATTING TABLE BORDERS

Formatting your table borders is a matter of selecting the cells (or the entire table) and then selecting the formatting parameters. After you've selected the appropriate cells, select the **Format** menu, and then select **Borders and Shading**.

TIP

> **Select the Entire Table**   A fast way to select the entire table is to place the insertion point in the table and then select **Table**, point at **Select**, and select **Table** again.

The Borders and Shading dialog box appears. Select the style of border that you want to place on the selected area of the table.

To select the border style, choose from one of the following:

- **Box**—This places a box around the outside of the table.

- **All**—This places a box around the table, gridlines inside the table, and also applies any shadow and color parameters that have been set in Word.

- **Grid**—This places a border around the table and places a border (grid) on the row and column lines.

- **Custom**—To change the style, color, and width of your border lines, use the **Style**, **Color**, and **Width** drop-down boxes to select the options for your border lines. When you have completed your selections, click **OK** to return to the table.

The border options that you selected are used to format the cells that you selected in the table.

AUTOMATICALLY FORMATTING THE TABLE

You can also format your table in a more automatic fashion using the Table AutoFormat feature. This feature enables you to select from a list of predetermined table formats that configure the borders and provide text and background colors in the cells. You can even select a particular font for the text contained in the cells.

To AutoFormat your table, click any cell of the table and then follow these steps:

1. Select **Table**, **AutoFormat**. The Table AutoFormat dialog box appears (see Figure 18.5).

2. To preview the various formats provided, click a format in the **Formats** scroll box. A preview of the format is shown.

3. When you have found the format that you want to use, select the format and then click **Apply**.

TIP

> **Select the Table Items You Want to Format with AutoFormat**
> The AutoFormat dialog box provides several check boxes
> (Borders, Shading, Font, Color, and so on) that can be
> deselected if you don't want your AutoFormat selection
> to format these particular items in your table.

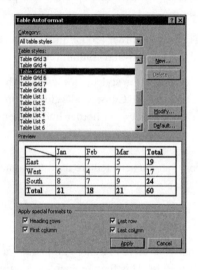

FIGURE 18.5
*The Table AutoFormat dialog box enables you to select and apply a format style
for your entire table.*

In this lesson, you learned how to create, edit, and format tables. In
the next lesson, you will learn how to create columns in your documents.

LESSON 19
Creating Columns in a Document

In this lesson, you learn how to create and edit column settings in your document.

UNDERSTANDING WORD COLUMNS

Word makes it very easy for you to insert and format columns for newsletters, brochures, and other special documents. It gives you complete control over the number of columns, column widths, and the space between the columns. You can insert columns for the entire page run of a document or place columns only in a particular document section.

The columns that you work with in Word are called newspaper or "snaking columns." This means that if you have two columns on a page and fill the first column, the text snakes over into the second column and continues there. This format is typical of your daily newspaper's columns.

TIP

> **For Side-by-Side Columns, Use a Table** If you want to create columns that allow you to place paragraphs of information side by side in a document, place the text in a table that is not formatted with a visible border. This gives you great control over the individual text blocks in the separate columns that you create (see Lesson 18, "Using Word Tables").

CREATING COLUMNS

You can format a new document for columns, or you can select text and then apply column settings to that specific text. When you apply column settings to any selected text, Word automatically places the text (now in the number of columns you selected) into its own document section with a section break above and below the text. This allows you to switch from text in regular paragraphs (which are basically one column that covers all the space between the left and right margins) to text placed in multiple columns. You can also turn off the columns and return to text in paragraphs with very little effort on your part. Figure 19.1 shows a document that contains a section of text in paragraphs, followed by text in columns, and again followed by text in paragraphs (three sections in the same document). Sections are covered in Lesson 21, "Working with Larger Documents."

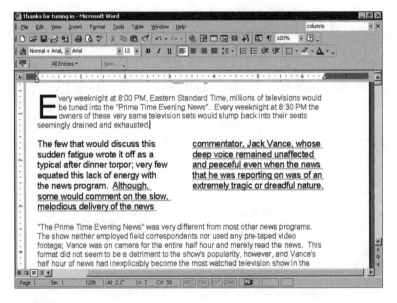

FIGURE 19.1
Documents can contain text in paragraphs and text in columns, as needed.

To place additional columns into a document, follow these steps:

1. Place the insertion point where you want the columns to begin or select the text that you want to format with the columns.

2. Select **Format, Columns**. The Columns dialog box appears (see Figure 19.2).

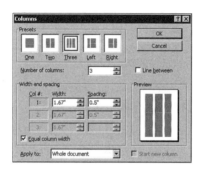

FIGURE 19.2
The Columns dialog box enables you to set the number of columns and column options for those that you place into your document.

3. To select the number of columns you want to place in the document, you can choose from several preset options or specify a number of custom columns. To use the presets select one of the following (all presets create columns separated by half-inch space):

   • **One**—The default setting; this removes columns from the document and places all text in the normal one-column configuration.

   • **Two**—Creates two equal columns.

   • **Three**—Creates three equal columns.

- **Left**—Creates two columns where the left column is half as wide as the right column.

- **Right**—Creates two columns where the right column is half as wide as the left column.

4. If you want to select a custom number of columns (rather than using the Presets), use the **Number of Columns** spinner box (or type a number in the box). Use the Width and Spacing box, located beneath the Number of Columns spinner box, to specify the width for each column and the distance between each of the columns.

5. If you want to place a vertical line between the columns, select the **Line Between** check box.

6. You can apply these new columns to the entire document (if you've selected text, it applies only to that particular text) or click the **Apply To** drop-down box and select **Whole Document** or **This Point Forward**. If you choose This Point Forward, the columns are placed in the document from the insertion point to the end of the document (in their own section).

7. When you have finished selecting your column options, click **OK**.

TIP

> 🔳 **Create Columns with a Click of the Mouse**   You can also create columns for currently selected text or insert columns into the text using the Columns button on the Standard toolbar. Click the **Columns** button and then select 1, 2, 3, or 4 columns from the drop-down box (you can choose **Cancel** if you change your mind). If you choose to create multiple columns using this method, columns of equal width are created.

Editing Column Settings

If you want to edit any of the column settings in your document, such as column number or column width, you can return to the Column dialog box to change any of the options.

1. Make sure that you click in the document section that contains the columns you want to modify.

2. Select **Format**, **Columns**. The Column dialog box appears.

3. Edit the various settings, described in the "Creating Columns" section, as needed. When you have completed your selections, click **OK**.

Inserting a Column Break

Because you are working with continuous, newspaper-type column settings, you might want to force a column break in a column. This allows you to balance the text between columns or end the text in a column at a particular point and force the rest of the text into the next column. To force a column break, follow these steps:

1. Place the insertion point in the column text where you want to force the break.

2. Select **Insert**, **Break**. The Break dialog box appears.

3. Select the **Column Break** option button.

4. Click **OK** to place the break in the column.

TIP

Use the Keyboard to Insert a Column Break   You can also quickly place a column break in a column by pressing **Ctrl+Shift+Enter**.

The text at the break is moved into the next column in the document. Column breaks in the Print Layout view appear the way they will print, and all the column borders show in this view. In the Normal view, multiple columns are displayed as a single continuous column. The column break appears as a dotted horizontal line labeled Column Break.

REMOVING COLUMN BREAKS

Removing column breaks is very straightforward. Methods do vary, however, depending on the view that you are currently in.

In Print Layout mode, place the insertion point at the beginning of the text just after the break, click **Columns**, and then drag to select one column. This removes the break from the document.

TIP

> ¶ **Use the Show/Hide Button to Reveal Column Breaks**
> You can also quickly show all your column breaks by clicking the **Show/Hide Button.** After you see the column breaks, just delete them.

In the Normal view, you can actually see the Column Break line (it appears as a dashed line). Select the break line with the mouse and then press **Delete**.

In this lesson, you learned to create and edit column settings in your documents. In the next lesson, you will learn to add graphics to your documents.

LESSON 20
Adding Graphics to a Document

In this lesson, you learn how to insert graphics, such as clip art, into your document and how to use the Word drawing tools to create your own graphics.

INSERTING A GRAPHIC

Adding a graphic to your document is really just a matter of identifying the place in the document where you want to place the picture and then selecting a specific graphic file. Word provides you with a large clip art gallery of ready-made graphics (in the metafile format .wmf). You can also place images into your document that you find on the Web, that you receive in to e-mail messages, that are imported from a scanner or digital camera, and more.

Word also embraces several graphic file formats, including the following file types:

- CompuServe GIF (.gif)
- Encapsulated PostScript (.eps)
- Various paint programs (.pcx)
- Tagged Image File format (.tif)
- Windows bitmap (.bmp)
- JPEG file interchange format (.jpg)
- WordPerfect graphics (.wpg)

To add a graphic file (a picture other than one of the Word clip art files), insert the image using the Insert menu.

Follow these steps to add a graphic to your document:

1. Place the insertion point where you want to place the graphic in the document.

2. Select **Insert**, **Picture**, and then select **From File** on the cascading menu. The Insert Picture dialog box appears.

3. Use the **Look In** box to locate the drive and folder that contains the picture file. After you locate the picture, click the file to view a preview (see Figure 20.1).

The Views drop-down arrow enables you to choose to see a list, preview, or thumbnails, among others.

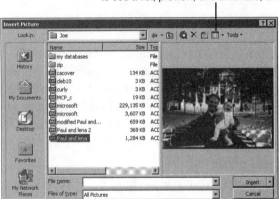

FIGURE 20.1
You can preview your graphical images before inserting them into your document.

4. After you select the picture you want to insert into the document, click **Insert** in the lower-right corner of the Insert Picture dialog box.

The picture is placed in your document and the Picture toolbar appears in the document window. The Picture toolbar provides several tools you can use to modify and edit the graphics in your document. See the "Modifying Graphics" section in this lesson.

Probably the first thing you will want to do to any graphic or picture that you insert into a document is size the image so it fits better on the page in relation to your text. Most inserted graphics, even those from the Office clip art library, tend to be inserted into a document in a fairly large size.

To size a graphic, click it to select it. Sizing handles (small boxes) appear on the border of the graphic. Place the mouse on any of these sizing handles. The mouse pointer becomes a sizing tool with arrows pointing in the directions in which you can change the size; drag to size the graphic. To maintain the height/width ratio of the image (so you don't stretch or distort the image), use the sizing handles on the corners of the image and drag diagonally.

TIP

> **Add a Graphic with Copy and Paste**   You can copy a
> graphic to the Windows Clipboard from any Windows
> graphic program that you are running and then paste it
> into your Word document.

USING THE WORD CLIP ART

If you don't have a collection of your own pictures and graphics to place in your document, don't worry; Word provides a large collection of clip art images you can use to liven up your documents. The clip art library is organized by theme. For example, if you want to peruse the animal clip art that Word provides, select the **Animal** theme.

To insert Word clip art into your document, follow these steps:

1. Place the insertion point where you want to place the graphic in the document.

2. Select **Insert, Picture**, and then select **Clip Art** on the cascading menu. The Insert Clip Art task pane appears (see Figure 20.2).

FIGURE 20.2
The Insert Clip Art task pane gives you access to the Word clip art gallery.

3. Type in a clip art theme, such as **Animals**, into the **Search Text** area.

4. (Optional) By default, the search will be conducted on all your media collections, including the Office Collections. If you want to preclude certain collections from the search (to speed up the search process), click the **All Collections** drop-down arrow and clear the check mark from any of the locations listed.

5. (Optional) If you want to preclude certain file types from the search (to speed up the search process), select the **All Media File Types** drop-down box and deselect any of the file types (ClipArt, Photographs, and so on) as required.

TIP

Sound and Action Imagery Available, Too   You can insert sound or movie clips into your document from the Clip Art task pane. By default, they are included in the results for any search you conduct.

6. Click the **Search** button and various clip art images that fit your search criteria appear.

7. When you have located the clip art you want to place in the document, click the image. An image drop-down box appears. Select **Insert** to place the image in your document (see Figure 20.3).

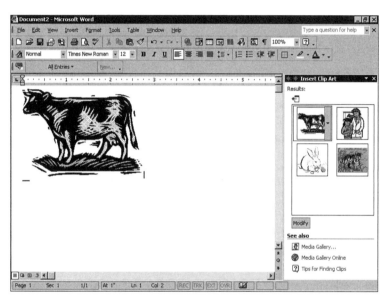

FIGURE 20.3
Click a particular clip art category to view the clip art images.

If used appropriately, pictures and clip art can definitely improve the look and feel of your documents—particularly special documents such as flyers, newsletters, and brochures. If you find the clip art library provided doesn't have what you need, click the **Media Gallery Online** link under the **See Also** section near the bottom of the task pane. Your Web browser opens and you go to Microsoft's online clip art library, which offers additional clip art images for your use.

CAUTION

Images and Copyright   Clip art images, such as those that ship with Microsoft Word, are considered "free" images and can be used in any of your Word documents. Other images that you find on the Web might be copyrighted. You are responsible for determining whether you have the right to use an image before copying it. Sometimes you can pay a fee for one-time use or make another agreement.

MODIFYING GRAPHICS

You can modify the images you place into your documents. An invaluable tool for modifying images is the Picture toolbar. It provides buttons that enable you to modify several picture parameters. You can also easily crop and resize your graphics.

When you click a picture (a picture file or Word clip art) in the document, the Picture toolbar automatically appears. You can use the toolbar to adjust the brightness or contrast of the image. You can also add a border to the graphic or adjust other picture properties. Word's Picture toolbar offers a large number of possibilities. Table 20.1 provides a listing and a description of the most commonly used buttons on the Picture toolbar.

TABLE 20.1   The Picture Toolbar Buttons and Their Purposes

Button	Click To
	Insert a new picture at the current picture position.
	Change the image to grayscale or black and white.
	Crop the image (after selecting, you must drag the image border to a new cropping position).
	Select a line style for the image border (you must first use the Borders and Shading command to add a border to the image).

TABLE 20.1   (continued)

Button	Click To
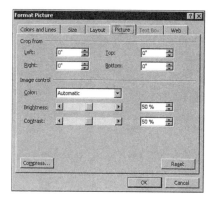	Control how text wraps around the image (square, tight, behind image, and so on).
	Open the Format Picture dialog box.
	Reset the image to its original formatting values.

You can select from several formatting options for your picture when you select the **Format Picture** button; this opens the Format Picture dialog box (see Figure 20.4).

FIGURE 20.4
The Format Picture dialog box offers several ways to modify your picture.

The Format Picture dialog box provides several tabs that can be used to control various formatting attributes related to the picture. These tabs are

- **Colors and Lines**—Enables you to change the fill color (or background color) for the picture. This tab also provides settings for line weight and color and the style of arrows used on lines. Line options are available only if you have created the image using the tools on the Drawing toolbar.

- **Size**—Enables you to specify the height and width of the image in inches. It also enables you to specify the height and width scale (in percentages) for the image.

- **Layout**—Enables you to specify how text should wrap around the image (see Figure 20.5). Other options enable you to place the image behind or in front of the text.

FIGURE 20.5
The Layout tab of the Format Picture dialog box enables you to select how text near the image is wrapped.

- **Picture**—Enables you to crop the picture (refer to Figure 20.4). It also provides an Image control area that lets you control the brightness and contrast of the image. You also can change the color of the image from the default (Automatic) to Grayscale, Black and White, or Washout using the Color drop-down box.

- **Web**—Enables you to include message text for the image that will appear as the image is loaded on a Web page. You need to use this option only if the Word document is going to be saved as a Web page for Web site.

CAUTION

Why Is the Text Box Tab Unavailable?   The Text box tab is available only when you are using the dialog box to change the format options on a text box that you have created using the Text Box tool on the Drawing toolbar.

After making formatting changes to the picture using the Format Picture dialog box, click **OK** to return to your document.

TIP

Formatting Drawings You Create   If you create your own image in a Word document using the tools on the Drawing toolbar, you can format the drawing using the Format Drawing Canvas dialog box that contains the same tabs as those found on the Format Picture dialog box. To open the Format Drawing Canvas dialog box, select the drawing you have created, and select **Format**, **Drawing Canvas**.

TIP

Resize or Crop with the Mouse   Select the picture, and then drag the resizing handles (the black boxes on the picture borders) to increase or decrease the size. If you want to crop the picture, hold down the **Shift** key as you drag any of the resizing handles.

You can delete a picture you no longer want in the document by clicking the picture and then pressing **Delete**. You can also move or copy the picture using the **Cut**, **Copy**, **Paste** commands (for general information about moving, copying, and pasting items in Word, see Lesson 4, "Editing Documents").

USING THE WORD DRAWING TOOLBAR

You can also create your own graphics in your documents using the drawing tools provided on the Word Drawing toolbar. This toolbar provides several tools, including line, arrow, rectangle, oval, and text box tools. You can also use the appropriate tools to change the fill color on a box or circle, change the line color on your drawing object, or change the arrow style on arrows you have placed on the page.

To display the Drawing toolbar, select **View**, point at **Toolbar**, and then select **Drawing** from the toolbar list.

TIP

> **Quickly Access Toolbars**   You can also right-click any toolbar in the Word window to access the toolbar list; to choose the Drawing toolbar, select **Drawing**.

The Drawing toolbar appears at the bottom of the document window just above the Word status bar. Figure 20.6 shows the Drawing toolbar and the tools available on it.

 Word provides you with an add-on program called WordArt that enables you to create special text effects in your document. You can create text that wraps around a circle, as well as a number of other special text "looks." In Word, click the **WordArt** button on the Drawing toolbar to start the WordArt program. WordArt can also be used in other Office programs, such as PowerPoint, to create visually exciting text items.

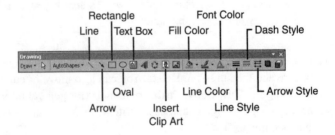

FIGURE 20.6
The Drawing toolbar makes it easy for you to create your own graphics in your documents.

CREATING A NEW OBJECT

To draw a particular object, click the appropriate button on the toolbar. Then, drag the mouse to create the object in your document. To draw a square or circle, click the **Rectangle** tool or the **Oval** tool and hold down the **Shift** key as you draw the object with the mouse. If you find that you aren't very good at actually drawing graphical objects, click the **AutoShapes** drop-down arrow (near the left side of the Drawing toolbar) and select a particular object shape from the list provided.

MODIFYING DRAWN OBJECTS

You can also control the various attributes for a particular object that you've drawn. You must first select the object using the selection pointer (click the **Select Objects** tool and then click the object). You can manipulate the object's line style, fill color, and line color. Just choose the appropriate tool on the toolbar and make your selection from the list of possibilities.

You can also size and move objects that you draw. Select an object and use the sizing handles to increase or decrease the size of the particular object. If you want to move the object to a new position, place the mouse pointer in the middle of the selected object and drag it to a new position.

If you draw several related objects, you can select all the objects at once and drag them together to a new location. Select the first object and then hold down the **Shift** key and select subsequent objects, as needed. When you drag any of the objects to a new location, all the selected objects move together.

At times you will want to delete a particular object from your document. Simply select the object and then press **Delete** to remove it.

You will find that the Drawing toolbar provides you with all the tools (except natural artistic ability) you need to create fairly sophisticated custom images. A little practice with the various tools goes a long way in helping you create objects that add interest to your documents.

INSERTING IMAGES FROM SCANNERS AND OTHER SOURCES

You can also place images into your Word documents that do not currently exist as a picture or clip art file. You can actually attach to a particular *input device*, such as a scanner or digital camera, and then have it scan an image or take a picture that is inserted into your document.

PLAIN ENGLISH

> **Input Device**   Any device, such as a scanner or a digital camera, that can be attached to your computer and used to acquire a picture.

Word enables you to acquire images from an attached scanner, a digital camera, or other device such as a video camera. All you have to do is set up the device so that it works on your computer (consult your device's documentation), and Word can use it to capture any image that device provides.

To insert an image from an attached device, follow these steps:

1. Place the insertion point in the document where you want to insert the image.

2. Select the **Insert** menu, point at **Picture**, and then click **From Scanner or Camera**. The Insert Picture from Camera or Scanner dialog box appears.

3. Click the **Device** drop-down box and select the device you want to capture the picture from (this is necessary only if you have more than one device attached).

4. Click the **Insert** button. The device scans the image or, in the case of a camera, downloads a particular image and places the image in your document.

In this lesson, you learned how to insert pictures and clip art and create graphics. In the next lesson, you will learn how to set up a mail merge in Word.

LESSON 21

Working with Larger Documents

In this lesson, you learn how to work with larger documents, including inserting section breaks and building a table of contents.

ADDING SECTIONS TO DOCUMENTS

When you work with larger documents, you might have several parts in the document, such as a cover page, a table of contents, and the body of the document. In most cases, these different parts of the document require different formatting and layout attributes. To divide a document into different parts that have different layouts, use sections. A *section* is a defined portion of the document that can contain its own set of formatting options. You can divide a document into as many sections as you need.

 TIP

> **Section** A portion of a document (defined with marks that you insert) that can be formatted differently from the rest of the document or other distinct sections of the document.

When you first begin a new document, the document consists of one section with consistent page formatting throughout the document. If you look at the status bar in a new document, you find that it reads "Sec 1," which means that the insertion point is currently in Section 1 of the document (which would be the entire document, in this case).

Sections are defined in your document by section breaks (which means a certain position in the document serves as the break between the existing section and the new section you insert). To place additional section breaks in a document, follow these steps:

1. Place the insertion point where you would like to insert the new section break.

2. Select **Insert, Break**. The Break dialog box appears. In the lower half of the Break dialog box, several section break types are available (see Figure 21.1).

FIGURE 21.1
Select your type of section break in the Break dialog box.

- **Next Page**—A page break is placed in the document and the new section begins on this new page.

- **Continuous**—The new section starts at the insertion point and continues for the rest of the document (or until it comes to the next defined section).

- **Even Page**—The new section starts on the next even-numbered page.

- **Odd Page**—The new section starts on the next odd-numbered page.

3. Select the option button for the type of section break you want to place in the document.

4. Click **OK** to insert the new section into the document.

Your new section break appears in the document. In the Normal view, the section break appears as a double horizontal line marked with the text "Section Break" followed by the type of section you selected. If you are working in the Print Layout view, the only way to see which section you're in is to look at the number displayed on the status bar (see Figure 21.2).

Section breaks are visible in the Normal View.

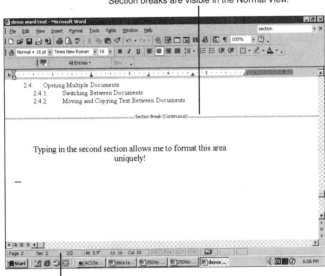

The status bar lists which section your pointer is in.

FIGURE 21.2
You can easily find out which section of a document you are in by reading the status bar or switching the document to Normal View.

After you have the new section in the document, you can apply page formatting to it as needed.

If you want to delete a section break, place the mouse pointer in the selection area and select the section break as you would any other line of text (this won't work in the Print Layout view). After the section break is selected, press the **Delete** key to remove it.

CREATING A TABLE OF CONTENTS

If you want to make it easy for the reader of a large document to find specific sections or parts of the document, you must include a table of contents. Creating a table of contents in Word relies heavily on using specific text styles to format and organize your document. As long as you do this, creating a table of contents is actually very straightforward.

For example, you can use either Word's built-in heading styles (Heading 1, Heading 2, Heading 3, and so forth) to format the different levels of headings in the document, or you can create your own styles to do so. Using these headings requires you to use methodology to break down the contents of your document, such as using section levels or chapter levels. The important thing is that you use them consistently to format the various headings in the document.

A good example is a document that is divided into parts and then further subdivided into chapters (each part contains several chapters). If you use Word's heading styles to format the different division levels in the document, you would use Heading 1 for the parts (Part I, Part II, and so forth) and Heading 2 for the chapter titles. By assigning these built-in styles (or your own) to your different headings, you can generate a table of contents that shows two levels: parts and chapters. This process works because Word can pinpoint a particular heading level by the style that you've assigned to it (for more about working with and creating styles, see Lesson 12, "Working with Styles").

After you've set your various headings for parts, chapters, or other divisions into your document and have assigned a particular style to each group of headings, you are ready to use the Word Table of Contents feature to generate the actual table of contents.

To create a table of contents using the Word heading styles—or unique styles that you have created—follow these steps:

1. Create a blank page at the beginning of your document for your table of contents (or create a new section in which to

place your table of contents) and place your insertion point in it.

2. On the **Insert** menu, choose **Reference, Index and Tables**.

3. When the Index and Tables dialog box appears, select the **Table of Contents** tab (see Figure 21.3).

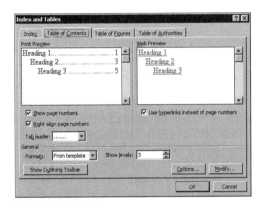

FIGURE 21.3
The Table of Contents tab on the Index and Tables dialog box is where you specify the options for your new table of contents. You see both a Print Preview and a Web Preview.

4. The Table of Contents tab provides you with a preview of the table of contents (TOC) hierarchy for Word's built-in heading styles. If you used the Word heading styles to format and specify the various division levels in your document, you can skip down to step 7. If you made your own unique heading or section styles, click the **Options** button.

5. The Table of Contents Options dialog box appears. This is where you specify the styles you used to format the various TOC levels in your document. Scroll down through the **Available Styles** list. To specify a style as a TOC hierarchical level, type the level number (1, 2, 3, and so on) into the appropriate style's TOC level box.

6. When you have selected the styles that serve as your various TOC levels, click **OK** to return to the Table of Contents tab.

7. To select a style for the TOC, click the **Formats** drop-down list. You can choose from several styles, such as Classic, Distinctive, and Fancy. After you select a format, a preview is provided in the Print Preview and Web Preview areas of the dialog box.

TIP

Open the Outlining Toolbar for Quick Access of TOC Features   If you will be editing headings in the document that will affect the TOC after you generate it, you might want to click the **Show Outlining Toolbar** button on the Table of Contents tab. This opens the Outlining toolbar. After generating the TOC and doing any editing in the document, you can use the Update TOC button on the Outlining toolbar to quickly regenerate the TOC. The toolbar also provides a Go to TOC button that can be used to quickly move from anywhere in the document back to the TOC.

8. Use the various check boxes on the tab to select or deselect options for formatting the table of contents. After you've specified options such as right align, page numbers, and the tab leader style, you are ready to generate the table of contents; click **OK**.

Your new table of contents appears in the document (see Figure 21.4). You can add a title to the table of contents and format the text as needed. If you want to remove the table of contents from the document, place the mouse pointer in the selection area to the left of the table of contents. Click to select the TOC. Press the **Delete** key to remove it from the document.

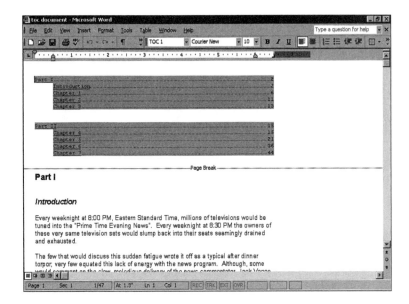

FIGURE 21.4
The table of contents is generated at the insertion point in your document. You can add your own title.

TIP

> **Use the TOC to Quickly Move to a Particular Chapter**   A
> real slick feature associated with the table of contents in
> your document is the ability to quickly jump to a partic-
> ular part of your document. For example, if you wanted
> to move to the beginning of Chapter 3 in the document
> from the TOC, press **Ctrl+click** on the Chapter 3 notation
> in the table of contents. You are linked directly to the
> beginning of Chapter 3.

In this lesson you learned how to insert sections into a document and
create a table of contents.

INDEX

T

Microsoft®
Excel™ 2002

MINUTE
GUIDE

201 West 103rd Street
Indianapolis, IN 46290

Joe Habraken

10 Minute Guide to Microsoft® Excel™ 2002

© 2002 by Que® Corporation

All rights reserved. No part of this book shall be reproduced,
stored in a retrieval system, or transmitted by any means, electronic, mechanical, photocopying, recording, or otherwise, without written permission from the publisher. No patent liability is
assumed with respect to the use of the information contained
herein. Although every precaution has been taken in the preparation of this book, the publisher and author assume no responsibility for errors or omissions. Nor is any liability assumed for
damages resulting from the use of the information contained
herein.

International Standard Book Number: 0-7897-2633-5

Library of Congress Catalog Card Number: 2001090286

Printed in the United States of America

First Printing: October 2001

04   03   8   7

Trademarks

All terms mentioned in this book that are known to be trademarks or service marks have been appropriately capitalized.
Que Corporation cannot attest to the accuracy of this information. Use of a term in this book should not be regarded as
affecting the validity of any trademark or service mark.

Microsoft is a registered trademark of Microsoft Corporation.

Excel is a trademark of Microsoft Corporation.

Warning and Disclaimer

Every effort has been made to make this book as complete and
as accurate as possible, but no warranty or fitness is implied.
The information provided is on an "as is" basis. The author and
the publisher shall have neither liability nor responsibility to
any person or entity with respect to any loss or damages arising
from the information contained in this book.

Associate Publisher
Greg Wiegand

Acquisitions Editor
Stephanie McComb

Managing Editor
Thomas F. Hayes

Project Editor
Tonya Simpson

Indexer
Mandie Frank

Proofreader
Plan-It Publishing

Technical Editor
Dallas Releford

Team Coordinator
Sharry Gregory

Interior Designer
Gary Adair

Cover Designer
Sandra Schroeder

Page Layout
Susan Geiselman

Contents

TABLE OF CONTENTS

DEDICATION

To my brother, Pete.

ACKNOWLEDGMENTS

Creating books like this takes a real team effort. I would like to thank
Stephanie McComb, our acquisitions editor, who worked very hard to
assemble the team that made this book a reality. Also, a tip of the hat
and a thanks to Dallas Releford, who, as the technical editor for the
project, did a fantastic job making sure that everything was correct
and suggested a number of additions that made the book even more
technically sound. Finally, a great big thanks to our project editor,
Tonya Simpson, who ran the last leg of the race and made sure the
book made it to press on time—what a great team of professionals.

Tell Us What You Think!

As the reader of this book, *you* are our most important critic and commentator. We value your opinion and want to know what we're doing right, what we could do better, what areas you'd like to see us publish in, and any other words of wisdom you're willing to pass our way.

As an associate publisher for Que, I welcome your comments. You can fax, e-mail, or write me directly to let me know what you did or didn't like about this book—as well as what we can do to make our books stronger.

Please note that I cannot help you with technical problems related to the topic of this book, and that due to the high volume of mail I receive, I might not be able to reply to every message.

When you write, please be sure to include this book's title and author, as well as your name and phone or fax number. I will carefully review your comments and share them with the author and editors who worked on the book.

Fax: 317-581-4666

E-mail: feedback@quepublishing.com

Mail: Greg Wiegand
            Que
            201 West 103rd Street
            Indianapolis, IN 46290 USA

Introduction

Microsoft Excel 2002 is an incredibly versatile and easy-to-use spreadsheet program that can help you calculate and analyze numerical data for both large and small businesses. You can create simple spreadsheets, invoices, and even complex ledger reports. You even can save Excel data for use on the World Wide Web.

THE WHAT AND WHY OF MICROSOFT EXCEL

Excel provides you with all the tools you need to quickly create many different types of business spreadsheets and reports. Whether you work at home or in a busy office, Microsoft Excel can help you do some heavy-duty number crunching. In Excel, you can

- Create spreadsheets that include formulas and built-in Excel functions
- Format numbers and text so that Excel printouts are easy to read
- Use clip art, pictures, borders, and colors to add interest to your spreadsheets
- Take Excel data and publish it to the World Wide Web

Additionally, Excel provides several features that make it easy for you to calculate the results of formulas and format your worksheets. You can

- Use the Excel Function Wizard to help you choose the right function to calculate the appropriate result.
- Use the Autoformat feature to quickly format an entire worksheet.
- Use the new speech feature for voice dictation and voice commands.

While providing you with many complex features, Microsoft Excel is easy to learn. This book will help you understand the possibilities awaiting you with Microsoft Excel 2002.

WHY QUE'S *10 MINUTE GUIDE TO MICROSOFT EXCEL 2002*?

The *10 Minute Guide to Microsoft Excel 2002* can save you precious time while you get to know the different features in Microsoft Excel. Each lesson is designed to be completed in 10 minutes or less, so you'll be up to snuff on basic and advanced Excel skills quickly.

Although you can jump around between lessons, starting at the beginning is a good plan. The bare-bones basics are covered first, and more advanced topics are covered later. If you need help installing Excel, see the next section for instructions.

INSTALLING EXCEL

You can install Microsoft Excel 2002 on a computer running Microsoft Windows 98, Windows NT 4.0, Windows 2000, or Windows XP. You can purchase Microsoft Excel as a standalone product on its own CD-ROM or as part of the Microsoft Office XP suite (which comes on a CD-ROM). Whether you are installing Excel as a standalone product or as part of the Microsoft Office XP suite, the installation steps are basically the same.

To install Excel, follow these steps:

1. Start your computer, and then insert the Excel 2002 or Microsoft XP Office CD in the CD-ROM drive. The CD-ROM should autostart, providing you with the opening installation screen (for either Excel or Office, depending on the CD with which you are working).

2. If the CD-ROM does not autostart, choose **Start**, **Run**. In the Run dialog box, type the letter of the CD-ROM drive, followed by **setup** (for example, **e:\setup**). If necessary, use the Browse button to locate and select the CD-ROM drive and the setup.exe program.

3. When the Setup Wizard prompts you, enter your name, organization, and CD key in the appropriate boxes.

4. Choose **Next** to continue.

5. The next wizard screen provides instructions to finish the installation. Complete the installation. Select **Next** to advance from screen to screen after providing the appropriate information requested by the wizard.

After you finish the installation from the CD, icons for Excel and any other Office applications you have installed will appear on the Windows Start menu. Lesson 2 in this book provides you with a step-by-step guide to starting Excel 2002.

CONVENTIONS USED IN THIS BOOK

To help you move through the lessons easily, commands, options, and icons you need to select, and keys you need to press appear in **bold** type.

In telling you to choose menu commands, this book uses the format *menu title*, *menu command*. For example, the statement "Choose **File**, **Properties**" means to open the File menu and select the Properties command.

In addition to those conventions, the *10 Minute Guide to Microsoft Excel 2002* uses the following sidebars to identify helpful information:

PLAIN ENGLISH

New or unfamiliar terms are defined in term sidebars.

TIP

Read these tips for ideas that cut corners and confusion.

CAUTION

This icon identifies areas where new users often run into trouble. These sidebars offer practical solutions to those problems.

LESSON 1
What's New in Excel 2002

This lesson introduces you to Microsoft Access, and you learn what's new in Access 2002.

INTRODUCING EXCEL 2002

Excel is a powerful spreadsheet program that can help you create worksheets and invoices and do both simple and sophisticated number crunching. It is designed to help you calculate the results of formulas and help you analyze numerical data. Excel also makes it easy for you to take numerical information and display the data in a variety of chart types. You even can add graphics and other objects to your Excel worksheets to create professional-looking printouts and business reports.

Excel provides several user-friendly features that make it easy for you to get your data into a worksheet and format the information. Excel also makes it easy for you to do calculations, whether you use formulas that you create or use any of the numerous functions (built-in formulas) that Excel provides. There are financial, statistical, logical, and even engineering functions (Excel functions are covered in Lesson 6, "Performing Calculations with Functions").

The following are some of the Excel features with which you will become familiar in this book:

- **Excel templates**—Excel provides several templates—such as a time card, expense sheet, and sales invoice—that provide you with a ready-made worksheet containing formulas and formatting. All you have to do is enter the appropriate information to create a complete worksheet. Excel templates are discussed in the next lesson.

- **Fill feature**—The Fill feature enables you to add series of numbers or quickly copy information from one cell to several cells. The Fill feature is discussed in Lesson 3.

- **Wizards**—Wizards help you use many Excel features. They guide you through a number of Excel processes, including the creation of functions (covered in Lesson 6) and the insertion of charts into a worksheet (charts are discussed in Lessons 17 and 18).

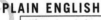

PLAIN ENGLISH

> **Wizard**   A feature that guides you step by step through a particular process in Excel, such as creating a new chart.

WHAT'S NEW IN EXCEL 2002

Excel 2002 is similar in look and feel to Excel 2000, the previous version of this powerful spreadsheet software. Excel 2002 provides the same adaptive menu and toolbar system found in Excel 2000 that customizes the commands and icons listed on your menus and toolbars based on the commands you use most frequently.

Excel 2002 also includes several new features, such as task panes and voice dictation, that make it even easier for you to create and maintain your Excel workbooks. Let's take a look at some of the important changes to the Excel 2002 software.

INTRODUCING TASK PANES

One of the biggest changes to the Excel environment (and all the Microsoft Office XP suite applications, such as Word 2002, Access 2002, and PowerPoint 2002) is the introduction of the Office task pane. The task pane is a special pane that appears on the right side of the Excel application window when you use certain Excel features (features that formerly were controlled using dialog boxes).

For example, when you start a new Excel workbook, the New Workbook task pane appears (see Figure 1.1). This task pane makes it easy for you to start a new blank workbook or create a workbook using one of the spreadsheet templates provided by Excel.

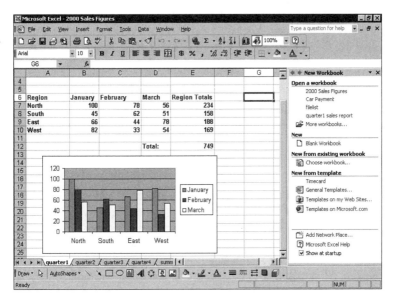

FIGURE 1.1
The New Workbook task pane makes it easy for you to create a new Excel workbook.

Other task panes that you will run across as you work in Excel are the Office Clipboard and the Clip Gallery. The Office Clipboard enables you to copy or cut multiple items from an Excel workbook and then paste them into new locations. The Clip Gallery enables you to insert clip art and other images into your Excel worksheets. Task panes are discussed in this book, when appropriate, as you explore the various Excel features.

INTRODUCING VOICE DICTATION AND VOICE COMMANDS

One of the most exciting new features in Excel 2002 (and the entire Office XP suite) is voice dictation and voice-activated commands. If your computer is outfitted with a sound card, speakers, and a microphone (or a microphone with an earphone headset), you can dictate information into your Excel worksheets. You also can use voice commands to activate the menu system and toolbars in Excel.

Before you can really take advantage of the Speech feature, you must train it so that it can easily recognize your speech patterns and intonation. After the Speech feature is trained, you can effectively use it to dictate text entries or access various application commands without using a keyboard or mouse.

CAUTION

> **Requirements for Getting the Most Out of the Speech Feature**   To make the Speech feature useful, you will need a fairly high-quality microphone. Microsoft suggests a microphone/headset combination. The Speech feature also requires a more powerful computer. Microsoft suggests using a computer with 128MB of RAM and a Pentium II (or later) processor running at a minimum of 400MHz. A computer that meets or exceeds these higher standards should be capable of getting the most out of the Speech feature.

If you are new to Excel, you might want to explore the other lessons in this book before you attempt to use the Speech feature. Having a good understanding of how Excel operates and the features that it provides will allow you to get the most out of the Speech feature.

TRAINING THE SPEECH FEATURE

The first time you start the Speech feature in Excel, you are required to configure and train the feature. Follow these steps to get the Speech feature up and running:

1. In Excel, select the **Tools** menu, point at **Speech**, and then select **Speech Recognition**. The Welcome to Office Speech Recognition dialog box appears. To begin the process of setting up your microphone and training the Speech feature, click the **Next** button.

2. The first screen of the Microphone Wizard appears. It asks you to be sure your microphone and speakers are connected to your computer. If you have a headset microphone, this screen shows you how to adjust the microphone for use. Click **Next** to continue.

3. The next wizard screen asks you to read a short text passage so that your microphone volume level can be adjusted (see Figure 1.2). When you have finished reading the text, click **Next** to continue.

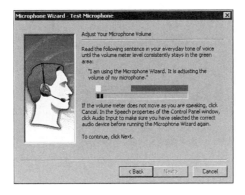

FIGURE 1.2
The Microphone Wizard adjusts the volume of your microphone.

4. On the next screen, you are told that if you have a headset microphone, you can click **Finish** and proceed to the speech recognition training. If you have a different type of microphone, you are asked to read another text passage. The text then is played back to you. This is to determine whether the microphone is placed at an appropriate distance from your mouth. When you get a satisfactory playback, click **Finish**.

When you finish working with the Microphone Wizard, the Voice
Training Wizard appears. This wizard collects samples of your speech
and, in essence, educates the Speech feature as to how you speak.

To complete the voice training process, follow these steps:

1. After reading the information on the opening screen, click
   Next to begin the voice training process.

2. On the next screen, you are asked to provide your gender and
   age (see Figure 1.3). After specifying the correct information,
   click **Next**.

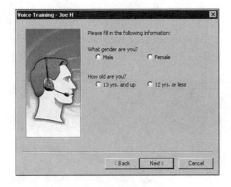

FIGURE 1.3
Supply the voice trainer with your gender and age.

3. On the next wizard screen, you see an overview of how the
   voice training will proceed. You also see directions for how
   to pause the training session. Click **Next**.

4. The next wizard screen reminds you to adjust your microphone. You also are reminded that you need a quiet room
   when training the Speech feature. When you are ready to
   begin training the speech recognition feature, click **Next**.

5. On the next screen, you are asked to read some text. Each
   word is highlighted as the wizard recognizes it. After finishing with this screen, continue by clicking **Next**.

6. You are asked to read text on several subsequent screens. Words are selected as the wizard recognizes them.

7. When you complete the training screens, your profile is updated. Click **Finish** on the wizard's final screen.

You now are ready to use the Speech feature. Using the Voice Dictation and Voice Command features are discussed in Lesson 3, "Entering Data into the Worksheet."

CAUTION

> **The Speech Feature Works Better Over Time**   Be advised that the voice feature's performance improves as you use it. As you learn to pronounce your words more carefully, the Speech feature tunes itself to your speech patterns. You might need to do additional training sessions to fine-tune the Speech feature.

This lesson introduced you to Excel 2002 and some of the new available features, such as task panes and the Speech feature. In the next lesson, you will learn how to start Excel and create a new workbook.

LESSON 2
Creating a New Workbook

In this lesson, you learn how to start and exit Excel and you become familiar with the Excel window. You also learn how to create new workbooks and open existing workbook files.

STARTING EXCEL

Excel provides you with all the tools you need to create both simple and complex spreadsheets. You also will find that Excel is a fairly typical Windows program and provides you with all the features, such as menu bars and toolbars, with which you are familiar from working in the Windows environment.

To start Excel from the Windows desktop, follow these steps:

1. Click the **Start** button, and the Start menu appears.

2. Choose **Programs**, and the Programs menu appears.

3. Choose **Microsoft Excel** to start the program.

UNDERSTANDING THE EXCEL WINDOW

When you click the Microsoft Excel icon, the Excel application window appears, displaying a blank workbook labeled Book1 (see Figure 2.1). On the right side of the Excel window is the New Workbook task pane. This task pane enables you to open existing Excel workbooks or create new blank workbooks or workbooks based on various Excel templates (which is discussed later in the lesson).

TIP

> **Close the Task Pane**   If you would like a little more room to work on the current workbook sheet in the Excel window, click the **Close** (**x**) button on the task pane.

When you work in Excel, you use workbook files to hold your numerical data, formulas, and other objects, such as Excel charts. Each Excel workbook can consist of several sheets; each sheet is called a worksheet.

PLAIN ENGLISH

> **Workbook**   An Excel file is called a workbook. Each workbook consists of several worksheets made up of rows and columns of information.

You enter your numbers and formulas on one of the workbook's worksheets. Each worksheet consists of 256 columns. The columns begin with A and proceed through the alphabet. The 27th column is AA, followed by AB, AC, and this convention for naming subsequent columns continues through the entire alphabet until you end up with the last column (column 256), which is designated IV.

Each worksheet also consists of 65,536 rows. The intersection of a column and a row on the worksheet is called a cell. Each cell has an address that consists of the column and row that intersect to make the cell. For example, the very first cell on a worksheet is in column A and row 1, so the cell's address is A1.

PLAIN ENGLISH

> **Worksheet**   One sheet in an Excel workbook. Each worksheet consists of 256 columns and 65,536 rows (plenty of space to create even the most enormous spreadsheet).

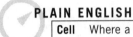

PLAIN ENGLISH

Cell   Where a row and column intersect, each cell has
an address that consists of the column letter and row
number (A1, B3, C4, and so on). You enter data and formulas in the cells to create your worksheets.

Figure 2.1 shows cell A1 highlighted in worksheet 1 (designated as
Sheet1 on its tab) of Workbook 1 (designated in the title bar as Book1;
this will change to a particular filename after you name the workbook
using the Save function).

Toolbars
    Menu bar   Formula bar   Column headings

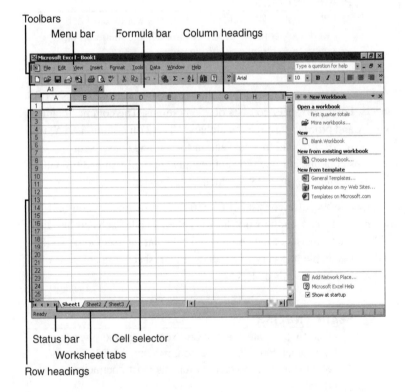

Status bar   Cell selector
    Worksheet tabs
Row headings

FIGURE 2.1
*Excel provides a new workbook and the menus and toolbars necessary for doing
some serious number crunching.*

The Excel window shown here includes many of the various elements available in other Office applications, such as Word or PowerPoint. These elements include a menu bar (from which you select commands), a status bar (which displays the status of the current activity), and toolbars (which contain buttons and drop-down lists that provide quick access to various commands and features).

In addition, the window contains several elements that are unique to Excel, as shown in Table 2.1.

Table 2.1 Elements of the Excel Window

Element	Description
Formula bar	When you enter information into a cell, it appears in the Formula bar. You can use the Formula bar to edit the data later. The cell's location also appears in the Formula bar.
Column headings	The letters across the top of the worksheet, which identify the columns in the worksheet.
Row headings	The numbers down the side of the worksheet, which identify the rows in the worksheet.
Cell selector	The dark outline that indicates the active cell. (It highlights the cell in which you are currently working.)
Worksheet tabs	These tabs help you move from worksheet to worksheet within the workbook.

Starting a New Workbook

As you've already seen, when you start Excel, it opens a new blank workbook. It is ready to accept data entry, which is discussed in Lesson 3, "Entering Data into the Worksheet."

The empty workbook that appears when you start Excel is pretty much a blank canvas, but Excel also enables you to create new workbooks based on a template. A *template* is a predesigned workbook that you can modify to suit your needs. Excel contains templates for creating invoices, expense reports, and other common business accounting forms.

To create a new workbook, follow these steps:

1. Open the **File** menu and select **New**. The New Workbook task pane appears on the right side of the Excel window (if you did not close it as outlined earlier, it should already be open).

2. The New Workbook task pane enables you to create new blank workbooks or create workbooks based on a template (see Figure 2.2).

FIGURE 2.2
The New Workbook task pane provides quick access to commands for creating new Excel workbooks.

3. To create a blank workbook, click the **Blank Workbook** icon. A new blank workbook opens in the Excel window.

PLAIN ENGLISH

> **Instant Workbook**   You also can quickly start a new blank workbook by clicking the **New** button on the Standard toolbar.

Blank templates are fine when you have a design in mind for the overall look of the workbook. However, for some help with workbook layout and formatting, you can base your new workbook on an Excel template. To use an Excel template, follow these steps:

1. Click the **General Templates** icon in the New from Template menu of the New Workbook task pane. The Templates dialog box appears.

2. Click the **Spreadsheet Solutions** tab on the Templates dialog box. The various workbook template icons appear (see Figure 2.3).

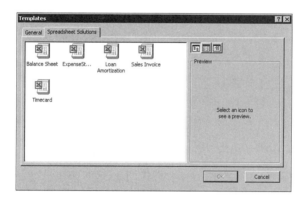

FIGURE 2.3
The Spreadsheet Solutions tab provides the different Excel templates.

3. Select a template by clicking its icon, and then click **OK** or press **Enter**. A new workbook opens onscreen with a default name based on the template you chose. For example, if you

chose the Timecard template, the new workbook is named
Timecard1, as shown at the top of Figure 2.4.

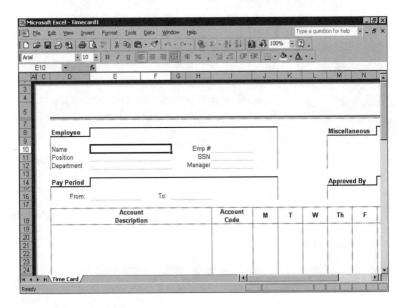

FIGURE 2.4
*A new workbook based on a template provides a basic layout for a particular
business form.*

SAVING AND NAMING A WORKBOOK

Whether you build your workbook from a blank template or use one
of the Excel templates, after you enter some data into the workbook,
you should save the file (you learn about data entry in Lesson 3,
"Entering Data into the Worksheet"). Also, because changes that you
make to the workbook are not automatically saved, you should occasionally save the edited version of your work.

The first time you save a workbook, you must name it and specify a
location where it should be saved. Follow these steps to save your
workbook:

1. Open the **File** menu and select **Save**, or click the **Save** button on the Standard toolbar. The Save As dialog box appears (see Figure 2.5).

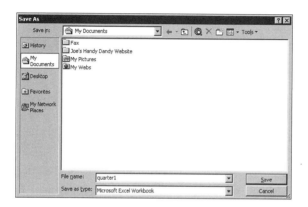

FIGURE 2.5
Specify the name and location for your new workbook in the Save As dialog box.

2. Type the name you want to give the workbook in the **File Name** text box. You can use up to 218 characters, including any combination of letters, numbers, and spaces.

3. Normally, Excel saves your workbooks in the My Documents folder. To save the file to a different folder or drive (such as a network drive), select a new location using the **Save In** list.

CAUTION

> **The Folder I Want to Save In Doesn't Exist!**   You can create a new folder from the Save As dialog box: Click the **Create New Folder** button on the toolbar of the Save As dialog box, type a name for the new folder, and then press **Enter**.

4. Click **Save** to save your workbook and close the Save As dialog box.

To save changes that you make to a workbook you previously saved, just click the **Save** button on the Standard toolbar. You also can press the shortcut key combination of **Ctrl+S** to save changes to your workbook.

SAVING A WORKBOOK UNDER A NEW NAME OR LOCATION

There might be an occasion when you want to save a copy of a particular workbook under a different name or in a different location. Excel makes it easy for you to make duplicates of a workbook. Follow these steps:

1. Select the **File** menu and select **Save As**. The Save As dialog box opens, just as if you were saving the workbook for the first time.

2. To save the workbook under a new name, type the new filename over the existing name in the **File Name** text box.

3. To save the new file on a different drive or in a different folder, select the drive letter or the folder from the **Save In** list.

4. To save the new file in a different format (such as Lotus 1-2-3 or Quattro Pro), click the **Save As Type** drop-down arrow and select the desired format.

5. Click the **Save** button or press **Enter**.

 TIP

> **Saving Excel Workbooks in Other File Formats**
> Occasionally, you might share Excel workbook data with co-workers or colleagues who don't use Excel. Being able to save Excel workbooks in other file formats, such as Lotus 1-2-3 (as discussed in step 4), enables you to provide another user a file that they can open in their spreadsheet program.

OPENING AN EXISTING WORKBOOK

If you have a workbook you've previously saved that you would like
to work on, you must open the file first, before you can make any
changes. Follow these steps to open an existing workbook:

1. Open the **File** menu and select **Open,** or click the **Open** button on the Standard toolbar. The Open dialog box shown in
   Figure 2.6 appears.

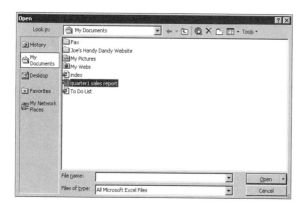

FIGURE 2.6
Use the Open dialog box to locate and open an existing Excel workbook.

2. If the file is not located in the current folder, open the **Look
   In** drop-down list box and select the correct drive and folder.

3. Select the file you want to open in the files and folders list.

4. To see a preview of the workbook before you open it, click
   the **Views** button and select **Preview**. Excel displays the contents of the workbook in a window to the right of the dialog
   box.

5. Click **Open** to open the currently selected workbook.

TIP

> **Recently Used Workbooks**   If the workbook you want to
> open is one of your four most recently used workbooks,
> you'll find it listed at the bottom of the File menu. It
> also will be listed at the top of the New Workbook task
> pane (if the task pane is active).

CLOSING WORKBOOKS

When you have finished with a particular workbook and want to continue working in Excel, you easily can close the current workbook.
Click the **Close** (x) button in the upper-right corner of the workbook.
(There are two Close buttons: The one on top closes Excel; the one
below it closes the current workbook window.) You also can close the
current workbook by selecting **File, Close**. If you have changed the
workbook since the last time you saved it, you will be prompted to
save any changes.

TIP

> **It's Closing Time!**   If you have more than one workbook
> open, you can close all of them at once by holding down
> the **Shift** key, selecting the **File** menu, and then selecting
> **Close All**.

EXITING EXCEL

When you have finished working with Excel, you need to exit the
application. This closes all workbooks that are currently open. To exit
Excel, select the **File** menu and select **Exit**. Or, you can click the
Close (x) button at the upper-right corner of the Excel window.

If you have changed any of the workbooks with which you were
working, you are prompted to save changes to these workbook files
before exiting Excel.

In this lesson, you learned how to start and exit Excel. You also learned how to open a new workbook and create a workbook on an Excel template. Finally, you were provided the ins and outs of opening and closing Excel workbooks. In the next lesson, you will learn how to enter different kinds of data into Excel when you build a workbook file.

LESSON 3

Entering Data into the Worksheet

In this lesson, you learn how to enter different data types into an Excel worksheet and use special features, such as AutoComplete and the Speech feature.

UNDERSTANDING EXCEL DATA TYPES

When you work in Excel, you enter different types of information, such as text, numbers, dates, times, formulas, and functions (which is a special built-in formula provided by Excel). Excel data basically comes in two varieties: labels and values.

A label is a text entry; it is called a label because it typically provides descriptive information, such as the name of a person, place, or thing. A label has no numerical significance in Excel; it's just there to describe accompanying values.

PLAIN ENGLISH

> **Label**   Any text entry made on an Excel worksheet.

A value is data that has numerical significance. This includes numbers, dates, and times that you enter on your worksheet. Values can be acted on by formulas and functions. Formulas are discussed in Lesson 4, "Performing Simple Calculations," and Excel functions are discussed in Lesson 6, "Performing Calculations with Functions."

PLAIN ENGLISH

Values Entries, such as numbers and dates, that have numerical significance and can be acted upon by formulas or functions.

ENTERING TEXT

Text is any combination of letters, numbers, and spaces. By default, text is automatically left-aligned in a cell, whereas numerical data is right-aligned.

To enter text into a cell, follow these steps:

1. Use your mouse or the keyboard arrows to select the cell in which you want to enter text.

2. Type the text. As you type, your text appears in the cell and in the Formula bar, as shown in Figure 3.1.

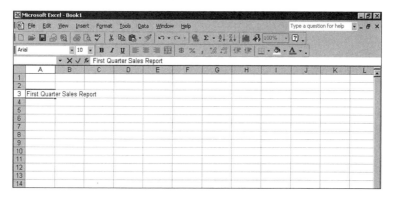

FIGURE 3.1
Data that you enter into a cell also appears in the Formula bar as you type it.

3. Press **Enter**. Your text appears in the cell, left-aligned. The cell selector moves down one cell. You also can press **Tab** or an arrow key to enter the text and move to the next cell to the right (or in the direction of the arrow).

CAUTION

> **But My Entry Doesn't Fit!**   When text does not fit into a cell (because of the column width set for that column), Excel displays the information in one of two ways: If the next cell is empty, the text overflows into that cell, allowing you to see your entire entry. If the cell to the right of your entry is not empty, you will be able to see only the portion of your entry that fits within the confines of the cell. This can easily be remedied by changing the column width. You'll learn about changing column widths in Lesson 14, "Inserting and Removing Cells, Rows, and Columns."

TIP

> **Entering Numbers As Text**   To enter a number that you want treated as text (such as a ZIP code), precede the entry with a single quotation mark ('), as in '46220. The single quotation mark is an alignment prefix that tells Excel to treat the following characters as text and left-align them in the cell. You do not have to do this to "text" numerical entries, but it ensures that they will not be mistakenly acted upon by formulas or functions.

TIPS ON ENTERING COLUMN AND ROW LABELS

Column and row labels identify your data. Column labels appear across the top of the worksheet beneath the worksheet title (if any). Row labels are entered on the left side of the worksheet.

Column labels describe what the numbers in a column represent. Typically, column labels specify time intervals such as years, months, days, quarters, and so on. Row labels describe what the numbers in each row represent. Typically, row labels specify data categories, such as product names, employee names, or income and expense items in a budget.

When entering your column labels, enter the first label and press the **Tab** key instead of pressing Enter. This moves you to the next cell on the right so that you can enter another column label. When entering row labels, use the down-arrow key instead of the Tab key. Figure 3.2 shows the various labels for a quarterly sales summary.

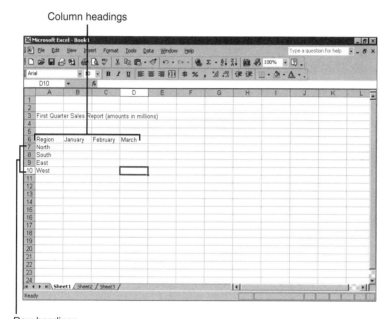

FIGURE 3.2
Column and row headings serve as labels for the data you enter on the work-sheet.

If you need to enter similar data (such as a series of months or years) as column or row labels, you can enter them quickly as a series; this technique is discussed later in this lesson.

ADDING COMMENTS TO CELLS

Although not really considered cell content (such as labels and values), you can add comments to particular cells. These comments allow you to associate information with a cell—information that does not appear (by default) with the worksheet when sent to the printer.

Comments are similar to placing a Post-it note on a cell, reminding you that an outstanding issue is related to that cell. For example, if you need to check the value that you've placed in a particular cell to make sure that it's accurate, you can place a comment in the cell (see Figure 3.3). Cells containing comments are marked with a red triangle in the upper-right corner of the cell. To view a comment, place the mouse pointer on the comment triangle.

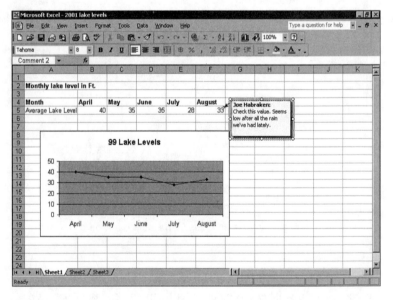

FIGURE 3.3
Comments can be added to cells as a kind of electronic Post-it note.

To insert a comment into a cell, follow these steps:

1. Click the cell in which you want to place the comment.

2. Select **Insert, Comment**. A comment box appears next to the cell.

3. Type your information into the comment box.

4. Click anywhere else in the worksheet to close the comment box.

You also can easily remove comments from cells. Select the cell, and then select **Edit** and point at **Clear**. On the cascading menu, select **Comments** to remove the comment.

ENTERING NUMBERS

Data that serves as the values in your workbooks can include the numeric characters 0–9. Because formulas also are considered values (you learn about simple calculations in Lesson 4, "Performing Simple Calculations"), other valid value characters include symbols such as +, – , /, and *. You also can use characters such as a comma (,), a percent sign (%), or a dollar sign ($) in your values. You will find, however, that you can save yourself a few data-entry keystrokes and add these characters using different Excel formatting options (you learn about Excel formatting in Lesson 11, "Changing How Numbers and Text Look").

For example, you could enter the dollar amount $700.00 including the dollar sign and the decimal point. However, it's probably faster to enter 700 into the cell and then format all the cells that contain dollar amounts after you have entered all the data.

To enter a value, follow these steps:

1. Click in the cell where you want to enter the value.

2. Type the value. To enter a negative number, precede it with a minus sign or surround it with parentheses.

3. Press **Enter** or the **Tab** key; the value appears in the cell
   right-aligned. Figure 3.4 shows various values entered into a
   simple worksheet.

	A	B	C	D	E	F
1						
2						
3	First Quarter Sales Report (amounts in millions)					
4						
5						
6	Region	January	February	March		
7	North	70	35	90		
8	South	100	56	66		
9	East	54	84	55		
10	West	66	33	70		
11						
12						
13						
14						

FIGURE 3.4
Values are right-aligned in a cell.

TIP

> **What Are All Those Pound Signs?**   If you enter a number
> and it appears in the cell as all pound signs (#######)
> or in scientific notation (such as 7.78E+06), the cell
> just isn't wide enough to display the entire number. To
> fix it, double-click the right border of the column's head-
> ing. The column expands to fit the largest entry in that
> column. See Lesson 14, "Inserting and Removing Cells,
> Rows, and Columns," for more information on working
> with column widths.

ENTERING DATES AND TIMES

Dates that you enter into an Excel workbook have numerical significance. Excel converts the date into a number that reflects the number
of days that have elapsed since January 1, 1900. Even though you
won't see this number (Excel displays your entry as a normal date),
the number is used whenever you use this date in a calculation. Times
also are considered values. Excel sees them as the number of seconds
that have passed since 12 a.m.

Follow these steps to enter a date or time:

1. Click in the cell where you want to enter a date or a time.

2. To enter a date, use the format MM/DD/YY or the format MM-DD-YY, as in 5/9/01 or 5-9-01.

   To enter a time, be sure to specify a.m. or p.m., as in 7:21 p or 8:22 a.

 TIP

> **A.M. or P.M.?**   Unless you type am or pm after your time entry, Excel assumes that you are using a 24-hour international clock. Therefore, 8:20 is assumed to be a.m., not p.m. (20:20 would be p.m.: 8 plus 12 hours). Therefore, if you mean p.m., type the entry as 8:20 pm (or 8:20 p). Note that you must type a space between the time and the am or pm notation.

3. Press **Enter**. As long as Excel recognizes the entry as a date or a time, it appears right-aligned in the cell. If Excel doesn't recognize it, it's treated as text and left-aligned.

After you enter your date or time, you can format the cells to display the date or time exactly as you want it to appear, such as September 16, 1998, or 16:50 (international time). If you're entering a column of dates or times, you can format the entire column in one easy step. To format a column, click the column header to select the column. Then open the **Format** menu and select **Cells**. On the **Numbers** tab, select the date or time format you want to use (you learn more about formatting text and numbers in Lesson 11).

COPYING (FILLING) THE SAME DATA TO OTHER CELLS

Another way to enter labels or values onto a sheet is to use the Fill feature. You can copy (fill) an entry into surrounding cells. For example, suppose you have a list of salespeople on a worksheet, and they will each get a $100 bonus. You can enter the 100 once and then use the Fill feature to insert multiple copies of 100 into nearby cells. To use the Fill feature for copying, follow these steps:

1. Click the fill handle of the cell (the small block in the lower-right corner of the cell) that holds the data that you want to copy (see Figure 3.5).

2. Drag the fill handle down or to the right to copy the data to adjacent cells. A data tag appears to let you know exactly what data is being copied into the cells.

	A	B	C	D	E	F
1						
2						
3						
4	Sales Force Data (First Quarter Totals)					
5						
6	First Name	Last Name	Total	Bonus		
7	Bob	Smith	800	100		
8	Alice	Tumey	500			
9	Alfred	Juarez	789			
10	Katie	Jones	680			
11	John	Roberts	780			
12					100	
13						
14						
15						

FIGURE 3.5
Drag the fill handle to copy the contents of a cell into neighboring cells.

3. Release the mouse button. The data is "filled" into the selected cells.

When you release the mouse, a shortcut box for Fill options appears at the end of the cells that you filled. Copy Cells is the default option for the Fill feature, so you can ignore the shortcut box for the moment. It does come into play when you enter a series in the next section.

CAUTION

Watch That Fill!   The data you're copying replaces any existing data in the adjacent cells that you fill.

ENTERING A SERIES OF NUMBERS, DATES, AND OTHER DATA

Entering a value *series* (such as January, February, and March or 1, 2, 3, 4, and so on) is accomplished using the Fill feature discussed in the preceding section. When you use the Fill feature, Excel looks at the cell holding the data and tries to determine whether you want to just copy that information into the adjacent cells or use it as the starting point for a particular series of data. For example, with Monday entered in the first cell of the series, Excel automatically inserts Tuesday, Wednesday, and so on into the adjacent cells when you use the Fill feature.

Sometimes, Excel isn't quite sure whether you want to copy the data when you use Fill or create a series. This is where the Fill options shortcut box comes in. It enables you to select how the Fill feature should treat the data that you have "filled" into the adjacent cells. Figure 3.6 shows the creation of a day series using Fill.

FIGURE 3.6
Fill also can be used to create a series of data in adjacent cells.

When you create a series using Fill, the series progresses by one increment. For example, a series starting with 1 would proceed to 2, 3, 4, and so on. If you want to create a series that uses some increment other than 1, you must create a custom series, which is discussed in the next section.

ENTERING A CUSTOM SERIES

If you want to create a series such as 10, 20, 30, where the series uses a custom increment between the values, you need to create a custom series. Excel provides two ways to create a custom series. To create a custom series using Fill, follow these steps:

1. Enter the first value of the series into a cell.

2. Enter the second value in the series into the next cell. For example, you might enter **10** into the first cell and then **20** into the second cell. This lets Excel know that the increment for the series is 10.

3. Select both cells by clicking the first cell and dragging over the second cell.

4. Drag the fill handle of the second cell to the other cells that will be part of the series. Excel analyzes the two cells, sees the incremental pattern, and re-creates it in subsequent cells.

You also can create a custom series using the Series dialog box. This enables you to specify the increment or step value for the series and even specify a stop value for the series.

1. Enter the first value of the series into a cell.

2. Select the cells that you want included in the series.

3. Select the **Edit** menu, point at **Fill**, and then select **Series**. The Series dialog box opens (see Figure 3.7).

FIGURE 3.7
The Series dialog box enables you to create a custom series.

4. Enter the Step Value for the series. You also can enter a Stop Value for the series if you did not select the cells used for the series in step 2. For example, if you want to add a series to a column of cells and have clicked in the first cell that will receive a value, using a Stop Value (such as 100 for a series that will go from 1 to 100) will "stop" entering values in the cells when it reaches 100—the Stop Value.

5. Click **OK** to create the series.

TIP

> **Different Series Types**   Not only can you create a linear series using the Series dialog box (as discussed in the steps in this section), but you also can create growth and date series. In a growth series, the data you're copying replaces any existing data in the adjacent cells that you fill.

Taking Advantage of AutoComplete

Another useful feature that Excel provides to help take some of the drudgery out of entering information into a workbook is the AutoComplete feature. Excel keeps a list of all the labels that you enter on a worksheet by column. For example, suppose you have a worksheet tracking sales in Europe and you are entering country names, such as Germany, Italy, and so on, multiple times into a particular column in the worksheet. After you enter Germany the first time, it becomes part of the AutoComplete list for that column. The next time you enter the letter G into a cell in that column, Excel completes the entry as "Germany."

You also can select an entry from the AutoComplete list. This allows you to see the entire list of available entries. Follow these steps:

1. Enter your text and value data as needed onto the worksheet.

2. If you want to select a text entry from the AutoComplete list to fill an empty cell, right-click that cell. A shortcut menu appears.

3. Select **Pick from List** from the shortcut menu. A list of text entries (in alphabetical order) appears below the current cell.

4. Click a word in the list to insert it into the current, empty cell.

TIP

> **Adding Data to Excel Using Voice Recognition**   The Office Speech Recognition feature also can be used to enter data into an Excel worksheet and to perform voice commands. If you have a computer that is set up with a sound card and microphone, you can use this feature. See Lesson 1, "What's New in Excel 2002," for more information on setting up the voice feature in Excel.

DICTATING WORKSHEET INFORMATION

If you have a microphone and have set up the Speech Recognition feature as discussed in Lesson 1, you also can dictate information into an Excel workbook. You can dictate both labels and values into the worksheet cells.

To dictate entries into an Excel worksheet, follow these steps:

1. To turn on voice dictation, select **Tools**, point at **Speech**, and then select **Speech Recognition**. The Language bar appears in the Excel window with the Dictation feature turned on (see Figure 3.8).

2. Dictate the contents of the cell. Use the Enter key or the arrow keys to move to the next cell you want to fill.

3. Dictate the contents of other cells as required.

4. To turn off the Dictation mode, click the **Microphone** on the Language bar.

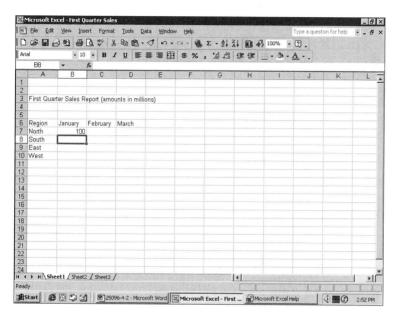

FIGURE 3.8
The Office Voice Recognition feature allows you to dictate information into a worksheet.

Dictating numerical values into a cell is a little trickier than dictating a text label. Numbers less than 20 are spelled as words in Excel. To force these values to be entered as actual numbers, say "force num," pause for a second, and then say the number, such as "6."

TIP

> **Turn on Dictation with a Voice Command**   If the Language bar is already present in the Excel workspace, you can say "dictation" to turn on the feature.

You also can use the Speech feature to issue voice commands. You can open and select menus in Excel and even navigate dialog boxes using voice commands.

To use voice commands, open the Language bar (click **Tools**, **Speech**). Click the **Microphone** icon, if necessary, to expand the Language bar. Then, click the **Voice Command** icon on the bar (or say "voice command").

To open a particular menu, such as the Format menu, say "format." Then, to open a particular submenu such as Font, say "font." In the case of these voice commands, the Font dialog box opens.

You then can navigate a particular dialog box using voice commands. In the Font dialog box, for example, to change the size of the font, say "size"; this activates the Size box that controls font size. Then, say the size of the font, such as "14." You also can activate other font attributes in the dialog box in this manner. Say the name of the area of the dialog box you want to use, and then say the name of the feature you want to turn on or select.

When you have finished working with a particular dialog box, say "OK" (or "Cancel" or "Apply," as needed). The dialog box closes and provides you with the features you selected in the dialog box. When you have finished using voice commands, say "microphone," or click the **Microphone** icon on the Language bar.

You also can activate buttons on the various toolbars using voice commands. For example, you could sort an Excel worksheet by a particular column by clicking in the column and then saying "sort ascending." The Sort Ascending button on the Excel toolbar becomes active and your data is sorted.

In this lesson, you learned how to enter different types of data and how to automate data entry with features such as AutoComplete and the Speech feature. In the next lesson, you learn how to perform simple calculations in a workbook.

Lesson 4
Performing Simple Calculations

In this lesson, you learn how to use formulas to calculate results in your worksheets.

Understanding Excel Formulas

One way to add calculations to an Excel workbook is to create your own formulas. Formulas typically are used to perform calculations such as addition, subtraction, multiplication, and division. More complex calculations are better left to Excel Functions, which is a built-in set of formulas that provide financial, mathematical, and statistical calculations. You learn more about functions in Lesson 6, "Performing Calculations with Functions."

Formulas that you create typically include cell addresses that reference cells on which you want to perform a calculation. Formulas also consist of mathematical operators, such as + (addition) or * (multiplication). For example, if you wanted to multiply two cells, such as C3 and D3, and then divide the product by 3, you would design a formula that looks like this:

`=(C3*D3)/3`

Notice that the formula begins with the equal sign (=). This lets Excel know that the information that you are placing in the cell is meant to do a calculation. The parentheses are used to let Excel know that you want C3 multiplied by D3 before the result is divided by 3. Creating appropriate formulas requires an understanding of the order of mathematical operations, or what is often called the rules of precedence. The natural order of math operations is covered in the next section.

As previously mentioned, you can create formulas that add, subtract, and multiply cells in the worksheet. Table 4.1 lists some of the operators that you can use and how you would use them in a simple formula.

Table 4.1   Excel's Mathematical Operators

Operator	Performs	Sample Formula	Result
^	Exponentiation	=A1^3	Enters the result of raising the value in cell A1 to the third power
+	Addition	=A1+A2	Enters the total of the values in cells A1 and A2
−	Subtraction	=A1–A2	Subtracts the value in cell A2 from the value in cell A1
*	Multiplication	=A2*A3	Multiplies the value in cell A2 by cell A3
/	Division	=A1/B1	Divides the value in cell A1 by the value in cell B1

Figure 4.1 shows some formulas that have been created for an Excel worksheet. So that you can see how I wrote the formulas, I've configured Excel so that it shows the formula that has been placed in a cell

rather than the results of the formula (which is what you would normally see).

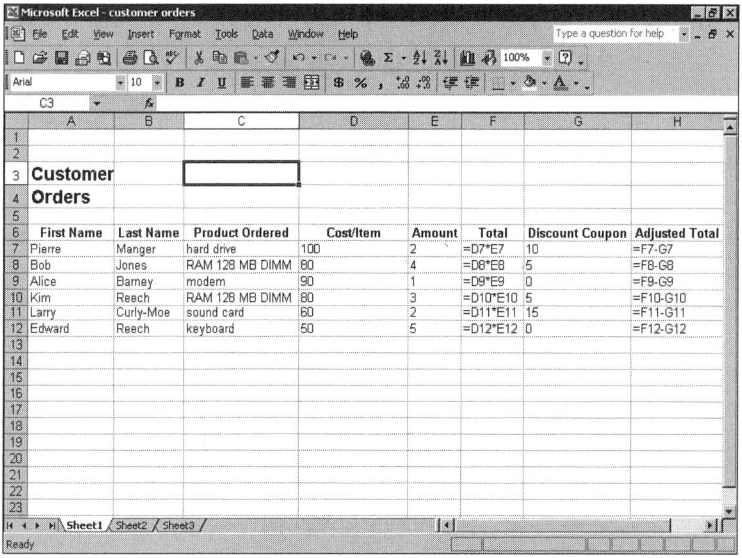

FIGURE 4.1
You can create formulas to do simple calculations in your worksheets.

ORDER OF OPERATIONS

The order of operations, or *operator precedence*, simply means that some operations take precedence over other operations in a formula. For example, in the formula =C2+D2*E2, the multiplication of D2 times E2 takes precedence, so D2 is multiplied by E2 and then the value in cell C2 is added to the result.

You can force the precedence of an operation by using parentheses. For example, if you want C2 and D2 added before they are multiplied by E2, the formula would have to be written =(C2+D2)*E2.

The natural order of math operators follows:

1st   Exponent (^) and calculations within parentheses

2nd   Multiplication (*)and division (/)

3rd   Addition (+) and subtraction (−)

In the case of operations such as multiplication and division, which operate at the same level in the natural order, a formula containing the multiplication operator followed by the division operator will execute these operators in the order they appear in the formula from left to right. If you don't take this order into consideration, you could run into problems when entering your formulas. For example, if you want to determine the average of the values in cells A1, B1, and C1, and you enter `=A1+B1+C1/3`, you'll get the wrong answer. The value in C1 will be divided by 3, and that result will be added to A1+B1. To determine the total of A1 through C1 first, you must enclose that group of values in parentheses: `=(A1+B1+C1)/3`.

ENTERING FORMULAS

You can enter formulas in one of two ways: by typing the entire formula, including the cell addresses, or by typing the formula operators and selecting the cell references. Take a look at both ways.

To type a formula, perform the following steps:

1. Select the cell where you will place the formula.

2. Type an equal sign (=) into the cell to begin the formula.

3. Enter the appropriate cell references and operators for the formula. Figure 4.2 shows a simple multiplication formula. The formula also appears in the Formula bar as you type it. The cells that you specify in the formula are highlighted with a colored border.

4. Press **Enter** when you have finished the formula, and Excel calculates the result.

TIP

Unwanted Formula   If you start to enter a formula and then decide you don't want to use it, you can skip entering the formula by pressing **Esc**.

	SUM	▾ ✕ ✓ ƒx	=D7*E7						
	A	B	C	D	E	F	G	H	I
1									
2									
3	**Customer**								
4	**Orders**								
5									
6	First Name	Last Name	Product Ordered	Cost/Item	Amount	Total	Discount Coupon	Adjusted Total	
7	Pierre	Manger	hard drive	100	2	=D7*E7	10		
8	Bob	Jones	RAM 128 MB DIMM	80	4		5		
9	Alice	Barney	modem	90	1		0		
10	Kim	Reech	RAM 128 MB DIMM	80	3		5		
11	Larry	Curly-Moe	sound card	60	2		15		
12	Edward	Reech	keyboard	50	5		0		
13									
14									
15									

FIGURE 4.2
The formula appears in the cell and in the Formula bar as you type it.

To enter a formula by selecting cell addresses, follow these steps:

1. Click in the cell where you will place the formula.

2. Type the equal sign (=) to begin the formula.

3. Click the cell whose address you want to appear first in the formula. You also can click a cell in a different worksheet or workbook. The cell address appears in the cell and in the Formula bar.

4. Type a mathematical operator after the value to indicate the next operation you want to perform. The operator appears in the cell and in the Formula bar.

5. Continue clicking cells and typing operators until the formula is complete.

6. Press **Enter** to accept the formula and have Excel place its results into the cell.

CAUTION

Error!   If ERR appears in a cell, you've likely made a mistake somewhere in the formula. Be sure you did not commit one of these common errors: dividing by zero, using a blank cell as a divisor, referring to a blank cell, deleting a cell used in a formula, or including a reference to the same cell in which the formula appears.

TIP

Natural Language Formulas   Excel also enables you to create what are called Natural Language formulas. You can refer to a cell by its column heading name and the corresponding row label. For example, if you had a column labeled Total and a column labeled Discount for each customer, you can write a formula such as =Smith Total–Smith Discount. You are referring to cells by the labels that you have placed in the worksheet rather than the actual cell addresses.

USING THE STATUS BAR AUTOCALCULATE FEATURE

Using a feature that Excel calls AutoCalculate, you can view the sum of a column of cells simply by selecting the cells and looking at the status bar. The values in the selected cells are added. You also can right-click the AutoCalculate area of the status bar and choose different formulas, such as average, minimum, maximum, and count.

This feature is useful if you want to quickly check the total for a group of cells or compute the average. It also allows you to "try out" an Excel function (discussed in Lesson 5) before actually entering it into a cell. You also can view the average, minimum, maximum, and count of a range of cells. To display something other than the sum, highlight the group of cells on which you want the operation performed, right-click the status bar, and select the option you want from the shortcut menu that appears (see Figure 4.3).

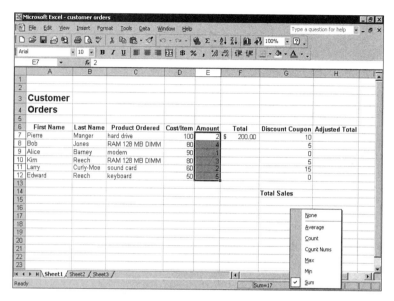

FIGURE 4.3
You can view the results of different built-in formulas in the status bar.

 TIP

> **Where's the Status Bar?**   If the status bar is not visible
> on your screen, you can display it by selecting the **View**
> menu and then selecting **Status Bar**.

DISPLAYING FORMULAS

Normally, Excel does not display the formula in a cell. Instead, it displays the result of the calculation. You can view the formula by selecting the cell and looking in the Formula bar. However, if you're trying to review all the formulas in a large worksheet, it would be easier if you could see them all at once (and even print them). If you want to view formulas in a worksheet, follow these steps:

1. Open the **Tools** menu and choose **Options**.

2. Click the **View** tab.

3. In the Window options area of the View tab (near the bottom of the tab), click to select the **Formulas** check box.

4. Click **OK**.

EDITING FORMULAS

Editing a formula is the same as editing any entry in Excel. The following steps show how to do it:

1. Select the cell that contains the formula you want to edit.

2. Click in the Formula bar to place the insertion point in the formula, or press **F2** to enter Edit mode (the insertion point is placed at the end of the entry in that cell).

TIP

> **In-Cell Editing**   To quickly edit the contents of a cell, double-click the cell. The insertion point appears inside the cell, and you can make any necessary changes.

3. Press the left-arrow key or the right-arrow key to move the insertion point within the formula. Then, use the **Backspace** key to delete characters to the left, or use the **Delete** key to delete characters to the right. Type any additional characters.

4. When you finish editing the data, click the **Enter** button on the Formula bar or press **Enter** to accept your changes.

In this lesson, you learned how to enter and edit formulas. In the next lesson, you learn how to copy formulas, when to use relative and absolute cell addresses, and how to change Excel's settings for calculating formulas in the worksheet.

LESSON 5

Manipulating Formulas and Understanding Cell References

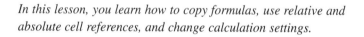

In this lesson, you learn how to copy formulas, use relative and absolute cell references, and change calculation settings.

COPYING FORMULAS

Copying labels and values in Excel is no big deal. You can use the Copy and Paste commands (discussed in Lesson 10, "Editing Worksheets") or you can use some of the Fill features discussed in Lesson 3, "Entering Data into the Worksheet." Copying or moving formulas, however, is a little trickier.

Suppose that you create the formula =D7*E7 and place it into cell F7, as shown in Figure 5.1. You have designed the formula to reference cells D7 and E7. However, Excel looks at these cell references a little differently. Excel sees cell D7 as the entry that is located two cells to the left of F7 (where the formula has been placed, in this example). It sees cell E7 as being the location that is one cell to the left of F7.

Excel's method of referencing cells is called *relative referencing*. The great thing about this method of referencing cells is that, when you copy a formula to a new location, it adjusts to the relative cell references around it and provides you with the correct calculation.

For example, you could copy the formula in cell F7 to cell F8, and Excel would use relative referencing to change the cell addresses in

the formula. The original formula =D7*E7 would appear as D8*D7
when copied to cell F8.

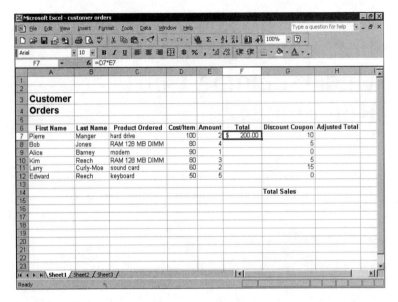

FIGURE 5.1

Formulas you place in Excel use relative referencing for calculations.

Relative referencing is very useful in most situations where you copy
a formula to several cells in the same column. However, it can get you
into trouble when you cut and paste a formula to a new location or
copy the formula to a location where it can no longer reference the
appropriate cells to provide you with the correct calculation. In these
situations, you must use absolute referencing so that the formula references only specified cells and does not change the cell references in
the formula when pasted to the new location. Absolute referencing is
discussed in the next section.

You can copy formulas using the Copy and Paste commands (see
Lesson 10); however, when you need to copy a formula to multiple
locations, you also can use the Fill feature discussed in Lesson 3.

Because Excel uses relative referencing by default, the formula adjusts to each of its new locations. An alternative way to "copy" a formula to multiple adjacent cells is to select all cells that will contain the formula before you actually write the formula in the first cell. Follow these steps:

1. Select all the cells that will contain the formula (dragging so that the cell that you will write the formula in is the first of the selected group of cells).

2. Enter the formula into the first cell.

3. Press **Ctrl+Enter** and the formula is placed in all the selected cells.

GET AN ERROR?

If you get an error message in a cell after copying a formula, verify the cell references in the copied formula. For more information on sorting out cell referencing, see the next section in this lesson.

USING RELATIVE AND ABSOLUTE CELL ADDRESSES

As mentioned at the beginning of this lesson, when you copy a formula from one place in the worksheet to another, Excel adjusts the cell references in the formulas relative to their new positions in the worksheet. There might be occasions when you don't want Excel to change the reference related to a particular cell that appears in a formula (or in an Excel function, which is discussed in Lesson 6, "Performing Calculations with Functions").

ABSOLUTE VERSUS RELATIVE

An *absolute reference* is a cell reference in a formula that does not change when copied to a new location. A *relative reference* is a cell reference in a formula that is adjusted when the formula is copied.

For example, suppose you have a worksheet that computes the commission made on sales by each of your salespeople. Sales have been so good that you've decided to give each person on the sales team a $200 bonus. Figure 5.2 shows the worksheet that you've created.

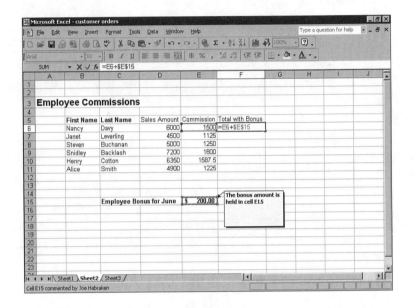

FIGURE 5.2
Some formulas require absolute references.

Notice that the bonus amount is contained in only one cell on the worksheet (cell E15). Therefore, when you create the formula that will be used in F6 and then copied to cells F7 through F11, you need to be sure that the bonus amount in cell E15 is always referenced by the formula. This is a case where you must "absolutely" reference the bonus amount in cell E15.

To make a cell reference in a formula absolute, add a $ (dollar sign) before the column letter and before the row number that make up the cell address. For example, in Figure 4.2, the formula in F6 must read as follows:

```
=E6+$E$15
```

The address, E15, refers to cell E15, meaning that cell E15 is absolutely referenced by the formula. This cell reference remains "locked" even when you copy the formula to the other cells in the E column.

To create an absolute reference in a formula (or a function, which is discussed in Lesson 6), create your formula as you normally would (as detailed in Lesson 4, "Performing Simple Calculations"). After typing or pointing out a cell address in a formula that needs to be an absolute reference, press **F4**. A dollar sign ($)is placed before the cell and row designation for that cell.

Some formulas might contain cell addresses where you will make the column designation absolute, but not the row (or vice versa). For example, you could have a formula $A2/2. You are telling Excel that the values always will be contained in column A (it is absolute), but the row reference (2) can change when the formula is copied. Having a cell address in a formula that contains an absolute designation and a relative reference is called a *mixed reference*.

PLAIN ENGLISH

Mixed References   A reference that is only partially absolute, such as A$2 or $A2. When a formula that uses a mixed reference is copied to another cell, only part of the cell reference (the relative part) is adjusted.

Absolute referencing and mixed references are required by some of Excel's built-in functions as well. You work with functions in the next lesson.

RECALCULATING THE WORKSHEET

Excel automatically recalculates the results in your worksheet every time you enter a new value or edit a value or formula. This is fine for most workbooks. However, if you have a computer with limited memory and processing power, you might find that having Excel recalculate all the results in a very large worksheet every time you make a change means that you are sitting and waiting for Excel to complete the recalculation.

You can turn off the automatic recalculation. However, this won't be necessary except in situations where you are working with huge workbooks that contain a large number of formulas, functions, and data. Turning off the automatic calculation feature also means that you must remember to manually recalculate the values in the worksheet before you print. To change the recalculation setting, take the following steps:

1. Open the **Tools** menu and choose **Options**.

2. Click the **Calculation** tab to display the options shown in Figure 5.3.

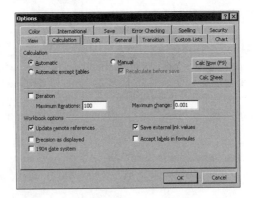

FIGURE 5.3
You can turn off the automatic recalculation feature.

3. Select one of the following Calculation options:

- **Automatic**—This is the default setting. It recalculates the entire workbook each time you edit or enter a formula.

- **Automatic Except Tables**—This automatically recalculates everything except formulas in a data table.

- **Manual**—This option tells Excel to recalculate only when you say so. To recalculate manually, press the **F9** key. When this option is selected, you can turn off or on the Recalculate Before Save option.

4. Click **OK**.

In this lesson, you learned how to copy formulas. You also learned when to use relative and absolute cell addresses and how to change the recalculation settings. In the next lesson, you learn how to use the Insert Function feature to insert Excel's special built-in formulas called functions.

Lesson 6

Performing Calculations with Functions

In this lesson, you learn how to perform calculations with functions and how to use the Insert Function feature to quickly insert functions into your worksheets.

What Are Functions?

You already learned in Lesson 4, "Performing Simple Calculations," how to create your own formulas in Excel. When you work with more complex calculations, you are better off using Excel's built-in formulas—functions.

Functions are ready-made formulas that perform a series of operations on a specified range of values. For example, to determine the sum of a series of numbers in cells A1 through H1, you can enter the function =SUM(A1:H1). Excel functions can do all kinds of calculations for all kinds of purposes, including financial and statistical calculations.

Every function consists of the following three elements:

- The = sign, which indicates that what follows is a function (formula).

- The function name, such as SUM, which indicates the operation to be performed.

- A list of cell addresses, such as (A1:H1), which are to be acted upon by the function. Some functions can include more than one set of cell addresses, which are separated by commas (such as A1,B1,H1).

You can enter functions into the worksheet by typing the function and cell references (as you did with your own formulas), or you can use the Insert Function feature, which walks you through the process of creating a function in a worksheet (you will work with the Insert Function feature in a moment). Table 6.1 lists some of the Excel functions that you probably will use most often in your worksheets.

Table 6.1 Commonly Used Excel Functions

Function	Example	Description
AVERAGE	=AVERAGE(B4:B9)	Calculates the mean or average of a group of cell values.
COUNT	=COUNT(A3:A7)	Counts the number of cells that hold values in the selected range or group of cells. This also can be used to tell you how many cells are in a particular column, which tells you how many rows are in your spreadsheet.
IF	=IF(A3>=1000,"BONUS", "NO BONUS")	Allows you to place a conditional function in a cell. In this example, if A3 is greater than or equal to 1000, the true value, BONUS, is used. If A3 is less than 1000, the false value, NO BONUS, is placed in the cell.

Table 6.1   (continued)

Function	Example	Description
MAX	=MAX(B4:B10)	Returns the maximum value in a range of cells.
MIN	=MIN(B4:B10)	Returns the minimum value in a range of cells.
PMT	=PMT(.0825/12,360, 180000)	Calculates the monthly payment on a 30-year loan (360 monthly payments) at 8.25% a year (.0825/12 a month) for $180,000.
SUM	=SUM(A1:A10)	Calculates the total in a range of cells.

TIP

> **Specify Text with Quotation Marks**   When entering text into a function, the text must be enclosed within quotation marks. For example, in the function =IF(A5>2000 "BONUS","NO BONUS"), if the condition is met (the cell value is greater than 2000), the word BONUS will be returned by the function. If the condition is not met, the phrase NO BONUS will be returned in the cell by the function.

Excel provides a large number of functions listed by category. There are Financial functions, Date and Time functions, Statistical functions, and Logical functions (such as the IF function described in Table 6.1). The group of functions that you use most often depends on the type of worksheets you typically build. For example, if you do a lot of accounting work, you will find that the Financial functions offer functions for computing monthly payments, figuring out the growth on an investment, and even computing the depreciation on capital equipment.

Although some commonly used functions have been defined in Table 6.1, as you become more adept at using Excel, you might want to explore some of the other functions available. Select **Help**, **Microsoft Excel Help**. On the Contents tab of the Help window, open the **Function Reference** topic. Several subtopics related to Excel functions and their use are provided.

USING AUTOSUM

Adding a group of cells probably is one of the most often-used calculations in an Excel worksheet. Because of this fact, Excel makes it very easy for you to place the SUM function into a cell. Excel provides the AutoSum button on the Standard toolbar. AutoSum looks at a column or row of cell values and tries to select the cells that should be included in the SUM function.

To use AutoSum, follow these steps:

1. Select the cell where you want to place the SUM function. Typically, you will choose a cell that is at the bottom of a column of values or at the end of a row of data. This makes it easy for AutoSum to figure out the range of cells that it should include in the SUM function.

2. Click the **AutoSum** button on the Standard toolbar. AutoSum inserts =SUM and the cell addresses that it thinks should be included in the function (see Figure 6.1).

3. If the range of cell addresses that AutoSum selected is incorrect, use the mouse to drag and select the appropriate group of cells.

4. Press the **Enter** key. AutoSum calculates the total for the selected range of cells.

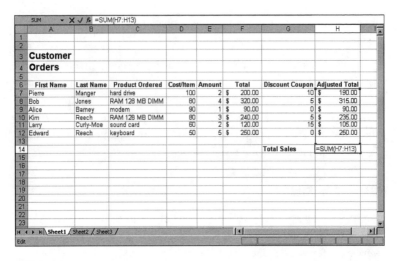

FIGURE 6.1
AutoSum inserts the SUM function and selects the cells that will be totaled by the function.

TIP

> **Quick AutoSum**   To bypass the step where Excel displays the SUM formula and its arguments in the cell, select the cell in which you want the sum inserted and double-click the **AutoSum** button on the Standard toolbar.

USING THE INSERT FUNCTION FEATURE

After you become familiar with a function or a group of functions, you place a particular function in an Excel worksheet by typing the function name and the cells to be referenced by the function (the same as you have done for formulas that you create as outlined in Lesson 4). However, when you are first starting out with functions, you will find it much easier to create them using the Insert Function feature. The Insert Function feature leads you through the process of inserting a function and specifying the appropriate cell addresses in the function.

For example, suppose you want to compute the average, maximum, and minimum of a group of cells that contain the weekly commissions for your sales force. Figure 6.2 shows how these three functions would look on a worksheet (the display has been changed in Excel to show you the functions rather than their results). You could use the Insert Function feature to create any or all of these functions.

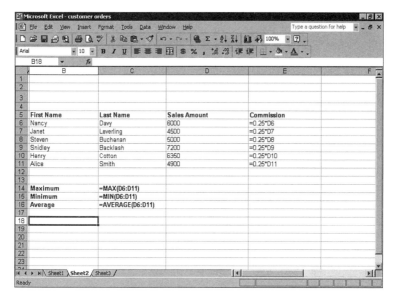

FIGURE 6.2
Functions can be placed into a worksheet using the Insert Function feature.

To use the Insert Function feature, follow these steps:

1. Click in the cell where you want to place the function.

2. Click the **Insert Function** button on the Formula bar. The Insert Function dialog box appears (see Figure 6.3).

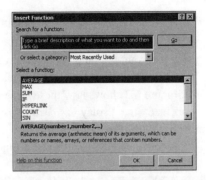

FIGURE 6.3
The Insert Function dialog box helps you select the function you want to use.

3. To search for a particular function, type a brief description of what you want to do in the Search for a Function box (for example, you could type **monthly payment** and Excel would show you financial functions that help you calculate monthly payments), and then click **Go** to conduct the search. You also can select a function category, such as Financial or Statistical, using the Select a Category drop-down box. In either case, a list of functions is provided in the Select a Function dialog box.

TIP

> **Recently Used Functions**   The Insert Function dialog box by default lists the functions that you have used most recently.

4. From the Functions list, select the function you want to insert. Then click **OK**. The Function Arguments dialog box appears. This dialog box allows you to specify the range of cells (some functions require multiple ranges of cells) that the function acts upon (see Figure 6.4).

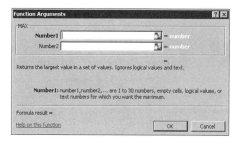

FIGURE 6.4

The Function Arguments dialog box is where you specify the cells that will be acted upon by the function. The argument specified in this case is for the Maximum function.

5. Next, you must enter the range of cells that will be acted upon by the function. Click the **Collapse** button on the far right of the Number1 text box in the Function Arguments dialog box. This returns you to the worksheet.

6. Use the mouse to select the cells that you want to place in the function (see Figure 6.5). Then click the **Expand** button on the right of the Function Arguments dialog box.

7. Click **OK**. Excel inserts the function and cell addresses for the function into the selected cell and displays the result.

If you find that you would like to edit the list of cells acted upon by a particular function, select the cell that holds the function and click the **Insert Function** button on the Formula bar. The Function Arguments dialog box for the function appears. Select a new range of cells for the function, as discussed in steps 4 and 5.

NOTE

What's This Function?   If you'd like to know more about a particular function, click the **Help on This Function** link at the bottom of the Function Arguments dialog box. The Help window will open with help on this specific function.

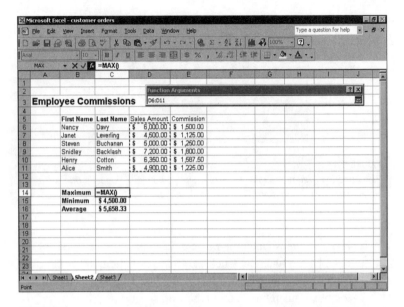

FIGURE 6.5
The Function Arguments collapses and allows you to select the cells that will be acted upon by the function.

In this lesson, you learned the basics of working with functions, and you learned how to use Excel's Insert Function feature to quickly enter functions. You also learned how to quickly total a series of numbers with the AutoSum tool. In the next lesson, you learn how to move around in an Excel worksheet.

LESSON 7
Getting Around in Excel

In this lesson, you learn the basics of moving around in a worksheet and within a workbook.

MOVING FROM WORKSHEET TO WORKSHEET

Now that you've taken a look at how to enter labels, values, formulas, and functions, you should take a look at how to navigate the space provided by Excel workbooks and worksheets. By default, each workbook starts off with three worksheets. You can add or delete worksheets from the workbook as needed. Because each workbook consists of one or more worksheets, you need a way of moving easily from worksheet to worksheet. Use one of the following methods:

- Click the tab of the worksheet you want to go to (see Figure 7.1). If the tab is not shown, use the tab scroll buttons to bring the tab into view, and then click the tab.

- Press **Ctrl+PgDn** to move to the next worksheet or **Ctrl+PgUp** to move to the previous one.

SWITCHING BETWEEN WORKBOOKS

Switching between the different workbooks that you have open on the Windows desktop is very straightforward. By default, each workbook has its own button on the Windows taskbar and opens in its own Excel application window (refer to Figure 7.1). To switch between workbooks, click the button for the workbook you want.

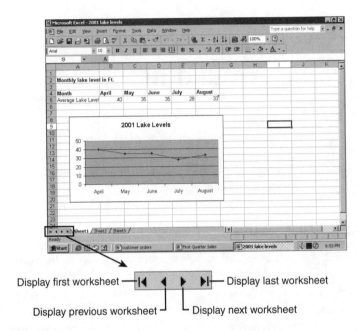

Display first worksheet — Display last worksheet

Display previous worksheet — Display next worksheet

FIGURE 7.1
Use the tabs to move from worksheet to worksheet.

If you don't want to have a separate taskbar entry for each open Excel workbook, you can turn off this feature using the Windows in Taskbar option on the View tab of the Options dialog box (click **Tools, Options**). Keep in mind, however, that disabling this feature means that you will have to use the Window menu to switch between Excel workbooks. To do so, select the Window menu, and then select the name of the workbook you want to make the current workbook in the Excel application window.

MOVING WITHIN A WORKSHEET

To enter your worksheet data, you need some way of moving to the various cells within the worksheet. Keep in mind that the part of the worksheet displayed onscreen is only a small piece of the actual worksheet.

USING THE KEYBOARD

To move around the worksheet with your keyboard, use the key combinations listed in Table 7.1.

Table 7.1   Moving Around a Worksheet with the Keyboard

To Move	Press This
Up one cell	Up-arrow key
Down one cell	Down-arrow key
Right one cell	Right-arrow key
Left one cell	Left-arrow key
Up one screen	Page Up
Down one screen	Page Down
Leftmost cell in a row (column A)	Home
Lower-right corner of the data area	Ctrl+End
Cell A1	Ctrl+Home
Last occupied cell to the right of a row	End+right-arrow key

You also can quickly go to a specific cell address in a worksheet using the Go To feature. Press **Ctrl+G** (or select **Edit**, **Go To**). Type the cell address you want to go to into the Reference box, and then click the **OK** button (see Figure 7.2).

FIGURE 7.2

The Go To feature can be used to move to a specific cell address on the worksheet.

The Go To feature keeps a list of cells to which you have recently moved using the Go To feature. To quickly move to a particular cell in the Go To list, double-click that cell address.

TIP

Even Faster Than Go To   To move quickly to a specific cell on a worksheet, type the cell's address (the column letter and row number; for example, **C25**) into the Name box at the left end of the Formula bar and press **Enter**.

USING A MOUSE

To scroll through a worksheet with a mouse, follow the techniques listed in Table 7.2.

Table 7.2   Moving Around a Worksheet with the Mouse

To Move	Click This
Move the selector to a particular cell.	Any cell.
View one more row, up or down.	Up or down arrows on the vertical scrollbar.
View one more column, left or right.	Left or right arrows on the horizontal scrollbar.
Move through a worksheet quickly.	The vertical or horizontal scrollbar; drag it up or down or right and left, respectively. As you drag, a ScreenTip displays the current row/column number.

TIP

Watch the Scroll Box   The size of the scroll box changes to represent the amount of the total worksheet that is currently visible. If the scroll box is large, you know you're seeing almost all of the current worksheet in the window. If the scroll box is small, most of the worksheet is currently hidden from view.

USING A WHEEL-ENABLED MOUSE

If you use the Microsoft IntelliMouse or any wheel-enabled mouse, you can move through a worksheet even faster than you can using the scrollbars and a conventional mouse. Here's how:

To:	Do This:
Scroll a few rows (scroll up and down)	Rotate the wheel in the middle of the mouse forward or backward.
Scroll faster (pan)	Click and hold the wheel button, and then drag the mouse in the direction in which you want to pan. The farther away from the origin mark (the four-headed arrow) you drag the mouse, the faster the panning action. To slow the pan, drag the mouse back toward the origin mark.
Pan without holding the wheel	Click the wheel once, and then move the mouse in the direction in which you want to pan. (You'll continue to pan when you move the mouse until you turn panning off by clicking the wheel again.)
Zoom in and out	Press the **Ctrl** key as you rotate the middle wheel. If you zoom out, you can click any cell you want to jump to. You then can zoom back in so you can see your data.

In this lesson, you learned how to move through a worksheet, and to move from workbook to workbook. In the next lesson, you learn how to get help in Excel.

LESSON 8
Getting Help in Microsoft Excel

In this lesson, you learn how to access and use the Help system in Microsoft Excel.

HELP: WHAT'S AVAILABLE?

Microsoft Excel supplies a Help system that makes it easy for you to look up information on Excel commands and features as you create your worksheets and work with the various Excel features. Because every person is different, the Help system can be accessed in several ways. You can

- Ask a question in the Ask a Question box.

- Ask the Office Assistant for help.

- Get help on a particular element you see onscreen with the What's This? tool.

- Use the Contents, Answer Wizard, and Index tabs in the Help window to get help.

- Access the Office on the Web feature to view Web pages containing help information (if you are connected to the Internet).

USING THE ASK A QUESTION BOX

The Ask a Question box is a new way to quickly open the Excel Help system. The Ask a Question box resides at the top right of the Excel application window.

For example, if you are working in Excel and wish to view information on how to create a new chart, type **How do I create a chart?** into the Ask a Question box. Then press the **Enter** key. A shortcut menu appears below the Ask a Question box, as shown in Figure 8.1.

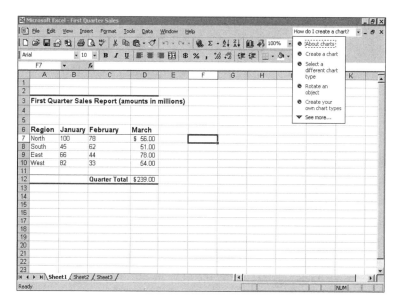

FIGURE 8.1
The Ask a Question box provides a list of Help topics that you can access quickly.

To access one of the Help topics supplied on the shortcut menu, click that particular topic. The Help window opens with topical matches for that keyword or phrase displayed.

In the case of the "new chart" question used in Figure 8.1, you could select **Create a chart** from the shortcut menu that appears. This opens the help window and displays help on how to create an Excel chart (see Figure 8.2).

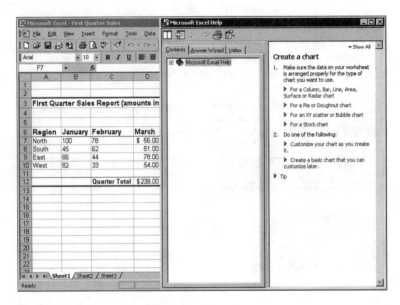

FIGURE 8.2
The Ask a Question box provides a quick way to access the Help window.

In the Help window, you can use the links provided to navigate the Help system. Click any of the content links to expand the information provided on that particular topic. You also can use the Contents, Answer Wizard, and Index tabs to find additional information or look for new information in the Help window. You learn more about these different Help window tabs later in this lesson.

USING THE OFFICE ASSISTANT

Another way to get help in Excel is to use the Office Assistant. The Office Assistant supplies the same type of access to the Help system as the Ask a Question box. You ask the Office Assistant a question, and it supplies you with a list of possible answers that provide links to various Help topics. The next two sections discuss how to use the Office Assistant.

TURNING THE OFFICE ASSISTANT ON AND OFF

By default, the Office Assistant is off. To show the Office Assistant in your application window, select the **Help** menu, and then select **Show the Office Assistant**.

You also can quickly hide the Office Assistant if you no longer want it in your application window. Right-click the Office Assistant and select **Hide**. If you want to get rid of the Office Assistant completely so it isn't activated when you select the Help feature, right-click the Office Assistant and select **Options**. Clear the **Use the Office Assistant** check box, and then click **OK**. You can always get the Office Assistant back by selecting **Help**, **Show Office Assistant**.

ASKING THE OFFICE ASSISTANT A QUESTION

When you click the Office Assistant, a balloon appears above it. Type a question into the text box. For example, you might type **How do I print?** for help printing your work. Click the **Search** button.

The Office Assistant provides some topics that reference Help topics in the Help system. Click the option that best describes what you're trying to do. The Help window appears, containing more detailed information. Use the Help window to get the exact information you need.

Although not everyone likes the Office Assistant because having it enabled means that it is always sitting in your Excel application window, it can be useful at times. For example, when you access particular features in Excel, the Office Assistant can automatically provide you with context-sensitive help on that particular feature. If you are brand new to Microsoft Excel, you might want to use the Office Assistant to help you learn the various features that Excel provides as you use them.

TIP

> **Select Your Own Office Assistant**   Several different Office
> Assistants are available in Microsoft Excel. To select
> your favorite, click the Office Assistant and select the
> **Options** button. On the Office Assistant dialog box that
> appears, select the **Gallery** tab. Click the **Next** button
> repeatedly to see the different Office Assistants avail-
> able. When you locate the assistant you want to use,
> click **OK**.

USING THE HELP WINDOW

You also can forego either the Type a Question box or the Office
Assistant and get your help directly from the Help window. To directly
access the Help window, select **Help** and then **Microsoft Excel Help**.
You also can press the **F1** key to make the Help window appear.

The Help window provides two panes. The pane on the left provides
three tabs: Contents, Answer Wizard, and Index. The right pane of the
Help window provides either help subject matter or links to different
Help topics. It functions a great deal like a Web browser window. You
click a link to a particular body of information and that information
appears in the right pane.

The first thing you should do is maximize the Help window by clicking its **Maximize** button. This makes it easier to locate and read the
information the Help system provides (see Figure 8.3).

When you first open the Help window, a group of links in the right
pane provides you with access to information about new Excel features and other links, such as a link to Microsoft's Office Web site.
Next, take a look at how you can take advantage of different ways to
find information in the Help window: the Contents tab, the Answer
Wizard tab, and the Index tab.

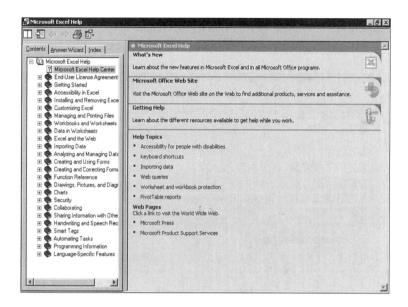

FIGURE 8.3
The Help window provides access to all the help information provided for Excel.

TIP

> **View the Help Window Tabs**   If you don't see the differ-
> ent tabs in the Help window, click the **Show** button on
> the Help window toolbar.

USING THE CONTENTS TAB

The Contents tab of the Help system is a series of books you can
open. Each book has one or more Help topics in it, which appear as
pages or chapters. To select a Help topic from the Contents tab, follow
these steps:

1. In the Help window, click the **Contents** tab on the left side of
   the Help window.

2. Find the book that describes, in broad terms, the subject for
   which you need help.

3. Double-click the book, and a list of Help topics appears below the book, as shown in Figure 8.4.

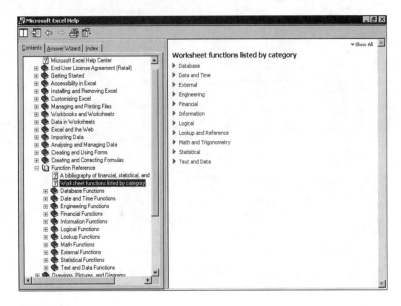

FIGURE 8.4
Use the Contents tab to browse through the various Help topics.

4. Click one of the pages (the pages contain a question mark) under a Help topic to display it in the right pane of the Help window. Expand any of the links provided to read more information as needed.

5. When you finish reading a topic, select another topic on the Contents tab or click the Help window's **Close** (**x**) button to exit Help.

USING THE ANSWER WIZARD

Another way to get help in the Help window is to use the Answer Wizard. The Answer Wizard works the same as the Ask a Question box or the Office Assistant; you ask the wizard a question and it supplies you with a list of topics that relate to your question. You click one of the choices provided to view help in the Help window.

To get help using the Answer Wizard, follow these steps:

1. Click the **Answer Wizard** tab in the Help window.

2. Type your question into the What Would You Like to Do? box. For example, you might type the question, **How do I copy a formula?**

3. After typing your question, click the **Search** button. A list of topics appears in the Select Topic to Display box. Select a particular topic, and its information appears in the right pane of the Help window, as shown in Figure 8.5.

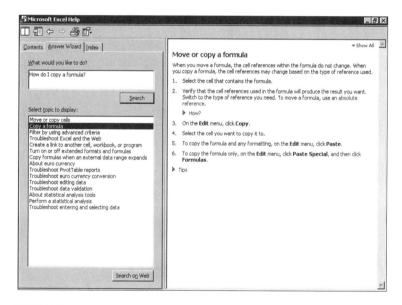

FIGURE 8.5

Search for help in the Help window using the Answer Wizard tab.

TIP

> **Print Help** If you want to print information provided in the Help window, click the **Print** icon on the Help toolbar.

USING THE INDEX

The Index is an alphabetical listing of every Help topic available. It's like an index in a book.

Follow these steps to use the index:

1. In the Help window, click the **Index** tab.

2. Type the first few letters of the topic for which you are look-ing. The Or Choose Keywords box jumps quickly to a key-word that contains the characters you have typed.

3. Double-click the appropriate keyword in the keywords box. Topics for that keyword appear in the Choose a Topic box.

4. Click a topic to view help in the right pane of the Help win-dow (see Figure 8.6).

TIP

> **Navigation Help Topics** You can move from topic to topic in the right pane of the Help window by clicking the various links that are provided there. Some topics are collapsed. Click the triangle next to the topic to expand the topic and view the help provided.

GETTING HELP WITH SCREEN ELEMENTS

If you wonder about the function of a particular button or tool on the Excel screen, wonder no more. Just follow these steps to learn about this part of Help:

1. Select **Help** and then **What's This?** or press **Shift+F1**. The mouse pointer changes to an arrow with a question mark.

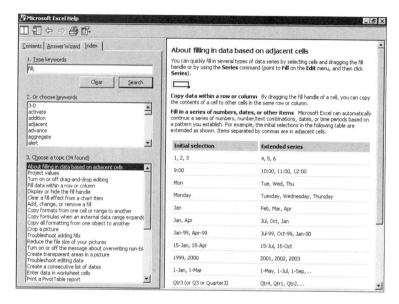

FIGURE 8.6
Use the Index tab to get help in the Help window.

2. Click the screen element for which you want help. A box
appears explaining the element.

TIP

> **Take Advantage of ScreenTips**   Another Help feature pro-
> vided by Excel is the ScreenTip. All the buttons on the
> different toolbars provided by Excel have a ScreenTip.
> Place the mouse on a particular button or icon, and the
> name of the item (which often helps you determine its
> function) appears in a ScreenTip.

In this lesson, you learned how to use the Excel Help feature. In the
next lesson, you learn how to use different views of your Excel
worksheets.

LESSON 9

Different Ways to View Your Worksheet

In this lesson, you learn about the various ways in which you can view your worksheets.

CHANGING THE WORKSHEET VIEW

There are many ways to change how your worksheet appears within the Excel window. Changing the view has no effect on how your worksheets look when printed (unless you choose to hide data onscreen). However, changing the view and getting a different perspective helps you to see the overall layout of the worksheet and allows you to view worksheet cells that might not appear in the default screen view. For example, you can enlarge or reduce the size of the worksheet so that you can view more or less of it at one time.

`100%` ▼ To enlarge or reduce your view of the current worksheet, use the Zoom feature. Simply click the **Zoom** button on the Standard toolbar and select the zoom percentage you want to use from the following: 25%, 50%, 75%, 100%, or 200%. If you want to zoom by a number that's not listed, just type the number into the Zoom box and press **Enter**.

You also can have Excel zoom in on a particular portion of a worksheet. This is particularly useful when you have created very large worksheets. Select the area of the worksheet you want to zoom in on, and then click the **Zoom** button list and click **Selection**. You then can select different zoom values on the Zoom list to zoom in or out on that particular portion of the worksheet. Keep in mind that Excel zooms in on the entire worksheet, not just the selected cells. (It just makes sure that you can see the selected cells when you change the zoom values.)

> **TIP**
>
> **Fast Zoom with a Wheel Mouse** If you use the Microsoft IntelliMouse or another compatible wheel mouse, you can zoom in and out quickly by holding down the **Ctrl** key as you move the wheel forward or back.

You also can display your worksheet so that it takes up the full screen. This eliminates all the other items in the Excel window, such as the toolbars, the Formula bar, the status bar, and so on. Figure 9.1 shows a worksheet in the Full Screen view. To use this view, select the **View** menu and select **Full Screen**. To return to Normal view, click **Close Full Screen**.

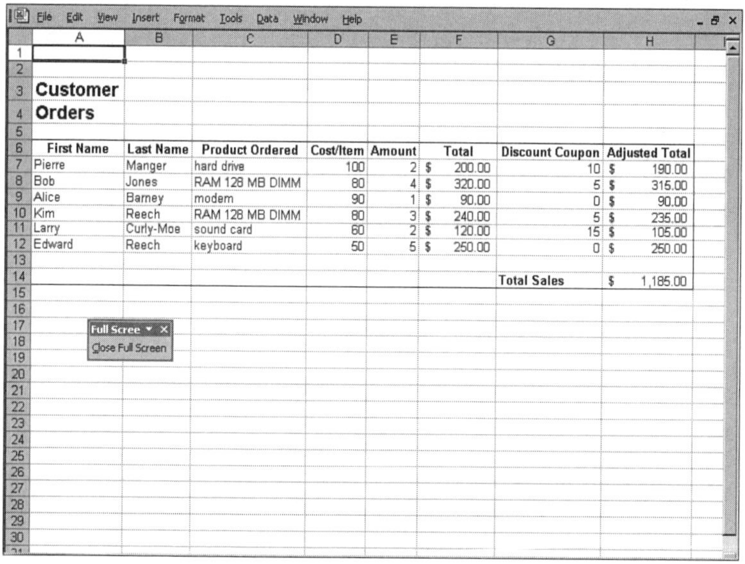

File Edit View Insert Format Tools Data Window Help
Customer Orders
First Name
Last Name
Product Ordered
Cost/Item
Amount
Total
Discount Coupon
Adjusted Total
Pierre Manger hard drive 100 2 $ 200.00 10 $ 190.00
Bob Jones RAM 128 MB DIMM 80 4 $ 320.00 5 $ 315.00
Alice Barney modem 90 1 $ 90.00 0 $ 90.00
Kim Reech RAM 128 MB DIMM 80 3 $ 240.00 5 $ 235.00
Larry Curly-Moe sound card 60 2 $ 120.00 15 $ 105.00
Edward Reech keyboard 50 5 $ 250.00 0 $ 250.00
Total Sales $ 1,185.00
Full Scree
Close Full Screen

FIGURE 9.1

View your worksheet on the entire screen.

FREEZING COLUMN AND ROW LABELS

When you work with very large worksheets, it can be very annoying as you scroll to the right or down through the worksheet when you can no longer see your row headings or column headings, respectively. For example, you might be entering customer data where the customer's name is in the first column of the worksheet, and when you scroll to the extreme right to enter data, you can no longer see the customer names.

You can freeze your column and row labels so that you can view them no matter how far you scroll down or to the right in your worksheet. For example, Figure 9.2 shows frozen row headings that allow you to see the customer names no matter how far you move to the right of the worksheet.

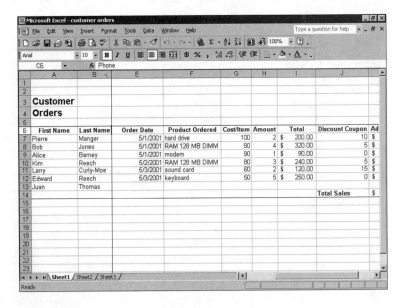

FIGURE 9.2
You can freeze row and column headings so they remain onscreen as you scroll.

To freeze row or column headings (or both), follow these steps:

1. Click the cell to the right of the row labels and/or below any column labels you want to freeze. This highlights the cell.

2. Select the **Window** menu, and then select **Freeze Panes**.

You might want to experiment on a large worksheet. Freeze the column and row headings, and then use the keyboard or the mouse to move around in the worksheet. As you do, the row and/or column headings remain locked in their positions. This enables you to view data in other parts of the worksheet without losing track of what that data represents.

When you have finished working with the frozen column and row headings, you easily can unfreeze them. Select the **Window** menu again and select **Unfreeze Panes**.

SPLITTING WORKSHEETS

When you work with very large worksheets, you might actually want to split the worksheet into multiple windows. This enables you to view the same worksheet in different windows. You then can scroll through the multiple copies of the same worksheet and compare data in cells that are normally far apart in the worksheet.

Figure 9.3 shows a worksheet that has been split into multiple panes. Each "copy" of the worksheet will have its own set of vertical and horizontal scrollbars.

To split a worksheet, follow these steps:

1. Click in the cell where you want to create the split. A split appears to the left of the selected cell and above the selected cell.

2. You can adjust the vertical or horizontal split bars using the mouse. Place the mouse on the split bar and drag it to a new location.

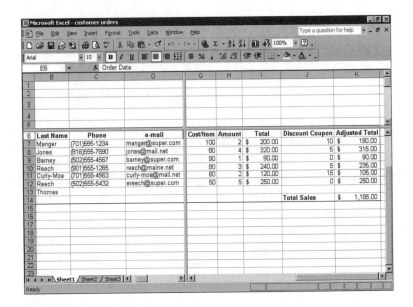

FIGURE 9.3
You can split a worksheet into two windows, making it easy to compare data in the worksheet.

3. You can use the scrollbars in the different split panes to view data in the worksheet (different data can be viewed in each pane).

To remove the split, select the **Window** menu and select **Remove Split**.

TIP

> **Create Splits with the Split Boxes**   You also can create a vertical or horizontal split in a worksheet by using the split boxes. A horizontal split box rests just above the vertical scrollbar, and a vertical split box rests on the far right of the horizontal scrollbar. Place your mouse on either of these split boxes and drag them onto the worksheet to create a split bar.

HIDING WORKBOOKS, WORKSHEETS, COLUMNS, AND ROWS

For those times when you're working on top-secret information (or at least information that is somewhat proprietary, such as employee salaries), you can hide workbooks, worksheets, columns, or rows from prying eyes. For example, if you have confidential data stored in one particular worksheet, you can hide that worksheet, yet still be able to view the other worksheets in that workbook. You also can hide particular columns or rows within a worksheet.

Use these methods to hide data:

- To hide a row or a column in a worksheet, click a row or column heading to select it (you can select adjacent columns or rows by dragging across them). Then, right-click within the row or column and select **Hide** from the shortcut menu that appears (see Figure 9.4). To unhide the row or column, right-click the border between the hidden item and rows or columns that are visible, and then select **Unhide** from the shortcut menu.

- To hide a worksheet, click its tab to select it. Then, open the **Format** menu and select **Sheet, Hide**. To unhide the worksheet, select **Format, Sheet**, and then **Unhide**. Select the worksheet to unhide in the Unhide dialog box that appears, and then click **OK**.

- To hide an entire workbook, open the **Window** menu and select **Hide**. This removes the workbook from the Excel window, even though the workbook is open. To unhide the workbook, select **Window, Unhide**.

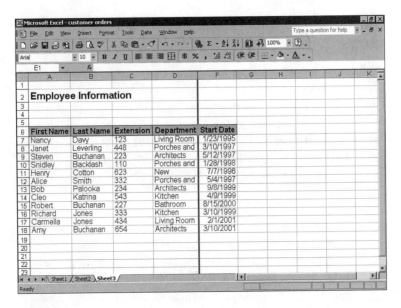

FIGURE 9.4
Column E, which contains employee salaries, has been hidden on a worksheet.

LOCKING CELLS IN A WORKSHEET

In some situations, you might create a worksheet or worksheets and someone else will enter the data. In these situations, you might want to lock cells that contain formulas and functions so that the person doing the data entry does not accidentally overwrite or delete the worksheet formulas or functions. Locking cells in a worksheet is a two-step process. You must first select and lock the cells. Then, you must turn on protection on the entire worksheet for the "lock" to go into effect.

Follow these steps to lock cells on a worksheet:

1. Select the cells in the worksheet that you want to lock. These are typically the cells that contain formulas or functions.

2. Select **Format** and then **Cells**. The Format Cells dialog box appears. Click the **Protection** tab on the dialog box (see Figure 9.5).

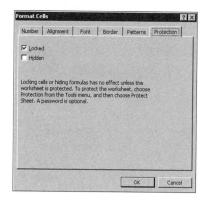

FIGURE 9.5

Cells can be locked using the Protection tab of the Format Cells dialog box.

3. Be sure the Locked check box is selected on the Protection tab. Then click **OK**.

4. Now you must protect the entire worksheet to have the lock feature protect the cells that you selected. Select the **Tools** menu, point at **Protections**, and then select **Protect Sheet**. The Protect Sheet dialog box appears (see Figure 9.6).

5. Enter a password if you want to require a password for "unprotecting" the worksheet. Then click **OK**.

The cells that you locked in steps 1, 2, and 3 no longer will accept data entry. Every time someone tries to enter data into one of those cells, Excel displays a message stating that data will not be accepted. The cells now are protected and you can pass the workbook on to the person who handles the data entry.

FIGURE 9.6
The worksheet must be protected if you want to lock cells containing formulas or functions.

In this lesson, you learned how to change the view of your worksheet, freeze column and row headings, and hide data. You also learned how to lock certain cells from data entry. In the next lesson, you will learn how to edit worksheets by correcting data. You also will learn to use the spell checker and AutoCorrect feature.

LESSON 10
Editing Worksheets

In this lesson, you learn how to change data and how to undo those changes if necessary. You also learn how to search for data and replace it with other data, how to spell check your work, and how to copy, move, and delete data.

CORRECTING DATA

You've taken a look at entering text, values, formulas, and functions. There will definitely be occasions when you need to edit information in a cell. One way to change an entry in a cell is to replace it by selecting the cell and then entering new data. Just press **Enter** after entering the information. If you just want to modify the existing cell content, you also can edit data within a cell.

To edit information in a cell, follow these steps:

1. Select the cell in which you want to edit data.

2. To begin editing, click in the Formula bar to place the insertion point into the cell entry. To edit within the cell itself, press **F2** or double-click the cell. This puts you in Edit mode; the word Edit appears in the status bar.

3. Press the right- or left-arrow key to move the insertion point within the entry. Press the **Backspace** key to delete characters to the left of the insertion point; press the **Delete** key to delete characters to the right. Then, type any characters you want to add.

4. Press the **Enter** key when you have finished making your changes.

If you change your mind and you no longer want to edit your entry, click the **Cancel** button on the Formula bar or press **Esc**.

> **TIP**
>
> **Moving to the Beginning or End of a Cell Entry**   In Edit mode, you can move quickly to the beginning or end of a cell's contents. Press **Home** to move to the beginning of the entry; press **End** to move to the end of the entry.

UNDOING AN ACTION

Although editing a worksheet is supposed to improve it, you might find that you've done something to a cell or range of cells that you had not intended. This is where the Undo feature comes in.

You can undo just about any action while working in Excel, including any changes you make to a cell's data. To undo a change, click the **Undo** button on the Standard toolbar (or select **Edit, Undo**).

You also can undo an undo. Just click the **Redo** button on the Standard toolbar.

> **TIP**
>
> **Undoing/Redoing More Than One Thing**   The Undo button undoes only the most recent action. To undo several previous actions, click the **Undo** button multiple times or click the drop-down arrow on the undo button and select the number of actions you want undone.

USING THE REPLACE FEATURE

Suppose you've entered a particular label or value into the worksheet and find that you have consistently entered it incorrectly. A great way to change multiple occurrences of a label or value is using Excel's

Replace feature; you can locate data in the worksheet and replace it with new data. To find and replace data, follow these steps:

1. Select the **Edit** menu, and then select **Replace**. The Find and Replace dialog box appears, as shown in Figure 10.1.

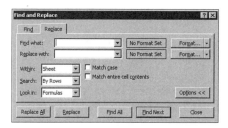

FIGURE 10.1
Find and replace data with the Find and Replace dialog box.

2. Type the text or value that you want to find into the **Find What** text box.

3. Click in the **Replace With** text box and type the text you want to use as replacement text.

4. To expand the options available to you in the dialog box, click the **Options** button (Figure 10.1 shows the dialog box in its expanded form).

5. If you want to match the exact case of your entry so that Excel factors in capitalization, click the **Match Case** check box. If you want to locate cells that contain exactly what you entered into the Find What text box (and no additional data), click the **Match Entire Cell Contents** check box.

6. To search for entries with particular formatting, click the **Format** button to the right of the Find What box. The Find Format dialog box appears (see Figure 10.2). You can search for entries that have been assigned number, alignment, font, border, patterns, and protection using the appropriate tab on

the Find Format dialog box. After making your selection,
click the **OK** button.

FIGURE 10.2
*The Find Format dialog box enables you to search for entries that have been
assigned a particular formatting.*

7. You also can replace your entries with a particular formatting. Click the **Format** button to the right of the Replace
With box. The Replace Format dialog box appears. It is the
same as the Find Format dialog box. Simply select any formats you want to assign to your replacement, and then click
OK.

8. Click **Find Next** to find the first occurrence of your specified
entry.

9. When an occurrence is found, it is highlighted. Click
Replace to replace only this occurrence and then click **Find
Next** to find the next occurrence.

10. If you want to find all the occurrences, click **Find All**; you
also can replace all the occurrences of the entry with
Replace All.

11. When you have finished working with the Find and Replace
dialog box, click **Close**.

NOTE

Search an Entire Workbook   If you want to search an entire workbook for a particular entry, click the **Within** drop-down list in the Find and Replace dialog box and select **Workbook**.

If you don't need to replace an entry but would like to find it in the worksheet, you can use the Find feature. Select **Edit**, **Find**, and then type the data you want to locate into the Find What text box and click **Find Next**.

Checking Your Spelling

Because worksheets also include text entries, you might want to make sure that you check for any misspellings in a worksheet before printing the data. Excel offers a spell-checking feature that finds and corrects misspellings in a worksheet.

To run the Spelling Checker, follow these steps:

1. Click the **Spelling** button on the Standard toolbar (or select **Tools**, **Spelling**). The Spelling dialog box appears. Excel finds the first misspelled word and displays it at the top of the Spelling dialog box. A suggested correction appears in the Suggestions box (see Figure 10.3).

2. To accept the suggestion in the Suggestions box, click **Change**, or click **Change All** to change all occurrences of the misspelled word.

3. If the suggestion in the Suggestions box is not correct, you can do any of the following:

   - Select a different suggestion from the Suggestions box, and then click **Change** or **Change All**.

   - Type your own correction into the Change To box, and then click **Change** or **Change All**.

- Click **Ignore Once** to leave the word unchanged.

- Click **Ignore All** to leave all occurrences of the word unchanged.

- Click **Add to Dictionary** to add the word to the dictionary so that Excel won't flag it as misspelled again.

- Click **AutoCorrect** to add a correctly spelled word to the AutoCorrect list so that Excel can correct it automatically as you type.

- If you make a mistake related to a particular entry, click the **Undo Last** button to undo the last change you made.

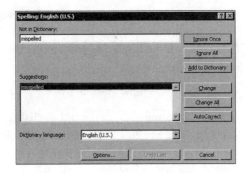

FIGURE 10.3
Correct spelling mistakes with the options in the Spelling dialog box.

4. You might see a message asking whether you want to continue checking spelling at the beginning of the sheet. If so, click **Yes** to continue. When the Spelling Checker can't find any more misspelled words, it displays a prompt telling you that the spelling check is complete. Click **OK** to confirm that the spelling check is finished.

NOTE

> **Setting Spelling Options** If you want to set options related to the Spelling feature, such as ignoring words in uppercase and words with numbers, click the **Options** button in the Spelling dialog box. This takes you to the Options dialog box for the Speller. Set options as needed and then click **OK** to return to the Spelling dialog box.

COPYING AND MOVING DATA

In Lesson 3, you learned how to use the Fill feature to copy a particular entry to multiple cells. In this section, you take a closer look at the Copy feature. When you copy or cut data in a cell, that data is held in a temporary storage area (a part of the computer's memory) called the Clipboard.

Excel 2002 makes it easy for you to work with the Clipboard because it can be viewed in the Office Clipboard task pane (you look at the Clipboard later in this lesson). This enables you to keep track of items that you have copied or cut to the Clipboard. The Clipboard not only enables you to copy or move data with Excel, but it enables you to place Excel data directly into another application such as Word.

PLAIN ENGLISH

> **Clipboard** The Clipboard is an area of memory that is accessible to all Windows programs. The Clipboard is used to copy or move data from place to place within a program or between programs.

When you copy data, you create a duplicate of data in a cell or range of cells. Follow these steps to copy data:

1. Select the cell(s) that you want to copy. You can select any range or several ranges if you want. (See Lesson 13, "Working with Ranges," for more information).

2. Click the **Copy** button on the Standard toolbar. The contents of the selected cell(s) are copied to the Clipboard.

3. Select the first cell in the area where you would like to place the copy. (To copy the data to another worksheet or workbook, change to that worksheet or workbook first.)

4. Click the **Paste** button. Excel inserts the contents of the Clipboard at the location of the insertion point.

> **CAUTION**
>
> **Watch Out!**   When copying or moving data, be careful not to paste the data over existing data (unless, of course, you intend to).

You can copy the same data to several places by repeating the **Paste** command. Items remain on the Clipboard until you remove them.

USING DRAG AND DROP

The fastest way to copy something is to drag and drop it. Select the cells you want to copy, hold down the **Ctrl** key, and drag the border of the range you selected (see Figure 10.4). When you release the mouse button, the contents are copied to the new location. To insert the data between existing cells, press **Ctrl+Shift** as you drag.

To drag a copy to a different sheet, press **Ctrl+Alt** as you drag the selection to the sheet's tab. Excel switches you to that sheet, where you can drop your selection into the appropriate location.

MOVING DATA

Moving data is similar to copying except that the data is removed from its original place and placed into the new location.

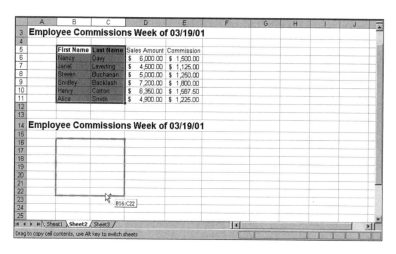

FIGURE 10.4
Dragging is the fastest way to copy data.

To move data, follow these steps:

1. Select the cells you want to move.

2. Click the **Cut** button.

3. Select the first cell in the area where you want to place the data. To move the data to another worksheet, change to that worksheet.

4. Click **Paste**.

USING DRAG AND DROP TO MOVE DATA

You also can move data using drag and drop. Select the data to be moved, and then drag the border of the selected cells to its new location. To insert the data between existing cells, press **Shift** while you drag. To move the data to a different worksheet, press the **Alt** key and drag the selection to the worksheet's tab. You're switched to that sheet, where you can drop your selection at the appropriate point.

USING THE OFFICE CLIPBOARD

You can use the Office Clipboard to store multiple items that you cut or copy from an Excel worksheet (or workbook). You then can paste or move these items within Excel or to other Office applications. The Office Clipboard can hold up to 24 items.

> **CAUTION**
>
> **What a Drag!** You can't use the Drag-and-Drop feature to copy or move data to the Office Clipboard.

The Office Clipboard is viewed in the Clipboard task Pane. Follow these steps to open the Office Clipboard:

1. Select the **Edit** menu, and then select **Office Clipboard**. The Clipboard task pane appears. Any items that you have cut or copied appear on the Clipboard (see Figure 10.5).

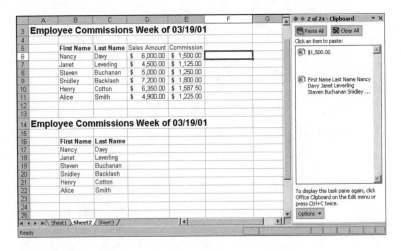

FIGURE 10.5
The Clipboard provides a list of items that you have cut or copied.

2. To paste an item that appears on the Clipboard, click in a cell on the worksheet, and then click the item on the Clipboard. It then is pasted into the selected cell.

You can remove any of the items from the Clipboard. Place the mouse pointer on an item listed on the Clipboard and click the drop-down arrow that appears. Click **Delete** on the shortcut menu that appears.

You also can clear all the items from the Clipboard. Click the **Clear All** button at the top of the Clipboard task pane.

TIP

> **Open the Clipboard from the System Tray**   You can quickly open the Office Clipboard in any Office application by double-clicking the Clipboard icon in the Windows System Tray (at the far right of the Windows taskbar).

DELETING DATA

To delete the data in a cell or range of cells, select them and press **Delete**. Excel also offers some additional options for deleting cells and their contents:

- With the **Edit**, **Clear** command, you can delete only the formatting of a cell (or an attached comment) without deleting its contents. The formatting of a cell includes the cell's color, border style, numeric format, font size, and so on. You'll learn more about this option in a moment.

- With the **Edit**, **Delete** command, you can remove cells and then shift surrounding cells over to take their place (this option is described in more detail in Lesson 14, "Inserting and Removing Cells, Rows, and Columns").

To use the Clear command to remove the formatting of a cell or a note, follow these steps:

1. Select the cells you want to clear.

2. Open the **Edit** menu and point at **Clear**. The Clear submenu appears.

3. Select the desired Clear option: **All** (which clears the cells of all contents, formatting, and notes), **Formats**, **Contents**, or **Comments**.

In this lesson, you learned how to edit cell data and undo changes. In addition, you learned how to spell check your worksheet and how to copy, move, and delete data. In the next lesson, you learn how to format your Excel labels and values.

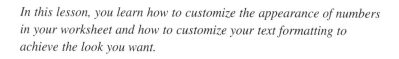

LESSON 11

Changing How Numbers and Text Look

In this lesson, you learn how to customize the appearance of numbers in your worksheet and how to customize your text formatting to achieve the look you want.

FORMATTING TEXT AND NUMBERS

When you work in Excel, you work with two types of formatting: value formatting and font formatting. Value formatting is where you assign a particular number style to a cell (or cells) that holds numeric data. You can assign a currency style, a percent style, and several other numeric styles to values.

Another formatting option available to you in Excel relates to different font attributes. For example, you can add bold or italic to the contents of a cell or cells. You also can change the font used for a range of cells or increase the font size.

Next, you take a look at numeric formatting, and then you look at how different font attributes are controlled in Excel.

USING THE STYLE BUTTONS TO FORMAT NUMBERS

The Formatting toolbar (just below the Standard toolbar) contains several buttons for applying a format to your numbers, including the following:

Button	Name	Example/Description
$	Currency Style	$1,200.90
%	Percent Style	20.90%
,	Comma Style	1,200.90
+.0 .00	Increase Decimal	Adds one decimal place
.00 +.0	Decrease Decimal	Deletes one decimal place

To use one of these buttons, select the cell or cells you want to format, and then click the desired button. If you would like more formatting options for numeric values, read on; they are covered in the next section.

NUMERIC FORMATTING OPTIONS

The numeric values that you place in your Excel cells are more than just numbers; they often represent dollar amounts, a date, or a percentage. If the various numeric style buttons on the Formatting toolbar (discussed in the previous section) do not offer the exact format you want for your numbers, don't worry. Excel's Format Cells dialog box offers a wide range of number formats and even allows you to create custom formats.

To use the Format Cells dialog box to assign numeric formatting to cells in a worksheet, follow these steps:

1. Select the cell or range that contains the values you want to format.

2. Select the **Format** menu and select **Cells**. The Format Cells dialog box appears.

3. Click the **Number** tab. The different categories of numeric formats are displayed in a Category list (see Figure 11.1).

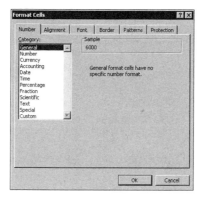

FIGURE 11.1
Apply a numeric format in the Number tab of the Format Cells dialog box.

4. In the Category list, select the numeric format category you want to use. The sample box displays the default format for that category.

5. Click **OK** to assign the numeric format to the selected cells.

As you can see from the Number tab on the Format Cells dialog box, Excel offers several numeric formatting styles. Table 11.1 provides a list of these different number formats.

Table 11.1   Excel's Number Formats

Number Format	Examples	Description
General	10.6 $456,908.00	Excel displays your value as you enter it. In other words, this format displays currency or percent signs only if you enter them yourself.

Table 11.1   (continued)

Number Format	Examples	Description
Number	3400.50 _120.39	The default Number format has two decimal places. Negative numbers are preceded by a minus sign, but they also can appear in red and/or parentheses.
Currency	$3,400.50 _$3,400.50	The default Currency format has two decimal places and a dollar sign. Negative numbers appear with a minus sign, but they also can appear in red and/or parentheses.
Accounting	$3,400.00 $978.21	Use this format to align dollar signs and decimal points in a column. The default Accounting format has two decimal places and a dollar sign.
Date	11/7	The default Date format is the month and day separated by a slash; however, you can select from numerous other formats.
Time	10:00	The default Time format is the hour and minutes separated by a colon; however, you can opt to display seconds, a.m., or p.m.
Percentage	99.50%	The default Percentage format has two decimal places. Excel multiplies the value in a cell by 100 and displays the result with a percent sign.

Table 11.1   (continued)

Number Format	Examples	Description
Fraction	1/2	The default Fraction format is up to one digit on each side of the slash. Use this format to display the number of digits you want on each side of the slash and the fraction type (such as halves, quarters, eighths, and so on).
Scientific	3.40E+03	The default Scientific format has two decimal places. Use this format to display numbers in scientific notation.
Text	135RV90	Use Text format to display both text and numbers in a cell as text. Excel displays the entry exactly as you type it.
Special	02110	This format is specifically designed to display ZIP codes, phone numbers, and Social Security numbers correctly so that you don't have to enter any special characters, such as hyphens.
Custom	00.0%	Use Custom format to create your own number format. You can use any of the format codes in the Type list and then make changes to those codes. The # symbol represents a number placeholder, and 0 represents a zero placeholder.

You also can open the Format Cell dialog box using a shortcut menu. Select the cell or cells that you want to assign a numeric format to, and then right-click those cells. On the shortcut menu that appears, select **Format Cells**. Then, select the **Number** tab to select your numeric format.

CAUTION

> **That's Not the Date I Entered!**   If you enter a date into a cell that is already formatted with the Number format, the date appears as a value that represents the number of days between January 1, 1900 and that date. Change the cell's formatting from a Number format to a Date format and select a date type. The entry in the cell then appears as an actual date.

TIP

> **How Do I Get Rid of a Numeric Format?**   To remove a number format from a cell (and return it to General format), select the cell whose formatting you want to remove, open the **Edit** menu, select **Clear**, and select **Formats**.

HOW YOU CAN MAKE TEXT LOOK DIFFERENT

When you type text into a cell, Excel automatically formats it in the Arial font with a text size of 10 points. The 12-point font size is considered typical for business documents (the higher the point size, the bigger the text is; there are approximately 72 points in an inch). You can select from several fonts (such as Baskerville, Modern, or Rockwell) and change the size of any font characters in a cell. You can also apply special font attributes, such as bold, italic, and underline.

PLAIN ENGLISH

> **Font**   A font is a set of characters that have the same typeface, which means they are of a single design (such as Times New Roman).

Before you take a look at applying different font attributes to the cells in a worksheet, take a look at how you change the default font for all your Excel workbooks. This enables you to select a different font and font size for your worksheets.

To change the default font, follow these steps:

1. Select **Tools** and then click **Options** to open the Options dialog box.

2. Click the **General** tab (see Figure 11.2).

3. In the Standard Font area, use the drop-down list to select a new font. Use the Size drop-down list to select a new default font size.

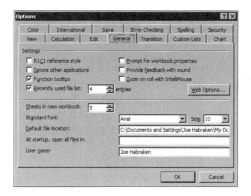

FIGURE 11.2
You can set a new default font and font size for your Excel workbooks.

4. When you click the **OK** button, Excel makes your preference the default font and size.

CHANGING TEXT ATTRIBUTES WITH TOOLBAR BUTTONS

When you are working on your various Excel worksheets, you probably will apply a variety of formatting options to the different cells in a particular worksheet. A fast way to assign text attributes, such as bold and italic, is to use the various font attribute buttons on the Excel Formatting toolbar.

To use the Formatting toolbar to change text attributes, follow these steps:

1. Select the cell or range that contains the text whose look you want to change.

2. To change the font, click the **Font** drop-down list, and select a new font name. To change the font size, click the **Font Size** drop-down list and select the size you want to use. You also can type the point size into the Font Size box and then press **Enter**.

3. To add an attribute such as bold, italic, or underlining to the selected cells, click the appropriate button: **Bold**, **Italic**, or **Underline**, respectively.

 TIP

> **Font Keyboard Shortcuts**   You can apply certain attributes quickly by using keyboard shortcuts. First select the cell(s), and then press **Ctrl+B** for bold, **Ctrl+I** for italic, **Ctrl+U** for single underline, or **Ctrl+5** for strikethrough.

You also can change the color of the font in a cell or cells. Select the cell or cells and click the **Font Color** drop-down arrow on the Formatting toolbar. Select a font color from the Color palette that appears.

ACCESSING DIFFERENT FONT ATTRIBUTES

If you would like to access a greater number of font format options for a cell or range of cells, you can use the Font tab of the Format Cells dialog box. It provides access to different fonts, font styles, font sizes, font colors, and other text attributes, such as strikethrough and super-script/subscript. To format cells using the Font tab of the Format Cells dialog box, follow these steps:

1. Select the cell or range that contains the text you want to format.

2. Select the **Format** menu and select **Cells**, or press **Ctrl+1**. (You can also right-click the selected cells and choose **Format Cells** from the shortcut menu.)

3. Click the **Font** tab. The Font tab provides drop-down lists and check boxes for selecting the various font attributes (see Figure 11.3).

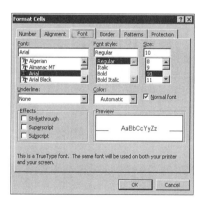

FIGURE 11.3
The Font tab provides access to all the font attributes.

4. Select the options you want.

5. Click **OK** to close the dialog box and return to your work-sheet.

ALIGNING TEXT IN CELLS

When you enter data into a cell, that data is aligned automatically.
Text is aligned on the left, and numbers are aligned on the right (values resulting from a formula or function are also right-aligned). Both text and numbers are initially set at the bottom of the cells. However, you can change both the vertical and the horizontal alignment of data in your cells.

Follow these steps to change the alignment:

1. Select the cell or range you want to align.

2. Select the **Format** menu and then select **Cells**. The Format Cells dialog box appears.

3. Click the **Alignment** tab (see Figure 11.4).

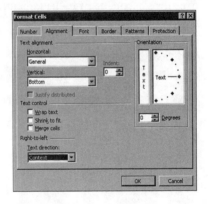

FIGURE 11.4
Select from the Alignment options on the Alignment tab of the Format Cells dialog box.

4. Choose from the following options to set the alignment:

   • **Horizontal**—Lets you specify a left/right alignment in the cells. (The **Center Across** selection centers a title or other text within a range of cells, which is discussed in a moment.)

- **Vertical**—Lets you specify how you want the text aligned in relation to the top and bottom of the cells.

- **Orientation**—Lets you flip the text sideways or print it from top to bottom instead of left to right.

- **Wrap Text**—Tells Excel to wrap long lines of text within a cell without changing the width of the cell. (Normally, Excel displays all text in a cell on one line.)

- **Shrink to Fit**—Shrinks the text to fit within the cell's current width. If the cell's width is adjusted, the text increases or decreases in size accordingly.

- **Merge Cells**—Combines several cells into a single cell. All data is overlaid, except for the cell in the upper-left corner of the selected cells.

5. Click **OK** when you have finished making your selections.

TIP

> **Changing Text Orientation**   The Alignment tab also provides an Orientation box that enables you to rotate text within a cell or a group of merged cells. Drag the degree dial on the Alignment tab or use the Degree box to specify the amount of rotation for the text.

ALIGNING TEXT FROM THE TOOLBAR

Like the font attributes such as bold and italic, you also can select certain alignment options directly from the Formatting toolbar. The following buttons enable you to align the text:

Button	Name	Description
	Align Left	Places data at left edge of cell
	Align Right	Places data at right edge of cell

Button	Name	Description
▤	Center	Centers data in cell
▦	Merge and Center	Centers data in selected cell range

Excel also enables you to indent your text within a cell. If you're typing a paragraph's worth of information into a single cell, for example, you can indent that paragraph by selecting **Left Alignment** from the Horizontal list box in the Format Cells dialog box (as explained earlier). After selecting Left Alignment, set the amount of indent you want with the Indent spin box in the Format Cells dialog box.

In addition, you can add an indent quickly by clicking the following buttons on the Formatting toolbar:

Button	Name	Description
▤	Decrease Indent	Removes an indent or creates a negative indent
▤	Increase Indent	Adds an indent

COMBINING CELLS AND WRAPPING TEXT

You can also center text across a range of cells or merge several cells to hold a sheet title or other text information. If you want to center a title or other text over a range of cells, select the entire range of blank cells in which you want the text centered. This should include the cell that contains the text you want to center (which should be in the cell on the far left of the cell range). Then, click the **Merge and Center** button on the Formatting toolbar.

Combining a group of cells also allows you to place a special heading or other text into the cells (this works well in cases where you use a large font size for the text). Select the cells that you want to combine. Then, select **Format, Cells** and select the **Alignment** tab of the Format Cells dialog box.

Click the **Merge Cells** check box and then click **OK**. The cells are then merged.

If you have a cell or a group of merged cells that holds a large amount of text (such as an explanation), you might want to wrap the text within the cell or merged cells. Click the cell that holds the text entry, and then select **Format, Cells**. Select the **Alignment** tab of the Format Cells dialog box.

Click the **Wrap Text** checkbox. Then click **OK**.

Copying Formats with Format Painter

After applying a numeric format or various font attributes to a cell or cell range, you can easily copy those formatting options to other cells. This works whether you're copying numeric or text formatting or shading or borders, as you'll learn in upcoming lessons. To copy a format from one cell to another, follow these steps:

1. Select the cells that contain the formatting you want to copy.

2. Click the **Format Painter** button on the Standard toolbar. Excel copies the formatting. The mouse pointer changes into a paintbrush with a plus sign next to it.

3. Click one cell or drag over several cells to which you want to apply the copied formatting.

4. Release the mouse button, and Excel copies the formatting and applies it to the selected cells.

TIP

Painting Several Cells   To paint several areas with the same formatting at one time, double-click the **Format Painter** button to toggle it on. When you're through, press **Esc** or click the **Format Painter** button again to return to a normal mouse pointer.

In this lesson, you learned how to format numbers and to copy formatting from one cell to another. You also learned how to customize your text formatting to achieve the look you want. In the next lesson, you learn how to add borders and shading to the cells in your worksheet.

LESSON 12
Adding Cell Borders and Shading

In this lesson, you learn how to add borders and shading to your worksheets.

ADDING BORDERS TO CELLS

As you work with your worksheet onscreen, you'll notice that each cell is identified by gridlines that surround the cell. By default, these gridlines do not print; even if you choose to print them, they don't look very good on the printed page. To create well-defined lines on the printout (and onscreen, for that matter), you can add borders to selected cells or entire cell ranges. A border can appear on all four sides of a cell or only on selected sides; it's up to you.

TIP

> **Printing the Gridlines** It's true that gridlines do not print by default. But if you want to try printing your worksheet with gridlines, just to see what it looks like, open the **File** menu, select **Page Setup**, click the **Sheet** tab, check the **Gridlines** box, and click **OK**.

To add borders to a cell or range, perform the following steps:

1. Select the cell(s) around which you want a border to appear.

2. Open the **Format** menu and choose **Cells**. The Format Cells dialog box appears.

3. Click the **Border** tab to see the Border options shown in Figure 12.1.

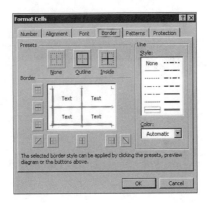

FIGURE 12.1
Choose Border options from the Format Cells dialog box.

4. Select the desired position, style (thickness), and color for the border. The position of the border is selected using the buttons along the left of the Border box. You also can click inside the **Border** box itself to place the border.

5. Click **OK** or press **Enter**.

When adding borders to a worksheet, hiding the gridlines onscreen gives you a preview of how the borders will look when printed. To hide gridlines, select the **Tools** menu, select **Options** (this opens the Options dialog box), and then select the **View** tab. Remove the check mark from the Gridlines check box, and then click **OK** to return to the worksheet. Selecting this option has no effect on whether the gridlines actually print, only on whether they are displayed onscreen.

 TIP

Add Borders from the Toolbar   You can use the Borders button on the Formatting toolbar to add a border to cells or cell ranges. Select the cells, and then click the **Borders** drop-down arrow on the Formatting toolbar to select a border type.

ADDING SHADING TO CELLS

Another way to offset certain cells in a worksheet is to add shading to those cells. With shading, you can add a color or gray shading to the background of a cell. You can add shading that consists of a solid color, or you can select a pattern as part of the shading options, such as a repeating diagonal line.

Follow these steps to add shading to a cell or range. As you make your selections, keep in mind that if you plan to print your worksheet with a black-and-white printer, the colors you select might not provide enough contrast on the printout to provide any differentiation between ranges of cells. You can always use the Print Preview command (as explained in Lesson 16, "Printing Your Workbook") to view your results in black and white before you print.

1. Select the cell(s) you want to shade.

2. Open the **Format** menu and choose **Cells**.

3. Click the **Patterns** tab. Excel displays the shading options (see Figure 12.2).

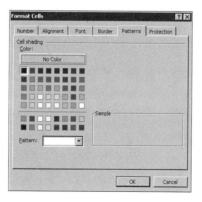

FIGURE 12.2
Choose colors and patterns from the Patterns tab of the Format Cells dialog box.

4. Click the **Pattern** drop-down arrow to see a grid that contains colors and patterns.

5. Select the shading color and pattern you want to use. The Color options let you choose a color for the overall shading. The Pattern options let you select a black or colored pattern that is placed on top of the cell-shading color you selected. A preview of the results appears in the Sample box.

6. When you have finished making your selections, click **OK**.

 TIP

> **Add Cell Shading with the Toolbar**   Select the cells you want to shade. Click the **Fill Color** drop-down arrow on the Formatting toolbar and then select the fill color from the Color palette that appears.

USING AUTOFORMAT

If you don't want to take the time to test different border types and shading styles, you can let Excel help you with the task of adding some emphasis and interest to the cells of your worksheet. You can take advantage of AutoFormat, which provides various predesigned table formats that you can apply to a worksheet.

To use predesigned formats, perform the following steps:

1. Select the cell(s) that contain the data you want to format. This could be the entire worksheet.

2. Select the **Format** menu, and then select **AutoFormat**. The AutoFormat dialog box appears (see Figure 12.3).

3. Scroll through the list to view the various AutoFormat styles provided. When you find a format that you want to use, click it to select it.

4. To prevent AutoFormat from overwriting certain existing formatting (such as numbers, alignment, or fonts), click the **Options** button and deselect the appropriate check boxes.

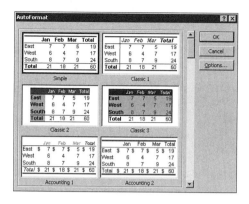

FIGURE 12.3
Select a format from the AutoFormat dialog box.

5. Click **OK**, and your worksheet is formatted.

TIP

> **Yuck! I Chose That?**   If you don't like what AutoFormat
> did to your worksheet, click the **Undo** button (or press
> **Ctrl+Z**).

APPLYING CONDITIONAL FORMATTING

Another useful formatting feature that Excel provides is conditional
formatting. Conditional formatting allows you to specify that certain
results in the worksheet be formatted so that they stand out from the
other entries in the worksheet. For example, if you wanted to track all
the monthly sales figures that are below a certain amount, you can use
conditional formatting to format them in red. Conditional formatting
formats only cells that meet a certain condition.

To apply conditional formatting, follow these steps:

1. Select the cells to which you want to apply the conditional
formatting.

2. Select the **Format** menu and select **Conditional Formatting**.
   The Conditional Formatting dialog box appears, as shown in
   Figure 12.4.

FIGURE 12.4
Apply formats conditionally to highlight certain values.

3. Be sure that **Cell Value Is** is selected in the Condition 1
   drop-down box on the left of the dialog box.

4. In the next drop-down box to the right, you select the condition. The default is Between. Other conditions include Equal
   To, Greater Than, Less Than, and other possibilities. Use the
   drop-down box to select the appropriate condition.

5. After selecting the condition, you must specify a cell or cells
   in the worksheet that Excel can use as a reference for the
   conditional formatting. For example, if you select Less Than
   as the condition, you must specify a cell in the worksheet
   that contains a value that can be used for comparison with
   the cells to which you are applying the conditional formatting. Click the **Shrink** button on the Conditional Formatting
   dialog box. You are returned to the worksheet. Select the reference cell for the condition.

6. Click the **Expand** button on the Conditional Formatting dialog box to expand the dialog box.

7. Now you can set the formatting that will be applied to cells
   that meet your condition. Click the **Format** button in the
   Conditional Formatting dialog box and select the formatting
   options for your condition in the Format Cells dialog box.

Then click **OK**. Figure 12.5 shows a conditional format that applies bold and italic to values that are less than the value contained in cell D6.

FIGURE 12.5
Set the various options for your conditional formatting.

8. After setting the conditions to be met for conditional formatting (you can click **Add** to set more than one condition), click **OK**.

You are returned to the worksheet. Cells that meet the condition you set up for conditional formatting will be formatted with the options you specified. Figure 12.6 shows cells that the settings used in Figure 12.5 conditionally formatted.

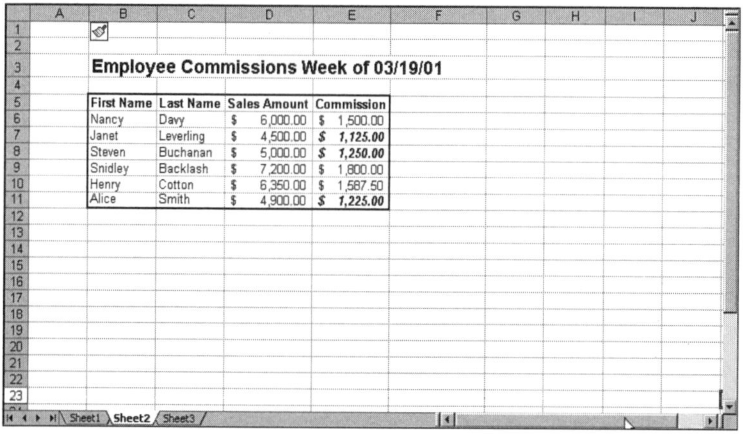

	A	B	C	D	E	F	G	H	I	J
1										
2										
3		**Employee Commissions Week of 03/19/01**								
4										
5		First Name	Last Name	Sales Amount	Commission					
6		Nancy	Davy	$ 6,000.00	$ 1,500.00					
7		Janet	Leverling	$ 4,500.00	*$ 1,125.00*					
8		Steven	Buchanan	$ 5,000.00	*$ 1,250.00*					
9		Snidley	Backlash	$ 7,200.00	$ 1,800.00					
10		Henry	Cotton	$ 6,350.00	$ 1,587.50					
11		Alice	Smith	$ 4,900.00	*$ 1,225.00*					
12										

FIGURE 12.6
Conditional formatting formats only the cells that meet your conditions.

TIP

> **Conditional Formatting Applied to Formulas**   You also can
> set up conditional formatting to highlight cells that con-
> tain a particular formula or function. Select **Formula Is**
> for Condition 1 in the Conditional Formatting dialog box
> and then type the formula or function in the box to the
> right.

In this lesson, you learned some ways to enhance the appearance of
your worksheets with borders and shading. In the next lesson, you
learn how to work with ranges and create range names.

LESSON 13

Working with Ranges

In this lesson, you learn how to select and name ranges.

WHAT IS A RANGE?

When you select a group of cells (which you have done numerous times in the various Excel lessons), you are in fact selecting a range. A cell range can consist of one cell or any group of contiguous cells.

Ranges are referred to by their anchor points (the upper-left corner and the lower-right corner). For example, a range that begins with cell C10 and ends with I14 is referred to as C10:I14.

PLAIN ENGLISH

Range   A group of contiguous cells on an Excel worksheet.

Although selecting ranges certainly is not rocket science (however, a few tricks for selecting cell ranges are discussed in the next section), you can do several things with a selected range of cells. For example, you can select a range of cells and print them (rather than printing the entire worksheet). You also can name ranges, which makes it much easier to include the cell range in a formula or function (you learn about range names and using range names in formulas later in the lesson).

SELECTING A RANGE

To select a range using the mouse, follow these steps:

1. Move the mouse pointer to the upper-left corner of a range.

2. Click and hold the left mouse button.

3. Drag the mouse to the lower-right corner of the range and release the mouse button. The cells are highlighted on the worksheet (see Figure 13.1).

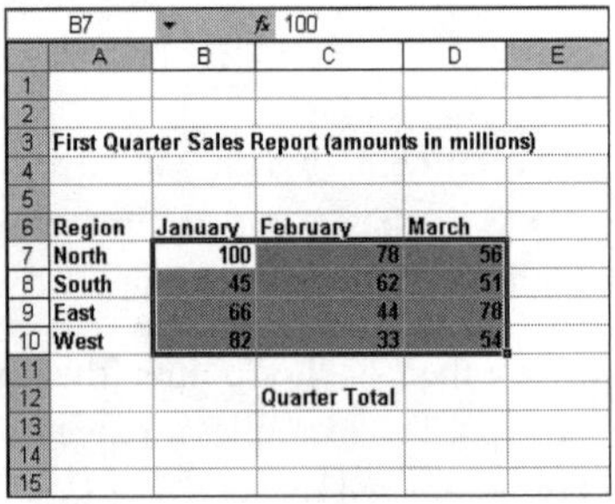

FIGURE 13.1
A range is any combination of cells that forms a rectangle or a square.

Techniques that you can use to quickly select a row, a column, an entire worksheet, or several ranges are shown in Table 13.1.

Table 13.1   Selection Techniques

To Select This	Do This
Several ranges	Select the first range, hold down the **Ctrl** key, and select the next range. Continue holding down the **Ctrl** key while you select additional ranges.
Row	Click the row heading number at the left edge of the worksheet. You also can press **Shift+Spacebar**. To select several adjacent rows, drag over their headers. To select nonadjacent rows, press **Ctrl** as you click each row's header.

Table 13.1   (continued)

To Select This	Do This
Column	Click the column heading letter at the top edge of the worksheet. You also can press **Ctrl+Spacebar**.
Entire worksheet	Click the **Select All** button (the blank rectangle in the upper-left corner of the worksheet, above row 1 and left of column A). You also can press **Ctrl+A**.
The same range on several sheets	Press and hold **Ctrl** as you click the worksheets you want to use, and then select the range in the usual way.
Range that is out of view	Press **Ctrl+G** (**Go To**) or click in the **Name** box on the Formula bar and type the address of the range you want to select. For example, to select the range R100 to T250, type **R100:T250** and press **Enter**.

TIP

> **Deselecting a Range**   To deselect a range, click any cell in the worksheet.

Selected cells are not highlighted in reverse video, as in previous versions of Excel, but in a slightly grayed tone, so you still can read your data.

Naming Ranges

Up to this point, when you have created formulas or functions or formatted cells in a worksheet, you have specified cells and cell ranges using the cell addresses. You also can name a cell or range of cells. For example, you could select a range of values and assign that range a name. You also could select a range of cells that includes your expenses and name that range EXPENSES. You then can name a range of cells that includes your income and name that range

INCOME. It would be very simple to then create a formula that subtracts your expenses from your income using the range names that you created. The formulas would be written as follows:

`=INCOME-EXPENSES`

Using range names in formulas and functions definitely can make your life easier. Range names are very useful when you create formulas or functions that pull information from more than one worksheet in a workbook or different workbooks. You can even use a range name to create a chart (you learn about charts in Lesson 17, "Creating Charts").

Follow these steps to name a range:

1. Select the range you want to name (the cells must be located on the same worksheet). If you want to name a single cell, simply select that cell.

2. Select the **Insert** menu, point at **Name**, and then select **Define**. The Define Name dialog box appears (see Figure 13.2).

FIGURE 13.2
Use the Define Name dialog box to name a cell range.

3. Type the name for the range in the box at the top of the dialog box. You can use up to 255 characters, and valid range names can include letters, numbers, periods, and underlines, but no spaces.

4. Click the **Add** button to name the range. The name is added to the list of range names.

5. Click **OK**.

TIP

> **Selecting a Different Range**   You can change the selected range from the Define Name dialog box. Click the **Shrink** button at the bottom of the dialog box, and then select the range on the worksheet. To return to the dialog box, click the **Expand** button on the Define Name dialog box.

You also can use the Define Name dialog box to delete any unwanted range names. Select **Insert**, point at **Name**, and then select **Define**. Select an unwanted range name from the list and click the **Delete** button. To close the dialog box, click **OK**.

TIP

> **Quickly Create a Range Name**   You also can create a range name by typing it into the Name box on the Formula bar. Select the cell range, click in the Name box, and type the name for the range. Then press **Enter**.

CREATING RANGE NAMES FROM WORKSHEET LABELS

You also can create range names using the column and row labels that you have created for your worksheet. The row labels are used to create a range name for each row of cells, and the column labels are used to create a range name for each column of cells. Follow these steps:

1. Select the worksheet, including the column and row labels.

2. Select the **Insert** menu, point at **Name**, and then select **Create**. The Create Names dialog box appears (see Figure 13.3).

FIGURE 13.3
Use the Create Names dialog box to create range names for the cells in the worksheet.

3. Click in the check boxes that define the position of the row and column labels in the worksheet.

4. After specifying the location of the row and column labels, click **OK**.

You can check the range names (and their range of cells) that were created using the Create Name feature in the Define Name dialog box. Select **Insert**, point at **Name**, and then select **Define**. All the range names that you created appear in the Names in Workbook list.

Inserting a Range Name into a Formula or Function

As previously discussed in this lesson, range names make it easy for you to specify a range of cells in a formula or function. To insert a range name into a formula or function, follow these steps:

1. Click in the cell where you want to place the formula or function.

2. Type the formula or function (begin the formula or function with the equal sign).

3. When you are ready to insert the range name into the formula or function, select the **Insert** menu, point at **Name**, and select **Paste**. The Paste Name dialog box appears (see Figure 13.4).

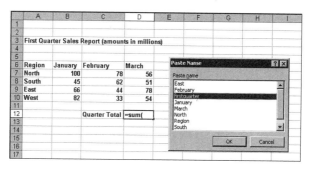

FIGURE 13.4
Use the Paste Name dialog box to insert a range name into a formula or function.

4. Select the range name you want to place in the formula or function, and then click **OK**.

5. Finish typing the formula or function (including the appropriate operators).

6. Press **Enter** to place the formula or function into the cell and return the calculated value.

In this lesson, you learned how to select and name ranges. You also learned how to insert a range name in a formula or function. In the next lesson, you learn how to manipulate cells, delete and add rows and columns, and work with column widths and row heights.

LESSON 14

Inserting and Removing Cells, Rows, and Columns

In this lesson, you learn how to rearrange the data in your worksheet by adding and removing cells, rows, and columns. You also learn how to adjust the width of your columns and the height of your rows to best use the worksheet space.

INSERTING ROWS AND COLUMNS

As you edit and enhance your worksheets, you might need to add rows or columns within the worksheet. Inserting entire rows and columns into your worksheet is very straightforward. Follow these steps:

1. To insert a single row or column, select a cell to the right of where you want to insert a column, or below where you want to insert a row.

   To insert multiple columns or rows, select the number of columns or rows you want to insert. To insert columns, drag over the column letters at the top of the worksheet. To insert rows, drag over the row numbers. For example, select three column letters or row numbers to insert three rows or columns.

2. Select the **Insert** menu, and then select **Rows** or **Columns**. Excel inserts rows above your selection and columns to the left of your selection. The inserted rows or columns contain the same formatting as the cells (or rows and columns) you

selected in step 1. Figure 14.1 shows a worksheet in which
additional columns have been added to a worksheet.

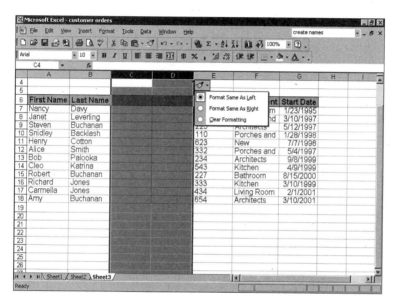

FIGURE 14.1
Columns can be inserted easily into an Excel worksheet.

As you can see, when you insert rows or columns, the Insert Options
shortcut icon appears to the right of the inserted columns, or below
inserted rows. Use the Insert Options menu to specify from where the
column or row should copy its formatting. For example, in the case of
inserted columns, you can choose to copy the formatting from the column to the right or left of the inserted column or columns, or you can
choose to clear the formatting in the inserted columns.

TIP

> **Fast Insert**   To quickly insert rows or columns, select
> one or more rows or columns, right-click one of them,
> and choose **Insert** from the shortcut menu.

REMOVING ROWS AND COLUMNS

When you delete a row in your worksheet, the rows below the deleted row move up to fill the space. When you delete a column, the columns to the right shift left.

Follow these steps to delete a row or column:

1. Click the row number or column letter of the row or column you want to delete. You can select more than one row or column by dragging over the row numbers or column letters.

2. Select the **Edit** menu, and then select **Delete**. Excel deletes the rows or columns and renumbers the remaining rows and columns sequentially. All cell references in formulas and functions are updated appropriately.

INSERTING CELLS

Although inserting rows and columns makes it easy to dramatically change the layout of a worksheet, occasionally you might need to insert only a cell, or cells, into a worksheet. Inserting cells causes the data in existing cells to shift down a row or over a column to create a space for the new cells.

CAUTION

> **Watch Your Formulas and Functions**   Inserting cells into a worksheet can throw off the cell references in formulas and functions. Double-check your formulas and functions after inserting cells to be sure the calculations are acting on the appropriate cell addresses.

To insert a single cell or a group of cells, follow these steps:

1. Select the area where you want the new cells inserted. Excel inserts the same number of cells as you select.

2. Select the **Insert** menu, and then select **Cells**. The Insert dialog box appears (see Figure 14.2).

3. Select **Shift Cells Right** or **Shift Cells Down** (or you can choose to have an entire row or column inserted).

4. Click **OK**. Excel inserts the cells and shifts the adjacent cells in the direction you specify.

You will find that inserting cells is useful if you have entered rows of information and have mismatched data, such as a customer's name with someone else's order information. Inserting a couple of cells enables you to quickly edit the data without having to delete data or insert a new row.

TIP

Drag Insert Cells   A quick way to insert cells is to select the number of cells you want, hold down the **Shift** key, and then drag the fill handle up, down, left, or right to set the position of the new cells.

REMOVING CELLS

You already learned about deleting the data in cells back in Lesson 10, "Editing Worksheets," and you learned that you also can delete cells from a worksheet. Eliminating cells from the worksheet, rather than just clearing their contents, means that the cells surrounding the deleted cells in the worksheet are moved to fill the gap that is created. Remove cells only if you want the other cells in the worksheet to shift to new positions. Otherwise, just delete the data in the cells or type new data into the cells.

If you want to remove cells from a worksheet, follow these steps:

1. Select the cell or range of cells you want to remove.

2. Open the **Edit** menu and choose **Delete**. The Delete dialog box appears (see Figure 14.3).

FIGURE 14.3
Use the Delete dialog box to specify how the gap left by the deleted cells should be filled.

3. Select **Shift Cells Left** or **Shift Cells Up** to specify how the remaining cells in the worksheet should move to fill the gap left by the deleted cells.

4. Click **OK**. Surrounding cells shift to fill the gap left by the deleted cells.

As with inserting cells, you should check the cell references in your formulas and functions after removing cells from the worksheet. Be sure that your calculations are referencing the appropriate cells on the worksheet.

Adjusting Column Width and Row Height with a Mouse

When you are working in Excel, it doesn't take long to realize that the default column width of 8.43 characters doesn't accommodate long text entries or values that have been formatted as currency or other numeric formats. You can adjust the width of a column quickly by using the mouse.

You also can adjust row heights using the mouse. However, your row heights will adjust to any font size changes that you make to data held in a particular row. Row heights also adjust if you wrap text entries within them. You probably will find that you need to adjust column widths in your worksheets far more often than row heights.

CAUTION

What Is ########?   When you format a value in a cell with a numeric formatting, and Excel cannot display the result in the cell because of the column width, Excel places ######## in the cell. This lets you know that you need to adjust the column width so that it can accommodate the entry and its formatting.

To adjust a column width with the mouse, place the mouse pointer on the right border of the column. A sizing tool appears, as shown in Figure 14.4. Drag the column border to the desired width. You also can adjust the column width to automatically accommodate the widest entry within a column; just double-click the sizing tool. This is called AutoFit, and the column adjusts according to the widest entry.

If you want to adjust several columns at once, select the columns. Place the mouse on any of the column borders, and drag to increase or decrease the width. Each selected column is adjusted to the width you select.

Changing row heights is similar to adjusting column widths. Place the mouse on the lower border of a row and drag the sizing tool to increase or decrease the row height. To change the height of multiple rows, select the rows, and then drag the border of any of the selected rows to the desired height.

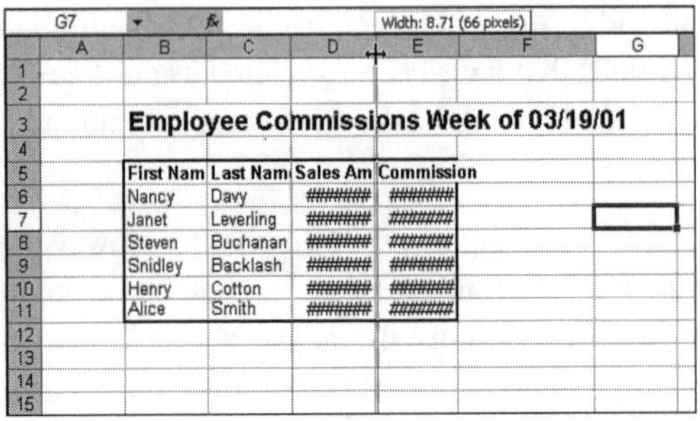

FIGURE 14.4
Use the column width sizing tool to adjust the width of a column.

USING THE FORMAT MENU FOR PRECISE CONTROL

If you want to precisely specify the width of a column or columns, or the height of a row or rows, you can enter specific sizes using a dialog box. This provides you with a little more control than just dragging a row height or column width.

To specify a column width, follow these steps:

1. Select the columns you want to change.

2. Select the **Format** menu, point at **Column**, and then select **Width**. The Column Width dialog box appears (see Figure 14.5).

3. Type the column width into the dialog box (the width is measured in number of characters).

4. Click **OK**. Your column(s) width is adjusted accordingly.

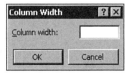

FIGURE 14.5
Column widths also can be specified in the Column Width dialog box.

Adjusting row heights is similar to adjusting column widths. Select the row or rows, and then select the **Format** menu, point at **Rows**, and select **Height**. In the Row Height dialog box that appears, type in the row height and click **OK**.

In this lesson, you learned how to insert and delete cells, rows, and columns. You also learned how to change row heights and column widths. In the next lesson, you will learn how to select, insert, delete, and move your Excel worksheets.

LESSON 15
Managing Your Worksheets

In this lesson, you learn how to add and delete worksheets within workbooks. You also learn how to copy, move, and rename worksheets.

SELECTING WORKSHEETS

By default, each workbook consists of three worksheets whose names appear on tabs at the bottom of the Excel window. You can add or delete worksheets as desired. One advantage of having multiple worksheets within a workbook is that it enables you to organize your data into logical chunks. Another advantage of having separate worksheets for your data is that you easily can reorganize the worksheets (and the associated data) in a workbook.

Before you learn about the details of inserting, deleting, and copying worksheets, you should know how to select one or more worksheets. Selecting a single worksheet is a method of moving from worksheet to worksheet in a workbook.

Selecting multiple worksheets in a workbook, however, is another story. Selecting multiple workbooks enables you to apply the same autoformatting, or cell formatting, to more than one worksheet at a time. This is particularly useful if you have several worksheets in a workbook that will end up looking very much the same. For example, you might have a workbook that contains four worksheets—each of the worksheets serving as a quarterly summary. Because the design of these worksheets is similar, applying formatting to more than one sheet at a time enables you to keep the sheets consistent in appearance.

To select a worksheet or worksheets, perform one of the following actions:

- To select a single worksheet, click its tab. The tab is highlighted to show that the worksheet is selected.

- To select several neighboring or adjacent worksheets, click the tab of the first worksheet in the group, and then hold down the **Shift** key and click the tab of the last worksheet in the group. Each worksheet tab will be highlighted (but only the first sheet selected will be visible).

- To select several nonadjacent worksheets, hold down the **Ctrl** key and click each worksheet's tab.

If you select two or more worksheets, they remain selected as a group until you ungroup them. To ungroup worksheets, do one of the following:

- Right-click one of the selected worksheets and choose **Ungroup Sheets**.

- Hold down the **Shift** key and click the tab of the active worksheet.

- Click any worksheet tab to deselect all the other worksheets.

INSERTING WORKSHEETS

When you create a new workbook, it contains three worksheets. You easily can add additional worksheets to a workbook.

Follow these steps to add a worksheet to a workbook:

1. Select the worksheet that you want to be to the right of the inserted worksheet. For example, if you select the quarter3

sheet shown in Figure 15.1, the new sheet will be inserted to
the left of quarter3.

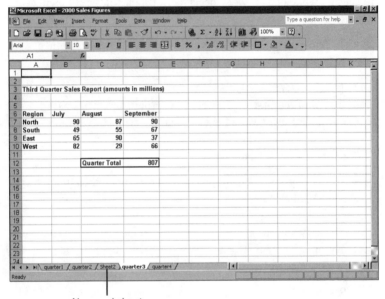

New worksheet

FIGURE 15.1
Excel inserts the new worksheet to the left of the active worksheet.

2. Select the **Insert** menu.

3. Select **Worksheet**. Excel inserts the new worksheet to the
   right of the previously selected worksheet.

TIP

> **Use the Shortcut Menu**   A faster way to work with work-
> sheets is to right-click the worksheet tab. This brings up
> a shortcut menu that lets you insert, delete, rename,
> move, copy, or select all worksheets.

TIP

> **Start with More Sheets** You can change the default
> number of worksheets Excel places in a new workbook
> by opening the **Tools** menu, selecting **Options**, clicking
> the **General** tab, and then changing the number in the
> **Sheets in New Workbook** option. Click **OK** to save your
> changes. The maximum value for the number of sheets
> in a workbook is determined by the amount of memory
> on your computer. You might find that using more than
> 20 sheets in a workbook that are full of data start to
> slow down Excel's overall performance.

DELETING WORKSHEETS

If you find that you have a worksheet you no longer need, or if you
plan to use only one worksheet of the three that Excel puts into each
workbook by default, you can remove the unwanted worksheets.
Here's how you remove a worksheet:

1. Select the worksheets you want to delete.

2. Select the **Edit** menu, and then select **Delete Sheet**.

3. If the sheet contains data, a dialog box appears, asking you to
   confirm the deletion. Click **Delete** to delete the sheet. You
   will lose any data that the sheet contained.

You can delete multiple sheets if you want. Use the techniques discussed earlier in this lesson to select multiple sheets, and then use
steps 2 and 3 in this section to delete the sheets.

MOVING AND COPYING WORKSHEETS

You can move or copy worksheets within a workbook, or from one
workbook to another. Copying a worksheet enables you to copy the

formatting of the sheet and other items, such as the column labels and
the row labels. Follow these steps:

1. Select the worksheet, or worksheets, you want to move or
   copy. If you want to move or copy worksheets from one
   workbook to another, be sure the target workbook is open.

2. Select the **Edit** menu and choose **Move or Copy Sheet**. The
   Move or Copy dialog box appears, as shown in Figure 15.2.

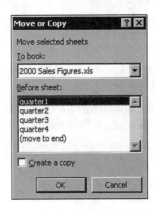

FIGURE 15.2
The Move or Copy dialog box asks where you want to copy or move a worksheet.

3. To move the worksheets to a different workbook, be sure that
   workbook is open, and then select that workbook's name
   from the To Book drop-down list. If you want to move or
   copy the worksheets to a new workbook, select **(New Book)**
   in the To Book drop-down list. Excel creates a new workbook
   and then copies or moves the worksheets to it.

4. In the Before Sheet list box, choose which worksheet you
   want to follow the selected worksheets.

5. To move the selected worksheet, skip to step 6. To copy the
   selected worksheets instead of moving them, select the
   Create a Copy option.

6. Select **OK**. The selected worksheets are copied or moved as specified.

MOVING A WORKSHEET WITHIN A WORKBOOK WITH DRAG AND DROP

A fast way to copy or move worksheets within a workbook is to use drag and drop. First, select the tab of the worksheet(s) you want to copy or move.

Move the mouse pointer over one of the selected tabs, click and hold the mouse button, and drag the tab where you want it moved. To copy the worksheet, hold down the **Ctrl** key while dragging. When you release the mouse button, the worksheet is copied or moved.

MOVING OR COPYING A WORKSHEET BETWEEN WORKBOOKS WITH DRAG AND DROP

You also can use the Drag-and-Drop feature to quickly copy or move worksheets between workbooks.

1. Open the workbooks you want to use for the copy or move.

2. Select **Window** and then **Arrange**. The Arrange dialog box opens.

3. You can arrange the different workbook windows horizontally, vertically, tiled, or cascaded in the Excel application window. For more than two open workbooks, your best selection is probably the **Tiled** option (see Figure 15.3).

4. After making your selection, click **OK** to arrange the workbook windows within the Excel application window.

5. Select the tab of the worksheet(s) you want to copy or move.

6. Move the mouse pointer over one of the selected tabs, click and hold the mouse button, and drag the tab where you want it moved. To copy the worksheet, hold down the **Ctrl** key while dragging.

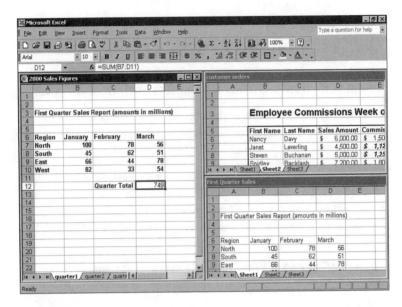

FIGURE 15.3
You can arrange multiple workbooks in the Excel window and then move or copy worksheets.

7. When you release the mouse button, the worksheet is copied or moved.

CHANGING WORKSHEET TAB NAMES

By default, all worksheets are named SheetX, where X is a number starting with the number 1. You should change the names that appear on the tabs so you'll have a better idea of the information each sheet contains. Here's how to do it:

1. Double-click the tab of the worksheet you want to rename. The current name is highlighted.

2. Type a new name for the worksheet and press **Enter**. Excel replaces the default name with the name you type.

In this lesson, you learned how to insert, delete, move, copy, and rename worksheets. In the next lesson, you learn how to preview and print your Excel workbooks.

LESSON 16
Printing Your Workbook

In this lesson, you learn how to preview your print jobs, repeat row and column headings on pages, and add headers and footers to your worksheets. You also learn how to print an entire workbook and large worksheets.

PREVIEWING A PRINT JOB

After you've finished a particular worksheet and want to send it to the printer, you might want to take a quick look at how the worksheet will look on the printed page. You will find that worksheets don't always print the way they look on the screen.

 To preview a print job, select the **File** menu, and then select **Print Preview**, or click the **Print Preview** button on the Standard toolbar. Your workbook appears in the same format in which it will appear when sent to the printer (see Figure 16.1).

LEAD IN HERE

> **A Close-Up View** Zoom in on any area of the preview by clicking it with the mouse pointer (which looks like a magnifying glass). Or, use the **Zoom** button on the Print Preview toolbar.

When you have finished previewing your worksheet, you can print the worksheet by clicking the **Print** button, or you can return to the worksheet by clicking **Close**.

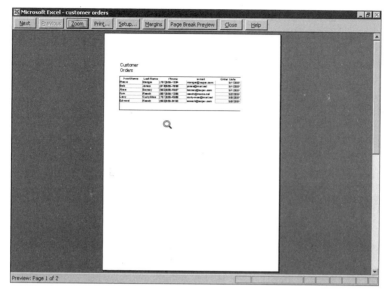

FIGURE 16.1
By previewing the worksheet, you can determine which page layout attributes need adjusting.

CHANGING THE PAGE SETUP

After you preview your worksheet, you might want to adjust page attributes, or change the way the page is set up for printing. For example, you might want to print the column and row labels on every page of the printout. This is particularly useful for large worksheets that span several pages; then, you don't have to keep looking back to the first page of the printout to determine what the column headings are.

Printing column and row labels and other worksheet page attributes, such as scaling a worksheet to print out on a single page or adding headers or footers to a worksheet printout, are handled in the Page Setup dialog box. To access this dialog box, select the **File** menu and select **Page Setup** (see Figure 16.2).

The following sections provide information on some of the most common page setup attributes that you will work with before printing your Excel worksheets.

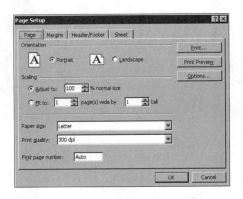

FIGURE 16.2
Access the Page Setup dialog box to be sure your worksheet page is set to print correctly.

PRINTING COLUMN AND ROW LABELS ON EVERY PAGE

Excel provides a way for you to select labels and titles that are located on the top edge and left side of a large worksheet and to print them on every page of the printout. This option is useful when a worksheet is too wide to print on a single page. If you don't use this option, the extra columns or rows are printed on subsequent pages without any descriptive labels.

Follow these steps to print column or row labels on every page:

1. Select the **File** menu, and then select **Page Setup**. The Page Setup dialog box appears.

2. Click the **Sheet** tab to display the Sheet options (see Figure 16.3).

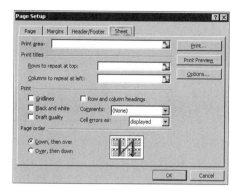

FIGURE 16.3
Use the Sheet tab to specify headings you want to repeat in the printout.

3. To repeat column labels and a worksheet title, click the **Shrink** button to the right of the Rows to Repeat at Top text box.

4. Drag over the rows that you want to print on every page. A dashed line border surrounds the selected area, and absolute cell references with dollar signs ($) appear in the Rows to Repeat at Top text box.

5. Click the **Expand** button on the collapsed dialog box to expand the Page Setup dialog box.

6. To repeat row labels that appear on the left of the worksheet, click the **Shrink** button to the right of the Columns to Repeat at Left text box. Excel reduces the Page Setup dialog box.

7. Select the columns that contain the row labels you want to repeat.

8. Click the **Expand** button to return again to the Page Setup dialog box.

9. To print your worksheet, click **Print** to display the Print dialog box. Then click **OK**.

NOTE

> **Select Your Print Area Carefully**   If you select rows or columns to repeat, and those rows or columns are part of your print area, the selected rows or columns might print twice. To fix this, select your print area again, leaving out the rows or columns you're repeating.

LEAD IN HERE

> **Access Print Preview from Other Dialog Boxes**   Page Setup and Print dialog boxes also include a Preview button, so you can check any last-minute changes you made in either dialog box without having to close the box first.

Scaling a Worksheet to Fit on a Page

If your worksheet is too large to print on one page even after you change the orientation and margins, consider using the **Fit To** option. This option shrinks the worksheet to make it fit on the specified number of pages. You can specify the document's width and height.

Follow these steps to scale a worksheet to fit on a page:

1. Select the **File** menu, and then select **Page Setup**. The Page Setup dialog box appears.

2. Click the **Page** tab to display the Page options.

3. In the Fit to XX Page(s) Wide by XX Tall text boxes, enter the number of pages into which you want Excel to fit your data.

4. Click **OK** to close the Page Setup dialog box and return to your worksheet, or click the **Print** button in the Page Setup dialog box to display the Print dialog box, and then click **OK** to print your worksheet.

TIP

> **Change the Page Orientation**   The Page tab of the Page
> Setup dialog box also enables you to change the orienta-
> tion of the worksheet from Portrait to Landscape.
> Landscape orientation is useful if you have a worksheet
> with a large number of columns.

ADDING HEADERS AND FOOTERS

Excel enables you to add headers and footers to your worksheets that
will appear at the top and bottom of every page of the printout
(respectively). The information can include any text, as well as page
numbers, the current date and time, the workbook filename, and the
worksheet tab name.

You can choose the headers and footers suggested by Excel, or you
can include any text plus special commands to control the appearance
of the header or footer. For example, you can apply bold, italic, or
underline to the header or footer text. You also can left-align, center,
or right-align your text in a header or footer (see Lesson 11,
"Changing How Numbers and Text Look," for more information).

To add headers and footers, follow these steps:

1. Select the **File** menu, and then select **Page Setup**. The Page
   Setup dialog box appears. Click the **Header/Footer** tab on
   the dialog box (see Figure 16.4).

2. To select a header, click the **Header** drop-down arrow. Excel
   displays a list of suggested header information. Scroll
   through the list and click a header you want. The sample
   header appears at the top of the Header/Footer tab.

TIP

> **Don't See One You Like?**   If none of the suggested head-
> ers or footers suit you, click the **Custom Header** or **Custom
> Footer** button and enter your own information.

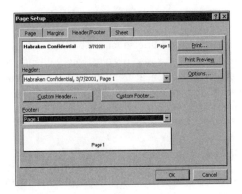

FIGURE 16.4
Add headers and footers with Header/Footer options.

3. To select a footer, click the **Footer** drop-down arrow. Excel displays a list of suggested footer information. Scroll through the list and click a footer you want. The sample footer appears at the bottom of the Header/Footer tab.

4. Click **OK** to close the Page Setup dialog box and return to your worksheet, or click the **Print** button to display the Print dialog box and click **OK** to print your worksheet.

TIP

> **Don't Want Headers or Footers Anymore?**   To remove the header and/or footer, choose **(None)** in the **Header** and/or **Footer** lists.

PRINTING YOUR WORKBOOK

After adjusting the page settings for the worksheet and previewing your data, it is time to print. You can print selected data, selected sheets, or the entire workbook.

To print your workbook, follow these steps:

1. If you want to print a portion of the worksheet, select the range of cells you want to print. To print only a chart, click it (you learn about creating charts in Lesson 17, "Creating Charts"). If you want to print one or more worksheets within the workbook, select the sheet tabs (see Lesson 15, "Managing Your Worksheets"). To print the entire workbook, skip this step.

2. Select the **File** menu, and then select **Print** (or press **Ctrl+P**). The Print dialog box appears, as shown in Figure 16.5.

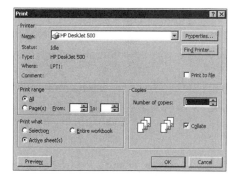

FIGURE 16.5
In the Print dialog box, select your printer and a page range to print.

TIP

Print Using the Default Settings   If you click the **Print** button (instead of using the **File** menu and clicking **Print**), Excel prints your current worksheet without letting you make any selections.

3. Select the options you would like to use:

   - **Print Range**—Lets you print one or more pages. For example, if the selected print area contains 15 pages and you want to print only pages 5–10, select **Page(s)**, and then type the numbers of the first and last page you want to print into the **From** and **To** boxes.

- **Print What**—Enables you to print the currently selected cells, the selected worksheets, or the entire workbook.

- **Copies**—Enables you to print more than one copy of the selection, worksheet, or workbook.

- **Collate**—Enables you to print a complete copy of the selection, worksheet, or workbook before the first page of the next copy is printed. This option is available when you print multiple copies.

4. Click **OK** to print your selection, worksheet, or workbook.

While your job is printing, you can continue working in Excel. If the printer is working on another job that you (or someone else, in the case of a network printer) sent, Windows holds the job until the printer is ready for it.

Sometimes, you might want to delete a job while it is printing or before it prints. For example, suppose you think of other numbers to add to the worksheet or realize that you forgot to format some text; you'll want to fix these things before you print the file. To display the print queue and delete a print job, follow these steps:

1. Double-click the **Printer** icon in the Windows system tray (at the far right of the taskbar), and the print queue appears.

2. Click the job you want to delete.

3. Select the **Document** menu, and then select **Cancel Printing**, or just press **Delete**.

   To delete all the files from the print queue, open the **Printer** menu and select **Purge Print Documents**. This cancels the print jobs but doesn't delete the files from your computer.

SELECTING A LARGE WORKSHEET PRINT AREA

You do not always have to print an entire worksheet; instead, you easily can tell Excel what part of the worksheet you want to print by selecting the print area yourself. If the area you select is too large to fit on one page, no problem; Excel breaks it into multiple pages. When you do not select a print area yourself, Excel prints either the entire worksheet or the entire workbook, depending on the options set in the Print dialog box.

To select a print area, follow these steps:

1. Click the upper-left cell of the range you want to print.

2. Drag downward and to the right until the range you want is selected.

3. Select the **File** menu, point at **Print Area**, and then select **Set Print Area**.

To remove the print area so you can print the entire worksheet again, select the **File** menu, select **Print Area**, and select **Clear Print Area**.

ADJUSTING PAGE BREAKS

When you print a workbook, Excel determines the page breaks based on the paper size, the margins, and the selected print area. To make the pages look better and to break information in logical places, you might want to override the automatic page breaks with your own breaks. However, before you add page breaks, try these options:

• Adjust the widths of individual columns to best use the space.

• Consider printing the workbook using the Landscape orientation.

• Change the left, right, top, and bottom margins to smaller values.

After trying these options, if you still want to insert page breaks, Excel offers you an option of previewing exactly where the page breaks appear, and then adjusting them. Follow these steps:

1. Select the **View** menu and select **Page Break Preview**.

2. If a message appears telling you how to adjust page breaks, click **OK**. Your worksheet is displayed with page breaks, as shown in Figure 16.6.

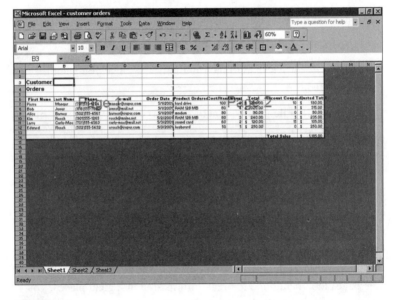

FIGURE 16.6
Check your page breaks before printing your worksheet.

3. To move a page break, drag the blue line to the desired location.

To delete a page break, drag it off the screen.

To insert a page break, move to the first cell in the column to the right of where you want the page break inserted, or move to the row below where you want the break inserted. For example, to insert a page break between columns G and H, move to cell H1. To insert a page break between rows 24 and 25, move to cell A25. Then, open the **Insert** menu and select **Page Break**. A dashed line appears to the left of the selected column or above the selected row.

4. To exit Page Break Preview and return to your normal worksheet view, open the **View** menu and select **Normal**.

In this lesson, you learned how to print all or part of your workbook, as well as how to print a large worksheet. You also learned to adjust page setup attributes, such as column and row labels and headers and footers. In the next lesson, you learn how to create Excel charts.

LESSON 17
Creating Charts

In this lesson, you learn how to create graphical representations (charts) of workbook data.

UNDERSTANDING CHARTING TERMINOLOGY

Charts enable you to create a graphical representation of data in a worksheet. You can use charts to make data more understandable to people who view your printed worksheets. Before you start creating charts, you should familiarize yourself with the following terminology:

- **Data Series**—The bars, pie wedges, lines, or other elements that represent plotted values in a chart. For example, a chart might show a set of similar bars that reflects a series of values for the same item. The bars in the same data series all would have the same pattern. If you had more than one pattern of bars, each pattern would represent a separate data series. For example, charting the sales for Territory 1 versus Territory 2 would require two data series—one for each territory. Often, data series correspond to rows of data in your worksheet (although they can correspond to columns of data if that is how you have arranged the information in your worksheet).

- **Categories**—Categories reflect the number of elements in a series. You might have two data series that compare the sales of two territories and four categories that compare these sales over four quarters. Some charts have only one category, and others have several. Categories normally correspond to the columns in your worksheet, with the category labels coming from the column headings.

- **Axis**—One side of a chart. A two-dimensional chart has an x-axis (horizontal) and a y-axis (vertical). The x-axis contains the data series and categories in the chart. If you have more than one category, the x-axis often contains labels that define what each category represents. The y-axis reflects the values of the bars, lines, or plot points. In a three-dimensional chart, the z-axis represents the vertical plane, and the x-axis (distance) and y-axis (width) represent the two sides on the floor of the chart.

- **Legend**—Defines the separate series of a chart. For example, the legend for a pie chart shows what each piece of the pie represents.

- **Gridlines**—Typically, gridlines appear along the y-axis of the chart. The y-axis is where your values are displayed, although they can emanate from the x-axis as well (the x-axis is where label information normally appears on the chart). Gridlines help you determine a point's exact value.

WORKING WITH DIFFERENT CHART TYPES

With Excel, you can create many types of charts. Some common chart types appear in Figure 17.1. The chart type you choose depends on the kind of data you're trying to chart and how you want to present that data. The following are the major chart types and their purposes:

- **Pie**—Use this chart type to show the relationship among parts of a whole.

- **Bar**—Use this chart type to compare values at a given point in time.

- **Column**—Similar to the bar chart. Use this chart type to emphasize the difference between items.

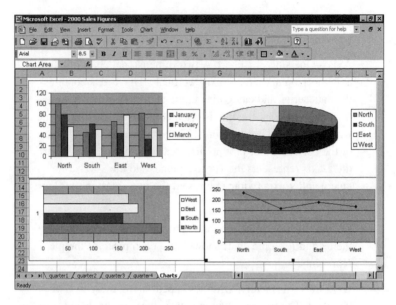

FIGURE 17.1
Excel chart types enable you to analyze and present your data.

- **Line**—Use this chart type to emphasize trends and the change of values over time.

- **Scatter**—Similar to a line chart. Use this chart type to emphasize the difference between two sets of values.

- **Area**—Similar to the line chart. Use this chart type to emphasize the amount of change in values over time.

Most of these basic chart types also come in three-dimensional varieties. In addition to looking more professional than the standard flat charts, 3D charts often can help your audience distinguish between different sets of data.

CREATING AND SAVING A CHART

You can place your new chart on the same worksheet that contains the chart data (an embedded chart) or on a separate worksheet (a chart sheet). If you create an embedded chart, it typically is printed side by side with your worksheet data. Embedded charts are useful for showing the actual data and its graphical representation side by side. If you create a chart on a separate worksheet, however, you can print it independently. Both types of charts are linked to the worksheet data that they represent, so when you change the data, the chart is updated automatically.

The **Chart Wizard** button on the Standard toolbar enables you to quickly create a chart. To use the Chart Wizard, follow these steps:

1. Select the data you want to chart. If you typed column or row labels (such as Qtr 1, Qtr 2, and so on) that you want included in the chart, be sure you select those, too.

2. Click the **Chart Wizard** button on the Standard toolbar.

3. The **Chart Wizard - Step 1 of 4** dialog box appears (see Figure 17.2). Select a **Chart Type** and a **Chart Sub-Type** (a variation on the selected chart type). Click **Next**.

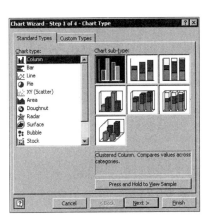

FIGURE 17.2
Choose the chart type using the Chart Wizard.

4. Next, Excel asks whether the selected range is correct. You can correct the range by typing a new range or by clicking

the **Shrink** button (located at the right end of the **Data Range** text box) and selecting the range you want to use.

5. By default, Excel assumes that your different data series are stored in rows. You can change this to columns, if necessary, by clicking the **Series in Columns** option. When you're ready for the next step, click **Next**.

6. Click the various tabs to change options for your chart (see Figure 17.3). For example, you can delete the legend by clicking the **Legend** tab and deselecting **Show Legend**. You can add a chart title on the **Titles** tab. Add data labels (labels that display the actual value being represented by each bar, line, and so on) by clicking the **Data Labels** tab. When you finish making changes, click **Next**.

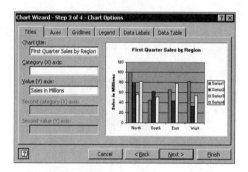

FIGURE 17.3
Select from various chart appearance options.

7. Finally, Excel asks whether you want to embed the chart (as an object) in the current worksheet (or any other existing worksheet in the workbook) or if you want to create a new worksheet for it. Make your selection and click the **Finish** button. Your completed chart appears.

TIP

Create a Chart Fast! To create a chart quickly, select the data you want to use and press **F11**. Excel creates a column chart (the default chart type) on its own sheet. You then can customize the chart as needed.

The charts you create are part of the current workbook. To save a chart, simply save the workbook that contains the chart.

MOVING AND RESIZING A CHART

To move an embedded chart, click anywhere in the chart area and drag it to the new location. To change the size of a chart, select the chart and drag one of its handles (the black squares that border the chart). Drag a corner handle to change the height and width, or drag a side handle to change only one dimension. (Note that you can't really resize a chart that is on a sheet by itself.)

PRINTING A CHART

If a chart is an embedded chart, it will print when you print the worksheet that contains the chart. If you want to print just the embedded chart, click it to select it, and then open the **File** menu and select **Print**. Be sure the **Selected Chart** option is turned on. Then, click **OK** to print the chart.

If you created a chart on a separate worksheet, you can print the chart separately by printing only that worksheet. For more information about printing, refer to Lesson 16, "Printing Your Workbook."

In this lesson, you learned about the different chart types and how to create them. You also learned how to save and print charts. In the next lesson, you will learn to enhance your Excel charts.

LESSON 18
Making Your Charts Look Better

In this lesson, you learn how to enhance your charts using the Chart toolbar and how to add titles, axis titles, and legends to a chart. You also learn how to manipulate text and colors on the chart.

SELECTING A CHART OBJECT

A chart is made up of several parts, or objects. For example, a chart can have a title, a legend, and different data series (data series appear on the y-axis, x-axis, or additional axes). To enhance these items on your chart, you first must select the item you want to fix up. To do this, simply click that part or select it from the Chart Objects box on the Chart toolbar (see the next section for help with the toolbar). When a part, such as the legend, is selected, handles (tiny black squares) appear around it, as shown in Figure 18.1.

TIP

> **Object**   Any one of the single items found on a chart, such as the legend or title.

When a chart object is selected, you can drag it to a new location. To resize an object, select it and drag one of its handles out to make the object larger, or drag it in to make it smaller. You actually can resize the whole chart by selecting it first and then dragging one of its handles.

Handles

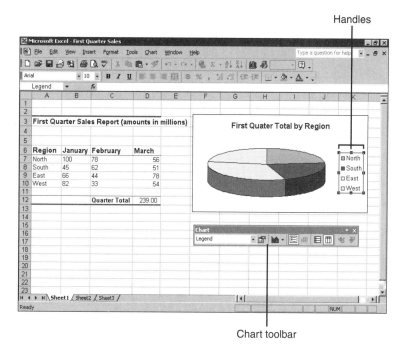

Chart toolbar

When a chart part is selected, it's surrounded by handles.

THE CHART TOOLBAR

You can use the Chart toolbar to quickly change chart attributes. Normally, the Chart toolbar is displayed whenever you select a chart object. If you don't see the Chart toolbar when the chart or any chart object is selected, select the **View** menu, select **Toolbars**, and then select **Chart**.

Table 18.1 describes each button on the **Chart** toolbar.

Table 18.1   Chart Toolbar Buttons

Button	Name	Use
Legend ▾	Chart Objects	Use this pull-down list to quickly select a particular object on the chart.
	Format Object	This button opens the format dialog box for the currently selected chart object.
	Chart Type	Use this pull-down menu to quickly change the type of chart.
	Legend	Use this button to display or hide the legend for the chart.
	Data Table	This button enables you to add a table of data to the chart or an axes that coincides with the data used to create the chart or that particular axis.
	By Row	Data used for the chart is held in your worksheet in either a row or a column. If the chart doesn't look correct, click this button to switch how the data is read from the worksheet (by row rather than by column) .

Table 18.1   (continued)

Button	Name	Use
▦	By Column	Use this button to switch how the data is read from the work-sheet. This button is used when data is arranged in columns.
✖	Angle Text	Use this button to angle Clockwise text in a title or label soit reads from bot-tom to top.
✖	Angle Text	Use this button to angle ounterclockwise text in a title or label so it reads from top to bottom.

CHANGING THE CHART TYPE

After you create your chart, you might find that a different chart type would be better suited for the type of data that you have in the work-sheet that was used to create the chart. To quickly change the chart type:

1. Click the chart to select it, or choose **Chart Area** from the Chart Objects drop-down list 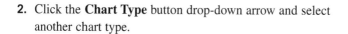 on the Chart toolbar. Selection handles will appear around the entire chart.

2. Click the **Chart Type** button drop-down arrow and select another chart type.

TIP

> **The Chart I Want Isn't Displayed!**   To change to a chart
> type that is not on the list, select the **Chart** menu, and
> then select **Chart Type**. The Chart Type dialog box opens.
> Choose the new chart type from the list provided.

ADDING A TITLE AND A LEGEND

Charts provide a great way to take numerical data and display it in a
"picture" format that most people can readily understand. However, a
title and legend will add clarity to your charts. The title tells you what
the chart is about, and legends are particularly useful because they
provide color coding of the different data ranges in the chart.

You also can add axis titles that appear along the x- and y-axes (and
the z-axis, if the chart is a 3-D chart). These titles provide additional
explanatory information related to the different chart axes. Follow
these steps:

1. Click the chart to select it, or choose **Chart Area** from the
   Chart Objects drop-down list on the Chart toolbar. Selection
   handles appear around the chart area.

2. Select the **Chart** menu, and then select **Chart Options**. The
   Chart Options dialog box appears.

3. Click the **Titles** tab (see Figure 18.2). Add a chart title and
   the different axes titles as needed. A sample chart is provided
   on the right to show you how your changes will look.

4. If you did not include a legend for the chart when you created the chart (as detailed in Lesson 17), click the **Legend**
   tab, and then click the **Show Legend** check box to select it.
   Use the different option buttons in the Placement box of the
   Legend tab to place the legend on the chart.

5. Click **OK** to close the dialog box and return to the chart.

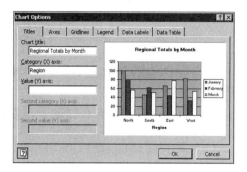

FIGURE 18.2
You can add axes titles to the chart.

FORMATTING CHART TEXT, COLORS, AND ALIGNMENT

Because the various text elements on a chart, such as the title or an axis title, are housed in their own text boxes, you can change the formatting for a particular object's text, including the color and alignment, by double-clicking that object. For example, if you double-click the chart title, the Format Chart Title dialog box opens, as shown in Figure 18.3.

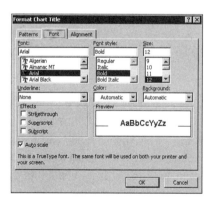

FIGURE 18.3
Double-click any text object in the chart to open its Format dialog box.

The Format dialog box for a particular chart object provides different tabs you can use to enhance the various elements of that object, such as the text font, borders and colors, and the text alignment. The following list describes each tab on the Format dialog box that you will run into when formatting various chart titles:

- **Font tab**—The Font tab enables you to change the font type and size, and add font attributes, such as bold, italic, and underline, to the text (refer to Figure 18.3).

- **Patterns tab**—The Patterns tab enables you to place a border around the text and select different fill colors for the box that surrounds the particular chart object. You can select the line type and fill color, and even place a shadow on the object's text box (see Figure 18.4).

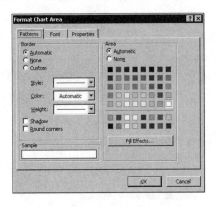

FIGURE 18.4
You can use the Patterns tab to add borders and fill colors to the chart object.

- **Alignment tab**—The Alignment tab enables you to control both the horizontal alignment (such as center or left) and vertical alignment (such as center or bottom) of the text in the chart object's text box. You can use the Orientation box on this tab to rotate the text in the box. Just drag the text alignment handle in the Orientation box to rotate the text.

When you have finished changing the attributes for a particular chart object text box, click the **OK** button in the dialog box. You will return to your worksheet, and the chart will display the enhancements that you selected.

LEAD IN HERE

> **Legends Have a Placement Tab**   Because legends provide color coding of the different data ranges in the chart, they do not include an Alignment tab as the other text object types do. The Format Legend dialog box includes a Placement tab that is used to place the legend on the chart area.

ENHANCING THE CHART AREA

Another way to enhance the overall look of your Excel chart is to change the color and pattern attributes of the chart area. This is the entire area enclosed within the chart's frame. To enhance the chart area, follow these steps:

1. Select the chart area (click on the chart or select **Chart Area** in the Chart Objects drop-down list on the Chart toolbar).

2. Click the **Format Chart Area** button on the Chart toolbar (or Select **Format**, **Selected Chart Area**).

3. To change the border and fill color for the entire chart, click the **Patterns** tab and use the drop-down lists and option buttons to select the line weight and color for the chart area.

4. To change the fonts used in the chart area, click the **Font** tab and make the appropriate selections.

5. When you have finished changing the various attributes of the chart area, click the **OK** button to close the dialog box.

In this lesson, you learned how to enhance your Excel charts. In the next lesson, you will learn how to save Excel worksheets for use on the World Wide Web.

LESSON 19
Adding Graphics and Other Objects to Worksheets

In this lesson, you learn how to add clip art and other images to your worksheets.

INSERTING CLIP ART INTO A WORKSHEET

Adding clip art or a picture to your worksheet is just a matter of identifying the place in the worksheet where you want to place the picture, and then selecting and inserting a specific picture file. Excel provides a large clip-art library, and you also can place images into your worksheets that you find on the World Wide Web, that you receive attached to e-mail messages, and that are imported from a scanner or digital camera.

Excel embraces several graphic file formats, including the following file types:

- CompuServe GIF (.gif)
- Encapsulated PostScript (.eps)
- Various paint programs (.pcx)
- Tagged Image File format (.tif)
- Windows bitmap (.bmp)
- JPEG file interchange format (.jpg)
- WordPerfect graphics (.wpg)

To insert an image from the Excel clip-art library, follow these steps:

1. Click in the worksheet cell where you would like to place the clip-art image.

2. Select **Insert**, **Picture**, and then select **Clip Art** on the cascading menu. The Insert Clip Art task pane appears (see Figure 19.1).

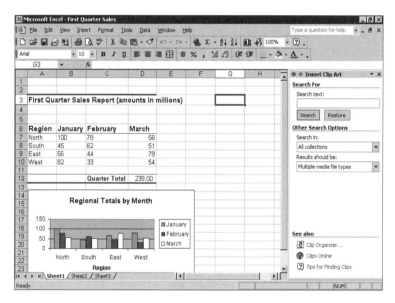

FIGURE 19.1
The Insert Clip Art task pane gives you access to the Excel clip-art gallery.

3. Type a clip-art theme, such as **animals**, into the **Search Text** area.

4. (Optional) If you want to preclude certain file types from the search to speed up the search process, select the **All Media File Types** drop-down box and deselect any of the file types (ClipArt, Photographs, and so on) as required.

TIP

> **Sound and Action Imagery Available, Too**   You can insert sound or movie clips into your worksheets from the Clip Art task pane. By default, they are included in the results for any search you conduct of the entire clip-art gallery.

5. Click the **Search** button, and various clip-art images that fit your search criteria appear.

6. When you have located the clip art you want to place in the worksheet, click the image. An image drop-down box appears (see Figure 19.2). Select **Insert** to place the image in your worksheet.

FIGURE 19.2
Click a particular clip-art image to insert it into the worksheet.

If used appropriately, pictures and clip art definitely can improve the look and feel of your worksheets, particularly if you want to add a company logo to your worksheet. If you find the clip-art library does-n't have what you need, click the **Media Gallery Online** link under the **See Also** section near the bottom of the task pane. Your Web browser opens, and you go to Microsoft's online clip-art library, which offers additional clip-art images for your use.

TIP

> **Add a Graphic with Copy and Paste**   You can copy a graphic to the Windows Clipboard from any Windows graphic program that you are running, and then paste it into your Excel worksheet.

SIZING AND MOVING A PICTURE

To size a graphic, click it to select it. Sizing handles (small circles) appear on the border of the image (see Figure 19.3). Place the mouse on any of these sizing handles. The mouse pointer becomes a sizing tool with arrows pointing in the directions in which you can change the size. Drag to size the graphic. To maintain the height/width ratio of the image so you don't stretch or distort the image, use the sizing han-dles on the corners of the image, and drag diagonally.

FIGURE 19.3
Use the sizing handles to change the size of the image.

To move the image to a new location in the worksheet, select the image and use the mouse to drag it to a new location. You can place it anywhere some whitespace appears on your worksheet.

Excel 2002 also makes it easy for you to rotate a graphic. Select the image, and then place the mouse pointer on the rotation handle that appears at the top of the graphic (it has a small green handle on the top). Rotate the handle in any direction to rotate the image.

INSERTING OTHER IMAGE FILE TYPES

As already mentioned, you can add images to your Excel files that you find on the Web, or that you have created using a scanner or digital camera. This enables you to place company logos and even employee pictures on an Excel worksheet. Pictures (other than clip-art files) are inserted using the Insert menu.

Follow these steps to add a picture file to an Excel worksheet:

1. Click in the cell where you want to place the picture.

2. Select **Insert**, **Picture**, and then select **From File** on the cascading menu. The Insert Picture dialog box appears.

3. Use the **Look In** box to locate the drive and folder that contains the picture file. After you locate the picture, click the file to view a preview (see Figure 19.4).

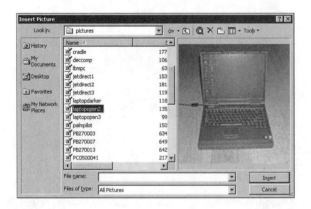

FIGURE 19.4
You can preview your graphical images before inserting them into your worksheet.

4. After you select the picture you want to insert, click **Insert** in the lower-right corner of the Insert Picture dialog box.

The picture is placed in your worksheet, and the Picture toolbar appears in the worksheet window. The next section provides information on using the Picture toolbar.

TIP

> **Deleting Unwanted Images**   Select the picture and press the **Delete** key. The image is removed from the worksheet.

USING THE PICTURE TOOLBAR

The Picture toolbar provides several tools you can use to modify and edit the images inserted into your worksheets (including clip art). If you don't see the Picture toolbar when an image is selected, right-click on any toolbar and select **Picture**.

Table 19.1 provides a listing and a description of the most commonly used buttons on the Picture toolbar.

Table 19.1   The Picture Toolbar Buttons and Their Purposes

Button	Click To
	Insert a new picture at the current picture position.
	Change the color of the image to grayscale or black and white.
	Crop the image (after selecting, you must drag the image border to a new cropping position).
	Rotate the image to the left (counter-clockwise).
	Select a line style for the image border (you first must use the Borders and Shading command to add a border to the image).

Table 19.1   (continued)

Button	Click To
	Open the Format Picture dialog box.
	Reset the image to its original formatting values.

To use one of the tools, select the image (if it is not already selected), and then select the appropriate button on the Picture toolbar. You can select from several formatting options for your picture when you select the **Format Picture** button; this opens the Format Picture dialog box. This dialog box provides tabs such as Color and Lines, Size, and Picture. For example, on the Picture tab, you can adjust the cropping and the brightness and contrast of the image (see Figure 19.5).

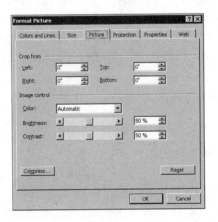

FIGURE 19.5
The Format Picture dialog box provides you with access to all the attributes of the selected image.

When you have finished working in the Format Picture dialog box, click OK. This closes the dialog box and returns you to your worksheet.

TIP

> **Cropping a Picture with the Mouse**   Select the picture,
> and then drag the resizing handles while you hold down
> the **Shift** key. This will crop the picture rather than resize
> it.

DRAWING YOUR OWN PICTURES

You can add additional graphic objects to your worksheets using the
Drawing toolbar. This toolbar provides several tools, including line,
arrow, rectangle, oval, and text box tools. You also can use the appropriate tools to change the fill color on a box or circle, change the line
color on your drawing object, or change the arrow style on arrows you
have placed on the worksheet.

To display the Drawing toolbar, select **View**, point at **Toolbar**, and
then select **Drawing** from the toolbar list. The Drawing toolbar
appears just above the Status bar at the bottom of the Excel window
(see Figure 19.6).

TIP

> **Quickly Access Toolbars**   You also can right-click any
> toolbar in the Word window to access the toolbar list;
> then select **Drawing**.

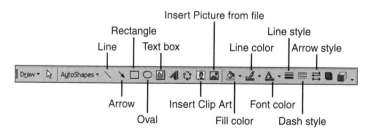

FIGURE 19.6
Use the Drawing toolbar to add graphical elements to your worksheets.

To draw a particular object, click the appropriate button on the toolbar. Then, drag the mouse to create the object on your worksheet. To draw a square or circle, click the **Rectangle** tool or the **Oval** tool and hold down the **Shift** key as you draw the object with the mouse. If you find that you aren't very good at actually drawing graphical objects, click the **AutoShapes** drop-down arrow (near the left side of the drawing toolbar) and select a particular object shape from the list provided.

You can control the various attributes for a particular object you've drawn. You first must select the object using the selection pointer (click the **Select Objects** tool, and then click the object). You can manipulate the object's line style, fill color, and line color. Just choose the appropriate tool on the toolbar, and make your selection from the list of possibilities.

You also can size and move objects that you draw. Select an object, and use the sizing handles to increase or decrease the size of the particular object. If you want to move the object to a new position, place the mouse pointer in the middle of the selected object and drag it to a new position.

If you draw several related objects, you can select all the objects at once and drag them together to a new location. Select the first object, and then hold down the **Shift** key and select subsequent objects as needed. When you drag any of the objects to a new location, all the selected objects move together.

At times, you will want to delete a particular object from your worksheet. Simply select the object and press **Delete** to remove it.

You will find that the Drawing toolbar provides you with all the tools (except natural artistic ability) you need to create fairly sophisticated custom images. A little practice with the various tools goes a long way in helping you create objects that add interest to your Excel worksheets and charts.

In this lesson, you learned how to add clip art, pictures, and drawing objects to your worksheets. In the next lesson, you will learn how to save an Excel worksheet for use on the Web.

LESSON 20

Saving and Publishing Files to the Web

In this lesson, you learn how to prepare worksheets for use on the World Wide Web. You also learn how to add hyperlinks to your Excel worksheets.

SAVING A WORKBOOK FOR THE WEB

You can save your Excel data to a Web site (or on your company's intranet) by converting your workbook to HTML format. When you save a workbook (or part of a workbook) in this way, it can be viewed through a Web browser.

PLAIN ENGLISH

HTML Short for HyperText Markup Language, HTML is the language in which data is presented on the World Wide Web. To display your Excel data on the Web, you must convert it to this format.

You can save your Excel worksheets for the Web in different ways. You can save them in the HTML format so that they can be viewed but not changed: In this scenario, the data is considered *static*. However, you can update the data yourself as needed simply by *republishing* the workbook (we discuss this later in the lesson).

You also can save the worksheet (or the workbook) so that your data is *interactive*; this means that a user can view it and change it right in their Web browser. They also will see the results of any formulas or functions that you have placed in the worksheet as they add data to the interactive Web worksheet.

CREATING AN FTP LOCATION

When you save your Excel workbook or worksheet for the Web, you can save the newly created HTML file directly to your Web site or to a location on your computer's hard drive. If you save the file to your hard drive, you can move it to the Web site later using Windows Explorer. If you are going to save the file directly to your Web site—or rather, to the Web server that hosts your Web site (on the Internet or your company's intranet)—you will need to create an FTP location. FTP stands for File Transfer Protocol, and it serves as a method of moving files from one computer to another (such as your Web server) on the Internet.

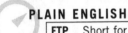

PLAIN ENGLISH

FTP   Short for File Transfer Protocol, FTP is used to move files from computer to computer on the Internet. Creating an FTP location on your computer enables you to save Web-ready content, such as Excel files, directly to your Web server.

Creating an FTP location enables you to save your Web-ready Excel files directly to the Web server that will host your Web site. To create an FTP location, follow these steps:

1. In Excel, select the **File** menu, and then select **Open**. The Open dialog box appears.

2. Click the **Save in** drop-down arrow at the top of the Open dialog box. Then, click **Add/Modify FTP Locations** on the drop-down list that appears. The Add/Modify FTP Locations dialog box appears (see Figure 20.1).

FIGURE 20.1

The Add/Modify FTP Locations dialog box enables you to create an FTP location for your Web server.

3. In the **Name of FTP Site** box at the top of the Add/Modify FTP Locations dialog box, type the name of the FTP site that coincides with your Web server. The FTP name for the Web server will be in the format ftp.Web site name.com. For example, if my Web site is Habraken.com, the correct FTP name would be ftp.habraken.com.

4. In the **Log on As** box, you must specify whether you log on to your Web server anonymously (Anonymous is the default) or whether a user name is required. Most Web sites hosted by an Internet service provider will require a user name and a password. Click the **User** option button, and then type the user name that you have been provided by your Internet service provider in the appropriate box.

5. If you specified a user name, click in the **Password** box and supply the password that is required for you to log on to your Web server (which is being specified as the FTP site).

6. Click the **Add** button to add the FTP location to the FTP sites list.

7. Click **OK** to close the Add/Modify FTP Locations dialog box.

8. You return to the Open dialog box. Click **Cancel** to close the Open dialog box.

Now that you have created an FTP location for your Web site, it will be available when you publish an Excel workbook or worksheet to your Web site. The next section discusses how to publish Excel content to a Web server.

Publishing an Excel Worksheet to the Web

After you have an FTP location setup that will allow you to save your Excel workbooks or worksheet to your Web server, you are ready to publish your Excel files to the Web. To publish your Excel worksheet (or the entire workbook), follow these steps:

1. If you're not publishing the entire workbook, select the cell range or item (such as a chart) that you want to publish.

2. Open the File menu and select **Save as Web Page**. The Save As dialog box appears, as shown in Figure 20.2. Notice that the Save As Type box says Web Page. This means that your worksheet will be saved in the HTML format.

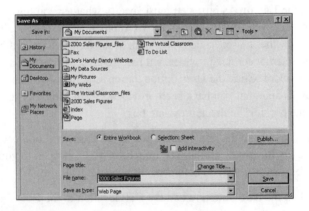

FIGURE 20.2
Use the Save As dialog box to save your Excel worksheet for the Web.

3. In the **Save in** list, select the FTP location that you created using the steps in the previous section (it will be at the very end of the list) or a folder on your hard drive where you want to save the HTML Excel file.

 TIP

Hey, Look Me Over!—Before publishing your data, you might want to save it to a local hard drive first. You then can view it in your Web browser. If the file needs editing, you can reopen it in Excel and make any necessary changes, or you can use an HTML editor, such as Microsoft FrontPage, to make changes as needed. You then can publish the HTML file to its permanent location on your company's intranet or the Internet.

4. Perform either of the following:

    To save the entire workbook, select **Entire Workbook, Save** (skip the remaining steps.)

    To save a part of the workbook (such as a worksheet or a chart), choose **Selection**.

5. Type a name for the HTML file in the **File Name** text box.

6. To specify the title for the HTML file that will be created, click **Change Title** and change the title for the Web page in the Set Title dialog box (the title appears in the title bar of a user's Web browser when your page is viewed). After editing the title, click **OK** to close the Set Title box. Now you are ready to publish the Excel content.

7. Click **Publish**. The Publish as Web Page dialog box appears, as shown in Figure 20.3.

8. If you are not going to publish all the items on a particular worksheet or workbook, use the Choose list to select the item you want to publish.

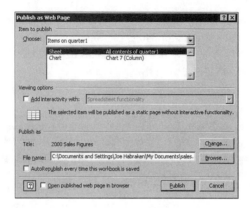

FIGURE 20.3
The Publish as Web Page dialog box enables you to set options related to your Excel Web content.

Before you leave the Publish as Web Page dialog box, you need to briefly learn about static versus interactive data, and then look at how you can have Excel data automatically updated to a Web page when you change the workbook or worksheet.

STATIC VERSUS INTERACTIVE DATA

As you learned at the very beginning of this lesson, you can save your Excel data as static Web information or you can make it interactive, allowing users on the Web to input their own data and take advantage of the formulas and functions you have placed in the worksheet. If you want to place a snapshot of data, such as a quarterly report, onto the Web, you will want to publish static data. If you refer to Figure 20.3, you will notice that static data is the default.

To publish interactive data, where the information in the worksheet can be changed by a user viewing the worksheet using a Web browser, click the **Add Interactivity With** check box on the Publish as Web Page dialog box. Also, be sure that the drop-down list next to the check box displays **Spreadsheet Functionality**, which allows users to enter, update, copy, move, delete, format, sort, or filter data in a Web browser window (you will look at an interactive worksheet in a Web browser later in this lesson).

COMPLETING THE PUBLISHING PROCESS

When you have determined whether the data will be static or interactive when published to the Web, you are ready to complete the Web publishing process. Follow these steps:

1. If you will be changing the contents of the Excel HTML file over time and want it automatically republished each time you save changes to the file, click the **AutoRepublish Every Time This Workbook Is Saved** check box. This will make it unnecessary for you to repeat the entire publishing process each time you change the contents of the Excel worksheet or workbook.

2. If you want, select the **Open Published Web Page in Browser** check box to launch your Web browser at the completion of the Web publishing process, so you can view the HTML file immediately.

3. When you have made all your selections in the Publish as Web Page dialog box, click **Publish**.

The Excel data will be published as an HTML file (Excel worksheets containing graphics and charts actually will be published as a group of files) to the location that you specified.

VIEWING EXCEL DATA IN A WEB BROWSER

After you have published your Excel worksheet or workbook to a Web server (or a location on your computer's hard drive), you can view the data in any Web browser. Excel data that you publish as interactive data is best viewed in Internet Explorer (4.0 or better).

To view the Excel data, open your Web browser. Then, specify the Web site to which you published the Excel data in the Address box. Or, in the case of data that you published to your local hard drive, select **File**, **Open** in your browser window. In the Open dialog box that appears, type the location and name of the file, or use the Browse button to browse for the file. Click **OK** to close the Open dialog box and view the file.

Figure 20.4 shows static Excel data that has been published. As already mentioned, static data only supplies information; the data cannot be manipulated in the browser window.

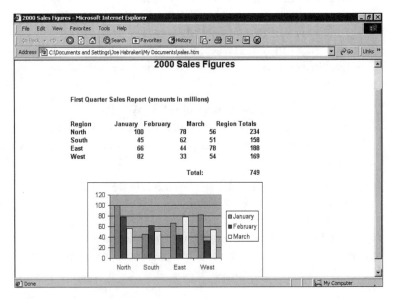

FIGURE 20.4
Static data published for the Web.

Excel workbooks or worksheets that have been published as interactive data actually can be manipulated within the browser window. This enables you to create worksheets that your clients can use on the Web. For example, you might create a worksheet that allows users to figure out how much a monthly car payment would be based on the car's principal (meaning the amount the car costs).

Figure 20.5 shows an interactive worksheet published to the Web. Users can input the price of a car and see what the monthly payment would be for a four-year loan at 8%.

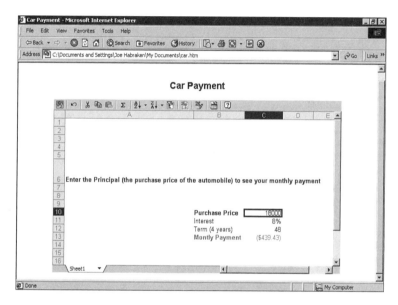

FIGURE 20.5
Interactive data published for the Web.

When you publish Excel data for use on the Web, you typically will want to incorporate the Web pages that you create into the series of other pages that are available on your Web site. This can be done using Web-page editing tools such as Microsoft FrontPage.

ADDING HYPERLINKS TO A WORKSHEET

A *hyperlink* is a cell containing text (or values) or a picture that, when clicked, takes the user to a Web page, to a file on your hard disk, or to a file on a local network. Adding hyperlinks to Excel worksheets that you then publish to the Web makes it easy for users viewing your Web content to jump to other pages on your Web site.

Using hyperlinks in Excel worksheets that you do not publish for the Web enable you to quickly jump to another worksheet or workbook that contains information related to the Excel data that is currently being viewed in Excel. To add a hyperlink, follow these steps:

1. Select the cell (containing descriptive text or a value related to the file or location that will open when the hyperlink is clicked) or image you want to use for the hyperlink.

2. Click the **Insert Hyperlink** button on the Standard toolbar.

3. If asked, be sure you save your workbook. The Insert Hyperlink dialog box appears, as shown in Figure 20.6.

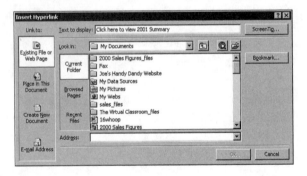

FIGURE 20.6
Use the Insert Hyperlink dialog box to create a hyperlink in your Excel work-sheet.

4. Perform one of the following:

   To link to a file or Web page, enter the address of the Web page or location of the file to which you want to link in the **Address** text box, or click **Browsed Pages** or **Recent Files** to select it from a list.

To link to a location within the workbook, click the **Place in This Document** button in the places bar. Then, enter the cell address in the **Type the Cell Reference** text box, or select it from the **Or Select a Place in This Document** list.

To create a link to a new workbook, click the **Create New Document** button in the places bar. Then, type a name for the document in the **Name of New Document** text box. To save the workbook in a directory other than the one shown, click the **Browse** button and select the directory you want to use.

To create a link to an e-mail address (so the link will open your e-mail program, display a message window, and automatically address the e-mail message), click the **E-Mail Address** button in the places bar. Then, type the e-mail address to which you want to link in the **E-Mail Address** text box, or select one from the **Recently Used E-Mail Addresses** list. If you want to enter a subject for the message, type one in the **Subject** text box.

5. To display a ScreenTip when the mouse pointer rests on the hyperlink, click **ScreenTip**, and enter the description you want to display. Click **OK**.

6. After you have made your selections in steps 4 and 5, click **OK** to close the dialog box. The text in the cell you selected becomes blue and underlined, meaning that it is now a hyperlink (images do not change color when they are used for hyperlinks).

When you move the mouse pointer over this link, it changes to a hand. Next to the hand, you can see the address of the link. Click the link, and you will jump to the appropriate worksheet, Web page, file, or e-mail program. The text of the link changes to purple to indicate that you have used the link.

If you need to change the text for a link later on, or to change the item to which the link points, right-click the link, and select **Hyperlink**

from the shortcut menu. Then, select **Edit Hyperlink**. The Edit
Hyperlink dialog box appears. Make your changes and click **OK**. To
delete the link, right-click, select **Hyperlink**, and then select **Remove
Link** from the shortcut menu.

In this lesson, you learned how to publish workbook files to the Web
and how to add hyperlinks to your Excel worksheets.

INDEX

T

U-V

Microsoft® Access 2002

10
M I N U T E
G U I D E

 201 West 103rd Street
Indianapolis, IN 46290

Joe Habraken

TEN MINUTE GUIDE TO MICROSOFT® ACCESS 2002

Copyright © 2002 by Que®

International Standard Book Number: 0-7897-2631-9

Library of Congress Catalog Card Number: 2001090285

Printed in the United States of America

First Printing: August 2001

05 04 03 02   8 7 6

TRADEMARKS

WARNING AND DISCLAIMER

Associate Publisher
Greg Wiegand

Acquisitions Editor
Stephanie J. McComb

Managing Editor
Thomas F. Hayes

Senior Editor
Susan Ross Moore

Indexer
Mandie Frank

Proofreaders
Kaylene Riemen
Juli Cook

Team Coordinator
Sharry Lee Gregory

Interior Designer
Gary Adair

Cover Designer
Alan Clements

Page Layout
Stacey Richwine-DeRome
Gloria Schurick

Table of Contents

ABOUT THE AUTHOR

Joe Habraken is a computer technology professional and best-selling author with more than fifteen years of experience in the information technology field as a network administrator, consultant, and educator. His recent publications include *Microsoft Office XP 8-in-1*, *The Absolute Beginner's Guide to Networking (Second Edition)*, and *Practical Cisco Routers*. Joe currently serves as the Director of UNEit, an IT training center for computer industry professionals at the University of New England in Portland, ME.

DEDICATION

To all the database users in the world who struggle with information overload.

ACKNOWLEDGMENTS

Creating books like this takes a real team effort. I would like to thank Stephanie McComb, our acquisitions editor, who worked very hard to assemble the team that made this book a reality. I would also like to thank our production editor, Susan Moore, who ran the last leg of the race and made sure the book made it to press on time—what a great team of professionals.

TELL US WHAT YOU THINK!

As the reader of this book, *you* are our most important critic and commentator. We value your opinion and want to know what we're doing right, what we could do better, what areas you'd like to see us publish in, and any other words of wisdom you're willing to pass our way.

As an Associate Publisher for Que, I welcome your comments. You can fax, email, or write me directly to let me know what you did or didn't like about this book—as well as what we can do to make our books stronger.

Please note that I cannot help you with technical problems related to the topic of this book, and that due to the high volume of mail I receive, I might not be able to reply to every message.

When you write, please be sure to include this book's title and author as well as your name and phone or fax number. I will carefully review your comments and share them with the author and editors who worked on the book.

Fax: 317-581-4666

E-mail: feedback@quepublishing.com

Mail: Associate Publisher
Que
201 West 103rd Street
Indianapolis, IN 46290 USA

Introduction

Microsoft Access 2002 is a powerful, relational database software
package that makes it easy for you to create and manage complex
databases. With Access, you can create a database quickly from
scratch or by using an Access Database Wizard. Once you've created
your database, Access provides all the tools you need to enter and
manipulate data.

THE WHAT AND WHY OF MICROSOFT ACCESS

Access can help you manage any size database, from simple contact
lists to complex business databases. Using Microsoft Access, you can
do the following:

- Quickly start a new database by using the Database Wizard

- Create tables from scratch or by using a wizard

- Add and edit database information by using both tables and
  forms

- Manipulate data in a number of tables by using queries and
  reports

While providing you with many advanced database features,
Microsoft Access is built so that even the novice database user can
build and maintain a database. This book will help you understand the
possibilities awaiting you with Microsoft Access 2002.

WHY *QUE'S 10 MINUTE GUIDE TO MICROSOFT ACCESS 2002*?

The 10 Minute Guide to Microsoft Access 2002 can save you precious
time while you get to know the different features that Microsoft Access

provides. Each lesson is designed to be completed in 10 minutes or less, so you'll be up to snuff on many Access features quickly.

Although you can jump around among lessons, starting at the beginning is a good plan. The bare-bones basics are covered first, and more advanced topics are covered later. If you need help installing Access, see the next section for instructions.

INSTALLING ACCESS

You can install Microsoft Access 2002 on a computer running Microsoft Windows 98, Windows NT 4.0, Windows 2000, and Windows XP. Microsoft Access can be installed as a stand-alone product and is also available as part of the Microsoft Office XP suite (both of these flavors of Access come on a CD-ROM).

To install Access, follow these steps:

1. Start your computer. Then insert the Microsoft Access or Microsoft XP Office CD in the CD-ROM drive. The CD-ROM should autostart, providing you with the opening installation screen.

2. If the CD-ROM does not autostart, choose Start, Run. In the Run dialog box, type the letter of the CD-ROM drive, followed by **setup** (for example, **e:\setup**). If necessary, use the Browse button to locate and select the CD-ROM drive and the setup.exe program.

3. When the Setup Wizard prompts you, enter your name, organization, and CD key in the appropriate box.

4. Choose **Next** to continue.

5. The next Wizard screen provides instructions to complete the installation. After providing the appropriate information on each screen, select **Next** to advance from screen to screen.

After you complete the installation from the CD, icons for Access and any other Office applications you might have installed will be provided on the Windows Start menu. Lesson 2 in this book provides you with a step-by-step guide to starting Access 2002.

CONVENTIONS USED IN THIS BOOK

To help you move through the lessons easily, these conventions are used:

On-screen text	On-screen text appears in bold type.
`Text you should type`	Information you need to type appears in a different bold, typeface.
Items you select	Commands, options, and icons you are to select and keys you are to press appear in bold type.

In telling you to choose menu commands, this book uses the format *menu title, menu command*. For example, the statement "choose File, Properties" means to "open the File menu and select the Properties command."

In addition to those conventions, the *10 Minute Guide to Microsoft Access 2002* uses the following icons to identify helpful information:

PLAIN ENGLISH

terms New or unfamiliar terms are defined in term sidebars.

TIP

Tips Read these tips for ideas that cut corners and confusion.

CAUTION

Cautions This icon identifies areas where new users often run into trouble; these cautions offer practical solutions to those problems.

LESSON 1
What's New in Access 2002

In this lesson, you are introduced to Microsoft Access and you learn what's new in Access 2002.

UNDERSTANDING ACCESS 2002

Strictly speaking, a *database* is any collection of information. Your local telephone book, for example, is a database, as is the shopping list that you take to the grocery store. Microsoft Access makes creating databases very straightforward and relatively simple.

The electronic container that Access provides for holding your data is called a *table* (see Figure 1.1). A table consists of rows and columns. Access stores each database entry (for example, each employee or each inventory item) in its own row; this is a *record*. Each record contains specific information related to one person, place, or thing.

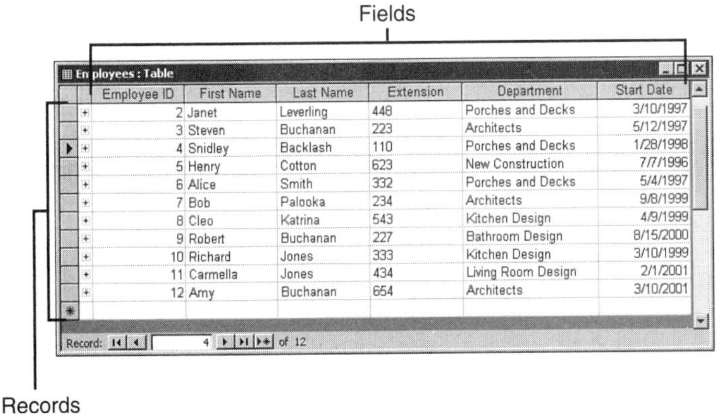

Fields

Employee ID	First Name	Last Name	Extension	Department	Start Date
2	Janet	Leverling	448	Porches and Decks	3/10/1997
3	Steven	Buchanan	223	Architects	5/12/1997
4	Snidley	Backlash	110	Porches and Decks	1/28/1998
5	Henry	Cotton	623	New Construction	7/7/1996
6	Alice	Smith	332	Porches and Decks	5/4/1997
7	Bob	Palooka	234	Architects	9/8/1999
8	Cleo	Katrina	543	Kitchen Design	4/9/1999
9	Robert	Buchanan	227	Bathroom Design	8/15/2000
10	Richard	Jones	333	Kitchen Design	3/10/1999
11	Carmella	Jones	434	Living Room Design	2/1/2001
12	Amy	Buchanan	654	Architects	3/10/2001

Record: 4 of 12

Records

FIGURE 1.1
A table serves as the container for your database information.

PLAIN ENGLISH

> **Table**   A container for your database information con-
> sisting of columns and rows.

Each record is broken up into discrete pieces of information, called
fields. Each *field* consists of a separate column in the table. Each field
contains a different piece of information that taken all together makes
up a particular record. For example, Last Name is a field. All the last
names in the entire table (all in the same column) are collectively
known as the Last Name field.

PLAIN ENGLISH

> **Record**   A row in a table that contains information
> about a particular person, place, or thing.

PLAIN ENGLISH

> **Field**   A discrete piece of information making up a
> record. Each column in the Access table is a different
> field.

INTRODUCING OTHER ACCESS OBJECTS

The table is just one type of object found in Access. You can also
work with forms, queries, and reports.

- A *form* is used to enter, edit, and view data in a table, one
  record at a time.

- A *query* enables you to ask your database questions. The
  answer to the query can be used to manipulate data in a table,
  such as deleting records or viewing the data in a table that
  meets only certain criteria.

- A *report* enables you to summarize database information in a
  format that is suitable for printing.

In essence, each of these different database objects allows you a different way of viewing and manipulating the data found in your tables. Each of these objects (including the table) should also be considered as you plan a new database. Planning a new database is discussed in Lesson 2, "Working in Access."

WHAT'S NEW IN ACCESS 2002

Access 2002 is similar in look and feel to Access 2000 the previous version of this powerful database software. Access 2002 provides the same adaptive menu and toolbar system found in Access 2000 that customizes the commands and icons listed on your menus and toolbars based on the commands you use most frequently.

Access 2002 also provides you with other useful tools and features that were available in previous versions of the Access software. For example, tools such as the Database and Tables Wizards make it easy for you to quickly create your databases and the tables that will contain your data.

PLAIN ENGLISH

Wizard   A feature that guides you step by step through a particular process in Access, such as creating a new table.

While providing you with the familiar tools and features found in earlier versions of Access, Access 2002 also supplies several new features. For example, Access 2002 now provides you with the ability to undo and redo multiple actions when you work with Access database objects such as tables and forms in the design view.

Other new features in Access 2002 such as Task panes and Voice dictation make it even easier for you to create and maintain your database files. Let's take a look at some of the important changes to the Access 2002 software.

INTRODUCING TASK PANES

One of the biggest changes to the Access environment (and all the Microsoft Office XP suite applications such as Word 2002, Excel 2002 and PowerPoint 2002) is the introduction of the Office task pane. The task pane is a special pane that appears on the right side of the Access application window when you use certain Access features (features that were formerly controlled using dialog boxes).

For example, when you choose to start a new database, the New File task pane appears (see Figure 1.2). This task pane makes it easy for you to start a new blank database or create a database using the different database templates provided by Access. Creating a new database in Access is covered in Lesson 3, "Creating a New Database."

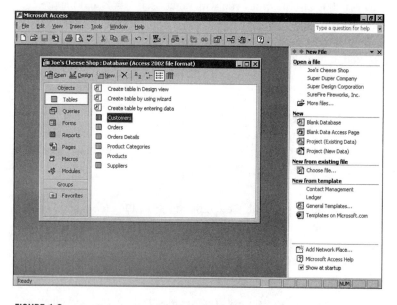

FIGURE 1.2
The New File task pane makes it easy for you to create a new Access database.

Other task panes that you will run across as you work in Access are the Office Clipboard and the Clip Gallery. The Office Clipboard allows you to copy or cut multiple items from an Access object such as a table and then paste them into new locations. The Clip Gallery provides you with the ability to insert clip art and other images into your Access tables, forms, or reports. Task panes are discussed in this book when appropriate as you explore the various Access features.

INTRODUCING VOICE DICTATION AND VOICE COMMANDS

One of the most exciting new features in Access 2002 (and the entire Office XP suite) is voice dictation and voice-activated commands. If your computer is outfitted with a sound card, speakers, and a microphone (or a microphone with an earphone headset), you can dictate information into your Access tables. You also can use voice commands to activate the menu system and toolbars in Access.

Before you can really take advantage of the Speech feature, you must provide it with some training so that it can more easily recognize your speech patterns and intonation. After the Speech feature is trained, you can effectively use it to dictate text entries or access various application commands without a keyboard or mouse.

CAUTION

Requirements for Getting the Most Out of the Speech Feature   To make the Speech feature useful, you will need a fairly high-quality microphone. Microsoft suggests a microphone/headset combination. The Speech feature also requires a more powerful computer. Microsoft suggests using a computer with 128MB of RAM and a Pentium II (or later) processor running at a minimum of 400MHz. A computer that meets or exceeds these higher standards should be capable of getting the most out of the Speech feature.

You may wish to explore the other lessons in this book if you are new to Access before you attempt to use the Speech feature. Having a good understanding of how Access operates and the features that it provides will allow you to then get the most out of using the Speech feature.

TRAINING THE SPEECH FEATURE

The first time you start the Speech feature in Access, you are required
to configure and train the feature. Follow these steps to get the Speech
feature up and running:

1. In Access, select the **Tools** menu and select **Speech**. The
   Welcome to Office Speech Recognition dialog box appears.
   To begin the process of setting up your microphone and train-
   ing the Speech feature, click the **Next** button.

2. The first screen of the Microphone Wizard appears. It asks
   you to make sure that your microphone and speakers are connected to your computer. If you have a headset microphone,
   this screen shows you how to adjust the microphone for use.
   Click **Next** to continue.

3. The next wizard screen asks you to read a short text passage
   so that your microphone volume level can be adjusted (see
   Figure 1.3). When you have finished reading the text, click
   Next to continue.

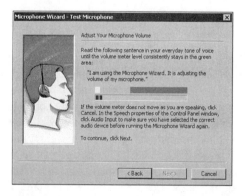

FIGURE 1.3
The Microphone Wizard adjusts the volume of your microphone.

4. On the next screen, you are told that if you have a headset microphone, you can click **Finish** and proceed to the speech recognition training. If you have a different type of microphone, you are asked to read another text passage. The text is then played back to you. This is to determine whether the microphone is placed at an appropriate distance from your mouth; when you get a satisfactory playback, click **Finish**.

When you finish working with the Microphone Wizard, the Voice Training Wizard appears. This wizard collects samples of your speech and, in essence, educates the Speech feature as to how you speak.

To complete the voice training process, follow these steps:

1. After reading the information on the opening screen, click **Next** to begin the voice training process.

2. On the next screen, you are asked to provide your gender and age (see Figure 1.4). After specifying the correct information, click **Next**.

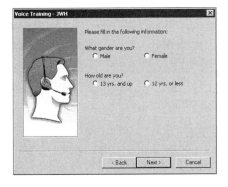

FIGURE 1.4
Supply the voice trainer with your gender and age.

3. On the next wizard screen, you are provided an overview of how the voice training will proceed. You are also provided with directions for how to pause the training session. Click **Next**.

4. The next wizard screen reminds you to adjust your microphone. You are also reminded that you need a quiet room
   when training the Speech feature. When you are ready to
   begin training the speech recognition feature, click **Next**.

5. On the next screen, you are asked to read some text. As the
   wizard recognizes each word, the word is highlighted. After
   finishing with this screen, continue by clicking **Next**.

6. You are asked to read text on several subsequent screens.
   Words are selected as the wizard recognizes them.

7. When you complete the training screens, your profile is
   updated. Click **Finish** on the wizard's final screen.

You are now ready to use the Speech feature. The next two sections
discuss using the Voice Dictation and Voice Command features.

CAUTION

> **The Speech Feature Works Better Over Time**   Be advised
> that the voice feature's performance improves as you use
> it. As you learn to pronounce your words more carefully,
> the Speech feature tunes itself to your speech patterns.
> You might need to do additional training sessions to
> fine-tune the Speech feature.

USING VOICE DICTATION

When you are ready to start dictating text into an Access table, put on
your headset microphone or place your standalone microphone in the
proper position that you determined when you used the Microphone
Wizard. When you're ready to go, select the **Tools** menu and then
select **Speech**. The Language bar appears, as shown in Figure 1.5. If
necessary, click the **Dictation** button on the toolbar (if the Dictation
button is not already activated or depressed).

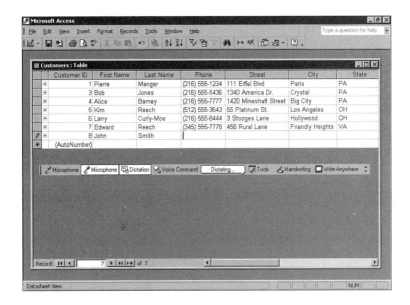

FIGURE 1.5
Dictating text into an Access table.

After you enable the Dictation button, you can begin dictating your text. Figure 1.5 shows text being dictated into an Access table. When you want to move to the next field in the record that you are dictating, say "tab." Numbers are dictated as they appear; for example, if you wished to enter the phone number prefix of 555, you would say "555." If you need to put a line break into the text, say "new line." Punctuation is placed into a table (in cases where you are creating a field that requires punctuation marks) by saying the name of a particular punctuation mark, such as "period" or "comma."

CAUTION

How Do I Insert the Word "Comma" Rather Than the Punctuation Mark?   Because certain keywords, such as "period" or "comma," are used to insert punctuation during dictation, you must spell these words out if you want to include them in the text. To do this, say "spelling mode," and then spell out the word, such as c-o-m-m-a. As soon as you dictate an entire word, the spelling mode is ended.

When you have finished dictating into the document, click the **Microphone** button on the Language bar (the second Microphone button from the left; the first is used to select the current speech driver, which you can leave as the default). When you click the **Microphone** button, the Language bar collapses, hiding the **Dictation** and the **Voice Command** buttons. You can also stop Dictation mode by saying "microphone."

You can minimize the Language bar by clicking the **Minimize** button on the right end of the bar. This sends the Language bar to the Windows System Tray (it appears as a small square icon marked EN, if you are using the English version of Office and Access).

With the Language bar minimized in the System Tray, you can quickly open it when you need it. Click the **Language Bar** icon in the System Tray, and then select **Show the Language Bar**.

Using the Dictation feature correctly requires that you know how to get the Speech feature to place the correct text or characters into your Access table. For more help with the dictation feature, consult the Microsoft Access Help system (discussed in Lesson 10).

USING VOICE COMMANDS

Another tool the Speech feature provides is voice commands. You can open and select menus in Access and even navigate dialog boxes using voice commands.

To use voice commands, open the Language bar (click **Tools**, **Speech**). Click the **Microphone** icon, if necessary, to expand the Language bar. Then, click the **Voice Command** icon on the bar (or say "voice command").

To open a particular menu such as the Format menu, say "format." Then, to open a particular submenu such as Font, say "font." In the case of these voice commands, the Font dialog box opens.

You can then navigate a particular dialog box using voice commands. In the Font dialog box, for example, to change the size of the font, say "size"; this activates the Size box that controls font size. Then, say the size of the font, such as "14." You can also activate other font attributes in the dialog box in this manner. Say the name of the area of the dialog box you want to use, and then say the name of the feature you want to turn on or select.

When you have finished working with a particular dialog box, say "OK," (or "Cancel" or "Apply," as needed) and the dialog box closes and provides you with the features you selected in the dialog box. When you have finished using voice commands, say "microphone," or click the **Microphone** icon on the Language bar.

Believe it or not, you can also activate buttons on the various toolbars using voice commands. For example, you could sort your Access table by a particular field by clicking in that field and then saying "sort ascending." The Sort Ascending button on the Table Datasheet toolbar becomes active and your table is sorted by the selected field.

In this lesson, you were introduced to Access 2002 and some of the new features available in this latest version of Microsoft Access such as task panes and the Speech feature. In the next lesson, you learn how to plan an Access database and start the Access software.

LESSON 2
Working in Access

In this lesson, you learn what a relational database is and how to plan your database. You also learn how to start Microsoft Access, become familiar with its toolbars, and then exit the software.

PLANNING A DATABASE

Access is a special kind of database called a *relational database*. A relational database divides information into discrete subsets. Each subset groups information by a particular theme, such as customer information, sales orders, or product information. In Access, these subsets of data reside in individual tables like the one described previously.

Access enables you to build relationships between tables. These relationships are based on a field that is common to two tables. Each table must have a field called the primary key (you learn how to specify a field as the primary key in Lessons 4 and 5). The primary key must uniquely identify each record in the table. So, the primary key field is typically a field that assigns a unique number (no duplicates within that table) to each record.

For example, a Customers table might contain a Customer Identification field (shown as CustomerID in Figure 2.1) that identifies each customer by a unique number (such as your Social Security number). You might also have a table that holds all your sales orders. To link the Sales table to the Customers table, you include the Customer Identification field in the Sales table. This identifies each sale by customer and links the Sales table data to the Customers table data.

PLAIN ENGLISH

Relational Database A collection of individual tables holding discrete subsets of information that are linked by common data fields.

You will find that even a simple database consists of several tables that are related. Figure 2.1 shows a database and the different table relationships. Lesson 11, "Creating Relationships Between Tables," provides information on creating table relationships.

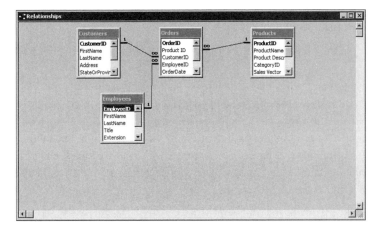

FIGURE 2.1
A relational database contains related tables.

When you do create a new database, you want to make sure that the database is designed not only to meet your data entry needs, but also to meet your needs for viewing and reporting the data that is held in the various tables that make up the database. Taking a little time to plan your database before you create it can save you from headaches down the road. The sections that follow provide some tips on planning a database.

DETERMINING YOUR TABLES

Technically, you need only one table to make a database. However, because Access is a relational database program, it's meant to handle many tables and create relationships among them. For example, in a database that keeps track of customer orders, you might have the following tables:

- Customers

- Orders

- Products

- Salespeople

- Shipping Methods

Using many tables that hold subsets of the database information can help you avoid making redundant data entries. For example, suppose you want to keep contact information on your customers along with a record of each transaction they make. If you kept it all in one table, you would have to repeat the customer's full name, address, and phone number each time you entered a new transaction. It would also be a nightmare if the customer's address changed; you would have to change the address in every transaction record for that customer.

A better way is to assign each customer an ID number. Include that ID number in a table that contains names and addresses, and then use the same ID number as a link to a separate transactions table. Basically, then, each table in your database should have a particular theme—for example, Employee Contact Information or Customer Transactions. Don't try to have more than one theme per table.

A table design requirement is to be sure that every table that you create uses the first field (the first column of the table) as a way to uniquely identify each record in the table. This field can then serve as the table's primary key. For example, customers can be assigned a customer number, or sales transactions can be assigned a transaction number. The primary key is the only way that you can then link the table to another table in the database.

It's a good idea to do some work on paper and jot down a list of tables that will be contained in the database and the fields that they will contain. Restructuring tables because of poor planning isn't impossible, but it isn't much fun, either.

DETERMINING YOUR FORMS

As already mentioned in Lesson 1, forms are used for data entry. They allow you to enter data one record at a time (see Figure 2.2). Complex forms can also be constructed that actually allow you to enter data into more than one table at a time (this is because fields can be pulled from several tables in the same database into one form).

FIGURE 2.2
A form allows you to enter data one record at a time.

Planning the forms that you use for data entry is not as crucial as planning the tables that make up the database. Forms should be designed to make data entry easier. They are great in that they allow you to concentrate on the entry or editing of data one record at a time. You might want to have a form for each table in the database, or you might want to create composite forms that allow you to enter data into the form that is actually deposited into more than one table.

The great thing about forms is that they don't have to contain all the fields that are in a particular table. For example, if you have someone else enter the data that you keep in an employee database, but you don't want that data entry person to see the employee salaries, you can design a form that does not contain the salary field.

DETERMINING YOUR QUERIES

Queries enable you to manipulate the data in your database tables. A query can contain criteria that allow you to delete old customer records, or it can provide you with a list of employees who have worked at the company for more than 10 years.

Deciding the queries that you will use before all the data is entered can be difficult. However, if you are running a store—a cheese shop, for example—and know that it is important for you to keep close tabs on your cheese inventory, you will probably want to build some queries to track sales and inventory.

Queries are an excellent way for you to determine the status of your particular endeavor. For example, you could create a query to give you total sales for a particular month. Queries are, in effect, questions. Use queries to get the answers that you need from your database information.

DETERMINING YOUR REPORTS

A report is used to publish the data in the database. It places the data on the page (or pages) in a highly readable format. Reports are meant to be printed (unlike tables and forms, which are usually used onscreen). For example, you might run a club and want a report of all people who haven't paid their membership dues or who owe more than $1,000 on their account.

A report is usually for the benefit of other people who aren't sitting with you at your computer. For example, you might print a report to hand out to your board of directors to encourage them to keep you on as CEO. A report can pull data from many tables at once, perform calculations on the data (such as summing or averaging), and present you with neatly formatted results. Figure 2.3 shows a database report.

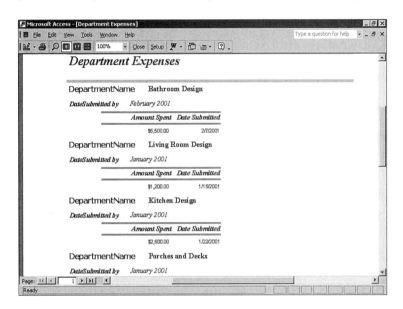

FIGURE 2.3
Reports allow you to organize and summarize database information.

You can create new reports at any time; you don't have to plan them before you create your database. However, if you know you will want a certain report, you might design your tables in the format that will be most effective for that report's use.

Designing good databases is an acquired skill. The more databases that you work with, the better each will be. Now that you've gotten your feet wet with database planning, take a look at how to start Access.

STARTING ACCESS

You can start Access in several ways, depending on how you've installed it. One way is to use the Start menu button. Follow these steps:

1. Click the **Start** button. A menu appears.

2. Highlight or point to **Programs**. A list of programs installed on your computer appears.

3. Click **Microsoft Access** in the list of applications. Access starts.

PLAIN ENGLISH

> **Moving Programs Around on the Start Menu**   If you prefer to have Access in a different program group, open the **Start** menu and drag the Access item to another location of your choice.

OTHER WAYS TO START ACCESS

Some other ways to start Access require more knowledge of Windows and Microsoft Office. If you're confused by them, stick with the primary method explained in the preceding section.

- You can create a shortcut icon for Access that sits on your desktop; you can then start Access by double-clicking the icon. To create the shortcut icon, drag the Access item from the **Start** menu to the desktop.

- When you're browsing files in Windows Explorer, you can double-click any Access data file to start Access and open that data file. Access data files have an .mdb extension and a little icon next to them that resembles the icon next to Microsoft Access on the Programs menu.

- If you can't find Access, you can search for it. Click the Start button and select **Find**, select **Files or Folders**, and then type msaccess.exe into the Named text box. Open the **Look In** list and select **My Computer**. Then click **Find Now**. When the file appears on the list at the bottom of the Find window, double-click it to start Access, or right-click and drag it to the desktop to create an Access shortcut.

PARTS OF THE ACCESS SCREEN

Access is much like any other Windows program: It contains menus, toolbars, a status bar, the Ask a Question box, and so on. Figure 2.4 provides a look at these different areas of the Access window. This view assumes that you have either created a new database or opened an existing database in the Access workspace. Creating a new database and opening an existing database are discussed in Lesson 3, "Creating a New Database."

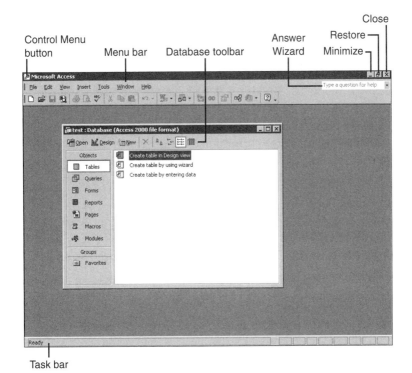

FIGURE 2.4
Access provides the familiar menu and toolbars found in all Microsoft Office applications.

You probably have noticed that most of the buttons on the toolbar are unavailable. That's because you haven't created any objects, such as tables or forms, for the new database. The toolbar currently displayed in the Access window is the Database toolbar. Access actually has a different toolbar for each database object such as a table or a form. In some cases, multiple toolbars exist for an object, depending on whether you are entering data into the object or changing the design parameters of the object.

For example, Access tables have two toolbars. The Table Datasheet toolbar provides you with tools that help you enter and manipulate the data in the table when you work with it in the Datasheet view. If you switch to the Design view of the table, a Table Design toolbar helps you manipulate the design settings for the table.

Because you will be working with each Access object type, you will also become familiar with each object toolbar. As you work with the various buttons on the toolbars, remember that you can place the mouse pointer on any toolbar button to receive a ToolTip. The ToolTip provides the name of the button, which usually is indicative of what the particular tool is used for.

One other thing that should be mentioned related to the Access window is that only one database at a time can be open in the Access window. It doesn't enable you to work on multiple databases at the same time, as you could work with multiple documents, or workbooks in Word or Excel.

PLAIN ENGLISH

Choose Your Toolbars   As you work in Access on the various objects, right-click any toolbar to view a shortcut menu that provides a list of available toolbars. Typically, you are limited to the toolbar specific to the object that you are working on.

EXITING ACCESS

Although you have only barely gotten your feet wet with Access, take a look at how you exit the application. You can exit Access in several ways:

- Select **File**, and then select **Exit**.

- Click the Access window's **Close** (x) button on the upper right of the Access window.

- Press **Alt+F4**.

In this lesson, you became familiar with what a relational database is and how to plan the various types of objects that would be placed in a new database. You also had a chance to open Access, take a look at the Access window and exit the application window. In the next lesson, we look at different ways to create a new Access database.

LESSON 3

Creating a New Database

In this lesson, you learn how to create a blank database. You also learn how to create a new database using a database template and the Database Wizard. You also learn how to close your database, open it, and how to find a misplaced database file.

CHOOSING HOW TO CREATE YOUR DATABASE

Before you can create your database tables and actually enter data, you must create a database file. The database is really just a container file that holds all the database objects, such as the tables, forms, and reports. You also have two options for creating a new database: You can create a blank database from scratch or create a new database based on a database template.

Creating a new database based on a template means that you take advantage of the Database Wizard, which not only creates your new database file but also helps you quickly create tables, forms, and other objects for the database.

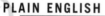

PLAIN ENGLISH

> **Database Wizard**   Access provides several templates for creating new database files, and the Database Wizard walks you through the process of creating objects, such as tables, for the new database.

Whether you create your new database from scratch or use one of the database templates depends on how closely one of the Access templates meets your database needs. If one of the templates provides you with the type of tables and other objects necessary for your project, it makes sense to use a template. For example, if you want to create a database that helps you manage your company's inventory, you can take advantage of the Inventory Control template that Access provides. This template provides you with the basic tables and other objects to start the process of getting a handle on your inventory database.

In some cases, the templates might not meet your needs. For example, if you want to create a complex database that allows you to track sales, customers, and employee performance, it might be easier to create a blank database and then create each table for the database from scratch. Let's start the overview of database creation with creating a blank database.

Selecting a Database File Type

One thing to discuss before you look at creating a new database is the database file format. By default, new databases created in Access 2002 are created in the Access 2000 file format. This makes your database files compatible with earlier versions of Access, such as Access 2000 and Access 97.

Saving the database in the Access 2000 file format does not negate you from using any of the tools or features available in Access 2002. If you use your database files only in Access 2002 and share the databases with co-workers who also use Access 2002, you can set the default file format for new databases to Access 2002. Select the **Tools** menu, and then select **Options**. The Options dialog box opens.

Select the **Advanced** tab on the Options dialog box. Click the **Default File Format** drop-down box and select **Access 2002**. Now take a look at creating new databases.

CREATING A BLANK DATABASE

Creating a blank database is very straightforward. As mentioned previously, you are just creating the container file that holds all the objects that actually make up the database. To create a blank database, follow these steps:

1. Open the Access window (click **Start**, **Programs**, **Access**).

 2. Select **Blank Database** in the task pane or click the **New** button on the Database toolbar. The File New Database dialog box appears (see Figure 3.1).

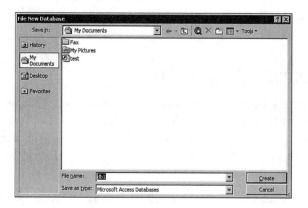

FIGURE 3.1
Provide a location and a name for the new database file.

3. Use the Save In drop-down box to locate the folder in which you want to save the new database. Type a name for the new file into the **File Name** text box.

4. When you are ready to create the database file, click **Create**. The new database window appears in the Access workspace (see Figure 3.2).

Object icons   Object pane

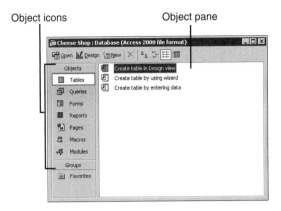

FIGURE 3.2
A new database window opens in Access.

The database window provides you with a set of icons that allows you to select a particular object type. For example, the Tables icon is selected by default after you create the new database (which makes sense, because you need to create at least one table before you can create any of the other object types such as a form or a report).

Shortcuts for different methods of creating tables are provided at the top of the Object pane on the right side of the database window. After you create a new table for the database, it is listed in this pane. In Lesson 4, "Creating a Table with the Table Wizard," and Lesson 5, "Creating a Table from Scratch," you take a look at creating tables.

The database window enables you to view the different objects that you've created for a particular database (or those that have been created when you use the Database Wizard). When you want to switch the database window's focus to a different Access object, all you have to do is click the appropriate icon in the Objects list.

TIP

> **Different Ways to View the Database Windows**   The tool-
> bar on the database window provides buttons for open-
> ing or creating a particular database object, such as a
> table or a form. The toolbar also provides buttons that
> can be used to change the view in the Object pane:
> **Large Icons, Small Icons, List** (the default view) and
> **Details** (which provides information such as when the
> object was last modified).

CLOSING A DATABASE

When you finish working with a database, you might want to close it
so that you can concentrate on creating a new database (such as you
do in the next section). However, because Access allows you to have
only one database open at a time, as soon as you begin creating a new
database the currently open database closes. Opening an existing database also closes the current database (which is something you do later
in this lesson).

If you want to close a database, there are a couple of possibilities: You
can click the **Close (x)** button on the database window, or you can
select **File, Close**. In either case, the database window closes, clearing
the Access workspace.

CREATING A DATABASE FROM A TEMPLATE

Another option for creating a new database is using one of the Access
database templates. Templates are available for asset tracking, contact
management, inventory control, and other database types. Another
perk of using an Access template to create a new database is that a
Database Wizard creates tables and other objects, such as forms and
reports, for the new database. The wizard also sets up the relationships
between the various tables (making your database relational).

Your interaction with the Database Wizard is somewhat limited; the
wizard allows you to select the fields that will be used in the tables

that it creates for the database. However, you don't have a say about which tables are initially created (tables can always be deleted later if you don't need them). You are, however, given the opportunity to select the format for screen displays (for forms and reports) and to select the format for printed reports.

To create a database from a template, follow these steps:

1. In the Access window, click **General Templates** on the task pane. If the task pane is not currently in the Access window, select **File, New** to open it.

TIP

> **Opening the Task Pane**   When you are working on a particular database and want to open the task pane, select the **View** menu, point at **Toolbars**, and then select **Task Pane**.

2. The Templates dialog box appears. If necessary, click the Databases tab on the dialog box to view the database templates (see Figure 3.3).

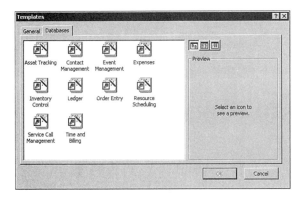

FIGURE 3.3
Access provides several database templates.

3. Click the database template you want to use (for example, the Contact Management template) and then click **OK**. The File New Database dialog box appears.

4. Specify a location for the database using the Save In drop-down list, type a name for the database, and then click **Create** to continue. A new database file is created, and then the Database Wizard associated with the template starts. For example, if you chose the Contact Management template, the wizard appears and explains the type of information that the database holds.

5. To move past the wizard's opening screen, click **Next**. On the next screen, a list of the tables that will be created appears (see Figure 3.4). The tables in the database are listed on the left of the screen and the selected table's fields appear on the right.

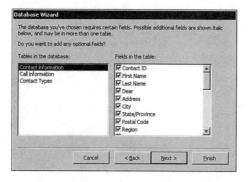

FIGURE 3.4
You can examine and deselect (or select) the fields that will be contained in each table.

6. Select a table to examine its fields. If you do not want to include a field in the table, clear the check box next to the field name. Optional fields are also listed for each field and are shown in italic. To include an optional field, click it to place a check mark next to it. When you have finished viewing the tables and their fields, click **Next** to continue.

CAUTION

Be Careful Deselecting Fields!   Because you are stuck with the tables that the Database Wizard creates, you must be very careful removing fields from the tables. This is especially true of fields that uniquely identify the records in a table, such as Contact ID. These fields are often used to relate the tables in the database. You might want to leave all the fields alone initially when you use the wizard.

7. The next screen asks you to select the screen display style you want to use. This affects how forms appear on the screen. Click a display style in the list to preview the style; after selecting the style you want to use, click **Next**.

8. On the next screen, the wizard asks you for a style for your printed reports. Click a report style and examine the preview of it. When you decide on a style, click it, and then click **Next**.

TIP

Report Background   The colored backgrounds used for some report styles look nice onscreen, but they don't print well on a black-and-white printer. Unless you have access to a color printer, stick to plain backgrounds for the best report printouts.

9. On the next wizard screen, you are asked to provide a title for the database. This title appears on reports and can be different from the filename. Enter a title as shown in Figure 3.5.

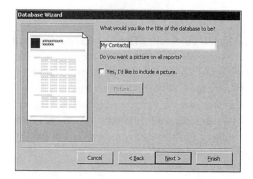

FIGURE 3.5
Enter a title for the database, and as an option, choose a graphic to use for a logo.

10. (Optional) To include a picture on your forms and reports (for example, your company's logo), click the **Yes, I'd Like to Include a Picture** check box. Then click the **Picture** button, choose a picture file from your hard drive (or other source), and click **OK** to return to the wizard.

11. Click **Next** to continue. You are taken to the last wizard screen; click **Finish** to open the new database. The wizard goes to work creating your database and its database objects.

When the wizard has finished creating the database, the database's Main Switchboard window appears (see Figure 3.6). The Main Switchboard opens automatically whenever you open the database.

All the databases created using one of the Access templates (other than the Blank Database template) include a Main Switchboard. The Switchboard is nothing more than a fancy form with some programming built in to it. It enables you to perform common tasks related to database management by clicking a button. It is very useful when a person is unfamiliar with how to manipulate the various objects in a database.

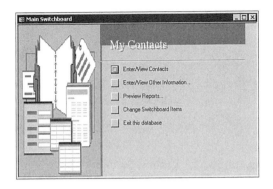

FIGURE 3.6
The Switchboard window is a database navigation tool provided by the Database Wizard.

Using the Main Switchboard is pretty much self-explanatory. After you become familiar with Access, you probably won't even use it. To close the Switchboard, click its **Close (x)** button.

TIP

I Hate That Switchboard! To prevent the Switchboard from opening when you open the database, choose **Tools**, **Startup**. In the Startup dialog box, select the **Display Form/Page** drop-down list and select **[None]**. Click **OK**.

After you close the Switchboard window, you will find that the database window has been minimized in the Access workspace. Just double-click its title bar (at the bottom-left corner of the screen) to open it. To see the tables that the wizard created, click the **Tables** object type. Click the other object types (such as forms) to see the other objects that were created by the wizard.

The tables that the wizard creates are, of course, empty. After you fill them with data (either inputting the data directly into the table or using a form), you will be able to run queries and create reports.

OPENING A DATABASE

You have already taken a look at how to close a database; next, you walk through the process of opening a database file. The next time you start Access or after you finish working with another database, you need to know how to open your other database files.

One of the easiest ways to open a database you've recently used is to select it from the File menu. Follow these steps:

1. Open the **File** menu. You'll see up to four databases that you've recently used listed at the bottom of the menu.

2. If the database you need is listed there, click it.

TIP

> **Want to See More Files?**   To increase the number of files displayed in this list, open the **Tools** menu and select **Options**. Then, from the **General** tab of the Options dialog box, select a number from 1 to 9 (the default is 4) in the **Recently Used Files** drop-down list.

A list of recently used databases also appears on the tip of the Access task pane. You can open any of the files by clicking the filename (to open the task pane, select **View**, **Toolbars**, **Task Pane**).

If a file you want to open is not listed either on the File menu or the task pane, you can open it using the Open command. Follow these steps:

1. Select **File**, **Open**, or click the toolbar's **Open** button. The Open dialog box appears (see Figure 3.7).

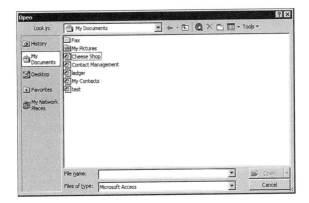

FIGURE 3.7
Use the Open dialog box to locate a database file you want to open.

2. If the file isn't in the currently displayed folder, use the Look In drop-down list to access the correct drive, and then double-click folders displayed in the dialog box to locate the file.

3. When you have located the database file, double-click the file to open it.

In this lesson, you learned how to create a database from scratch and how to create a database from a template. You also learned how to close and open a database. In the next lesson, you learn how to create a table using the Table Wizard.

Lesson 4

Creating a Table with the Table Wizard

In this lesson, you learn how to create a table by using the Table Wizard.

Tables Are Essential

As discussed in Lesson 1, your tables really provide the essential framework for your database. Tables not only hold the data that you enter into the database, but they are designed so that relationships can be established between the various tables in the database. Tables can be created from scratch, as discussed in the next lesson, or they can be created using the Table Wizard.

Working with the Table Wizard

The Table Wizard can save you a lot of time by supplying you with all the needed fields and field formats for entering your database information. Access provides a large number of different kinds of tables that you can create with the wizard. The wizard is also fairly flexible, allowing you to select the fields the table will contain and the way in which they will be arranged. You can also change the name of a field during the process. If the wizard doesn't provide a particular field, you can always add it to the table later, as discussed in Lesson 6, "Editing a Table's Structure."

To create a table using the Table Wizard, follow these steps:

1. In the database window, click the **Tables** object icon, and then double-click **Create Table by Using Wizard**. The Table Wizard opens.

TIP

> **Alternative Routes** You can also start the Table Wizard by clicking the **New** button in the database window or choosing **Insert, Table**. In both cases, the New Table dialog box opens. Then, choose **Table Wizard** and click **OK**.

2. On the first Table Wizard screen, you can select from two categories of table types: **Business** or **Personal**. Your choice determines the list of sample tables that appears (see Figure 4.1).

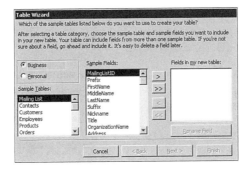

FIGURE 4.1
Select either the Business or Personal category to view a list of tables.

3. Select a table in the Sample Tables list; its fields appear in the Sample Fields list.

4. To include a field from the Sample Fields list in the table, select the field and click the **Add (>)** button to move it to the **Fields in My New Table** list. You can include all the fields in Sample Fields list by clicking the **Add All (>>)** button.

5. If you want to rename a field that you have added, click the **Rename Field** button, type a new name into the Rename field box, and then click **OK**.

TIP

> **Remove Unwanted Fields**   If you add a field that you don't want in the table, select the field in the **Fields in My New Table** list and click the **Remove (<)** button. To remove all the fields and start over, click **Remove All (<<)**.

6. Repeat steps 3 and 4 as needed to select more fields for the table. You can select fields from more than one of the sample tables for the table that you are creating (remember that you want fields in the table related only to a particular theme, such as customer information). When you're finished adding fields, click **Next** to continue.

7. The next screen asks you to provide a name for the table (see Figure 4.2). Type a more descriptive name if necessary to replace the default name.

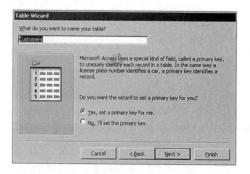

FIGURE 4.2
Provide a name for the table and allow the wizard to select a primary key for the table.

8. This dialog box also asks whether you want the wizard to create a primary key for the table or allow you to select the primary key yourself. The *primary key* is the field that uniquely identifies each of the records in the table. For example, CustomerID is an excellent primary key because each customer is assigned a different ID number. In this case, click **Yes, Set a Primary Key for Me** to have the wizard choose your primary key field. You can learn to set your own primary keys in Lesson 5, "Creating a Table from Scratch."

PLAIN ENGLISH

Primary Key   The field that uniquely identifies each record in the table. Every table must have a primary key. This is usually an ID number because most other fields could conceivably hold the same data for more than one record (for example, you might have several people with the last name of Smith).

9. Click **Next** to continue. Because you're allowing the wizard to select the primary key, you are taken to the last wizard screen. On the last wizard screen, you have the options of modifying the table's design, entering data directly into the new table, or having the wizard create a data entry form for you. To see the table the wizard created, go with the default: Enter Data Directly into the Table (see Figure 4.3).

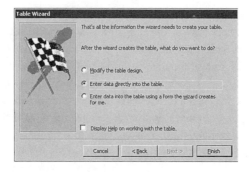

FIGURE 4.3
After completing the table, you can have the wizard open it so that you can enter data.

10. Click **Finish**.

The new table appears in the Access workspace (see Figure 4.4). From here you can enter data into the table, the specifics of which are discussed in Lesson 7, "Entering Data into a Table." When you close the table, it appears in the Object pane of the database window (you must also select the Tables object icon).

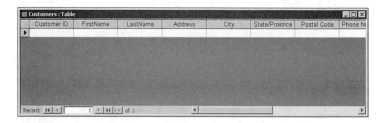

FIGURE 4.4
Your new table appears in the Access workspace when you close the Table Wizard.

In this lesson, you learned how to create a new table by using the Table Wizard. In the next lesson, you learn how to create a table in the design and datasheet views.

LESSON 5
Creating a Table from Scratch

In this lesson, you learn how to create a table in the Table Design view and the Datasheet view.

CREATING TABLES WITHOUT THE WIZARD

Although the Table Wizard provides an easy method for quickly creating tables, it does not provide you with complete control over all the aspects of creating the table. It does allow you to select the fields used in the table from a set list, but it restricts you to only those predefined fields (there are also several types of fields, each used for a different data type). Creating tables from scratch in the Design view allows you to build the table from the bottom up and gives you complete control over all aspects of the table's design.

> **PLAIN ENGLISH**
>
> **Design View**   This view allows you to enter field names, select the data type that a field will hold, and customize each field's properties. A Design view is available for all the Access objects, including tables, forms, queries, and reports.

The Design view isn't the only way to create a table from scratch in Access. You can also create a table in the Datasheet view by labeling your field columns directly on the table's datasheet, which is similar to creating a worksheet in Excel. Take a look at both methods for creating a new table.

TIP

> **Datasheet View** This view places each record in a separate row and each field in a separate column (column headings are provided by the field names). This view is used to enter data directly into the table. You will use the Datasheet view whenever you want to view the records in the table or add or edit records.

CREATING A TABLE IN TABLE DESIGN VIEW

When you create a table in the Design view, you are creating the structure for the table; you create a list of the fields that will be in the table. You also select the data type for each field. (Fields can hold text, numbers, even graphics—you learn the types of fields that can be created later in this lesson.) You also have the option of entering a description for each field. Field descriptions are useful in that they provide a quick summary of the type of data that goes into the field.

Another issue that relates to creating a table in the Design view (or editing a table's structure in the Design view) is that any changes you make must be saved before closing the table. If you have worked in other applications, such as Word or Excel, you might think that saving your work is just common sense. However, when you actually start working on entering data into a table or a form, Access automatically saves your records as you enter them. Therefore, in Access, you need to remember to save only the changes that you make to the structure of a table, form, query, or report. You learn more about this in Lesson 6, "Editing a Table's Structure."

TIP

> **Field Naming Rules** Field names in Access can be up to 64 characters long and can contain spaces and both alphanumeric and numeric characters. You can't use periods or exclamation points in your field names. Also, avoid special characters (such as $, %, or #) in field names because some of these characters have special meanings in Access code.

To create a table in Table Design view, follow these steps:

1. In the database window (of a particular database) click the **Tables** icon if necessary, and then double-click **Create Table in Design View**. The Table Design view opens (see Figure 5.1).

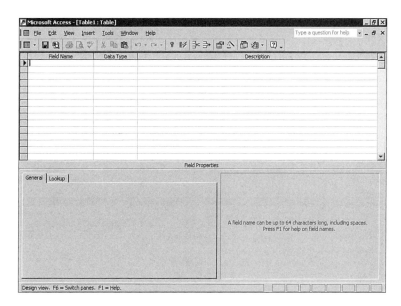

FIGURE 5.1
The Table Design view allows you to create the structure for your table.

2. Be sure that the insertion point is in the first row of the Field Name column. Type the field name for the first field in your table. Then, press **Tab** or **Enter** to move to the Data Type column.

3. When you move to the Data Type column, an arrow appears for a drop-down list. The default data type setting is Text; several other data types are available, such as AutoNumber, which automatically numbers each of your records. This field type is excellent for customer number fields or employee ID fields. Click the **Data Type** drop-down list and select a field

type. The different data types are discussed later in this lesson, in the section "Understanding Data Types and Formats."

4. After selecting the data type, press **Enter** to move to the Description column; type a description for the field. (This is optional; the table will work fine without it.)

TIP

> **Deleting a Field**　If you enter a field and decide that you don't want it in the table's structure, select the field (its entire row) and press the **Delete** key.

5. Enter other fields and their field types (descriptions are optional) as needed. Figure 5.2 shows the structure for a table that will be used to enter product information.

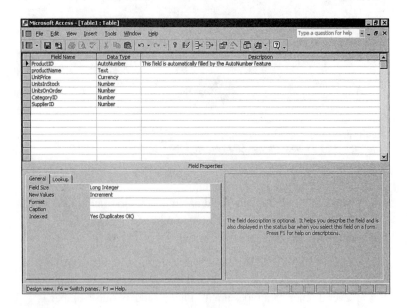

FIGURE 5.2
A table's structure consists of several fields; fields may differ by field type.

SETTING THE PRIMARY KEY

An important aspect of table structure design is that each table must have a field that is used to uniquely identify the records in the table. This field is called the *primary key*. Setting an appropriate key is trickier than it appears because no two records can have the same key value. In a table of customers, for example, you might think the Last Name field would be a good key, but this theory falls flat as soon as you find that you have more than one customer with the same last name. A more appropriate primary key for your customers is a Social Security number (although people don't like to give these out) because it uniquely identifies each customer.

A good general rule is to create an identification field, such as a customer number, that allows you to assign a sequential number to each customer as you add them to your database table. Access can even help you out with the assigning of numbers to the customers because you can make the field type for the Customer Number field AutoNumber. An AutoNumber field type assigns a number to each record starting with the number 1.

TIP

Creating the Primary Key   Typically, the first field in the table serves as the primary key.

To set a primary key, follow these steps:

1. In Table Design view, select the field that you want for the primary key.

2. Select **Edit**, **Primary Key**, or click the **Primary Key** button on the toolbar. A key symbol appears to the left of the field name, as shown in Figure 5.3.

Primary Key

Field Name	Data Type	Description
ProductID	AutoNumber	This field is automatically filled by the AutoNumber feature
productName	Text	
UnitPrice	Currency	
UnitsInStock	Number	
UnitsOnOrder	Number	
CategoryID	Number	
SupplierID	Number	

FIGURE 5.3
The primary key field is marked by a key symbol.

3. After you select the primary key and have finished entering your table fields, you should save the table. Click the **Save** button on the Table Design toolbar to open the Save As dialog box.

4. Enter a name for the table, and then click **OK**.

5. After saving the table, you can either switch to the Datasheet view (to enter data) by clicking the **View** button on the toolbar, or you can choose to close the table by clicking the table's **Close** (**x**) button.

PLAIN ENGLISH

No Primary Key!   If you attempt to close your new table in the Design view without specifying a primary key (even if you have saved the table), a message appears, letting you know that no primary key has been assigned. Click **Yes** on the message box to have Access assign a primary key to the table. If you have set up your table to contain an AutoNumber field, Access will make this field the primary key. Otherwise, Access creates a new AutoNumber field in the table and specifies it as the primary key. You can change the name of this new field as needed.

Understanding Data Types and Formats

To assign appropriate data types to the fields you create in a table, it is necessary for you to know what differentiates the different data types available for use with your table fields. When you create a field, you want to assign it a data type so that Access knows how to handle its contents. The following are the different data types you can choose:

- **Text**—Text and numbers up to 255 characters (numbers that are not going to be used in calculations).

- **Memo**—Lengthy text.

- **Number**—Numbers used in mathematical calculations.

- **Date/Time**—Date and time values.

- **Currency**—Numbers formatted for currency.

- **AutoNumber**—Sequentially numbers each new record. Only one AutoNumber field can be placed in a table. This field type is typically used for the primary key field.

- **Yes/No**—Lets you set up fields with a true/false data type.

- **OLE (Object Linking and Embedding)**—A picture, spreadsheet, or other item from another software program.

- **Hyperlink**—A link to another file or a location on a Web page. This field type lets you jump from the current field to information in another file.

- **Lookup Wizard**—This field type chooses its values from another table.

In addition to a field type, each field has other formatting options you can set. They appear in the bottom half of the dialog box, in the Field Properties area. The formatting options change depending on the field type; there are too many to list here, but Table 5.1 shows some of the most important ones you'll encounter.

TABLE 5.1   Formatting Options for Data Types

Formatting Option	Description
Field Size	The maximum number of characters a user can input in that field (applies only to text fields).
Format	A drop-down list of the available formats for that field type. You can also create custom formats.
Decimal Places	For number fields, you can set the default number of decimal places that a number shows.
Default Value	If a field is usually going to contain a certain value (for example, a certain ZIP code for almost everyone), you can set that as the Default Value option. It always appears in a new record, but you can type over it in the rare instances when it doesn't apply.
Required	Choose **Yes** if a particular field is required to be filled in each record.

The best general rule for setting the data type for the field is to take a moment to consider what kind of data will go into that field. For example, if you are working with the monetary value of a product, you will probably want to use currency.

The different formatting options provided for a field in the Field Properties box are often used to help make sure that data is entered correctly. For example, the Field Size option can be used to limit a Number data type field to only a single or double digit. In the case of the default value, you can actually save data entry time because you use this option when a particular field almost always has a certain value or text entry.

CREATING A TABLE IN THE DATASHEET VIEW

After you feel comfortable creating new tables in the Design view, you might want to dive right in and create tables in the Datasheet view. Creating tables this way immediately creates a table with 20 field columns and 30 record rows. This method still requires, however, that you enter the Table Design view to specify the key field, the field data types, field descriptions, and any field property changes.

Creating tables in the Datasheet view is really useful only if you feel the need to quickly enter some data into the table before setting up the table's properties. To create a table in the Datasheet view, follow these steps:

1. In the database window (with the Table icon selected), double-click **Create Table by Entering Data**. A new table in Data-sheet view appears in the Access workspace (see Figure 5.4).

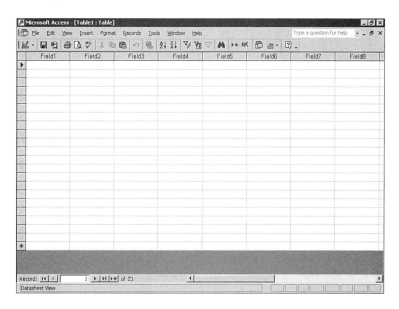

FIGURE 5.4
Tables can be created in the Datasheet view.

2. To enter the field names, double-click any field column heading (Field1, Field2, and so on). Then, type in the field name.

3. After you have placed the field names, you can begin entering data.

Creating a table in the Datasheet view might be fine for quickly entering data, but you will still probably need to switch to the Table Design view at some point and set up the various field data types and properties.

 You can switch to the Design view from the Datasheet view by clicking the **View** icon on the Table Datasheet toolbar. Remember to save any changes to the table's design that you make in the Design view.

In this lesson, you learned to create a table in the Design view and the Datasheet view. You also learned about the different field data types. In the next lesson, you learn how to edit and enhance your table's structure.

LESSON 6
Editing a Table's Structure

In this lesson, you learn how to change your table structure by adding and removing fields and hiding columns.

EDITING FIELDS AND THEIR PROPERTIES

After you've created a table with the Table Wizard or from scratch, you might find that you want to fine-tune the table's structure. This requires that you edit your fields and their properties.

You can delete fields, add new fields, or change the order of fields in the table. You also can change a field's data type. Because the table's structure is discussed here and not the data, you need to work in the Table Design view.

> **CAUTION**
>
> **Get the Table's Structure Down Before Entering Data**   You should try to finalize the table's field structure and properties before you enter data. Changing data types or other field properties can actually delete data that you've already entered into the table.

You can open an existing table in the Table Design view in several ways:

- In the database window, click the **Table** object icon, select the table you want to work with in the right pane of the database window, and then click the **Design** button on the database window's toolbar.

- Right-click the table in the database window and select **Design View** from the shortcut menu that appears.

- If you are in the table's Datasheet view, click the **View** button on the Table Datasheet view toolbar.

CHANGING FIELD NAMES AND DATA TYPES

When you are in the Design view (see Figure 6.1), you can enhance or rework your table's structure. For example, you can change a field's name. Just double-click the field's current name and type in a new one.

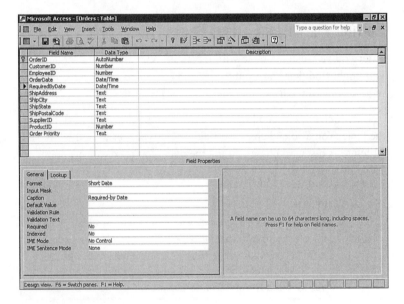

FIGURE 6.1
A table's existing structure can be edited in the Design view.

You can also change the data type for an existing field. Click the field's Data Type box and select a new data type from the drop-down list. Remember that when you change a field name or a field's data type, you must save the changes that you've made to the table's structure.

Setting Field Properties

Field properties can also be edited for each field using the various Properties boxes found in the Field Properties pane. Lesson 5, "Creating a Table from Scratch," provides a quick overview of some of the properties that are available.

Another very useful field property, particularly for fields that use text entries (remember that text entries can include numbers) is an *input mask*. An input mask is used to format that data as you enter it into a field. For example, you might want to enter a date in a particular format, such as the format xx/xx/xx. The input mask can be used so that when you enter the data into the date field, all you need to enter is the two-digit input for the month, day, and year. Access automatically places the slashes in the field for you.

PLAIN ENGLISH

Input Mask   A field property that limits the number of characters that can be entered in a field.

Input masks are also very useful for entering ZIP codes. The input mask limits the number of characters that can be entered (such as those in a ZIP code), and if you use the 5-4 ZIP code format, the input mask can place the dash into the ZIP code for you.

To create an input mask for a field (such as a date field or a Design view field), follow these steps:

1. Click in the Field Name box to select the field for which you want to create the input mask.

2. In the Field Properties pane, click in the Input Mask box. The Input Mask Wizard button appears in the box.

3. Click the **Input Mask Wizard** button to open the dialog box shown in Figure 6.2.

FIGURE 6.2
The Input Mask Wizard helps you create an input mask for a field.

4. The Input Mask Wizard offers a list of possible masks for the field based on the field's data type. For example, Figure 6.2 shows the Input Mask Wizard used for a field with the Date data type. Select one of the mask formats listed, and then click **Next**.

5. The next wizard screen shows you the input mask you have chosen and gives you the opportunity to change the format. You can also test the input mask format by typing some data into the Try It box. Edit the input mask format if necessary and then click **Next** to continue.

6. You are taken to the last wizard screen. Click **Finish** to create the input mask. The input mask appears in the Input Mask box in the Field Properties pane (see Figure 6.3).

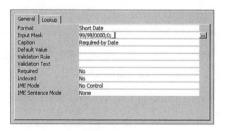

FIGURE 6.3
The input mask appears in the Input Mask box.

7. Click the **Save** button to save changes that you have made to the table structure.

Adding, Deleting, and Moving Fields

You can also add additional fields to your table's structure. All you have to do is add a new row to the field list and then enter the new field name and data type. Follow these steps:

1. Click the record selector (the gray square to the left of the field name) to select the field that will follow the new field that you create (in the field list).

2. Select **Insert**, **Row**. A blank row appears in the Field Name list.

3. Enter a name, a data type, a description, and so on for the new field.

You can also delete any unwanted fields. Click the record selector for the field and then press the **Delete** key on the keyboard. A message box appears that requires you to confirm the field's deletion. Click **Yes** to delete the field.

CAUTION

Don't Remove Important Fields!   Be very careful about deleting fields after you start entering records into your table. When you delete a field, all the information stored for each record in that field is gone, too. The best time to experiment with deleting fields is before you enter any data into the table.

You can also rearrange the fields in the table. Click the record selector for the field to select the field. Then, use the mouse to drag the field to a new position in the field list. Remember to save any changes that you have made to the table's structure.

DELETING A TABLE

No matter how hard you work on a table's design, you might find as
you design the other tables for your database that you just don't need
a particular table. It's easy to delete a table (although it might not
be easy to forget the time that you spent creating the table); simply
follow these steps:

1. In the database window, click the **Tables** object type.

2. In the right pane of the database window, select the table you
   want to delete.

3. Select **Edit**, **Delete**, or press the **Delete** key on your keyboard.

4. A message appears asking whether you're sure you want to
   do this. Click **Yes**.

In this lesson, you learned how to modify your table's properties in
the Design View. You also learned how to create an input mask for a
field. Adding and removing fields was also covered. In the next lesson,
you learn how to enter data into the table in the Datasheet view and
navigate the table.

LESSON 7
Entering Data into a Table

In this lesson, you learn how to add records to a table, print the table, and close it.

ENTERING A RECORD

After you've created the table and fine-tuned its structure, you are ready to enter data into the table. This means that you should have access to all the data that you need to enter. Then, all you have to do is open the table and input the data records.

TIP

> **Using Forms to Enter Data**   Access doesn't limit you to entering data directly into the table. You can also enter data using a form. Form creation and data entry using a form are covered in Lesson 13, "Modifying a Form."

First, from the database window, double-click the table in which you want to enter the records. The table opens in the Datasheet view (see Figure 7.1). If this is the first time you have entered data into the table, only one empty record appears in the table. As you complete each record, a new blank record (a new row) appears.

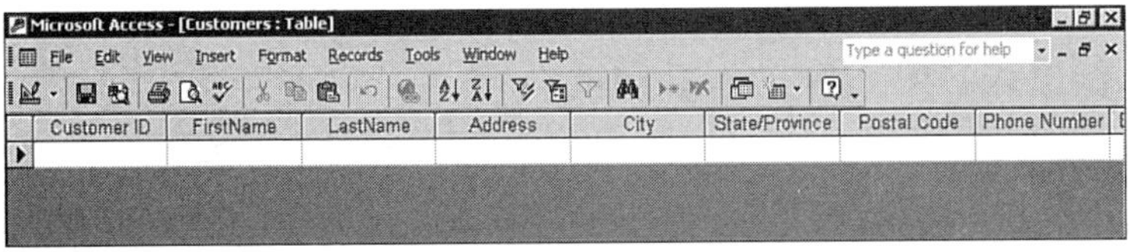

FIGURE 7.1
A table's existing structure can be edited in the Design view.

To enter records into the table, follow these steps:

1. Click in the first field of the first blank record (if necessary). If the first field is an identification field, such as Customer ID, and you selected the AutoNumber data type for the field, press **Tab** to advance to the next field (the AutoNumber field is automatically filled in for you).

2. Type the value for that field.

3. Press **Tab** to move to the next field and enter that field's data.

4. Continue pressing **Tab** and entering data until you complete the last field in the record. When you press **Tab** in the last field, a new record (a new row) appears, and the insertion point moves to the first field in the new record.

5. Continue entering records as required.

TIP

> **Data Entry Tricks**   Access offers some hotkey combina-
> tions for entering dates and data found in the same field
> in a previous record. To insert the current date, press
> **Ctrl+;** (semicolon). To insert the current time, press
> **Ctrl+:** (colon). To repeat the value from the same field in
> the previous record, press **Ctrl+'** (apostrophe).

You should be aware that, as you enter each field's data and move onto the next field, Access automatically saves your table data. This is very different from other Office applications, such as Word or Excel, where you must save your data after entering it.

MOVING AROUND IN A TABLE

So far, you've used the Tab key only to move from field to field in the table. You might have also used the mouse to move the insertion point from a field in one record to another field in that record, or to a field in a different record. Because you do your data entry from the keyboard, Access provides several keystrokes that can be used to navigate the various fields in the table. For example, you can back up one field in a record by pressing **Shift+Tab**. Table 7.1 summarizes the various keyboard shortcuts for moving around in a table.

TABLE 7.1   Table Movement Keys

To Move To	Press
Next field	Tab
Previous field	Shift+Tab
Last field in the record	End
First field in the record	Home
Same field in the next record	Down-arrow key
Same field in the previous record	Up-arrow key
Same field in the last record	Ctrl+down-arrow key
Same field in the first record	Ctrl+up-arrow key
Last field in the last record	Ctrl+End
First field in the first record	Ctrl+Home

HIDING A FIELD

When you are entering data into the table, you might find that you have not actually collected the data that you need to enter into a particular field. This means that you must skip this field in all the records as you enter your data (until you come up with the data).

You can hide a field or fields in the table datasheet. This doesn't delete the field column or disrupt any of the field properties that you set for that particular field. It just hides the field from your view as you enter your data. To hide a field, follow these steps:

1. In the Datasheet view, select the field or fields that you want to hide (click a field's column heading, as shown in Figure 7.2). To select multiple contiguous fields, click the first field, and then hold down the **Shift** key and click the last field.

FIGURE 7.2
You can select a column and then hide it.

2. Select **Format** and then **Hide Columns,** or right-click the column and select **Hide Columns**. The column or columns disappear.

3. Enter your data records into your table; the hidden column is skipped as you move from column to column.

4. When you have finished entering data into the other fields in the table, you can unhide the column. Select **Format, Unhide Columns**. The Unhide Columns dialog box appears (see Figure 7.3). Fields with a check mark next to them are unhidden; fields without a check mark are hidden.

5. Click the check box of any hidden field to "unhide" the field.

6. Click **Close**. The hidden column (or columns) reappear in the table.

FIGURE 7.3
The Unhide Columns dialog box shows you which columns are currently hidden.

FREEZING A COLUMN

Another useful manipulation of the field columns in an Access table that can make data entry easier is freezing a column. For example, if a table has a large number of fields, as you move to the right in the table during data entry, fields in the beginning of the table scroll off the screen. This can be very annoying if you lose your place, because you might not remember for which customer you were entering data.

You can freeze columns so that they remain on the screen even when you scroll to the far right of a table record. Follow these steps:

1. Click the column heading of the field column you want to freeze. This selects the entire column of data.

2. Click the **Format** menu; then click **Freeze Columns**.

3. The frozen field column moves over to the first field position in the table. Click anywhere in the table to deselect the field column.

4. When you move through the fields in a record toward the far right of the table, the frozen field column remains on the screen. This allows you to see important data such as the customer's name as you attempt to enter other data into a particular record.

You can freeze multiple columns if you want, such as the Last Name field and the First Name field. When you want to unfreeze the column or columns in the table, select the **Format** menu, and then select **Unfreeze All Columns**.

USING THE SPELLING FEATURE

To ensure your data entry accuracy, you can quickly check the spelling of the data that you have input into your table. This should help you clear up any typos that might have happened during your entry of the table records.

The Spelling feature, obviously, won't be able to check the numerical information that you input or help you enter proper names, but it can help you avoid embarrassing misspellings. To check the spelling in a table, follow these steps:

1. Click the **Spelling** button on the Table Datasheet toolbar, or you can select **Tools**, **Spelling** to open the Spelling dialog box (see Figure 7.4).

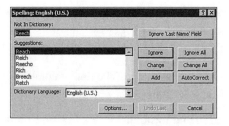

FIGURE 7.4
The Spelling feature enables you to quickly check for typos and misspellings in your Access table.

2. Words flagged as misspelled appear in the dialog box. A list of suggestions also appears from which you can choose a correct spelling. You can either correct the misspellings manually or click one of the suggestions. When you're ready,

click **Change** to correct the spelling. The Speller then moves to the next misspelled word.

3. If you want to add the flagged word to the dictionary, click the **Add** button. If a flagged word is correctly spelled, click the **Ignore** button to ignore the word and continue with the spell check.

4. If the field containing the flagged word is a field that typically holds proper names or other values that the Spelling feature will always flag as misspelled, click the **Ignore "Field Name"** button.

CLOSING A TABLE

After you have finished entering data into a particular table and checking the spelling, you should close that table. Because the table is just like any other window, click the table's **Close (x)** button to close the table. You are then returned to the database window.

In this lesson, you learned how to enter records into a table, navigate the table from the keyboard, and hide columns in the table. You also learned to check the spelling in the table and close the table. In the next lesson, you learn how to edit data in a table.

LESSON 8
Editing Data in a Table

In this lesson, you learn how to edit information in a field, select records, and insert and delete records.

CHANGING A FIELD'S CONTENT

After you enter the records in a table, you will probably find that you need to make some changes; sometimes data is entered incorrectly or the data for a particular record might actually change. Editing a field's content is easy. You can replace the old field content entirely or edit it.

REPLACING A FIELD'S CONTENT

If the data in a field must be updated or has been entered incorrectly, the easiest way to replace this data is to enter the new data from scratch. To replace the old content in a field, follow these steps:

1. You can use the **Tab** key to move to the field you want to edit (the contents of the field will be selected), or select the contents of a field with the mouse. To use your mouse, place the mouse pointer on the upper-left or right edge of the field. The mouse pointer becomes a plus sign (+) as shown in Figure 8.1. Click the field to select its content.

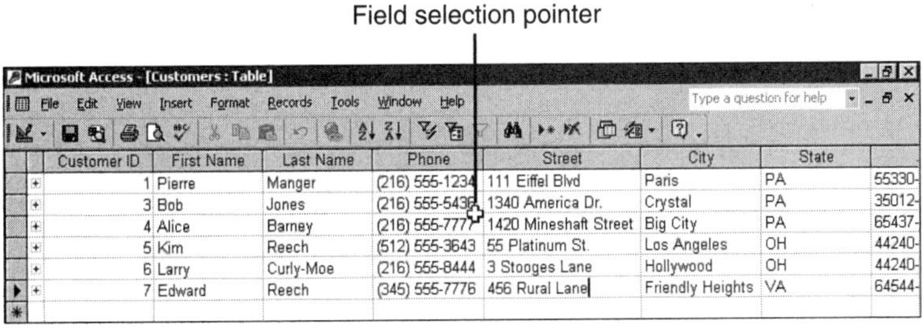

Field selection pointer

FIGURE 8.1
To select a field's entire contents, make sure that the mouse pointer is a plus sign when you click.

2. Type the new data, which replaces the old data.

3. You can the use the **Tab** key or the mouse to move to the next field you need to edit.

EDITING A FIELD'S CONTENT WITH A MOUSE

Replacing the entire contents of a field is kind of a heavy-handed way to edit a field if you need to correct the entry of only one or two characters. You can also fine-tune your entries by editing a portion of the data in the field. Follow these steps:

1. Place the mouse pointer over the position in the field where you want to correct data. The mouse pointer should become an I-beam.

2. Click once to place the insertion point at that position in the field (see Figure 8.2). Now you can edit the content of the field.

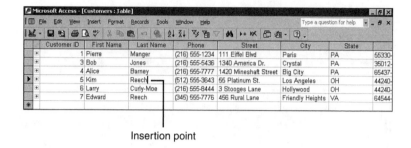

Insertion point

FIGURE 8.2
Place the insertion point into a field to edit its content.

3. Press **Backspace** to remove the character to the left of the insertion point or **Delete** to remove the character to the right of the insertion point.

4. Enter new text into the field as needed. New entries in the field are inserted, meaning they displace the current entry but do not overwrite it.

MOVING AROUND A FIELD WITH A KEYBOARD

Although the mouse provides a quick way to place the insertion point into a field, you might want to be able to navigate inside a field using the keyboard, especially when you are editing a fairly long field entry. Access provides several keyboard possibilities for moving inside a cell. Table 8.1 lists these keyboard-movement keys.

TABLE 8.1 Moving Within a Field

To Move	Press
One character to the right	Right-arrow key
One character to the left	Left-arrow key
One word to the right	Ctrl+right-arrow key
One word to the left	Ctrl+left-arrow key

To Move	Press
To the end of the line	End
To the beginning of the line	Home

MOVING AND COPYING DATA

As in any Office application, you can use the Cut, Copy, and Paste commands to copy and move data in your table fields. This is particularly useful if you want to quickly copy a ZIP code that is the same for more than one customer, or you want to cut data that you put in the wrong field, so that you can paste it into the appropriate field. To use copy, cut, and paste, follow these steps:

1. Select the entire field or the portion of a field's content that you want to cut or copy.

2. Select **Edit**, and then **Cut** (to move) or **Copy** (to copy). Or press **Ctrl+X** to cut or **Ctrl+C** to copy.

3. Position the insertion point where you want to insert the cut or copied material.

4. Select **Edit**, **Paste,** or press **Ctrl+V** to paste.

TIP

Toolbar Shortcuts   You can also use the Cut, Copy, and Paste buttons on the Table Datasheet toolbar to manipulate text in the table fields.

INSERTING AND DELETING FIELDS

You can also insert and delete fields in the Table Datasheet view. This allows you to quickly enter the data into a new field or delete an unneeded field. It is preferable, however, to insert new fields into the table in the Design view and then enter data. This is because you will eventually have to switch to Table Design view to specify the data type or other properties of the new field.

To insert a field, follow these steps:

1. Select the existing field column in which you want to insert the new field. The new field column is inserted to the left of the currently selected field column.

2. Select **Insert, Column**. The new column appears in the table (see Figure 8.3).

Customer ID	FirstName	LastName	Phone	Address	City	State	Field1	
1	Pierre	Manger	(216) 555-1234	111 Eiffel Blvd	Paris	PA		6
2	Bob	Jones	(216) 555-5436	1340 America D	Crystal	PA		3
3	Alice	Barney	(216) 555-7777	1420 Mineshaft	Big City	PA		6
4	Kim	Reech	(512) 555-3643	55 Platinum St.	Los Angeles	OH		4
5	Larry	Curly-Moe	(216) 555-8444	3 Stooges Lane	Hollywood	OH		4
6	Edward	Reech	(345) 555-7776	456 Rural Lane	Friendly Heights	VA		6

FIGURE 8.3
New field columns can be added to the table in the Datasheet view.

3. To name the new field, double-click the field heading (such as Field1) and type the new name for the field.

4. Enter data into the new field as needed.

Deleting a field or fields is also very straightforward. Remember, however, that deleting a field also deletes any data that you have entered into that field. Select the field that you want to delete and then select **Edit, Delete Column**. You are asked to verify the deletion of the field. If you're sure, click **Yes**.

INSERTING NEW RECORDS

As your customer base increases or other new data becomes available for your database, you will definitely be adding records to the various tables in the database. New records are inserted automatically. As soon as you begin to enter data into a record, a new blank record appears at the bottom of the table (see Figure 8.4).

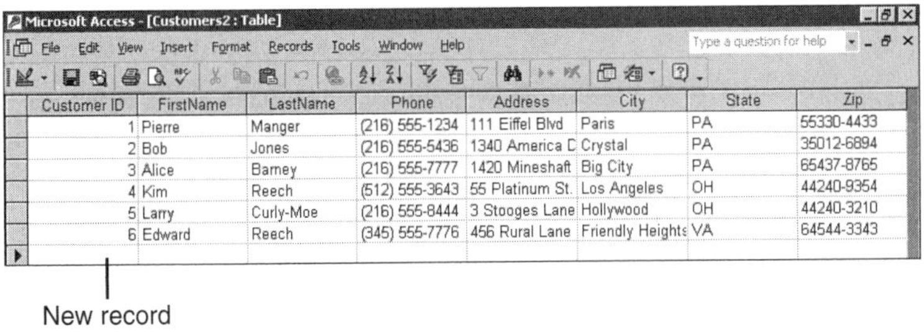

Microsoft Access - [Customers2 : Table]
File Edit View Insert Format Records Tools Window Help
Type a question for help
Customer ID FirstName LastName Phone Address City State Zip
1 Pierre Manger (216) 555-1234 111 Eiffel Blvd Paris PA 55330-4433
2 Bob Jones (216) 555-5436 1340 America C Crystal PA 35012-6894
3 Alice Barney (216) 555-7777 1420 Mineshaft Big City PA 65437-8765
4 Kim Reech (512) 555-3643 55 Platinum St. Los Angeles OH 44240-9354
5 Larry Curly-Moe (216) 555-8444 3 Stooges Lane Hollywood OH 44240-3210
6 Edward Reech (345) 555-7776 456 Rural Lane Friendly Heights VA 64544-3343
New record

FIGURE 8.4
New records are automatically inserted at the bottom of the table.

This process is re-created every time you complete a record and then start a new record. Inserting information into the first field of the new record inserts another new record below the one on which you are working.

You can't insert new records between existing ones or at the top of the table. New records are always entered at the bottom of the table, below the last completed record.

TIP

What If I Want the Records in a Different Order? Although you can enter new records only at the bottom of the table, you can rearrange the order of your records if you want. This can be done using the sorting feature discussed in Lesson 17, "Creating a Simple Query."

Deleting Records

You will probably find that certain records in the table become outdated or no longer pertinent to the database (such as an employee who has left your company but still has a record in the Employee table). You can delete a record or several records at a time.

To delete a record or records, follow these steps:

1. To select the record that you want to delete, click the record selector button (the small gray box to the left of the record, as shown in Figure 8.5). If you want to select multiple records, click and drag the record selector buttons of the contiguous records.

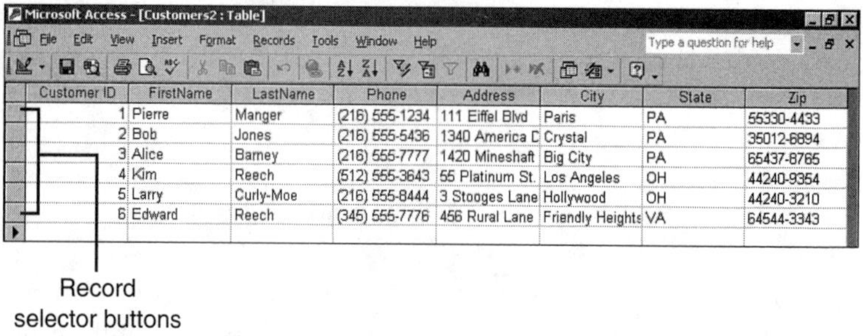

Record selector buttons

FIGURE 8.5
Select the record or records you want to delete.

2. To delete the record or records, perform any of the following:

   • Click the **Delete Record** button on the toolbar.

   • Press the **Delete** key on the keyboard.

   • Select the **Edit, Delete Record**.

3. A dialog box appears, letting you know that you are deleting a record and will not be able to undo this action. To delete the record or records, click **Yes**.

CAUTION

Deleting Records Affects the AutoNumber Sequence
When you delete records in the table that were assigned an identification number using the AutoNumber data type, that number (or numbers) will be lost from the sequence. For example, if you delete a customer with

the AutoNumber customer ID of 3, the number 3 is removed from the sequence. When listing your customers, the customer numbers would then appear as 1, 2, 4, 5, and so on.

In this lesson, you learned how to edit data in a field, how to insert and delete fields, and how to copy and move data from place to place. You also learned how to insert and delete records in the table. In the next lesson, you learn how to format your table.

LESSON 9
Formatting Access Tables

In this lesson, you learn how to improve the look of a table by adjusting the row and column sizes, changing the font, and choosing text alignment options.

CHANGING THE LOOK OF YOUR TABLE

Most people don't spend a lot of time formatting Access tables because they don't always use the table for data entry; instead, they use a form. Most people also don't typically print their tables. They use data-entry forms to see the records onscreen and reports to print their records. The tables are merely holding tanks for the raw data.

However, creating forms and reports might be more work than you want to tackle right now. And formatting a table so that data entry is a little less tedious (and less hard on the eyes) or so you can quickly print a copy of a table (covered in Lesson 22, "Printing Access Objects") is certainly no crime. Making a table more readable onscreen is certainly nice for the person using the table to enter data.

CHANGING COLUMN WIDTH AND ROW HEIGHT

One common problem with a table is that you can't see the complete contents of the fields. Fields often hold more data than will fit across a column's width. This causes the data in your table to appear to be cut off.

You can fix this problem in two ways: make the column wider so it can display more data, or make the row taller so it can display more than one line of data.

CHANGING COLUMN WIDTH

Access offers many ways to adjust column width in a table; you can
choose the method you like best. One of the easiest ways to adjust the
column width is to drag the column headings. Follow these steps:

1. Position the mouse pointer between two field names (column
   headings) so that the pointer turns into a vertical line with
   left- and right-pointing arrows; this is the sizing tool (see
   Figure 9.1). You'll be adjusting the column on the left; the
   column on the right will move to accommodate it.

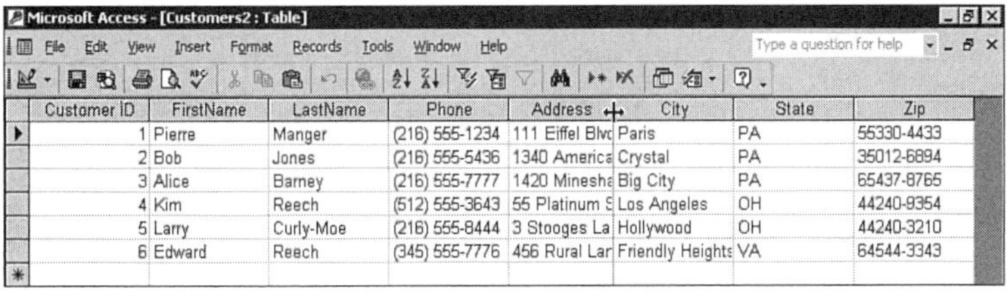

FIGURE 9.1
Position the mouse pointer between two column headings.

2. Click and hold the mouse button and drag the edge of the
   column to the right or left to increase or decrease the width.

3. Release the mouse button when the column is the desired
   width.

Alternatively, you can double-click the column's vertical border when
the sizing tool is showing, which automatically adjusts the width of
the column on the left so that it accommodates the largest amount of
data entered in that particular field.

Another, more precise, way to adjust column width is to use the
Column Width dialog box. Follow these steps:

1. Select the column(s) for which you want to adjust the width.

2. From the **Format** menu, choose **Column Width**, or right-click and choose **Column Width** from the shortcut menu. The Column Width dialog box appears (see Figure 9.2).

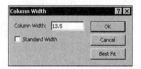

FIGURE 9.2
Adjust the column width precisely in the Column Width dialog box.

3. Do one of the following to set the column width:

- Adjust the column to exactly the width needed for the longest entry in it by clicking **Best Fit**.

- Set the width to a precise number of field characters by typing a value in the **Column Width** text box.

- Reset the column width to its default value by selecting the **Standard Width** check box.

4. Click **OK** to apply the changes.

Because changing the width of a field column in the table is actually changing the field's length (which you designated in the Design view when you created the table), you do need to save these changes. Click the **Save** button on the Table Datasheet toolbar.

CHANGING ROW HEIGHT

You can also change the height of the rows or records in the table. This allows you to see more text in a field that contains a large amount of data, such as a memo field.

CAUTION

> **Adjusting One Row Height Adjusts Them All**   If you change the height of one row, it changes the height of all the rows or records in the table. Edit the row height only in cases where it allows you to see more data in a particular field for each record.

One way to make rows taller (or shorter) is to drag a particular row's border, enlarging the record's row. Position the mouse pointer between two rows in the row selection area, and then drag up or down. Remember that this changes the height of all the rows in the table (meaning all the records).

Another way is to use the Row Height dialog box. It works the same as the Column Width dialog box, except that no Best Fit option is available. Select the **Format** menu and then choose **Row Height**. The Row Height dialog box appears.

Enter the height for the table's rows into the dialog box (or click **Standard Height** to return the rows to the default height) and click **OK**.

Changing the Font and Font Size

Unlike other Access views (such as Report and Form), you can't format individual fields or portions of the data that are entered in a particular view. You can format the font style only for the entire table. Font changes are automatically applied to all data in the table, including the field column headings.

Font changes that you make in Datasheet view won't affect the way your data looks in other Access objects, such as your reports, queries, or forms. They affect only the table itself.

There are some good reasons for changing the font style in a table. For example, you might want to increase the font size so that the field contents are easier to read. Or you might bold the data in the table so that you get a nice, crisp printout when you print the table (see Lesson 22).

CHANGING THE DEFAULT FONT STYLE

If the default style used in Access for tables has been bugging you
from the beginning, you can change the default font used in Datasheet
view for all the tables you create in Access.

Select **Tools,** and then **Options**. Select the **Datasheet** tab of the
Options dialog box (see Figure 9.3).

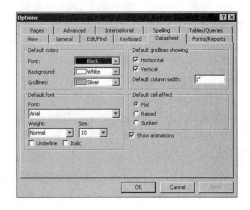

FIGURE 9.3
You can change the default Datasheet font properties in the Options dialog box.

Use the different drop-down menus in the Default Font box of the
Datasheet tab to select the font name, font weight, or font size. When
you have finished making your changes, click **OK**.

CHANGING THE FONT STYLE FOR A TABLE

Font changes that you make to a specific table override the default
font settings. To choose a different font for a currently open table
datasheet, follow these steps:

1. From the **Format** menu, choose **Font**. The Font dialog box
   appears (see Figure 9.4).

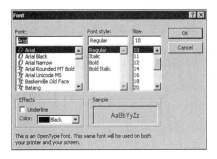

FIGURE 9.4
Select the different font options in the Font dialog box.

2. Select a font from the **Font** list box.

3. Select a style from the **Font Style** list box.

4. Select a size from the **Size** list box.

5. Select a color from the **Color** drop-down list.

6. (Optional) Click the **Underline** check box if you want under-lined text.

7. You can see a sample of your changes in the Sample area. When you're happy with the look of the sample text, click **OK**.

Another way you can change the look of your table is with the Datasheet Formatting dialog box (choose **Format**, **Datasheet**). You can change the cell special effects, background color, the color of the grid lines between each row and column, and whether the lines show.

In this lesson, you learned how to format column widths and table heights. You also worked with changing the font attributes for a table. In the next lesson, you learn how to get help in Access.

LESSON 10
Getting Help in Microsoft Access

In this lesson, you learn how to access and use the Help system in Microsoft Access.

HELP: WHAT'S AVAILABLE?

Microsoft Access supplies a Help system that makes it easy for you to look up information on Access commands and features as you create database tables and other objects and enter information into your database. Because every person is different, the Help system can be accessed in several ways. You can

- Ask a question in the Ask a Question box.

- Ask the Office Assistant for help.

- Get help on a particular element you see onscreen with the What's This? tool.

- Use the Contents, Answer Wizard, and Index tabs in the Help window to get help.

- Access the Office on the Web feature to view Web pages containing help information (if you are connected to the Internet).

USING THE ASK A QUESTION BOX

The Ask a Question box is a new way to quickly open the Access Help system. The Ask a Question box resides at the top right of the Access application window.

For example, if you are working in Access and wish to view information on how to create a new table, type `How do I create a table?` into the Ask a Question box. Then press the **Enter** key. A shortcut menu appears below the Ask a Question box, as shown in Figure 10.1.

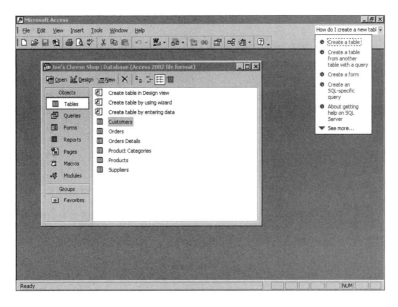

FIGURE 10.1
The Ask a Question box provides a list of Help topics that you can quickly access.

To access one of the Help topics supplied on the shortcut menu, click that particular topic. The Help window opens with topical matches for that keyword or phrase displayed.

In the case of the "new table" question used in Figure 10.1 you could select **Create a table** from the shortcut menu that appears. This opens the Help window and displays help on how to create a new Access table (see Figure 10.2).

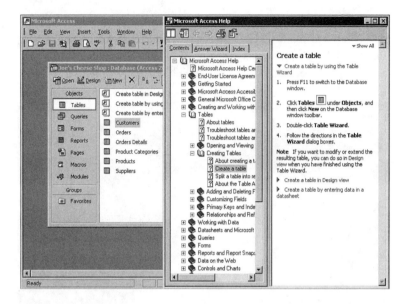

FIGURE 10.2
The Ask a Question box provides a quick way to access the Help window.

In the Help window, you can use the links provided to navigate the Help system. Click any of the content links to expand the information provided on that particular topic. You can also use the Contents, Answer Wizard, and Index tabs to find additional information or look for new information in the Help window. You learn more about these different Help window tabs later in this lesson.

USING THE OFFICE ASSISTANT

Another way to get help in Access is to use the Office Assistant. The Office Assistant supplies the same type of access to the Help system as the Ask a Question box. You ask the Office Assistant a question, and it supplies you with a list of possible answers that provide links to various Help topics. The next two sections discuss how to use the Office Assistant.

TURNING THE OFFICE ASSISTANT ON AND OFF

By default, the Office Assistant is off. To show the Office Assistant in your application window, select the **Help** menu and then select **Show the Office Assistant**.

You can also quickly hide the Office Assistant if you no longer want it in your application window. Right-click the Office Assistant and select **Hide**. If you want to get rid of the Office Assistant completely so it isn't activated when you select the Help feature, right-click the Office Assistant and select **Options**. Clear the **Use the Office Assistant** check box, and then click **OK**. You can always get the Office Assistant back by selecting **Help**, **Show Office Assistant**.

ASKING THE OFFICE ASSISTANT A QUESTION

When you click the Office Assistant, a balloon appears above it. Type a question into the text box. For example, you might type **How do I print?** for help printing your work. Click the **Search** button.

The Office Assistant provides some topics that reference Help topics in the Help system. Click the option that best describes what you're trying to do. The Help window appears, containing more detailed information. Use the Help window to get the exact information that you need.

Although not everyone likes the Office Assistant because having it enabled means that it is always sitting in your Access application window, it can be useful at times. For example, when you access particular features in Access, the Office Assistant can automatically provide you with context-sensitive help on that particular feature. If you are brand-new to Microsoft Access, you might want to use the Office Assistant to help you learn the various features that Access provides as you use them.

TIP

> **Select Your Own Office Assistant** Several different Office Assistants are available in Microsoft Office. To select your favorite, click the Office Assistant and select the **Options** button. On the Office Assistant dialog box that appears, select the **Gallery** tab. Click the **Next** button repeatedly to see the different Office Assistants that are available. When you locate the assistant you want to use, click **OK**.

USING THE HELP WINDOW

You can also forgo either the Type a Question box or the Office Assistant and get your help directly from the Help window. To directly access the Help window, select **Help** and then **Microsoft Access Help**. You can also press the **F1** key to make the Help window appear.

The Help window provides two panes. The pane on the left provides three tabs: Contents, Answer Wizard, and Index. The right pane of the Help window provides either help subject matter or links to different Help topics. It functions a great deal like a Web browser window. You click a link to a particular body of information and that information appears in the right pane.

The first thing that you should do is maximize the Help window by clicking its **Maximize** button. This makes it easier to locate and read the information that the Help system provides (see Figure 10.3).

When you first open the Help window, a group of links in the right pane provides you with access to information about new Access features and other links, such as a link to Microsoft's Office Web site. Next, take a look at how you can take advantage of different ways to find information in the Help window: the Contents tab, the Answer Wizard tab, and the Index tab.

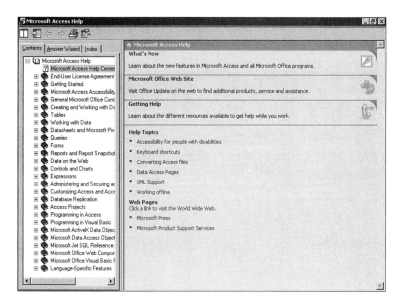

FIGURE 10.3
The Help window provides access to all the help information provided for Access.

TIP

> **View the Help Window Tabs**   If you don't see the differ-
> ent tabs in the Help window, click the **Show** button on
> the Help window toolbar.

USING THE CONTENTS TAB

The Contents tab of the Help system is a series of books you can
open. Each book has one or more Help topics in it, which appear as
pages or chapters. To select a Help topic from the Contents tab, follow
these steps:

1. In the Help window, click the **Contents** tab on the left side of
   the Help window.

2. Find the book that describes, in broad terms, the subject for
   which you need help.

3. Double-click the book, and a list of Help topics appears below the book, as shown in Figure 10.4.

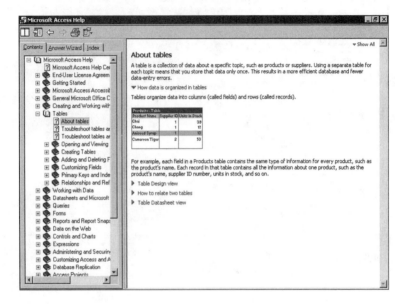

FIGURE 10.4
Use the Contents tab to browse through the various Help topics.

4. Click one of the pages (the pages contain a question mark) under a Help topic to display it in the right pane of the Help window.

5. When you finish reading a topic, select another topic on the Contents tab or click the Help window's **Close** (**x**) button to exit Help.

USING THE ANSWER WIZARD

Another way to get help in the Help window is to use the Answer Wizard. The Answer Wizard works the same as the Ask a Question box or the Office Assistant; you ask the wizard questions and it supplies you with a list of topics that relate to your question. You click one of the choices provided to view help in the Help window.

To get help using the Answer Wizard, follow these steps:

1. Click the **Answer Wizard** tab in the Help window.

2. Type your question into the What Would You Like to Do? box. For example, you might type the question, **How do I filter a table?**

3. After typing your question, click the **Search** button. A list of topics appears in the Select Topic to Display box. Select a particular topic, and its information appears in the right pane of the Help window, as shown in Figure 10.5.

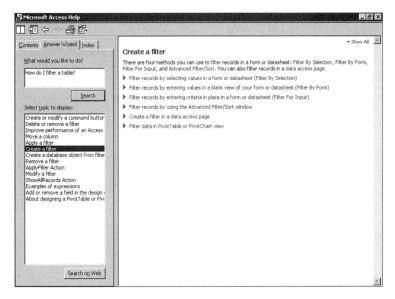

FIGURE 10.5
Search for help in the Help window using the Answer Wizard tab.

TIP

| Print Help | If you want to print information provided in the Help window, click the **Print** icon on the Help toolbar. |

USING THE INDEX

The Index is an alphabetical listing of every Help topic available. It's like an index in a book.

Follow these steps to use the index:

1. In the Help window, click the **Index** tab.

2. Type the first few letters of the topic for which you are looking. The Or Choose Keywords box jumps quickly to a keyword that contains the characters you have typed.

3. Double-click the appropriate keyword in the keywords box. Topics for that keyword appear in the Choose a Topic box.

4. Click a topic to view help in the right pane of the Help window (see Figure 10.6).

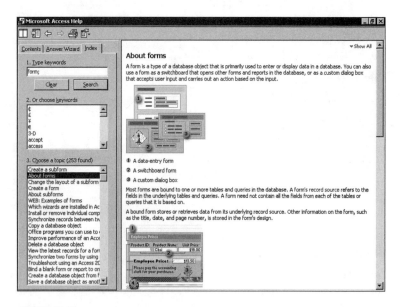

FIGURE 10.6
Use the Index tab to get help in the Help window.

TIP

> **Navigation Help Topics**   You can move from topic to topic in the right pane of the Help window by clicking the various links that are provided there. Some topics are collapsed. Click the triangle next to the topic to expand the topic and view the help provided.

GETTING HELP WITH SCREEN ELEMENTS

If you wonder about the function of a particular button or tool on the Access screen, wonder no more. Just follow these steps to learn about this part of Help:

1. Select **Help** and then **What's This?** or press **Shift+F1**. The mouse pointer changes to an arrow with a question mark.

2. Click the screen element for which you want help. A box appears explaining the element.

TIP

> **Take Advantage of ScreenTips**   Another Help feature provided by Access is the ScreenTip. All the buttons on the different toolbars provided by Access have a ScreenTip. Place the mouse on a particular button or icon, and the name of the item (which often helps you determine its function) appears in a ScreenTip.

In this lesson you learned how to use the Access Help feature. In the next lesson you learn how to create relationships between database tables.

LESSON 11

Creating Relationships Between Tables

In this lesson, you learn how to link two or more tables using a common field and create a relational database.

UNDERSTANDING TABLE RELATIONSHIPS

You've already learned in Lesson 2, "Working in Access," that the best way to design a database is to create tables that hold discrete types of information. For example, one table can contain customer information, and another table can hold order information. By creating relationships between tables, you enable forms, queries, and reports to combine information from the tables to produce meaningful results.

Suppose that you have two tables in your database. One table, Customers, contains names and addresses; the other, Orders, contains orders the customers have placed. The two tables both contain a common field: Customer ID. All records in the Orders table correspond to a record in the Customers table. (This is called a one-to-many relationship because one customer could have many orders.)

The secret to creating relationships revolves around the primary keys for your tables. For example, in a Customers table, the primary key is the Customer ID. It uniquely identifies each customer record. Then, when you design an Orders table, you make sure that you include the Customer ID field. In the Orders table, the Customer ID is not the primary key (it is actually called the foreign key); a field such as Order Number would be the primary key field. You include the Customer ID field in the Orders table so that order information can be linked to customer information in the Customers table.

PLAIN ENGLISH

Foreign Key   A primary key field in a table that is duplicated in a second table (where it is not the primary key) and used to link the tables together.

CREATING A RELATIONSHIP BETWEEN TABLES

To create a relationship between tables, open the Relationships window. Before you can create relationships between tables, you must first add the tables to the Relationships window. Follow these steps:

1. In the database, select **Tools**, **Relationships**, or click the **Relationships** button on the toolbar to open the Relationships window.

2. If you haven't selected any tables yet, the Show Table dialog box appears automatically (see Figure 11.1). If it doesn't appear, choose **Relationships**, **Show Table**.

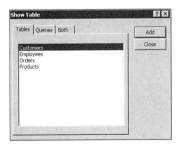

FIGURE 11.1
Add tables to your Relationships window with the Show Table dialog box.

3. Click a table that you want to include in the Relationships window, and then click the **Add** button.

TIP

> **Well-Designed Databases and Relationships**   In a well-designed database, every table in the database is related to at least one other table in the database. So, you might want to add all your tables to the Relationships window.

4. Repeat step 3 to select all the tables you require in the Relationships window, and then click **Close**. Each table appears in its own box in the Relationships window, as shown in Figure 11.2. Each table box lists all the fields in that table.

TIP

> **Enlarge the Table Box**   If you can't see all the fields in a table's box, drag the table border to make it large enough to see all the fields.

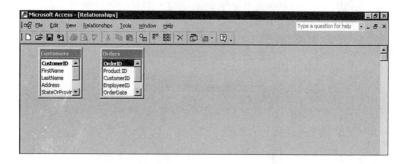

FIGURE 11.2
Tables in the Relationships window.

5. After you have the tables available in the relationships window, you can create the relationships between the table. Remember that you must link the tables using a common field. For example, you can link the Customers table to the

Orders table using the Customer ID field, as shown in Figure
11.2. Select the common field in the table where it is the primary key (in this case, the Customer table). Drag the field
and drop it on its counterpart (the same field name) in the
other table (in this case Orders). The Edit Relationships window opens (see Figure 11.3).

CAUTION

> **Field Type Matters** The fields to be linked must be of
> the same data type (date, number, text, and so on). The
> only exception is that you can link a field with an
> AutoNumber format to another field with a number for-
> mat; AutoNumber fields are considered long-integer
> number fields.

FIGURE 11.3
The Edit Relationships dialog box asks you to define the relationship you're
creating.

6. The Edit Relationships dialog box shows the fields that will
   be related. It also allows you to enforce referential integrity,
   which you learn about in the next section. For now, click
   Create. A relationship is created, and you'll see a join line
   between the two fields in the Relationships window (see
   Figure 11.4).

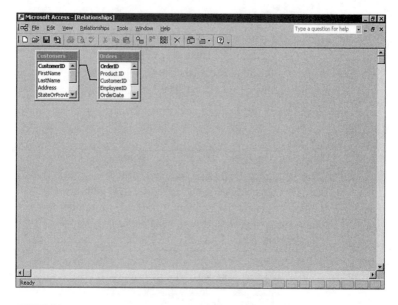

FIGURE 11.4
The join line represents a relationship between the two fields.

 When you create relationships between tables, it's important that you save them. Click the **Save** button on the Relationships toolbar to save the current relationships (and the list of tables available in the Relationships window).

ENFORCING REFERENTIAL INTEGRITY

In the Edit Relationships box is a check box called Enforce Referential Integrity. What does this mean? *Referential integrity* means that data entered in a field that is used to link two tables must match from one table to another. Actually, the data entered in the table where the field does not serve as the primary key must match the entries that are in the table where the field serves as the primary key.

PLAIN ENGLISH

Referential Integrity   The data contained in a primary key field used in a table relationship must be matched in that same field in the secondary table. Otherwise, Access returns an error message.

For example, you could link a Customers table that has a Customer ID field as its primary key to an Orders table that also holds the Customer ID field, where it does not serve as the primary key (the Customer ID is providing the link for the relationship). If you enforce referential integrity, values entered into the Order table's Customer ID field must match values already entered into the Customers table's Customer ID field. Enforcing referential integrity is a way to make sure that data is entered correctly into the secondary table.

When referential integrity is breached during data entry, (meaning a value is entered into the secondary table in the relationship that was not in the linking field of the primary table), an error message appears (see Figure 11.5). This error message lets you know that the field value you have entered in the linking field is not contained in a record in the other table in the relationship (where the field is the primary key).

FIGURE 11.5
Enforcing referential integrity means that values entered in the linking field must be contained in the field in the table where it serves as the primary key.

Two other options are possible when data entered into a field violates referential integrity. Figure 11.6 shows the Edit Relationships with the Enforce Referential Integrity box selected. The two additional options provided are

- **Cascade Update Related Fields**—If this check box is selected, any data changes that you make to the linking field in the primary table (Customers, in this example) are updated to the secondary table. For example, if you had a customer in the Customers table listed with Customer ID 5 and you changed that to Customer ID 6, any references to Customer ID 5 would be updated to Customer ID 6 in the Orders table.

- **Cascade Delete Related Fields**—If this check box is marked and you change the linking field's data in the primary table so that it no longer matches in the secondary table, the field information is deleted from the secondary table. Therefore, if you changed a Customer ID number in the Customers table, the field data in the Customer ID field in the Orders table would be deleted.

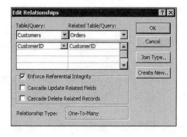

FIGURE 11.6
The Edit Relationships dialog box is used to change the options related to a particular relationship.

You should probably set up your relationships and enforce referential integrity before you do any data entry in the related tables. You should also typically enter the data first into the table where the linking field is the primary key. For example, you should fill in as much of your Customers table information as possible before you try to fill the data fields in the related Orders table.

EDITING A RELATIONSHIP

You can edit any of the relationships that you create between your tables. Just double-click the relationship line and the Edit Relationships dialog box appears (refer to Figure 9.6). For example, you might want to enforce referential integrity on an existing relationship or change other options related to the relationship as discussed in the previous section.

When you have finished editing the relationship, click **OK** to close the Edit Relationships box. This returns you to the Relationships window.

REMOVING A RELATIONSHIP

To delete a relationship, just click it in the Relationships window (the line between the tables turns bold to indicate that it is selected), and then press **Delete**. Access asks for confirmation; click **Yes**, and the relationship disappears.

If you delete relationships between tables, you are affecting how information in the tables can be combined in a query, form, or report. It is a good practice to design your tables so that they can be related. Remember that each table is supposed to hold a subset of the database information. If each table is set up correctly, it should have at least one other table in the database to which it can be related.

In this lesson, you learned how to create, edit, and delete relationships between tables. In the next lesson, you learn how to create forms using a wizard or from scratch.

LESSON 12
Creating a Simple Form

In this lesson, you learn how to create a form using the AutoForm, the Form Wizard, and from scratch.

CREATING FORMS

As discussed in Lesson 7, "Entering Data into a Table," entering data directly into a table has its downside. It can become difficult to concentrate on one record at a time, and if you are working with a large number of fields, information is constantly scrolling on and off the screen.

An alternative to entering data into the table is to use a form. With a form, you can allot as much space as you need for each field, you get to concentrate on one record at a time, and you can create forms that simultaneously enter data into more than one table. You can create a form in three ways:

- AutoForms provide very quick, generic forms that contain all the fields in a single table.

- The Form Wizard helps you create a form by providing a series of screens in which you can choose the fields and style for the form.

- Creating a form from scratch means that you work in the Form Design view and select the fields from the appropriate table or tables. This is the most difficult way to create a new form (at first), but it also provides the most control.

CREATING A FORM WITH AUTOFORM

The easiest way to create a form is with AutoForm. AutoForm takes the fields from a specified table and creates a form; it's not very flexible, but it is very convenient. To use the AutoForm feature, follow these steps:

1. From the database window, click the **Forms** object type.

2. Click the **New** button on the database window toolbar. The New Form dialog box appears (see Figure 12.1).

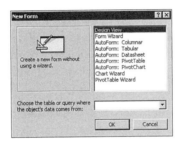

FIGURE 12.1
Choose how you want to create your form.

3. You can click several types of forms, including

   - **AutoForm:Columnar**—A columnar form (the most popular kind). This creates a form that contains your fields in a single column, from top to bottom.

   - **AutoForm:Tabular**—A form that resembles a table.

   - **AutoForm:Datasheet**—A form that resembles a datasheet.

4. Open the drop-down list at the bottom of the dialog box and choose the table or query you want to use as the source of the form's fields.

5. Click **OK**. The form appears, ready for data entry (see Figure 12.2).

FIGURE 12.2
AutoForm creates a form based on a single table.

Forms created with AutoForm can be edited using the Form Design view, which is discussed later in this lesson. When you attempt to close the AutoForm, you are asked whether you want to save it. If you do, click **Yes**. Then, enter a name for the form into the Save As box and click **OK**.

TIP

 Create an AutoForm in the Table Datasheet View You can also create an AutoForm while you are working on a table in the Datasheet view. Click the **AutoForm** button on the Table Datasheet toolbar. A new form appears, based on the table's fields.

CREATING A FORM WITH THE FORM WIZARD

The Form Wizard offers a good compromise between the automation of AutoForm and the control of creating a form from scratch. The wizard allows you to select the fields for the form and select the layout and look for the form. Follow these steps to use the Form Wizard:

1. From the database window, click the **Forms** object type.

2. Double-click **Create Form by Using Wizard** to open the Form Wizard (see Figure 12.3).

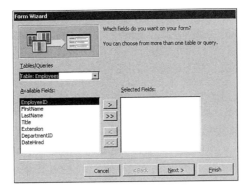

FIGURE 12.3
The Form Wizard enables you to choose which fields you want to include from as many different tables in the database as you like.

3. From the Tables/Queries drop-down list, choose a table or query from which to select fields. (By default, the first table in alphabetical order is selected, which probably isn't what you want.)

4. Click a field in the Available Fields list that you want to include on the form, and then click the **Add** (>) button to move it to the Selected Fields list.

5. Repeat step 4 until you've selected all the fields you want to include from that table. If you want to include fields from another table or query, go back to step 3 and choose another table.

PLAIN ENGLISH

Selecting All Fields   You can quickly move all the fields from the Available Fields list to the Selected Fields list by clicking the **Add All** (>>) button. If you make a mistake, you can remove a field from the Selected Fields list by clicking it and then clicking either the **Remove** (<) button or the **Remove All** (<<) button.

6. Click **Next** to continue. You're asked to choose a layout: **Columnar**, **Tabular**, **Datasheet**, or **Justified**. Click each button to see a preview of that type (Columnar is the most common). Select the layout you want to use, and then click **Next**.

7. The next screen asks you to select a style for your form (see Figure 12.4). Click each style listed to see a preview of it; click **Next** when you've selected a style.

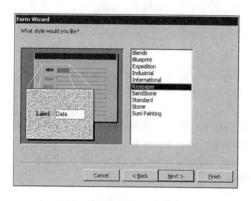

FIGURE 12.4
You can select from several form styles.

8. On the last screen, enter a title for the form into the text box at the top of the dialog box (if you want a title other than the default).

9. Click the **Finish** button. The form appears, ready for data entry (see Figure 12.5).

FIGURE 12.5
The Form Wizard creates a usable form using the fields, format, and style that you selected.

If your form's field labels are cut off or need some additional layout work, you can fix them in the Form Design view. You learn about modifying a form in Lesson 13, "Modifying a Form."

CREATING A FORM FROM SCRATCH

You can also create a form from scratch in the Form Design view. This method might seem difficult at first, but Access provides tools, such as the Field list and the Toolbox, to help you create your form. The most powerful and difficult way to create a form is with Form Design view. In this view, you decide exactly where to place each field and how to format it.

To open the Form Design view and create a new form, follow these steps:

1. From the database window, click the **Forms** object type.

2. Click the **New** button. The New Form dialog box appears.

3. Click **Design View**.

4. Select a table or query from the drop-down list at the bottom of the dialog box. This table provides a Field list that makes it easy to place fields on the form.

5. Click **OK**. A Form Design window appears (see Figure 12.6). You're ready to create your form.

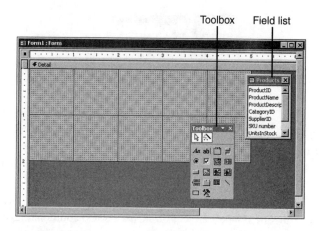

FIGURE 12.6
Form Design view presents a blank canvas for your new form.

Notice that a Field list and Toolbox appear in the Form Design view. You work with creating form controls (the equivalent of a field in a table) using these tools in the next section.

You can also start the process of building a form in the Design view by double-clicking the **Create Form in Design View** link in the database window. Because you are not specifying a table for the Field list to use (as you did in the steps outlined in this section), however, that Field list won't be available. Instead, you must specify a table for the Field list.

To do this, click the **Properties** button on the Form Design toolbar. The form's properties dialog box appears (see Figure 12.7).

FIGURE 12.7
The properties dialog box enables you to set a number of properties for the form.

In the properties dialog box, be sure that the **All** tab is selected. Click in the Record Source box, and then use the drop-down arrow that appears to specify the table that will serve as the field source for the form. The Field list appears. Close the properties dialog box.

TIP

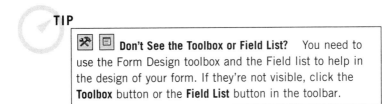

Don't See the Toolbox or Field List?   You need to use the Form Design toolbox and the Field list to help in the design of your form. If they're not visible, click the **Toolbox** button or the **Field List** button in the toolbar.

ADDING CONTROLS TO A FORM

The basic idea of the Form Design window is simple: It's similar to a light table or a paste-up board where you place the elements of your form. The fields you add to a form appear in the form's Detail area. The Detail area is the only area visible at first; you'll learn how to add other areas in the next lesson.

PLAIN ENGLISH

Controls and Fields When you are working with a table, you work directly with fields of data. On forms and reports, you work with controls, which are elements that display data from a field, hold informative text (such as titles and labels), or are purely decorative (such as lines and rectangles).

To add a control displaying a field to the form, follow these steps:

1. Display the Field list if it's not showing. Choose the **Field List** from the **View** menu to do so.

2. Drag a field from the Field list onto the Detail area of the form. The mouse pointer changes to show that a field is being placed.

3. Repeat step 2 to add as many fields as you like to the form (see Figure 12.8).

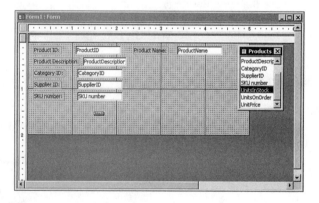

FIGURE 12.8
Drag fields from the Field list to the form grid.

When you drag a field to a form from the Field list, it becomes a control that displays data from that table field on the form. It is basically a link between the table field and the control on the form. You can drag more than one field to the form at once using the steps described earlier. However, in step 2, rather than clicking and dragging a single field, do one of the following before dragging:

- To select a block of adjacent fields, click the first one you want and hold down the **Shift** key while you click the last one.

- To select nonadjacent fields, hold down the **Ctrl** key as you click each one you want.

- To select all the fields on the list, double-click the **Field List** title bar.

You can move objects around on a form after you initially place them; you'll learn how to do this in the next lesson. Don't worry if your form doesn't look very professional at this point; in the next several lessons, you see how to modify and improve your form.

 TIP

> **Using Snap to Grid**   If you find it hard to align the fields neatly, choose **Snap to Grid** from the **Format** menu to place a check mark next to that command. This forces the borders of the fields included on your form to "snap" to the grid that appears in the Design view. If you want to align the fields on your own, select **Snap to Grid** again to turn it off.

 After you have placed all the controls on the form that relate to the fields in a particular table or tables, you are ready to do some data entry. First, however, you must save the form's structure. Click the **Save** button on the Form Design toolbar. Type a name for the form into the Save As dialog box. Then click **OK**.

ENTERING DATA INTO A FORM

The point of creating a form is so that you can enter data more easily into your tables. The form acts as an attractive mask that shields you from the stark reality of the table's Datasheet view. To enter data into a form, follow these steps:

1. Open the form. In the database window, click the **Form** tab, and then double-click the form's name.

2. Click in the field with which you want to begin and type your data.

3. Press **Tab** to move to the next field. If you need to go back, you can press **Shift+Tab** to move to the previous field. When you reach the last field, pressing **Tab** moves you to the first field in a new, blank record.

   To move to the next record before you reach the bottom field or to move back to previous records, click the right- and left-arrow buttons on the left end of the navigation bar at the bottom of the window.

4. Repeat steps 2 and 3 to enter all the records you like. They're saved automatically as you enter them.

In this lesson, you created a form using AutoForm, the Form Wizard and from scratch in the Design view. In the next lesson, you learn how to modify and fine-tune your forms.

LESSON 13
Modifying a Form

In this lesson, you learn how to modify a form's design.

CLEANING UP YOUR FORM: AN OVERVIEW

After you've created a form, you might find that it doesn't quite look as good as you like. Controls might need realignment, or you might want to resize the label for a particular control or controls. You also might want to expand the form grid areas so that you can rearrange the form controls or add additional controls to the form.

All these actions can be accomplished in the Form Design view. Using this view, you can edit the structure of any form that you create, regardless of whether you created the form using AutoForm, the Form Wizard, or the Design view.

MOVING FIELD CONTROLS

The most common change to a form is to reposition a control. For example, you might want to move several controls down so you can insert a new control, or you might want to rearrange how the controls appear on the grid.

If you placed controls on the form to begin with (rather than using AutoForm or the Form Wizard), you have probably noticed that the control consists of two parts: a label and the actual control. You can manipulate various aspects of the label and the control independently (such as their sizes or the distance between them). You work with label and control sizing later in this lesson.

TIP

> **More Space**   If you want to create extra space at the
> bottom of the controls so that you have more room to
> move them around, drag the Form Footer pane down so
> that more of the Detail area is visible. You can also drag
> the right side of the grid to make the form wider. If you
> need more space at the top of the form, highlight all the
> controls and move them down as a group.

Follow these steps:

1. From the database window, select a form in the Form list,
   and then click the **Design** button on the database window
   toolbar. The form is opened in Design view.

2. Click a control's label to select it. Selection handles appear
   around the label (a displacement handle also appears on the
   control, but you don't want to touch that right now). You can
   select several controls by holding down **Shift** as you click
   each control's label.

3. Position the mouse pointer on the edge of the control's label
   so that the pointer becomes a hand (see Figure 13.1). If
   you're moving more than one selected control, you can position the mouse pointer on any selected control's label.

4. Drag the control's label and the control to a new location.

5. Release the mouse button when the control is at the desired
   new location.

CAUTION

> **The Label Moved Without the Control Attached!**   When
> you position the mouse pointer over the control to be
> moved, be sure the pointer changes to an open hand, as
> shown in Figure 13.1. If you see a pointing finger, you
> are on the control's displacement box. The pointing fin-
> ger is used to move controls and labels independently,
> as you'll learn in the next section.

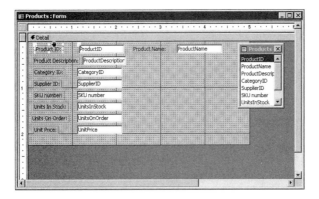

FIGURE 13.1
To move a control, first select it. Then, drag it by its label using the hand pointer.

MOVING CONTROLS AND FIELD LABELS INDEPENDENTLY

Depending on how you are laying out the controls in your form, you might want to separate the control label from the control. For example, you might want to arrange the form in a tabular format where the control names are positioned over the controls. Separating controls and labels also allows you to move the control so that the field label isn't cut off. Then you can resize the label.

> **PLAIN ENGLISH**
>
> **Field Controls: The Most Commonly Used Controls**   Controls related to fields in a table and their attached labels are discussed in this lesson, but the same methods can be used with other controls that have attached labels, such as combo boxes and list boxes (which are discussed in Lesson 14, "Adding Special Controls to Forms").

To move a control or its attached label by itself, follow these steps:

  1. Click the control that you want to separate from its label.

2. Position the mouse pointer over the displacement handle at the top left of the label or the control (the large box handle on the top left of the label or the control). The mouse pointer becomes a pointing finger (see Figure 13.2).

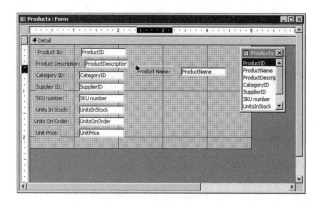

FIGURE 13.2
Drag the displacement handle to move the control or label independently.

3. Drag the label or the control to a new position.

TIP

> **Deleting Labels**   If a certain control is self-explanatory (such as a picture), you might want to delete its attached label. To do so, select the label and press **Delete**.

Separating the label from a control allows you to arrange your controls in all kinds of tabular and columnar arrangements on the form grid. Just make sure that you keep the correct label in close proximity to the appropriate control.

CHANGING LABEL AND CONTROL SIZES

You can also change the width or height of a label or control. Separating a label from its control, as discussed in the previous section, provides you with the room to resize the label or the control independently. To change a label's or control's width (length), follow these steps:

1. Click the label or the control to select it. If you are going to resize the control itself, be sure you click the control. Selection handles (small boxes) appear around it.

2. Position the mouse pointer on either the right or left of the label or control until the mouse pointer becomes a sizing tool (a horizontal double-headed arrow, as shown in Figure 13.3).

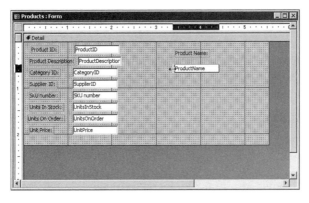

FIGURE 13.3
You can change the size of a label or control by dragging a sizing box.

3. Drag the label's or control's sizing handle to increase or decrease the length as needed. Then release the mouse button.

VIEWING HEADERS AND FOOTERS

So far, you have been working in the main part of the form grid called the Detail area. The Detail area is where you place the various field controls for the form (and additional controls, such as those discussed in the next lesson).

There are other areas of a form. For example, a form header can be used to include a title for the form (header information appears at the top of the form). The other form areas are

- **Form Header**—An area at the top of the form that can be used for repeating information, such as a form title.

- **Form Footer**—An area at the bottom of the form that can be used for repeating information, such as the current date or explanatory information related to the form.

- **Page Header**—Forms that are built to add data to multiple tables can consist of multiple pages. You can also include a Page Header area on a form that enables you to include information that you want to repeat on each page of the form when it is printed out, such as your name or company information.

- **Page Footer**—This area enables you to place information, such as page numbering, that appears on every page when the form is printed.

These different areas of the form grid aren't displayed by default; to display these areas, such as the Form Header/Footer, use the View menu. To show the Form Header/Footer, for example, select **View**, **Form Header/Footer**.

When you create a form with the Form Wizard, the Form Header and Form Footer areas appear in Design view, but nothing is in them. To make some room to work in the Form Header, click the **Detail Header** bar to select it, position the mouse pointer between the bars, and drag downward (see Figure 13.4).

The Detail section contains controls whose data changes with every record. As already mentioned, the Form Header contains text you want repeated on each onscreen form. This makes the Form Header a great place to add a label that contains a title for the form.

Sizing tool   Form Header

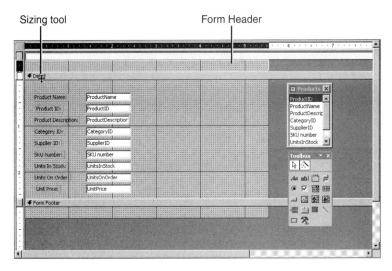

FIGURE 13.4
Drag the Detail Header bar down to create space to add text in the Form header.

ADDING LABELS

You can add a label to any of the areas in the form. Adding labels to
the form enables you to place titles, subtitles, or explanatory text on
the form. Because you will want these types of labels to repeat at the
top or bottom of the form, the best place to add them is to the form's
header or footer. To add titles and other general information to a
header or a footer or to add information specific to particular controls
to the Detail area, follow these steps:

1. If the toolbox isn't displayed, choose **Toolbox** from the **View**
   menu, or click the **Toolbox** button on the toolbar.

2. Click the **Label** tool in the toolbox (the one with the itali-
   cized letters *Aa* on it). The mouse pointer changes to a capital
   A with a plus sign next to it.

3. Place the Label pointer on an area of the form grid, such as the Form Header area. Drag to create a box or rectangle for text entry (see Figure 13.5).

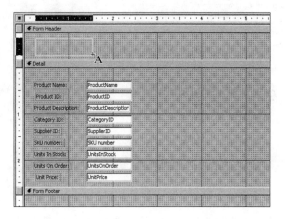

FIGURE 13.5
Select the Label tool in the toolbox.

4. When you release the mouse button, a new label box appears with an insertion point inside it. Type the text you want the label box to contain.

PLAIN ENGLISH

You Must Type the Text Now   If you don't type anything before you go on to step 5, the box disappears as soon as you click away from it.

5. Click anywhere outside the control's area to finish, or press **Enter**.

Don't worry about positioning the label as you create it; you can move a label control in the same way that you move other controls. Just click it, position the mouse pointer so that the hand appears, and then drag it to where you want it to go.

FORMATTING TEXT ON A FORM

After you place all your information on the form (that is, the controls you want to include and labels to display any titles or explanatory text), the next step is to make the form look more appealing.

All the formatting tools you need are on the Formatting toolbar (the top toolbar in the Form Design view). Table 13.1 describes several of the formatting tools. To format a control or label, select it, and then click the appropriate formatting tool to apply the format to the control or label.

TABLE 13.1   Tools on the Formatting Toolbar

Tool	Purpose
B	Toggles bold on/off
I	Toggles italic on/off
U	Toggles underline on/off
≣	Left-aligns text
≣	Centers text
≣	Right-aligns text
◇ ▾	Fills the selected box with the selected color
A	Colors the text in the selected box
◢	Colors the outline of the selected box
▢	Adds a border to the selected box
▭	Adds a special effect to the selected box

Some tools, such as the Font and Size tools, are drop-down lists. You click the down arrow next to the tool and then select from the list. Other tools are simple buttons for turning bold and italic on or off. Still other tools, such as the Color and Border tools, combine a button and a drop-down list. If you click the button, it applies the current value. You can click the down arrow next to the button to change the value.

You can change the color of the form background, too. Just click the header for the section you want to change (for example, **Detail**) to select the entire section. Then right-click and choose **Fill/Back** color to change the color.

 **PLAIN ENGLISH**

> **AutoFormat**   You can use a shortcut for formatting your form. Choose **Format**, **AutoFormat**. You can choose from among several premade color and formatting schemes. If you don't like the formatting after you apply it, press **Ctrl+Z** to undo.

CHANGING TAB ORDER

When you enter data on a form, press **Tab** to move from control to control in the order they're shown in the form. The progression from control to control on the form is the *tab order*. When you first create a form, the tab order runs from top to bottom.

When you move and rearrange controls, the tab order doesn't change automatically. For example, suppose you had 10 controls arranged in a column and you rearranged them so that the tenth one was at the beginning. It would still require 10 presses of the **Tab** key to move the insertion point to that control, even though it's now at the top of the form. This makes it more difficult to fill in the form, so you'll want to adjust the tab order to reflect the new structure of the form.

TIP

Tab Order Improvements   To make data entry easier, you might want to change the tab order to be different from the obvious top-to-bottom structure. For example, if 90% of the records you enter skip several controls, you might want to put those controls last in the tab order so that you can skip over them easily.

Follow these steps to adjust the tab order:

1. Choose **View**, **Tab Order**. The Tab Order dialog box appears (see Figure 13.6).

FIGURE 13.6
Use the Tab Order dialog box to decide what tab order to use on your form.

2. Choose the section for which you want to set tab order. The default is Detail.

3. The controls appear in their tab order. To change the order, click a control and then drag it up or down in the list.

4. To quickly set the tab order based on the controls' current positions in the form (top to bottom), click the **Auto Order** button.

5. Click **OK**.

When you have finished making different enhancements to your form, you must save the changes. Click the **Save** button on the Form Design toolbar.

In this lesson, you learned how to improve a form by moving controls, adding text labels, adding formatting, and adjusting the tab order. In the next lesson, you learn about special controls that you can add to a form.

Lesson 14
Adding Special Controls to Forms

In this lesson, you learn about some special controls you can include on your forms.

Using Special Form Controls

So far, you've taken a look at adding controls to a form that directly relate to fields on a table or tables. This means that unless the control is linked to a field in a table that uses the AutoNumber data type, you are going to have to type absolutely all the data that you enter into the form (exactly as you would in the table).

Fortunately, Access offers some special form controls that can be used to help you enter data. For example, a list box can contain a list of entries for a control. All you have to do is select the appropriate entry from the list. Other special controls also exist that can make it easier to get your data into the form. These controls are

- **List Box**—Presents a list from which you choose an item.

- **Combo Group**—Like a list box, but you can type in other entries in addition to those on the list.

- **Option Group**—Provides you with different types of input buttons (you can select only one type of button when you create an Option group). You can use option buttons, toggle buttons, or check boxes.

- **Command Button**—Performs some function when you click it, such as starting another program, printing a report, saving the record, or anything else you specify.

Figure 14.1 shows some special controls in the Form view. In this lesson, you create each of these control types.

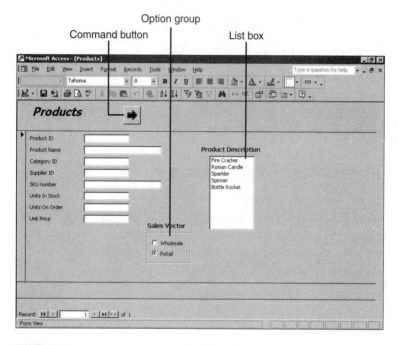

FIGURE 14.1
Special controls can make data entry easier.

All these special controls can be created using the buttons on the Toolbox. Wizards are also available that walk you through the steps of creating each of these special control types. To use the wizard for a particular special control, make sure that the Control Wizards button is activated on the Toolbox. Figure 14.2 shows the Toolbox and the buttons that you are working with in this lesson.

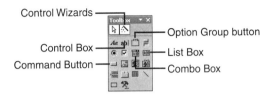

Control Wizards

Option Group button

Control Box

List Box

Command Button

Combo Box

FIGURE 14.2
To use wizards, make sure that the Control Wizards button is selected.

CREATING A LIST BOX OR A COMBO BOX

A *list box* or a *combo box* can come in handy if you find yourself
repeatedly typing certain values into a field. For example, if you have
to enter the name of one of your 12 branch offices each time you use a
form, you might find it easier to create a list box containing the branch
office names, and then you can click to select a particular name from
the list. With a list box, the person doing the data entry is limited to the
choices that display on the list.

A combo box is useful when a list box is appropriate, but when it's
possible that a different entry might occasionally be needed. For
example, if most of your customers come from one of six states, but
occasionally you get a new customer from another state, you might
use a combo box. During data entry, you could choose the state from
the list when appropriate and type a new state when it's not.

Follow these steps to create a list box or combo box from Form
Design view:

1. Make sure that the **Control Wizards** button on the Toolbox
   is selected.

2. Click the **List Box** or **Combo Box** button in the Toolbox.
   The mouse pointer changes to show the type of box you
   selected.

3. Drag your mouse to draw a box on the grid where you want
   the new element to be placed. When you release the mouse
   button, the list or combo box wizard starts.

4. On the wizard's first screen (see Figure 14.3), click the
option button **I Will Type In the Values That I Want**. Then
click **Next**.

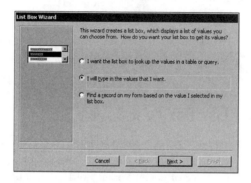

FIGURE 14.3
The wizard walks you through the steps of creating a list box or a combo box.

 TIP

> **Another Way to Enter Values** List boxes and combo
> boxes can also be set up so that they pull their list of
> values from an existing table in the database (or a query
> that you've created). Select **I Want the List Box to Look Up
> the Values in a Table or Query** on the first wizard screen,
> and then specify the table or query that should supply
> the values for the list.

5. On the next screen, a column of boxes (only one box shows
before you enter your values) is provided that you use to
enter the values that you want to appear in the list. Type them
in (as shown in Figure 14.4), pressing the **Tab** key after each
one. Then click **Next**.

6. On the next screen, you choose the option of Access either
remembering the values in the list for later use (such as in a
calculation) or entering a value selected from the list in a

particular field. Because you are using this box for data entry, select **Store That Value in This Field**, and then choose a field from the drop-down list that is supplied. For example, if you want this list to provide data from your Product Description field, select it in the drop-down list. Click **Next** to continue.

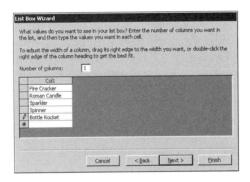

FIGURE 14.4
Type the values for the list or combo box.

TIP

> **Tying a List or Combo Box to a Field**   The best way to approach list and combo boxes is to create a form that includes all the fields from a particular table. Then, you can delete the controls for fields in the Form Design view that you want to "re-create" as list or combo boxes. You then store the values from the list or combo box in one of the fields that you removed from the form.

7. On the next screen, type the label text for the new list or combo box control.

8. Click **Finish**. Your new list or combo box appears on your form (see Figure 14.5).

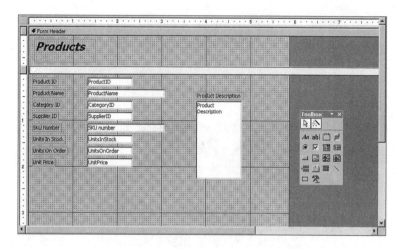

FIGURE 14.5
Your list or combo box appears on the form grid.

> **CAUTION**
>
> **Where Are My Values?**   Don't be alarmed that the values
> you entered for the control don't appear in the box in
> the Design view. The values will be available when you
> switch to the Form view and do data entry on the form.

> **TIP**
>
> **I Picked the Wrong Box Type!**   You can easily switch
> between a list box and a combo box, even after you cre-
> ate it. In Form Design view, right-click the control, click
> **Change To** from the shortcut menu that appears, and
> select a new control type.

CREATING AN OPTION GROUP

Another useful special control is the *option group*. An option group
provides different types of buttons or input boxes that can be used to
quickly input information into a form. An option group can use one of
the following types of buttons:

- **Option buttons**—A separate option button is provided for each choice you supply on the form. To make a particular choice, click the appropriate option button.

- **Check boxes**—A separate check box is provided for each item you place in the option group. To select a particular item, click the appropriate check box.

- **Toggle buttons**—A button is provided for the response required, which can be toggled on and off by clicking the button.

Option groups work best when a fairly limited number of choices is available, and when you create your option group, you should select the type of button or box that best suits your need. If you have several responses where only one response is valid, use option buttons. If you have a situation in which more than one response is possible, use check boxes. Toggle buttons are used when only one response is possible, and it responds to a yes or no type question. The option button is then turned on or off with a click of the mouse.

TIP

 Other Options   You can create a series of option buttons or check boxes using the Option Group button, or you can opt to directly create option buttons or check boxes by clicking the required button (the **Option** button or the **Check Box** button, respectively) on the Toolbox.

To create an Option Group control (you will create a control that uses option buttons), follow these steps:

1. Make sure that the **Control Wizards** button in the Toolbox is selected.

 2. Click the **Option Group** button on the Toolbox. Your mouse pointer changes to show the Option Group icon.

3. Drag your mouse pointer on your form to draw a box where you want the option group to appear. When you release the mouse button, the wizard starts.

4. The wizard prompts you to enter the labels you want for each button (or check box or toggle button), as shown in Figure 14.6. You will need a label for each button that will appear in the group. These labels should be the same as the type of data you would normally insert into the field for which you are building the option group (which is specified in step 7). Enter the labels needed, pressing **Tab** after each one; then click **Next**.

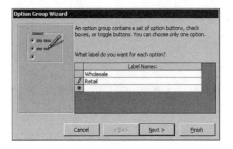

FIGURE 14.6
Enter the labels you want for each option here.

5. On the next screen, you can select one of the labels that you input in step 4 as the default choice for the option group. Specify the label, and then click **Yes, the Default Choice Is**. Or click **No, I Don't Want a Default As the Other Possibility**. Then click **Next**.

6. On the next screen, the wizard asks what value you want to assign to each option (such as 1, 2, and so on). These values provide a numerical equivalent for each label you listed in step 4 and are used by Access to store the response provided by a particular option button or check box. You should use the default values that Access provides. Click **Next** to continue.

7. On the next screen, you decide whether the value that you assigned to each of your option labels is stored in a particular field or saved by Access for later use. Because you are using the option group to input data into a particular field, be sure the **Store the Value in This Field** option button is selected. This stores the data that the option group provides in a particular field. Select the field from the drop-down list provided. Then, click **Next** to continue.

8. On the next screen, select the type of control (option button, check box, or toggle button—see Figure 14.7) you want to use and a style for the controls; then click **Next**.

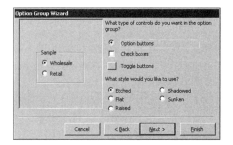

FIGURE 14.7
You can choose different input controls for your Option group.

9. On the last screen, type a label for the new control. Then click **Finish**.

Your new Option control appears on the grid area of the form. All the different option values that you entered appear in the control. When you switch to the Form view to enter data, you can use the various option buttons or check boxes to select an actual value for that particular field.

ADDING COMMAND BUTTONS

Another special control type that you can add to your form is a command button. Command buttons are used to perform a particular action. For example, you could put a command button on a form that enables you to move to the next record or to print the form. Access offers different command button types that you can place on your forms:

- **Record Navigation**—You can add command buttons that allow you to move to the next, previous, first, or last record.

- **Record Operations**—You can make buttons that delete, duplicate, print, save, or undo a record.

- **Form Operations**—Command buttons can print a form, open a page (on a multiple page form), or close the form.

- **Application**—Command buttons can exit Access or run some other application.

- **Miscellaneous**—Command buttons can print a table, run a macro, run a query, or use the AutoDialer to dial a phone number specified on a form.

TIP

> **Placing Command Button**   Form headers or footers make a great place to put any command buttons that you create. Placing them in the header makes it easy for you to go to the top of the form and click a particular command button.

To place a command button on a form, follow these steps:

1. Be sure that the **Control Wizards** button in the Toolbox is selected.

2. Click the **Command Button** in the Toolbox. Your mouse pointer changes to show the Command Button icon.

3. Click your form where you want the command button to appear (such as the header of the form). The Command Button Wizard opens.

4. On the first wizard screen, select an action category in the Categories list, and then in the Actions box (see Figure 14.8), select the action that the button should perform. Then click **Next**.

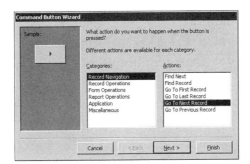

FIGURE 14.8
Choose what action you want the command button to execute.

5. On the next screen, you can select to have either text or a picture appear on the command button. For text, choose **Text** and then enter the text into the appropriate box. To place a picture on the button, select **Picture** and then select a picture from the list provided (you can use your own bitmap pictures on the buttons if they are available; use the **Browse** button to locate them). Then click **Next**.

6. On the next screen, type a name for your new button. Then click **Finish**. The button appears on your form. You can move it around like any other control.

In this lesson, you learned how to create list and combo boxes, option groups, and command buttons. In the next lesson, you learn how to search for data in a table and replace it with the Find and Replace features.

LESSON 15

Searching for Information in Your Database

In this lesson, you learn how to search for data in a database using the Find feature and how to find and replace data using the Replace feature.

USING THE FIND FEATURE

Whether you are viewing the records in the table using the Datasheet view or a form, the Find feature is useful for locating a particular record in a table. For example, if you keep a database of customers, you might want to find a particular customer's record quickly by searching using the customer's last name. You can search the table using a specific field, or you can search the entire table (all the fields) for a certain text string.

Although the Find feature is designed to find information in a table, you can use the Find feature in both the Table Datasheet view and the Form view. The results of a particular search display only the first match of the parameters, but you can repeat the search to find additional records (one at a time).

TIP

> **Finding More Than One Record** If you need to find several records at once, Find is not the best tool because it locates only one record at a time. A better tool for locating multiple records is a filter, discussed in the next lesson.

To find a particular record, follow these steps:

1. Open your table in the Datasheet view or open a form that is used to enter data in the table that you want to search.

2. Click in the field that contains the data for which you want to search.

3. Select **Edit**, **Find**, or press **Ctrl+F**. The Find and Replace dialog box appears (see Figure 15.1) with the Find tab on top.

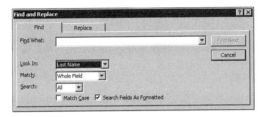

FIGURE 15.1
Use the Find and Replace dialog box to find data in a record.

4. Type the data string that you want to find into the **Find What** text box.

5. The default value for Look In is the field you selected in step 2. If you want to search the entire table, click the **Look In** list drop-down box and select the table's name.

6. From the **Match** drop-down list, select one of the following:

    -   **Whole Field**—Select this to find fields where the specified text is the only thing in that field. For example, "Smith" would not find "Smithsonian."

    -   **Start of Field**—Select this to find fields that begin with the specified text. For example, "Smith" would find "Smith" and "Smithsonian," but not "Joe Smith."

    -   **Any Part of Field**—Select this to find fields that contain the specified text in any way. "Smith" would find "Smith," "Smithsonian," and "Joe Smith."

7. To limit the match to entries that are the same case (upper-
   case or lowercase) as the search string, select the **Match
   Case** check box.

8. To find only fields with the same formatting as the text you
   type, select **Search Fields As Formatted** (this option can
   slow down the search on a large table, so don't use it unless
   you think it will affect the search results).

9. When you are ready to run the search, click **Find Next**.

10. If needed, move the Find and Replace dialog box out of the
    way by dragging its title bar so that you can see the record
    it found. If Access finds a field matching your search, it
    highlights the field entry containing the found text (see
    Figure 15.2).

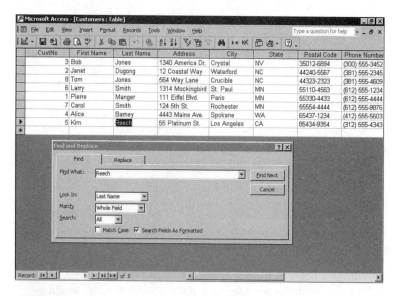

FIGURE 15.2
Access finds records, one record at a time, that contain the search text.

11. To find the next occurrence, click **Find Next**. If Access can't find any more occurrences, it tells you the search item was not found. Click **OK** to clear that message.

12. When you finish finding your data, click the Find and Replace dialog box **Close** (**x**) button.

USING THE REPLACE FEATURE

The Replace feature is similar to the Find feature, except that you can stipulate that a value, which you specify, replace the data found during the search. For example, if you found that you misspelled a brand name or other value in a table, you could replace the word with the correct spelling. This is useful for correcting proper names because the Spelling Checker doesn't help correct those types of spelling errors.

To find and replace data, follow these steps:

1. Select **Edit**, **Replace**, or press **Ctrl+H**. The Find and Replace dialog box appears with the Replace tab displayed (see Figure 15.3).

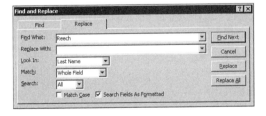

FIGURE 15.3
You can find specific text in a table and then replace it using the Replace feature.

2. Type the text you want to find into the **Find What** text box.

3. Type the text you want to replace it with into the **Replace With** text box.

4. Select any options you want using the Match drop-down list or the check boxes on the Search tab. They work the same as the options discussed on the Find tab (in the previous section).

5. To start the search, click **Find Next**. Access finds the first occurrence of the search string.

6. Click the **Replace** button to replace the text.

7. Click **Find Next** to find other occurrences, if desired, and replace them by clicking the **Replace** button.

8. If you decide that you would like to replace all occurrences of the search string in the table, click the **Replace All** button.

9. When you have found the last occurrence of the search string (Access lets you know that the string can no longer be located, which means you are at the end of the table), click the **Close** (x) button on the Find and Replace dialog box.

The Find and Replace feature works well when you want to work with data in a particular field, but it is limited because you can work with only one record at a time. Other, more sophisticated ways exist to locate records that contain a particular parameter. For example, you can filter records (discussed in the next lesson) using a particular field's content as the filter criteria. This provides you with a subset of the current table, showing you only the records that include the filter criteria.

Queries also provide you with a method for creating a subset of records found in a database table. Queries are discussed in Lesson 17, "Creating a Simple Query," and Lesson 18, "Creating Queries from Scratch."

In this lesson, you learned how to find and replace data in a database. In the next lesson, you learn how to sort, filter, and index records in a database table.

LESSON 16
Sorting, Filtering, and Indexing Data

In this lesson, you learn how to find data by sorting and filtering and how to speed up searches with indexing.

FINDING AND ORGANIZING YOUR DATA

You've already had a chance to work with the Find and Replace features (in the previous lesson). Find and Replace are great features when you're working with individual instances of a particular value and want to search for it in a particular field. This lesson takes a look at other ways to organize the data in the table, including the Sort and Filter features.

SORTING DATA

Although you probably entered your records into the table in some kind of logical order, perhaps by employee number or employee start date, being able to change the order of the records in the table based on a particular field parameter can be extremely useful. This is where the Sort feature comes in.

Using Sort, you can rearrange the records in the table based on any field in the table (more complex sorts can also be created that allow you to sort by more than one field, such as Last Name and then First Name). You can sort in either ascending (A to Z, 1 to 10) or descending (Z to A, 10 to 1) order.

PLAIN ENGLISH

Which View?   You can sort either in Form view or Data-sheet view, but the Datasheet view is better because it shows you all the records in the table in their new sort order.

The fastest way to sort is to use either the **Sort Ascending** or **Sort Descending** button on the Table toolbar. However, this easy road to sorting limits you to sorting by one field or adjacent fields.

Follow these steps to sort records:

1. Place the insertion point in the field by which you want to sort the table (if you want to sort by more than one adjacent field, select the field columns by clicking and dragging the Field Column names). Figure 16.1 shows a Customers table where the insertion point has been placed in the Country field.

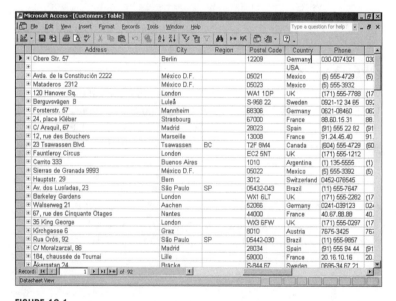

FIGURE 16.1

Place the insertion point in the field by which you want to sort that table.

2. To sort the records in the table by that field in ascending order (alphabetically from A to Z), click the **Sort Ascending** button. Figure 16.2 shows the results of an ascending sort by Country field on the table that was shown in Figure 16.1.

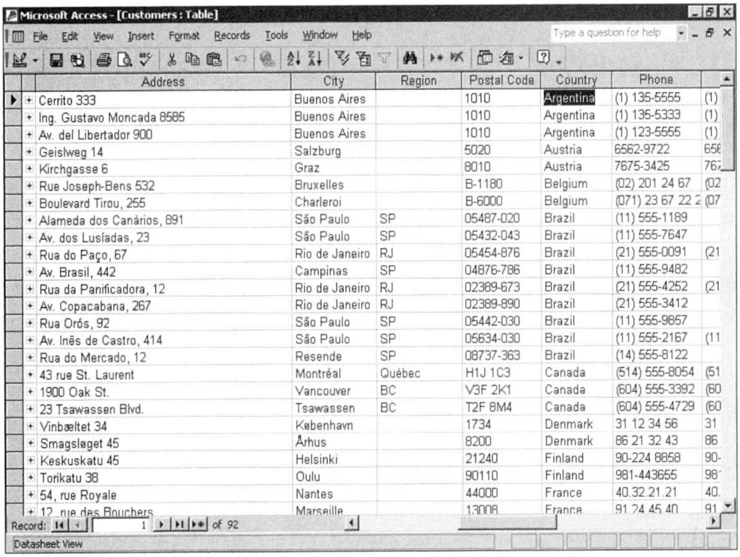

Address	City	Region	Postal Code	Country	Phone	
Cerrito 333	Buenos Aires		1010	Argentina	(1) 135-5555	(1)
Ing. Gustavo Moncada 8585	Buenos Aires		1010	Argentina	(1) 135-5333	(1)
Av. del Libertador 900	Buenos Aires		1010	Argentina	(1) 123-5555	(1)
Geislweg 14	Salzburg		5020	Austria	6562-9722	656
Kirchgasse 6	Graz		8010	Austria	7675-3425	767
Rue Joseph-Bens 532	Bruxelles		B-1180	Belgium	(02) 201 24 67	(02
Boulevard Tirou, 255	Charleroi		B-6000	Belgium	(071) 23 67 22 2	(07
Alameda dos Canàrios, 891	São Paulo	SP	05487-020	Brazil	(11) 555-1189	
Av. dos Lusíadas, 23	São Paulo	SP	05432-043	Brazil	(11) 555-7647	
Rua do Paço, 67	Rio de Janeiro	RJ	05454-876	Brazil	(21) 555-0091	(21
Av. Brasil, 442	Campinas	SP	04876-786	Brazil	(11) 555-9482	
Rua da Panificadora, 12	Rio de Janeiro	RJ	02389-673	Brazil	(21) 555-4252	(21
Av. Copacabana, 267	Rio de Janeiro	RJ	02389-890	Brazil	(21) 555-3412	
Rua Orós, 92	São Paulo	SP	05442-030	Brazil	(11) 555-9857	
Av. Inês de Castro, 414	São Paulo	SP	05634-030	Brazil	(11) 555-2167	(11
Rua do Mercado, 12	Resende	SP	08737-363	Brazil	(14) 555-8122	
43 rue St. Laurent	Montréal	Québec	H1J 1C3	Canada	(514) 555-8054	(51
1900 Oak St.	Vancouver	BC	V3F 2K1	Canada	(604) 555-3392	(60
23 Tsawassen Blvd.	Tsawassen	BC	T2F 8M4	Canada	(604) 555-4729	(60
Vinbæltet 34	København		1734	Denmark	31 12 34 56	31
Smagsløget 45	Århus		8200	Denmark	86 21 32 43	86
Keskuskatu 45	Helsinki		21240	Finland	90-224 8858	90-
Torikatu 38	Oulu		90110	Finland	981-443655	98
54, rue Royale	Nantes		44000	France	40.32.21.21	40.
12, rue des Bouchers	Marseille		13008	France	91 24 45 40	91

FIGURE 16.2

The table records are sorted based on the field that you selected.

3. To sort the records in descending order, click the **Sort Descending** button.

4. To place the records back in their presorted order, select the **Records** menu, and then select **Remove Filter/Sort**.

As already mentioned, you can sort a table by adjacent fields using the sort buttons. All you have to do is select the field headings for those particular field columns, and then click the correct sort button. For example, if you wanted to sort a customer table by last name and then first name, the last name would have to be in the column that is directly to the left of the First Name field.

FILTERING DATA

Although sorting rearranges the records in the table, you might need
to see a subset of the records in a table based on a particular criterion.
Filtering is used for this purpose. The Filter feature temporarily hides
records from the table that do not meet the filter criteria.

For example, you might want to view the records in an employee table
where the employees have exceeded their sales goal for the year. Or in
an order table, you might want to find orders that were placed on a
particular date. Filters can help you temporarily narrow down the
records shown in the table based on your criteria.

You can apply a filter in three ways: Filter by Selection (or Filter Excluding Selection), Filter by Form, and Advanced Filter/Sort. The first
two methods are very easy ways to quickly filter the records in a table.

The Advanced Filter/Sort feature uses a Design view that is almost the
same as the Query Design view (covered in Lesson 18, "Creating
Queries from Scratch"). If you learn how to create queries (which are
really nothing more than advanced filters/sorts), you will be able to
work with the Advanced Filter/Sort feature.

This section covers Filter by Selection and Filter by Form. Next, take
a look at how you filter by selection.

FILTER BY SELECTION

Filtering by selection is the easiest method of filtering, but before you
can use it, you must locate a field that contains the value that you
want to use to filter the table. For example, if you want to filter a customer table by a country, such as Germany, you must locate a field in
a record that contains the text "Germany."

To filter by selection, follow these steps:

1. Locate a field in a record that contains the value you want to
   use to filter the table. For example, if you want to see all the
   customers in Germany, you would find a field in the Country
   field column that contains "Germany."

2. Select the data in the field.

3. Click the **Filter by Selection** button on the toolbar, or select **Records**, point at **Filter**, and then choose **Filter by Selection**. The records that match the criteria you selected appear as shown in Figure 16.3.

TIP

Fine-Tuning Filter by Selection You can also filter the table by selecting only a portion of an entry in a field. For example, if you want to filter the records by last names beginning with the letter S, select the S in a last name that appears in the Last Name field in a record.

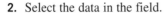

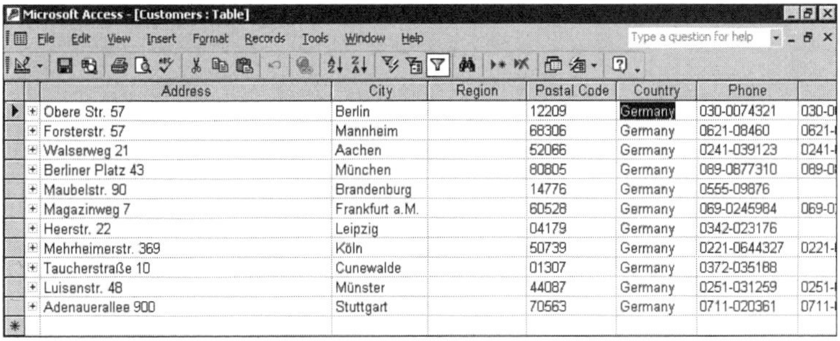

Address	City	Region	Postal Code	Country	Phone	
Obere Str. 57	Berlin		12209	Germany	030-0074321	030-0
Forsterstr. 57	Mannheim		68306	Germany	0621-08460	0621-
Walserweg 21	Aachen		52066	Germany	0241-039123	0241-
Berliner Platz 43	München		80805	Germany	089-0877310	089-0
Maubelstr. 90	Brandenburg		14776	Germany	0555-09876	
Magazinweg 7	Frankfurt a.M.		60528	Germany	069-0245984	069-0
Heerstr. 22	Leipzig		04179	Germany	0342-023176	
Mehrheimerstr. 369	Köln		50739	Germany	0221-0644327	0221-
Taucherstraße 10	Cunewalde		01307	Germany	0372-035188	
Luisenstr. 48	Münster		44087	Germany	0251-031259	0251-
Adenauerallee 900	Stuttgart		70563	Germany	0711-020361	0711-

FIGURE 16.3

The table will be filtered by the field data you selected.

With Filter by Selection, you can filter by only one criterion at a time. However, you can apply successive filters after the first one to further narrow the list of matching records.

You can also filter for records that don't contain the selected value. Follow the same steps as outlined in this section, but choose **Records**, point at **Filter**, and choose **Filter Excluding Selection** in step 3.

After you have finished viewing the records that match your filter criteria, you will want to bring all the table records back on screen. Select **Records**, **Remove Filter/Sort**.

FILTER BY FORM

Filtering by form is a more powerful filtering method than filtering by selection. With Filter by Form, you can filter by more than one criterion at a time. To filter by form, follow these steps:

1. With the table open in the Datasheet view, click the **Filter by Form** button on the toolbar, or select **Records**, point at **Filter**, and then select **Filter by Form**. A blank form appears, resembling an empty datasheet with a single record line.

2. Click in the field for which you want to set a criterion. A down arrow appears for a drop-down list. Click the arrow and select the value you want from the list (see Figure 16.4). You also can type the value directly into the field if you prefer.

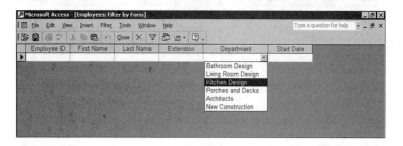

FIGURE 16.4
Set the criteria for the filter using the drop-down list in each field.

3. Enter additional criteria for the filter as needed using the drop-down lists provided by the other fields in the table.

4. After you enter your criteria, click the **Apply Filter** button on the toolbar. Your filtered data appears in the Table window.

As in Filter by Selection, you can remove a filter by clicking the **Remove Filter** button or by selecting **Records**, **Remove Filter/Sort**.

SAVING YOUR FILTER AS A QUERY

If you design a filter that you would like to keep, you can save it as a query. After it is saved as a query, it resides on the Query list in the database window. You will work with queries in Lessons 17 and 18.

To save a filter as a query, follow these steps:

1. Display the filter in Filter by Form view.

2. Select **File, Save As Query**. Access asks for the name of the new query.

3. Type a name and click **OK**. Access saves the filter as a query.

INDEXING DATA

Although not a method of manipulating data like a sort or a filter, indexes provide a method for speeding up searches, sorts, and filters by cataloging the contents of a particular field. The primary key field in a table is automatically indexed. If you have a large database table and frequently search, sort, or filter by a field other than the primary key field, you might want to create an index for that field.

> **CAUTION**
>
> **Can't Be Indexed**   You can't index a field whose data type is Memo, Hyperlink, or OLE Object. There is no way for Access to verify the content of fields containing these types of entries, making it impossible to create an index.

To index a field, follow these steps:

1. Open the table in Design view.

2. Select the field that you want to index.

3. In the Field Properties pane on the General tab, click in the **Indexed** box.

4. From the Indexed field's drop-down list, select either **Yes (Duplicates OK)** or **Yes (No Duplicates)**, depending on whether that field's content should be unique for each record (see Figure 16.5). For example, in the case of indexing a last name field, you would want to allow duplicates (Duplicates OK), but in the case of a Social Security number field where you know each entry is unique, you would not want to allow duplicates (No Duplicates).

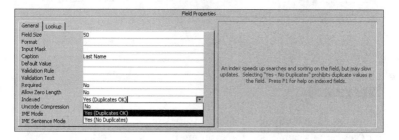

FIGURE 16.5
To index a field, set its Indexed value to one of the Yes choices.

5. Save your changes to the table's structure by clicking the **Save** button on the Design toolbar.

6. Close the Design view of the table.

Indexes aren't glamorous. They work behind the scenes to speed up your searches and filters. They don't really have any independent functions of their own.

In this lesson, you learned how to sort, filter, and index your database tables. In the next lesson, you learn how to create a query using the Query Wizard.

LESSON 17
Creating a Simple Query

In this lesson, you create a simple query.

UNDERSTANDING QUERIES

As you learned in the previous lesson, Access offers many ways to help you narrow down the information you're looking at, including sorting and filtering. The most flexible way to sort and filter data, however, is using a query.

A *query* is a question that you pose to a database table or tables. For example, you might want to know which of your customers live in a specific state or how many of your salespeople have reached a particular sales goal. The great thing about queries is that you can save queries and use them to create tables, delete records, or copy records to another table.

Queries enable you to specify

- The table fields that appear in the query
- The order of the fields in the query
- Filter and sort criteria for each field in the query

> **PLAIN ENGLISH**
>
> **Query** A query enables you to "question" your database using different criteria that can sort, filter, and summarize table data.

Queries are a powerful tool for analyzing and summarizing database information. In this lesson, you take a look at the queries you can create using a wizard. Creating queries in the Design view is covered in Lesson 18, "Creating Queries from Scratch."

USING THE SIMPLE QUERY WIZARD

The easiest way to create a query is with the Simple Query Wizard, which enables you to select the table fields you want to include in the query. A simple query is useful when you want to weed out extraneous fields but still want to see every record in the database table. The Simple Query Wizard helps you create a *select query*.

PLAIN ENGLISH

> **Select Query**   The select query is used to select certain data from a table or tables. It not only filters the data, but it can also sort the data. It can even perform simple calculations on the results (such as counting and averaging).

To create a select query with the Simple Query Wizard, follow these steps:

1. In the Access window, open the database with which you want to work and select the **Queries** icon in the database window.

2. Double-click **Create Query by Using Wizard**. The first dialog box of the Simple Query Wizard appears (see Figure 17.1).

3. Choose the table from which you want to select fields from the Tables/Queries drop-down list.

4. Click a field name in the Available Fields list; then click the **Add (>)** button to move the field name to the Selected Fields list. Add fields as needed, or move them all at once with the **Add All (>>)** button.

5. (Optional) Select another table or query from the Tables/Queries list and add some of its fields to the Selected Fields list (this enables you to pull data from more than one table into the query). When you have finished adding fields, click **Next**.

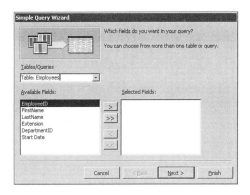

FIGURE 17.1
The Simple Query Wizard first asks what fields you want to include in the query.

CAUTION

> **Relationships Required**   If you're going to use two or more tables in your query, they must be joined by a relationship. See Lesson 11, "Creating Relationships Between Tables," for more information.

6. On the next screen, enter a title for the query. Then, click **Finish** to view the query results. Figure 17.2 shows the results of a simple query.

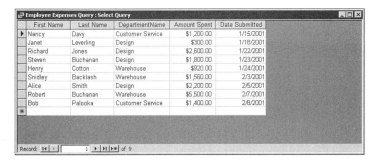

FIGURE 17.2
Queries created using the Simple Query Wizard list the data from the fields you selected.

The problem with queries created using the Simple Query Wizard is that you aren't supplied with the option of setting sort parameters for the records or the capability to filter them by particular criteria. Simple queries just allow you to select the fields. For this query to provide a little more manipulation of the table data, you would have to edit this Query Design view, which is discussed in the next lesson. Building queries from scratch provides you with a lot more control over how the data is filtered, sorted, and summarized.

SAVING A QUERY

When you create a query, Access saves it automatically. You don't need to do anything special to save it. When you are finished viewing the results of the query, click its **Close (x)** button. The new query is then listed in the Query list that the database window provides.

RERUNNING A QUERY

At any time, you can rerun your query. If the data has changed in the table fields that you included in a query, rerunning the query provides you with an updated set of results.

To rerun a query, follow these steps:

1. Open the database containing the query.

2. Select the **Queries** icon in the database window.

3. In the Query list, double-click the query you want to run, or click it once and then click the **Open** button.

TIP

Queries Look Like Tables   Queries can be manipulated in the Datasheet view just like a table. You can use the Sort and Filter features on a query, or you can delete records from the query.

USING OTHER QUERY WIZARDS

Access's different query features are quite powerful; they can do amazingly complicated calculations and comparisons on data from several tables. Queries also can do calculations to summarize data or arrange the query data in a special format called a crosstab. Creating more advanced queries means that your database tables must be joined by the appropriate relationships; otherwise, the query cannot pull the data from multiple tables.

You can create very complex queries from the Query Design view, which you learn about in the next lesson. However, Access also provides some wizards that can be used to create some of the more complex query types. These wizards include the following:

- **Crosstab Query Wizard**—This wizard displays summarized values, such as sums, counts, and averages, from a field. One field is used on the left side of the Query datasheet to cross-reference other field columns in the Query datasheet. For example, Figure 17.3 shows a Crosstab table that displays the different products that a customer has ordered, sorted on the customer's first name.

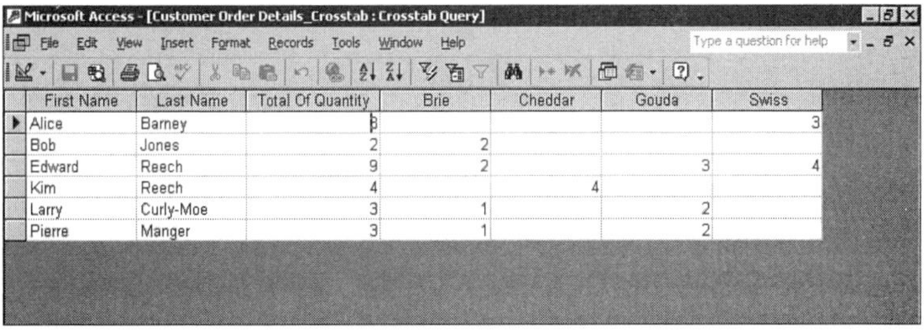

First Name	Last Name	Total Of Quantity	Brie	Cheddar	Gouda	Swiss
Alice	Barney	3				3
Bob	Jones	2	2			
Edward	Reech	9	2		3	4
Kim	Reech	4		4		
Larry	Curly-Moe	3	1		2	
Pierre	Manger	3	1		2	

FIGURE 17.3
Crosstab queries allow you to cross-tabulate information between table fields.

- **Find Duplicates Query Wizard**—This query is used to compare two tables and find duplicate records.

- **Find Unmatched Query Wizard**—This wizard compares two tables and finds all records that don't appear in both tables (based on comparing certain fields).

You can access any of these query wizards from the database window. With the Query icon selected, click the **New** button on the database window toolbar. The New Query dialog box appears, as shown in Figure 17.4.

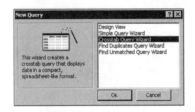

FIGURE 17.4
The other query wizards can be accessed from the New Query dialog box.

Select the wizard that you want to use for your query and click **OK**. Work with the wizard as it walks you through the steps for creating your new query.

UNDERSTANDING ACCESS QUERY TYPES

Before this lesson ends, you should spend a little time learning about the different types of queries that Access offers. In this lesson, you created a select query that "selects" data from a table or tables based on your query criteria. You can also build other types of queries. The different query types are

- **Make Table Query**—This type of query is similar to a select query, but it takes the data pulled together by the criteria and creates a new table for the database.

- **Update Query**—This query updates field information in a record. For example, you might have placed a certain credit

limit for customers and want to update it in all the records.
You would use an Update query.

- **Append Query**—This type of query is used to copy records
  from one table and place them (append them) into another
  table. For example, you might want to append employee
  records from an Active Employee table to a Former
  Employee table.

- **Delete Query**—This type of query is used to delete records
  from a table. For example, you might want to delete old
  records from a table based on particular criteria.

Now, you might be thinking that all these query types are a little too
much to handle. However, you create different query types just as you
would a select query.

As a matter of fact, you actually design each of these different query
types as a select table (using a wizard, Query Design view, or a combination of both), and then you change the query type in the Query
Design view. It's just a matter of selecting the query type from the
Query menu.

In this lesson, you learned how to create a simple query and how to
save, edit, and print query results. You also learned about the different
query wizards and the different types of queries. In the next lesson
you work in the Query Design view.

LESSON 18
Creating Queries from Scratch

In this lesson, you learn how to open a query in Design view, how to select fields to include in it, and how to specify criteria for filtering the records.

INTRODUCING QUERY DESIGN VIEW

In Lesson 17, "Creating a Simple Query," you created a simple query using the Simple Query Wizard. This wizard allowed you to select the fields from a particular table and then create a standard select query. Although the Simple Query Wizard makes it easy to create a query based on one table, you will find that building more sophisticated queries is best done in the Query Design view.

The Query Design view provides two distinct areas as you work. A Table pane shows you the tables currently being used for the query. The bottom pane, the Query Design grid (see Figure 18.1) enables you to list the fields in the query and select how these fields will be sorted or the information in them filtered when you run the query.

OPENING A QUERY IN QUERY DESIGN VIEW

One thing that you can do in the Query Design view is edit existing queries, such as the simple query that you created in the previous lesson. You can change the fields used in the query and change the action that takes place on that field (or fields) when you run the query. To open an existing query in Query Design view, follow these steps:

1. Open the database that contains the query you want to edit (select **File, Open**).

2. In the database window, click the **Queries** icon.

3. In the Query list, select the query you want to edit.

4. Click the **Design** button on the database window toolbar.

The query opens in the Query Design window.

Table pane   Query Design grid

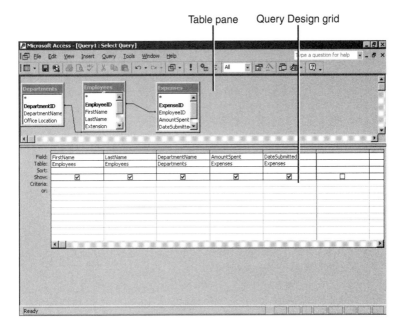

FIGURE 18.1
The Query Design view is divided into a Table pane and a Query Design grid.

STARTING A NEW QUERY IN QUERY DESIGN VIEW

Creating a new query from scratch in the Query Design view allows you to select both the tables and the fields that you use to build the query. To begin a new query in Query Design view, follow these steps:

1. Open the database that holds the table or tables that you will use to build the query.

2. Click the **Queries** icon in the database window.

3. In the Query list, double-click **Create Query in Design View**. The Show Table dialog box appears, listing all the tables in the database (see Figure 18.2).

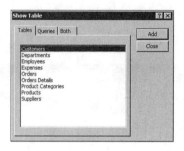

FIGURE 18.2
Choose which tables you want to include in the query.

4. Click a table that contains fields you want to use in the query, and then click the **Add** button. Repeat for each table you want to add.

5. Click **Close** when you finish adding tables. The Query Design view window opens.

The tables chosen for the query appear in the top pane of the Query Design view. Field names do not appear in the Query Design grid until you add them. Adding fields to the query is covered in the next section.

PLAIN ENGLISH

> **Create Table Relationships**   When you create queries
> from multiple tables, these tables must be related. See
> Lesson 11, "Creating Relationships Between Tables" for
> more information.

ADDING FIELDS TO A QUERY

Whether you create your query from scratch or modify an existing query, the Query Design view provides the capability to add the table fields that will be contained in the query. Be sure that the tables that contain the fields for the query are present in the design window.

> **TIP**
>
> **Adding More Tables**   You can add tables to your query at any time. Click the **Show Table** button on the toolbar, or select **Query, Show Table**. Then, select the tables you want and click **Add**. Click **Close** to return to your query design.

To add a field to the query, follow these steps:

1. In the first field column of the query grid, click in the **Field** box. A drop-down arrow list appears.

2. Click the drop-down list and select a field (see Figure 18.3). Because all the fields available in the tables you selected for the query are listed, you might have to scroll down through the list to find the field you want to use.

3. Click in the next field column and repeat the procedure. Add the other fields that you want to include in the query as needed.

As you add the fields to the query from left to right, be advised that this will be the order in which the fields appear in the query when you run it. If you need to change the field that you've placed in a particular field column, use the Field drop-down list in the column to select a different field.

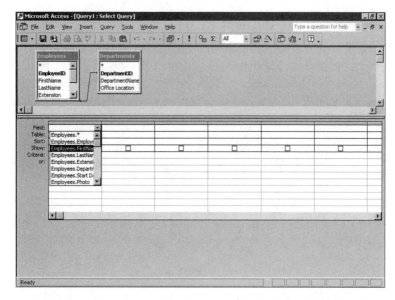

FIGURE 18.3
Scroll through the Field list to locate the field you want to place in the query.

TIP

> **Quickly Add Fields to the Query**   You can also add fields to
> the query directly from the tables that appear in the Table
> pane of the Query Design view. In one of the tables,
> locate the field that you want to place in the first field
> column and double-click the field name (in the table
> itself). The field appears in the Field box in the first field
> column of the query grid. To add the next field, locate it
> in a table, and then double-click it. This method enables
> you to select the fields from specific tables rather than
> scrolling through a long, continuous list of field names.

DELETING A FIELD

If you place a field that you don't want into a field column, you can
replace it using the drop-down list in the Field box (of that column) to
select a different field. If you don't want a field in that field column at

all, you can delete the field from the query. Deleting the field deletes the entire field column from the query. You can use two methods for deleting a field column from the query:

- Click anywhere in the column and select **Edit, Delete Columns**.

- Position the mouse pointer directly above the column so that the pointer turns into a downward-pointing black arrow. Then click to select the entire column. To delete the selected field column, press **Delete**.

After you have the fields selected that you will use in the table, you are ready to set the criteria for the query.

ADDING CRITERIA

The criteria that you set for your query determines how the field information found in the selected fields appears in the completed query. You set criteria in the query to filter the field data. The criteria that you set in a query are similar to the criteria that you worked with when you used the filtering features in Lesson 16, "Sorting, Filtering, and Indexing Data."

For example, suppose you have a query where you have selected fields from an Employee table and a Department table (which are related tables in your company database). The query lists the employees and their departments. You would also like to list only employees that were hired before March 1999. This means that you would set a criteria for your Start Date field of <03/01/99. Using the less-than sign (<) simply tells Access that you want the query to filter out employee records where the start date is before (less than) March 1, 1999.

To set criteria for a field in your query, follow these steps:

1. In Query Design view, click the **Criteria** row in the desired field's column.

2. Type the criteria you want to use (see Figure 18.4).

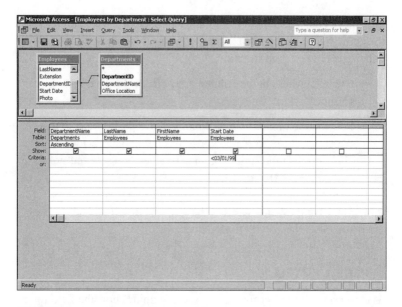

FIGURE 18.4
Enter your criteria into the Criteria row of the appropriate field's column.

3. Queries can contain multiple criteria. Repeat steps 1 and 2 as needed to add additional criteria to field columns in the query.

Query criteria can act both on alphanumeric field data (text) and numeric data (dates are seen by Access as numerical information). For example, suppose you have a Customer table that lists customers in two states: Ohio (OH) and Pennsylvania (PA). Criteria used to filter the customer data in a query so that only customers in PA are shown in the query results would be PA. It's that simple.

When you work with criteria, symbols are used (such as the less-than sign that appears in the criteria in Figure 18.4) to specify how the query should react to the data string that you place in the Criteria box. Table 18.1 provides a list of some of these symbols and what you use them for.

Table 18.1   Sample Criteria for Queries

Symbol	Used For
< (less than)	Matching values must be less than (or before in the case of dates) the specified numerical string.
> (greater than)	Matching values must be greater than (or after in the case of dates) the specified numerical string.
<= (less than or equal to)	Matching values must be equal to or less than the value used in the criteria.
>= (greater than or equal to)	Matching values must be equal to or greater than the value used in the criteria.
= (equal to)	Matching values must be equal to the criteria string. This symbol can be used both with text and numeric entries.
Not	Values matching the criteria string will not be included in the results. For example, Not PA filters out all the records in which PA is in the state field.

USING THE TOTAL ROW IN A QUERY

You can also do calculations in a query, such as totaling numeric information in a particular field or taking the average of numeric information found in a particular field in the query. To add calculations to a query, you must add the Total row to the Query Design grid.

After the Total row is available in the query grid, different calculations can be chosen from a drop-down list in any of the fields that you have chosen for the query. For example, you can sum (total) the numeric information in a field, calculate the average, and even do more intense statistical analysis with formulas such as minimum, maximum, and standard deviation.

To add a calculation to a field in the query grid, follow these steps:

1. In Query Design view, click the **Totals** button on the Query Design toolbar. The Total row is added to the Query Design grid (just below the Table row).

2. Click in the Total row for a field in the Query Design grid that contains numerical information. A drop-down arrow appears.

3. Click the drop-down arrow (see Figure 18.5) to select the formula you want to place in the field's Total box. The following are some of the more commonly used formula expressions:

   - **Sum**—Totals the values found in the field.

   - **Avg**—Calculates the average for the values found in the field.

   - **Min**—Displays the lowest value (the minimum) found in the field.

   - **Max**—Displays the highest value (the maximum) found in the field.

   - **Count**—Calculates the number of entries in the field; it actually "counts" the entries.

   - **StDev**—Calculates the standard deviation for the values in the field. The standard deviation calculates how widely values in the field differ from the field's average value.

4. Repeat steps 2 and 3 to place formulas into other field columns.

When you use the Total row, you can summarize the information in a particular field mathematically when you run the query. For example, you might want to total the number of orders for a particular product, so you would use the sum formula provided by the Total drop-down list.

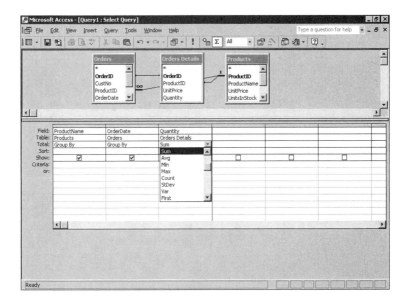

FIGURE 18.5
Calculations added to the Total row are chosen from a drop-down list.

VIEWING QUERY RESULTS

After you have selected the fields for the query and have set your field criteria, you are ready to run the query. As with tables created in the Design view and forms created in the Design view, you should save the query after you have finished designing it.

 Just click the **Save** button on the Query Design toolbar. Supply a name for the query and then click **Yes**.

 Now, you are ready to run the query. Click the **Run** button on the Query Design toolbar, or choose **Query, Run**. The query results appear in a datasheet that looks like an Access table (see Figure 18.6).

 After you have reviewed the results of your query, you can quickly return to the Query Design view to edit the query fields or criteria. Just click the **Design View** button on the toolbar.

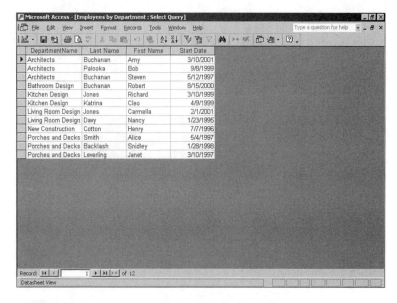

FIGURE 18.6
The results of the query appear as a table datasheet.

In this lesson, you learned how to choose the fields for a query and specify criteria in the Query Design view. In the next lesson, you learn how to create reports in Access by using the AutoReport feature and the Report Wizard.

LESSON 19
Creating a Simple Report

In this lesson, you learn how to create reports in Access by using the AutoReport feature and the Report Wizard.

UNDERSTANDING REPORTS

So far, the discussion of Access objects has centered on objects that are used either to input data or manipulate data that has already been entered into a table. Tables and forms provide different ways of entering records into the database, and queries enable you to sort and filter the data in the database.

Now you are going to turn your attention to a database object that is designed to summarize data and provide a printout of your database information—an Access report. Reports are designed specifically to be printed and shared with other people.

You can create a report in several ways, ranging from easy to difficult. An AutoReport, the simplest possibility, takes all the records in a table and provides a summary that is ready to print. The Report Wizard, an intermediate possibility, is still simple to use but requires more decisions on your part to select the fields and the structure of the report. Finally, the most difficult method of creating a report is building a report from scratch in the Report Design view. You learn about the Report Design view in the next lesson.

USING AUTOREPORT TO CREATE A REPORT

The fastest way to take data in a table and get it into a format that is appropriate for printing is AutoReport. The AutoReport feature can create a report in a tabular or columnar format. A tabular report resembles a datasheet in that it arranges the data from left to right on the page. A columnar report resembles a form in that it displays each record in the table from top to bottom. The downside of AutoReport is that it can create a report from only one table or query.

To use the AutoReport feature to create a simple report, follow these steps:

1. Open the database containing the table or query that you will use to create the report.

2. Click the **Reports** icon in the left pane of the database window.

3. Click the **New** button on the database toolbar. The New Report dialog box appears (see Figure 19.1).

FIGURE 19.1
Choose one of the AutoReport formats in the New Report dialog box.

4. Select **AutoReport:Columnar** or **AutoReport:Tabular**.

5. In the drop-down list at the bottom of the dialog box, select the table or query on which you want to base the report.

6. Click **OK**. The report appears in Print Preview. The Print Preview mode allows you to examine your report before printing. You learn more about Print Preview later in this lesson.

TIP

 Create an AutoReport from an Open Table   You can also create an AutoReport directly from an open table. With the table open in the Access window, click the **New Object** drop-down list on the Table Datasheet toolbar and select AutoReport. This creates a simple columnar report.

AutoReport produces fairly simple-looking reports. To have more control over the report format and layout, you can create a report using the Report Wizard.

CREATING A REPORT WITH THE REPORT WIZARD

The Report Wizard offers a good compromise between ease-of-use and control over the report that is created. With the Report Wizard, you can build a report that uses multiple tables or queries. You can also choose a layout and format for the report. Follow these steps to create a report with Report Wizard:

1. Open the database containing the table or query on which you want to report.

2. Click the **Reports** icon in the database window.

3. In the Reports pane of the database window, double-click **Create Report by Using Wizard** to start the Report Wizard (see Figure 19.2). The first wizard screen enables you to choose the fields to include in the report.

4. From the Tables/Queries drop-down list, select a table or query from which you want to include fields.

5. Click a field in the Available Fields list, and then click the **Add (>)** button to move it to the Selected Fields list. Repeat this step to select all the fields you want, or click **Add All (>>)** to move all the fields over at once.

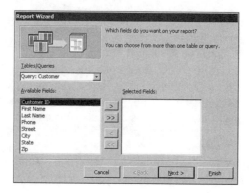

FIGURE 19.2
The first Report Wizard screen enables you to select the fields for the report.

6. For a report using fields from multiple tables, select another table or query from the Tables/Queries list and repeat step 5. To build the report from more than one table, you must create a relationship between the tables. When you finish selecting fields, click **Next** to continue.

7. On the next wizard screen, Access gives you the option of viewing the data by a particular category of information. The wizard provides this option only when you build a report from multiple tables. For example, if you have a report that includes fields from a Customer table, a Products table, and an Orders table, the information in the report can be organized either by customer, product, or order information (see Figure 19.3). Select the viewpoint for the data from the list on the left of the wizard screen; then select **Next** to continue.

8. On the next wizard screen, you can further group records in the report by a particular field. To group by a field, click the field and then click the > button. You can select several grouping levels in the order you want them. Then click **Next** to move on.

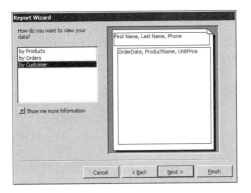

FIGURE 19.3
Data in the report can be arranged from a particular viewpoint based on the tables used to create the report.

PLAIN ENGLISH

Grouping?   By default, the field data in the report are not grouped. By selecting different group levels, you can group information by department, product, or any field that you select. Grouping the data enables you to create a report that has been divided into logical subsections.

9. The wizard asks whether you would like to sort the records in the report (see Figure 19.4). If you want to sort the records by a particular field or fields (you can sort by more than one field, such as by last name and then first name), open the top drop-down list and select a field by which to sort. From the drop-down lists, select up to four fields to sort by, and then click **Next**.

10. On the next wizard screen, choose a layout option from the Layout section. When you click an option button for a particular layout, the sample in the box changes to show your selection.

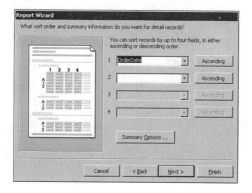

FIGURE 19.4
Set the sort order for your records.

 PLAIN ENGLISH

Where Are All the Layouts?   If you don't choose any group-
ings in your report, you are limited to three layout choices:
Columnar, Tabular, and Justified. More layouts are available when you have set grouping options for the report.

11. In the next wizard dialog box, choose a report style. Several
    are listed; click one to see a sample of it, and then click **Next**
    when you're satisfied with your choice.

12. On the last wizard screen, you're asked for a report title.
    Enter one into the Report text box, and click **Finish** to see
    your report in Print Preview.

VIEWING AND PRINTING REPORTS IN PRINT PREVIEW

When you create a report with either AutoReport or the Report
Wizard, the report appears in Print Preview (as shown in Figure 19.5).
From there, you can print the report if you're happy with it or go to
Report Design view to make changes. (You'll learn more about the
Report Design view in Lesson 20, "Customizing a Report.")

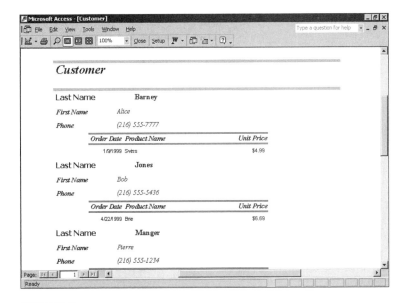

FIGURE 19.5
Either AutoReports or reports created with the wizard automatically open in Print Preview.

 In the Print Preview mode, you can zoom in and out on the report using the **Zoom** tool (click once to zoom in and click again to zoom out). Using the appropriate button on the Print Preview toolbar, you can also display the report as one page, two pages, or multiple pages.

 If you want to print the report and specify any print options (such as the number of copies), choose **File, Print**. If you want a quick hard copy, click the toolbar's **Print** button.

If you click the **Close (x)** button on the Print Preview toolbar, you are taken directly to the Report Design view. You learn about the Report Design view in the next lesson.

In this lesson, you learned how to create an AutoReport and a report using the Report Wizard. You also learned how to use Print Preview and print the report. In the next lesson, you learn how to work in Report Design view to customize your report.

LESSON 20
Customizing a Report

In this lesson, you learn how to use Report Design view to make your reports more attractive.

ENTERING REPORT DESIGN VIEW

You've already seen that you can create reports using AutoReport and the Report Wizard. After you've created a report using either of these methods, you can edit or enhance the report in the Report Design view. You can also create Reports from scratch in the Report Design view.

The Report Design view is similar to the Form Design view that you worked with in Lesson 13, "Modifying a Form," and Lesson 14, "Adding Special Controls to Forms." Like forms, reports are made up of controls that are bound to fields in a table or tables in the database.

To edit an existing report in the Design view, follow these steps:

1. Click the **Reports** icon in the database window.

2. In the list of reports provided, select the report you want to modify.

3. Click the **Design** button on the database toolbar. The report appears in Design view, as shown in Figure 20.1.

As you can see in Figure 20.1, the report's underlying structure contains several areas. The Detail area contains the actual controls that relate to the table fields included in the report. Above the Detail area is the Page Header, which contains the labels that are associated with the controls in the Detail area. At the very top of the report is the Report Header. It contains a text box that displays the name of the report.

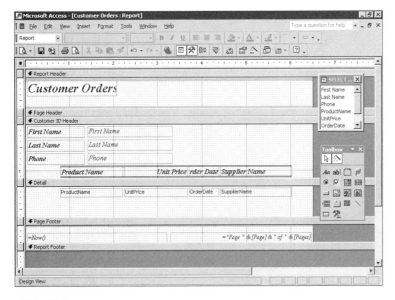

FIGURE 20.1
The report is divided into several areas in the Design view.

At the bottom of the report are two footers. The Page Footer contains formulas that display the current date and print the page number of the report. At the very bottom of the report is the Report Footer. The Report Footer is blank in Figure 20.1. It can be used, however, to insert a summary formula or other calculation that works with the data that appears in the Detail area (you will add a calculation to a report later in the lesson).

As already mentioned, the Report Design view is similar to Form Design view. The Report Design view also supplies the Toolbox, which is used to add text boxes and special controls to the report. The Field list allows you to add field controls to the report.

CAUTION

Using Special Controls on a Report   Access enables you to place any type of control on a report, even command buttons or combo boxes. These won't do you much good on a report, however. It's better to stick to text boxes, labels, and graphics on reports—items that enhance the overall look of the report when it is printed.

WORKING WITH CONTROLS ON YOUR REPORT

Working with report controls in Report Design view is the same as working with controls in Form Design view. You might want to turn back to Lesson 11 to review how you manipulate controls and their labels. The following is a brief review:

- **Selecting Controls**—Click the control to select it. Selection handles appear around the control.

- **Moving Objects**—To move a control, first select it. Next, position the mouse pointer over a border so that the pointer turns into an open hand. Then, click and drag the control to a new location.

PLAIN ENGLISH

Moving Between Report Areas   You can't drag a control from one section of the report to another, but if you do need to move it, you can use cut and paste. Select the control (or label) and press **Ctrl+X** to cut it. Then, click the title of the section where you want to move it and press **Ctrl+V** to paste it into the newly selected section.

- **Resizing Objects**—First, select the object. Then, position the mouse pointer over a selection handle and drag it to resize the object.

- **Formatting Text Objects**—Use the **Font** and **Font Size** drop-down lists on the toolbar to choose fonts; then use the **Bold**, **Italic**, and **Underline** toolbar buttons to set special attributes.

You can add any controls to the report that the Toolbox provides. For example, you might want to add a graphic to the report, such as a company logo. The next section discusses adding an image to a report.

ADDING AN IMAGE TO A REPORT

You can add graphics, clip art, or even images from a digital camera to your Access reports. For example, if you want to add a company logo to a report, all you need is access to the logo image file on your computer (or a company's network). If you want to include an image, such as a company logo, on the very first page of the report, you will want to add it to the Report Header. Any information or graphics placed in the Report Header will appear at the very top of the report. Images that you want to use to illustrate information in the report should go in the Details area.

To add an image to a report, follow these steps:

1. Expand the area of the report (such as the Report Header) in which you want to place the image. For example, to expand the Report Header, drag the Page Header's title bar downward using the mouse (the mouse becomes a sizing tool when you place it on an area's border).

2. Click the **Image** button on the Toolbox. The mouse pointer becomes an image drawing tool.

3. Drag to create a box or rectangle that will contain the image in the appropriate area of the report. When you release the mouse, the Insert Picture dialog box appears (see Figure 20.2).

4. Use the Look In drop-down list to locate the drive that contains the image file, and then open the appropriate folder by double-clicking.

FIGURE 20.2
Use the Insert Picture dialog box to locate and insert your picture into the report.

5. When you locate your image, click the filename to select it, and then click **OK**. The image is inserted into the report.

You might find that the image file is larger than the image control that you have created. To make the image fit into the control, right-click the Image control and select **Properties** from the shortcut menu that appears. In the Properties dialog box, select the **Format** tab. Then, click in the Size Mode box and select **Zoom** from the drop-down list. This automatically sizes the graphic to fit into the control (which means that it typically shrinks the image to fit into the control). You can then close the Properties box.

TIP

> **Check Your Report Design in Print Preview**   As you work on the structure of your report in the Design view, you can check to see how things will look by switching to the Print Preview mode. Click the **Print Preview** button on the Report Design toolbar.

ARRANGING AND REMOVING CONTROLS

As already mentioned, you can move or resize the controls on the report. This also goes for any new controls that you add from the Toolbox or by using the Field list. You can also remove unwanted controls from the report.

To delete a control, select it by clicking it, and then press **Delete**. Deleting a control from the report doesn't delete the field from the associated table.

ADDING TEXT LABELS

You can also add descriptive labels to your report. For example, you might want to add a text box containing descriptive text to the Report Header.

 Click the **Label** button on the Toolbox. The mouse pointer becomes a label drawing tool. Drag with the mouse to create a text box in any of the areas on the report. When you release the mouse, you can begin typing the text that will be contained in the text label.

PLACING A CALCULATION IN THE REPORT

Controls (also called text boxes in a report) most commonly display data from fields, as you've seen in the reports that you have created. However, text boxes can also hold calculations based on values in different fields.

Creating a text box is a bit complicated: First, you must create an unbound control/text box (that is, one that's not associated with any particular field), and then you must type the calculation into the text box. Follow these steps:

1. Click the **Text Box** tool in the Toolbox, and then click and drag on the report to create a text box.

2. Change the label to reflect what's going in the text box. For example, if it's sales tax or the total of your orders multiplied

by the price of your various products, change the label accordingly. Position the label where you want it.

3. Click in the text box and type the formula that you want calculated. (See the following list for guidance.)

4. Click anywhere outside the text box when you finish.

Figure 20.3 shows a control that provides the total value of the orders for each item. This control multiplies the Quantity control (which is tied to a field that supplies the number of orders for each item) by the UnitPrice control (which provides the price of each item).

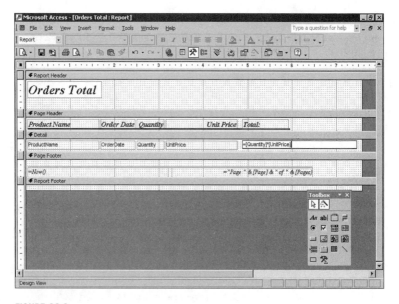

FIGURE 20.3
You can add controls to the report that do math.

The formulas you enter into your calculated text box use standard mathematical symbols:

+   Add

-     Subtract

*   Multiply

/   Divide

All formulas begin with an equal sign (=), and all field names are in parentheses. The following are some examples:

- To calculate a total price where a control called Quantity contains the number of items and a control called Price holds the price of each item, you would multiply these data in these two controls. The formula would look like this: **=[Quantity]*[Price]**.

- To calculate a 25% discount off the value in the field, such as a field called Cost, you would type the formula **=[Cost]*.075**.

- To add the total of the values in three fields, enter **[Field1]+ [Field2]+[Field3]** (where Field# is the name of the field).

PLAIN ENGLISH

More Room   If you run out of room in the text box when typing your formula, press **Shift+F2** to open a Zoom box, which gives you more room.

In this lesson, you learned how to customize your report by adding and removing controls, moving them around, and creating calculations. In the next lesson, you learn how to take advantage of table relationships in forms, queries, and reports.

LESSON 21

Taking Advantage of Database Relationships

In this lesson, you learn how to view related table data and use related tables in forms and reports.

REVIEWING TABLE RELATIONSHIPS

When we first discussed creating a database earlier in this book, we made a case for creating tables that held discrete subsets of the data that would make up the database. We then discussed the importance of creating relationships between these tables, as discussed in Lesson 11, "Creating Relationships Between Tables." In this lesson, you take a look at how you can take advantage of related tables when creating other Access objects, such as forms, queries, and reports.

As previously discussed in Lessons 2 and 11, tables are related by a field that is common to each table. The common field serves as the primary key in one of the tables and as the foreign key in the other table. (The foreign key is the same field, but it is held in a table where it does not serve as the primary key.)

For example, in Figure 21.1, an Employees table is linked to two other tables: Expenses and Departments. The Employees table and the Expenses table are related because of the EmployeeID field. The Employees table and the Departments table are related by the DepartmentID field.

The more complex your database, the more tables and table relationships the database contains. For example, Figure 21.2 shows a complex company database that contains several related tables.

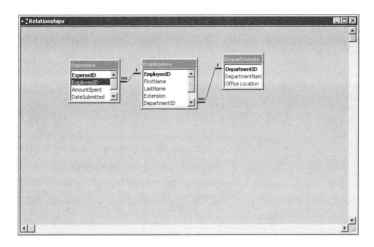

FIGURE 21.1
Related tables share a common field.

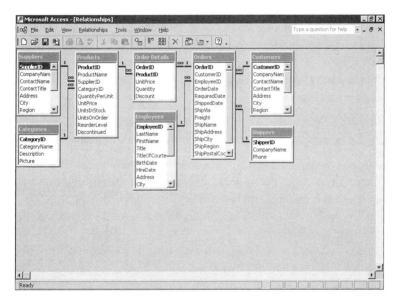

FIGURE 21.2
Complex databases contain many related tables.

More important to the discussion in this lesson is how you take advantage of related tables to create complex forms and reports. First, take a look at how related table data can be viewed in the Table Datasheet view.

VIEWING RELATED RECORDS IN THE DATASHEET VIEW

When working with a table in the Datasheet view, you can view data held in a related table. The information that can be viewed is contained in any table that is subordinate to the table you currently have open in the Datasheet view. Tables subordinate to a particular table hold the foreign key (which is the primary key in the top-level table in the relationship).

For example, suppose you are viewing the Departments table that was included in the table relationships shown in Figure 21.1. A plus sign appears to the left of each record in the table (see Figure 21.3). To view related data for each record, click the plus sign. A table appears that contains the related data for that record. In this example, the Employees table provides the related data (which, if you look back at Figure 21.1, was related subordinately to the Departments table).

When related records are displayed, the plus sign turns into a minus sign. Click that minus sign to hide the related records again.

As you can see in Figure 21.3, even the related records can have linked information. For example, clicking any of the plus signs next to the records containing employee information shows data pulled from the Expenses table (which, again referring to Figure 21.1, is related to the Employees table).

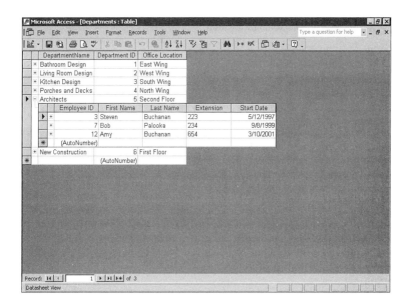

FIGURE 21.3
Display related records in the linked table by clicking a plus sign next to a record.

CREATING MULTI-TABLE QUERIES

The real power of relational databases is to use the related tables to create other Access objects, such as queries. Multi-table queries enable you to pull information from several related tables. You can then use this query to create a report or a form.

The easiest way to create a multi-table query is in the Query Design view. Follow these steps:

1. From the database window (with the Query icon selected), double-click **Create Query in Design View**. The Show Table dialog box appears.

2. In the Show Table dialog box (see Figure 21.4), select the
    related tables that you want to include in the query. For
    example, using the tables shown in Figure 21.4, you could
    create a query using the Employees, Departments, and
    Expenses tables that would show you each employee, the
    department, and any expenses that the employee has incurred.

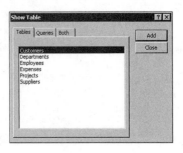

FIGURE 21.4
Select the tables that will be used to create the multi-table query.

3. After you have selected the tables for the query, click **Close**
    to close the Show Table dialog box. The tables and their rela-
    tionships appear at the top of the Query Design window.

4. Add the fields to the Query grid that make up the query. The
    fields can come from any of the tables that you have included
    in the query. Figure 21.5 shows a multi-table query that
    includes fields from the Employees, Departments, and
    Expenses tables.

5. When you have finished designing the multi-table query, you
    can run it. Click the **Run** button on the toolbar.

The query results appear in the Datasheet view. Combining data from
related tables into one query allows you to create other objects from
that query, such as forms or reports.

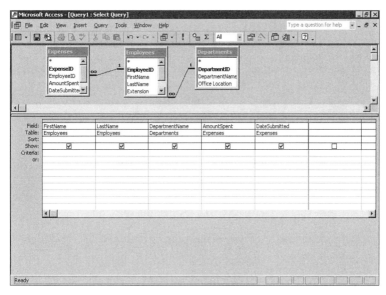

FIGURE 21.5
Multi-table queries enable you to pull data from fields on more than one table.

CREATING MULTI-TABLE FORMS

Forms can be created from more than one table using the Form Wizard or the Form Design view. Creating a form from fields that reside in more than one table allows you to enter data into more than one table using just the single form.

A very simple way to create a multi-table form is to add a *subform* to an existing form. For example, you might have a form that is based on a Customers table. If you would also like to be able to view and enter order information when you work with the Customers form, you can add an Orders subform to it. It is important that the tables used to create the two forms (the main form and the subform) are related tables.

PLAIN ENGLISH

Subform   A form control that actually consists of an entire form based on another table or tables.

The easiest way to create a subform is to actually drag an existing form onto another form in the Design view. The following steps describe how you do it:

1. Use the AutoForm feature, the Form Wizard, or the Form Design view to create two forms: the form that serves as the main form and the form that serves as the subform. These forms should be based on tables that are related.

2. In the Form Design view, open the form that will serve as the main form.

3. Size the Form Design window so that you can also see the database window in the Access workspace (see Figure 21.6).

4. In the database window, be sure that the Forms list is showing. Then, drag the form that will serve as the subform onto the main form that is open in the Design view. When the mouse pointer enters the Design view, it becomes a control pointer. Release the mouse button when you are in the general area where you want to place the subform. The subform control appears on the main form.

5. Maximize the Form Design window. Reposition or size the subform in the Design view until you are happy with its location (see Figure 21.7).

6. Save the changes that you have made to the main form (specifically, the addition of the subform).

7. To change to the Form view to view or add data to the composite form, click the **View** button on the Form Design toolbar.

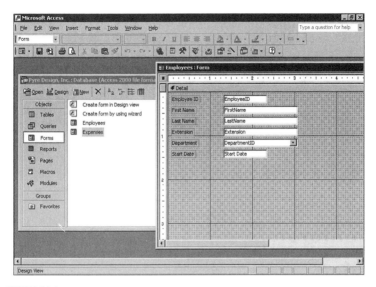

FIGURE 21.6
The subform is dragged from the database window onto the Design view of the main form.

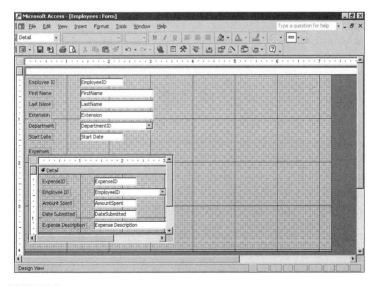

FIGURE 21.7
The subform becomes another control on the main form.

Figure 21.8 shows the main form and the subform in the Form view.
The form can be used to view or enter data into two tables at once.

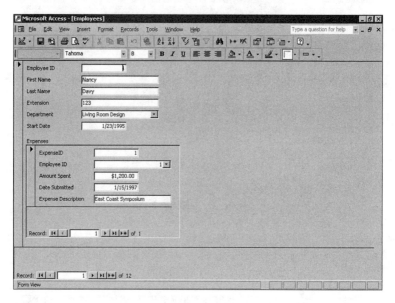

FIGURE 21.8
The composite form can be used to view and enter data into more than one table.

CREATING MULTI-TABLE REPORTS

You can also create reports that include information from more than
one table or query. The process is the same as the procedure that you
used in Lesson 19, "Creating a Simple Report," when you used the
Report Wizard to create a report. All you have to do is select fields
from related tables during the report creation process. This allows the
report to pull information from the related tables.

An alternative to creating reports that contain fields from more than
one table is to create a report that contains a *subreport*. The procedure
is similar to the procedure discussed in the previous section, when you
created a main form that held a subform.

PLAIN ENGLISH

Subreport A report control that consists of an entire report based on another table or tables.

To create a report that contains a subreport, follow these steps:

1. Use the AutoReport feature, the Report Wizard, or the Report Design view to create two reports: the report that serves as the main report and the report that serves as the subreport. These reports should be based on tables that are related.

2. In the Report Design view, open the report that will serve as the main report. Size the area in which you will place the subreport. For example, you might want to place the subreport in the Report Header area so that it can be viewed on any page of the printed report.

3. Size the Report Design window so that you can also see the database window in the Access workspace.

4. In the database window, be sure that the Reports list is showing. Then, drag the report that will serve as the subreport onto the main report in the Design view window. Don't release the mouse until you have positioned the mouse pointer in the area (such as the Report Header) where you want to place the subreport.

5. Size or move the subreport control as needed and then save any changes that you have made to the main report.

When you view the composite report in the Print Preview mode, the subreport appears as part of the main report. Figure 21.9 shows the composite report in the Print Preview mode. Placing subreports on a main report enables you to include summary data that can be referenced while data on the main report is viewed either on the screen or on the printed page.

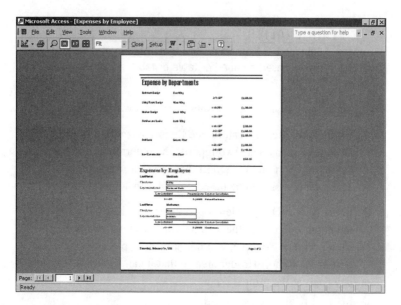

FIGURE 21.9
Composite reports enable you to report the data in different ways on the same report.

In this lesson, you learned how to create queries, forms, and reports based on more than one related table. In the next lesson, you learn how to print Access objects.

Lesson 22
Printing Access Objects

In this lesson, you learn how to print Access tables, forms, queries, and reports.

Access Objects and the Printed Page

You have probably gotten a feel for the fact that tables, forms, and queries are used mainly to view and manipulate database information on your computer's screen, whereas the report is designed to be printed. This doesn't mean that you can't print a table or a form; it's just that the report provides the greatest amount of control in placing information on the printed page.

First, this lesson discusses printing Access objects with the report. Then, you look at printing some of the other Access objects, such as a table or form.

Printing Reports

As you learned earlier in this book, the Access report is the ideal format for presenting database information on the printed page. Using reports, you can add page numbering controls and other header or footer information that repeat on each page of the report.

Whether you create a report using AutoReport or the Report Wizard, the completed report appears in the Print Preview mode, as shown in Figure 22.1.

 You can immediately send the report to the default printer by clicking the **Print** button on the Print Preview toolbar. If you find that you would like to change the margins on the report or change how the report is oriented on the page, click the **Setup** button on the Print Preview toolbar. The Page Setup dialog box appears (see Figure 22.2).

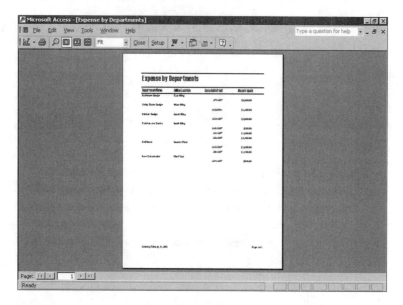

FIGURE 22.1
Reports created using AutoReport or the Report Wizard open in the Print Preview mode.

FIGURE 22.2
The Page Setup dialog box enables you to control the margins and page orientation of the printed report.

Three tabs are on the Page Setup dialog box:

* **Margins**—This tab enables you to set the top, bottom, left, and right margins. To change one of the default settings (1 inch), type the new setting in the appropriate margin box.

* **Page**—This tab enables you to change the orientation of the report on the printed page. Portrait, which is the default setting, orients the report text from top to bottom on a regular 8 1/2-inch by 11-inch page. Landscape turns the page 180 degrees, making it an 11-inch by 8 1/2-inch page. Landscape orientation works well for reports that contain a large number of fields placed from left to right on the report. This tab also enables you to select the type of paper that you are going to use for the printout (such as letter, legal, and so on).

* **Columns**—This tab enables you to change the number of columns in the report and the distance between the columns. Because the columns for the report are determined when you create the report using AutoReport or the Report Wizard, you probably won't want to tamper with the column settings. It's easier to change the distance between field controls in the Report Design view.

TIP

🖼 **Use the Report Design View to Make Design Changes**
If you find that the report needs some major structural changes, click the **View** button to go to the Design view.

After you have finished making your choices in the Page Setup dialog box, click **OK** to close the dialog box. You can now print the report.

PRINTING OTHER DATABASE OBJECTS

The fastest way to print a database object, such as a table, form, or query, is to select the object in the database window. Just select the appropriate object icon in the database window and select an object in the object list, such as a table.

After the object is selected, click the **Print** button on the database toolbar. Your database object is sent to the printer.

If you would like to preview the printout of a table, form, or query, either select the particular object in the database window or open the particular object and then click the **Print Preview** button. The object is then displayed in the Print Preview mode, such as the table shown in Figure 22.3.

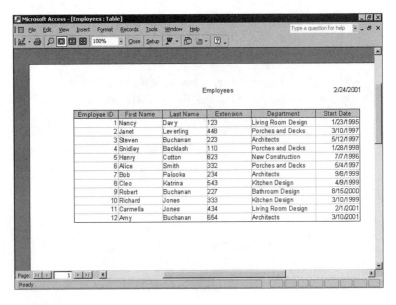

FIGURE 22.3
Any database object, such as a table, can be viewed in Print Preview.

When you print tables, forms, or queries, the name of the object and the current date are placed at the top of the printout. Page numbering is automatically placed at the bottom of the printout. You can control the margins and the page layout (portrait or landscape) for the table printout (or other object) using the Page Setup dialog box (discussed earlier in this lesson).

USING THE PRINT DIALOG BOX

So far, this discussion of printing in Access has assumed that you want to print to your default printer. You can also print a report or other database object to a different printer and control the range of pages that are printed or the actual records that are printed. These settings are controlled in the Print dialog box.

From the Print Preview mode or with a particular object open in the Access window, select **File**, **Print**. The Print dialog box appears (see Figure 22.4).

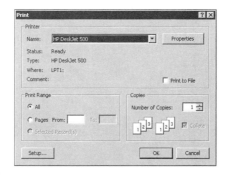

FIGURE 22.4
The Print dialog box enables you to select a different printer or specify a print range.

To select a different printer (one other than the default), click the **Name** drop-down list and select a printer by name. If you want to select a range of pages to print (such as a range of pages in a report), click the **Pages** option button and then type the page range into the page boxes.

In the case of tables and queries, you can also print selected records. Before you open the Print dialog box, select the records in the table or query. Then, when you open the Print dialog box, click the **Selected Record(s)** option button.

When you have finished changing the default printer or specifying a page range or the printing of select records, you are ready to print the object. Click the **OK** button. This closes the Print dialog box and sends the object to the printer.

In this lesson you learned how to print the various Access objects.

INDEX

W-X

Y-Z

Microsoft® Outlook® 2002

10 MINUTE GUIDE

201 West 103rd Street
Indianapolis, IN 46290

Joe Habraken

10 Minute Guide to Microsoft® Outlook® 2002

Copyright © 2002 by Que® Corporation

All rights reserved. No part of this book shall be reproduced, stored in a retrieval system, or transmitted by any means, electronic, mechanical, photocopying, recording, or otherwise, without written permission from the publisher. No patent liability is assumed with respect to the use of the information contained herein. Although every precaution has been taken in the preparation of this book, the publisher and author assume no responsibility for errors or omissions. Nor is any liability assumed for damages resulting from the use of the information contained herein.

International Standard Book Number: 0-7897-2638-6

Library of Congress Catalog Card Number: 20-01090289

Printed in the United States of America

First Printing: August 2001

06   05   04   03   12   11   10   9   8

Trademarks

All terms mentioned in this book that are known to be trademarks or service marks have been appropriately capitalized. Que cannot attest to the accuracy of this information. Use of a term in this book should not be regarded as affecting the validity of any trademark or service mark.

Warning and Disclaimer

Every effort has been made to make this book as complete and as accurate as possible, but no warranty or fitness is implied. The information provided is on an "as is" basis. The author and the publisher shall have neither liability nor responsibility to any person or entity with respect to any loss or damages arising from the information contained in this book.

Acquisitions Editor
Stephanie J. McComb

Development Editor
Stephanie J. McComb

Project Editor
Tricia Liebig

Indexer
Mandie Frank

Proofreaders
Angela Boley
Amy Jay

Team Coordinator
Sharry Lee Gregory

Interior Designer
Gary Adair

Cover Designer
Alan Clements

Page Layout
Lizbeth Patterson

Contents

DEDICATION

To my Aunt Donna; enjoy your retirement!

ACKNOWLEDGMENTS

Creating books like this takes a real team effort. I would like to thank
Stephanie McComb, our acquisitions editor, who worked very hard to
assemble the team that made this book a reality and also served as the
development editor for this book—coming up with many great ideas
for improving the content of the book. Also, a great big thanks to our
project editor, Tricia Liebig, who ran the last leg of the race and made
sure the book made it to press on time—what a great team of professionals.

TELL US WHAT YOU THINK!

As the reader of this book, *you* are our most important critic and commentator. We value your opinion and want to know what we're doing right, what we could do better, what areas you'd like to see us publish in, and any other words of wisdom you're willing to pass our way.

As an Associate Publisher for Que, I welcome your comments. You can fax, e-mail, or write me directly to let me know what you did or didn't like about this book—as well as what we can do to make our books stronger.

Please note that I cannot help you with technical problems related to the topic of this book, and that due to the high volume of mail I receive, I might not be able to reply to every message.

When you write, please be sure to include this book's title and author as well as your name and phone or fax number. I will carefully review your comments and share them with the author and editors who worked on the book.

Fax: 317-581-4666

E-mail: feedback@quepublishing.com

Mail: Greg Wiegand
            Que
            201 West 103rd Street
            Indianapolis, IN 46290 USA

Introduction

Microsoft Outlook 2002 is a personal information manager (PIM). With Outlook, you can communicate throughout your office or over the Internet with e-mail, and you can also schedule meetings, create task lists for yourself and others and keep track of all your important appointments. Outlook provides accessibility and flexibility for you and your coworkers and friends.

THE WHAT AND WHY OF MICROSOFT OUTLOOK

Outlook can help you organize your work on a day-to-day basis. Using Microsoft Outlook, you can do the following:

- Create task lists

- Manage your calendar

- Log phone calls and other important events in your journal

- Make notes to remind yourself of important tasks

Additionally, Outlook can help you communicate with others and share your workload. When you and your coworkers use the combined features of Microsoft Outlook and Microsoft Office, you can

- Schedule meetings and invite coworkers

- Communicate with others using e-mail

- Import and export files

While providing you with many communication and organizational features, Microsoft Outlook is easy to learn. This book will help you understand the possibilities awaiting you with Microsoft Outlook 2002.

WHY QUE'S *10 MINUTE GUIDE TO MICROSOFT OUTLOOK 2002*?

The 10 Minute Guide to Microsoft Outlook 2002 can save you precious time while you get to know the different features provided by Microsoft Outlook. Each lesson is designed to be completed in 10 minutes or less, so you'll be up to snuff on basic and advanced Outlook features quickly.

Although you can jump around among lessons, starting at the beginning is a good plan. The bare-bones basics are covered first, and more advanced topics are covered later. If you need help installing Outlook, see the next section for instructions.

WHO SHOULD USE THIS BOOK?

The *10 Minute Guide to Microsoft Outlook 2002* is for anyone who

- Has Microsoft Outlook 2002 installed on their PC.

- Needs to learn Microsoft Outlook 2002 quickly.

- Wants to explore some of the advanced features of Outlook.

- Wants a quick way to select, learn, and perform tasks in Microsoft Outlook.

CONVENTIONS USED IN THIS BOOK

The *10 Minute Guide to Microsoft Outlook 2002* includes step-by-step instructions for performing specific tasks. To help you as you work through these steps and help you move through the lessons easily, additional information is included and identified by the following icons.

PLAIN ENGLISH

New or unfamiliar terms are defined to help you as you work through the various steps in the lesson.

TIP

> Read these tips for ideas that cut corners and confusion.

CAUTION

> This icon identifies areas where new users often run into
> trouble; these hints offer practical solutions to those
> problems.

LESSON 1
What's New in Outlook 2002?

In this lesson, you are introduced to Outlook's powerful organizing features, and you learn what's new in Outlook 2002.

GETTING ORGANIZED WITH OUTLOOK 2002

Outlook 2002 is the latest version of Microsoft's popular personal information manager (PIM). Outlook can help you manage incoming and outgoing e-mail messages and help you keep organized by providing a personal calendar, a contacts list, and a personal to-do list. Since Outlook's ultimate purpose is to keep you organized, its basic "look and feel" makes it easy for you to manage your e-mail, contacts, and appointments.

PLAIN ENGLISH

> **Personal Information Manager (PIM)**   A PIM is a software package that helps you keep track of your appointments, meetings, contacts, and messages, such as e-mail and faxes.

Outlook provides an environment that's very much like a filing cabinet. Items of information are kept in folders, which you can access with one click of the mouse. For instance, your new e-mail messages can be found in the Inbox. Appointments, meetings, and events are stored in the Calendar folder. The names of your contacts, their e-mail addresses, business addresses, and phone numbers are stored in the

Contacts folder. Folders are also provided for your Tasks, Journal Entries, and Notes.

NEW FEATURES IN OUTLOOK 2002

On the surface Outlook 2002 looks very similar to the previous version of Outlook, Outlook 2000. For example, Outlook 2002 uses the same adaptive menu and toolbar system found in Outlook 2000 that customizes the commands listed on the menu system and icons available on toolbars based on the commands you use most frequently.

You will find, however, that Outlook 2002 offers a number of improvements over previous versions of Outlook. These improvements range from an easier setup procedure for your e-mail accounts to the availability of AutoCorrect to automatically detect and correct spelling errors and typos in your messages and other entries. Let's take a look at some of the new enhancements available in Outlook 2002.

EASIER E-MAIL CONFIGURATION

In Outlook 2000, the Outlook Startup Wizard required that you selected the type of network environment that Outlook would be used in: either a corporate network that used a Microsoft Exchange Server to handle e-mail or a stand-alone computer connected to the Internet. Outlook 2002 no longer requires that you make the distinction between Outlook on a corporate network or as an Internet e-mail client.

Outlook 2002 also makes it much easier for you to add different kinds of e-mail accounts and access them from the Outlook Inbox. Not only are Exchange Server e-mail accounts and Internet e-mail accounts supported, but you can now use Outlook as your e-mail client for World Wide Web e-mail services such as Microsoft Hotmail. Once you have Outlook 2002 up and running, your e-mail accounts can be added, edited, or removed using the new E-mail Accounts Wizard. Adding and configuring e-mail accounts is covered in Lesson 3, "Understanding the Outlook E-mail Configurations."

FRIENDLY NAMES DISPLAYED IN E-MAILS

When you add contacts to your Contacts folder, you can now enter a "friendly name" for the contact. This friendly name, which is entered in the Display As box in the Contact's window (see Figure 1.1), will then appear in the To: box when you send an e-mail to the contact.

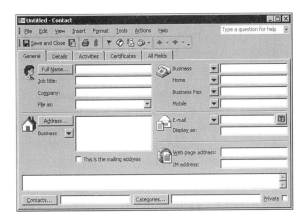

FIGURE 1.1
Friendly names can be specified for your contacts.

Using friendly names to identify contacts allows you to make sure that you are sending a particular e-mail message to the correct contact. Creating a Contacts list is covered in Lesson 13, "Creating a Contacts List."

OTHER OUTLOOK 2002 ENHANCEMENTS

Outlook 2002 also provides other enhancements that make it easier to use than previous versions of Outlook. Some of these enhancements are:

- **Microsoft Word Is the Default E-mail Editor**   If you have Microsoft Word 2002 installed on your computer, Outlook is configured to use Word as its default e-mail editor. This allows you to take advantage of Word's powerful word-processing features to create your e-mails. E-mails are created by default as HTML documents, which allow you to format text in the message and even include images directly in the e-mail message.

- **AutoCorrect Available**   AutoCorrect automatically detects and correct typos, misspellings, and incorrect capitalization. Even if you decide not to use Word as your e-mail editor, Outlook still allows you to take advantage of the AutoCorrect feature as you compose your e-mail messages.

- **Extra Line Breaks Removed from Text Messages**   Many text messages that you receive as e-mail will contain extra line breaks that make the message difficult to read. Outlook 2002 automatically removes these extra line breaks; this makes it easier for you to read the text-only messages that you receive in your Inbox.

- **Preview Pane Can Be Used to Open Attachments and Follow Links**   The Preview pane in Outlook 2002 now allows you to click on links contained in e-mail messages and follow these links to Web addresses. Attachments contained in an e-mail message can also be opened directly from the Preview pane.

CAUTION

Outlook 2002 No Longer Emphasized As Fax Manager   An additional change that you will find in Outlook 2002 is that it does not include a new version of WinFax. While previous versions of WinFax included as part of earlier versions of Outlook are supported, Outlook 2002 is probably no longer your best tool for sending, receiving, and managing fax messages. A third party fax service will provide you greater flexibility when working with faxes.

Outlook 2002 provides more features and greater ease of use than previous versions of this powerful PIM. This book will provide you with step-by-step lessons that you can use to familiarize yourself with the various organizational features provided by Outlook.

In this lesson, you learned how Outlook can help you stay organized. You were also introduced to some of the new features found in Outlook 2002. In the next lesson, you will take a first look at the Outlook window and learn how to start and exit the software.

LESSON 2
Getting Started in Outlook

In this lesson, you learn how to start and exit Outlook, identify parts of the Outlook window, and use the mouse to get around the program.

STARTING OUTLOOK

You start Outlook from the Windows desktop. After starting the program, you can leave it open, or you can minimize it to free up the desktop for other applications. Either way, you can access it at any time during your day.

> **CAUTION**
>
> **Outlook and System Performance** If you leave Outlook open on your desktop, it still requires a certain amount of your system resources. This means that if you normally run multiple applications, such as Word and Excel, you might see some loss of performance as you work. If this becomes a problem, close Outlook (or any program not being used) to free up your system's memory. Adding memory to your system, of course, also is an alternative for increasing performance. The suggested amount of memory for running Office XP is 64MB for Windows 98, Me, and Windows NT. For Windows 2000, 128MB is suggested.

To start Microsoft Outlook, follow these steps:

1. From the Windows desktop, click the **Start** button, choose **Programs,** and then select **Microsoft Outlook**.

○ **TIP**

Shortcuts to Launching Outlook   You can also double-
click the **Outlook** shortcut icon on the desktop to start
Outlook, or you can click the **Outlook** icon on the Quick
Launch toolbar on the Windows taskbar (next to the
Start button).

2. If your PC is set up for multiple users, the Choose Profile
   dialog box appears; click **OK** to accept the default profile, or
   choose your profile and open Microsoft Outlook. Figure 2.1
   shows the Outlook screen that appears.

○ **PLAIN ENGLISH**

Profile   The profile includes information about you and
your e-mail accounts and is created automatically when
you install Outlook (the e-mail accounts are added to
the profile when Outlook is set up for the first time, as
discussed in Lesson 3, "Understanding the Outlook E-
mail Configurations"). Multiple profiles become an issue
only if you share your computer with other users.

In situations where you connect to the Internet using a modem dial-up
connection, the Connection Wizard attempts to make a dial-in connection as Outlook opens. This enables Outlook to check your e-mail
server.

○ **CAUTION**

The First Time You Start Outlook   The very first time
you start Outlook on a computer that has not had a
previous version of the software installed, you will be
required to configure the e-mail accounts that you use.
Setting up your e-mail accounts is discussed in
Lesson 3.

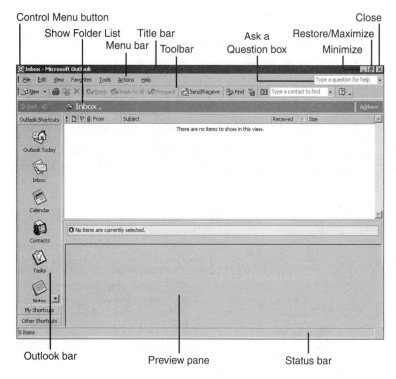

FIGURE 2.1
The Outlook window includes all the icons and items you need to access its various features.

UNDERSTANDING THE OUTLOOK WINDOW

The Outlook window includes items you can use to navigate in and operate the program. If you do not see some of the items listed in Figure 2.1 on your screen, open the **View** menu and select the command for the appropriate element (such as **Toolbars**, **Status Bar**, **Folder List**, or **Outlook Bar**). A check mark in front of an item means the item is currently showing. If you find the Preview pane distracting when you first open the Outlook window, click the **View** menu and click **Preview Pane** to close the Preview pane.

Table 2.1 describes the elements you see in the opening screen.

TABLE 2.1   Elements of the Outlook Window

Element	Description
Title bar	Includes the name of the application and current folder, plus the Minimize, Maximize, and Close buttons.
Control Menu button	Opens the Control menu, which provides such commands as Move, Size, Minimize, and Close.
Minimize button	Reduces the Outlook window to a button on the taskbar; to restore the window to its original size, click the button on the taskbar.
Maximize button	Enlarges the Outlook window to cover the Windows desktop. When the window is maximized, the Maximize button changes to a Restore button you can click to return the window to its previous size.
Close (x) button	Closes the Outlook program window.
Menu bar	Contains menus of commands you can use to perform tasks in the program.
Toolbar	Includes icons that serve as shortcuts for common commands, such as creating a new message or printing a message.
Show Folder List	Displays the current folder. Click this to display a list of personal folders you can open.
Outlook bar	Displays icons representing folders: Inbox, Calendar, Contacts, and so on. Click an icon to change to the folder it names. The Outlook Shortcuts, My Shortcuts, and Other Shortcuts buttons on the bar list specific groups of folders (for example, the My Shortcuts button lists icons related to your e-mail, such as the Drafts, Outbox, and Sent items).

TABLE 2.1   (continued)

Element	Description
Status bar	Displays information about the items currently shown in the Information Viewer.
Preview pane	Displays a preview of the currently selected item in your Outlook Inbox or other selected folder.
Ask a Question box	This box allows you to quickly ask the Outlook Help system a question. It also allows you to forgo using the Office Assistant to access the Help system.

TIP

Finding a Toolbar Button's Purpose   You can place the mouse pointer on any toolbar button to view a description of that tool's function.

USING THE MOUSE IN OUTLOOK

Like most Windows-based programs, you can use the mouse in Outlook to select items, open e-mail and folders, move items, and so on. In general, clicking selects an item, and double-clicking selects it and performs some action on it (for example, displaying its contents). In addition to clicking and double-clicking, there are some special mouse actions you can use in Outlook:

- **Drag**—To move an object to another position on the screen (to transfer a mail message to another folder, for example), you can drag the object with the mouse. To drag an object to a new location onscreen, point to the object and press and hold down the left mouse button. Move the mouse pointer to the new location and then release the mouse button.

- **Right-click**—You can display a shortcut menu by clicking the right mouse button when pointing to an item. For example, you can right-click a folder in the Outlook bar or a piece of e-mail. A shortcut menu appears, which usually contains common commands relating to that particular item.

- **Multiselect**—You can act on multiple items at once by selecting them before issuing a command. To select multiple contiguous items, hold down the **Shift** key and click the first and last items you want to select. To select noncontiguous items (those that are not adjacent to each other), hold down the **Ctrl** key and click each item.

If you have a mouse, such as the Microsoft IntelliMouse, that includes a scroll wheel, you can use it in Outlook. Turn the wheel toward you to move down through any list in Outlook, such as your Contacts list, or move the wheel up to scroll up in a list.

TIP

> **Keyboard Shortcuts**   You can use the keyboard to move around Outlook and to access many, but not all, of its features. For example, to open a menu with the keyboard, press the **Alt** key and then press the underlined letter in the menu name (press **Alt+F** to open the File menu, for instance).

WORKING OFFLINE

In cases where you use a modem connection to access your e-mail server, you can close the connection while still working in Outlook. This allows you to free up your phone line or, if you pay for your connection based on the time you are connected, save on connection time. Working offline in Outlook does not affect any Outlook features or capabilities. E-mail that you create while working offline is held in the Outbox until you reconnect to your Internet connection.

To work offline, select the **File** menu and then select **Work Offline**. If you are prompted to confirm the closing of your dial-in connection, click **Yes**.

EXITING OUTLOOK

When you are finished working in Outlook, you can exit the application in a couple of ways. You can use the File menu: select **File**, **Exit**. Or you can close Outlook by clicking the Outlook window's **Close (x)** button. In cases where you are connected to the Internet using a dial-up connection, you are prompted as to whether you want to log off your connection. If you want to close the dial-up connection, select **Log Off** in the message box.

In this lesson, you learned about the Outlook window, how to start and exit Outlook, and how to use the mouse to get around the program. In the next lesson, you will learn about the different Outlook e-mail account types and how to add them to the Outlook configuration. You also will learn how to access e-mail accounts to edit their settings and how to delete unneeded e-mail accounts.

LESSON 3

Understanding the Outlook E-mail Configurations

In this lesson, you learn how to set up Outlook for different types of electronic mail.

TYPES OF OUTLOOK E-MAIL CONFIGURATIONS

The type or flavor of e-mail that you use in Outlook depends on who provides your e-mail account. Outlook contains support for the three most common providers of e-mail service:

- **ISP**—When you sign up for an Internet service provider (ISP), the company usually provides you with at least one e-mail account.

- **Exchange**—In networked environments (most offices, for example), an e-mail server such as Microsoft Exchange may control delivery of e-mail.

- **Web**—Outlook also provides you with the capability to connect to Web-based e-mail services, such as Microsoft's Hotmail or Yahoo!'s Yahoo! mail.

Because Outlook serves not only as your e-mail client, but also as your personal information manager (allowing you to build a contacts list and keep track of your appointments and tasks), it is designed to operate either in a standalone environment or in a corporate service environment. As a standalone application, your contacts, appointments, and tasks are stored locally on your computer and you access your e-mail through the Internet. However, in a corporate environment, your calendar and tasks folders are kept on a corporate communication server (typically Microsoft Exchange Server) where your information can be shared with other users.

PLAIN ENGLISH

E-mail Client   Software that is configured on a user's computer to connect to e-mail services on a company's network or on the Internet.

Making Your E-mail Choice

The first time you start Outlook (double-click its desktop icon), you must communicate to Outlook the type of e-mail account that you use on your computer. Outlook assists you in this task by launching the Outlook Startup Wizard. Click **Next** to move past the opening screen. The E-mail Accounts screen appears as shown in Figure 3.1.

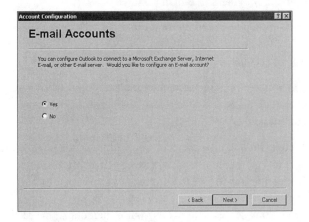

FIGURE 3.1
The Outlook Startup Wizard helps you set up your e-mail accounts.

To configure an e-mail account for use in Outlook, make sure that the **Yes** option button is selected, and then click **Next** to continue. The

next screen presents a selection of different e-mail servers, as shown
in Figure 3.2.

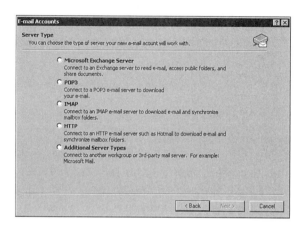

FIGURE 3.2
Outlook can function as an e-mail client for several e-mail types.

How your e-mail functions depends on which option you select to
configure Outlook as a specific e-mail client. The possibilities are

- **Microsoft Exchange Server**—This type of account makes
  Outlook an Exchange Server client; mailboxes and other
  resources, such as shared public folders, are managed on the
  Exchange Server computer. If this is what your Outlook
  installation requires, your network system administrator
  should provide these settings for you.

- **POP3**—POP3 is a protocol that most ISPs use, which allows
  a POP3 e-mail server to function as a mail drop.

  This means that your Internet e-mail is forwarded to the
  POP3 server and sits there until you connect with your e-mail
  client (Outlook) and download the mail to your computer.

PLAIN ENGLISH

> **POP3 (Post Office Protocol Version 3)**   A set of software protocols or rules used to download mail to your computer. Your e-mail resides on the POP3 server until you connect and download it to your computer.

- **IMAP**—IMAP is a protocol that allows Outlook to download e-mail from an IMAP mail server. IMAP differs from POP3 in that your e-mail is not removed from the mail server when you connect to the server with your e-mail client (Outlook). Instead, you are provided a list of saved and new messages, which you can then open and read. IMAP is particularly useful when one e-mail account may be accessed by more than one computer, allowing the messages to be available from more than one computer.

  You might think that IMAP is a good idea because it leaves the e-mail on the mail server. However, you can use IMAP only if your ISP or company provides an IMAP mail server. In most cases, ISPs don't want your mail on their server, so they use POP3, which sends the mail to your computer when you connect.

PLAIN ENGLISH

> **IMAP (Internet Message Access Protocol)**   A set of software rules used by an e-mail client to access e-mail messages on a shared mail server as if the messages were stored locally.

- **HTTP**—The Hypertext Transfer Protocol is the protocol and set of rules that enables you to browse Web sites using a Web browser. HTTP e-mail is accessed through a Web site, and your inbox actually resides on a server that is hosted by the provider of the e-mail Web site. Common providers of this type of e-mail include Microsoft (in the case of Hotmail) and Yahoo! (in the case of Yahoo! mail). Normally, such e-mail is accessed from the provider's Web site; however, Outlook can be configured to act as your e-mail client with HTTP mail providers.

- **Additional Server Types**—This selection allows you to configure Outlook as a mail client for other e-mail server types, such as Microsoft Mail or third-party e-mail server software. It also provides you with the capability to create a special e-mail account that allows you to receive faxes in the Outlook Inbox.

Even though Outlook pretty much demands that you configure an e-mail account during the initial Outlook setup, it doesn't easily provide for the fact that you might want to set up more than one account. However, it is very easy to add additional e-mail accounts as needed, which is discussed later in this lesson. The two most common uses for Outlook are as a Microsoft Exchange Server e-mail client or as an Internet e-mail client using POP3, IMAP, or HTTP. In the following sections, you take a closer look at the configuration steps for setting up your first POP3 or HTTP account. You can then learn how to add additional accounts after Outlook has been initially configured.

 TIP

> **Importing E-mail Settings**   If you are already using an e-mail client, such as Outlook Express, you can import all the e-mail messages and the settings for your e-mail accounts into Outlook. Outlook actually prompts you to perform this import when you start it for the first time. If you import mail settings, you won't be required to add an e-mail account as outlined in this section. You can use the information in this lesson, however, to add any additional e-mail accounts that you might need.

Internet POP3 E-mail

If you connect to the Internet using a modem, a DSL router, or a broadband cable modem, your Internet connection is of the type that an Internet service provider (ISP) provides. Most ISPs provide e-mail to their users in the form of a POP3 account. This means that the ISP's e-mail server holds your e-mail until you connect and download your messages to Outlook.

PLAIN ENGLISH

ISP (Internet Service Provider)   A commercial, educational, or government institution that provides individuals and companies access to the Internet.

ISPs that provide e-mail service also must have some mechanism for you to send e-mail to other users on the Internet. A computer called an SMTP server handles the sending of e-mail from your computer, over the Internet, to a final destination. That destination is typically the POP3 server that serves as the mail drop for the person to whom you are sending the Internet e-mail.

PLAIN ENGLISH

SMTP (Simple Mail Transfer Protocol)   A set of rules used to transfer Internet mail; your ISP goes through an SMTP host, or relay, server to get your mail to you.

If you do not use an e-mail account (such as a POP3 account) that your ISP supplies to you, you can still use Outlook for Internet e-mail. In this case, sign up for an HTTP e-mail account on the Web and configure Outlook to use it. Configuring HTTP e-mail is discussed in a moment, but first take a look at the steps required to configure a POP3 e-mail account as Outlook's initial e-mail account.

The first thing Outlook needs you to provide is information related to the POP3 account, such as your username, password, and SMTP and

POP3 servers, all of which your ISP must provide. To complete the configuration of your POP3 account, follow these steps:

1. Select the **POP3** button on the E-mail Accounts screen, and then click **Next** to continue.

2. On the next screen, shown in Figure 3.3, enter your name, your e-mail address, your username, and your password. You also must provide the name of your ISP's POP3 (incoming server) and SMTP server (outgoing server) in the appropriate box. If your ISP uses Secure Password Authentication, which provides a second layer of authentication for their mail servers, click the Log on using Secure Password Authentication (SPA). (If SPA is used, you are provided a second username and password, other than your e-mail username, to log onto the servers; most ISPs do not use SPA.)

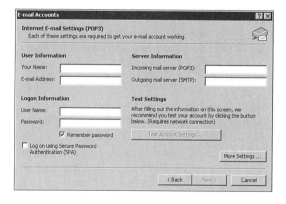

FIGURE 3.3

You must supply all the information listed on the Internet E-mail Settings (POP3) screen.

3. You can test your new account settings to make sure that they work; be sure you are connected to the Internet, and then click the **Test Account Settings** button. Outlook tests the user account and the servers listed. A Test Account Settings

dialog box appears, as shown in Figure 3.4. To close the dialog box, click **Close**.

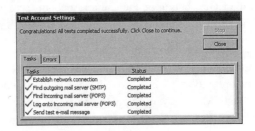

FIGURE 3.4
You can check your Internet e-mail settings after entering the appropriate information.

4. When you have completed your POP3 configuration settings (and tested them), click the **Next** button.

5. A final screen appears, letting you know that you have provided all the necessary information. Click **Finish** to end the process and open the Outlook Inbox.

PLAIN ENGLISH

Configuring for IMAP   The steps to configure an IMAP account are the same as those listed to configure the POP3 Internet e-mail account. The only differences are that you select IMAP on the initial setup screen and then make sure that the IMAP server name is provided on the configuration screen rather than the POP3 server name.

HTTP E-MAIL ACCOUNTS

Although most people use either an Exchange Server (configured by a system administrator) or a POP3 account as their primary e-mail account, Web-based HTTP accounts, such as Microsoft Hotmail, are convenient for checking personal e-mail from any computer.

Typically, you must log on to the appropriate Web site and provide a username and password to access your HTTP e-mail account. Although this offers a degree of flexibility that is appealing to many users, others are often put off because, in the past, this has prevented them from checking their e-mail using Outlook.

Fortunately, Outlook now has the capability to access HTTP e-mail accounts directly from Outlook. Before you can configure the HTTP account, however, you must sign up for an account on the site of HTTP mail service provider that you want to use. Assuming that you have an active account, follow these steps to configure an HTTP e-mail account:

1. Rather than selecting POP3, as you did in the previous section, select the **HTTP** option button on the E-mail Accounts dialog box (shown previously in Figure 3.2). Click **Next** to continue.

2. On the next screen, shown in Figure 3.5, enter your name, your e-mail address, your username, and your password (supplied by your mail provider). If you use an HTTP provider other than Hotmail, select **Other** in the HTTP Mail Service Provider dialog box, and then provide the URL of your HTTP service (you are providing the Web page address of the service).

3. Click **Next** after entering all the necessary information. On the final screen that appears, click **Finish**.

You are then returned to the Outlook window. When you add an HTTP account, such as a Hotmail account, to Outlook, a second set of folders appears in the Outlook folder listings, including Deleted Items, Inbox, Outbox, and Sent Items. Figure 3.6 shows this new set of folders.

Because a second set of folders is created, you can access the HTTP account from Outlook, but you manage received, sent, or deleted mail in their own set of folders. Mail received on any other accounts you

might have, such as a POP3 account, are still located in your main
Outlook Inbox.

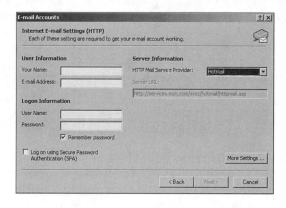

FIGURE 3.5
You must supply all the information listed on the HTTP E-mail Settings screen.

FIGURE 3.6
The HTTP mail folders, such as Hotmail, appear in the Outlook Folders list.

ADDING OTHER TYPES OF E-MAIL ACCOUNTS

As previously mentioned, Outlook is typically used as an e-mail client for either Exchange Server environments or for Internet e-mail where an ISP supplies either a POP3, an IMAP, or an HTTP e-mail account. However, many users find that they have more than one type of account at their disposal. Very often, users get one or more accounts through their ISP, but also sign up for an HTTP account that they can have easy access to from multiple locations (these HTTP accounts are usually free).

TIP

Configuring Exchange Server E-mail Accounts   If you are using Outlook on a corporate network that uses an Exchange Server as the e-mail server, your account will typically be set up on your computer by the network administrator. The name of the Exchange Server and your network user name are required to complete the configuration. If you use Outlook on a corporate network, consult your network administrator for help in configuring Outlook. Using Outlook for e-mail on an Exchange Server network enables several e-mail features that are not available when you use Outlook for Internet e-mail, such as a POP3 account. On a network, you can redirect replies, set message expirations, and even grant privileges to other users who can then monitor your e-mail, calendar, contacts, and tasks.

You can use the following steps to add e-mail accounts to the Outlook settings after you have already made your initial configuration, as discussed in the previous sections of this lesson. Remember, you can add any type of e-mail account to Outlook after the fact.

In the Outlook window:

1. Select **Tools, E-mail Accounts**. The E-mail Accounts dialog box opens, as shown in Figure 3.7.

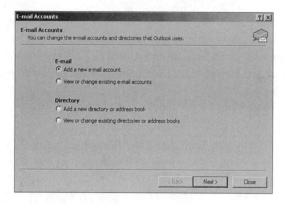

FIGURE 3.7
E-mail accounts are added using the E-mail Accounts dialog box.

2. Select the **Add a New E-mail Account** option button, and click **Next** to continue.

3. The Server Type screen opens with a list of the different types of e-mail accounts (this is the same screen provided during the initial e-mail configuration for Outlook, shown earlier in Figure 3.2).

4. Select the type of e-mail account you want to add to the Outlook configuration, and then click the **Next** button.

The information needed to configure a particular e-mail type is requested on the next screen, as previously discussed in this lesson.

DELETING E-MAIL ACCOUNTS

As you've seen in this lesson, configuring Outlook with different types of e-mail accounts is a pretty straightforward process. You might also find, on occasion, that you want to delete an e-mail account from the Outlook configuration. To do so, follow these steps:

1. Select **Tools, E-mail Accounts**. In the E-mail Accounts dialog box, select the **View or Change Existing E-mail Accounts** option button, and then click **Next**.

2. The E-mail Accounts dialog box appears as shown in Figure 3.8. To delete an account, select the account, and then click the **Remove** button.

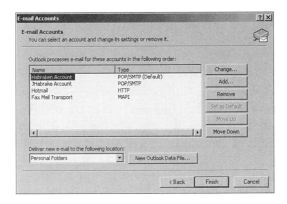

FIGURE 3.8
E-mail accounts are managed in the E-mail Accounts dialog box.

3. You are asked to confirm the deletion of the account. Click **Yes** to continue.

You can also use the E-mail Accounts dialog box to edit the settings for any of the e-mail accounts that you have created. Select the appropriate account, and then select the **Change** button. A dialog box for that specific account opens as shown in Figure 3.9, and you can change settings as required.

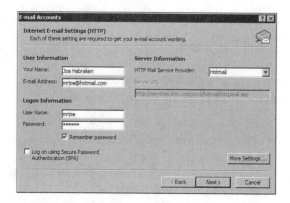

FIGURE 3.9
E-mail accounts settings can be edited using their settings dialog box.

In some cases, you might need to configure special settings for an
e-mail account, such as how your computer connects to the Internet
when you are using a particular e-mail account. Select the **More
Settings** button on the e-mail accounts settings dialog box. The
E-mail Settings dialog box appears for the e-mail account (see
Figure 3.10).

The E-mail Settings dialog box has a series of tabs that differ depending on the type of e-mail account you are editing. In most cases
(unless your ISP has provided you with special settings information),
the only settings you will want to adjust are on the Connection tab,
which allows you to specify how Outlook connects to the Internet
when you are checking this particular account for e-mail.

After completing the addition of any special settings to the E-mail
Settings dialog box, click **OK** to close it. You are returned to the dia-
log box for the e-mail account. Click **Next** to return to the E-mail
Accounts dialog box, and then click **Finish** to return to Outlook.

In this lesson, you learned how to configure the initial Outlook e-mail
account and how to add additional accounts. You also learned how to
delete e-mail accounts from the Outlook configuration. In the next lesson, you will learn how to use the various Outlook tools, such as the
Outlook bar.

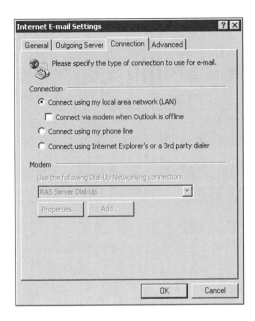

FIGURE 3.10

Special settings related to an e-mail account can be reached by clicking the More Settings button.

LESSON 4
Using Outlook's Tools

In this lesson, you learn how to change views in Outlook, how to use the Outlook bar, and how to use the Folder list.

USING THE OUTLOOK BAR

Each Outlook organizational tool has its own folder. You have a folder for e-mail (Inbox), a folder for the calendar (Calendar), and so on. The Outlook bar is a tool you can use to quickly change folders in Outlook. The icons in the Outlook bar represent all the folders available to you and provide shortcuts to getting to the contents of those folders. Figure 4.1 shows the Outlook bar and other areas of the Outlook window.

Three shortcut groups are located within the Outlook bar: Outlook Shortcuts, My Shortcuts, and Other Shortcuts. Each group contains related folders in which you can work.

- **Outlook Shortcuts**—This group contains folders for working with the different organizational tools in Outlook, such as Inbox, Calendar, Tasks, and so on.

- **My Shortcuts**—This group contains folders for organizing and managing e-mail you compose and send, such as the Outbox and the Sent Items folder. This group also provides access to the Journal (which keeps track of Office documents that you open and e-mail that you send) and an icon that takes you online to the Outlook Update Web page.

- **Other Shortcuts**—This group contains folders on your computer, such as My Computer, My Documents, and Favorites, which is a list of your favorite Web sites. You can use each of these folders to work with files and folders outside Outlook.

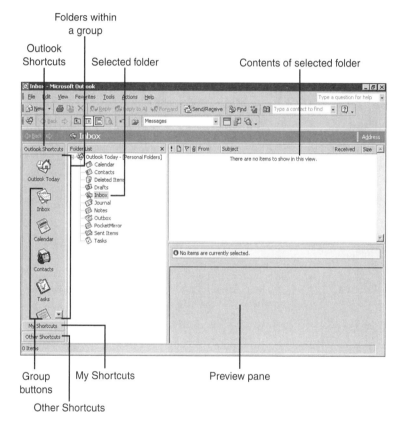

Folders within a group

Outlook Shortcuts

Selected folder

Contents of selected folder

Group buttons

My Shortcuts

Preview pane

Other Shortcuts

FIGURE 4.1

Use the Outlook bar to view various items in your work.

To switch from one group to another, click the **Outlook Shortcuts**, **My Shortcuts**, or **Other Shortcuts** button on the Outlook bar. The

Outlook shortcuts group is displayed by default, providing you with quick access to tools such as your Inbox, Calendar, and Contacts list.

THE OUTLOOK SHORTCUTS FOLDERS

The Outlook Shortcuts group's folder icons in the Outlook bar enable you to access your work in Outlook. That includes your e-mail messages, appointments, contact list, and so on. Table 4.1 describes each of the folders within the Outlook Shortcuts group.

TABLE 4.1   Outlook Shortcuts Group Folders

Folder	Description
Outlook Today	Although not really a folder, the Outlook Today icon on the Outlook bar provides a summary of Calendar events, tasks, and new messages for the current day (today).
Inbox	Includes messages you've received by e-mail and fax.
Calendar	Contains your appointments, events, scheduled meetings, and so on.
Contacts	Lists names and addresses of the people with whom you communicate.
Tasks	Includes any tasks you have on your to-do list.
Notes	Lists notes you write to yourself or others.
Deleted Items	Includes any items you've deleted from other folders.

THE MY SHORTCUTS FOLDERS

The My Shortcuts group folders provide a method of organizing your incoming and outgoing e-mail messages (see Figure 4.2). Table 4.2 describes each folder in the Mail group.

TABLE 4.2   My Shortcuts Folders

Folder	Description
Draft	Contains messages you have started but not sent.
Sent Items	Stores all messages you've sent.
Outbox	Contains messages to be sent.
Journal	Keeps track of your activities in Outlook, such as the logging of e-mail sent to specific contacts. The Journal also can keep track of your activities in other Office applications, such as Word or Excel.

FIGURE 4.2

The My Shortcuts folder icons give you access to your e-mail and fax messages that have been saved as drafts, that have been sent, or that are waiting to be sent.

CAUTION

I See Other Folders in My Groups   You can add additional folders and folder icons very easily to Outlook. If you find folders other than the ones described here, folders have probably been added to your particular installation of Outlook.

THE OTHER SHORTCUTS FOLDERS

The Other Shortcuts group contains folders that are on your computer but not within Outlook: My Computer, My Documents, and Favorites. You can access a document or information in any of those areas so that you can attach it to a message, add notes to it, or otherwise use it in Outlook.

For example, with My Computer, you can view the contents of both hard and floppy disks, CD-ROM drives, and so on (see Figure 4.3). Double-click a drive in the window to view its folders and files. Double-click a folder to view its contents as well. Then, you can attach files to messages or otherwise use the files on your hard drive with the Outlook features.

KEEPING TRACK

Moving Up a Level   Use the **Back** button on the Advanced toolbar (right-click the Outlook toolbar and select **Advanced** on the shortcut menu) to return to a folder or drive after you've double-clicked to expand it and view its contents.

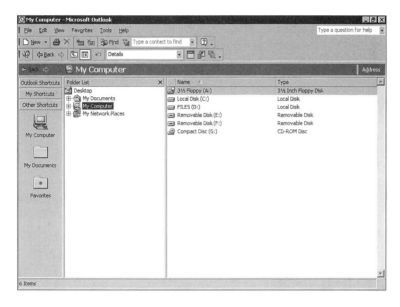

FIGURE 4.3
View your entire system through the My Computer folder in Outlook.

USING THE FOLDER LIST

Outlook provides another method of viewing the folders within
Outlook and your system: the Folder List. The Folder List displays the
folders within any of the three groups (Outlook Shortcuts, My
Shortcuts, or Other Shortcuts). From the list, you can select the folder
you want to view.

To use the Folder List, first select the group (such as Outlook
Shortcuts or Other Shortcuts) that contains the folders you want to
view, and then select a particular folder (using the appropriate shortcut) from the Outlook bar to display the list (see Figure 4.4).

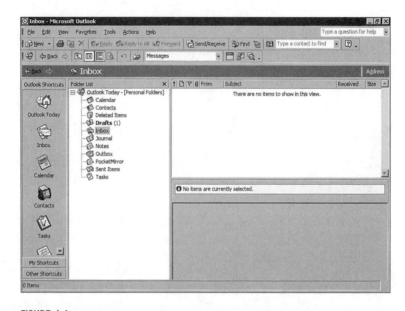

FIGURE 4.4
The Folder List shows all folders in the group you selected.

TIP

> **Pinning Down the Folder List**   When you open the
> Folder List button on a particular folder's name, the
> Folder List floats on top of the current folder window.
> Click the **Push Pin** button in the upper-right corner of
> the Folder List to pin down the list in the Outlook win-
> dow. If you want to close the Folder List, click its **Close**
> (**x**) button.

Choose any folder from the list, and the Information Viewer changes
to reflect your selection. If you want to display another folder in the
Information screen, click the folder to display its contents.

CHANGING VIEWS

In Outlook, you are provided with different views that enable you to look at the information in your various folders from a particular perspective. Each view presents the information in a different format and organizational structure.

The easiest way to select the different views provided for each of your Outlook folders is to use a Current View drop-down box that is present on the Advanced toolbar for each folder type (Inbox, Calendar, Contacts, and so on). To open the Advanced toolbar (it doesn't matter which Outlook folder you currently have selected), follow these steps:

1. Point to the Standard toolbar for an Outlook folder (such as the Inbox) and click the right mouse button.

2. A shortcut menu appears, as shown in Figure 4.5. Click **Advanced**. The Advanced toolbar appears.

FIGURE 4.5
Right-click the Standard toolbar to access the Outlook Advanced toolbar.

3. If you find later that you would like to close the Advanced toolbar, repeat steps 1 and 2 to remove the check mark next to Advanced on the shortcut menu that appears.

 TIP

> **You Must Open the Advanced Toolbar Only Once** After you've opened the Advanced toolbar for a folder, such as the Calendar or Inbox, it will be available for all the other Outlook folders.

Each folder, such as the Inbox, Calendar, Contacts, and so on, has a different set of buttons on the Standard and Advanced toolbars. This is because the commands and features that you access on a toolbar are particular to the folder that you currently have selected.

After you have the Advanced toolbar open, you can change the current view of any folder by clicking the **Current View** drop-down box, as shown in Figure 4.6. Each Current View box contains views that are appropriate for the currently selected folder on the Outlook bar.

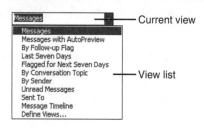

FIGURE 4.6
Select a view to change the format of the information.

As you can see in Figure 4.6, you can change your view of the Inbox so that you can see the following:

- **Messages**—All messages

- **Messages with AutoPreview**—Messages and their first three lines of text

- **By Follow-Up Flag**—Messages that have been tagged with a follow-up flag

- **Last Seven Days**—Messages from the last seven days

- **Flagged for Next Seven Days**—Messages tagged with a flag for the next seven days

- **By Conversation Topic**—Messages organized by topic

- **By Sender**—Messages organized by sender

- **Unread Messages**—Unread messages only

- **Sent To**—Messages by recipient

- **Message Timeline**—Messages arranged in a timeline

Similarly, the Calendar folder, which is arranged in the Day/Week/ Month view type by default, enables you to view your appointments and events by Active Appointments, Day/Week/Month with Auto-Preview, Events, Recurring Appointments, and several other view types.

You can also change the view type for any of your folders by selecting the **View** menu and then pointing at **Current View**. The View list appears at the top of the Current View submenu.

As you work your way through the Outlook part of this book, you'll see examples of some of the different view types as they are used when you are working in Outlook. When you change folders in Outlook, take a quick look at the available views in the Current View drop-down list.

CREATING CUSTOM VIEWS

In addition to Outlook's many presupplied views, you can also create custom views of the information in your Outlook folders. To create a custom view for one of your Outlook folders, follow these steps:

1. Click the **View** menu and then point at **Current View**. Select **Define Views** (near the bottom of the Current View submenu). A Define Views dialog box for the currently selected folder opens.

2. Click the **New** button in the Define Views box. The Create a New View dialog box appears, as shown in Figure 4.7.

FIGURE 4.7
You can create custom views for your Outlook folders.

3. Enter a name for your new view and select a view type from the list in the Type of View box.

   You can select different view types for a custom view:

   - **Table**—Presents items in a grid of sorts in rows and columns. Use this view type to view mail messages, tasks, and details about any item.

   - **Timeline**—Displays items as icons arranged in chronological order from left to right on a time scale. Use this to view journal entries and other items in this type of view.

   - **Card**—Presents items such as cards in a card file. Use this to view contacts.

   - **Day/Week/Month**—Displays items in a calendar view in blocks of time. Use this type for meetings and scheduled tasks.

   - **Icon**—Provides graphical icons to represent tasks, notes, calendars, and so on.

4. After you've selected the type of view you want to create, click the **OK** button. A View Settings dialog box appears

based on your selection. In this box, you determine which
fields you want to have in the view and the fonts and other
view settings you want to use.

5. After you've selected the fields and view settings, click
   Apply View. The items in the current folder appear in the
   new view.

TIP

> **Using the Create a New View Option Buttons**   If you
> work on a network where Outlook folders are shared on
> an Exchange Server, you can create your new view so
> that you see only the information in the view. Alter-
> natively, you can share the view with other users that
> access the information. The default option in the Create
> a New View dialog box is **This folder, visible to everyone**.
> To reserve the custom view for yourself, click the **This
> folder, visible only to me** option button. If you want to
> use the new view for all your mail folders, click the **All
> Mail and Post folders** option button.

PLAIN ENGLISH

> **Fields**   A specific type of information that you want to
> appear in your custom view. For a custom Inbox view
> using the Timeline view type, the fields include
> Received (when the message was received), Created
> (when the message was created), and Sent (when the
> message was sent).

Your newly created view appears on the Current View list on the
Advanced toolbar. You can select it by clicking the list's drop-down
arrow and then clicking the custom view's name.

CAUTION

Should I Design My Own Views?   Designing your own views can be complicated. Outlook provides several views for each folder on the Outlook bar. You might want to explore all these possibilities before you begin to create your own views.

USING OUTLOOK TODAY

Outlook Today is a great way to get a snapshot view of your day. This feature provides a window that lists all your messages, appointments, and tasks associated with the current day.

To open the Outlook Today window, click the **Go** menu and select **Outlook Today**. Icons for your Calendar, Messages, and Tasks appear in the Outlook Today window, as shown in Figure 4.8. Items for the current day are listed below the icons.

You can click any of the listed items (a particular appointment or task) to open the appropriate folder and view the details associated with the items. You can even update the items.

The Outlook Today Standard toolbar also provides a Type a Contact to Find box that you can use to quickly find people in your Contacts folder. Type a name into the Type a Contact to Find box (on the left of the Standard toolbar) and then press **Enter**. A Contact window appears for the person. You can edit the person's information or close the Contact box by clicking the **Close** button.

After you have viewed the items in the Outlook Today window, you can return to any of your folders by clicking their icons on the Outlook bar. Outlook Today is an excellent way to get a handle on what your day has in store for you.

In this lesson, you learned to use the Outlook Bar, change and create views in Outlook, use the Folder List, and take advantage of the Outlook Today feature. In the next lesson, you will learn to get help in Outlook.

FIGURE 4.8

Outlook Today provides a list of all the items associated with the current day.

LESSON 5

Getting Help in Microsoft Outlook

In this lesson, you learn how to access and use the Help system in Microsoft Outlook.

HELP: WHAT'S AVAILABLE?

Microsoft Outlook supplies a Help system that makes it easy for you to look up information on Outlook commands and features as you compose e-mail messages and work with other Outlook features such as the Contacts list and the Calendar. Because every person is different, the Help system can be accessed in several ways. You can

- Ask a question in the Ask a Question box.

- Ask the Office Assistant for help.

- Get help on a particular element you see onscreen with the What's This? tool.

- Use the Contents, Answer Wizard, and Index tabs in the Help window to get help.

- Access the Office on the Web feature to view Web pages containing help information (if you are connected to the Internet).

Using the Ask a Question Box

The Ask a Question box is a new way to access the Outlook Help system. It is also the easiest way to quickly get help. An Ask a Question box resides at the top right of the Outlook window.

For example, if you are working in Outlook and wish to view information on how to create a new appointment, type **How do I schedule a meeting?** into the Ask a Question box. Then press the **Enter** key. A shortcut menu appears below the Ask a Question box, as shown in Figure 5.1.

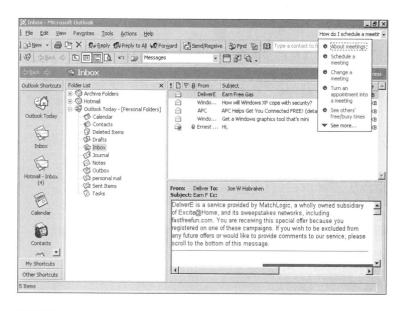

FIGURE 5.1

The Ask a Question box provides a list of Help topics that you can quickly access.

To access one of the Help topics supplied on the shortcut menu, click that particular topic. The Help window opens with topical matches for that keyword or phrase displayed.

In the case of the "meeting" question used in Figure 5.1, you could select **Schedule a meeting** from the shortcut menu that appears. This opens the help window and displays help on how to create a meeting (see Figure 5.2).

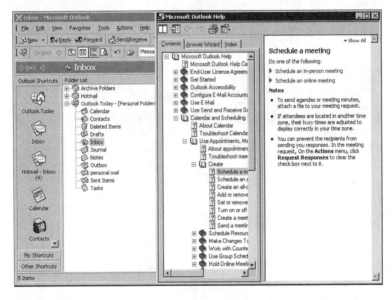

FIGURE 5.2
The Ask a Question box provides a quick way to access the Help window.

In the Help window, you can use the links provided to navigate the Help system. You can also use the Contents, Answer Wizard, and Index tabs to find additional information or look for new information in the Help window. You learn more about these different Help window tabs later in this lesson.

USING THE OFFICE ASSISTANT

Another way to get help in Outlook is to use the Office Assistant. The Office Assistant supplies the same type of access to the Help system as the Ask a Question box. You ask the Office Assistant a question, and it supplies you with a list of possible answers that provide links to various Help topics. The next two sections discuss how to use the Office Assistant.

TURNING THE OFFICE ASSISTANT ON AND OFF

By default, the Office Assistant is off. To show the Office Assistant in your application window, select the **Help** menu and then select **Show the Office Assistant**.

You can also quickly hide the Office Assistant if you no longer want it in your application window. Right-click the Office Assistant and select **Hide**. If you want to get rid of the Office Assistant completely so it isn't activated when you select the Help feature, right-click the **Office Assistant** and select **Options**. Clear the **Use the Office Assistant** check box, and then click **OK**. You can always get the Office Assistant back by selecting **Help, Show Office Assistant**.

ASKING THE OFFICE ASSISTANT A QUESTION

When you click the Office Assistant, a balloon appears above it. Type a question into the text box. For example, you might type **How do I print?** for help printing your work. Click the **Search** button.

The Office Assistant provides some topics that reference Help topics in the Help system. Click the option that best describes what you're trying to do. The Help window appears, containing more detailed information. Use the Help window to get the exact information that you need.

Although not everyone likes the Office Assistant because having it enabled means that it is always sitting in your Outlook window, it can be useful at times. For example, when you access particular features in Outlook, the Office Assistant can automatically provide you with context-sensitive help on that particular feature. If you are brand new to Microsoft Outlook, you might want to use the Office Assistant to help you learn the various features that Outlook provides as you use them.

TIP

> **Select Your Own Office Assistant**   Several different Office Assistants are available in Microsoft Office. To select your favorite, click the Office Assistant and select the **Options** button. On the Office Assistant dialog box that appears, select the **Gallery** tab. Click the **Next** button repeatedly to see the different Office Assistants that are available. When you locate the assistant you want to use, click **OK**.

USING THE HELP WINDOW

You can also forgo either the Type a Question box or the Office Assistant and get your help directly from the Help window. To directly access the Help window, select **Help** and then **Microsoft Outlook Help.** You can also press the **F1** key to make the Help window appear.

The Help window provides two panes. The pane on the left provides three tabs: Contents, Answer Wizard, and Index. The right pane of the Help window provides either help subject matter or links to different Help topics. It functions a great deal like a Web browser window. You click a link to a particular body of information and that information appears in the right pane.

The first thing that you should do is maximize the Help window by clicking its **Maximize** button. This makes it easier to locate and read the information that the Help system provides (see Figure 5.3).

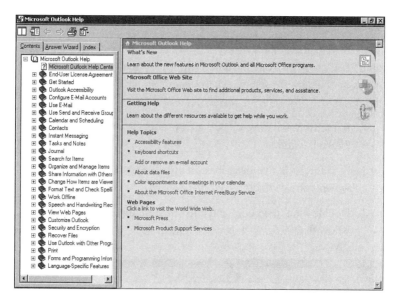

FIGURE 5.3
The Help window provides access to all the help information provided for Outlook.

When you first open the Help window, a group of links in the right pane provides you with access to information about new Outlook features and other links, such as a link to Microsoft's Office Web site. Next, take a look at how you can take advantage of different ways to find information in the Help window: the Contents tab, the Answer Wizard tab, and the Index tab.

TIP

View the Help Window Tabs   If you don't see the different tabs in the Help window, click the **Show** button on the Help window toolbar.

USING THE CONTENTS TAB

The Contents tab of the Help system is a series of books you can
open. Each book has one or more Help topics in it, which appear as
pages or chapters. To select a Help topic from the Contents tab, follow
these steps:

1. In the Help window, click the **Contents** tab on the left side of
   the Help window.

2. Find the book that describes, in broad terms, the subject for
   which you need help.

3. Double-click the book, and a list of Help topics appears
   below the book, as shown in Figure 5.4.

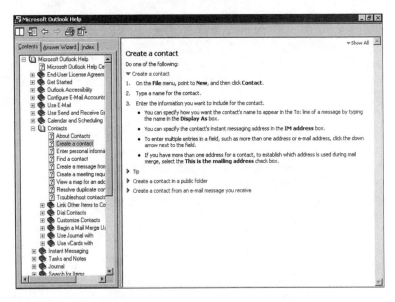

FIGURE 5.4
Use the Contents tab to browse through the various Help topics.

4. Click one of the pages (the pages contain a question mark) under a Help topic to display it in the right pane of the Help window.

5. When you finish reading a topic, select another topic on the Contents tab or click the Help window's **Close** (**x**) button to exit Help.

USING THE ANSWER WIZARD

Another way to get help in the Help window is to use the Answer Wizard. The Answer Wizard works the same as the Ask a Question box or the Office Assistant; you ask the wizard questions and it supplies you with a list of topics that relate to your question. You click one of the choices provided to view help in the Help window.

To get help using the Answer Wizard, follow these steps:

1. Click the **Answer Wizard** tab in the Help window.

2. Type your question into the What Would You Like to Do? box. For example, you might type the question, **How do I create a new contact?**

3. After typing your question, click the **Search** button. A list of topics appears in the Select Topic to Display box. Select a particular topic, and its information appears in the right pane of the Help window, as shown in Figure 5.5.

TIP

> **Print Help**   If you want to print information provided in the Help window, click the **Print** icon on the Help toolbar.

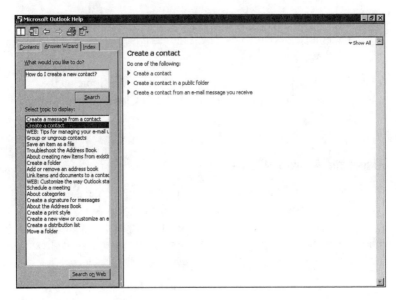

FIGURE 5.5
Search for help in the Help window using the Answer Wizard tab.

USING THE INDEX

The Index is an alphabetical listing of every Help topic available. It's like an index in a book.

Follow these steps to use the index:

1. In the Help window, click the **Index** tab.

2. Type the first few letters of the topic for which you are look-ing. The Or Choose Keywords box jumps quickly to a key-word that contains the characters you have typed.

3. Double-click the appropriate keyword in the keywords box. Topics for that keyword appear in the Choose a Topic box.

4. Click a topic to view help in the right pane of the Help win-dow (see Figure 5.6).

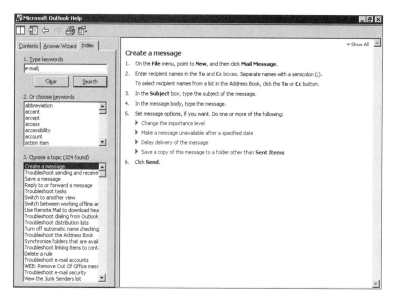

FIGURE 5.6
Use the Index tab to get help in the Help window.

TIP

Navigation Help Topics   You can move from topic to topic in the right pane of the Help window by clicking the various links that are provided there. Some topics are collapsed. Click the triangle next to the topic to expand the topic and view the help provided.

GETTING HELP WITH SCREEN ELEMENTS

If you wonder about the function of a particular button or tool on the Outlook screen, wonder no more. Just follow these steps to learn about this part of Help:

1. Select **Help** and then **What's This?** or press **Shift+F1**. The mouse pointer changes to an arrow with a question mark.

2. Click the screen element for which you want help. A box
   appears explaining the element.

TIP

Take Advantage of ScreenTips   Another Help feature
provided by Outlook is the ScreenTip. All the buttons on
the different toolbars provided by Outlook have a
ScreenTip. Place the mouse on a particular button or
icon, and the name of the item (which often helps you
determine its function) appears in a ScreenTip.

In this lesson, you learned how to access the Outlook Help feature. In
the next lesson, you will learn how to create and send e-mail messages.

LESSON 6
Creating Mail

In this lesson, you learn how to compose a message, format text, check your spelling, and send e-mail. You also learn how to use different e-mail formats such as plain text and HTML.

COMPOSING A MESSAGE

You can send an e-mail message to anyone for whom you have an e-mail address, whether that address is in your list of contacts or scribbled on a Post-it note. In addition to sending a message to one or more recipients, in Outlook you can forward or copy messages to individuals in your Contacts list. You can even e-mail groups of people who are listed in your various distribution lists.

TIP

Compose Your Messages Offline If you connect to an Internet service provider and don't want to waste precious connect time while you compose e-mail messages, you can create new messages in Outlook without being connected to the Internet. New messages you send are placed in your Outbox until you connect to the Internet and actually send them on to their final destination. When you are connected to the Internet, all you have to do is click the **Send/Receive** button on the Standard toolbar (or **Tools**, **Send/Receive**, **Send All**) to send any messages held in the Outbox.

New ▾   To open format the text of a new e-mail message while in the Outlook Inbox, select **File**, point at **New**, and then select **Mail Message** in the Outlook Inbox window. (You can also click the **New** button on the Standard toolbar.) A new message window appears (see Figure 6.1).

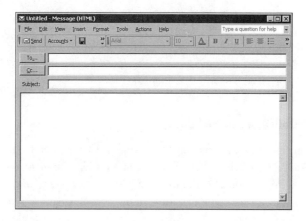

FIGURE 6.1
Compose a new message in the Untitled Message window.

E-mail addresses can be placed in the To box of a message that you want to send (a message you create from scratch or an existing message that you are forwarding) in several ways. You can

- Use your Outlook Contacts list.

- Use your Outlook Address Book.

- Type in an e-mail address that you don't currently have in any of your lists.

In the case of e-mail messages that you reply to, the e-mail address of the person who sent you the message is automatically placed in the To box, making it ready to be sent.

Having e-mail addresses listed in either your Contacts list or the Outlook Address Book is the easiest way to add an e-mail address to a list. It also helps you keep organized, and that is probably one of the reasons why you're using Outlook in the first place. You will also find that having e-mail addresses readily available in an Outlook list makes it easier to send carbon copies (duplicate e-mails) or blind carbon copies of messages when you are composing a particular message.

PLAIN ENGLISH

Blind Carbon Copy   A blind carbon copy (Bcc) of a message is a copy sent to someone in secret; the other recipients have no way of knowing that you are sending the message to someone as a blind carbon copy.

You can find more information on using Outlook's Personal Address Book in Lesson 12, "Using the Outlook Address Books." Lesson 13, "Creating a Contacts List," shows you how to use contacts.

To address a new e-mail message, follow these steps:

1. In the message window, click the **To** button to display the Select Names dialog box. Names that have been entered in your Contacts list appear on the left side of the dialog box. If you want to switch to a different list, such as the Outlook Address Book, click the drop-down list on the upper-right corner of the dialog box and make a new selection.

    If the e-mail address you want isn't in your Contacts list, instead of clicking the **To** button, type the e-mail address directly into the To text box (if you do this, you can then skip steps 3 through 7).

2. From the list of addresses that appears on the left of the dialog box, choose the name of the intended recipient and select the **To** button (or you can double-click the name). Outlook

copies the name to the Message Recipients list. You can also
add any distribution lists to the To box that appear in your
address list. To send a carbon copy or blind carbon copy to a
recipient, use the **Cc** or **Bcc** buttons.

Figure 6.2 shows a message that is addressed to an individual
whose address was contained in the Contacts list and also to
a group of people who are listed in a distribution list (you can
enter as many addresses as you want).

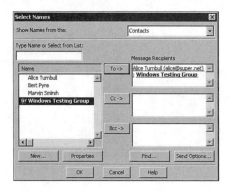

FIGURE 6.2
*Add e-mail addresses or distribution list names quickly with the Select Names
dialog box.*

3. Click **OK** to return to the message window. Click in the
   Subject box and type the subject of your message.

4. Click in the text area, and then enter the text of the message.
   You do not have to press the Enter key at the end of a line;
   Outlook automatically wraps the text at the end of a line for
   you. You can use the Delete and Backspace keys to edit the
   text you enter.

5. When you finish typing the message, you can send the message, or you can format the message or check the spelling as
   detailed later in this lesson. To send the message, click the
   Send button on the message's Standard toolbar.

CAUTION

> **No Address**   If you try to send a message without enter-
> ing an address, Outlook displays a message that at least
> one e-mail address must be in the To box. Type in an
> address or select an address from your Contacts list or
> Address Book.

FORMATTING TEXT

You can enhance the format of the text in your message to make it
more attractive, to make it easier to read, or to add emphasis. Any formatting you do transfers to the recipient with the message if the recipient has Outlook or another e-mail client that can work with HTML or
Rich Text Format messages. However, if the recipient doesn't have an
e-mail client that can handle these special message formats, formatting might not transfer and the message will be received in plain text.

PLAIN ENGLISH

> **HTML**   Hypertext Markup Language is used to design
> Web pages for the World Wide Web. Outlook can send
> messages in this format, providing you with several text
> formatting options. Graphics can even be pasted into an
> HTML message.

PLAIN ENGLISH

> **Rich Text Format**   A special e-mail format developed by
> Microsoft for use with Microsoft mail systems. Outlook
> can send and receive messages in Rich Text Format.
> This enables you to send and receive messages with
> special formatting, such as bold, italic, various fonts,
> and other special characters and graphics.

You format text in two ways. You can format the text after you type it
by selecting it and then choosing a font, size, or other attribute; or you

can select the font, size, or other attribute to toggle it on, and then enter the text, which will be formatted as you type.

To format the text in your message, first make sure the Formatting toolbar is showing. On the menu system provided by the message window, select **View**, and then select **Toolbars** and click **Formatting**. Figure 6.3 shows a message with the Formatting toolbar displayed. Formatting options have also been applied to the text in the message. Table 6.1 explains the buttons found on the Formatting toolbar.

> **CAUTION**
>
> **The Formatting Toolbar Buttons Don't Work**   Only messages sent in HTML or Rich Text Format can be formatted. Plain-text messages don't supply you with any formatting options. So, even if the Formatting toolbar appears at the top of a plain-text message, the formatting options will not be available. Selecting the message type (such as HTML or plain text) is discussed in the section "Selecting the E-mail Message Format," found later in this lesson.

Formatting toolbar

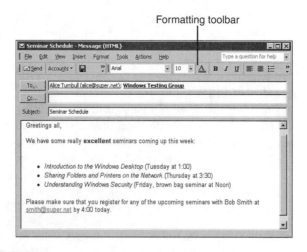

FIGURE 6.3
Use the Formatting toolbar to modify format of your message text.

TABLE 6.1   Formatting Toolbar Buttons

Button	Name
A	Font Color
B	Bold
I	Italic
U	Underlineformat of the text
≣	Align Left
≣	Center
≣	Align Right
≔	Bullets
≔	Numbering
信	Decrease Indent
信	Increase Indent
—	Insert Horizontal Line

CAUTION

My Toolbars Look Completely Different!   If you are using
Microsoft Word as your e-mail editor, the toolbars that are
present in the new message window reflect those you
have selected in your Word installation. The Word and
Outlook toolbars have many of the same buttons.

1. To apply a new font to format the selected text, on the Formatting toolbar, click the down arrow in the **Font** box. Scroll through the font list, if necessary, to view all fonts on the system, and then click the font you want to apply to the text. You can also apply a style to selected text in the message. On the Formatting toolbar, click the **Style** drop-down arrow. The styles available range from a set of predefined heading styles to special styles such as Numbered list and Bulleted list.

2. Assign a size by clicking the down arrow beside the **Font Size** drop-down list and choosing the size; alternatively, you can type a size into the Font Size text box.

3. To choose a color, click the **Color** button and select a color from the palette box that appears.

4. Choose a type style to apply to text by clicking the **Bold**, **Italic**, and/or **Underline** buttons on the Formatting toolbar.

5. Choose an alignment by selecting the **Align Left**, **Center**, or **Align Right** button from the Formatting toolbar.

6. Add bullets to a list by clicking the **Bullets** button on the Formatting toolbar. If you prefer a numbered list, click the **Numbering** button.

7. Create text indents or remove indents in half-inch increments by clicking the **Increase Indent** or **Decrease Indent** buttons. (Each time you click the Indent button, the indent changes by one-half inch.)

8. If you want to divide the text in the message using a horizontal line, place the insertion point at the appropriate place in the text and then click the **Add Horizontal Line** button.

TIP

> **Yuck, No Thanks!**   If you assign formatting to your text and don't particularly like it, click **Edit** and select **Undo** to remove the last formatting that you assigned.

Selecting the E-mail Message Format

The default message format in Outlook is HTML. If you send most of your messages to individuals who don't have mail clients that can read the HTML format, you might want to change the default to plain text. On corporate networks, you might find an advantage to using the Rich Text Format as the default text format for your messages. This file format was developed for the Exchange Server mail environment used on most business networks.

The default format is set in the Outlook Options dialog box on the Mail Format tab. Fortunately, Outlook makes it very easy for you to switch the format of a mail message while you are composing the message. First, take a look at how to set the default mail type, and then look at how to change the message format while composing the message.

To set the default message format:

1. Click **Tools**, **Options**. The Options dialog box appears.

2. Click the **Mail Format** tab (see Figure 6.4).

TIP

> **Include Hyperlinks**   If you use the HTML or Rich Text Format message formats, you can include hyperlinks in your e-mails. Hyperlinks are Web addresses and e-mail addresses that can be accessed by clicking them in the message. Just type the Web address or e-mail address, and the hyperlink is created automatically in the message.

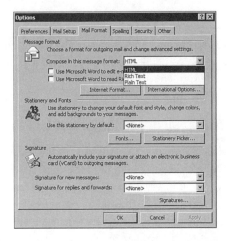

FIGURE 6.4
You can send your messages in HTML, Rich Text Format, or plain-text format.

3. To select the message format, click the **Compose in This Message Format** drop-down box. Select **HTML**, **Rich Text**, or **Plain Text**. If you want to use Microsoft Word as your e-mail editor, click the **Use Microsoft Word to Edit E-Mail Messages** check box.

PLAIN ENGLISH

Using HTML Stationery   If you use the HTML format for your messages, you can also select to use a particular stationery on the Mail Format tab. Stationery types can be previewed using the **Stationery Picker** button. Be advised that HTML stationery will slow down the loading of e-mail messages on the recipient's computer, and not everyone will have a mail client that can view the stationery. You probably should use the stationery only for personal messages to friends and family members who also use Outlook as their e-mail client.

CHECKING SPELLING

Because you don't want to look like you wedged a crayon in your brain during your childhood years, and you generally want to maintain your professional image, you should check the spelling in your mail messages before you send them. Outlook includes a spelling checker you can use for that purpose. If you are using Word as your e-mail editor, you will use the Word Spelling and Grammar features.

To check the spelling in a message, follow these steps:

1. In a message window, choose **Tools**, and then select **Spelling** or press **F7**. If the spelling checker finds a word whose spelling it questions, it displays the Spelling dialog box (shown in Figure 6.5). (If no words are misspelled, a dialog box appears saying that the spelling check is complete; choose **OK** to close the dialog box.)

FIGURE 6.5
Check your spelling before sending a message.

2. Your response to the word Outlook questions in the Spelling dialog box will vary. If you recognize that Outlook has correctly flagged a misspelled word, choose one of the following:

   • **Suggestions**—Select the correct spelling in this text box, and it automatically appears in the Change To text box.

- **Change**—Click this button to change this particular occurrence of the word in question to the spelling in the Change To text box.

- **Change All**—Click this button to change the word in question to the spelling listed in the Change To text box every time the spelling checker finds the word in this message.

If Outlook checks a word that you know is already spelled correctly (such as a proper name), choose one of the following:

- **Not in Dictionary**—Enter the correct spelling into this text box.

- **Ignore**—Click this button to continue the spelling check without changing this occurrence of the selected word.

- **Ignore All**—Click this button to continue the spelling check without changing any occurrence of the word in question throughout this message.

- **Add**—Click this button to add the current spelling of the word in question to the dictionary so that Outlook will not question future occurrences of this spelling.

- **Undo Last**—Click this button to undo your last spelling change and return to that word.

3. Continue until the spelling check is complete (or click **Cancel** to quit the spelling check).

4. Outlook displays a message box telling you that the spell check is complete. Click **OK** to close the dialog box.

TIP

> **Set Your Spelling Options**   Click the **Options** button in
> the Spelling dialog box to set options that tell Outlook to
> do such things as ignore words with numbers, ignore
> original message text in forwarded messages or replies,
> always check spelling before sending, and so on.

ADD A SIGNATURE

You can further personalize your e-mails by adding a signature to the
message. A signature can be as simple as just your name, or the signature can include your phone number or extension or other information.
Some people even add a favorite quote to their signature. If you use
HTML as your message format, you can even include signature files
that contain graphics. Plain-text signatures (for use with plain-text
messages) will consist only of text characters.

First, take a look at how you can create a signature. Then you can take
a look at how you apply it to a message.

CREATING A SIGNATURE

1. Choose **Tools**, **Options** to open the Options dialog box, and
   then select the **Mail Format** tab.

2. Click the **Signatures** button at the bottom of the dialog box.
   The Create Signature dialog box opens.

3. Click the **New** button; the Create a New Signature dialog box
   opens as shown in Figure 6.6.

4. Type a name for your new signature, and then click **Next**.

5. The Edit Signature dialog box appears. Enter the text you
   want included in the signature. You can use the Paragraph or
   Font buttons to add formatting to the text in the signature.

6. When you have finished creating your signature, click the
Finish button. Click **Close** to close the Create Signatures dialog box, and then click **OK** to close the Options dialog box.

FIGURE 6.6
Outlook walks you through the steps of creating a signature.

TIP

> **You Can Edit Signatures**   To edit a signature, select the
> signature in the Create Signatures dialog box and then
> click **Edit**.

INSERTING THE SIGNATURE

After you've created a signature or signatures, you can quickly add it
to any message by placing the insertion point where you want to place
the signature, choosing **Insert**, and then choosing **Signature**; all the
signatures that you have created appear on the menu. Select the signature from the list you want to use in the message you are currently
composing.

You can also preview the signatures before inserting them; choose
Insert, **Signature**, and then select **More** from the cascading menu.
The Select a Signature dialog box opens. Select any of your signatures
to view a preview of the signature. When you find the signature you
want to use, click **OK**.

SENDING MAIL

You probably know that after you add recipient addresses, compose
your message, format the text, spell check the message, and insert a
signature in the e-mail, you are ready to send the message. But you
can use a couple of ways to actually send the message on its way.

The fastest way to send the message using the mouse is to click the
Send button on the Message toolbar. If you prefer, press **Ctrl+Enter**.
In either case, your message is heading out to its destination. If you
are working offline, the message is placed in the Outbox until you
connect to the Internet and send and receive your messages.

RECALLING A MESSAGE

If you use Outlook as an e-mail client in a Microsoft Exchange Server
environment, you can actually recall or replace e-mail messages that
you have sent. But you can recall or replace only messages that have
not been opened by the recipient or moved to another folder by a
recipient.

If the Folder List is not visible, click the **View** menu, and then click
Folder List.

1. Click the **My Shortcuts** button on the Outlook bar, and then
   select the **Sent Items** folder.

2. Double-click to open the message that you want to recall.

3. In the message window, click the **Actions** menu, and then
   click **Recall This Message**. The Recall This Message dialog
   box opens as shown in Figure 6.7.

4. To recall the message, click the **Delete Unread Copies of
   This Message** option button, and then click **OK**. A notice
   appears in the message window informing you that you
   attempted to recall this message on a particular date and at a
   particular time.

FIGURE 6.7
Messages that have not been read can be recalled or replaced.

5. If you want to replace the message with a new message, click the **Delete Unread Copies and Replace with New Message** option button. When you click **OK**, a new message window opens with a copy of the message you want to recall in it. Just change the message text or address and then send the message.

6. You eventually receive a notification in your Inbox (as new mail) notifying you whether the recall was successful.

In this lesson, you learned to compose a message, format text, check your spelling, and send mail. You also learned how to select different e-mail formats such as HTML and Plain Text and add a signature to an e-mail message. You also learned how to recall a message. In the next lesson, you will learn to work with received e-mail.

LESSON 7
Working with Received Mail

In this lesson, you learn how to read your mail, save an attachment, answer mail, and close a message.

READING MAIL

When you log on to Outlook, your Inbox folder appears, and any new messages you've received are downloaded from your ISP's (or your company's) mail server. If you use Internet mail and a dial-up connection (in contrast to DSL or cable modem connections, which are always connected), a dial-up connection must be made before Outlook can check the mail server for new mail.

No matter what the connection situation, after you download any new e-mail to your computer, the new mail appears in the Outlook Inbox (see Figure 7.1). If you watch closely when you connect to your network or Internet service provider, a downloading mail icon appears in the lower right of the Outlook window, showing you that new mail is being received.

As you can see in Figure 7.1, the Inbox provides important information about each message. For example, one message has been labeled as high priority and one message has an attachment. Messages that have already been replied to are marked with a curved reply arrow. You'll learn about file attachments in Lesson 9, "Attaching Files and Items to a Message," and mail priorities in Lesson 11, "Setting Mail Options."

Additional information about a particular message, such as the actual reply date, is contained at the top of the Preview pane when that

particular message is selected. At the bottom of the Outlook status bar
(on the left), information such as how many items are in the Inbox and
how many message are unread is also provided.

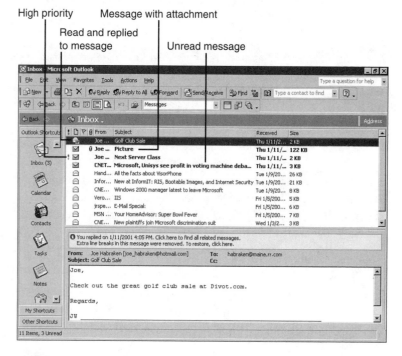

FIGURE 7.1
*The Inbox provides information related to your received messages: the sender,
the subject, the date received, and priority and attachment icons.*

To read a message, you can select it, and its contents appear in the
Outlook Preview pane. You can also open a message in its own window; double-click a mail message to open it. Figure 7.2 shows an
open message.

To read the next or previous mail message in the Inbox when you have
opened a mail message, click either the **Previous Item** or the **Next
Item** button on the message window toolbar. To access more view
choices, select the **View** menu, and then point at **Previous** or **Next**;

submenu choices are provided for each of these choices that allow you to jump to another item, an unread item, or to a message that has been assigned a particular priority or that has been flagged.

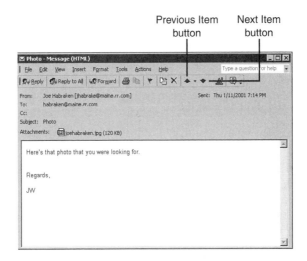

FIGURE 7.2
The message window displays the message and tools for responding to the message or moving to the previous or next message in the Inbox.

PLAIN ENGLISH

Item Outlook uses the word *item* to describe a mail message, an attached file, an appointment or meeting, a task, and so on. Item is a generic term in Outlook that describes the currently selected element.

After you open a message in the Inbox, it is marked as read (notice that the envelope that represents the message is opened). You can also mark messages as read or unread by selecting **Edit** and then selecting either **Mark As Read** or **Mark As Unread**. Additionally, you can mark all the messages in the Inbox as read by choosing **Edit**, **Mark All As Read**. You might want to mark mail messages as read so you don't read them again; you might want to mark important mail as unread so you'll be sure to open it and read it again.

TIP

 No Mail?   Maybe Outlook is not configured to check for mail automatically. To force Outlook to
look for mail, click the **Send and Receive** button on the
toolbar, or choose **Tools**, point at **Send/Receive**, and
then select **Send/Receive All**. Any new messages are
placed in the Inbox.

SAVING AN ATTACHMENT

You often receive messages that have files or other items attached to
them, such as graphical images. In the Inbox list of messages, an
attachment is represented by a paper clip icon beside the message.
Save any attachments sent to you so that you can open, modify, print,
or otherwise use the attached document or image. Messages can contain multiple attachments.

CAUTION

What About Viruses?   Unfortunately, there is a chance
that an attachment to a message can be a virus or other
malicious software. Computer viruses can really wreak
havoc on your computer system. When you receive an
e-mail message from someone you don't know and that
message has an attachment, the best thing to do is
delete the message without opening it or the attachment. Because viruses can read your address book and
send themselves to the people it contains, even e-mail
from known parties bears at least some scrutiny. If you
save an attachment to your computer, you might want to
check the file with an antivirus program before you actually open the file. Be especially cautious if the file that
you receive as an attachment has an .exe or .vba extension. These extensions, which virus creators commonly
use to get you to unleash a virus on your own computer,
mark that the attachment is an actual program.

To save an attachment, follow these steps:

1. Open the message containing an attachment by double-clicking the message. The attachment appears as an icon below the subject area of the message (see Figure 7.3).

FIGURE 7.3
An icon represents the attached file.

2. (Optional) You can open the attachment from within the message by double-clicking the attachment icon. A message appears, as shown in Figure 7.4, warning you that attachments can contain viruses. To open the file, click the **Open It** option button and then click **OK**. The attachment will be opened in the application in which it was created (such as Word or Excel). When you have finished looking at the attachment, you can return to the e-mail message by closing the open application.

    If you choose **Save the File to Disk**, a Save Attachment dialog box appears, allowing you to save the file to your hard drive.

3. You probably noticed in the Opening Mail Attachment message box that you also had the option to save the attachment (see Figure 7.4). There is another way to save your

attachments, and it actually makes it easier when you have to
save multiple attachments attached to the same e-mail message. In the message window, select **File**, **Save Attachments**.
The Save Attachment dialog box appears (see Figure 7.5).

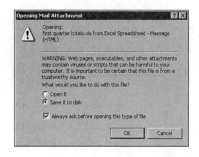

FIGURE 7.4
You can open or save an attachment by double-clicking its icon.

FIGURE 7.5
Save the attachment to a convenient folder.

4. Choose the folder in which you want to save the attachment
   or attachments and click **Save**. The dialog box closes and
   returns to the message window. You can change the name of
   the file in the File Name box, if you want. After you save the

attachment, you can open the attachment, which is now like
any other saved file on your computer, at any time from the
application in which it was created.

TIP

> **Use the Right Mouse Button**   You can also quickly save
> an attachment by right-clicking the attachment icon. On
> the shortcut menu that appears, click **Save As**, and then
> save the attachment to an appropriate folder.

ANSWERING MAIL

You might want to reply to a message after you read it. The message
window enables you to answer a message immediately, or at a later
time if you prefer. To reply to any given message, follow these steps:

1. Select the message in the Inbox window, and then click the
   Reply button on the Inbox toolbar.

   If you have the message open, click the **Reply** button in the
   message window. The Reply message window appears, with
   the original message in the message text area and the sender
   of the message already filled in for you (see Figure 7.6).

TIP

> **Reply to All**   If you receive a message that
> has also been sent to others—as either a message or a
> carbon copy (Cc)—you can click the **Reply to All** button
> to send your reply to each person who received the mes-
> sage.

2. The insertion point is automatically placed above the message
   text that you are replying to. Enter your reply text.

3. When you finish your reply, click the **Send** button. Outlook
   sends the message.

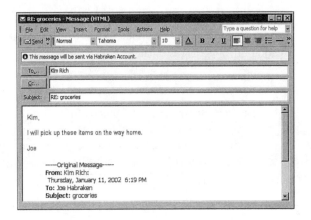

FIGURE 7.6
You can reply to a message quickly and easily.

The next time you open a message to which you've replied, there is a reminder at the top of the message window telling you the date and time you sent your reply. Don't forget that the purple arrow next to a message in the Inbox window shows that the message has been replied to.

PRINTING MAIL

You can print mail messages, either directly from the Inbox when they have been selected or from a message window when you have opened a particular message. To print an unopened message, select the message in the message list of the Inbox or other folder and choose **File**, **Print**. The Print dialog box opens; click **OK** to send the message to the printer. If the message is already open, you can follow these steps:

1. Open the message in Outlook.

2. Choose **File** and then select **Print**, or press **Ctrl+P** to view the Print dialog box.

3. In the Print dialog box, click **OK** to print one copy of the entire message using the printer's default settings. See Lesson

19, "Printing in Outlook," for detailed information about configuring pages and changing printer options.

TIP

> 🖨 **Toolbar Shortcut**   Click the **Print** button on the toolbar to print an unopened or opened message using the default print settings.

When you finish reading or printing a message, click the **Close** button on the message window.

In this lesson, you learned to read your mail, save an attachment, answer mail, and print a message. In the next lesson, you will learn to delete and forward messages and create folders to store your messages.

LESSON 8
Managing Mail

In this lesson, you learn how to delete and undelete messages, forward messages, and create folders. You also learn how to move messages to these folders.

DELETING MAIL

Although you might want to store certain important messages and perhaps even create folders to store them in, which is discussed in Lesson 10, "Saving Drafts and Organizing Messages," you'll definitely want to delete much of the mail that you receive after reading it. You can easily delete messages in Outlook when you're finished reading and sending replies to them.

 The easiest way to delete a selected message is to click the **Delete** button on the Outlook toolbar. If the message is open, just click the **Delete** button on the message window toolbar instead.

If you want to delete several messages in the Inbox, just select the messages using the mouse. To select several contiguous messages, click the first message, and then hold down the **Shift** key when you click the last message in the series. To select noncontiguous messages, hold down the **Ctrl** key and click each message. When you have all the messages selected that you want to delete, click the **Delete** button (or you can select the **Edit** menu and then select **Delete**).

UNDELETING ITEMS

If you change your mind and want to get back items you've deleted, you can usually retrieve them from the Deleted Items folder. By default, when you delete an item, it doesn't disappear from your computer; it merely moves to the Deleted Items folder. Items stay in the Deleted Items folder until you delete them from that folder—at which point they are unrecoverable. Typically, when you exit Outlook, the Deleted Items folder is emptied automatically. To retrieve a deleted item from the Deleted Items folder, follow these steps:

1. Click the scroll-down arrow on the Outlook bar to locate the Deleted Items folder.

2. Click the **Deleted Items** icon in the Outlook bar to open the folder.

3. Select the items you want to retrieve; you can then drag them back to the Inbox by dragging them and dropping them onto the Inbox icon in the Outlook bar. Or if you don't like dragging messages, select the files you want to move from the Deleted Items folder, and then select **Edit**, **Move to Folder**. The Move Items dialog box appears as shown in Figure 8.1.

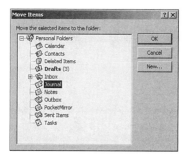

FIGURE 8.1
Deleted messages can be moved out of the Deleted Items folder back into the Inbox.

4. Select the folder you want to move the items into (such as the Inbox) and then click the **OK** button.

TIP

Use Undo Immediately   If you want to undelete a message or messages that you just deleted, select the **Edit** menu, and then select **Undo Delete**.

EMPTYING THE DELETED ITEMS FOLDER

If you're sure you want to delete the items in the Deleted Items folder, empty the contents of the folder. To delete items in the Deleted Items folder, follow these steps:

1. On the Outlook bar, choose **Outlook Shortcuts**, and then select the **Deleted Items** folder. All deleted items in that folder appear in the message list, as shown in Figure 8.2.

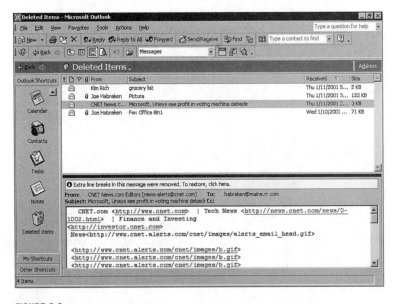

FIGURE 8.2
Deleted messages remain in the Deleted Items folder until you permanently delete them.

2. To permanently delete an item or items, select it (or them) in the Deleted Items folder.

3. Click the **Delete** button, or choose **Edit** and then select **Delete**. Outlook displays a confirmation dialog box asking whether you're sure you want to permanently delete the message. Choose **Yes** to delete the selected item.

4. To switch back to the Inbox or another folder, select the folder from either the Outlook bar or the Folder List.

> **TIP**
>
> **Automatic Permanent Delete**   You can set Outlook to permanently delete the contents of the Deleted Items folder every time you exit the program. To do so, in the Outlook window choose **Tools**, and then click **Options**. Select the **Other** tab of the Options dialog box and click the **Empty the Deleted Items Folder Upon Exiting** check box. Then click **OK**.

FORWARDING MAIL

You can forward mail that you receive to a co-worker or anyone else with an e-mail address. When you forward a message, you can also add comments to the messages if you so desire.

> **PLAIN ENGLISH**
>
> **Forward Mail**   When you forward mail, you send a copy of a message you have received to another person; you can add your own comments to the forwarded mail, if you want.

You can forward an open message or a message selected in the message list in the Inbox in the same way. To forward mail, follow these steps:

1. Select or open the message you want to forward. Then click the **Forward** button. The FW Message window appears (see Figure 8.3).

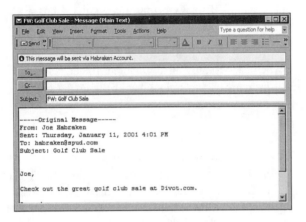

FIGURE 8.3
When you forward a message, the original message appears at the bottom of the message window.

2. In the To text box, enter the addresses of the people to whom you want to forward the mail. If you want to choose an address or addresses from a list, click the **To** button to display the Select Names dialog box, and then select the address or addresses from your Contacts list.

3. (Optional) In the Cc text box, enter the addresses of anyone to whom you want to forward copies of the message.

4. In the message area of the window, enter any message you want to send with the forwarded text.

PLAIN ENGLISH

> **Attachments Are Forwarded, Too** If the message that you forward contains attached files, the attachments are also forwarded.

5. When you are ready to send the message, click the **Send** button.

CREATING FOLDERS

Although Outlook provides you with an Inbox, an Outbox, a Sent Items folder, and a Deleted Items folder, you might find it advantageous to create your own folders. This provides you with alternative places to store items and can make finding them in the future easier (rather than just having all your messages languish in the Inbox). Folders can also be used to store items other than messages, so you could even create subfolders for your Contacts folder or Calendar.

TIP

> **Folders Aren't the Only Way to Get Organized**   Although the creation of folders can help you organize messages and other items that you want to store in Outlook, another tool called the Organizer has been designed to help you move, delete, and even color code received e-mail messages. You will take a look at the Organizer in Lesson 10.

To create a folder, follow these steps:

1. Click the **Folder List** drop-down button , and then click the **Folder List pin** to "pin it down" to the Outlook window.

2. To create a folder in the Folder List, right-click the folder, such as the Inbox, that will serve as the parent folder for the new folder.

3. On the shortcut menu that appears (see Figure 8.4), select New Folder. The Create New Folder dialog box appears.

4. In the Create New Folder dialog box, type a name for the folder into the Name box.

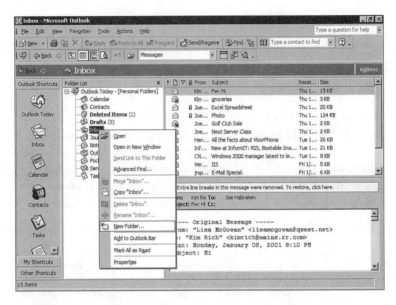

FIGURE 8.4
Folders can be created anywhere in the Folder List.

TIP

> **Create Folders from the File Menu**   You can also open the
> Create New Folder dialog box from the File menu. Just
> select **File**, point at **New**, and then select **Folder**.

5. Use the icons in the New Folder dialog box main pane area
   to select the type of folder that you want to create. For example, if you want to hold mail messages in the folder, select
   the **Mail and Post** icon (see Figure 8.5).

6. Select the **Location** drop-down list to select the location for
   the new folder. If you want to nest the new folder in an existing folder, such as the Inbox, select that folder on the list. If
   you want to create the new folder as a first-level folder, select
   Personal Folders.

FIGURE 8.5
Folders can be created to hold mail messages, contacts, and even calendar appointments.

7. When you have finished making your entries and selections in the New Folder dialog box, click **OK** to create the folder.

8. You are asked whether you want to add a shortcut icon for the new folder to the Outlook bar. If you want to create the icon, click **Yes**.

The new folder appears on the Outlook bar and in the Folder List.

TIP

> **Add an Outlook Bar Shortcut for a Folder**   Even if you choose not to add a shortcut for the folder to the Outlook bar when you create the folder, you can add it later. Right-click any folder you've created in the Folder List and select **Add to Outlook Bar** from the shortcut menu that appears.

CAUTION

> **I Want to Delete a Folder**   If you add a folder and then decide you don't want it, right-click the folder in the Folder List and select **Delete** from the shortcut menu. You then must verify the deletion; click **Yes**.

MOVING ITEMS TO ANOTHER FOLDER

You can move items from one folder in Outlook to another; for example, you can create a folder to store all messages pertaining to a specific account or just make a folder that holds personal messages instead of business-related messages. You can easily move any messages to a new folder and then open them later to read them or to reply to them.

To move an item to another folder, follow these steps:

1. From the Inbox or any Outlook folder, select the message or messages you want to move.

2. Select **Edit**, **Move to Folder**. The Move Items dialog box appears (see Figure 8.6).

FIGURE 8.6
Choose the folder in which you want to store the message or messages.

3. In the Move Items dialog box, select the folder to which you want to move the message or messages.

4. Click **OK**. The message or messages are moved to the destination folder.

 TIP

> **Quickly Move Items**   You can quickly move any message or other Outlook item by dragging it from the open folder in which it resides to any folder icon in the Outlook bar.

In this lesson, you learned to forward messages, delete messages, and create new folders and move items to those folders. In the next lesson, you will learn to attach files and other items to an e-mail message.

LESSON 9

Attaching Files and Items to a Message

In this lesson, you learn how to attach a file and Outlook items to an e-mail message.

ATTACHING A FILE

You can attach any type of file to an Outlook message, which makes for a convenient way of sending your files to your co-workers or sending pictures to family members across the country who use Internet e-mail. You can send Word documents, Excel spreadsheets, a family photo (taken from a digital camera or scanned from a photograph), or any other file you have on your hard drive.

When you attach a file, it appears as an icon in an attachment box that resides in the message window right below the Subject box, as shown in Figure 9.1. A button to the left of the attached file can be used to quickly access the Insert File dialog box if you want to change the attached file or add additional attachments before sending the message.

You can also open or view any files that you attach to your e-mail messages (before or after you send them) by double-clicking the file. Next, you take a look at attaching and viewing attachments, such as files created in other applications and picture files. Then, you can take a look at attaching an Outlook item such as a contact or appointment to an e-mail message.

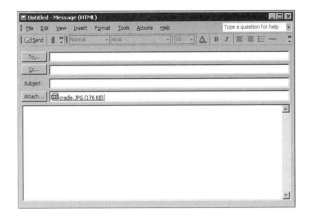

FIGURE 9.1
Attached files appear as icons in the Attach box.

> **PLAIN ENGLISH**
>
> **E-Mail Attachments and E-Mail Clients**   Depending on the
> e-mail client they are using, the way recipients of your
> file attachments retrieve them will vary. For example,
> some e-mail packages do not show the attachment as an
> icon, but save the attachment directly to a specific
> folder on the recipient's computer after the e-mail mes-
> sage is downloaded.

To attach a file to a message, follow these steps:

1. In the new message window, choose Insert and then select
   File, or click the Insert File button on the toolbar. The Insert
   File dialog box appears (see Figure 9.2).

2. From the **Look In** drop-down list, choose the drive and
   folder that contain the file you want to attach.

3. Select the file you want to attach.

4. Click **OK** to insert the file into the message.

FIGURE 9.2
Select the file you want to attach to a message.

An Attach box appears below the Subject box on the message, and an icon and the filename are inserted.

PLAIN ENGLISH

> **Large Files Take Time** Sending an extremely large file can take a great deal of time, depending on your connection speed. Some ISPs, such as America Online, set a limit for attachment file size for sent or received attachments. Using tools that reduce the size of files—applications such as WinZip or Microsoft Compressed Folders—you can compress larger files. However, the recipient of a message in which you have included a "zipped" attachment needs the appropriate tool, such as WinZip, to uncompress the attached file.

ATTACHING OUTLOOK ITEMS

In addition to attaching files from other programs, you can also attach an Outlook item to a message. An Outlook item can be any item saved in one of your personal folders, including an appointment, a contact, a note, and so on. You can attach an Outlook item in the same manner you attach a file.

Follow these steps to attach an Outlook item:

1. In the message window, choose **Insert**, **Item**. The Insert Item dialog box appears (see Figure 9.3).

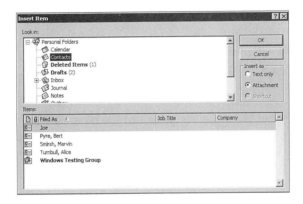

FIGURE 9.3
Select items from any folder in Outlook, such as a contact's information from the Contacts folder.

2. From the **Look In** list, choose the folder containing the item you want to include in the message.

3. Select from the items that appear in the **Items** list when you have the appropriate folder selected. To select multiple adjacent items, hold down the **Shift** key and click the first and last desired items; to select multiple nonadjacent items, hold down the **Ctrl** key and click the items.

4. In the Insert As area, choose from the following option buttons:

   • **Text Only**—Inserts the file as text into the message, such as the contact's information or the text in an e-mail message.

- **Attachment**—Attaches the e-mail message or Contact record as an attachment to the current e-mail message.

- **Shortcut**—If you are using Outlook in a networked environment where Exchange Server is used and all your folders, such as Contacts, are stored on the network, you can attach shortcuts to your e-mail message. Then, another user on the network can double-click the shortcut to access its information.

5. Click **OK**, and Outlook inserts the selected items into your message (either as an attachment or as inserted text).

Figure 9.4 shows an attached contact record in an Outlook e-mail message. When the e-mail recipient receives the message, he or she can access the contact information by double-clicking the attachment icon. The recipient can then save the contact information to their Contacts folder.

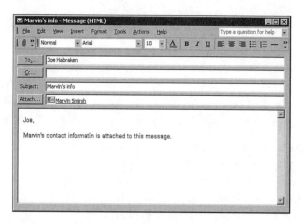

FIGURE 9.4
Select an item from any folder in Outlook, such as a contact's information, and attach it to your e-mail message.

PLAIN ENGLISH

It Doesn't Work Without Outlook   If recipients don't have Outlook on their computers, they will not be able to view the attached item, such as an Outlook contact record. If you know that a recipient doesn't have Outlook, insert the contact information into the message as text using the Text Only option in the Insert Item dialog box.

In this lesson, you learned how to attach files and Outlook items to an Outlook e-mail message. You also learned how to insert an object into an Outlook item. In the next lesson, you will learn to save draft messages and work with the Outlook Organizer.

LESSON 10

Saving Drafts and Organizing Messages

In this lesson, you learn how to save a draft, view messages that you've sent, and manage messages by creating rules using the Outlook Organizer.

SAVING A DRAFT

Suppose you start a message but you are called away or need to do something else before you can finish it. You don't have to lose the message by canceling, forcing you to start over again later; you can save the message in the Drafts folder and then open it later to complete it.

To save a draft, open and begin composing a new message. Then, follow these steps:

1. In the message window, click the **Close** button. A dialog box appears, asking whether you want to save changes, as shown in Figure 10.1.

FIGURE 10.1
Click Yes to save the message in the Drafts folder for later completion.

2. Click **Yes**. Outlook places the current message into the Drafts Folder.

To open the message and continue working on it at another time, follow these steps:

1. Click the **Drafts** folder icon in the My Shortcuts group on the Outlook bar, or choose **Drafts** from the Folder List.

2. Double-click the message to open it. At the top of the Message tab, you'll see a reminder that reads: This Message Has Not Been Sent.

3. Continue your work on the message. If you need to store it again before you're finished, click the **Close** button and answer **Yes** to the message box that asks you to save the file. Alternatively, you can choose to save changes that you have made to the message by clicking the **Save** button on the message toolbar and then closing the message. The message remains in the Drafts folder until you move or send it.

4. When you've actually completed the entire message and are ready to send it, click the **Send** button to send the message.

TIP

> **Create an Outlook Bar Icon for Drafts**   If you would like to place a Drafts folder icon on the Outlook bar when you are in the Outlook Shortcuts group, open the Folder List, pin the Folder List down (click on the push pin that appears when you open the Folders list), and then right-click the **Drafts** folder. On the shortcut menu that appears, select **Add to Outlook Bar**. An icon appears on the Outlook bar for the Drafts folder.

VIEWING SENT ITEMS AND CHANGING DEFAULTS

By default, Outlook saves a copy of all e-mail messages that you send. It keeps these copies in the Sent Items folder, which can be opened

using the Sent Items icon found in the My Shortcuts group on the
Outlook bar. You can view a list of sent items at any time, and you can
open any message in that list to review its contents.

VIEWING SENT ITEMS

To view sent items, follow these steps:

1. In the Outlook bar, choose the **My Shortcuts** group.

TIP

> **Save Time Using the Folder List**   You can select the Sent
> Items folder from the Folder List instead of using the
> icon in the My Shortcuts group.

2. On the Outlook bar, click the **Sent Items** icon; Outlook displays a list of the contents of that folder. Figure 10.2 shows
   the Sent Items list. All messages you send remain in the Sent
   Items folder until you delete or move them.

3. (Optional) To view a sent item, select it to view its contents
   in the Preview pane, or double-click it to open it. When you
   have finished viewing its contents, click the **Close** (**x**) button.

TIP

> **Open the Preview Pane**   If you don't see the Preview
> pane when you are working in the Sent Items folder,
> select the **View** menu, and then select **Preview Pane**.

CHANGING SENT E-MAIL DEFAULTS

You can control whether Outlook saves copies of your sent messages
(this is also true for unsent messages that are, by default, saved to the
Drafts folder). Follow these steps:

1. Select **Tools**, **Options**, and the Options dialog box appears.

2. Select the **Preferences** tab on the Options dialog box.

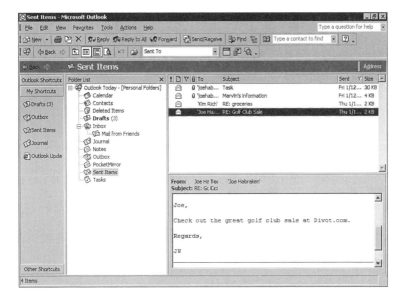

FIGURE 10.2
You can open any sent message by double-clicking it.

3. Click the **E-mail Options** button. The E-mail Options dialog box appears (see Figure 10.3). This dialog box provides a series of check boxes that you can use to toggle several e-mail–related features on and off; to make sure that saved copies of messages are placed in the Sent Items folder, click the **Save Copies of Messages in Sent Items Folder** check box. To have e-mail that is not sent automatically saved in the Outbox, click the **Automatically Save Unsent Messages** check box.

The E-mail Options tab also gives you control over several other features related to the management of your e-mail. More mail option settings are discussed in the next lesson.

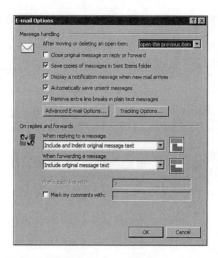

FIGURE 10.3
The E-mail Options dialog box gives you control over various features related to sending and saving unsent e-mail messages.

Using the Organize Tool

You have already learned how to create folders and move e-mail messages to folders to help keep your Outlook information organized (look back at Lesson 9, "Attaching Files and Items to a Message," for more info). Outlook also provides an easy-to-use tool, called the Organize tool, that can help you move, delete, or color code received and sent mail. The Organize tool can even help you deal with annoying junk e-mail that you receive. The Organize feature is able to read the e-mail address of the sender of a particular message and use it to find all the messages in the Inbox that this person has sent. The Organize feature can also use other criteria, such as keywords, to help organize e-mail that you receive. It can actually be configured to delete certain junk mail as soon as you receive it.

The Organize tool provides the Move Message and Create a Rule commands for getting messages out of a particular folder, such as the

Inbox, and placing these items into a different folder. Each of these avenues for moving messages to a particular Outlook folder has its own set of commands in the Organize pane.

MOVING MESSAGES WITH THE ORGANIZER

Suppose that you decide to move a message or messages from a particular person to a new location in Outlook. You can use the Move Message command and place the items into a different folder. However, if you receive additional messages from this individual at a later time, you would have to again manually move the messages to the new location. Wouldn't it be easier to have Outlook move these messages automatically?

To automatically manage future messages from an individual, you can use the Create a Rule command. This creates a rule that moves new messages from an individual to the new location automatically. That way, you can find all the messages from a particular person in the same place when you need them.

PLAIN ENGLISH

Rules   Rules are a set of conditions (such as a particular e-mail address or message content) that you identify to move, delete, or manage incoming e-mail messages.

PLAIN ENGLISH

Rules and Attachments   The rules you create to organize your messages can look at the sender, receiver, message subject, and message text. Attachments to a message are not governed by the rules that you create, so the content of file attachments to a message do not govern how they are handled by the Organize tool or rules.

To use the Organize tool to manage messages from a particular sender, follow these steps:

1. In your Inbox, select a message that you want to work with.

2. Click the **Tools** menu and then click **Organize**, or click the **Organize** button on the toolbar. The Organize window appears (see Figure 10.4).

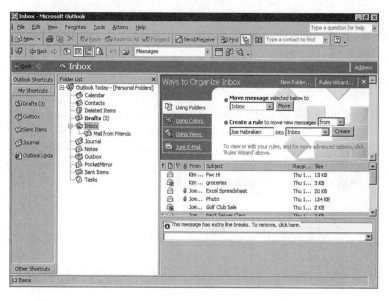

FIGURE 10.4
The Organize tool helps you manage messages using folders, colors, and views.

The Organize tool helps you manage and organize your messages using these methods:

- **Using Folders**—This method is used to move or delete messages; they can be moved to a folder that you create or moved to the Deleted Items folder.

- **Using Colors**—This option enables you to color code messages according to the rule you create.

- **Using Views**—This option uses the rule to categorize messages by their view (Flagged, By Sender, and so on).

- **Junk E-mail**—An option is also provided that helps you deal with junk e-mail.

To manually move the currently selected message in your Inbox, follow these steps:

1. Click **Using Folders**. The e-mail address of the person who sent you the selected e-mail appears in the From box.

2. In the Move Message Selected Below To box, click the drop-down arrow and select the Outlook folder to which you would like to move the message.

3. Click the **Move** button, and the message is moved to the new location.

4. If you want to move other messages, select the message in the Message list and repeat steps 2 and 3.

As already mentioned, you can manage any new messages you receive from a particular individual by creating a rule that automatically moves these new messages to a folder of your choice. To create a new rule for the sender of the currently selected message in your Inbox, follow these steps:

1. Click **Using Folders**. The e-mail address of the person who sent you the selected e-mail appears in the From box.

2. In the Create a Rule to Move New Messages drop-down box, make sure **From** is selected.

3. In the **Into** box, click the drop-down arrow and select the name of the folder to which you want to move the messages.

If you want to move the messages to a folder that is not listed on the drop-down list, click **Other Folder**. The Select Folder list dialog box appears. Double-click the folder that you want to use.

4. When you have selected the folder that the messages are placed in by the rule, click **Create**.

A message box appears in the Organize window (see Figure 10.5).

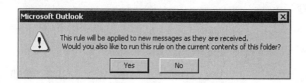

FIGURE 10.5
The new rule can act on existing messages or just new messages.

To run the rule on messages already in the folder (they will be moved by the rule), click **Yes**. If you want the rule to act only on new messages received, click **No**.

That's all there is to creating the new rule. Now, whenever you receive a message from that particular person, the message will be moved to the new location as soon as you receive the message.

USING ORGANIZER TO MANAGE JUNK E-MAIL

When you browse the World Wide Web, you will often come across Web sites that ask you to register with the site using your e-mail address. This is very common with Web sites that provide special content or allow you to enter various contests. After you provide a site with your e-mail address, chances are that they will sell your e-mail address to other Web sites and companies (it's not unlike having your home address placed on a mailing list). This means that it doesn't take very long before you begin to receive junk e-mail messages in Outlook.

The Organize tool also provides you with an automatic strategy for dealing with annoying junk mail. Click **Junk E-mail** in the Organize window (see Figure 10.6). The Organize tool enables you to either color code junk mail and adult-content e-mail or move these kinds of e-mail to a folder of your choice. In most situations, junk e-mail and other unwanted e-mail can be moved directly to the Deleted Items folder, and the items can then be easily discarded. Outlook automatically identifies these types of mail messages as you receive them by using a list of keywords as identifiers.

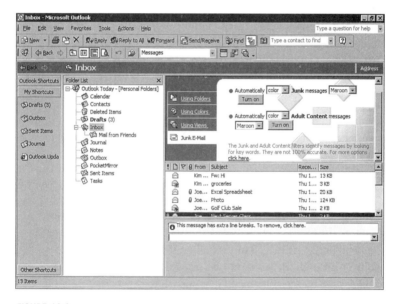

FIGURE 10.6
The Organize tool's Junk E-mail manager can help you deal with incoming junk mail.

To color code junk messages or adult-content messages, make sure the Automatically drop-down box for each junk-mail type (junk messages or adult content) contains the choice **Color**. Then, use the appropriate color drop-down box to select the color you want to use to code these messages as they are received. After you have selected the color, click the **Turn On** button to begin color coding all new messages that are identified as junk mail or adult-content mail by Outlook.

To send junk messages or adult-content messages directly to a specific folder (such as Deleted Items), select **Move** in the Automatically drop-down box for either type of message. In the Messages To drop-down box for either message type, select **Junk Mail** or **Deleted Items** to send mail messages directly to either of these folders. You can also send these messages directly to an alternative folder of your choice by clicking **Other Folder**. After you have selected the folder you want to send these messages to, click the **Turn On** button. Messages that Outlook identifies as junk mail or adult content are sent directly to the folder you specified.

You can also click the **For More Options Click Here** selection at the bottom of the Organize pane to access additional options related to junk mail and adult content. Links are provided so that you can access the list of e-mail addresses that you have identified as sources of junk mail or adult content. Any e-mail address on these lists is used to identify incoming e-mail that should be color coded or moved to a specific folder by the Organize tool. After you have completed your selections in the Organize window, click its **Close** button.

You can quickly add e-mail addresses to the Junk E-mail or Adult Content list by right-clicking any message in your Inbox. A shortcut menu appears; point at Junk E-mail on the menu, and then select either **Add to Junk Senders List** or **Add to Adult Content Senders List** from the cascading menu that opens. This adds this e-mail to the list, marking it as a source of junk mail or adult-content messages.

CREATING ADVANCED RULES WITH THE WIZARD

If the Organize tool isn't able to manage your e-mail to the degree you desire, you can create more advanced rules for managing messages using the Outlook Rules Wizard. The Rules Wizard enables you to create pretty sophisticated rules using simple sentences.

To open the Rules Wizard, follow these steps:

1. Click **Tools, Rules Wizard**. The Rules Wizard dialog box
   appears (see Figure 10.7).

   All the rules previously created using the Organize tool
   appear in the Rules Description box. You can copy, modify,
   rename, or delete a rule in this dialog box. You can also
   change a rule's priority by selecting a rule and then moving it
   up or down using the Move Up or Move Down buttons.

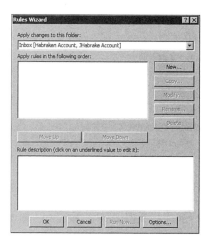

FIGURE 10.7
The Rules Wizard helps you create rules for managing mail messages.

2. To create a new rule, click the **New** button. The Rules Wizard
   walks you through the rule-creation process. The first screen
   asks you to choose either to create the rule from an existing
   template or create a new, blank rule. Step 3 describes creating
   a rule from scratch (although both possibilities offer similar
   options from the wizard).

3. Click the **Start from a Blank Rule** option button. Now you
   can select the type of rule you want to create, such as **Check**

Messages When They Arrive (see Figure 10.8), and then click **Next**.

FIGURE 10.8
In the Rules Wizard, you select the type of rule you want to create.

4. Select the type of rule you want to create, and then click **Next**.

5. The next screen asks you to select conditions that are to be used by the new rule (see Figure 10.9). These conditions range from messages sent directly to you, to e-mail addresses that you have placed on your junk e-mail list. Use the check boxes provided to select the condition or conditions for your new rule. Click Next to continue.

TIP

Conditions That Require Input from You Some conditions such as From People or Distribution List or Specific Words require that you provide a list of people for the condition to use or certain words. Conditions requiring additional information have an underlined selection for you to click.

FIGURE 10.9
You select the conditions that are to be used by the rule.

6. The next screen asks you to decide what the rule should do to
   a message that meets the rules criteria. Several choices are
   provided, such as Move It to the Specified Folder or Delete It
   (see Figure 10.10). Make your selections in the check boxes
   provided. Click **Next** to continue.

7. The next screen provides you with the opportunity to add any
   exceptions to the rule. These exceptions can include Except
   If Sent Only to Me or Except Where My Name Is in the To
   Box. You add the exceptions by clicking the check box next
   to a particular exception. You can select multiple exceptions
   or choose to have no exceptions to the rules. Then, click
   Next to continue.

8. The Rules Wizard's final screen asks you to type a name for
   your new rule. After you've done that, click **Finish**. The new
   rule appears in the Rules Wizard dialog box. You can create
   more new rules or click **OK** to close the dialog box.

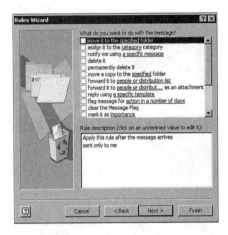

FIGURE 10.10
You determine the type of action you want Outlook to take when it finds a message that meets the rule's criteria.

TIP

> **Delete "Bad" Rules**   If you find that a rule or rules that you have created are actually doing things to messages that you hadn't planned, you can delete the rules. Rules created with the Organize tool can also be deleted in this manner. Open the Rules Wizard (click **Tools**, then **Rules Wizard**). In the Rules Wizard dialog box, select rules that you want to delete and then select **Delete**. They will be removed from the rule list.

When you use the Rules Wizard for the first time, you may want to create a simple rule or two that handle messages that you do not consider extremely important. A poorly designed rule could delete important messages that you receive. A good general rule is to use the Organize tool first and let it create simple rules, and if you need more advanced message-management help, use the Rules Wizard.

In this lesson, you learned to save a draft and view sent items. You also learned how to use the Organize tool and the Rules Wizard to manage Outlook messages. In the next lesson, you will learn to set various Outlook e-mail options and work with message flags.

LESSON 11
Setting Mail Options

In this lesson, you learn how to set options for messages related to message priority and the delivery of messages. You also learn how to work with message flags.

WORKING WITH MESSAGE OPTIONS

Outlook provides options that enable you to mark any message with certain options that emphasize a certain aspect of the message's importance. You can use Priority status so that the recipient knows you need a quick response. Using a sensitivity rating makes it so that not just anyone can change your message after it is sent. With other options you can enable the recipients of your message to vote on an issue by including voting buttons in your message and having the replies sent to a specific location.

You also can set delivery options. For example, you can schedule the delivery of a message for a specified delivery time or date if you don't want to send it right now.

CAUTION

Recognizing Priority Flags   Not all e-mail packages recognize the priority flags that you place on messages you send. These priority flags work ideally in a network situation, where Outlook is the e-mail client for all users. Microsoft's Outlook Express e-mail client also has the capability to recognize priority flags that you use on sent messages.

To set message options, open a new e-mail and click the **Options** button on the toolbar (or select **View**, **Options**). As you can see in Figure
11.1, the Message Options dialog box is separated into four areas. The
next four sections discuss each group of options in detail.

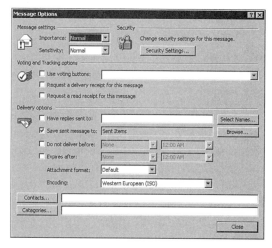

FIGURE 11.1
Use the Message Options dialog box to govern how your message is sent.

MESSAGE SETTINGS

In the Message Settings area, set any of the following options for your
message:

- Click the **Importance** drop-down arrow and choose a priority
  level of **Low**, **Normal**, or **High** from the list. (Alternatively,
  you could click the **Importance High** or **Importance Low**
  button on the message's toolbar when you compose the message.) When importance isn't specified, the message is given
  Normal importance.

- Click the **Sensitivity** drop-down arrow and choose one of the following options:

    - **Normal**—Use this option to indicate that the message contents are standard or customary.

    - **Personal**—Use this option to suggest that the message contents are of a personal nature.

    - **Private**—Use this option to prevent the message from being edited (text changes, copy, paste, and so on) after you send it.

    - **Confidential**—Use this option to indicate that the message contents are restricted or private. Confidential messages can be edited by the recipient. Marking the message Confidential is only to suggest how the recipient should handle the contents of the message.

TIP

> **Mark All Messages As Private** You can mark all your new messages as private automatically. Choose **Tools**, **Options**. On the **Preferences** tab, click the **E-Mail Options** button. In the E-Mail Options dialog box, click the **Advanced E-Mail Options** button. Use the **Sensitivity** drop-down box at the bottom of the Advanced E-Mail Options dialog box to set the default sensitivity for all your new e-mail messages.

Outlook also supplies you with options related to the security settings for a message. You can choose to encrypt the contents of your message or add a digital signature to the message.

To set the security option for the message, click the **Security Settings** button. This opens the Security Properties dialog box, as shown in Figure 11.2.

If you want to encrypt the message, click the **Encrypt Message Contents and Attachments** check box. If you want, you can also add a digital signature to the message that verifies you are the sender; click the **Add Digital Signature to This Message** check box.

FIGURE 11.2
You can set security options for a message, such as encryption and the use of a digital signature.

KEEPING TRACK

Encryption   Messages are coded so that they remain secure until the recipient opens them.

KEEPING TRACK

Digital Signature   A digital ID that is electronically stamped on messages that you send. This allows recipients of the message to verify that the message is truly sent by you.

Before you can use either the encryption or the digital-signature features, you must obtain a digital ID, which is also often called a certificate. Digital IDs are issued by an independent certifying authority.

Microsoft's certifying authority of choice is VeriSign Digital ID. For a fee, you can obtain, download, and install your digital ID from VeriSign by following the steps on their Web page at `http://digitalid.verisign.com/`.

Most e-mail traffic doesn't really require encryption or the use of digital signatures. You will have to determine for yourself whether your e-mails require extra security precautions such as encryption and digital signatures.

VOTING AND TRACKING OPTIONS

The Voting and Tracking Options enable you to control special features such as voting buttons (these allow recipients of the message to reply with a click of the mouse), which supply you with the means to track the receipt of your message. The delivery and read notification options allow you to receive notification that the recipient of the message has received the message or opened and read it, respectively.

- Select the **Use Voting Buttons** check box to add the default choices (Approve and Reject) to your message. You can also add Yes and No choices or Yes, No, and Maybe choices using the drop-down list to the right of the Use Voting Buttons check box. If you want to provide other choices, enter your own text into the text box (using semicolons to break up your choices). When you send a message with voting buttons to several people, you can view a summary of all the voting results by clicking the voting summary message on any of the e-mail responses.

- Select **Request a Delivery Receipt for This Message** to receive an e-mail notification that the intended recipient has received the message.

- Select **Request a Read Receipt for This Message** to receive e-mail confirmation that the recipient has opened the message.

Delivery Options

In addition to voting and tracking options, you can set certain delivery
options, such as having replies sent to individuals you select. You can
also choose a folder where a copy of the message is saved, or schedule
the time of the delivery. In the Delivery Options area of the Message
Options dialog box, choose any of the following check boxes:

- Normally, a reply to an e-mail message returns to the e-mail
  address of the sender. Sometimes, especially if you have multiple e-mail accounts, you might want replies to your message to go to a different e-mail address than the one you're
  sending from. Choose the **Have Replies Sent To** check box
  and specify in the text box the e-mail address to which you
  want the replies sent (see Figure 11.3). You can use the
  Select Names button to view your Contacts or Outlook
  Address Book and choose an e-mail address or addresses
  from the selected list.

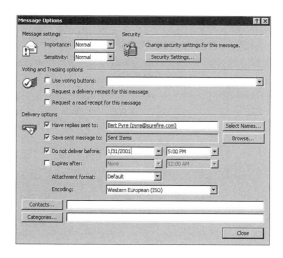

FIGURE 11.3
*You can specify that responses to a message be sent to specific e-mail
addresses (including or excluding your own).*

- Select the **Save Sent Message To** check box to save your message to a folder other than the Sent Items folder. The Sent Items folder is specified by default, but you can choose to save the sent message to any folder in Outlook. Use the **Browse** button and the resulting Select Folder dialog box to specify a particular folder.

- Select the **Do Not Deliver Before** option to specify a delivery date. Click the down arrow in the text box beside the option to display a calendar on which you can select the day. This option enables you to send out e-mail even when you are not at your computer (or in the office). The message will be held in your Outbox folder until the specified time. If you are using Internet e-mail, your computer and Outlook must be up and running for the e-mail to be sent. In a corporate environment where Exchange Server is used, the e-mail is stored on the mail server and is sent automatically on the delivery date.

- Select the **Expires After** check box to include a day, date, and time of expiration. You can click the down arrow in the text box to display a calendar from which you can choose a date, or you can enter the date and time yourself. Messages marked to expire are made unavailable after the expiration date. This means the message is basically recalled from any computer where the message has not been read (this feature works only in networked environments using Microsoft Exchange Server).

The delivery options are really great in cases where someone other than you needs to keep track of the responses related to an e-mail message that you sent or in cases where you don't want to immediately deliver a message using the Do Not Deliver Before option. Using the Expire option means that people who have been on vacation won't have to read old messages that you have sent; they will no longer be available because of the expiration date.

ASSIGNING CONTACTS AND CATEGORIES TO A MESSAGE

The Message Options dialog box also enables you to link a contact or contacts to a message. Linking a contact (or contacts) to a message allows you to view the message on that contact's Activities tab (when you are viewing the contact's actual record in the Contacts folder). The use of the Activities tab on a contact's record is discussed in Lesson 13, "Creating a Contacts List."

> **CAUTION**
>
> **Do Contact Links and Categories Appear on Sent Messages?**
> When you link contacts and categories to messages, you are actually just applying organizational tags to the e-mails. You can then view all the e-mail sent to a particular contact in the Contacts folder or sort sent e-mail by a particular category. The recipient of e-mail that you have tagged in this manner does not know that you created the link.

To assign a contact link to the message, click the **Contacts** button in the Message Options dialog box. The Select Contacts dialog box opens, showing all your contacts. Double-click a contact to add it to the Contacts box on the Message Options dialog box. Now the sent message is linked to a particular contact or contacts and can be accessed for later consideration when you are working with that contact or contacts in the Contacts folder.

Another option that Outlook provides for organizing sent messages is the use of categories. You can assign your messages to different categories, such as Business, Goals, Hot Contacts, Phone Calls, and so on. You set the category for a message in the Categories dialog box.

To assign a category, follow these steps:

1. In the Message Options dialog box, click the **Categories** button. The Categories dialog box appears (see Figure 11.4).

FIGURE 11.4
Organize your messages with categories.

2. To assign an existing category, select the category or categories that best suit your message from the Available
   Categories list. To assign a new category, enter a new category into the **Item(s) Belong to These Categories** text box,
   and then click the **Add to List** button.

3. Click **OK** to close the Categories dialog box and return to the
   Message Options dialog box.

TIP

> **Create Your Own Categories**   If you want to create a new
> category to assign to your e-mail messages, click the
> **Master Category List** button on the Categories dialog box.
> The Master Category List dialog box appears. Type the
> name of the new category in the New category box, and
> then click **Add** (repeat as necessary). To return to the
> Categories dialog box, click **OK**. Your new categories
> appear in the Categories dialog box.

When you have set all the options for the current message, click the
Close button to close the Message Options box and return to the message window.

The whole point of tagging sent messages with categories is so that
you can view messages by category when you open the Sent Items
folder. For example, you might want to quickly check the messages
that have been tagged with the Competition category. Changing the
view of a particular folder, such as the Sent Items folder, is handled
using the View menu.

1. Use the Folder List to open the Sent Items folder.

2. To view the messages by category, select the **View** menu,
   point at **Current View**, and then select **Customize Current
   View**. The View Summary dialog box opens.

3. Click the **Group By** button on the View Summary dialog
   box. The Group By dialog box opens as shown in Figure
   11.5.

4. Click the **Group Items By** drop-down list and select
   Categories, and then click **OK** to close the dialog box.

5. Click **OK** to close the View Summary dialog box.

6. When you return to the Sent Items folder, a list of the categories that you have assigned to your sent messages appear.

To view the messages listed under a particular category, click the **plus** (+) symbol to the left of a particular category.

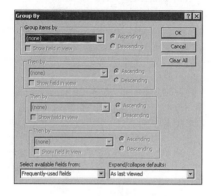

FIGURE 11.5
View your messages by category.

CAUTION

Now My View Is All Messed Up!   To remove the custom view, repeat steps 2–5; in step 4 select **None** in the Group By drop-down box. This returns your view of the folder to the default view.

USING MESSAGE FLAGS

Another tool for tagging messages is a message flag. A message flag enables you to mark a message as important, either as a reminder for yourself or as a signal to the message's recipient. When you send a message flag, a red flag icon appears in the recipient's message list, and Outlook adds text at the top of the message telling which type of flag you are sending. In addition, you can add a due date to the flag, and that date appears at the top of the message.

The following list outlines the types of flags you can send in Outlook:

Call	No Response Necessary
Do Not Forward	Read

Follow Up	Reply
For Your Information	Reply to All
Forward	Review

Using these various flags is like sticking a brief note on the message that provides you with a clue as to what type of follow-up might be required by a particular message. To use a message flag, follow these steps:

1. Open a new message or existing message that you want to flag. In the message window, click **Actions** and then select **Follow Up**. The Flag for Follow Up dialog box appears (see Figure 11.6).

FIGURE 11.6
Flag a message to show its importance or as a reminder for your follow-up.

2. Click the **Flag To** drop-down arrow, and choose the flag type you want to add to the message.

3. Click the **Due By** drop-down arrow and use the calendar that appears to enter a date into the text box. Use the **Time** drop-down box to set a specific time. Assigning a due date and time makes you act on the message as dictated by the flag by a particular date.

4. Click **OK** to return to the message window.

Figure 11.7 shows the Inbox with some flagged messages.

Marking messages with the Follow Up flag is a great way to remind
yourself that you need to attend to a particular issue. Flagging messages for your e-mail recipients helps them prioritize responses, so
you receive the needed reply within a particular time frame.

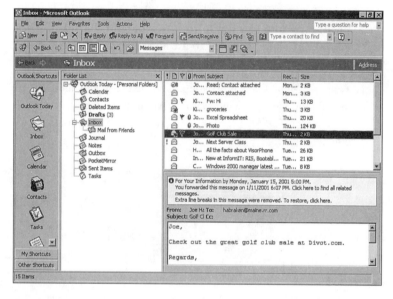

FIGURE 11.7
*Flagged messages "pop out" of a particular folder, reminding you to deal with
them.*

When you double-click a flagged message and open it in a message
window (see Figure 11.8), the flag type appears at the top of the message, just above the From box.

Viewing the flag type on the message provides you with a quick
reminder as to what your next action should be regarding the particular message.

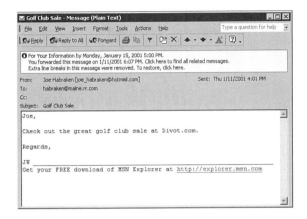

FIGURE 11.8

To view the type of flag attached, open the message.

In this lesson, you learned to set options for messages including options related to the delivery and tracking of messages. You also learned how to flag messages. In the next lesson, you will learn to use the Contact and Outlook address books.

LESSON 12

Using the Outlook Address Books

In this lesson, you learn about different Outlook address books and how to import lists to Outlook from other applications.

UNDERSTANDING THE OUTLOOK ADDRESS BOOKS

Outlook has the capability to access different stores or lists of information that can provide you with people's e-mail addresses and other contact information, such as phone numbers and addresses. The address books that you can access include the Personal Address Book, your Contacts list, and other directory lists that are provided by other e-mail systems and communication servers. For example, in a corporate network, a Microsoft Exchange Server can provide you with a Global Address list that is shared by all users on the Exchange network. The e-mail address of any users on the network are then easily found in one resource.

KEEPING TRACK

> **The Contacts List**   You might notice contacts in the list of address books; this list contains entries you create in your Contacts list. For more information about the Contacts list, see Lesson 13, "Creating a Contacts List."

Where your e-mail addresses and other contact information are stored depends on whether you are using Outlook on a corporate network that uses Active Directory, a network that uses Exchange Server, or as a standalone product where you use an Internet e-mail account.

However, no matter where your contact information is kept, Outlook makes it easy for you to access your different address books using the Address Book feature.

Using the Address Book

The Address Book is basically a launch pad that allows you to access information lists (they are all considered address books) that contain e-mail addresses and other contact information. Because you create your own Contacts list, you always have this resource available, even if you aren't connected to a special network server and you access your e-mail by connecting to the Internet. You can find more information about building your Contacts list in Lesson 13. Outlook also has the capability to access Web-based address directories such as Bigfoot and InfoSpace, which are both Web directories that can help you find people's e-mail addresses.

You can open the Address Book feature by clicking the **To** button or **Cc** button on a new message or by clicking the **Address Book** icon on the Outlook toolbar. After the Address Book dialog box is open, as shown in Figure 12.1, you can use the **Show Names from the** drop-down list to select the specific address book (such as your Personal Address Book or Contacts list) that you want to view.

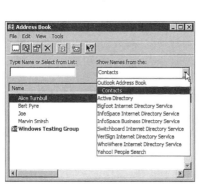

FIGURE 12.1
The Address Book enables you to access any of your address books.

Finding Records in an Address Book

The Address Book dialog box also makes it easy for you to search through a particular address book for a particular person. In the Type Name box, begin to type the name of a contact you want to find in the list; as soon as you type enough of the contact's name for Outlook to find that particular contact, it will be highlighted in the list provided.

In cases where you want to search for a record or records by a particular character string (such as all records in the address book that have the last name of Smith), the Address Book provides you with a Find dialog box.

 Click the **Find Items** button on the Address Book toolbar. The Find dialog box appears as shown in Figure 12.2.

FIGURE 12.2
You can search a particular address book by keywords or text strings using the Find dialog box.

Type your search string into the Find Names Containing box. Then, click **OK** to run the search. The search results appear in the Address Book dialog box. Only the records that match your search parameters appear in the list.

ADDING RECORDS TO AN ADDRESS BOOK

You can also add records to any of the address books that you have access to. For example, you can add records to your Personal Address book or to your Contacts list directly in the Address Book window. Keep in mind that in a corporate environment, your network administrator likely controls some address books, such as the Global Address Book. This means that you won't be able to add information to these address books; you can use them only as resources to find information such as e-mail addresses.

To add a record to an address book that you do control:

1. In the Address Book dialog box, make sure that you have the address book selected that you want to add the new record to.

2. Click the **New Entry** button on the Address Book toolbar. The New Entry dialog box appears (see Figure 12.3).

FIGURE 12.3
You can add new records to address books using the New Entry dialog box.

3. Use the **Put This Entry in the** drop-down box at the bottom of the New Entry dialog box to make sure that your new record ends up in the correct address book. To add a new record (a new contact, for example), click **New Contact** and then click **OK**.

PLAIN ENGLISH

> **Distribution List**   A distribution list allows you to create a record that includes the e-mail addresses for several people. This makes it easy to send e-mails to a group of people. You can create distribution lists in the New Entry dialog box. You will learn how to create distribution lists in the next lesson.

4. A blank record appears for your new entry. Enter the appropriate information for the new record, such as the person's name, e-mail address, and so on into the appropriate text boxes. When you have finished entering the information, click **OK** to save the new entry. In the case of new contacts added to the Contacts list, click the **Save and Close** button.

The blank records that open for your new entries will look slightly different, depending on the address book in which you are creating the new record. In the case of new contacts (which is discussed in the next lesson), you can enter information for the new entry that includes the person's address, phone number, fax number, and even a Web page address. Some address books may allow you to enter only the name and e-mail address of the person.

TIP

> 🗐 **Create a New Message from the Address Book Dialog Box**   If you opened the Address Book using the **Address Book** icon on the Outlook toolbar (or selected **Tools, Address Book**), you can open a new message for any of the contacts listed in one of the address books. Select the particular person, and then click the **New Message** icon on the Address Book icon. A new message opens addressed to that particular person.

IMPORTING ADDRESS BOOKS AND CONTACT LISTS

If you are migrating from another personal information manager or
e-mail client and want to import your address book or Contacts list,
Outlook contains different conversion filters for this purpose. Outlook
even provides you with an Import/Export Wizard that walks you
through the steps of importing address lists and address books from
these other software packages.

To start the Outlook Import/Export Wizard, follow these steps:

1. Click **File**, and then select **Import and Export**. The Outlook
   Import and Export Wizard opens (see Figure 12.4).

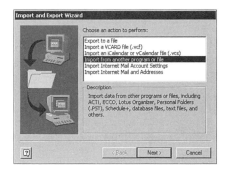

FIGURE 12.4
*The Import and Export Wizard walks you through the process of importing your
old address books or information from other applications.*

2. On the first wizard screen, you can choose to import e-mail
   and contacts information from another e-mail client, such as
   Outlook Express or Netscape, by selecting **Import Internet
   Mail and Addresses**. Then, click **Next**.

3. On the next screen, select the e-mail client, such as Outlook
   Express, that holds the information that you will import to

Outlook (remember that this feature imports e-mail messages and address information from the e-mail client to Outlook). Then, click **Next**.

4. The next wizard screen asks you to select the Outlook address book that will hold the imported information. Select the **Personal Address Book** option button or the **Outlook Contacts Folder** option button to specify the destination for the imported records. Additional option buttons on this screen allow you to specify how duplicate records are handled; select one of the following:

   - Replace duplicates with items imported; this option replaces any records currently in the address book with duplicates from the imported file.

   - Allow duplicates to be created; any duplicates currently in the address book are not overwritten during the import, and duplicate records are placed in the address book.

   - Do not import duplicate items; any duplicate items found in the address book that is being imported are not imported into Outlook.

5. After making your selections, click **Finish**.

The e-mail messages and the e-mail address records are imported into the Outlook address book that you chose. A message appears letting you know how many records were imported. The address records are placed in the address book that you chose. Imported e-mail is placed in the appropriate Outlook folder, such as your Inbox and Sent Items folders.

TIP

> **Importing Information from Database Programs**   If you
> want to import address records or other information from
> programs such as Microsoft Access or Lotus Notes,
> select the Import from another program or file option on
> the initial Import and Export Wizard screen. You are
> then walked through the steps of selecting the program
> and file that holds the data that you want to import. You
> will have the option of selecting the Outlook Contacts
> list or another address book, such as the Personal
> Address Book, to hold the information after it is
> imported.

EXPORTING OUTLOOK ADDRESS RECORDS

There might be occasions where you would like to take the records in
one of your Outlook address books, such as the Contacts list, and
export this information to another software package. For example, you
may want to place all the records in your Contacts list in an Access
database file (this is particularly useful in cases where you might be
using Outlook to hold information about your customers or clients).
Outlook records can be exported using the Import and Export Wizard.

Follow these steps:

1. Click **File**, and then select **Import and Export**. The Outlook
   Import and Export Wizard opens.

2. Select **Export to a File**, and then click **Next**.

3. On the next screen, you are provided with a list of file types
   that you can use for your export file (see Figure 12.5). Select
   a file type, such as Microsoft Access, and then click **Next**.

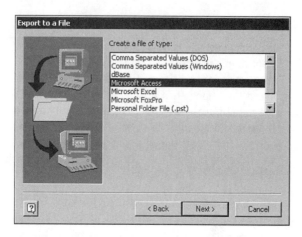

FIGURE 12.5
The Import and Export Wizard walks you through the process of importing your old address books or information from other applications.

4. On the next screen, you are asked to select the Outlook folder that contains the information that you will export. Select the appropriate folder such as **Contacts**. Then, click **Next**.

5. On the next screen, type a name for the file in the Save Exported File As: box. If you want to specify a specific location on your computer for the file to be saved, use the **Browse** button to open the Browse dialog box. When you have returned to the wizard (click **OK** to close the Browse dialog box), click **Next**.

6. The next screen lists the folder that will be exported. Click **Finish**. The export file is created.

After the information has been exported to the new file (it is actually copied to the new file; your Contacts list remains intact in Outlook), you can open the file using the destination application. For example, if you created an Access database using the export feature, you can open the file created using Microsoft Access.

In this lesson, you learned to use the Address Book feature to find records and to create new entries in your various address books. You also learned how to import address books from other software programs. In the next lesson, you will learn to work with the Outlook Contacts feature.

LESSON 13
Creating a Contacts List

In this lesson, you learn how to create and view a Contacts list and how to send mail to someone on your Contacts list. You also learn how to create a distribution list.

CREATING A NEW CONTACT

You use the Contacts folder to create, store, and access your Contacts list. You can enter any or all of the following information about each contact:

- Name
- Job title
- Company name
- Address (street, city, state, ZIP code, and country)
- Phone (business, home, business fax, mobile)
- E-mail address
- Web page address
- Comments, notes, or descriptions
- Categories

> **Contact**   In Outlook, a contact is any person or company for which you've entered a name, address, phone number, or other information. You can communicate with a contact in Outlook by sending an e-mail message, scheduling a meeting, sending a letter, and so on.

You also can edit the information at any time, add new contacts, or delete contacts from the list. To open the Contacts folder and create a new contact, follow these steps:

1. To open the Contacts folder, click the **Contacts** shortcut on the Outlook bar. The Contacts folder opens.

2. To create a new contact, select **Actions** and then choose **New Contact**, or click the **New Contact** button on the Standard toolbar. The Contact dialog box appears, with the General tab displayed (see Figure 13.1).

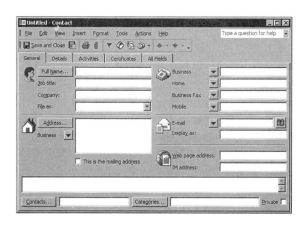

FIGURE 13.1
You can enter as much or as little information about each contact as you need.

3. Enter the contact's name into the Full Name text box. If you want to add more detailed information for the name, click the **Full Name** button to display the Check Full Name dialog box, and then enter the contact's title and full name (including first, middle, and last names) and any suffix you want to include. Click **OK** to close the Check Full Name dialog box and return to the Contact dialog box.

4. Press the **Tab** key to navigate from one field in this dialog box to the next. After the name field, the insert point moves down to the contact's job title and then the company name. This information is optional.

5. In the **File As** drop-down box, enter or select the method by which you want to file your contact's names. You can choose **Last Name First** or **First Name First**, or you can enter your own filing system, such as by company or state.

TIP

> **Keep It Simple**   The default filing method for contacts is last name first, which makes it easy to quickly find the contact when you need it.

6. Enter the address into the Address box and choose whether the address is **Business**, **Home**, or **Other**. Alternatively, you can click the **Address** button to enter the street, city, state, ZIP code, and country in specified areas instead of all within the text block. You can add a second address (the Home address, for example) if you want. Address information is optional.

7. In the **Phone** drop-down lists, choose the type of phone number—Business, Callback, Car, Home Fax, ISDN, Pager, and so on—and then enter the number. You can enter up to 19 numbers into each of the four drop-down boxes in the Phone area of the dialog box.

8. You can enter up to three e-mail addresses into the **E-Mail** text box. The box below the e-mail address allows you to enter how the e-mail address appears when you send a message to a person (for example, smith@mail.com could appear as Bob Smith); in the **Web Page Address** text box, enter the address for the company or contact's URL on the World Wide Web.

If you have more than one e-mail address for a contact, the first number or address in the list serves as the default. For example, when e-mailing a contact, the first e-mail address in the list is placed in the To box on the new message. If you want to use a different e-mail address for the contact, double-click the contact's name in the Message To box and select one of the other e-mail addresses in the contact's Properties box. When you want to call a contact for whom you have multiple numbers, a drop-down list appears in the New Call dialog box that enables you to choose the appropriate number.

PLAIN ENGLISH

URL (Uniform Resource Locator)   The address for a Web page on the World Wide Web. A typical URL is written `http://www.companyname.com`, such as `http://www.mcp.com`.

9. In the comment text box, enter any descriptions, comments, or other pertinent information. Then, select or enter a category to classify the contact.

10. After you have finished entering the new contact information, click the **Save and Close** button to return to the Contacts folder. You can also save the new contact by opening the **File** menu and choosing one of the following commands:

   • **Save**—Saves the record and closes the Contact dialog box.

- **Save and New**—Saves the record and clears the Contact dialog box so that you can enter a new contact.

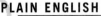

PLAIN ENGLISH

Other Tabs in the Contacts Window   Most of the information that you need to enter for a contact is contained on the General tab. You can also add additional information, such as the person's nickname or spouse's name, on the Details tab. The Certificates tab allows you to specify a certificate to use to send encrypted e-mail to this particular contact (Certificates are discussed in Lesson 11, "Setting Mail Options").

You can edit the information for a contact at any time by double-clicking the contact's name in the Contacts list; this displays the contact's information window. Alternatively, you can work on the fields in a record directly in the Contacts list window. Click within the information listed below a contact's name (such as the phone number or address) to position the insertion point in the text and then delete or enter text. Press **Enter** to complete the modifications you've made and move to the next contact in the list.

Viewing the Contacts List

By default, you see the contacts in Address Cards view (Address Cards appear in the Current View list on the Outlook Advanced toolbar). The information you see displays the contact's name and other data, such as addresses and phone numbers. The contact's company name, job title, and comments, however, are not displayed by default. Figure 13.2 shows the Contacts list in the default Address Cards view.

You can use the horizontal scrollbar to view more contacts, or you can click a letter in the index (on the right side of the screen) to display contacts beginning with that letter in the first column of the list.

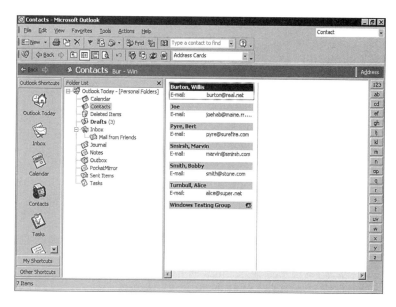

FIGURE 13.2
View your contacts in Address Cards view.

You can change how you view the contacts in the list by choosing one of these options from the Current View drop-down list on the Standard toolbar:

- **Address Cards**—Displays full name, addresses, and phone numbers of the contacts, depending on the amount of information you've entered, in a card format.

- **Detailed Address Cards**—Displays full name, job title, company, addresses, phone numbers, e-mail addresses, categories, and comments in a card format.

- **Phone List**—Displays full name, job title, company, File As name, department, phone numbers, and categories in a table, organizing each entry horizontally in rows and columns.

- **By Category**—Displays contacts in rows by categories. The information displayed is the same as what's displayed in a phone list.

- **By Company**—Displays contacts in rows, grouped by their company. The information displayed is the same as what's displayed in a phone list.

- **By Location**—Displays contacts grouped by country. The information displayed is the same as what's displayed in a phone list.

- **By Follow-Up Flag**—Displays contacts grouped by follow-up flags. The view also displays the due date for the follow-up that you specified when you marked the contact with a flag (flags are discussed in Lesson 10, "Saving Drafts and Organizing Messages," and can be assigned to Contacts the same as they are assigned to e-mail messages).

VIEWING A CONTACTS ACTIVITIES TAB

Although the Contacts folder provides different views for perusing the actual contacts in the Contacts list, these views really don't give you any indication of the messages that you have sent to a particular contact or the tasks that you might have assigned to a particular contact (assigning a task to a contact is covered later in this lesson).

You can view all the activities related to a particular contact on the contact's Activities tab. With the Contacts folder open, follow these steps:

1. Double-click a contact in the Contacts folder to open the contact.

2. Click the **Activities** tab on the contact's window. All the activities, such as sent and received e-mails and any assigned tasks, appear in the Activities pane (see Figure 13.3).

FIGURE 13.3
You can view all the activities related to a particular contact.

3. To see a subset of the Activities list, click the **Show** drop-down box. You can choose to view only E-mail, Notes, or Upcoming Tasks/Appointments related to that particular contact (any items that you delete in the Activities list are removed from the list and the folder that contained them).

4. You open any of the items on the Activities list by double-clicking that item. Close an opened item by clicking its **Close** (**x**) button.

5. When you have finished viewing the activities related to a particular contact, you can close the contact's window.

USING DISTRIBUTION LISTS

If you find that you are sending e-mail messages or assigning tasks to multiple recipients, you might want to create a distribution list. A distribution list enables you to group several contacts. Then, to send an e-mail to all the contacts in the distribution list, you address the e-mail with the name of the distribution list.

The distribution lists that you create are listed in your Contacts folder. You can open an existing distribution list by double-clicking it. You can then add or delete members of the list.

To create a distribution list, follow these steps:

1. Select the **Actions** menu, and then select **New Distribution List**, or you can right-click an empty space of the Contacts folder and select **New Distribution List** from the shortcut menu that appears. The Distribution List window appears (see Figure 13.4).

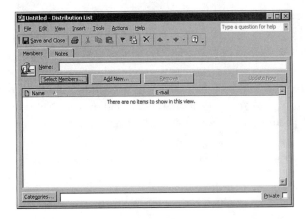

FIGURE 13.4
You can add contacts to a distribution list for mass e-mail mailings.

2. To enter a name for the distribution list, type the name into the Name box.

3. To add contacts to the distribution list, click the **Select Members** button, which opens the Select Members dialog box. Use the **Show Names from the** drop-down list to select the address book, such as the Contacts list, that you want to use to add names to the distribution list.

4. Select a contact to add to the distribution list, and then click the **Members** button to add the contact to the list (see Figure 13.5).

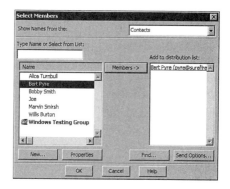

FIGURE 13.5
Add your contacts to the list from any of your address books.

5. To select multiple contacts at once, hold down the **Ctrl** key, click the mouse on each contact, and then click the **Members** button.

6. When you have finished adding the contacts to the distribution list, click the **OK** button on the Select Members dialog box. You are returned to the Distribution List window.

7. To save the distribution list, click the **Save and Close** button on the list's toolbar.

After you have saved the distribution list, it appears as a contact listing in your Contacts folder. You can use the distribution list's name in the To box of an e-mail message to send the message to all the contacts listed in the distribution list.

If you find that you want to remove names from a distribution list, open the distribution list from the Contacts folder. In the Distribution List window, select the name or names you want to remove from the list. Then, click the **Remove** button. Make sure that you save the changes that you have made to the distribution list.

> **TIP**
>
> **Add People to the Distribution List Who Are Not Current Contacts**   If you want to add names and associated e-mail addresses for people who are not in an address book to a distribution list, click the **Add New** button in the Distribution List window. The Add New dialog box allows you to enter a name and e-mail address for a new member of the distribution list.

COMMUNICATING WITH A CONTACT

You can send messages to any of your contacts, arrange meetings, assign tasks, or even send a letter to a contact from within Outlook (this also includes any distribution lists that you have created in the Contacts folder). To communicate with a contact, make sure you're in the Contacts folder. You do not need to open the specific contact's information window to perform any of the following procedures.

SENDING MESSAGES

To send a message to a contact, you must make sure you've entered an e-mail address in the General tab of the Contact dialog box for that particular contact. If Outlook cannot locate the e-mail address, it displays a message dialog box letting you know.

To send a message from the Contacts folder, select the contact, select **Actions**, and then select **New Message to Contact** (or you can right-click the contact or the distribution list and select **New Message to Contact** from the shortcut menu that appears).

 In the Untitled - Message dialog box, enter the subject and message and set any options you want. When you're ready to send the message, click the **Send** button.

SCHEDULING A MEETING WITH A CONTACT

To schedule a meeting with a contact (or with contacts contained in a distribution list), you must first select the contact or distribution list (as with sending mail messages, the contacts involved must have an e-mail address). After you've selected the contact or list, select **Actions**, and then select **New Meeting Request to Contact** to open the Untitled - Meeting dialog box.

Enter the subject, location, time, date, and other information you need to schedule the meeting, and then notify the contact by sending an invitation (invitations are sent automatically during the process of creating the meeting). For more information about scheduling meetings, see Lesson 15, "Planning a Meeting."

ASSIGNING A TASK TO A CONTACT

As with mail messages and meetings, a contact must have an e-mail address to assign that individual a task. To assign a task to a contact, select the contact (tasks cannot be assigned to distribution lists), select **Actions**, and then select **New Task for Contact**. The Task dialog box appears. Enter the subject, due date, status, and other information, and then send the task to the contact, just click the Send Task button on the task's toolbar. For detailed information about assigning tasks, see Lesson 16, "Creating a Task List."

SENDING A LETTER TO A CONTACT

If you want to create a hard copy letter and send it using "snail mail" (meaning sending it using the postal system), Outlook can help you create the letter based on the information in a particular Contact's record. Outlook uses the Microsoft Word Letter Wizard to help you create a letter to send to a contact. Within the Word Letter Wizard, you follow directions as they appear onscreen to complete the text of the letter. (You must have Microsoft Word installed on your computer to use this feature.)

To send a letter to the contact, select the contact in the Contacts folder
and choose **Actions**, and then select **New Letter to Contact**. Word
opens the Letter Wizard onscreen. The Letter Wizard helps you format
and complete the letter (see Figure 13.6). Just follow the onscreen
directions to create the letter.

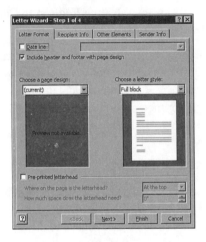

FIGURE 13.6
Use Word's Letter Wizard to create a letter to a contact.

CALLING A CONTACT

Another obvious way to communicate with a contact is over the telephone. For Outlook to dial the phone number for you, you must have a
modem hooked to your computer that can dial out for you. With the
right equipment, Outlook makes it easy for you to make a phone call
to a contact by dialing the phone number for you.

For Outlook to manage your calls, you must have a modem hooked to
your computer that can dial out for you. If you're in a networked environment that has access to a network modem pool, you can also dial
out using your computer. The line you dial out on, however, must also
be accessible by your telephone.

To initiate a phone call to a contact, select the contact in the Contact list and follow these steps:

1. Select **Actions**, point at **Call Contact**, and then select the appropriate phone number from the cascading menu that appears (all the phone numbers for the selected contact appear, including business, home, and fax). You can also click the **Dial** button on the Standard toolbar and select the appropriate phone number from the drop-down list. In both cases, the New Call dialog box appears (see Figure 13.7).

FIGURE 13.7
You can quickly initiate a telephone call to a contact using the Actions menu or the Dial button.

2. Click the **Start Call** button to allow Outlook to dial the contact's phone number using your modem.

3. The Call Status dialog box appears. Pick up your phone and click the **Talk** button in the Call Status dialog box. This engages the phone, and you can speak to your contact when they answer your call.

Viewing a Map of a Contact's Address

A useful feature Outlook offers is the capability to view an area map based on the address of a particular contact (requires an active Internet connection). This can be incredibly useful when you aren't sure where a particular contact is located.

To view a map of a contact's address, double-click the contact in the Contact list. The contact's record opens in the Contact dialog box.

 Click the **Display Map of Address** button on the Contacts toolbar. Microsoft Internet Explorer opens to the Microsoft Expedia Web site and displays a map based on the contact's address, as shown in Figure 13.8.

FIGURE 13.8
You can view a map of a contact's address.

You can zoom in and out on the map, and you can print a hard copy. When you are finished viewing the map and want to return to Outlook, simply close the Internet Explorer window.

In this lesson, you learned to create a Contacts list, view the list, and send mail to someone on your Contacts list. You also learned how to create a distribution list and view a map of a contact's address. In the next lesson, you will learn to navigate the Calendar, create an appointment, and plan events using the Outlook calendar.

Lesson 14
Using the Calendar

In this lesson, you learn how to navigate the Calendar, create appointments, and save appointments. You also learn how to insert an Office object, such as an Excel workbook, in an appointment.

Navigating the Calendar

You can use Outlook's Calendar to schedule appointments and create a task list. If necessary, Outlook can also remind you of appointments and daily or weekly tasks. You can schedule appointments months in advance, move appointments, cancel appointments, and so on. The Calendar makes it very easy to identify the days on which you have appointments.

To open the Outlook Calendar, click the **Calendar** icon in the Outlook bar, or select the **Calendar** folder from the Folder List. Figure 14.1 shows the Calendar in Outlook.

Outlook provides multiple ways for you to move around in the Calendar and view specific dates:

- Scroll through the Schedule pane to view the time of an appointment.

- In the Monthly Calendar pane, click the left and right arrows next to the names of the months to go backward and forward one month at a time. Click a date to display that day's information in the Schedule pane.

Monthly Calendar pane

Today's date

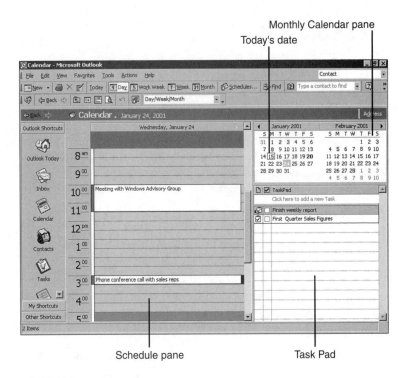

Schedule pane   Task Pad

FIGURE 14.1
You can view all appointments and tasks at a glance.

TIP

Changing Calendar Views   You can change to different views of the Calendar by clicking the **Current View** drop-down arrow on the Advanced toolbar. Views including Active Appointments, Recurring Appointments, and By Category are available.

- In the monthly calendar pane, click a particular date on one of the months shown to display that date in the schedule pane.

- To view a different month in the Monthly Calendar pane, click the current month in the Monthly Calendar pane and select the name of the month from the shortcut list. Or you can use the **Back** or **Forward** arrows to the left and right of the shown months (respectively) to go back or forward on the calendar.

- To view a week or multiple days in the Schedule pane, select them in the Monthly Calendar pane.

- To add a task to the Task Pad, click where you see **Click Here to Add a New Task** on the Task Pad.

- Use the scrollbars for the Task Pad to view additional tasks, if necessary.

TIP

Change the Date Quickly   To quickly go to today's date or to a specific date without searching through the Monthly Calendar pane, right-click in the Schedule pane and choose either **Today** or **Go to Date**.

CREATING AN APPOINTMENT

You can create an appointment on any day in the Outlook Calendar. When you create an appointment, you can add the subject, location, starting time, category, and even an alarm to remind you ahead of time.

Follow these steps to create an appointment:

1. In the Monthly Calendar pane, select the month and the date for which you want to create an appointment.

2. In the Schedule pane, double-click next to the time at which the appointment is scheduled to begin. The Untitled - Appointment dialog box appears, with the Appointment tab displayed (see Figure 14.2).

3. Enter the subject of the appointment in the **Subject** text box (you can use a person's name, a topic, or other information).

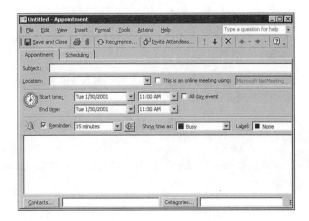

FIGURE 14.2
Enter all the details you need when scheduling an appointment.

4. In the **Location** text box, enter the meeting place or other text that will help you identify the meeting when you see it in your calendar.

5. Enter dates and times in the **Start Time** and **End Time** boxes (or click the drop-down arrows and select the dates and times).

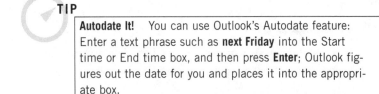

TIP

Autodate It!   You can use Outlook's Autodate feature: Enter a text phrase such as **next Friday** into the Start time or End time box, and then press **Enter**; Outlook figures out the date for you and places it into the appropriate box.

6. If you want your PC to let you know when you're due for the appointment, select the **Reminder** check box and enter the amount of time before the appointment occurs that you want to be notified. If you want to set an audio alarm, click the **Alarm Bell** button and browse your hard drive to select a specific sound file for Outlook to play as your reminder.

7. From the **Show Time As** drop-down list, you can select how the appointment time block should be marked on the calendar. The default is Busy. But you can also block out the specified time as Free, Tentative, or Out of Office. The drop-down list uses different colors and patterns to specify each of the different appointment types.

8. In the large text box near the bottom of the Appointment tab, enter any text that you want to include, such as text to identify the appointment, reminders for materials to take, and so on.

9. Click the **Categories** button and assign a category (or categories) to the appointment.

10. Click the **Save and Close** button to return to the Calendar.

The Scheduling tab enables you to schedule a meeting with co-workers and enter the meeting on your calendar. See Lesson 15, "Planning a Meeting," for more information.

SCHEDULING A RECURRING APPOINTMENT

Suppose you have an appointment that comes around every week or month or that otherwise occurs on a regular basis. Instead of scheduling every individual occurrence of the appointment, you can schedule that appointment in your calendar as a recurring appointment.

To schedule a recurring appointment, follow these steps:

1. In the Calendar folder, choose the **Actions** menu, and then **New Recurring Appointment**. The Appointment dialog box appears, and then the Appointment Recurrence dialog box appears on top of the Appointment dialog box (as shown in Figure 14.3).

2. In the Appointment Time area, enter the **Start** and **End** times for the appointment. Outlook calculates the duration of the appointment for you.

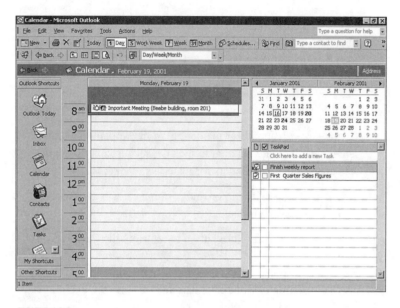

FIGURE 14.3
Schedule a recurring appointment once, and Outlook fills in the appointment for you throughout the Calendar.

3. In the Recurrence Pattern area, indicate the frequency of the appointment: **Daily**, **Weekly**, **Monthly**, or **Yearly**. After you select one of these options, the rest of the Recurrence Pattern area changes to provide you with appropriate options, such as days of the week for a weekly recurring appointment or day-of-the-month options for a monthly recurring appointment.

4. Enter the day and month, as well as any other options in the Recurrence Pattern area that are specific to your selection in step 3.

5. In the Range of Recurrence area, enter appropriate time limits according to the following guidelines:

   • **Start**—Choose the date on which the recurring appointments begin.

   • **No End Date**—Choose this option if the recurring appointments are not on a limited schedule.

- **End After**—Choose this option and enter the number of appointments if there is a specific limit to the recurring appointments.

- **End By**—Choose this option and enter an ending date to limit the number of recurring appointments.

6. Click **OK** to close the Appointment Recurrence dialog box. The Appointment dialog box appears.

7. Fill in the Appointment dialog box using the steps in the "Creating an Appointment" section already discussed in this lesson. When you finish providing all the details for the recurring appointment, click the **Save and Close** button to return to the Calendar.

The recurring appointment appears in your calendar on the specified date and time. A recurring appointment contains a circular double-arrow icon to indicate that it is recurring.

TIP

> **Make Any Appointment Recurring**   If you have already started creating an appointment and then would like to make it recurring, click the **Recurrence** button on the appointment's toolbar. The Appointment Recurrence dialog box opens.

PLANNING EVENTS

In the Outlook Calendar, an *event* is any activity that lasts at least 24 hours, such as a trade show or a conference. You can plan an event in the Calendar program to block off larger time slots than you would for normal appointments. In addition, you can schedule recurring events (such as a monthly seminar you attend that lasts all day).

To schedule an event, choose **Actions**, and then select **New All Day Event**. The Event dialog box appears (see Figure 14.4; it looks similar to the New Appointment dialog box).

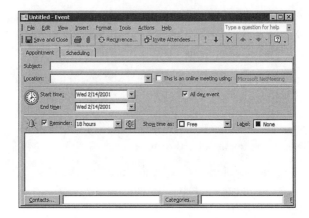

FIGURE 14.4
You can block out an entire day on the Calendar by scheduling an All Day Event.

Fill in the **Subject**, **Location**, **Start Time**, and **End Time** text boxes. Make sure the **All Day Event** check box is checked (that's the only difference between an event and an appointment). Click the **Save and Close** button to return to the Outlook Calendar. The appointment appears in gray at the beginning of the day for which you scheduled the event.

To schedule a recurring event, open a New All Day Event window and fill in the information as described earlier. To make the event recurring, click the **Recurrence** button in the Event window. The Event Recurrence dialog box opens; fill in the appropriate information and click **OK** (this dialog box is similar to the one for recurring appointments). Complete the information in the Event window, and then click the **Save and Close** button.

To edit an event or a recurring event, double-click the event in your calendar. Like a mail message or appointment, Outlook opens the event window so that you can change times, dates, or other details of the event.

INSERTING AN OBJECT

Outlook has the capability to insert an object, such as an Excel workbook or a file from any other Office application, into any Outlook item such as an appointment. For example, you might have an appointment to discuss some tax issues with your accountant and you have an Excel worksheet that details some of the information you want to go over. You can insert the Excel workbook right into the appointment. This makes it easy for you to view the data before you attend your appointment or even print the information.

You can insert an existing object into an appointment, or you can create an object within a message using the source application. For example, you could place an existing Excel workbook in an existing appointment.

To attach an existing object to an appointment in the Calendar, follow these steps:

1. Click the **Calendar** icon in the Outlook bar. Select **File, New, Appointment**. The new appointment will appear in the Outlook workspace. Position the insertion point in the appointment text box. This is where you will insert the Excel object.

2. In the appointment window, select **Insert**; then select **Object**. The Insert Object dialog box appears.

3. Choose the **Create from File** option (see Figure 14.5).

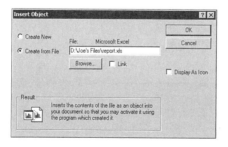

FIGURE 14.5
Insert an object, such as an Excel worksheet, into an Outlook task.

4. In the **File** text box, enter the path and the name of the file you want to insert. (You can use the **Browse** button and the resulting dialog box to search for the file, if necessary.)

5. Click **OK**. Outlook inserts the object into the Outlook item. The workbook or other inserted object actually resides inside a frame.

To edit an object, double-click within the frame, and the source application opens from within Outlook. Note that you'll still see your Outlook item and Outlook toolbars; however, you'll also see tools associated with the object's source application, which you can use to edit the object.

Figure 14.6 shows an Excel spreadsheet object within an Outlook appointment. Notice that the Excel toolbar and icons appear at the top of the Outlook window because an Excel object requires Excel's capabilities for editing.

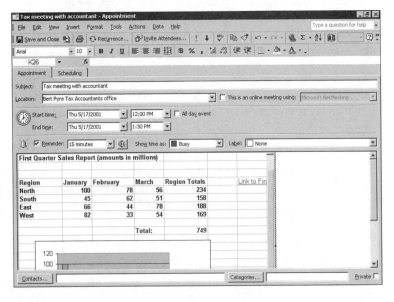

FIGURE 14.6
You can edit the object from within your Outlook appointment.

You can resize the object to suit your needs. First, select it, and a frame appears with eight small black boxes (called *handles*) on the corners and along the sides. To resize the object, position the mouse pointer over one of the black handles; the mouse pointer becomes a two-headed arrow. Click and drag the handle to resize the object.

When you change data in an embedded object, such as an Excel worksheet, remember to save the changes. Just click the **Save** button on the Excel toolbar (or the toolbar of the application that you are using to create the object). If you have resized an object in an item or inserted an object, remember to save the Outlook item (select **File**, **Save**).

Objects can also be inserted in tasks and meetings. Inserting objects enables you to have information related to a particular appointment, task, or meeting right at your fingertips.

In this lesson, you learned to navigate the Calendar, create appointments, and save appointments. You also worked with recurring appointments and the scheduling of events. In the next lesson, you will learn to create and schedule a meeting.

LESSON 15
Planning a Meeting

In this lesson, you learn how to schedule a meeting, enter attendees for a planned meeting, set the meeting date and time, and invite others to the meeting.

SCHEDULING A MEETING

Outlook enables you to plan the time and date of a meeting, identify the subject and location of the meeting, invite others to attend the meeting, and identify resources that will be needed for the meeting. You use the Calendar folder to plan and schedule meetings.

PLAIN ENGLISH

Meeting   In Outlook, a meeting is an appointment to which you invite people and plan for the inclusion of certain resources.

PLAIN ENGLISH

Resources   Any equipment you use in your meeting, such as a computer, a slide projector, or even the room itself.

To plan a meeting, follow these steps:

1. Click the icon for the Calendar folder on the Outlook bar. Then, in the Month pane, select the date on which you want to hold the meeting. To open a new meeting, select **Actions** and select **Plan a Meeting**. The Plan a Meeting dialog box appears (see Figure 15.1).

Attendees list   Green bar is starting time.

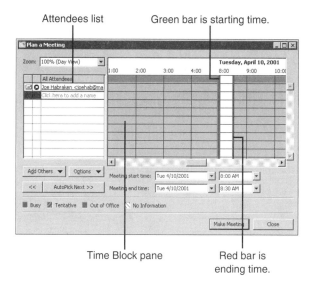

Time Block pane   Red bar is
                         ending time.

FIGURE 15.1

Choose the date and time of your meeting as well as the attendees.

2. To enter the names of the attendees, click in the **All Attendees** list where it reads Type Attendee Name Here. You can type a name into the box and then press **Enter**. Continue adding new names as necessary. Names that you type into the list do not have to coincide with records in your Contacts list, but if you include new names, Outlook will not have an e-mail address for those particular attendees when invitations are sent for the meeting.

3. A better way to invite attendees to your meeting is to click the **Add Others** button and choose the attendees from your Contacts list or other address book. This opens the Select Attendees and Resources dialog box, as shown in Figure 15.2. You can add attendees and any resources needed for the meeting in this dialog box. When you have finished adding attendees and resources, click **OK**.

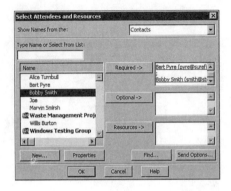

FIGURE 15.2
Attendees of the meeting and resources that will be needed can be added using the Attendees and Resources dialog box.

PLAIN ENGLISH

A Word About Adding Resources   The Select Attendees and Resources dialog box enables you to add attendees and resources to a meeting. Because you probably don't list resources, such as overhead projectors, in your Contacts folder, you will have to type the resource names for the meeting as detailed in step 1 of this section (placing them in the Attendees list). In the case of resources, click the e-mail icon that appears to the left of the resource and select **Don't Send Meeting to This Attendee**. This keeps Outlook from trying to e-mail the resource. You can also use this option if you have listed attendees for the meeting who are not contained in your Contacts list.

4. To set a date for the meeting, open the **Meeting Start Time** drop-down list and select the date from the calendar, or just type the date into the text box. The ending date (in the **Meeting End Time** drop-down list) automatically shows the same date you set in the Meeting Start Time date box; you can change the End Time date if you want.

5. To set a start time for the meeting, do one of the following:

    - Open the **Meeting Start Time** drop-down list and select the time.

    - Type a time into the text box.

    - Drag the green bar in the Time Block pane to set the start time.

6. To set an end time for the meeting, do one of the following:

    - Open the **Meeting End Time** drop-down list and select the end time.

    - Type a time into the text box.

    - Drag the red bar in the Time Block pane of the dialog box to change the ending time of the meeting.

    After you select the date and time for the meeting, notice that the time grid to the right of each attendee's name shows the currently scheduled appointments that they have on the day of the meeting. The times blocked out in each attendee's grid are based on appointments and meetings in their Outlook Calendar. Outlook is able to check your corporate network and check attendee availability by using their calendars. If you have a conflict between your meeting time and an attendee's appointment, you can adjust the time of your meeting and avoid availability conflicts.

7. When you finish planning the meeting, click the **Make Meeting** button. The Meeting window appears, allowing you to refine the meeting details. Details on using this dialog box are described in the next section.

TIP

Check the Availability of Internet Colleagues On a corporate network that uses Exchange Server, it's easy for Outlook to check other people's calendars to see whether they have a conflict with a meeting that you are planning. If you aren't using Outlook in an Exchange Server environment, you can also avoid scheduling conflicts by having people you invite use Internet e-mail to subscribe to Microsoft's Office Free/Busy Service. Outlook then periodically publishes a person's schedule to the service. All users that have subscribed can check the availability of participants using the service.

For more information about this service, go to `http://www.microsoft.com/office/` on the Web.

TIP

Use AutoPick to Shift the Meeting Time Frame You can click the **AutoPick Next** or **AutoPick Back** buttons to shift the meeting time (including the beginning and ending) to a half hour later or earlier, respectively. Each time you click one of the AutoPick buttons, the meeting shifts another half hour.

WORKING OUT MEETING DETAILS

After you plan a meeting, Outlook enables you to send invitations, identify the subject of the meeting, and specify the meeting's location. You enter these details in the Meeting dialog box.

When you schedule a meeting, as described in the previous section, you finish by clicking the **Make Meeting** button in the Plan a Meeting dialog box. When you do that, Outlook displays the Meeting dialog box with the Appointment tab in front (see Figure 15.3).

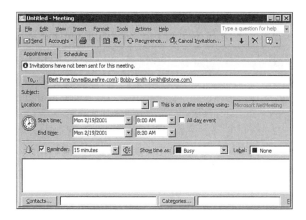

FIGURE 15.3
Specify the details related to the meeting in the Appointment tab of the Meeting dialog box.

Follow these steps to specify meeting details for a meeting you've already scheduled:

1. If you did not list the attendees in the Plan a Meeting dialog box, either click in the **To** text box and enter the names of the people that you want to attend the meeting, or click the **To** button to select the attendees from an address book or Contacts list.

2. In the **Subject** text box, enter a subject for the meeting.

3. In the **Location** text box, enter a location for the meeting.

4. (Optional) You can change the starting and ending dates and/or times in the Appointment tab. You also can choose the Attendee Availability tab to view the meeting in a format similar to that of the Plan a Meeting dialog box; make any changes to attendees, time, dates, and so on in the Attendee Availability tab.

5. (Optional) Select the **Reminder** check box and enter a time for Outlook to sound an alarm to remind you of the meeting. See Lesson 14, "Using the Calendar," for more information on using the Reminder feature.

6. (Optional) Enter any special text you want to send the attendees in the text box provided beneath the Reminder fields.

7. (Optional) If you plan to hold your meeting online using Microsoft NetMeeting, select the **This Is an Online Meeting Using** check box on the Appointment tab of the Meeting dialog box. Online meetings are scheduled the same as a face-to-face meeting; an online meeting, however, requires that you specify a Directory Server (this drop-down box is enabled when you select the online meeting check box) that will be used to connect the participants. In most cases, online meetings are held using Microsoft NetMeeting.

8. After you have entered all the required information for the new meeting, you can send invitations. However, before you send the invitations, you might want to make sure that the recipients reply to your meeting invitation. Select the **Action** menu and make sure that a selection check mark is next to **Request Responses**. If there isn't, click this selection to place a check mark next to it.

9. Now you can send the invitations; click the **Send** button. The meeting is saved and the Meeting window closes.

EDITING MEETING DETAILS AND ADDING ATTENDEES

You can edit the details of a meeting and change the date and time of the meeting at any time by opening the Meeting window. Opening the Meeting window also allows you to add attendees to the meeting.

Follow these steps:

1. In the Calendar folder, select the meeting date in the Monthly Calendar pane (any date that has scheduled appointments or meetings will be in bold on the Monthly Calendar pane). After you've opened the appropriate day, locate your appointment and double-click it to open it.

2. You can edit any information on the Appointment or Scheduling tabs.

 TIP

> **Any Responses?**   Choose the **Tracking** tab of the Meeting window to see whether the people you invited to the meeting have responded to your invitation.

3. You can also add additional attendees to your meeting. On either the Appointment tab or the Scheduling tab of the Meeting dialog box, use the **To** or **Add Others** buttons, respectively, to open the Select Attendees and Resources dialog box.

4. Open the **Show Names from the** drop-down list and choose either **Contacts** or another address book (you can also add a new record to the selected address book by clicking the **New** button; see Lesson 12, "Using the Outlook Address Books," for more information).

5. Select any name in the list on the left side of the dialog box and click the **Required** or **Optional** button to specify attendance requirements.

6. Click the **New** button to add resources to the list; then remember to notify the person who is in charge of those resources of your meeting.

7. Click **OK** to close the dialog box and add the new attendees to your list.

When you have finished editing the meeting and/or adding new attendees, click the **Save and Close** button on the meeting's toolbar. A message box appears as shown in Figure 15.4, asking you whether you want to send the new meeting details to your original and added attendees.

FIGURE 15.4
Updating meeting details requires that you send new invitations to the meeting participants.

Because changing meeting details means that you also need to inform the attendees of any changes, click **Yes** to send the updated invitations. Attendees will be required to respond to the new invitation if the Request Responses option is selected on the Actions menu.

In this lesson, you learned to schedule a meeting, enter attendees for a planned meeting, set the meeting time, and invite others to the meeting. You also learned how to edit meeting details and invite new attendees. In the next lesson, you will learn to create a Task list.

Lesson 16
Creating a Task List

In this lesson, you learn how to enter a task and record statistics about the task. You also learn how to assign tasks to other users.

Entering a Task

You can use the Tasks folder to create and manage tasks that you need to accomplish and don't want to forget about. You can list due dates, the status of a task, task priorities, and even set reminder alarms so your PC can keep you from forgetting a task entered in the list. To open the Tasks folder, click the Task shortcut in the Outlook Bar.

> **PLAIN ENGLISH**
>
> **Task List**   A task list is a list of things you must do to complete your work, such as plan for a meeting, arrange an event, and so on. Various tasks might include making a phone call, writing a letter, printing a spreadsheet, or making airline reservations.

To enter a task, follow these steps:

 1. In the Tasks folder, click the **New Task** button on the toolbar or double-click any empty space on the Task list. The Untitled - Task dialog box appears (see Figure 16.1).

> **TIP**
>
> **Use the Menu to Start a New Task**   To start a new task from the Task folder menu, select **Actions, New Task**.

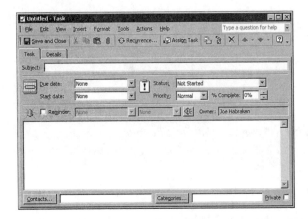

FIGURE 16.1
Enter data such as the subject of the task, due dates, and the task's priority.

2. On the Task tab, enter the subject of the task into the **Subject** box.

3. Enter a date on which the task should be complete, or click the down arrow to open the **Due Date** drop-down calendar, and then choose a due date.

4. Enter a start date, or click the down arrow to open the **Start Date** drop-down calendar, and then choose a start date.

5. From the Status drop-down list, choose the current status of the project: **Not Started**, **In Progress**, **Completed**, **Waiting on Someone Else**, or **Deferred**.

6. In the Priority drop-down list, choose **Normal**, **Low**, or **High** priority.

7. In the % Complete text box, type a percentage or use the spinner arrows to enter one.

8. (Optional) To set an alarm to remind you to start the task or complete the task, select the **Reminder** check box and enter a date and a time in the associated text boxes.

9. Enter any comments, descriptions, or other information related to the task in the comments text box located beneath the Reminder fields.

10. Click the **Categories** button and choose a category, if you want to assign the task to a particular category, or enter your own category in the text box.

TIP

> **Keeping a Task Private**   If you are using Outlook on a corporate network that uses Exchange Server, your folders are kept on the Exchange Server and, to a certain extent, their contents can be viewed by other users. Select the **Private** check box if you don't want others to see information about a task that you are creating.

11. Click the **Save and Close** button when you're finished.

TIP

> **Create Tasks in the Calendar Folder**   You can also create tasks on the Task Pad of the Calendar folder. Double-click the Task Pad to start a new task.

CREATING A RECURRING TASK

You can also create recurring tasks. For example, you might always have to hand in a weekly report every Friday; so why not schedule a recurring task that always reminds you to get that Friday report completed?

1. Double-click the Task Pad to open a new task window.

2. Enter the subject and other details of the task into the appropriate boxes.

3. To make the task a recurring task, click the **Recurrence** button on the Task toolbar. The Task Recurrence dialog box opens.

4. You can set the recurrence of the task for Daily, Weekly, Monthly, or Yearly. After selecting an appropriate recurrence, such as Weekly, select how often the recurrence of the task occurs (see Figure 16.2).

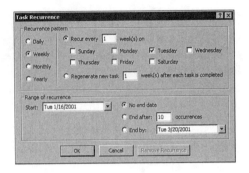

FIGURE 16.2
Set the recurrence pattern for a recurring appointment.

5. When you have finished setting the recurrence options, click **OK** to return to the task window.

6. Click **Save and Close** to save the new task. Recurring tasks are labeled in the task folder by a small circular arrow icon (letting you know that the task recurs).

ASSIGNING TASKS TO OTHERS

You can also assign tasks to others, such as co-workers or subordinates. Assigned tasks appear in your Task folder; however, the person you assign the task to has control over the task or the changing of the task parameters. To assign a task, follow these steps:

1. Double-click the Task pane to open a new task window.

2. Enter the subject and other details of the task into the appropriate boxes.

3. Click the **Assign Task** button on the Task toolbar. A To line is added at the top of the task window (see Figure 16.3).

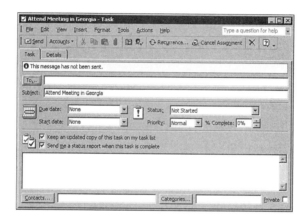

FIGURE 16.3
Use the To button to assign the task to people in your Contacts list.

4. Click the **To** button on the task and the Select Task Recipient dialog box opens.

5. Select the appropriate address book, such as your Contacts list, and then assign the task to a person or persons. Click **OK** to close the Recipient dialog box after you have finished assigning the task.

6. Click **Send** on the Task toolbar to send the task to the recipient or recipients. A message appears saying that, because you no longer own this task (because you have assigned it), no reminder will be assigned to the task (meaning you are not reminded if the task becomes past due). Click **OK** to close the message box.

Outlook sends the new task to the recipient or recipients. The task is actually sent as an e-mail message. When the recipient opens the

e-mail message in their Outlook Inbox, two buttons appear at the top
of the message, Accept and Decline (see Figure 16.4).

Accept task

    Decline task

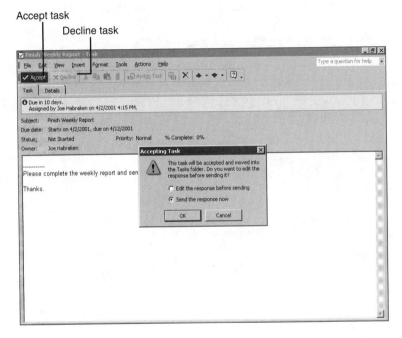

FIGURE 16.4
When a task recipient accepts the task it is moved to their Task list.

When the **Accept** button is selected, a message box appears (see Figure
16.4). This message box lets the recipient know that a response will be
sent to the originator of the task and that the task will be moved to the
Task Folder. To clear the message box, click **OK**. Now, when the recipient looks in the Outlook Task folder, they will find the task in the list.

If the task is declined (by clicking the Decline button), a message box
appears saying that the task will be moved to the Deleted Items folder
and that a message declining the task will be sent to the originator of
the task (which in this case was you) and will appear in the originator's Inbox. Because a copy of the task is kept in your Task folder, you
can open the task and assign it to another user.

VIEWING TASKS

As in any Outlook folder, you can change how you view tasks in the list using the Current View drop-down list in the Standard toolbar. By default, the Tasks folder displays tasks in a Simple List view. Following is a description of the views you can use to display the Tasks folder:

- **Simple List**—Lists the tasks, completed check box, subject, and due date.

- **Detailed List**—Displays the tasks, priority, subject, status, percent complete, and categories.

- **Active Tasks**—Displays the same information as the detailed list but doesn't show any completed tasks.

- **Next Seven Days**—Displays only those tasks you've scheduled for the next seven days, including completed tasks.

- **Overdue Tasks**—Shows a list of tasks that are past due.

- **By Category**—Displays tasks by category; click the button representing the category you want to view.

- **Assignment**—Lists tasks assigned to you by others.

- **By Person Responsible**—Lists tasks grouped by the person who assigned the tasks.

- **Completed Tasks**—Lists only those tasks completed, along with their due dates and completion dates.

- **Task Timeline**—Uses the Timeline view to display tasks by day, week, or month. Figure 16.5 shows the tasks assigned within one week.

CAUTION

Save What Settings?   Depending on the changes you make to a view, Outlook might display the Save View Settings dialog box asking whether you want to save the view settings before you switch to a different view. Generally, you'll want to discard the current view settings and leave everything the way you found it.

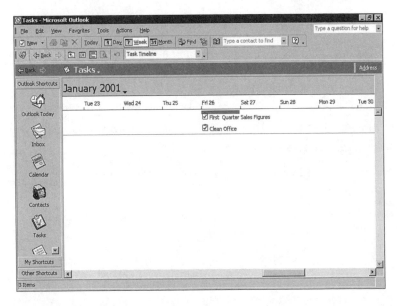

FIGURE 16.5
You can view your tasks in different views, such as the Task Timeline view.

MANAGING TASKS

When working with a task list, you can add and delete tasks, mark tasks as completed, and arrange the tasks within the list. You also can perform any of these procedures in most of the task views described in the previous sections. For information about printing a task list, see Lesson 19, "Printing in Outlook."

- To edit a task, double-click the task in the list. The Task dialog box appears.

- To mark a task as completed, click the check box in the second column from the left, or right-click the task and choose **Mark Complete** from the shortcut menu. Outlook places a line through the task.

- To delete a task, right-click the task and choose **Delete** from the shortcut menu.

- To assign an existing task to someone else, right-click the task and choose **Assign Task** from the shortcut menu. Fill in the name of the person to whom you want to assign the task (or use the To button to bring up the Select Task Recipient dialog box); after assigning the task, click the **Send** button to send the task to the recipient or recipients.

RECORDING STATISTICS ABOUT A TASK

You can record statistics about a task, such as time spent completing the task, billable time, as well as other information, for your own records or for reference when sharing tasks with your co-workers. This feature is particularly helpful when you assign tasks to others; you can keep track of assigned tasks and find out when they're completed.

To enter statistics about a task, open any task in the task list and click the **Details** tab. Figure 16.6 shows a completed Details tab for a sample task.

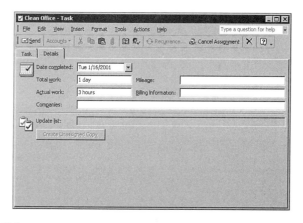

FIGURE 16.6
Fill in the statistics related to the completion of the task for later reference.

The following list describes the text boxes in the Details tab and the types of information you can enter:

- **Date Completed**—Enter the date the task was completed, or click the arrow to display the calendar and choose the date.

- **Total Work**—Enter the amount of time you expect the task to take.

- **Actual Work**—Enter the amount of time it actually took to complete the job. You can then compare the estimated time that you placed in the Total Work box with the actual time that it took (entered in the Actual Work box).

- **Mileage**—Enter the number of miles you traveled to complete the task.

- **Billing Information**—Enter any specific billing information, such as hours billed, resources used, charges for equipment, and so on.

- **Companies**—Enter the names of any companies associated with the contacts or with the project in general. Use semicolons to separate multiple names.

- **Update List**—Automatically lists the people whose task lists are updated when you make a change to your task. This is available only in situations where you are working in a Microsoft Exchange Server environment.

- **Create Unassigned Copy**—Copies the task so that it can be reassigned; use the button to send a task to someone other than an original recipient. This button is available only on tasks that you have assigned to other people.

TRACKING TASKS

Outlook also enables you to track tasks that you assigned to others. You can even receive status reports related to a task that you have assigned to another person or persons. To track tasks, follow these steps:

1. On the **Tools** menu, click **Options**; the Options dialog box appears. Click the **Preferences** tab.

2. On the Preferences tab, click the **Task Options** button. The Task Options dialog box opens (see Figure 16.7).

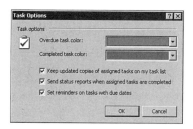

FIGURE 16.7
Make sure that you set task options so that you receive updated tasks and status reports for assigned tasks.

3. To automatically track the progress of new tasks you assign to others, make sure a check mark appears in the **Keep Updated Copies of Assigned Tasks on My Task List** check box.

4. To automatically receive notification when an assigned task is complete, select the **Send Status Reports When Assigned Tasks Are Completed** check box.

5. After you've made your selections, click **OK** to close the Task Options dialog box, and then click **OK** to close the Options dialog box.

TIP

Color Your Task List You can also set color options for overdue and completed tasks on the Task Options dialog box. Click the **Tools** menu, select **Options**, and from the Preferences tab, click the **Task Options** button.

In this lesson, you learned to enter a task and record statistics about the task. You also learned to edit tasks and assign tasks to others. In the next lesson, you will learn to use the Journal.

LESSON 17
Using the Journal

In this lesson, you learn how to create Journal entries manually and automatically and how to change views in the Journal.

CREATING A JOURNAL ENTRY

You can create a record of various actions so that you can track your work, communications, reports, and so on. In the Journal, you can manually record any activities, items, or tasks you want. For example, you might want to record the results of a telephone conversation.

You also can automatically record e-mail messages, meeting requests, meeting responses, task requests, and task responses. Additionally, you can automatically record activity related to documents created in the other Office applications: Access, Excel, PowerPoint, and Word.

The Journal is especially useful for recording information related to phone calls to and from people in your Contacts list. You can record information about the call, and you can also time the conversation and enter its duration (which is very useful information when you need to record billable-hours information for a particular client).

PLAIN ENGLISH

Journal   A folder within Outlook that you can use to record interactions, phone calls, message responses, and other activities important to your work.

Turning On the Journal

As already mentioned, you can automatically or manually record items in your Journal. Before you can take advantage of the Journal, however, you must turn it on.

The first time you open the Journal folder (using the icon in the Folder List or the Journal icon in the My Shortcuts list on the Outlook bar), a message appears, asking whether you want to turn the Journal feature on. Click **Yes**. The Journal Options dialog box appears as shown in Figure 17.1.

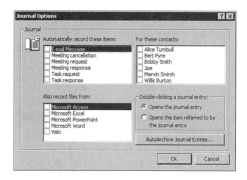

FIGURE 17.1
Click the check boxes in the Journal Options dialog box to have actions and events recorded automatically.

In this dialog box, you can specify what type of events you want to have automatically recorded in the Journal. Check boxes are provided to include e-mail messages, meeting requests, and other events that are received from people in your Contacts folder. To specify the items that you want automatically recorded, follow these steps:

1. In the **Automatically Record These Items** list, check those items you want Outlook to automatically record in your Journal. (The items recorded correspond with the people selected in the list of contacts in step 2.)

2. In the **For These Contacts** list, check any contacts you want automatically recorded in the Journal. Outlook records any items selected in step 1 that apply to the selected contacts.

3. In the **Also Record Files From** list, check the applications for which you want to record Journal entries. Outlook records the date and time you create or modify files in the selected programs.

4. When you have completed your selections, click the **OK** button. The Journal opens. It is now ready to automatically record the items that you chose in the Journal Options dialog box.

Suppose that you wanted Excel sessions to be automatically recorded in the Task list. You would make sure that Excel was selected in step 3. Then, whenever you work in Excel, that event is recorded. Figure 17.2 shows a Journal entry for an Excel event.

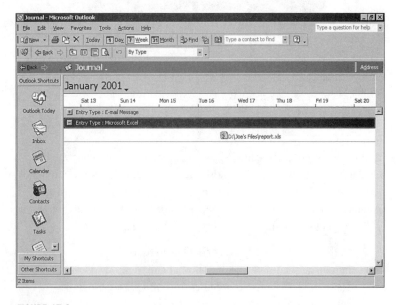

FIGURE 17.2
Journal entries for applications, such as Excel, are recorded automatically when you work in that application.

Recording an Entry Manually

You can also record items in the Journal manually using existing items such as e-mail messages. For example, you might add an e-mail message to the Journal that is not normally recorded (because you didn't select messages from that particular contact as something you want automatically recorded in the Journal).

To create a Journal entry manually, follow these steps:

1. In the Inbox folder (or any other folder in Outlook), select the item you want to record in the Journal and drag it onto the Journal folder icon in the Folder List (or drag it onto the Journal icon on the Outlook bar). The Journal Entry dialog box appears (see Figure 17.3).

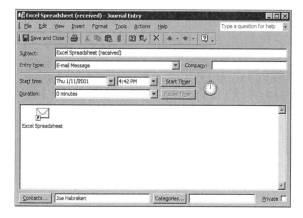

FIGURE 17.3
Drag an item onto the Journal icon, and the Journal Entry dialog box opens.

2. The information in the Subject, Entry Type, Contact, and Company boxes and some other information is entered for you from the selected task, contact, or other selected item. However, you can change any of the statistics you want by entering new information into the following text boxes:

- **Subject**—Displays the title or name of the Journal item.

- **Entry Type**—Describes the item based on its point of origin, such as a Word document, a meeting or appointment, and so on.

- **Company**—Lists the company or companies associated with the contacts.

- **Start Time**—Displays the date and time of the meeting, appointment, or other item.

- **Start Timer**—Like a stopwatch, the timer records the time that passes until you click the Pause Timer button.

- **Pause Timer**—Stops the timer.

- **Duration**—Enter the amount of time for completing the item.

- **Shortcut box**—Displays a shortcut to the item you originally dragged onto the Journal icon to create a new entry (such as a Calendar appointment, a contact, or a message). You can actually open the item by double-clicking the shortcut icon.

- **Contacts**—Lists the name(s) of any attendees, contacts, or other people involved with the selected item.

- **Categories**—Enter or select a category that you want to assign to the Journal entry.

3. Click **Save and Close** to complete the Journal entry.

If you want to create a new Journal entry, but you don't have a contact, a task, an e-mail, or other item that you want to use to create the entry, you can create a Journal entry from scratch (meaning it is not associated with any existing Outlook item such as an e-mail message). For example, you might want to create a Journal entry that holds information related to a phone call that you have made. Follow these steps:

1. Change to the Journal folder.

2. Choose **Actions**, and then select **New Journal Entry** or double-click any empty portion of the Journal pane. The Journal Entry dialog box appears.

3. Enter the subject for your new journal entry.

4. Select the type of entry you want to make; in this case, the default is already set to Phone Call. Leave the Journal Entry window open on your desktop.

5. Make your phone call; you can actually have Outlook dial the phone call for you using the **AutoDialer** icon, which can be accessed on the toolbar in the Contacts folder (click the **AutoDialer** icon, and then select **New Call**; use the **Contacts** drop-down list in the New Call dialog box to specify the contact that you want to call, and then click **Start Call**).

6. When your call is answered, click the **Start Timer** button in the Journal Entry window. Type any notes that you want to record during the phone conversation in the entry's text box.

7. When you finish the call, click the **Pause Timer** button. Notice that the duration of the call is entered in the Duration box. To save the Journal entry, click the **Save and Close** button.

CHANGING JOURNAL SETTINGS

You might find that when you started the Journal for the first time, you didn't configure that many events to be automatically recorded by the Journal. No problem; you can return to the Journal settings and change the options related to the automatic recording items in the Journal.

In the Journal folder, choose **Tools**, **Options**. The Options dialog box appears. Click the **Preferences** tab if necessary, and then click the **Journal Options** button. The Journal Options dialog box appears.

You can also choose to have your Journal entries AutoArchived. Click the **AutoArchive Journal Entries** button, and then choose a folder on your computer where you want to have the Journal Archive file stored (selecting the default folder is your best bet). Then, click **OK** to complete the process.

When you have finished making changes to the Journal options, click **OK** to close the Journal Options dialog box. Then, click **OK** to close the Options dialog box.

VIEWING JOURNAL ENTRIES

By default, the Journal folder displays information in the Timeline view and By Type, as shown in Figure 17.4. However, you can display the entries in various views, as described in the following list. To select a particular view, click the **Current View** drop-down button on the Advanced toolbar.

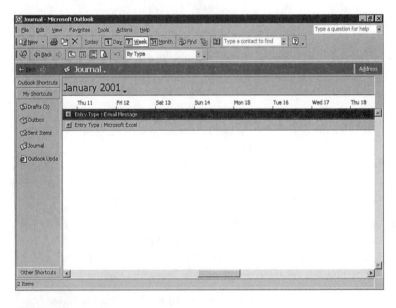

FIGURE 17.4
The default Journal view is the Timeline view.

KEEPING TRACK

> **Save Settings?** As in other views, Outlook might display the Save View Settings dialog box to ask whether you want to save the view settings before you switch to a different view. You're probably getting used to this dialog box by now.

- **By Type**—In Timeline view, this option groups Journal entries by type, such as e-mail messages, meetings, Word documents, and so on. Double-click a type to display its contents, and then position the mouse pointer over an entry to view its contents or name. When you switch to the Journal in the Type view, a Journal Options dialog box appears. This dialog box allows you to specify which e-mail messages will be recorded in the Journal, based on the contact they are received from. This dialog box also allows you to select which application use will also be recorded in the Journal, such as Excel, Word, or Access.

- **By Contact**—In Timeline view, this displays the name of each contact that you selected in the Options dialog box. Double-click any contact's name to view recorded entries.

- **By Category**—If you've assigned categories to your Journal entries and other items, you can display your Journal entries by category in the Timeline view.

- **Entry List**—Displays entries in a table with columns labeled Entry Type, Subject, Start, Duration, Contact, and Categories.

- **Last Seven Days**—Displays entries in an entry list but includes only those entries dated within the last seven days.

- **Phone Calls**—Lists all entries that are phone calls.

In this lesson, you learned to create Journal entries manually and automatically and to change views in the Journal. In the next lesson, you will learn to create notes.

LESSON 18
Using Outlook Notes

In this lesson, you learn how to create, sort, and view notes.

CREATING NOTES

If you've ever used a Post-it note to remind yourself of tasks, ideas, or other brief annotations, Outlook's Notes are for you. Notes are similar to paper sticky notes. You can use Notes to write down reminders, names, phone numbers, directions, or anything else you need to remember. In Outlook, all notes are kept in the Notes folder. You'll have to remember to look at the folder so you can view your notes.

TIP

> **The Long and Short of It**   You can enter pages and pages of text if you want. As you type, the page scrolls for you; use the arrow keys and the Page Up and Page Down keys to move through the note's text. Keep in mind, however, that the purpose of the note is a quick reminder, or information that you will eventually transfer to one of the other Outlook items, such as an appointment or task.

To create a note, click the **Notes** folder on the Outlook bar and then follow these steps:

1. In the Notes folder, choose **Actions**, and then select **New Note** or double-click an empty spot in the Notes pane. A new note appears, ready for you to type your text.

2. Enter the text for your note (see Figure 18.1).

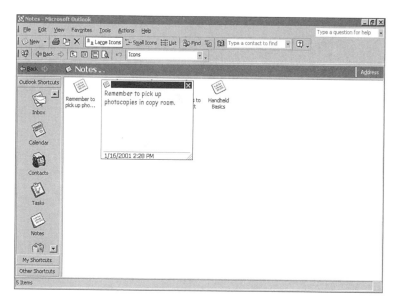

FIGURE 18.1
A note automatically includes the date and time it was created.

3. When you finish, click the **Close** (**x**) button to close the note. You can reopen a note and edit the text as you need to.

If you press Enter after entering text in the note, you create a line break and you create a title, of sorts, at the same time. Only the text before the hard return displays when the note is closed. If you do not add a hard return but enter the note text so that it automatically wraps from line to line, the entire note text appears below the note in Icons view.

SETTING NOTE OPTIONS

You can change the default color and size of your notes. You also can change the default font used for your notes. To set note options, follow these steps:

1. In the Notes folder (or in any of the Outlook folders), choose **Tools**, **Options**. The Options dialog box appears. On the

Preferences tab, click **Notes Options**; the Notes Options dialog box appears (see Figure 18.2).

FIGURE 18.2
You can customize your notes.

2. The Notes Options dialog box enables you to change the color, size, and font for your notes. Using the Color drop-down box, you can change the color to yellow, blue, green, pink, or white. The default is yellow.

3. Open the **Size** drop-down list and choose **Small**, **Medium**, or **Large** for the size of the notes. The default is Medium.

4. To change the font, click the **Font** button. The Font dialog box appears. Change the font, font style, size, color, and other options, and then click **OK**.

MANAGING INDIVIDUAL NOTES

To open an existing note, double-click it in the Notes folder. You can edit the text in an open note the same as you would edit any text. To move a note, drag its title bar. You can delete, forward, or print notes; you can change the color of individual notes; and you can specify categories for your notes. You can also drag the notes to the Windows desktop and arrange them there.

Click an open note's Control Menu button (click the very upper left of the note) to display a menu with the following commands:

- **New Note**—Creates a new note but leaves the first note open.

- **Save As**—Enables you to save the note and its contents.

- **Delete**—Deletes a note and its contents. (You also can delete a note by selecting it in the Notes list and pressing the **Delete** key.)

- **Forward**—Enables you to send the note as an attachment in an e-mail message.

- **Cut, Copy, Paste**—Enables you to select text from the note and cut or copy it to the Clipboard. The Paste command enables you to paste items on the Clipboard at the insertion point in the note.

- **Color**—Choose another color for the individual note.

- **Categories**—Enter or choose a category.

- **Print**—Print the contents of the note.

- **Close**—Closes the note. (You can also click the **Close** (x) button in the note's title bar.)

Viewing Notes

The Notes folder provides various views for organizing and viewing your notes. The default view is Icons, but you can change the view using the Current View drop-down list on the Advanced toolbar. Figure 18.3 shows the Notes folder in the default view.

You can choose to display your Notes folder in any of the following views:

- **Icons**—Displays the notes as note icons with the message (or a portion of the message) displayed below the icon.

- **Notes List**—Displays the notes in a list, showing the title and note contents in the Subject column, the creation date and time, and the categories.

- **Last Seven Days**—Displays all notes written in the last seven days, by subject, creation date, and categories.

- **By Category**—Displays the categories; double-click a category to show its contents.

- **By Color**—Displays notes by their color. Double-click a color to display the notes.

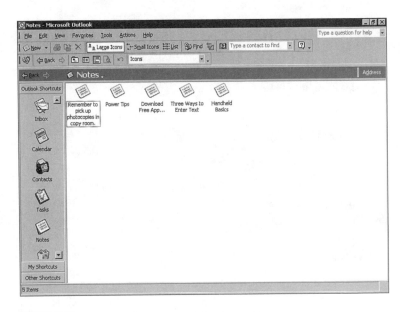

FIGURE 18.3
This view displays the notes in Icons view.

In this lesson, you learned to create and view notes. In the next lesson, you will learn to print in Outlook.

LESSON 19
Printing in Outlook

In this lesson, you learn how to print items in Outlook, change the page setup, preview an item before printing it, and change printer properties.

CHOOSING PAGE SETUP

In Outlook, before you print, you choose the print style you want to use. Each folder—the Inbox, Calendar, Contacts, and so on—offers different print styles, and each style displays the data on the page in a different way.

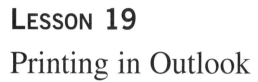

> **PLAIN ENGLISH**
>
> **Page** In Outlook, this is the area of the paper that will actually be printed on. You might, for example, print two or four pages on a single sheet of paper.

> **PLAIN ENGLISH**
>
> **Print Style** The combination of paper and page settings that control printed output.

You can choose from Outlook's built-in print styles, modify the default print styles, or create your own print styles. These lists show the default print styles available for each folder. To access the print styles for a particular item, select **File**, **Print**. The Inbox, Contacts, and Tasks use the Table style and the Memo style; the Journal and Notes use only the Memo style.

- 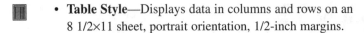 • **Table Style**—Displays data in columns and rows on an 8 1/2×11 sheet, portrait orientation, 1/2-inch margins.

- • **Memo Style**—Displays data with a header of information about the message and then straight text on an 8 1/2×11 sheet, portrait orientation, 1/2-inch margins.

The Calendar folder provides the Memo style as well as the following styles:

- • **Daily Style**—Displays one day's appointments on one page on an 8 1/2×11 sheet, portrait orientation, 1/2-inch margins.

- • **Weekly Style**—Displays one week's appointments per page on an 8 1/2×11 sheet, portrait orientation, 1/2-inch margins.

- • **Monthly Style**—Displays one month's appointments per page on an 8 1/2×11 sheet, landscape orientation, 1/2-inch margins.

- • **Tri-fold Style**—Displays the daily calendar, task list, and weekly calendar on an 8 1/2×11 sheet, landscape orientation, 1/2-inch margins.

- • **Calendar Details Style**—Shows the currently displayed Calendar items and the body text of each item (such as an appointment) in a list format.

The Contacts folder provides the Memo style as well as the following styles:

- • **Card Style**—Two columns and headings on an 8 1/2×11 sheet, portrait orientation, 1/2-inch margins.

- • **Small Booklet Style**—One-column pages that print the contacts in a format similar to mailing labels by placing multiple contacts on a page. This style can be printed in Portrait or Landscape mode.

- • **Medium Booklet Style**—One column that equals 1/4 of a sheet of paper. Four pages are on one 8 1/2×11 sheet of paper, portrait orientation, with 1/2-inch margins.

- **Phone Directory Style**—One column, 8 1/2×11 sheet of paper, portrait orientation with 1/2-inch margins.

> **CAUTION**
>
> **Will Page Setup Change My View?**   No matter how you set up your pages, it will not affect your view of tasks, calendars, or other Outlook items onscreen. Page setup applies only to a print job.

You can view, modify, and create new page setups in Outlook. To view or edit a page setup, follow these steps:

1. Change to the folder for which you're setting the page.

2. Choose **File** and then point at **Page Setup**. A secondary menu appears that lists the available print types.

3. Select the print type you want to view or edit, and the Page Setup dialog box appears (see Figure 19.1).

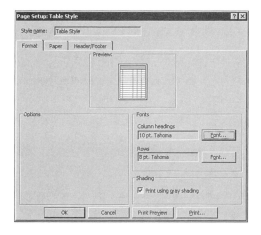

FIGURE 19.1
Customize the print style to suit yourself.

4. Click the **Format** tab to view and/or edit the page type, to choose options (in some cases), and to change fonts.

5. Click the **Paper** tab to view and/or edit paper size, page size, margins, and orientation.

6. Click the **Header/Footer** tab to view and/or edit headers for your pages.

PREVIEWING BEFORE PRINTING

To make sure an item looks the way you want it to look, you can choose to preview it before printing it. If you do not like the way an item looks in preview, you can change the page setup.

Open the folder that contains the item that you want to print preview. You can then open the item in the Print Preview view in any of the following ways:

- Click the **Print Preview** button in the Page Setup dialog box.

- Choose **File** and then select **Print Preview**.

- Click the **Print Preview** button on the Advanced toolbar.

- Click the **Preview** button in the Print dialog box.

Figure 19.2 shows a calendar and task list in Print Preview. You can change the page setup by clicking the **Page Setup** button; the Page Setup dialog box appears. Click the **Print** button to send the job to the printer. Click the **Close** button to exit Print Preview and return to the Outlook folder.

TIP

> **Enlarge the View**   When the mouse pointer looks like a magnifying glass with a plus sign in it, you can click to enlarge the page. When the mouse pointer looks like a magnifying glass with a minus sign in it, you can click to reduce the view again.

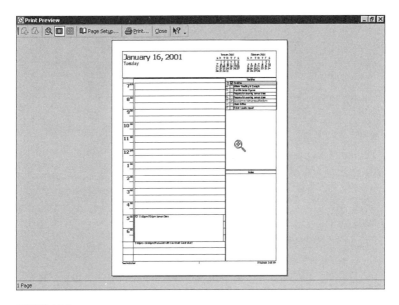

FIGURE 19.2
Preview the item before printing it.

Printing Items

After you choose the print style and preview an item to make sure it's
what you want, you can print the item. You can indicate the number of
copies you want to print, select a printer, change the print style or
page setup, and set a print range.

When you're ready to print an item, follow these steps:

1. Choose **File**, and then select **Print** or click the **Print** button
   on the Standard toolbar. The Print dialog box appears, as
   shown in Figure 19.3.

2. Your default printer appears in the Printer area of the dialog
   box. If you have a different printer connected to your system
   that you would like to use, choose a different printer from the
   Name drop-down list.

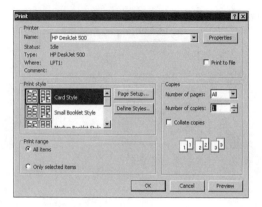

FIGURE 19.3
Set the printing options before printing the item.

3. In the Print Style area, choose a print style from the list. You also can edit the page setup (with the **Page Setup** button) or edit or create a new style (with the **Define Styles** button).

4. In the Copies area of the dialog box, choose **All**, **Even**, or **Odd** in **Number of Pages**, and enter the number of copies you want to print. This function is useful if you are going to print on both sides of the paper (this is called manual duplexing). You print the even pages, and then flip the sheets over in your printer and print the odd pages. Click the **Collate Copies** check box if you want Outlook to automatically assemble multiple copies.

5. Set the print range with the options in that area. (The Print Range options vary depending on the type of item you're printing.)

6. Click **OK** to print the item.

PRINTING LABELS AND ENVELOPES

A handy Outlook feature is the capability to print mailing labels and envelopes from your Contacts list. To take advantage of this feature, you also need to have Microsoft Word installed on your computer. Creating form letters, mailing labels or envelopes is called a *mail merge*. Basically, in Word, you create some type of main document (such as mailing labels, envelopes, and so on) that holds field codes that relate to the information you keep on each contact, such as name or address.

To actually start the merge process, open your Contacts folder and select **Tools, Mail Merge**. The Mail Merge Contacts dialog box opens (see Figure 19.4) and allows you to specify both the contacts for the merge and the Word document into which the contact information is merged. Using the option buttons at the top of the dialog box, you can specify that all the contacts or selected contacts are included in the mail merge. If you want to have only certain fields included in the mail merge, you can create a custom view of your Contacts folder (discussed in Outlook Lesson 4, "Using Outlook's Tools") before starting the Mail Merge.

After you specify the various options in the Mail Merge Contacts dialog box (see tip that follows) and click **OK**, you are taken to Word, where the mail merge is completed. To use this feature, you will need to have Microsoft Word installed on your computer. Just follow the steps provided by the Word Mail Merge Wizard to complete the merge process.

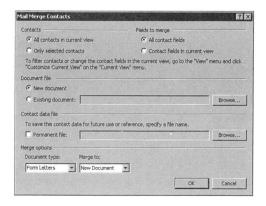

FIGURE 19.4
Contact data can be merged with a document in Word for mass mailings.

TIP

> **Setting Up a Mail Merge from Outlook**   The Mail Merge
> Contacts dialog box (refer to Figure 19.4) provides sev-
> eral options for customizing your mail merge using your
> Outlook Contacts. If you select the **Permanent File** check
> box, you can specify a filename and have your Contacts
> list saved as a data document for use in future Word
> mail merges (you won't have to start the merge from
> Outlook in the future if you select this option). You can
> also specify the type of document that Word creates dur-
> ing the mail merge using the Document type drop-down
> list. You can create form letters, mailing envelopes, and
> mailing labels.

SETTING PRINTER PROPERTIES

Whether you're printing to a printer connected directly to your computer or to a printer on the network, you can set printer properties. The
properties you set apply to all print jobs you send to the printer until
you change the properties again.

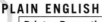

PLAIN ENGLISH

> **Printer Properties**   Configurations specific to a printer
> connected to your computer or to the network. Printer
> properties include paper orientation, paper source,
> graphics settings, fonts, and print quality.

CAUTION

> **Access Denied?**   If you cannot change the printer prop-
> erties to a network printer, it's probably because the net-
> work administrator has set the printer's configuration
> and you're not allowed access to the settings. If you
> need to change printer properties and cannot access the
> printer's Properties dialog box, talk to your network
> administrator.

To set printer properties, open the Print dialog box (by choosing **File, Print**). In the Printer area, select a printer from the Name drop-down list, and then click the **Properties** button. The printers' Properties dialog boxes differ depending on the make and model.

Most likely, you'll be able to set paper size, page orientation, and paper source using options on a Paper tab in the dialog box. In addition, you might see a Graphics tab, in which you can set the resolution, intensity, and graphics mode of your printer. A Fonts tab enables you to set options on TrueType fonts, font cartridges, and so on. You might also find a Device Options tab, in which you can set print quality and other options. For more information about your printer, read the documentation that came with it.

In this lesson, you learned to print items in Outlook, change the page setup, preview an item before printing it, and change printer properties.

INDEX

T